Formal and Empirical Issues
in Optimality Theoretic Syntax

Studies in Constraint-Based Lexicalism

A series edited by
Miriam Butt, *University of Konstanz*
Andreas Kathol, *University of California, Berkeley*
Tracy Holloway King, *Xerox Palo Alto Research Center*
Jean-Pierre Koenig, *State University of New York at Buffalo*
Sam Mchombo, *University of California, Berkeley*

The aim of this series is to make work in various nonderivational, lexicalist approaches to grammar available to a wide audience of linguists. In approaches of this kind, grammar is seen as the interaction of constraints from multiple dimensions of linguistic substance, including information about syntactic category, grammatical relations, and semantic and pragmatic interpretation.

Studies in
Constraint-Based Lexicalism

Formal and Empirical Issues
in Optimality Theoretic Syntax

edited by
Peter Sells

CSLI
PUBLICATIONS
Center for the Study of
Language and Information
Stanford, California

Copyright © 2001
CSLI Publications
Center for the Study of Language and Information
Leland Stanford Junior University
Printed in the United States
05 04 03 02 01   1 2 3 4 5

Library of Congress Cataloging-in-Publication Data

Formal and empirical issues in optimality theoretic syntax / [edited by]
Peter Sells.
    p. cm. – (Studies in constraint-based lexicalism ; 5)
    Includes bibliographical references and index.
    ISBN 1-57586-243-3 (alk. paper) – ISBN 1-57586-244-1 (pbk. : alk.
    paper)
    1. Grammar, Comparative and general–Syntax. 2. Optimality theory
(Linguistics) 3. Lexical-functional grammar.   I. Sells, Peter,
1957-   . II. Series.
    P291 .F58 2001
    415–dc21

                                                              2001032478

Please visit our web site at
http://cslipublications.stanford.edu/
for comments on this and other titles, as well as for changes
and corrections by the authors, editors and publisher.

Contents

Contributors

ASH ASUDEH: Department of Linguistics, Stanford University, Stanford, CA 94305-2150, USA, asudeh@csli.stanford.edu

GEORGE AARON BROADWELL: Department of Anthropology, SUNY Albany, Albany, NY 12222, USA, g.broadwell@albany.edu

HYE-WON CHOI: Department of Modern Languages and Literatures, SUNY Buffalo, Buffalo, NY 14260-4620, USA, hwchoi@acsu.buffalo.edu

ANETTE FRANK: DFKI, Stuhlsatzenhausweg 3, D-66123 Saarbrücken, Germany, frank@dfki.de

TRACY HOLLOWAY KING: NLTT/ISTL, Xerox PARC, 3333 Coyote Hill Road, Palo Alto, CA 94304, USA, thking@parc.xerox.com

JONAS KUHN: Institut für maschinelle Sprachverarbeitung, Universität Stuttgart, Azenbergstraße 12, 70174 Stuttgart, Germany, jonas@ims.uni-stuttgart.de

HANJUNG LEE: Department of Linguistics, Stanford University, Stanford, CA 94305-2150, USA, hanjung@csli.stanford.edu

JOHN T. MAXWELL III: NLTT/ISTL, Xerox PARC, 3333 Coyote Hill Road, Palo Alto, CA 94304, USA, maxwell@parc.xerox.com

YUKIKO MORIMOTO: Department of Linguistics, California State University, Fresno, 5245 N. Backer Ave. PB 92, Fresno, CA 93740-8001, ymorimot@csufresno.edu

PETER SELLS: Department of Linguistics, Stanford University, Stanford, CA 94305-2150, USA, sells@csli.stanford.edu

DEVYANI SHARMA: Department of Linguistics, Stanford University, Stanford, CA 94305-2150, USA, sharma@csli.stanford.edu

Preface and Acknowledgements

In 1999, we decided to put together a volume of representative and innovative work in the emerging Optimality-Theoretic Lexical-Functional Grammar (OT-LFG) approach to morphology, syntax, interpretation, and linguistic application. The eight papers collected here, combined, provide a relatively comprehensive overview of where research in OT-LFG is going, and of what major research issues in the coming years will be.

There are many people to be thanked for their part in bringing this volume to completion. I am grateful to several anonymous reviewers, who provided critical feedback on the papers here, and to Joan Bresnan, who gave feedback and advice all along the way. The entire production of the volume has been overseen by Tracy Holloway King and Miriam Butt, whose practical and editorial help went far beyond the call of duty. They and I were aided by Christine Kaschny, who proofread most of the papers and created the indices.

Peter Sells, Stanford, California, April 2001

1

Introduction

PETER SELLS

The papers collected here all explore aspects of the OT-LFG approach, pioneered by Joan Bresnan (see e.g. Bresnan (2000a), Bresnan (2000b)). OT-LFG brings together Lexical-Functional Grammar, as the representational basis of the grammatical information and structures, with the Optimality Theory approach to linguistic study. In this brief introduction,[1] I will outline some of the main features of OT syntax, and of the OT-LFG approach, and then consider a few of the major theoretical points in OT syntax that the papers collected here address.[2]

The papers are grouped thematically, as follows: the first three, by Choi, Lee, and Morimoto, are concerned with different surface orderings of clausal constituents under the influence of interacting factors, such as discourse-based information (Choi, Lee), or clause-external syntactic constraints (Morimoto). These papers and Broadwell's all have a theme of alignment or linear precedence as one empirical focus. The following two papers, by Sharma and Asudeh, consider how arguments of predicates are expressed: Sharma's paper looks specifically at case-marking expressed by clitics, while Asudeh's paper is concerned with argument-function linking patterns, some of which allow optionality as to which argument of a transitive predicate links to subject, and which to object. The final two papers, by Kuhn, and by Frank, King, Kuhn, and Maxwell, are concerned with more formal and computational aspects of OT-LFG, ranging from foundational and decidability issues to practical applications of the OT-LFG approach.

---

[1] I am grateful to Miriam Butt for comments on this introduction.

[2] The main sources for LFG are Bresnan (1982), Bresnan (2001) and Dalrymple et al. (1995); the defining statement for OT is Prince and Smolensky (1993).

Formal and Empirical Issues in Optimality Theoretic Syntax.
Peter Sells (ed.).
Copyright © 2001, CSLI Publications.

1.1 OT Syntax

OT as such is not a linguistic theory, but rather it is a way of interpreting constraints, as might be expressed in the elements of any theory.[3] The fundamental idea is that constraints are not interpreted in an all-or-nothing fashion, as in most previous generative approaches to linguistics, but rather, constraints are ranked with respect to each other, such that lower-ranking constraints may be violated in order for higher-ranking ones to be respected. To illustrate, let us consider the familiar phenomenon of second-position clitics—clitics which take the second-position in a finite clause.[4] Such clitics can be analyzed in OT by two constraints: one that asks for clitics to be leftmost in the relevant domain, and one that bars clitics from being in absolute initial position (see e.g., Anderson (2000) and Legendre (2001)). Let me refer to these constraints as Align-Left(X) and Non-Initial(X). No element chosen for X can satisfy them both. We count violations of the former constraint in a gradient fashion, effectively treating it as "Align as far to the left as possible," while the latter is simply satisfied or violated. The OT analysis predicts two types of language, depending only on the ranking. With the ranking Align-Left(X) ≫ Non-Initial(X), clitics meeting the description of X will be initial in their domain: satisfaction of the higher constraint is the most important. With the other ranking, clitics will be in second position: not initial, but then aligning as far to the left as possible. Due to the gradient nature of Align-Left(X), a clitic in second position represents a lower degree of violation than a clitic in third position, and so on.

This very simple example illustrates several important aspects of the OT approach to syntax. First, constraints represent important linguistic generalizations, even if they conflict when taken all together. This leads to the possibility of a syntactic theory which directly represents typological generalizations which are robust, but not absolute. Second, the constraint set is universal, and variation in grammars comes via different rankings of the constraints, predicting a typology of languages or language types. Third, constraints which are violated nevertheless have predictive force: constraints which have gradient interpretations always prefer a best-case form, even if it is not perfect. In the case of clitics, the important aspect of the analysis sketched above is that there is no 'Second-Position' constraint per se: if there was, then we would also expect constraints requiring First-Position, Third-Position, and so on. Such a constraint system would have no predictive power—clitics could be ordered anywhere. On the other hand, the approach sketched above predicts just two positions for clitics, first or

---

[3]See, for instance, the OT illustration of the calculation of leap years at `http://ifla.uni-stuttgart.de/~heck/ot/leapyear.html`.

[4]I am excluding here clitics which require designated elements, such as verbs, as their hosts, and therefore distribute in a clause wherever their hosts are.

second, which corresponds to a first approximation to the situation we find, cross-linguistically.

1.2 OT-LFG

In this section I will present the outlines of input-output relations as cast in OT-LFG, followed by a brief consideration of the formal nature of candidate evaluation.

1.2.1 Inputs and Outputs

As a constraint-based declarative grammatical formalism, LFG lends itself directly to an OT interpretation. In the first instance, the INPUT is taken to be an underspecified f-structure which represents the main grammatical information that a given sentence expresses, but without any representation of surface (and therefore language-specific) features of expression. This is exactly what the characterization of f-structures is in LFG—representations of language-invariant grammatical information—especially once morphological information is properly factored out (see Frank and Zaenen (1998)). For example, the INPUT representation of a transitive clause would include the predicate, its argument structure, semantic information about the arguments of the predicate, and tense and aspect information.

(1) shows the general architecture of input-output relations in OT-LFG, based on Bresnan (2000a, 26):

(1) INPUT   CANDIDATES

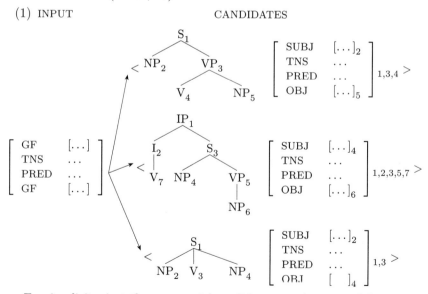

For simplicity, just three potential candidates are shown, each having an f-structure that is subsumed by the INPUT (they contain the same or more information, but no conflicting information), and each having a different c-structure form. From this point, the evaluation constraints determine an

OUTPUT winning candidate relative to an INPUT. The candidates for evaluation in OT-LFG are c-structure/f-structure pairs, which are the standard representations in LFG syntactic analysis. Faithfulness constraints relate the INPUT to the f-structure part of a given candidate, while structural markedness constraints and alignment constraints dictate the form of the c-structure part (see Kuhn's paper in particular for detailed discussion about these relationships).

Many aspects of surface syntactic variation across and within languages are correlated with discourse or contextual features, which are arguably not directly represented in f-structure. For example, the expression of topic and focus leads to surface variation in some languages in the form of scrambling or null expression (zero pronouns), and this information has to be represented for the constraint system to see it. Some researchers use the construct of 'information structure' (i-structure; see Vallduví (1992)); this is what characterizes the simplified INPUT representations in Choi's paper, where features of discourse-newness and discourse-prominence are posited. Lee's paper also relies on contextual information in the INPUT, and implicit there is a richer representations of contextual information (see section 5.2 in her paper); this has also been a feature of Kuhn's work (especially Kuhn (2001)). Lee and Kuhn have both explored the role in syntactic explanation of Birectional Optimization (see below), and this involves, as a matter of fact, a quite rich representation of context.[5]

In addition to information structure, argument structure may also be considered in the INPUT, in those cases where it is relevant. The representation in (28) in Lee's paper (section 3.3) is representative: there is functional and semantic information, discourse information (discourse-prominence and discourse-newness), as well as rich argument-structure information, showing volitionality, causality and sentience properties for Proto-Agent and Proto-Patient arguments. Note, though, that the INPUT does not specify which argument is subject and which is object: this is a matter for individual languages to choose, in their candidate evaluation.

Asudeh's paper is especially relevant in its study of argument-function linking. Thematic properties of arguments, along with semantic properties such as volitionality or animacy may all be correlated with differences in surface expression in some language(s), whether those differences are manifest through surface order, grammatical functions, case morphology, head-marking agreement, or any other morpho-syntactic device.

In considering the relations between the parts of the system in (1), Kuhn's paper addresses several formal and computational topics in the OT-LFG system: the nature of INPUT–OUTPUT relations, and complexity and decidability issues. Kuhn proposes that the relation between the IN-

---

[5]For practical convenience, INPUTs are not always formally represented as skeletal f-structures (attribute-value matrices), but are simplified in various ways, and sometimes even omitted altogether.

PUT and the f-structure part of the candidates in (1) is one of subsumption: each candidate's f-structure contains the same or more non-conflicting information relative to the INPUT. Thus, in a formal system for decidability, starting with a given INPUT, only those candidates which meet the subsumption requirement need to be considered, thereby avoiding the need to consider all logically possible candidates.

1.2.2 Candidate Evaluation

Another aspect of OT-LFG work concerns the nature of the constraint system: how the evaluation of candidates relative to each other works formally, and how this information can be used in various practical applications.

One goal of Kuhn's paper is to develop a formal system for expressing OT constraints, and for counting and keeping track of their violations, with regard to both scalar (gradient) and non-scalar (absolute) constraints. For example, an alignment constraint like HEAD-Left is interpreted in a scalar fashion: if the head is leftmost in its domain, there are 0 violations, and if it is not leftmost, there are n violations if there are n constituents preceding the head. On the other hand, *LEX-F is non-scalar: it forbids a lexical head in a functional head position (e.g., a lexical V in the I head of IP),[6] and it is either violated or not violated. Additionally, FAITHfulness violations—where the informational content of the INPUT and candidate f-structure do not match—are also given a formal construction (Kuhn, section 7.5).[7]

Formal and practical parsing considerations are taken up in the paper by Frank, King, Kuhn, and Maxwell, which explores ideas inspired by OT as part of a practical large grammar system built on LFG. For example, in parsing text, LFG grammar rules can be augmented to be sensitive to different possibilities in the parsing analysis or in the text itself. One such case is the function associated with a postverbal PP in English: once identified, is it given the role of oblique argument or adjunct? Frank, King, Kuhn, and Maxwell show how these two options can be associated with different weightings, using a formal construct of MARKs, to give the parsing grammar a preference for one over the other. This is one instantiation of a family of closely-related OT approaches which allow variable rankings to deal with the problem of optionality; this general issue is taken up in the Typological Predictions subsection below.

Extending the notion of MARKs, Frank, King, Kuhn, and Maxwell also note that for truly robust parsing, it may be necessary to parse text that is strictly speaking ungrammatical, though with some record kept of the fact that the text was not actually grammatical. They argue that there are two distinct theoretical notions, which they model with the labels UN-

---

[6]This constraint, which allows auxiliary verbs but not main verbs in functional head positions, is used in both Morimoto's and Kuhn's papers.

[7]Inspired by Kuhn's work (especially Kuhn (2001)), OT-LFG also offers a new view of the syntax-morphology interface (see Sells (2001a)).

GRAMMATICAL and NOGOOD. The former is associated with rules which can parse text even though it is ungrammatical (for example, text containing incorrect subject-verb agreement), while the latter is for text that is too ungrammatical to be parsed. In these ways, a robust parser can recover information from text that is ambiguous, partly ungrammatical, or possibly incomplete in other ways, while keeping track of the linguistic status of the forms that expressed that information.

1.3 Themes in OT Analysis

In this section, I focus on a few of the main themes that run through the papers in this volume. These involve ways in which aspects of the OT system have been developed to give accounts of empirical phenomena which go beyond the results of previous approaches to syntax (Positional Alignment, Bidirectional Optimization) and other properties of the OT approach which give predictions about markedness and typological implication, also largely lacking in previous generative work (Harmonic Alignment, Markedness, Typological Prediction). I can only briefly highlight the main analytical ideas and empirical predictions, without doing full justice to the motivation or coverage of any particular paper.

1.3.1 Positional Alignment

The surface structure of a given example is represented in the papers here by the c-structure part of the representation. Several papers address the question of constituent ordering, building mainly on the ideas of Generalized Alignment introduced by McCarthy and Prince (1993), as applied to syntax. The influential ideas in Grimshaw (1997) suggested an approach to the particular alignment constraints that syntax should concern itself with, and in some of my own work (in particular Sells (2001b)) I have explored alignment constraints specifically within the OT-LFG approach.

The papers by Choi, Lee, and Morimoto all address issues of ordering as expressed through alignment constraints, investigating differing and possibly conflicting ordering requirements on information in i-structure (e.g., [+Prom] aligns left), in f-structure (e.g., SUBJ aligns left), and locally within the c-structure (e.g., the c-structure X^0 head aligns left).

Three aspects of the analysis of constituent ordering are still open to further investigation: the domain(s) of alignment, the direction(s) of alignment, and the nature of alignment constraints as opposed to precedence constraints. The domains question has been answered in various ways, by different authors: some alignment constraints are defined to apply only within a local sub-tree (i.e., only among sisters), some apply within a full projection of XP, and some apply within the clause. Next comes the issue of whether alignment contraints come in symmetric sets (e.g., Head-Left, Head-Right), as suggested in Grimshaw (1997) and pursued in recent work (e.g., Grimshaw (2001)) to derive certain 'economy' results, or whether alignment constraints may have some asymmetry in them (e.g., TOPIC-Left but no TOPIC-Right, based on the fact that no languages seem to put topics at the right; see Sells (2001b)). Finally, some phenomena seem to be much more naturally captured by precedence constraints (of the form A≺B) rather than alignment constraints (A-Left ≫ B-Left); Broadwell's paper explicitly uses precedence constraints for the analysis of complex *wh*-phrases in San Dionicio Zapotec. Naturally, specific decisions in any of these areas lead to different empirical and typological predictions.

In addition to these three research areas, Morimoto's paper presents another: the issue of a different kind of alignment, termed 'Abutment' (though this type of alignment does fall under the overall scheme of Generalized Alignment proposed by McCarthy and Prince). In abutment, one element in a given domain tries to get as close to another element in that same domain as possible: their opposite edges try to align. Morimoto argues that certain syntactic elements are constrained to abut with the head of their domain, but whether that is left- or right-looking alignment is determined by the typological properties of head-positioning in the language in question, and not by left- or right-alignment constraints as such. For example, the canonical position of objects is immediately post-verbal in head-initial languages but immediately pre-verbal in head-final languages, and this would follow from just a single constraint Abut-OBJ(V).

Much of the work in OT syntax looking at i-structure influence on constituent ordering has focussed on (apparent) freedom of ordering possibilities, driven by different discoursal properties. In certain circumstances, though, languages with relatively flexible word order show 'freezing' effects, where only a canonical word order is possible. Lee illustrates freezing effects in Hindi and Korean, and shows that certain potential scrambling configurations are so marked that they are disallowed: in these cases, the unmarked order emerges. How these markedness predictions emerge in OT analyses is taken up in the next section.

1.3.2 Harmonic Alignment

A rather different kind of alignment—Harmonic Alignment—also plays a crucial role in some of the papers here, especially those by Lee, Sharma, and Asudeh. Harmonic alignment is used to generate sets of OT constraints with built-in relative rankings, and from this major typological predictions follow. The key idea is that various scales of different kinds of markedness align with each other to express 'regions' of markedness in grammars, which in turn can generate OT markedness constraints, using the formal mechanism of Harmonic Alignment from Prince and Smolensky (1993). This technique is presented with many insightful and important consequences in Aissen (1999) and Aissen (2000). Harmonic alignment also directly provides an account of 'markedness reversal', the situation where what is marked for one type of element (say, subjects) is unmarked for another (say, objects).

Let us consider the abstract situation of markedness as we find it in linguistics; the chart in (2) summarizes it. First, with regard to the least marked grammatical configuration, its linguistic expression takes the least marked form. In more marked configurations, a more marked form in the morpho-syntactic expression is called for: Passive is a canonical example of this, where a marked morphosyntactic form represents the marked configuration of an argument that is not the highest argument of the predicate being linked to the highest grammatical function, the subject. This contrasts with the least marked situation of the highest thematic argument being the subject, in an unmkarked Active construction. Finally, in highly marked configurations, there may be no possible expression at all. For example, Aissen's papers cited above analyze languages where arguments of transitive predicates with certain marked person/number combinations simply do not allow one of those arguments to be a Passive subject.

(2)   Scale of Markedness and Correlating Linguistic Expression:

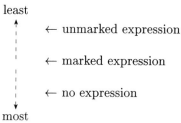

least

← unmarked expression

← marked expression

← no expression

most

Grammatical theory needs a way to formalize these intuitive ideas of markedness, and of marked configurations which are expressible, but only by marked morpho-syntactic forms. Within OT, the mechanism of Constraint Conjunction (also known as 'Local Conjunction', introduced by Smolensky (1995)) serves this purpose. It has been used to account for morphological marking of marked configurations (e.g., active is unmarked, passive is marked), and also to account for 'the worst of the worst' situations, where configurations become too marked to be expressible.

To illustrate, in Lee's paper, the markedness generalizations in (3) are proposed.

(3)   Markedness Generalizations:

    a. Honorific verbs are marked with respect to non-honorific verbs.

    b. Oblique subjects are marked with respect to non-oblique subjects.

    c. Subjects in non-initial position are marked with respect to subjects in initial position.

These constraints are developed for Korean, and while perhaps not so many languages have honorific forms of verbs, all three statements in (3) are clearly quite robust as cross-linguistic generalizations. These generalizations can be expressed as OT constraints in respective sub-hierachies, as in (4), which are the formalization of the statements in (3):

(4) a. *HON$_V$ ≫ *NON-HON$_V$
     b. *Su/Obl ≫ Su/Non-Obl
     c. *Su/Non-Initial ≫ *Su/Initial

For example, (4a) indicates that it is worse (i.e., more marked) to have a verb marked for honorification than a verb not marked for honorification. The notion of the 'worst of the worst' mentioned above is when more than one of the relatively marked configurations cooccurs with another marked one. In this context, what Lee shows is that while Korean has honorific verbs, oblique subjects, and subjects in non-initial position (i.e. scrambling), the combination of these marked configurations is not allowed: a sentence cannot have a non-initial oblique subject with an honorific verb form. The cumulative effect of the constraints is derived via Constraint Conjunction, the result of which is shown in (5), which represents notationally what the previous sentence describes. Formally, (5) is the conjunction of the three relatively higher constraints in (4). Each line in (4) represents a certain kind of markedness relation, while the conjunction in (5) represents the most marked combined situation.

(5) [*HON$_V$ & *Su/Obl] & *Su/Non-Initial

Lee argues that this constraint is part of Korean grammar, and if it outranks alignment constraints for discourse information (e.g., TOPIC-Left), leftmost positioning for topic non-subjects will be ruled out if those subjects are oblique with an honorific-marked verb: that is a configuration which the language just can not tolerate. In other less marked circumstances, topics will be leftmost, as the high ranking constraint (5) will be inapplicable. This is the freezing effect referred to above: constituent ordering in Korean usually responds to topic and focus information, but not in extremely marked grammatical circumstances (such as described by (5)).

1.3.3   Markedness in Morphological Expression

In (2), three different linguistic possibilities are given: morphologically unmarked expression, morphologically marked expression, and no expression at all. The simplest OT competition between candidates favors one candidate expression over another, which effectively covers the situation of expression vs. no expression: certain expressions are just impossible (ungrammatical), as described in the previous section.

For marked vs. unmarked expression, Aissen proposed the technique of local conjunction with *∅, a constraint which disprefers null morphological structure—in other words, a constraint which prefers morphological marking. Let us consider again Active vs. Passive: Passive is a marked morpho-syntactic form with respect to Active, and the argument-function linking is also marked, for the subject is not the thematically highest argument. To illustrate the effect of *∅ more directly, let us think of a simple transitive input with Agent and Patient arguments. If the evaluation grammar contains a constraint like *Su/Pat which says "avoid Patient subjects," this would block passive-like outputs completely. In contrast, the constraint [*Su/Pat & *∅] says "avoid Patient subjects in the absence of morphological marking" and has a different effect on output: it allows passive-like outputs just in case the form has some overt morphological (or morpho-syntactic) marking. This is how OT syntax captures the intermediate case shown in (2) above. Completing the picture, there is a countervailing force in the grammar, the constraint *STRUC, which prefers the absence of (morphological) structure. This allows the requirement of overt marking to be "turned off" at certain points, as I now illustrate with an example from Sharma's paper.

Sharma uses this technique to analyze patterns of subject and object registration by case clitics in Kashmiri. To choose just one part, there is the familiar phenomenon that subjects in perfective clauses are specially registered, by Ergative case, while subjects in non-perfective clauses are not, and take the default Nominative case. Sharma proposes the constraints in (6a) which reflect the intuition which she develops that perfective clauses (with subjects) are more marked than imperfective clauses; conjoining these constraints with *∅ gives the constraints in (6b):

(6) a. *SU/PERF ≫ *SU/IMPERF

  b. [*SU/PERF & *∅$_C$] ≫ [*SU/IMPERF & *∅$_C$]

The second line here says that it is more marked for perfective clauses with subjects to have no morpho-syntactic registration than it is for imperfective clauses: in other words, if any form is marked, it will be the one expressing a perfective clause. If the constraint *STRUC is interpolated between the two constraints in (6b), giving the ranking [*SU/PERF & *∅$_C$] ≫ *STRUC ≫ [*SU/IMPERF & *∅$_C$], there is special registration of the subject when the verb is in perfective aspect, but otherwise every morphological marker is penalized. So this means that subjects are registered—by clitics, in the case of Kashmiri—in perfective but not imperfective clauses, and as the relative ranking of the two constraints [*SU/PERF & *∅$_C$] and [*SU/IMPERF & *∅$_C$] is fixed in that order by Harmonic Alignment, a typology of just three language types emerges: languages in which there is no overt registration of subjects, regardless of clause type (*STRUC is ranked highest), languages like Kashmiri, and languages in which subjects are registered in both clause types (*STRUC is ranked lowest).

1.3.4 Typological Predictions

As I noted above, a key aspect of OT work is the prediction of typologies which arise from different constraint rankings. Typological predictions are brought out most directly in the papers here by Choi, Morimoto and

Sharma, but are implicit in most of them. Choi discusses how different rankings of constraints referring to i-structure alignment, pure structural alignment, and pure structural markedness give different possibilities for how languages express i-structure information. For example, in her rankings (section 2.4.2), the i-structure constraints for new information (NEW-R and NEW-L) are ranked very low in English,[8] below the canonical clause structure constraints. This means that English does not have any special syntax to express new information. That is, it is more important in English to respect the canonical syntactic configurations of the language than to alter the canonical syntax to express properties of i-structure.

Other languages are less rigid in this regard. German allows a limited interaction of the expression of complement ordering and new information, in that new information can optionally be rightmost (but necessarily before the clause-final verb) even if that disturbs the usual complement order. So for example with double-object verbs, the non-canonical order may emerge just in case the linearly second object represents new information. This limited interaction is predicted in Choi's account by the floating ranking { CMPL, NEW-R }, which says that ordering can either respond to the canonical pattern for complements or to the requirement that new information is expressed as far to the right as possible.

In contrast to English and German, other languages are much more flexible in their surface syntax. One of the major results of Valldu ví's work was how he showed that while Catalan is underlyingly VOS, surface ordering is most directly determined by the expression of new information, which is placed in front of the verb, regardless of the grammatical function of the new information constituent. In Choi's analysis, this means that NEW-L ranks very high, so that the language orders new information initially, in preference to following the canonical ordering within the clause.

These kinds of variation in major constituent order find natural accounts in the OT model with differential weights given to interacting factors from different structures in the grammar. It should be noted that the OT analysis does not blindly generate structural alternatives as output forms, but rather each specific ranking shows why and how constituent order variation is preferred: non-canonical orders will only be licensed by information structure factors, or whatever other perceptible influences on order there are. For instance, a different kind of typology with respect to positioning is addressed in Morimoto's paper. She focusses on a typology of verb and relative-marker positions in relative clauses, considering variation in whether a relative clause is introduced or closed off by a relative marker, and whether that marker is an independent functional element in a peripheral position or whether the verb appears in that peripheral position. She contrasts the OT approach with the full 'anti-symmetric' view of Kayne

---

[8] In Choi's rankings, only one constraint or the other is shown; the one shown outranks the other, and as such, the one not shown has no effect on the OT competitions.

(1994), which derives a typology by having sets of different movement operations. Crucial to her argument is the fact that some languages show more than one (typological) option, suggesting that a parameter-setting view, or its equivalent, is inappropriate for this kind of variation. By allowing total rankings for some languages, and partial rankings for others, the OT approach directly accounts for languages with single and with multiple options, drawn from a universal set of options defined by the constraint system.

The typological variation analyzed in Sharma's work (see section 6.7) was discussed above as it relates to harmonic alignment, which restricts the reranking possibilities, as constraints derived by harmonic alignment have a necessary relative ranking. The overall approach lays out the domain for a variety of different possibilities for morphological marking of grammatical features, via inflection, case, or clitics, and crucially embodies predictions about markedness. As described above, local conjunction of content constraints and local conjunction of constraints with *∅ also leads to the direct prediction that what is impossible in one language will be possible but morpho-syntactically marked in another, again providing a direct and broad-ranging typological dimension that has typically not been part of mainstream theoretical syntax.

Moving beyond typology to the more general phenomenon of variation, one major impact of OT work has been in the way it has allowed formally and theoretically sophisticated models of syntax to be applied to data sets with inherent variability. Recently a body of work has emerged in the style known as 'Stochastic OT', based on the original proposals of Boersma (1997).[9] This line of work directly addresses the fact that it really is an idealization to treat any data set in syntax as being free from internal variation or variability, by producing analyses which embrace the variation and model it to increasing levels of precision. Boersma's approach gives a precise foundation to the idea of 'floating constraints'—rankings which are not total, and where two (or more) contraints can float in their relative rankings. Floating constraints appear in several of the papers here, while the stochastic approach is more specifically considered in Asudeh's paper; after introducing the technique, Asudeh's formal ranking statement reflects the stochastic ranking, which effectively allows a probabilistic re-ranking of the relevant contraints for a given evaluation (section 7.6). This allows the potential of multiple outputs, with relative frequency determined by the probabilistic weights, and a much more accurate theoretical construction of complex and variable data.

Consequently, the OT view has a very rich approach to typology which goes far beyond what has standardly been accomplished in generative grammatical research: from any logically possible set of options for variation,

---

[9]See also, for example, Anttila (1997), Boersma (1998), Boersma and Hayes (2001), Bresnan and Deo (2000), and Keller (1998).

some will be ruled out by the constraint system (due to inherent rankings derived by harmonic alignment from robust typological and functional observations); of those remaining, there may simply be different options chosen in different languages, or some languages may allow multiple options, to varying degrees, via the stochastic approach. As emphasized by Bresnan and Deo (2000), the kinds of variation one finds within a language and across languages are quite similar.

1.3.5 Bidirectional Optimization: Ambiguity and Optionality

Although I have concentrated in this introduction on a 'production-oriented' approach to OT syntax, starting with an INPUT containing grammatical and semantic information which stands in correspondence to output surface forms, other approaches are possible, and, going in the 'comprehension' direction from overt form to semantic interpretation has also been the focus of a considerable amount of work in OT. A model of grammar which has both production and comprehension optimizations is a bidirectional model (see e.g., Wilson (2001)), which has many important empirical consequences. As Lee shows, it is the bidirectional OT approach that allows clear predictions to be made about the avoidance of ambiguous strings in certain circumstances, and more generally about how semantic information can be recovered from surface forms that are potentially ambiguous.[10] Both Lee and Kuhn show how a bidirectional model can account for other instances of word order freezing in scrambling languages, in addition to those above derived via Constraint Conjunction.

Issues of ambiguity and optionality have been considered to be potentially problematic for OT approaches—the nature of OT seems to be that there will always be exactly one winning candidate, which is at odds with optionality, for example (within the specific context of OT-LFG, see e.g., Johnson (1998)). However, Asudeh's paper shows how an OT account can predict when optionality will emerge, and also when it will not. As Asudeh notes, ambiguity is optionality in the comprehension-oriented direction: a given string has more than one option for its interpretation. Kuhn (2001) and Lee (2001) take the analysis of ambiguity far beyond the initial cases mentioned in their contributions here (see also Blutner (1999)). More generally, the papers here by Lee, Kuhn, and Frank, King, Kuhn, and Maxwell show how the OT-LFG model can encompass analyses of both optionality (in generation) and ambiguity (in parsing) which embody significant linguistic generalizations.

---

[10]Lee (2001) shows that the amount of ambiguity that different languages tolerate varies, showing that syntactic theory must allow constraints on production and recoverability to have different rankings, and to be part of the 'competence' grammar.

1.4 Conclusion

To conclude, it is probably worth pointing out that in comparison to other styles of OT syntax, based on the Minimalist syntax model of Chomsky (1995) and involving a serial derivation of each candidate, such as the 'derivation-and-evaluation' model (e.g., Broekhuis and Dekkers (2000), Broekhuis (2000)), or the 'local optimization' model (e.g., Heck and Müller (2000), Müller (2001)), the OT-LFG model of syntax is a much purer instantiation of the original OT conception: a constraint-based direct evaluation of direct INPUT-OUTPUT relations.

As illustrated in the papers here, the model directly brings in results and insights from functionalist and typological work in linguistics, discourse and contextual information, and more recently probabilistic information drawn from large corpora and/or practical applications. In this way, the OT-LFG model is the foundation of a syntactic system which sets as its goal a much broader outreach into all aspects of linguistic competence than has traditionally been in the vision of syntactic theory.

References

Aissen, Judith. 1999. Markedness and Subject Choice in Optimality Theory. *Natural Language and Linguistic Theory* 17:673–711.

Aissen, Judith. 2000. Differential Object Marking: Iconicity vs. Economy. MS., University of California, Santa Cruz.

Anderson, Stephen R. 2000. Towards an Optimal Account of Second-Position Phenomena. In *Optimality Theory: Phonology, Syntax and Acquisition*, eds. Joost Dekkers, Frank van der Leeuw, and Jeroen van de Weijer. Oxford: Oxford University Press, 302–333.

Anttila, Arto. 1997. Deriving variation from grammar: A study of Finnish genitives. In *Variation, change, and phonological theory*, eds. Frans Hinskens, Roeland van Hout, and W. Leo Wetzels. Amsterdam: John Benjamins, 35–68.

Blutner, Reinhard. 1999. Some Aspects of Optimality in Natural Language Interpretation. In *Papers in Optimality Theoretic Semantics*, eds. Helen de Hoop and Henriëtte de Swart. Utrecht University, Utrecht Institute of Linguistics OTS, 1–21.

Boersma, Paul. 1997. How we learn variation, optionality, and probability. In *IFA Proceedings 21*. University of Amsterdam: Institute of Phonetic Sciences, 43–58. ROA-221-109.

Boersma, Paul. 1998. *Functional Phonology: Formalizing the interactions between articulatory and perceptual drives*. The Hague: Holland Academic Graphics.

Boersma, Paul and Bruce Hayes. 2001. Empirical tests of the gradual learning algorithm. *Linguistic Inquiry* 32:45–86.

Bresnan, Joan (ed.). 1982. *The Mental Representation of Grammatical Relations*. Cambridge, Massachusetts: The MIT Press.

Bresnan, Joan. 2000a. Explaining Morphosyntactic Competition. In *Handbook of Contemporary Syntactic Theory*, eds. Mark Baltin and Chris Collins. Oxford:

Blackwell Publishers, 11–44.

Bresnan, Joan. 2000b. Optimal Syntax. In *Optimality Theory: Phonology, Syntax and Acquisition*, eds. Joost Dekkers, Frank van der Leeuw, and Jeroen van de Weijer. Oxford: Oxford University Press, 334–385.

Bresnan, Joan. 2001. *Lexical Functional Syntax*. Oxford: Blackwell.

Bresnan, Joan and Ashwini Deo. 2000. 'Be' in the *Survey of English Dialects*: A Stochastic OT Account. MS., Stanford University.

Broekhuis, Hans. 2000. Against Feature Strength: The Case of Scandinavian Object Shift. *Natural Language and Linguistic Theory* 18:673–721.

Broekhuis, Hans and Joost Dekkers. 2000. The Minimalist Program and Optimality Theory: Derivations and Evaluations. In *Optimality Theory: Phonology, Syntax and Acquisition*, eds. Joost Dekkers, Frank van der Leeuw, and Jeroen van de Weijer. Oxford: Oxford University Press, 386–422.

Chomsky, Noam. 1995. *The Minimalist Program*. Cambridge, Massachusetts: The MIT Press.

Dalrymple, Mary, Ronald M. Kaplan, John T. Maxwell, and Annie Zaenen (eds.). 1995. *Formal issues in Lexical-Functional Grammar*. Stanford, California: CSLI Publications.

Frank, Anette and Annie Zaenen. 1998. Tense in LFG: Syntax and Morphology. MS., Xerox Research Centre Europe.

Grimshaw, Jane. 1997. Projection, Heads, and Optimality. *Linguistic Inquiry* 28:73–422.

Grimshaw, Jane. 2001. Economy of Structure and Movement in OT. Colloquium handout, University of California, Santa Cruz, March 2001.

Heck, Fabian and Gereon Müller. 2000. Successive cyclicity, long-distance superiority, and local optimization. In *Proceedings of WCCFL 19*, eds. Roger Billerey and Brooke Danielle Lillehaugen. Somerville, Massachusetts: Cascadilla Press, 218–231. (available at http://merlin.philosophie. uni-stuttgart.de/~heck/ot/papers/).

Johnson, Mark. 1998. Optimality-theoretic Lexical Functional Grammar. In *Proceedings of the 11th Annual CUNY Conference on Human Sentence Processing*.

Kayne, Richard. 1994. *The Antisymmetry of Syntax*. Cambridge, Massachusetts: The MIT Press.

Keller, Frank. 1998. Gradient Grammaticality as an Effect of Selective Constraint Re-Ranking. In *Papers from the 34th Annual Meeting of the Chicago Linguistic Society*, eds. M. Catherine Gruber, Derrick Higgins, Kenneth Olson, and Tamara Wysocki, volume 2: The Panels. Chicago, Illinois.

Kuhn, Jonas. 2001. *Formal and Computational Aspects of Optimality-theoretic Syntax*. Ph.D. thesis, Institut für maschinelle Sprachverarbeitung, Universität Stuttgart.

Lee, Hanjung. 2001. *Optimization in Argument Expression and Interpretation: A Unified Approach*. Ph.D. thesis, Stanford University.

Legendre, Géraldine. 2001. Masked Second-Position Effects and the Linearization of Functional Features. In *Optimality-Theoretic Syntax*, eds. Géraldine Legendre, Jane Grimshaw, and Sten Vikner. Cambridge, Massachusetts: The MIT Press, 241–277.

McCarthy, John and Alan Prince. 1993. Generalized alignment. In *Yearbook of Morphology*, eds. Geert Booji and Jaap van Marle. Dordrecht: Foris, 79–153.

Müller, Gereon. 2001. Order Preservation, Parallel Movement, and the Emergence of the Unmarked. In *Optimality-Theoretic Syntax*, eds. Géraldine Legendre, Jane Grimshaw, and Sten Vikner. Cambridge, Massachusetts: The MIT Press, 279–313.

Prince, Alan and Paul Smolensky. 1993. Optimality Theory: Constraint Interaction in Generative Grammar. Technical Report RuCCS Technical Report #2, Center for Cognitive Science, Rutgers University, Piscataway, New Jersey. To be published by the MIT Press.

Sells, Peter. 2001a. The Morphological Expression of Syntactic Information. MS., Stanford University.

Sells, Peter. 2001b. *Structure, Alignment and Optimality in Swedish*. To appear, Stanford, California: CSLI Publications.

Smolensky, Paul. 1995. On the Internal Structure of the Constraint Component Con of UG. ROA-86-0000. Rutgers Optimality Archive. http://ruccs.rutgers.edu/roa.html.

Vallduví, Enric. 1992. *The Informational Component*. New York, New York: Garland.

Wilson, Colin. 2001. Bidirectional Optimization and the Theory of Anaphora. In *Optimality-Theoretic Syntax*, eds. Géraldine Legendre, Jane Grimshaw, and Sten Vikner. Cambridge, Massachusetts: The MIT Press, 465–507.

2

Phrase Structure, Information Structure, and Resolution of Mismatch

HYE-WON CHOI

2.1 Introduction

It has long been observed that discourse-contextual information plays a significant role in syntax, presumably more so in some languages than in others (Li and Thompson, 1976; Sgall et al., 1986; Givón, 1990; Kiss, 1995; to name only a few).[1] Discourse-pragmatic information such as topic and focus has been argued to be represented in a separate level of grammar, namely, 'information structure' (Vallduví, 1992; Lambrecht, 1994) and to interact directly with syntax especially in word order variation. With the introduction of Optimality Theory in syntax (Prince and Smolensky, 1993; Grimshaw, 1997; Legendre et al., 1998; Bresnan, 1998), this interaction between syntax and information structure has been pursued in terms of ranking between syntactic constraints and information-structural constraints (Choi 1996;Samek-Lodovici 1996; Costa 1998; Müller 1998). The purpose of this paper is to further pursue this line of approach in some of the word order phenomena in Catalan, English, and German.

---

[1] This paper has been built and developed upon the earlier work presented at the 1997 LFG Conference in San Diego. I thank Joan Bresnan, Tracy Holloway King, Knud Lambrecht, Peter Sells, and the audience at the conference, for their helpful questions, comments and discussions. I am grateful, especially for later development of the paper, to two anonymous reviewers and the editor of the volume, Peter Sells, for their invaluable comments and criticisms. Also, I owe thanks to David Fertig, Cristina Guijarro, Robert Hoeing, and Reinhild Steingrover-McRae for their judgments and discussions of some German and Catalan data. Of course, I alone am responsible for any errors and misinterpretations.

Formal and Empirical Issues in Optimality Theoretic Syntax.
Peter Sells (ed.).
Copyright © 2001, CSLI Publications.

In LFG (Lexical Functional Grammar), the grammar consists of several parallel and copresent structures such as c-structure (for categorial and constituent representation), f-structure (for representation of grammatical features and functions), a(rgument)-structure, s(emantic)-structure, and i(nformation)-structure (Bresnan, 1982, 2001; Bresnan and Kanerva, 1989; Bresnan and Moshi, 1990; Alsina, 1993; Halvorsen and Kaplan, 1988; Dalrymple et al., 1993; Choi, 1996; King, 1997). In the OT-LFG framework developed by Bresnan (1996, 2001), Choi (1996, 1999), Lee (1998, 2001), Sells (1998, 2000), Morimoto (1999), Asudeh (2001), and Kuhn (2001), the information flow between any two of these parallel structures is governed by a set of correspondence constraints, which are ranked and violable. For example, the correspondence between the information about grammatical functions or features and that about phrase structural constituency is governed by a set of f-structure/c-structure correspondence constraints. Likewise, the relationship between the discourse-contextual information and the phrase structural configuration will be governed by some i-structure/c-structure mapping constraints. Therefore, the interaction between syntax and discourse-pragmatics in the word order variation can be viewed as the interaction between the f-s/c-s constraints and the i-s/c-s constraints.

In fact, the syntactic information coming from the f-structure may not converge with the discoursal information coming from the i-structure, which then will cause mismatches in the c-structural representation (Choi, 1997b). In other words, the ideal c-structural configuration based on the syntactic information may not be identical to the ideal c-structural configuration based on the discoursal information. This paper investigates this type of mismatch in some of the informationally triggered syntactic constructions such as scrambling, detachment, and topicalization in Catalan, English, and German.

2.2 Phrase Structure and Information Structure

Discourse-pragmatic information is encoded in the surface sentential representation, although languages differ in how and to what degree they incorporate such information in phrase structure (section 2.2.1). We will discuss how the discourse-contextual information can be represented in terms of information structure (section 2.2.2).

2.2.1 Phrase Structure Flexibility

Languages like German and Catalan enjoy more freedom in word order than more rigidly structured languages like English. As such, some languages have more flexibility than others in phrase structural descriptions, but even in these relatively flexible languages, there is usually a particular phrase structural description which is considered to be unmarked, default, or canonical, while others are regarded as more marked or non-canonical. The marked or non-canonical structures are often associated with certain discourse functions so that these structures appear only in certain discourse contexts (cf. 'discourse configurationality' (Kiss, 1995)).

The default or canonical order is the one that is preferred when no discourse context is provided or when the context demands that the whole sentence be focused, i.e. of new information, for instance, when the sentence is uttered out of context or when it is an answer to a question like *What's up?, Any news?* or *What happened?* Example (1) shows a default-ordered sentence in English, German, and Catalan respectively, with the intended semantic meaning of [put(John,the knife,on the table)].

(1) a. English: John put the knife on the table.
   b. German: Hans hat das Messer auf den Tisch gelegt.
             Hans has the knife   on the table   put
             'Hans put the knife on the table.'
   c. Catalan: Va ficar   el ganivet damunt la taula el Joan.
             3-past-put the knife on the table   the Joan
             'Joan put the knife on the table.'

English has the SVO order as shown in (1a), and the PP argument follows the NP argument in default order. German is known to have the SOV-turned-SVO order (which will be discussed in section 2.3), and it is SVO in matrix clauses, as shown in (1b). Here too, as well as in Catalan, the oblique PP argument follows the object NP argument. Finally, Catalan is argued to be a VOS language (Rigau, 1988; Bonet, 1990; Vallduví, 1992) with the *pro*-drop property. When the whole sentence is presented as new information, the subject is sentence-final, although the sentence-final subject is often *pro*-dropped when it is given information, which produces the VO order.

These three languages differ in the way and the degree to which their word order reacts to discourse context. Take for example a focus context where the object NP is new information or focus, for instance, when the sentence is uttered as an answer to a question like *What did John put on the table?* The focused part is bracketed in the following examples.

(2) English:
   a. What did John put on the table?
   b. He put [the KNIFE] on the table.
   b'. *He put on the table [the KNIFE].

In English, as in (2), the word order does not change at all in this context. The change is only in prosody, where the focused part gets a pitch accent. This prosodic shift also happens in German and Catalan but German and Catalan show phrase structural variations as well. This is illustrated in (3) and (4) respectively.

(3) German:
   a. What did Hans put on the table?
   b. Hans hat [das MESSER] auf den Tisch gelegt.
      Hans has the knife   on the table   put
      'Hans put the knife on the table.'
   b'. Hans hat auf den Tisch [das MESSER] gelegt.
      Hans has on the table   the knife   put
      'Hans put the knife on the table.'

(4) Catalan:
   a. What did Joan put on the table?
   b. *Hi$_i$ va ficar   [el GANIVET] damunt la taula$_i$.
      cl 3-past-put the knife   on the table
      'He put the knife on the table.'
   b'. [El GANIVET], hi$_i$ va ficar   damunt la taula$_i$.
      the knife   cl 3-past-put on the table
      'He put the knife on the table.'

German and Catalan show an interesting split, though. As illustrated in (3), German actually has two options. One, as in (3b), is to maintain the default phrase structure but only modify the prosodic structure just like English. The other is to alter the phrase structure as well, by means of 'scrambling', as in (3b'). In Catalan, on the other hand, the default phrase structure is not a possibility even with the prosodic difference, as shown in (4b). It always alters its phrase structure in such a way that all the non-focal items are 'detached' rightward so that only the focal part remains in situ (Vallduví, 1992). This is shown in (4b').[2] Catalan is a clitic language, so all the arguments that are non-focal or given information except for the subject leave clitics right before the verb, for example, *hi* for *damunt la taula* in (4b').

To summarize, English, German, and Catalan vary in how their phrase structure responds to discourse context. More specifically, in a focus context which distinguishes the 'new' information from the 'given/ground' information as shown above, English does not respect this informational split in any phrase structural way, whereas German and Catalan react to it by reshaping their phrase structures, Catalan more aggressively than German. In the remaining part of this paper, I will investigate how and to what degree this phrase structural reaction to the discoursal information takes place in each language.

---

[2]In fact, (4b') could be analyzed such that the focal part moves 'leftward' or is focus-fronted instead of the non-focal part moving rightward. For arguments against the first view, see Vallduví (1992). This will be discussed in section 2.4.1.

2.2.2 Information Structure

Information structure is a domain of grammar where the discourse-contextual information is reflected at the sentence level (Vallduví, 1992; Lambrecht, 1994). It shows how a sentence is partitioned or structured according to the information coming from the discourse context, such as 'what the sentence is about', 'what the new or informative part of the sentence is', 'what the most important information of the sentence is', etc. The type of information that the information structure provides is distinguishable from the type of information that some syntactic representations provide such as 'what the subject or the object of the sentence is', or 'what composes the verb phrase (VP)'.

Topic and focus are the terms which show up most frequently when we talk about discourse context or information structure. However, neither topic nor focus is a uniform notion and often creates confusion. Topic is often defined as something that the sentence is 'about' (Kuno, 1972; Reinhart, 1982), but differences have been pointed out, for instance, between 'continuing' topic and 'shifted' topic (Herring, 1990; Aissen, 1992). Likewise, focus is the new or informative part of the sentence, but 'completive' or 'presentational' focus has been argued to behave differently from 'contrastive' focus (Dik et al., 1981; Herring, 1990; Rochemont and Culicover, 1990). Contrastive focus is sometimes called 'topical' and shifted topic is often noted as 'contrastive'.

Therefore, instead of the discretely named, often confusing terms like topic and focus, two discourse-information features, i.e. 'discourse-newness ([New])' and 'discourse-prominence ([Prom])' are used in this paper, as proposed in Choi (1996, 1999). [New] distinguishes what is 'new' or 'informative' from what is 'given', and [Prom] picks out what is 'important' or 'urgent' in the sentence. These two binary features may crosscut some of the existing notions of topic and focus. This is illustrated in (5).

(5)

	+PROM	−PROM
−NEW	(shifted) topic, link	continuing topic, tail
+NEW	contrastive/emphatic focus	completive/ presentational focus

A sentence can be structured in a variety of ways by these two dimensions of information features. For example, consider the focus context introduced earlier.

(6) a. What did you put on the table?
   b. I put [the knife]$_{[+New]}$ on the table.

One thing obvious in this context is that 'the knife' is [+New], namely, that it is the new information or the focus in (6b). However, depending on what kind of conversation has preceded or what kind of assumptions and understanding of the context the speaker and the hearer have, this sentence can have different information structure profiles.

For example, if the answer is mainly intended to provide the unknown information in the question, as in (7), 'the knife' will be marked simply as [+New] ('completive focus'), but not [+Prom]. In contrast, if the answer is not only to provide the information that is lacking but also to carry some extra information such as unexpectedness, contrastiveness, surprise, etc., the new information will also be marked as [+Prom] ('contrastive focus'), as shown in (8).

(7) a. Did you set the table yet? What did you put on the table?
　　b. I put [the knife]$_{[-Prom,+New]}$ on the table.

(8) a. We're having noodle soup for dinner. What did you put on the table?
　　b. I put [the knife]$_{[+Prom,+New]}$ on the table!

The rest of the sentence, that is, [I put (x) on the table], may have different profiles too. It is the ground or given information and therefore [−New], as opposed to [the knife] being [+New]. However, it may or may not make up a single informational unit. If the question is about what 'I' did as opposed to somebody else, as demonstrated in (9), then 'I' is not only 'given' information but also rather 'prominent'. Thus, [I] gets a [+Prom,−New] marking, whereas [put (x) on the table] gets [−Prom,−New]. So this difference in [Prom] splits the [−New] domain [I put (x) on the table] further into [I] and [put (x) on the table]. This is shown in (9).

(9) a. What about you? What did you put on the table?
　　b. [I] put [the knife] on the table.
　　b'. [I]$_{[+Prom,−New]}$ [the knife]$_{[+New]}$ [put on the table]$_{[-Prom,−New]}$

Note also that even without the distinction in [Prom], the [−New] domain can split into two or more parts. If the conversation continues to be about what 'I' did yesterday, namely, if 'I' is the 'continuing topic', then we will get the similar split between [I] and [put (x) on the table] even though both receive the same feature assignment, i.e. [−Prom,−New]. This is illustrated in (10).

(10) a. What did you do last night?
　　 b. I set the table for the party.
　　 a. What did you put on the table?
　　 b. [I] put [the knife] on the table.
　　 b'. [I]$_{[-Prom,−New]}$ [the knife]$_{[+New]}$ [put on the table]$_{[-Prom,−New]}$

Similarly, [put (x) on the table] may or may not form a single informational unit. When properly contextualized, [on the table] may form a separate unit from [put], although both will be assigned [−Prom,−New].

We can also think of the reverse case where [the knife] is the given information. A question like 'What happened to the knife?' will split [the knife] as [−New] and [I put (x) on the table] as [+New]. Likewise, a question like 'What did you do with the knife?' will further divide the [−New] domain into [I] and [the knife], and so forth. As such, there are quite a few possibilities of information structuring, as demonstrated in (11).

(11) a. [I put the knife on the table]
  b. [I] [put the knife on the table]
  c. [I] [put the knife] [on the table]
  d. [I] [put on the table] [the knife]
  e. [I put on the table] [the knife]
  f. [I put the knife] [on the table]
  g. [I] [put] [the knife] [on the table]
  h. [I] [put] [the knife on the table]
  i. . . .

Theoretically, all of these are conceivable, but of course, some are more common and others are harder to come by. Notably, many of these bracketings based on the information structure are unexpected from the syntactic point of view, for example, (d), (e), (f), and (h). In other words, the information structuring does not always match the syntactic structuring. We will further investigate the nature of this mismatch in the next section in terms of Optimal Syntax.

2.3 Structural Mismatches in Optimal Syntax

The mismatch between syntactic structure and information structure is, however, not totally unexpected considering the nature of the information that the two modules of grammar provide. The principles that tell us how grammatical features or functions are to be realized in the surface phrase structure, i.e. c(onstituent)-structure, and the principles that tell us how the information structure is to be realized in the c-structure may impose conflicting requirements on the c-structure. These potentially conflicting requirements are proposed in this paper to be OT constraints, which are violable and ranked.

2.3.1 Harmonic Alignment and Mismatches between Structures

As briefly mentioned at the beginning of the paper, the information flow between the parallel and copresent structures in LFG is governed by correspondence mapping constraints. Many of these parallel structures are defined by 'prominence' hierarchies, for example, the thematic hierarchy at a(rgument)-structure, the grammatical-functional hierarchy at f(unctional)-

structure (Bresnan, 2001), and the structural hierarchy defined by precedence and dominance at c-structure. If these different prominence relations correspond so that prominence on one level matches prominence on another, we have cases of 'harmonic alignment ' (Prince and Smolensky, 1993; Bresnan, 1998, 2000; Aissen, 2001; Morimoto, 1999; Lee, 2001). Therefore, the job of the correspondence constraints, in ideal situations, would be to ensure this harmonic alignment .

In word order phenomena, such lexical and grammatical information as case, thematic roles, grammatical functions, definiteness, and animacy, has been argued to play a role (Uszkoreit, 1984; Büring, 1997; Müller, 1998; Lee, 2001). Each kind of information has a certain prominence hierarchy associated with it, as illustrated in (12).

(12) 'Lexico-Grammatical Prominence' Hierarchies:
    a. Role: Agent > Beneficiary > Theme/Patient > Locative
    b. Case: Nominative > Accusative > Dative ...
    c. Definiteness: Definite > Indefinite
    d. Animacy: Human > Animate > Inanimate
    e. Grammatical Function: Subject > Object > Object$_\theta$ > Oblique > Adjunct

Suppose we have a sentence with two arguments. If one argument is nominative, agent, definite, and animate, and the other argument is accusative, patient, indefinite, and inanimate, then the first argument being the subject and the second the object would be an instance of harmonic alignment . Furthermore, if the first argument is mapped to a more prominent position than the second argument at c-structure, by the first being in a Specifier position and thus c-commanding the second in the Complement position, this would be an ideal case which generates the unmarked, canonical, or default order.

In fact, the lexical and grammatical information, as mentioned above, may not be represented in a single grammatical structure, but in several structures such as a-structure, f-structure, and probably also, s(semantic)-structure.[3] Each structure may have a direct correspondence relationship with the c-structure and could demand non-uniform requirements on the c-structure if arguments contain mismatching profiles of lexico-grammatical information. Suppose that we have agent and patient arguments in a sentence and the patient is the subject and the agent is an adjunct, that is, a passive sentence. In languages like English, the grammatical-functional hierarchy is more prominent than other lexico-grammatical hierarchies and therefore, the patient subject will take the more prominent c-structural po-

---

[3]It has also been argued that semantic information such as specificity and scope plays an important role in word order (Moltmann, 1990; Diesing, 1992; de Hoop, 1992; Büring, 1997). This type of information may be represented at a separate level such as s-structure and may directly interact with c-structure. This domain, though, is not investigated in this paper.

sition than the agent adjunct although the thematic hierarchy may demand the opposite. On the other hand, in languages such as German, Hindi, and Korean, the thematic hierarchy is as important (if not more so) as the grammatical functional hierarchy and thus the patient subject does not necessarily take the most prominent c-structural position (Lenerz, 1977; den Besten, 1982; Abraham, 1986; Webelhuth, 1992; Lee, 2001). Likewise, definiteness and animacy information can further complicate the mapping to the c-structure (Lenerz, 1977; Uszkoreit, 1984; Büring, 1997; Müller, 1998). Of course, all of these complications can be handled by different rankings of correspondence constraints in Optimality Theory (see Aissen (2001), Morimoto (1999), Asudeh (2001), and Lee (2001) for mismatch resolution of this kind). However, for the purposes of this paper, we will look only at the cases where all of these kinds of information converge (thus causing no mismatches) so that we can concentrate on the mismatches between the sentence-internal lexico-grammatical requirements on one hand and the discourse-contextual requirement on the other. Therefore, I will abstract away a little and assume that all of the lexico-grammatical information as shown in (12) is collected and converged in the f-structure, and use the following grammatical prominence hierarchy among arguments.[4]

(13) Grammatical Prominence Hierarchy:
    Subject > Dative Object (IO) > Accusative Object (DO) > Oblique

Now let us consider an example of correspondence between the lexico-grammatical information and the phrase structural configuration, represented here as the f-structure/c-structure correspondence. Recall the default-order examples in (1). In all three languages, the verb forms a VP with its complements separately from its subject, and the subject is in the most prominent position, c-commanding the other arguments of the sentence, although there exist some directional differences (for arguments for configurationality, see Webelhuth (1985) and Vallduví (1992) for German and Catalan respectively, among many others). This is illustrated in (14).

(14) a. English: [[John] [put [the knife] [on the table]]]
    b. German: [[Hans] hat [[das Messer] [auf den Tisch] gelegt]]
    c. Catalan: [[Va ficar [el ganivet] [damunt la taula]] [el Joan]]

The prominence hierarchy between the subject and the complements, and also between the complements is captured via the c-command or precedence relations. Also, the constituency of the predicate and the internal arguments is captured in terms of VP.

Conflicts may arise when discourse-contextual information comes into play. The conflicts can come from two sources. One comes from the mismatch in constituency and the other from the mismatch in prominence re-

---

[4]This hierarchy is not equivalent to the grammatical functional hierarchy in that the Dative Object is higher than the Accusative Object. This is to incorporate the thematic role hierarchy in part.

lations. That is, the prominence hierarchy at the i(information)-structure may be different from that of the f-structure, and also the constituency that the i-structure imposes on the c-structure may not be identical to the one that the grammatical relation demands on the c-structure, as briefly shown in section 2.2.2.

Of course, there are cases of further harmonic alignment where the i-structural demands either match or are compatible with the f-structural requirements. For example, in the all-focus context, there is no informational partition because the sentence is presented as a whole, i.e. as the single informational unit [+New]. Therefore, this i-structure does not cause any incompatibility with the f-structure requirements. This is illustrated in (15).

(15) a. What happened?
    b. i-s: [I put the knife on the table].

Also, a context like (16), in which the subject is [−New] and the VP is [+New], does not cause any conflict because the informational constituents match the syntactic constituents too.

(16) a. What did you do?
    b. i-s: [I] [put the knife on the table].

This structure could also represent the case where the subject is the topic, namely, where the syntactic prominence matches the informational prominence.[5]

However, there are many other contexts which give rise to mismatches, as demonstrated earlier in (11). For example, when the object is presented as given information as in (17), the informational constituency would be drastically different from the syntactic constituency. In the c-structure based on the grammatical information, as shown in (14), the subject NP [I] is one constituent and the VP [put the knife on the table] is another. In contrast, in the i-structure, which is illustrated in (17b), [the knife] is one ([−New]), and [I put on the table] forms another constituent, a focus domain ([+New]).

(17) a. What about the knife? What happened to the knife?
    b. i-s: [the knife]$_{[-New,+Prom]}$ [[I]$_{sbj}$ put on the table]$_{[+New,-Prom]}$

Furthermore, the informational prominence does not match the grammatical prominence in this example. In terms of f-structure, the subject 'I' is the most prominent information, but in terms of information structure, the object 'the knife' is the most prominent, being the topic of the sentence. The f-structure information would favor putting the subject [I]

---

[5]In Catalan, informational prominence requires a different type of c-structural prominence from what the f-structural prominence requires. Therefore, for a case like (16), the c-structural realization would not be the same. This is discussed in section 2.4.

in the most prominent c-structure position, but the i-structure information would demand us to put [the knife] there instead.

Languages differ in how they resolve these conflicts. Some languages are rather insensitive to the informational requirements and thus maintain their canonical phrase structures based on grammatical information throughout many different contexts. Other languages react fairly sensitively to the informational requirements and reshape their c-structures so that they closely resemble the given informational configuration. Among these languages, some are more sensitive to constituency and other languages more to the prominence hierarchy; some are more sensitive to [Prom] and others to [New]. In the remainder of this paper, we will examine how English, German, and Catalan differ in this respect.[6]

2.3.2 Optimal Syntax

The correspondence requirements or principles holding between the f-structure and the c-structure, and also between the i-structure and the c-structure, can be easily recast into Optimality-Theoretic constraints. Considering that the i-s/c-s correspondence is often inevitably conflicting with the f-s/c-s correspondence, the violability and rankedness of constraints (Prince and Smolensky, 1993) makes it easier to understand the interstructural correspondences and their mismatch resolution process. The 'optimal' output may not be perfect in that it may not satisfy all the constraints, and yet it is the 'best' possible that satisfies the constraints in a better way than any other candidates. Different rankings of the constraints in different languages allow us to have different 'optimal' results of the mismatch resolution.

We can think of the input as a combination of the lexico-grammatical information represented in primitive f-structure (Bresnan, 1996, 2000; Choi, 1996, 1999) and the discourse-contextual information reflected in i-structure. Note that the lexico-grammatical information is abstracted away and simplified such that all the information is converged as grammatical functions such as Subject, Object, etc., in the f-structure (section 2.3.1). The informational side of the input varies from context to context (section 2.2.2). Some possible i-structures are shown in (18).

---

[6]The mismatch resolution may not only be resolved by syntactic measures. Prosody is another domain which has a close connection with information structure and may have direct relevance to phrase structure (Reinhart, 1995; Zubizarreta, 1998; Büring, 1999). Morphological marking is also used for some languages. In this paper, I will put aside the morphological or prosodic realizations and only look at the syntactic realizations.

(18)   Input:

    a. $[\text{Sbj}]_{[+Prom,-New]}$, $[\text{Obj Obl V}]_{[-Prom,+New]}$

    b. $[\text{Sbj}]_{[+Prom,-New]}$, $[\text{Obj V}]_{[-Prom,-New]}$, $[\text{Obl}]_{[-Prom,+New]}$

    c. $[\text{Sbj}]_{[-Prom,-New]}$, $[\text{Obj}]_{[-Prom,+New]}$, $[\text{Obl}]_{[+Prom,-New]}$,
       $[\text{V}]_{[-Prom,-New]}$

    d. ...

One thing we should note here is that the grammatical information would not vary from speaker to speaker, but the i-structural information could vary even in the "same" discourse context, depending on the speaker's perception or intention. For example, consider a context where the object 'the knife' is presented as [−New] information, as in (19).

(19) a. What did you do with the knife?

    b. i-s1: $[\text{the knife}]_{[-Prom,-New]}$ $[\text{I put on the table}]_{[-Prom,+New]}$

    b′. i-s2: $[\text{the knife}]_{[+Prom,-New]}$ $[\text{I put on the table}]_{[-Prom,+New]}$

Suppose that the speaker of (a) presents 'the knife' non-prominently in (19). The speaker of (b) can perceive of it as non-prominent as the speaker of (a) intends it to be. Then the input will be (19b). Alternatively, however, the speaker of (b) could take 'the knife' as prominent, or deliberately intend it to be prominent for various reasons. Then, the input would have the [+Prom] marking for the 'knife', as in (19b′), instead of (19b), and the sentence will be produced according to such information. This variability in the i-structure input may be why people speak in different ways, namely, in different word orders, even in the "same" context.

F-s/C-s Constraints

As noted earlier, we have two separate types of constraints, one for the f-s/c-s correspondence and the other for the i-s/c-s correspondence. The f-s/c-s constraints would take care of the c-structure configuration based on the lexico-grammatical information such as Subject and Object provided in the f-structural input, whereas the i-s/c-s constraints would deal with the c-structural instantiation based on the information given in the i-structural input such as [Prom] and [New].

First of all, the f-s/c-s constraints in (20) will ensure that the arguments align with c-structure positions according to their lexico-grammatical prominence hierarchies which are demonstrated in (12) in section 2.3.1. For the purposes of this paper, this has been simplified and equated with the 'grammatical prominence' hierarchy in (13) (recall that the f-s/c-s correspondence is abstracted away from complications caused by mismatches in different hierarchies).

(20) F-s/C-s Constraints:
    a. SBJ: The subject aligns with the most prominent
                c-structure position.
    b. CMPL: Complements align according to the
                'grammatical prominence' hierarchy.

The basic idea of these constraints is that the 'grammatical' prominence
should match the 'structural' prominence. For example, constraint SBJ in
(20a) requires that the subject, the highest in the grammatical prominence
hierarchy, takes the most prominent c-structure position. The most prominent c-structure position, however, may vary from language to language,
defined by dominance and/or linear precedence depending on the language-
specific phrase structural organization. Similarly, constraint CMPL requires
the complement arguments to be positioned according to their 'grammatical' prominence.

To capture the basic phrase structural differences among the three languages, we first look at some c-structure constraints relevant to the X'-
theoretic tree structures. Recall the examples of sentences in default order
in (1) again, repeated here in (21). I assume the following tree structures
in (22) for each language.[7]

(21) a. English: John put the knife on the table.
     b. German: Hans hat das Messer auf den Tisch gelegt.
              Hans has the knife   on the table   put
              'Hans put the knife on the table.'
     c. Catalan: Va ficar   el ganivet damunt la taula el Joan.
              3-past-put the knife on the table   the Joan
              'Joan put the knife on the table.'

(22) a. English:

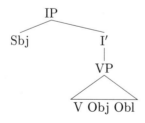

---

[7]For arguments for the phrase structures assumed here, see Bresnan (2001) for English, Choi (1996, 1999) for German and Vallduví (1992) for Catalan.

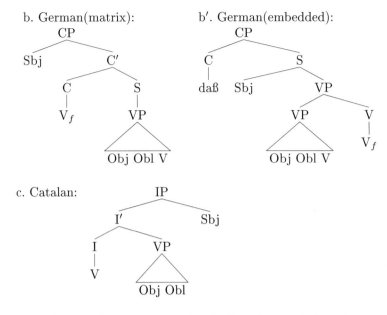

b. German(matrix):
CP

b'. German(embedded):
CP

c. Catalan:
IP

For the basic ordering between Head, Specifier, and Complement for each language under discussion, I propose the following alignment constraints in (23) (cf. Grimshaw, 1998; Vikner, 2001; Sells, 1998, 2000).

(23) C-structure Constraints:
a. SPEC-L: Specifier aligns left in its projection.
b. SPEC-R: Specifier aligns right in its projection.
c. HEAD-L: X^0 Head aligns left in its projection.
d. HEAD-R: X^0 Head aligns right in its projection.

The ranking between SPEC-L and SPEC-R will determine whether the Specifier (Spec) is on the left or right of the projection, and the ranking between HEAD-L and HEAD-R will further decide the alignment of the X^0 Head with respect to the Complement. Finally, the ranking between SPEC-L and HEAD-L or between SPEC-R and HEAD-R determines the order between the Spec and the X^0 Head, if there is competition between them.

Schematically speaking, English is an SVO language, Catalan is a VOS language, and German is basically SOV but turned to SVO (we will get to this shortly). Table (24) shows how the default order in each language would violate these constraints. (Note that this is not a regular tableau and constraints are not ranked in the table.) Accordingly, the constraints are ranked for each language in the last column.

(24)

V(S,O)		SP-L	SP-R	HD-L	HD-R
a.	SVO (Eng.)		**	*	*
b.	SOV (Ger.)		**	**	
c.	VOS (Cat.)	**			**
d.	OVS	**		*	*

SVO ranking: SP-L ≫ HD-L ≫ {SP-R, HD-R}
SOV ranking: {SP-L, HD-R} ≫ {SP-R, HD-L}
VOS ranking: {SP-R, HD-L} ≫ {SP-L, HD-R}
OVS ranking: SP-R ≫ HD-R ≫ {SP-L, HD-L}

As noted above, German has the SVO order (Verb Second) in matrix clauses, as shown in (21b), but SOV in embedded clauses, as illustrated in (25). This matrix/embedded asymmetry has been analyzed such that German is basically an SOV language but in matrix clauses, the finite verb is placed in the Head position (C) of the higher projection CP because of the Verb Second requirement. However, the Verb Second is blocked in embedded clauses because the head position (C) is already filled by a complementizer (Haider, 1985; Platzack, 1985; Taraldsen, 1985; Weerman, 1989; Vikner, 1995).

(25) a. Hans **hat** das Messer auf den Tisch gelegt. [SVO]
Hans has the knife on the table put
'Hans put the knife on the table.'

b. **daß** Hans das Messer auf den Tisch gelegt **hat**. [SOV]
that Hans the knife on the table put has
'that Hans put the knife on the table.'

The basic SOV order is captured by the ranking in (24b), but we need a few more constraints to handle the matrix/embedded difference. The main job of the constraints is to generate a left-headed functional projection, i.e. CP and to fill its Head with the finite verb for matrix clauses. The ranking among these and the ones above is given in (27).

(26) a. HEAD-L/fp: The Head of a functional projection aligns left.
b. OB-HD/fp: The Head of a functional projection (e.g., CP) should be filled.
c. COMP-L: Complementizer is the leftmost in its projection.

(27) German:
COMP-L ≫{SPEC-L, OB-HD/fp} ≫ HEAD-L/fp ≫ HEAD-R ≫ {SPEC-R, HEAD-L}

The constraint HEAD-L/fp requires that a functional Head be the leftmost, but since it is ranked lower than SPEC-L, we get the order of a Spec followed by a functional Head. Being ranked higher than HEAD-R (which is ranked higher than HEAD-L), HEAD-L/fp guarantees a functional projection (i.e. CP) to be left-headed while all the lower Heads are right-headed. Then, constraint OB-HD/fp requires that the Head of this highest projection be filled (cf. Ob-Hd/exp in Grimshaw (1998)). The obvious candidate for this position is the finite verb in a matrix clause and a complementizer in an embedded clause, each resulting in the existence or the lack of V2.

I assume that matrix clauses are all CP's (left-headed functional projection) in German, whether they are subject-initial or non-subject 'topic'-initial.[8] The higher ranking of SPEC-L over HEAD-L/fp provides us with a leftmost Spec position. As will be seen later in section 2.4.2, subject and 'topic' compete for this highest Spec position ([Spec,CP]), and if there is no topic ([+Prom]), the subject will take up this position. For embedded clauses, however, we would like the Spec position to be empty, which is true for other languages as well. Constraint COMP-L in (26c), which requires the complementizer to be the leftmost and is ranked higher than SPEC-L, will take care of this (cf. LeftEdge(CP) in Pesetsky (1997) or Lee (1998), 'the first (leftmost) pronounced word in CP must be the complementizer'). Due to this constraint, the default filler of this position, namely, the subject, will stay within S in embedded clauses, not filling the Spec of CP (*s that o v).[9]

Now, having set the basic c-structures, we can identify the most prominent c-structure position for the most prominent grammatical information, namely, the subject. Recall that the f-s/c-s constraint SBJ, introduced in (20), requires the subject to be in the most prominent c-structure position. For the languages under consideration, which are all configurational, the most prominent position is the highest Spec position which c-commands everything else. For English and German, which have SPEC-L ranked higher than SPEC-R, the highest Spec is the leftmost position. For Catalan, on the other hand, the highest Spec is the rightmost position since Catalan has SPEC-R ranked higher than SPEC-L. Therefore, we can reinterpret SBJ as a clause-level alignment constraint (Sells, 2000), that is, SBJ-L for English

---

[8]I do not assume the intermediate functional projection IP for subject-initial clauses in German. German is different from Icelandic or Scandinavian languages, which allow embedded V2 and thus seem to call for another functional projection (or two) below CP. German does not allow Verb Second in embedded clauses. Therefore, there is only one functional projection in the current account, which is CP, but it would not matter what we call it. The general constraint of 'economy of projection' would prohibit the generation of any unnecessary projections unless required by a higher-ranked constraint. However, the CP analysis is not crucial to the overall analysis of the paper. Vikner's (1995, 2001) analysis of V2, which assumes IP for the subject-initial sentence and CP for a non-subject topic-initial clause, would be compatible with the overall analysis. Then, of course, we need to explain why IP is left-headed in matrix clauses while it is right-headed in embedded clauses, which Vikner just assumes to be the case.

[9]Note that the ranking of COMP-L over SPEC-L does not lead to generating the Spec of CP on the right edge of CP due to the higher ranking of SPEC-L over SPEC-R. The subject in the right-edge Spec (*that o v s) would violate SPEC-L more seriously than the subject in [Spec,S] (that s o v).

and German, and SBJ-R for Catalan.[10] On the other hand, the other f-s/c-s constraint in (20) CMPL requires that complement arguments also align according to the 'grammatical prominence' hierarchy. Given the hierarchy of IO ≫ DO ≫ OBL, as shown in (13), it means that the dative object should precede (or c-command) the accusative object, and the accusative object, the oblique argument.[11] This constraint can also be expressed as clause-level alignment constraints as in Sells (2000). Then, CMPL is a group of alignment constraints ranked as follows: IO-L ≫ DO-L ≫ OBL-L. For considerations of space, though, I will put CMPL in the tableaux of this paper and add a mark * whenever the order of [IO DO Obl] is disturbed.

To summarize, the c-structure constraints demonstrated in (23) and (26) would set up the skeletal c-structures, and the f-s/c-s correspondence constraints as in (20) fill in the arguments according to their lexico-grammatical prominence hierarchies, which will give us the default or canonical structure as shown in (28) for each language.

(28) Output (c-s):
    a. English: [[Sbj] [V Obj Obl]]
    b. German: [[Sbj] V_f [Obj Obl (V)]]
    c. Catalan: [[V Obj Obl] [Sbj]]

However, if there are other types of prominence hierarchies than the grammatical prominence hierarchy, such as informational prominence hierarchies, and if these also put pressure on the arguments to align according to their hierarchies, then the argument positions could change. We will explore this issue in what follows.

I-s/C-s Constraints

Parallel to the f-s/c-s correspondence constraints that we have just seen, there are i-s/c-s correspondence constraints which would handle the mapping between i-structure and c-structure. This set of constraints may conflict with the f-s/c-s constraints and yield informationally-motivated non-canonical c-structures. I propose that these i-s/c-s alignment constraints are to align the informational prominence in the i-structure with the structural prominence in the c-structure. Suppose we have two kinds of informational hierarchies based on the features [Prom] and [New], as in (29).

---

[10]This does not mean, however, that SBJ replaces SPEC because obviously the subject is not the only element that can take a Spec position. What the SPEC-L/R constraint does is to generate a Spec position in the right direction for a particular language whenever it is needed, for example, for a *wh*-word or a topic/focus element. We will address this issue in section 2.4.2 when we discuss topicalization.

[11]In the current framework, the grammatical functions or the case relations are not defined by the c-structural configuration. Therefore, the arguments are mapped to the c-structural positions according to their prominence hierarchies. However, in a framework in which the grammatical and case relations are defined by the c-structural positions, constraints that govern the argument positions are defined through case requirements. See, for example, CASEADJ in Samek-Lodovici (2001), SUBJ-CASE and OBJ-CASE in Costa (1996, 2001), and NOM/SPECIP and ACC/COMPLV in Legendre (1998).

(29) a. [+Prom] > [−Prom]
    b. [+New] > [−New]

Languages may differ as to which direction they take to align these 'prominent' elements, i.e. [+Prom] and [+New]. I propose the following four constraints in (30).

(30) I-s/C-s Alignment Constraints:
    a. Prom-L: [+Prom] aligns left in the clause.
    b. Prom-R: [+Prom] aligns right in the clause.
    c. New-L: [+New] aligns left in the clause.
    d. New-R: [+New] aligns right in the clause.

Similar constraints have been proposed elsewhere. For example, Top-First in Costa (2001) and Top-L in Sells (2000) are close kins to Prom-L, the only difference being that Prom-L would include 'contrastive focus' ([+Prom,+New]) as well as 'topic' ([+Prom,−New]). All three languages we are looking at in this paper have Prom-L rather than Prom-R. New-R can find resemblance in Foc in Müller (1998), and AlignFocus in Samek-Lodovici (1996), Grimshaw and Samek-Lodovici (1998), Legendre (1998), and Costa (2001).[12] Some languages align 'focus' leftward (New-L), including Catalan, as we will see shortly. Some languages like Kanakuru even align 'focus' in both directions as suggested by Samek-Lodovici (2001) (cf. AF_{left}, AF_{right}).

It is clear how these alignment constraints will be interpreted if each element bears an individual information feature assignment. Suppose that

---

[12]Aligning [New] or 'focus' rightward is often captured by prosodic constraints rather than discourse constraints as proposed here, such as AccentAlign in Keller and Alexopoulou (1999). Assuming that every [+New] information gets pitch accent (e.g., [+Ń] in Choi (1996,1999)) and that [+New] aligns rightward, the same range of data can be captured either by discourse constraints or by prosodic constraints. However, there are cases in which 'accenting' does not converge with 'focus'. These are wider focus cases, where a bigger unit than an individual word or phrase is in focus. In such cases, the accent seems to fall on the right edge of the [+New] domain, for vo languages like English and Catalan, as shown below. This will be handled if we posit a constraint like AlignAccent requiring that 'the accent be aligned with the right edge of the [+New] domain.'

  (i) a. I [put the knife on the TABLE]$_{[+New]}$.
     b. I [put the KNIFE]$_{[+New]}$ on the table.
     c. I [PUT]$_{[+New]}$ the knife on the table.

For ov languages like German, the accent seems to fall on the penultimate element when the whole VP is the [+New] domain, but when the V′, [put the knife], is the [+New] domain, things are not as straightforward because of the possibility like (iib′). Some deaccenting mechanism seems necessary for such a case, e.g., *[−Ń].

  (ii) a. Ich habe [das Messer auf den TISCH gelegt]$_{[+New]}$.
      b. Ich habe auf den Tisch [das MESSER gelegt]$_{[+New]}$.
      b′. Ich habe [das MESSER [auf den Tisch]$_{[−New]}$ gelegt]$_{[+New]}$.

This issue certainly calls for a closer look, which is beyond the scope of this paper. For more prosodically-oriented accounts of word order variation, see Reinhart (1995) and Büring (1999) for German, and Zubizarreta (1998) for Romance languages.

we have three elements X Y Z in a sentence and each is assigned [New] as in the input in (31), namely, Y is [+New] and X and Z each is [−New]. Take constraint NEW-L, for example. NEW-L requires Y to be the leftmost, so (31c) is the candidate that does not violate this constraint at all. In (31a), however, Y is in the middle, so it violates this constraint once. In (31b), Y is sentence-final and has two elements ahead of it, so it violates NEW-L twice.

(31)

input: $X_{[-New]}$ $Y_{[+New]}$ $Z_{[-New]}$	NEW-L
a. $[\ X\ ]_{[-New]}$ $[\ Y\ ]_{[+New]}$ $[\ Z\ ]_{[-New]}$	*
b. $[\ X\ ]_{[-New]}$ $[\ Z\ ]_{[-New]}$ $[\ Y\ ]_{[+New]}$	**
c. $[\ Y\ ]_{[+New]}$ $[\ X\ ]_{[-New]}$ $[\ Z\ ]_{[-New]}$	

Now, what if [+New] is a domain and contains more than one element? Suppose that [X Y] is [+New]. Since the domain is assigned the information features as a whole, no individual element, neither X nor Y, has an independent feature marking. So, in a situation like (32b), where the [+New] domain is interrupted by a [−New] element [Z], it is not clear whether this violates NEW-L at all, or NEW-R, since neither X nor Y has any feature assignment.

(32)

input: $[X\ Y]_{[+New]}$ $Z_{[-New]}$	NEW-L
a. $[\ X\ Y\ ]_{[+New]}$ $[\ Z\ ]_{[-New]}$	*
b. $[\ X\ [\ Z\ ]_{[-New]}\ Y\ ]_{[+New]}$	**
c. $[\ Z\ ]_{[-New]}$ $[\ X\ Y\ ]_{[+New]}$	***

Thus, for an information domain, I will interpret the i-s alignment constraints in (30) such that 'a domain aligns if and only if every member of the domain aligns'. In other words, $[\ X\ Y\ ]_{[+New]}$ will be interpreted in practice as if it were $[\ X\ ]_{[+New]}$ $[\ Y\ ]_{[+New]}$. If we compare (32a) and (32b), the candidate with the broken i-structure domain, namely, (32b) violates the constraint more seriously than candidate (32a) with the unbroken domain. This interpretation of alignment constraints can provide a way of securing an i-structure domain also as a c-structure constituent as far as the direction of alignment conforms. However, if the direction of alignment is the opposite as in (32c), the candidate is penalized most seriously even if it has its i-s domain [X Y] unbroken. NEW-L, after all, is a leftward alignment constraint. In the languages we are considering in this paper, we do not find instances where candidate (32c) with the unbroken domain in the wrong direction wins over (32b), which has the domain broken but does better in alignment. If we had such a case, we would need a 'domain' constraint such as NEW-DOM, apart from the alignment constraints, which would penalize (32b) more than (32c) (Choi, 1997b).

2.4 Optimal Resolutions

The c-s and f-s/c-s constraints are potentially in conflict with the i-s/c-s constraints because the syntactic information may not converge with the discourse information in i-structure. As noted earlier in section 2.3.1, syntactic constituents may not be identical to i-s constituents; or the grammatically most prominent element may not be the i-structurally most prominent. Given the constraints proposed in section 2.3.2, these mismatches between the syntactic information and the discourse-contextual information can be resolved in the Optimality-Theoretic manner, via language-specific constraint rankings.

The most ideal or harmonic case would be the case where the nominative, agentive subject is also the topic of the sentence and the VP is the focus, and thus the subject, which is also the topic, takes the most prominent position (e.g., highest Spec) in phrase structure and the VP remains intact. Then, we get the most harmonic topic-comment/ground-focus partition, which also matches the syntactic partition, as illustrated in (33).

(33)   Subject   [Verb Object Oblique]$_{VP}$
       Topic [+Prom]   Comment [−Prom]
       Ground [−New]   Focus [+New]

This parallelism and the naturalness of the context is probably the reason that sometimes the subject-topic structure, instead of the all-focus or no-context case, is regarded as unmarked, default, or canonical.[13] However, things do not always fall out this way. We will examine the resolution process of some of the mismatch cases via language-particular rankings among the c-s, f-s/c-s, and i-s/c-s constraints introduced in section 2.3. The most relevant constraints are listed again below.

(34) Constraints:
      a. HEAD: HEAD-L, HEAD-R, HEAD-L/fp, OB-HD/fp
      b. SPEC: SPEC-L
      c. SBJ: SBJ-L, SBJ-R
      d. CMPL: IO-L, DO-L, OBL-L
      e. PROM: PROM-L
      f. NEW: NEW-L, NEW-R

First, we will examine the scrambling and detachment phenomena as instances of c-structural instantiations of [New] information. Therefore, this will be viewed as a ranked interaction between the syntactic constraints in (34a,b,c,d) and the NEW constraints in (34f). Then, topicalization and focus-preposing will be investigated as cases of c-structural realizations of the [Prom] information. Accordingly, the rankings of PROM and the rest will be examined.

---

[13]This may be why SVO (subject-topic structure), instead of VOS (all-focus structure), is often claimed as the default order in Catalan.

2.4.1 Scrambling and Detachment

We have seen how English, German, and Catalan behave differently in a focus context, i.e. when the sentence is partitioned by [New]. Referring back to examples (2), (3), and (4) again and describing the situation schematically with respect to [New] information: English does not allow a non-canonical c-structure (2b′); German allows both the canonical and a non-canonical structure (3b, 3b′); and finally, Catalan only allows a non-canonical structure (4b′). This tells us, even before looking more closely, that in English, the i-s/c-s constraint relevant to the [New] information, generically represented as NEW, is ranked lower than the f-s/c-s constraints SBJ or CMPL. In contrast, the ranking of the constraints is the reverse in Catalan. German appears to tie NEW and CMPL to get both orders in (3b) and (3b′) but to rank SBJ higher, as we will see below. Also, Catalan and German differ in terms of the direction they align [+New]: Catalan aligns [+New] to the left while German aligns [+New] to the right. In terms of constraint ranking, this means that Catalan ranks NEW-L higher than NEW-R, whereas German ranks NEW-R higher than NEW-L.

(35) Constraint Rankings:
   a. English: SBJ-L ≫ HEAD-L ≫ CMPL ≫ NEW-R
   b. German: SBJ-L ≫ HEAD-L/fp ≫ HEAD-R ≫ {NEW-R, CMPL} ≫ NEW-L
   c. Catalan: NEW-L ≫ HEAD-L ≫ SBJ-R ≫ CMPL ≫ NEW-R

Another noticeable point in the behavior of these languages is the flexibility of the verb position. In German, for instance, the verb *gelegt* 'put', unlike the PP or NP arguments, cannot scramble (i.e. left-adjoined to VP or S), as shown in (3b′), even if the i-structure demands so (NEW-R). In contrast, the verb *va ficar* 'put' in Catalan is detached (i.e. right-adjoined to IP) along with other arguments, as shown in (4b′). This difference can be accounted for by a ranking between NEW and HEAD constraints. Recall that in German, HEAD-R, which is ranked higher than HEAD-L, requires that the Head aligns to the right. This constraint HEAD-R is ranked higher than NEW-R in German so that even if the verb is [−New], it will maintain its rightmost position in VP because a violation of HEAD-R is more serious than a violation of NEW-R. Of course, the higher ranking of HEAD-L/fp (and OB-HD/fp) over HEAD-R would always keep the finite verb in the left-headed Head C in matrix clauses regardless of its [New] status. On the other hand, Catalan has HEAD-L ranked higher than HEAD-R so that the verb aligns left in its local projection. In contrast to German, Catalan has NEW-L higher than HEAD-L so that if the verb is [−New], then it loses its leftmost position and scrambles rightward.

With this much of an overview, let us examine each case more closely now. Due to space limitations, we will focus only on the crucial competitions and thus we may not see all the effects that have been described above and implied in each ranking of the constraints. Note that in this section, we look only at the cases in which the sentence is i-structured only by the [New] feature and no part of the sentence is [Prom]. The [Prom] cases will be discussed in section 2.4.2.

Catalan Right Detachment

We will first look at the most dramatic case, the Catalan right detachment. First, let us go back to example (4) again, which is repeated below as (36). In this example, [el ganivet] is the focus, that is, [+New], and other elements of the sentence are each marked [−New]. Note that the subject *el Joan* or the pronoun 'he' is *pro*-dropped. A [−New] subject is most likely to *pro*-drop in Catalan but does not leave a clitic unlike other arguments. In example (36), *hi* is a locative clitic coindexed with the [−New] PP *damunt la taula*, right-detached in this case.

(36) a. What did Joan put on the table?
    b. [El GANIVET], hi$_i$ va ficar   damunt la taula$_i$.
       the knife   cl 3-past-put on the table
       'He put the knife on the table.'

Having the ranking of New-L higher than any other syntactic constraints as established in (35), this case is rather straightforward: the [+New] element, [el ganivet] 'the knife', aligns left in the clause. If we follow Vallduví (1992), this is an extreme case of the rightward detachment. Everything that is [−New] moves out and is right-adjoined to IP and thus leaves [el ganivet], the [+New], alone in IP.[14]

(37)

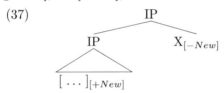

Note that even the verb cannot stay in IP. This shows that Head-L is ranked lower than New-L. Look at the tableau below.

(38) Input: [put]$_{[-New]}$ [the knife]$_{[+New]}$ [on the table]$_{[-New]}$

	New-L	Hd-L	Sbj-R	Cmpl	New-R
a.	*!				*
b.	*!*			*	
☞ c.		*			**

a. = [Hi va ficar el ganivet damunt la taula]$_{IP}$
b. = [[Hi va ficar damunt la taula]$_{IP}$ el ganivet]
c. = [[El ganivet]$_{IP}$ hi va ficar damunt la taula]

---

[14] I assume that each [−New] element in (36b) is adjoined to IP separately, resulting in a series of IP adjunctions. This is supported by the fact that the order among the right-detached items is free (Vallduví, 1992).

Candidate (a) is in the default order, or it may be the case that the [−New] [damunt la taula] 'on the table' is right-detached, i.e. right-adjoined to IP. But in either case, candidate (a) has the same violation profile. This candidate satisfies Head-L by leaving the verb in situ, but hence violates New-L. Similarly, candidate (b) satisfies Head-L but violates New-L. Here, the [+New] [el ganivet], instead of the [−New] elements, is detached. If Catalan aligned 'focus' rightward (that is, if Catalan ranked New-R higher than New-L), this would be the winning candidate. Candidate (c) is the winner in which all the [−New] are detached rightward including the verb so that it perfectly satisfies New-L. This violates Head-L, but since it is ranked lower than New-L in this language, (c) is the optimal output.

As illustrated above, the c-structure in Catalan responds aggressively to the i-structural requirement on [New]. Any non-focal, i.e. [−New], element should be detached rightward so that the focal ([+New]) element can be the leftmost. In fact, this narrow focus case such as (36) could be analyzed as an instance of focus-preposing, in which the [+New] is detached leftward, i.e. left-adjoined to IP, instead of all the others being right-adjoined. Actually, New-L itself would not have a preference either way, namely, whether [+New] is detached leftward or [−New] is detached rightward. However, this can be a problem for syntax in a wider-focus example, as we will see later. Therefore, I adopt the right-detachment analysis for the [+New] alignment, following Vallduví (1992). I do not claim, however, that there is no left-adjunction in Catalan. As we will see in section 2.4.2, topicalization and focus-preposing are cases of left-adjunction in Catalan. One thing to note is that Catalan focus-preposing (which preposes a [+Prom] focus) is not distinguishable from the regular ([−Prom]) focus case on the surface because both [+New] and [+Prom] align to the same direction, that is, to the left.[15] This issue will be discussed in section 2.4.2

Now, what about the subject focus case? As can be seen in (39), the subject does not behave any differently in Catalan. All the [−New] elements are detached rightward so that the [+New] subject can stay within IP and align on the left.

(39) a. Who will set the table?
   b. La COIA, la$_i$ pararà la taula$_i$.
   Coia   cl fut-set the table
   'Coia will set the table.'

In Catalan, New-L not only outranks Head-L but also Sbj-R. Therefore, candidate (c) in (40) is the optimal output because it satisfies New-L although it violates Sbj-R and Head-L.

---

[15] Vallduví (1992) argues against the existence of focus-preposing ([+Prom] focus) in Catalan. The surface similarity of the two constructions in Catalan is probably the reason that the contrastive focus ([+Prom,+New]) is not distinguished from the completive focus ([−Prom,+New]) in Vallduví's information packaging system.

(40)   Input: [Coia]$_{[+New]}$ [set]$_{[-New]}$ [the table]$_{[-New]}$

	New-L	Hd-L	Sbj-R	Cmpl	New-R
a.	*!*				
b.	*!		*		*
☞ c.		*	**		**

a. = [La parará la taula la Coia]$_{IP}$
b. = [[La parará la Coia]$_{IP}$ la taula]
c. = [[La Coia]$_{IP}$ la parará la taula]

Now, let's see a wider focus example. (41) is a context where the object is given information ([−New]) and the remaining part of VP is focus ([+New]). Here again, the [−New] subject 'I' is *pro*-dropped. This is a situation where an i-structural domain [put on the table] is not a syntactic constituent.[16]

(41) a. What did you do with the knife?
   b. *El$_i$ vaig ficar   [el ganivet]$_i$ damunt la TAULA.
      cl   1-past-put the knife   on the table
      'I put the knife on the table.'
   b'. El$_i$ vaig ficar   damunt la TAULA, [el ganivet]$_i$.
      cl   1-past-put on the table   the knife
      'I put the knife on the table.'

(42) Input: [I]$_{[-New]}$ [put on the table]$_{[+New]}$ [the knife]$_{[-New]}$

	New-L	Hd-L	Sbj-R	Cmpl
a.	**!			
☞ b.	*			*
c.	**!*	*		

a. = [El vaig ficar el ganivet damunt la taula]$_{IP}$
b. = [[El vaig ficar damunt la taula]$_{IP}$ el ganivet]
c. = [El ganivet [el vaig ficar damunt la taula]$_{IP}$]

Candidate (a) is the case in which [el ganivet], the [−New], is in the middle of the [+New] domain, breaking the i-structure domain of [put on the table]. Recall how constraint New-L applies to a domain as discussed in section

---

[16] If we take the left-adjunction analysis, we should say that [put on the table] is left-adjoined to IP rather than [the knife] being adjoined to the right. This is not plausible because, first of all, [put on the table] is not even a c-structure constituent to be involved in a syntactic operation. An alternative in which *put* and *on the table* each is left-adjoined separately may not be very plausible either. This latter option would be possible if [put] and [on the table] each were an independent informational unit and hence separately had an individual feature assignment, under the assumption that informationally-motivated operations target informational units only. However, unlike the [−New] case, where each element can be assigned an individual feature marking depending on the context, e.g., [put]$_{[-New]}$ [on the table]$_{[-New]}$, as seen above (see footnote 14), the [+New] domain hardly breaks (see the discussion in section 2.2.2 again). In other words, [put]$_{[+New]}$ [on the table]$_{[+New]}$ would not be a possible i-s structuring option.

2.3.2. Among the components of the [+New] domain, the finite verb *vaig ficar* is the leftmost, hence satisfying NEW-L, but the PP argument *damunt la taula* is preceded by two elements, thus causing two violations of NEW-L. Actually, due to the way we interpret the constraint, the optimal candidate (b) also incurs a violation to NEW-L because *damunt la taula* incurs one violation while *vaig ficar* incurs none. Yet this candidate is the optimal output since it incurs the fewest number of violations of NEW-L among the three candidates. On the other hand, candidate (c), where [el ganivet] is left-adjoined to IP, violates NEW-L most seriously because none of the [+New] domain aligns left.[17] This candidate has the i-s domain intact but the alignment is in the wrong direction. As a result, we have the candidate that leaves the information domain unbroken and also aligns it to the left as the optimal output without positing a separate domain constraint. In other words, due to the high ranking of the NEW constraint, Catalan can keep its informational domain intact and aligned, which is in contrast with the German case, as we will see shortly.

To summarize, the Catalan c-structure highly resembles the i-structure configuration with respect to the [New] feature: it keeps [+New] (whether individual or domain) in front of [−New], as far as [Prom] is not involved. It is due to the higher ranking of the i-s/c-s constraint NEW-L over all the relevant syntactic constraints, i.e. HEAD-L, SBJ-R, and CMPL.

German Scrambling

German scrambling is different from Catalan detachment in several aspects. As shown in (35), the i-s/c-s NEW constraint does not completely outrank (but ties) the f-s/c-s constraint CMPL.[18] Also, it is outranked by SBJ. Thus, as far as the [New] feature is concerned, the surface c-structures are fairly close to the canonical c-structure with minor variations between complements. In addition, NEW-R does not outrank HEAD-R either, let alone the V2 constraints such as HEAD-L/fp, and therefore, the positions of verb(s) are rather fixed. I will assume that the V2 structure is taken care of in the following examples but will not show the V2 constraints in the tableaux due to space limitations.

The well-known 'focus constraint' which prohibits a [+New] phrase from scrambling (Lenerz, 1977; Abraham, 1986; Webelhuth, 1992) can be easily accounted for if we have an alignment constraint NEW-R ranked higher than NEW-L, the reverse of the Catalan case. This is shown in (44) below. Whatever the ranking is between NEW-R and CMPL, leftward scrambling of the [+New] element, [das Buch] would not be motivated because this move violates both NEW-R and CMPL.

---

[17] I assume that [put on the table] cannot right-adjoin to IP as a single constituent especially when it is [+New]. See the past few footnotes.

[18] 'Tied' constraints may be represented in different ways in Optimality Theory. See Boersma (1997) and Asudeh (2001) for different ways of handling "ties".

(43) a. What did you give to the child?

 b. Ich habe dem Kind das BUCH geschenkt.

  I have the child the book given

  'I gave the child the book.'

 b'. *Ich habe das BUCH dem Kind geschenkt.

  I have the book the child given

  'I gave the book to the child.'

(44) Input: $[I]_{[-New]}$ [the child]$_{[-New]}$ [given]$_{[-New]}$ [the book]$_{[+New]}$

		SBJ-L	HD-R	NEW-R	CMPL
☞ a.				*	
b.				*!*	*
c.			*!		

a. = [Ich habe [dem Kind das Buch geschenkt]]

b. = [Ich habe [das Buch [dem Kind geschenkt]]]

c. = [Ich habe [dem Kind [geschenkt [das Buch]]]]

In this competition for the optimal order, the default-order candidate (a), (43b), is the winner. Candidate (b), seen also in (43b'), loses to this candidate because (b) adds a violation mark to NEW-R and also to CMPL by scrambling the [+New] [das Buch] leftward. Candidate (c) aligns [+New] on the right edge by scrambling the [−New] verb *geschenkt* and hence satisfies NEW-R. However, since HEAD-R is ranked higher than NEW-R, candidate (c) loses to (a) too. Note that the violation of HEAD-R by the finite verb *habe* is omitted in the tableau for simplicity. Candidate (c) is the mirror-image of the optimal candidate in the Catalan counterpart, shown in (36), only the direction of [+New] alignment being opposite (recall that in Catalan, both HEAD-L and CMPL are ranked lower than NEW). The reverse ranking of HEAD and NEW makes this candidate a dispreferred choice in German.

 Example (45) is an instance which shows the ranking between NEW-R and CMPL. This is essentially parallel to example (3) which was introduced earlier. In this case, both the default-order candidate (45b) and the scrambled candidate (45b') are acceptable. This implies that neither NEW-R nor CMPL is ranked higher (or lower) with respect to each other.

(45) a. Who did you give the book to?

 b. Ich habe dem KIND das Buch geschenkt.

  I have the child the book given

  'I gave the child the book.'

 b'. Ich habe das Buch dem KIND geschenkt.

  I have the book the child given

  'I gave the book to the child.'

(46) Input: $[\text{I}]_{[-New]}$ [the child]$_{[+New]}$ [the book]$_{[-New]}$ [given]$_{[-New]}$

		SBJ-L	HD-R	NEW-R	CMPL
☞	a.			**	
☞	b.			*	*
	c.			*!	*

a. = [Ich habe [dem Kind das Buch geschenkt]]
b. = [Ich habe [das Buch [dem Kind geschenkt]]]
c. = [Ich habe [das Buch [geschenkt [dem Kind]]]]

Candidate (c) is immediately eliminated from consideration because it violates the highest-ranking constraint where the candidates conflict, that is, HEAD-R. As mentioned above, this would be a winning candidate in the Catalan counterpart although the direction of scrambling is opposite due to NEW-L. Candidate (a) incurs two violation marks on NEW-R because the [−New], both [das Buch] and [geschenkt], follow the [+New]. On the other hand, candidate (b) incurs only one mark on NEW-R since the [−New] [das Buch] is scrambled leftward, but by doing so, this candidate incurs a mark on CMPL. However, as NEW-R and CMPL are not ranked with respect to each other, both candidates emerge as optimal.

The next question is whether the [New] domain is respected in German as it is in Catalan. Consider an example where 'the book' is [−New] and [give to the child] composes a [+New] domain. Then, in the canonical structure, the [−New] [das Buch] is in the middle of [+New] domain. This is shown in (47) below.

(47) a. What did you do with the book?
  b. Ich habe dem KIND das Buch geschenkt.
  I   have the child   the book given
  'I gave the child the book.'
  b′. Ich habe das Buch dem KIND geschenkt.
  I   have the book the child   given
  'I gave the book to the child.'

Here again, we see that both the canonical and the scrambled structures are acceptable. It is because the NEW constraint NEW-R in German does not outrank CMPL, which is unlike the case in Catalan. Therefore, we get two optimal outputs in this context too.

(48) Input: $[\text{I}]_{[-New]}$ [the book]$_{[-New]}$ [the child given]$_{[+New]}$

		SBJ-L	HD-R	NEW-R	CMPL
☞	a.			**	
☞	b.			*	*
	c.			***	
				*!	

 a. = [Ich habe [dem Kind das Buch geschenkt]]
 b. = [Ich habe [das Buch [dem Kind geschenkt]]]
 c. = [Ich habe [dem Kind [geschenkt [das Buch]]]]

Candidate (c) is ruled out because it violates HEAD-R most seriously. Candidate (a), which breaks the [+New] domain because the [−New] [das Buch] is in the middle of the [+New] domain, violates NEW-R twice due to *dem Kind* not being on the right edge. But since this is the default-order candidate, it does not violate CMPL. Candidate (b), on the other hand, violates NEW-R less seriously by scrambling [das Buch] leftward and thus putting *dem Kind* together with *geschenkt*, which also makes the [+New] domain nicely align right. However, by doing so, it violates CMPL. If NEW-R were ranked higher than CMPL, the candidate (b), which keeps the [+New] domain unbroken, would be the only optimal output, just as it is the case in Catalan. However, NEW-R is not ranked higher than CMPL, so candidate (a) is also optimal. In other words, the [New] domain is not necessarily respected in German, due to the low ranking of NEW.

 Finally, we will examine a subject case to see if the subject is affected by [New] in this language. Suppose that the subject is [+New], the focus, as in (49). Provided that no other constituent is [+Prom], namely, in a topic-less context, only the default-structure candidate is the optimal output.

(49) a. Who read the book?
  b. Hans hat das Buch gelesen.
   Hans has the book read
   'Hans read the book.'
  b′. *Das Buch hat Hans gelesen.
   the book has Hans read
   'The book Hans read.'

(50) Input: [Hans]$_{[+New]}$ [read]$_{[-New]}$ [the book]$_{[-New]}$

	SBJ-L	HD-L/fp	HD-R	NEW-R
☞ a.		*	**	***
b.	*!*	*	**	*
c.	*!**	*	***	

 a. = [Hans hat [das Buch gelesen]]
 b. = [Das Buch hat [Hans gelesen]]
 c. = [Das Buch hat [gelesen [Hans]]]

The choice in this competition can be rather simply explained if we rank the f-s/c-s constraint SBJ-L higher than the i-s/c-s constraints, NEW-R. In other words, the subject is not influenced by the [New] feature at all and keeps its prominent c-structure position whether it is [−New] or [+New] because of the higher ranking of SBJ-L. The situation changes, though, if the [Prom] feature is considered. We will see this in the next section.

To summarize, the c-structure in German is not as faithful to the i-structural input on [New] as the c-structure in Catalan is. First of all, German does not allow any repositioning of the verb. This is because Head-R is ranked higher than New-R, as we have seen above. Thus, no verbs will be scrambled. Second, since the f-s/c-s constraint Sbj-L is ranked higher than the New-R constraints, the subject would also be in its initial position regardless of its status as [New]. Finally, New-R interacts with Cmpl, but does not outrank it, so that German always allows the canonical-order candidate as optimal, at least in the [New] contexts. Also, for this reason, the [+New] domain is not maintained intact.

2.4.2 Topicalization and Focus-Preposing

Topicalization and focus-preposing (or focus-topicalization) share the same c-structural instantiation in many languages including English, German, and Catalan. All three languages place the topic and also a contrastive or emphatic focus at the left edge of the sentence, whether it is a Spec position or an adjoined position depending on the c-structural requirements of the particular language. The feature-based information structure adopted here enables us to handle these two constructions in a uniform manner as motivated by the same driving force, namely, the [Prom] feature. As briefly discussed in section 2.2.2, topic and contrastive/emphatic focus share the [+Prom] property in this model even if they differ in the [New] property: topic is [−New] and contrastive/emphatic focus is [+New] (see Choi (1996,1999) for motivations and discussions of the proposal).

I argue that topicalization and focus-preposing are driven by the i-structure/c-structure correspondence constraint Prom-L in all three languages.[19] This constraint is ranked higher than the New constraints and also than the f-s/c-s constraints such as Sbj so that a [+Prom] element, whether [−New] or [+New], wins over the subject and takes the most prominent c-structure position, i.e. the leftmost position. I propose the following revisions to the rankings for each language, and we will see each case below.

(51)　　Constraint Rankings:

    a. English: Prom-L ≫ Sbj-L ≫ Spec-L ≫ Head-L ≫ Cmpl ≫ New-R

    b. German: Spec-L ≫ Prom-L ≫ Sbj-L ≫ Head-L/fp ≫ Head-R ≫ {Cmpl, New-R}

    c. Catalan: Prom-L ≫ New-L ≫ Head-L ≫ Sbj-R ≫ Cmpl

---

[19]See Vikner (2001), for example, for a different account of topicalization in German. His constraint V2, which requires that 'a topic/operator should be in the specifier posi tion of CP or higher', is comparable to Prom-L in the current account but a difference lies in that Prom-L does not specify the position to be a Spec and thus allows a leftward adjunction as well as a left Spec to satisfy the constraint, and thus can capture the focus-preposing as well as scrambling by the same account.

Note that the relative ranking of the c-structure constraint SPEC-L with respect to PROM-L and SBJ-L plays a significant role in determining whether a [+Prom] will be adjoined or be in a Spec position. In German, for example, SPEC-L as well as PROM-L is ranked higher than SBJ-L so that whatever is the leftmost should be in a Spec position, barring a leftmost adjunction. It is this ranking that makes the subject and the [+Prom] compete for a single position, i.e. the leftmost Spec position. In English, in contrast, SPEC-L is ranked lower than PROM-L and SBJ-L. Therefore, the [+Prom] does not need to be in a Spec position. The contrast is illustrated in (52) and (53) below.

(52)   Input: [dem Kind]$_{[+Prom]}$ [ich]$_{[-Prom]}$

	SP-L	PROM-L	SBJ-L	HD-L/fp
a.		*!		*
b.	*!		*	**
☞ c.			**	*

a. = [$_{CP}$ Ich habe [dem Kind das Buch geschenkt]]
b. = [$_{CP}$ Dem Kind [$_{CP}$ ich habe [das Buch geschenkt]]]
c. = [$_{CP}$ Dem Kind habe [ich das Buch geschenkt]]

(53)   Input: [the knife]$_{[+Prom]}$ [I]$_{[-Prom]}$

	PROM-L	SBJ-L	SP-L	HD-L
a.	*!*			*
☞ b.		*	*	**
c.		*!*		*

a. = [$_{IP}$ I put the knife on the TABLE]
b. = [$_{IP}$ The knife [$_{IP}$ I put on the TABLE]]
c. = [$_{CP}$ The knife did [$_{IP}$ I put on the TABLE]]

The subject-initial clause (a) is out in both languages because of the higher ranking of PROM-L over SBJ-L. In German, candidate (c) with the [+Prom] in [Spec,CP] wins over candidate (b) with the [+Prom] adjoined to CP because of the higher ranking of SPEC-L. In English, on the other hand, the choice will be (b), the adjoined structure, due to the lower ranking of SPEC-L than SBJ-L.

English Topicalization

As noted earlier in section 2.3.2, the [Prom] marking is variable according to the individual speaker's intention or perception of the context. Even to the same question like (54a), speaker (b) could have three different ways of answering it according to her/his speech purposes.

(54) a. Where did you put the knife?
     b. I put [the knife] [on the TABLE].

b'. [The knife] I put [on the TABLE].

b''. [On the TABLE] I put [the knife].

What is invariable in the answers is that [on the table] is [+New] and all other constituents are [−New] (assume that this is a context which calls for an individual [−New] assignment for each element instead of [I put the knife] as a whole). What differs in each answer is the [Prom] configuration, namely, the information about which element is to be presented prominently. This can be seen in the various [Prom] configurations in (55).

(55)

	[I]	[put]	[the knife]	[on the table]
	[−New]	[−New]	[−New]	[+New]
a.	[−Prom]	[−Prom]	[−Prom]	[−Prom]
b.	[+Prom]	[−Prom]	[−Prom]	[−Prom]
c.	[−Prom]	[−Prom]	[+Prom]	[−Prom]
d.	[−Prom]	[−Prom]	[−Prom]	[+Prom]

First, as in (a), the speaker could intend to present no element of the sentence with any prominence. She/he would still present [on the table] as [+New], but in English, [+New] is instantiated only by a prosodic measure, not changing the c-structural configuration. Therefore, the default order in (54b) would be the optimal output for this input. For an input like (b) also, the canonical-structure (54b) would be the choice, because the subject is to be presented as [+Prom] here and the subject is already in the prominent c-structure position in (54b), that is, at the left edge of the sentence (SBJ-L, PROM-L).

In contrast, in (c) and (d), the speaker is presenting a non-subject prominently. In (c), the [+Prom] is a [−New], [the knife], whereas in (d), it is the [+New], [on the table]. The input (c) would yield a 'topic'-topicalization as in (54b') and the input (d) would yield a 'focus'-topicalization as in (54b'') (Gundel, 1974), both driven by PROM-L. Note that the current approach is based on the assumption that no two answers in (54) are exactly identical in its informational import. In other words, (54b) and (54b') differ from each other in the informational import of [the knife], while (54b) and (54b'') differ in the informational import of [on the table].[20]

The 'topicalized' examples (54b') and (54b'') can be explained by the following two tableaux. In (54b'), the [−New], [the knife], is [+Prom]. So in (56), candidate (b), which aligns this [+Prom] on the left, is the winner, even though this candidate violates SBJ-L in so doing. In (54b''), on the other hand, the [+New], [on the table] is [+Prom]. Similarly, candidate (c),

---

[20] It appears that to some speakers, the default-order sentence (54b) can be informationally identical to a topicalized one, say, (54b'') if an appropriate accenting is in place, e.g., a heavy pitch accent on the [+New] in (54b). In other words, the p-structural (prosodic) measure, i.e. accenting, does the job that the c-structural measure, i.e. preposing, would otherwise do. For these speakers, PROM-L probably ties with SBJ-L and the p-structure constraint that controls the accenting must be interacting with theses constraints in terms of ranking. I leave open the solution for this issue for future research.

in (57), is the optimal output because it satisfies Prom-L, which is ranked higher than any other constraints. Note that New-R requires [on the table] to align on the right because it is [+New], but it nevertheless aligns to the left since Prom-L outranks New-R.

(56) Input: [(55c)]

$[I]_{[-Prom,-New]}$ $[put]_{[-Prom,-New]}$ $[the\ knife]_{[+Prom,-New]}$ $[on\ the\ table]_{[-Prom,+New]}$

	Prom-L	Sbj-L	Sp-L	Hd-L	Cmpl	New-R
a.	*!*			*		
☞ b.		*	*	**		
c.	*!**	*	*	**	*	***

a. = [I put the knife on the TABLE]
b. = [The knife [I put on the TABLE]]
c. = [On the TABLE [I put the knife]]

(57) Input: [(55d)]

$[I]_{[-Prom,-New]}$ $[put]_{[-Prom,-New]}$ $[the\ knife]_{[-Prom,-New]}$ $[on\ the\ table]_{[+Prom,+New]}$

	Prom-L	Sbj-L	Sp-L	Hd-L	Cmpl	New-R
a.	*!**			*		
b.	*!**	*	*	**		
☞ c.		*	*	**	*	***

a. = [I put the knife on the TABLE]
b. = [The knife [I put on the TABLE]]
c. = [On the TABLE [I put the knife]]

As shown above, I assume that topicalization/preposing in English is an adjunction, not a placement in a higher Spec. Unlike *wh*-questions or other focus constructions initiated by negation or *so*, which call for a separate functional projection, topicalization does not evoke inversion. In fact, Culicover (1991) argues for the structural difference between the 'topic'-topicalization (IP adjunction) and the 'focus'-topicalization (a substitution in Spec/CP). One of his arguments is that 'topic'-topicalization creates an island for extraction while 'focus'-topicalization does not, as shown in the contrast in (58) (Culicover, 1991, 61). The second argument comes from the weak crossover facts that the topic-topicalization does not create a weak crossover effect, as shown in (59a), while the focus-topicalization does, as shown in (59b).

(58) a. *This book to Robin [I gave].
      b. This book to ROBIN [I gave].

(59) a. $Robin_i$ his_i mother really appreciates.
      b. *$ROBIN_i$ his_i mother really appreciates.

The current analysis can account for these differences without resorting to a phrase structural distinction such as IP-adjunction vs. [Spec,CP]. First, I argue that the contrast shown in (58) does not come from a syntactic island effect but from i-structural differences between the two. A double topicalization means that we have two [+Prom] elements in the current account. Considering that English aligns focus rightward (NEW-R), the only order possible between the two [+Prom]'s is [+Prom,−New] [+Prom,+New], which is the case in (58b). In generative terms, this means that only a 'focus-topicalized' sentence allows another topicalization out of it.

The difference in weak crossover can also be accounted for informationally, if not semantically. Simply put, the referential dependence in a binding relation between the binder and the bindee should be compatible with their informational status. In (59a), the binder [Robin] is the 'topic-topic', which is [−New] (namely, old, given, or established in discourse), provides reference to the bindee. In contrast, in (59b), the binder [Robin] is the 'focus-topic', which is [+New], and the bindee [his mother] is [−New] (or part of [−New]). In other words, the bindee, which is referentially dependent on the binder, is given information (established in discourse), while the binder, which is supposed to provide reference to the bindee, is new information (not established in discourse yet). I argue that this incompatibility is what makes (59b) unacceptable (see Choi (1997a) for a similar proposal for German weak crossover phenomena).

To summarize, the topicalization ('topic-topicalization') and the focus-preposing ('focus-topicalization') in English are explained uniformly by the ranking of constraints, PROM-L, SBJ-L, SPEC-L, and NEW-R. It has also been argued that their c-structural realizations do not differ. In the next two subsections, we will see similar constructions in Catalan and German. Essentially, they are captured by the same mechanism, but their c-structural realizations may differ because of their language-particular c-structural requirements.

Catalan Left Detachment

Topicalization or left detachment in Catalan is a little different from that in English or in German. The f-s/c-s constraints such as SBJ and CMPL are already outranked by NEW in Catalan, as we have seen earlier, and thus the crucial ranking is not between PROM and SBJ (or CMPL), but rather between PROM and NEW. Also, the direction of [New] alignment in Catalan is the opposite of that of English or German, that is, [−New] goes right, due to NEW-L. Therefore, the key issue here is not whether the contrastive/emphatic focus ([+Prom,+New]) would be topicalized to the left because even a [−Prom,+New] focus aligns to the left anyway, but whether the topic ([+Prom,−New]) would. The answer is yes and indeed, topic is left-detached, which indicates that PROM-L is ranked higher than NEW-L in Catalan.

An example of a topic case is (60), where [the knife] is [+Prom,−New], i.e. the speaker intends to present [the knife] prominently. The crucial conflict lies in that NEW-L demands [the knife] to align rightward while PROM-L requires it to align leftward. PROM-L rules, so [the knife] is detached leftward. Following Vallduví (1992), I assume that this is an instance of adjunction too. This resolution process is demonstrated in tableau (61).

(60) a. What about the knife? What did you do with the knife?

    b. [El ganivet]$_i$, el$_i$ va ficar   damunt la taula.

       the knife   cl 3-past-put on the table

       'The knife I put on the table.'

(61) Input:

$[I]_{[-Prom,-New]}$ [put on the table]$_{[-Prom,+New]}$
[the knife]$_{[+Prom,-New]}$

	PROM-L	NEW-L	HD-L	CMPL
a.	*!	**		
b.	*!*	*		*
☞ c.		**	*	

a. = [El va ficar el ganivet damunt la taula]
b. = [[El va ficar damunt la taula]$_{IP}$ el ganivet]$_{IP}$
c. = [$_{IP}$ El ganivet [$_{IP}$ el va ficar damunt la taula]]

We can compare this 'topic' ([+Prom,−New]) with the [−Prom,−New] case in (41). When [the knife] is [−Prom,−New], as in (41), the right-detached candidate (b), in which [+New] aligns to the left, is the winner.

The subject behaves the same way as other arguments in Catalan. The canonical position of the subject is sentence-final due to SBJ-R, as shown in (62a) (Vallduví, 1992, 93). As with other elements of the sentence, the subject is right-detached if it is [−New] (although it may be string-vacuous, as shown in (62b)), aligned left if it is [+New] (as a result of the [−New] being right-detached), or left-detached if it is [+Prom], as illustrated in (62c) and (62d) respectively. This means that both NEW-L and PROM-L outrank SBJ-R. The subject-topic case will be captured by basically the same tableau as in (61) above, except that SBJ-R is involved now.

(62) a. [Pararà la taula la COIA]$_{[-Prom,+New]}$.

    b. [Pararà la TAULA]$_{[-Prom,+New]}$, [la Coia]$_{[-Prom,-New]}$.

    c. [La COIA]$_{[-Prom,+New]}$ [la$_i$ pararà]$_{[-Prom,-New]}$
      [la taula]$_{[-Prom,-New]}$.

    d. [La Coia]$_{[+Prom,-New]}$ [pararà la TAULA]$_{[-Prom,+New]}$.

      Coia=Coia; pararà=will set; la taula=the table

Now, we can examine a [+Prom,+New] case in Catalan, where [the knife] is an emphatic/contrastive focus. An illustration is (63) below. In this situation, PROM-L and NEW-L do not have conflicting interests because both constraints would opt for [the knife] to align to the left. As a result, the candidate (c), where [the knife] is sentence-initial, is the favored candidate in (64). Since Catalan aligns both [+Prom] and [+New] on the left edge of the sentence, the 'topic-topicalized' sentence as in (60) and 'focus-topicalized' sentence in (63) are identical in terms of word order. But of course, the accent placement and cliticization (only a [−New] is cliticized) can distinguish the two.

(63) a. What is it that you put on the table?
      b. [El GANIVET], hi$_i$ va ficar damunt la taula$_i$.
        the knife   3-past-put on the table
        'The KNIFE I put on the table.'

(64) Input:
      [the knife]$_{[+Prom,+New]}$ [I]$_{[-Prom,-New]}$ [put]$_{[-Prom,-New]}$
      [on the table]$_{[-Prom,-New]}$

	PROM-L	NEW-L	HD-L	CMPL
a.	*!	*		
b.	*!*	**		*
☞ c.			*	

      a. = [Hi va ficar el ganivet damunt la taula]
      b. = [[Hi va ficar damunt la taula]$_{IP}$ el ganivet]$_{IP}$
      c. = [$_{IP}$ El ganivet [$_{IP}$ hi va ficar damunt la taula]]

Compare this with the regular focus case in (36). The two constructions are virtually indistinguishable in Catalan unlike the situation in English or German. It is because English and German have NEW-R ranked higher than NEW-L so that NEW-R conflicts with PROM-L, whereas the ranking is the reverse in Catalan so that NEW-L and PROM-L go together with regard to contrastive/emphatic focus. This indistinguishability of the two focus phenomena is probably why Vallduví (1992) argues against focus-preposing in Catalan. In the current analysis, we do not need to say that there is no focus-preposing. The lack of structural distinction between regular and contrastive focus naturally follows from the informational decomposition of focus, i.e. to [+Prom,+New] and [−Prom,+New], and the same direction of alignment driven by constraints PROM-L and NEW-L.

The fact that [+Prom] and [+New] are aligned in the same direction makes a prediction that there can be competition for the first position between a topic phrase and a focus phrase. The higher ranking of PROM-L over NEW-L makes another prediction that the topic ([+Prom]) will precede the focus ([+New]). This prediction is borne out indeed, as seen in examples in (65) and (66) from Vallduví and Engdahl (1996, (82), (86)).

(65) a. What about the boys? What did they eat?

    b. [El Pere] [els fesols], [es va menjar].
      Pere   the beans ate
      'Pere ate the beans.'

    c. input:
      $[\text{Pere}]_{[+Prom,-New]}$ $[\text{the beans}]_{[-Prom,+New]}$ $[\text{ate}]_{[-Prom,-New]}$

(66) a. What about the veggie dishes? Who ate them?

    b. [Els fesols] [el Pere], [se'ls va menjar].
      the beans Pere   cl   ate
      'The beans Pere ate.'

    c. input:
      $[\text{Pere}]_{[-Prom,+New]}$ $[\text{the beans}]_{[+Prom,-New]}$ $[\text{ate}]_{[-Prom,-New]}$

As predicted, the topic ([+Prom]) precedes the focus ([+New]) in this language. This is illustrated below in (67). Due to space limitations, I will only show the second example.

(67) Input:
    $[\text{Pere}]_{[-Prom,+New]}$ $[\text{the beans}]_{[+Prom,-New]}$ $[\text{ate}]_{[-Prom,-New]}$

	PROM-L	NEW-L	HD-L	SBJ-R
a.	*!	**		
b.	*!*		*	**
c.	*!		**	**
☞ d.		*	**	*

    a. = [Es va menjar] [els fesols] [el Pere]
    b. = [El Pere] [es va menjar] [el fesols]
    c. = [El Pere] [el fesols] [es va menjar]
    d. = [El fesols] [el Pere] [es va menjar]

To summarize, Catalan topicalization/focus-preposing is handled by the same constraint PROM-L, aligning a [+Prom] on the left edge. Due to the relatively high ranking of NEW-L and the direction of the [+New] alignment in this language, focus-preposing ([+Prom,+New]) is not easily distinguished from a regular focus alignment ([−Prom,+New]).

German Topicalization

Unlike English and Catalan, the position for the [+Prom] is a Spec in German, as shown earlier in section 2.4.2. I argue that it is not because German has a different constraint which requires a [+Prom] to be in a Spec (e.g., PROM-SPEC), but because German has the SPEC-L constraint (and also OB-HD/fp) fairly high in the ranking, which makes a Spec position always available on the left edge of the sentence (see also section 2.3.2). When there is no [+Prom] element in the sentence, the subject will take this position, being the most prominent grammatical function. The f-s/c-s constraint SBJ-L does this job. However, if there is a [+Prom] element, whether [−New] or [+New], the [+Prom] will take this position because PROM-L outranks SBJ-L in German just as in English.[21] In what follows, I will not show SPEC-L, OB-HD/fp, HEAD-L/fp, and HEAD-R in the tableaux for space limitations, assuming that the V2 issue has been taken care of.

Consider first a non-subject topic example as in (68), where the object [the book] is presented as [+Prom].

(68) a. What about the book? Who did you give the book to?
b. Das Buch habe ich dem Kind geschenkt.
    the book have I   the child   given
    'The book I gave to the child.'

(69) Input:
$[\text{I}]_{[-Prom,-New]}$ $[\text{given}]_{[-Prom,-New]}$ $[\text{to the child}]_{[-Prom,+New]}$
$[\text{das Buch}]_{[+Prom,-New]}$

	PROM-L	SBJ-L	NEW-R	CMPL
a.	*!*		**	
b.	*!*	**	***	
☞ c.		**	*	*

a. = [Ich habe dem Kind das Buch geschenkt]
b. = [Dem Kind habe [ich das Buch geschenkt]]
c. = [Das Buch habe [ich dem Kind geschenkt]]

This works more or less like the English example. The [+Prom] takes the most prominent position winning over the subject. The only difference is that SPEC-L and OB-HD/fp are higher in German so that we always have a Spec followed by a finite verb, and also that NEW-R is not ranked lower than CMPL in German, but this will not matter for topicalization.

The [+New] case is not different from the [−New]. Being [+Prom], it also takes the highest Spec position. Just as in English, PROM-L conflicts with NEW-R, because a [+Prom,+New] would create bidirectional pressure. However, the ranking of PROM-L over NEW-R resolves this conflict.

(70) a. What is it that you gave to the child?
b. Das BUCH habe ich dem Kind geschenkt.
    the book   have I   the child given
    'The BOOK I gave to the child.'

---

[21]Note that we can capture [Prom]-related scrambling in embedded clauses by the same constraint PROM-L (see Choi (1996,1999) for a detailed account of German scrambling in embedded clauses). Since the higher Spec is not available in embedded clauses (COMP-L, see section 2.3.2 again), a [+Prom] ends up in an adjoined position, not in a Spec. Thus, the [Prom]-motivated topicalization in matrix clauses and the scrambling in embedded clauses can be captured by the interaction of c-structure constraints and PROM-L.

(71) Input:

$[I]_{[-Prom,-New]}$ $[given]_{[-Prom,-New]}$ $[to\ the\ child]_{[-Prom,-New]}$
$[das\ Buch]_{[+Prom,+New]}$

	Prom-L	Sbj-L	New-R	Cmpl
a.	*!*		*	
b.	*!*	**	*	
☞ c.		**	***	*

a. = [Ich habe dem Kind das Buch geschenkt]
b. = [Dem Kind habe [ich das Buch geschenkt]]
c. = [Das Buch habe [ich dem Kind geschenkt]]

Before closing, let us look at a unique feature of German topicalization. In German, a bigger unit than an individual phrase, e.g., a VP, can topicalize. Moreover, even a partial VP can topicalize, which is often referred to as 'remnant' VP topicalization (Webelhuth and den Besten, 1987; Uszkoreit, 1987). As seen in (72), the topicalized part may not be a whole VP but only part of it. In (72a), only [V + Accusative Object] is topicalized, leaving the Dative Object behind. In (72b), [V + Dative Object] is topicalized, leaving the Accusative Object behind, and so on (Uszkoreit, 1987).

(72) a. [Den Brief zustecken] sollte   der Kurier nachher [dem Spion].
          the note   slip   should the courier later   the spy

      b. [Dem Spion zustecken] sollte   der Kurier nachher [den Brief].
          the spy   slip   should the courier later   the note

      c. [Nachher dem Spion zustecken] sollte   der Kurier [den Brief].
          later   the spy   slip   should the courier the note

I argue that we can account for remnant VP topicalization in the current analysis without any additional measures. Suppose a context like (73), in which [dem Kind geschenkt] forms an informational unit as [+Prom,+New].

(73) a. What is it that you did with the book?
      b. [Dem Kind geschenkt] habe ich das Buch.

(74) Input:

$[I]_{[-Prom,-New]}$ $[the\ book]_{[-Prom,-New]}$ $[the\ child\ given]_{[+Prom,+New]}$

	Prom-L	Sbj-L	New-R	Cmpl
a.	**!****		**	
b.	**!***	**	**	
c.	**!*****		*	*
☞ d.	*	**	*******	

a. = Ich habe [dem Kind [das Buch] geschenkt]
b. = [[Das Buch] geschenkt] habe ich dem Kind
c. = Ich habe das Buch [dem Kind geschenkt]
d. = [Dem Kind geschenkt] habe ich das Buch

Just as NEW is applied to a domain, PROM-L is applied such that it is satisfied if every member of the [+Prom] domain aligns to the left. In this case, [dem Kind geschenkt] is the [+Prom] domain. Candidate (a) and (b), which have the [+Prom] domain broken, violate PROM-L seriously, so lose out of competition. We can then compare candidates (c) and (d), which keep the [+Prom] domain unbroken. In fact, candidate (c) violates PROM-L most seriously by aligning the [+Prom] domain to the right rather than to the left. Therefore, candidate (d) is the optimal output where the [+Prom] domain, [dem Kind geschenkt], is aligned left in the best possible way, namely, as a c-structurally unbroken i-structure domain.

It is interesting to note that a [+Prom,+New] domain behaves differently from a [−Prom,+New] one. Recall that German does not maintain the [+New] domain intact. Refer to example (47) again, where the [New] domain is [−Prom]. As illustrated in the discussion of the scrambling in section 2.4.1, NEW-R and CMPL tie so that two orders are acceptable, one of which does not respect the [+New] domain. In contrast, a [+Prom,+New] domain is respected, as shown above. In other words, topicalization can also be used as a way of keeping an informational domain (i.e. [+Prom] domain) syntactically unbroken, which is not otherwise guaranteed.

Now, let me move on to another case of remnant topicalization, a [−New] one. Suppose that [give to the child] forms an information unit here as [+Prom,−New].

(75) a. Talking about giving to the child, what did you give to the child?
     a′. Talking about giving to the child, who gave the book to the child?
      b. [Dem Kind geschenkt] habe ich das Buch.

If [dem Kind geschenkt], a [−New], were also [−Prom], then this domain would not have been preserved at all. Remember the well-known 'focus' constraint in German scrambling that a [+New] cannot be scrambled (due to the effects of NEW-R and CMPL), as discussed in section 2.4.1. Interestingly, if this domain is [+Prom] as in (75), then [dem Kind geschenkt] can topicalize as an unbroken unit, as shown in (76).

(76) Input:
$[I]_{[-Prom,-New]}$ [the book]$_{[-Prom,+New]}$ [the child given]$_{[+Prom,-New]}$

	PROM-L	SBJ-L	NEW-R	CMPL
a.	**!****		*	
b.	**!*****		**	*
☞ c.	*	**		

  a. = Ich habe [dem Kind [das Buch] geschenkt]
  b. = Ich habe das Buch [dem Kind geschenkt]
  c. = [Dem Kind geschenkt] habe ich das Buch

The topicalized candidate (c) is again the optimal output in this competition for optimality. Candidate (a) and candidate (b) lose to candidate

(c) because they violate the highest-ranking Prom-L more seriously than candidate (c). Candidate (a) would be the optimal choice if the [−New] domain, [dem Kind geschenkt], were [−Prom]. As we have seen in the past two examples, the remnant topicalization in German shows an interesting aspect that topicalization is motivated not only to place a 'prominent' part of the sentence in the 'prominent' position, but also to maintain a certain informational domain to be a syntactic domain as well.

To summarize, we have examined the topicalization and focus-preposing (or focus-topicalization) constructions in English, Catalan, and German. Each language shows examples of interesting interactions between the c-structure and f-s/c-s constraints (Spec-L, Sbj-L, Sbj-R, Cmpl, Head-L, Head-L/fp, Head-R) and the i-s/c-s constraints (Prom-L, New-R, New-L). Properly ranked, these constraints select the 'optimal' instantiations of the grammatical and informational inputs, and therefore, provide resolutions to various types of mismatches.

2.5 Concluding Remarks

In this paper, I have examined some of the informationally-motivated constructions such as scrambling, detachment, topicalization, and focus-preposing in Catalan, German, and English. These constructions have been analyzed as instances of optimal resolutions of the c-structural mismatches caused by the differences in the 'grammatical' information (in f-structure) and the discourse-contextual information (in i-structure). The resolutions in different languages have been analyzed to be reached by proper rankings of the c-s, f-s/c-s, and i-s/c-s correspondence constraints. Naturally, the different rankings in each language result in different types of c-structural instantiations.

Although I have concentrated on the type of mismatches caused by information-structural input in this paper, I do not claim that all word order variations are driven by i-structural motivations. Some may be caused by other syntactic reasons such as structural requirements on binding relations (e.g., 'binder should take a more prominent c-s position than bindee') (Choi, 2001). Some may be driven semantically, for instance, by requirements on semantic scope (e.g., 'the element with wider scope should be placed in a structurally higher position'; or 'the element that is inside the scope should be placed within a certain c-structure domain'). Prosody may also play a role. This domain overlaps substantially with the i-structure because of its close connection to the 'focus' phenomena. As argued by Reinhart (1995), Büring (1999), and Zubizarreta (1998), some reordering facts can be explained by prosodic motivations (e.g., 'a phrase of given information should scramble to avoid the default sentential stress'), although not all can be explained by prosody alone. Although it was beyond the scope of this paper, the relationship between the information structure and the prosodic structure is certainly a highly related topic which calls for further research.

Let me conclude by addressing one of the important issues raised in this type of Optimality-Theoretic approach. It is the issue of 'grammaticality' and 'markedness'. Namely, in Optimality Theory, only the 'optimal' output is "grammatical" and the suboptimal outputs are "ungrammatical". However, most of the suboptimal candidates in word order competition are not 'ungrammatical' but simply *more* marked. For example, there is a clear distinction between the sentences in (a) through (c) and the one in (d): the former is 'grammatical' (although the markedness grows as we move from (a) to (c)) and the latter is 'ungrammatical'.

(77) a. I gave this book to ROBIN.
   b. This book I gave to ROBIN.
   c. This book to ROBIN I gave.
   d. *Gave I to ROBIN this book.

The direction that this paper pursues is that we adhere to the original definition of 'grammaticality' as 'optimality', that only the optimal output is grammatical. Then, the grammar has the burden of successfully generating all the grammatical outputs as the optimal ones, however marked they may be in general. For example, even Culicover's (1991) multiply-topicalized example (77c) should occur as the 'best' or 'optimal' output in some competition. We can get this example as the optimal output as we did in this paper, because grammaticality is the optimality *relative to the input*. Then, where does the markedness come from? It comes from the markedness in the input, in a sense. An example like (77c) is highly marked because the input which leads to this output is highly marked, hardly common, and very difficult to come by. Meanwhile, an example like (77a) is unmarked because this output is optimal not only with the input with minimally available information (e.g., with f-s information only and no i-s information), but also with many other different types of inputs including the one in the highly common (frequently showing) context (e.g., subject-topic context). Therefore, we hear the unmarked output much more often than marked ones. Finally, we get ungrammaticality as a collective result of suboptimality. An ungrammatical example such as (77d) is the one which would *never* show up as the optimal output with any type of input, because the constraint(s) which rule out this candidate are so highly ranked in that particular language that there would always be another candidate which does better than this in the competition.

One of the alternative ways of handling the issue of grammaticality and markedness would be the one proposed by Müller (1998). He proposes two types of constraint hierarchies, one matrix hierarchy and the other subhierarchy. If a candidate turns out to be suboptimal in the competition based on the constraints in the matrix hierarchy, it will be 'ungrammatical'. However, if a candidate proves to be suboptimal in the competition based on the constraints in the subhierarchy, it would be 'marked' but not 'ungrammatical'. Similarly, Büring (1999) distinguishes 'structural markedness' from 'pragmatic markedness': the former will result in ungrammaticality while the latter in markedness. I do not adopt this line of approach because of the following unanswered questions that arise with this type of approach. Is this subdivision part of universal grammar so that every language has it? How is it determined whether a certain constraint belongs to matrix hierarchy or subhierarchy? Are there inherent features in the constraints that will determine their destiny? Is it syntactic versus pragmatic? Yet, some languages seem to violate syntactic constraints like case requirements more easily than some pragmatic constraints. Would we allow reranking of the constraints only within the particular hierarchy or between hierarchies? Could a matrix constraint in one language be a sub-constraint in another language? These certainly call for further research in the future.

References

Abraham, Werner. 1986. Word Order in the Middle Field of the German Sentence. In *Topic, Focus, and Configurationality*, eds. Werner Abraham and Sjaak de Meij. Amsterdam: John Benjamins, 15–38.

Aissen, Judith. 1992. Topic and Focus in Mayan. *Language* 68:43–80.

Aissen, Judith. 2001. Markedness and Subject Choice in Optimality Theory. In *Optimality-Theoretic Syntax*, eds. Géraldine Legendre, Jane Grimshaw, and Sten Vikner. Cambridge, Massachusetts: The MIT Press, 61–96.

Alsina, Alex. 1993. *Predicate Composition: A Theory of Syntactic Function Alternations*. Ph.D. thesis, Stanford University.

Asudeh, Ash. 2001. Linking, Optionality, and Ambiguity in Marathi. This volume.

Boersma, Paul. 1997. How we learn variation, optionality, and probability. In *IFA Proceedings 21*. University of Amsterdam: Institute of Phonetic Sciences, 43–58. ROA-221-109.

Bonet, Eulalia. 1990. Subjects in Catalan. In *MIT Working Papers in Linguistics 13*. MIT: Department of Linguistics, 1–26.

Bresnan, Joan (ed.). 1982. *The Mental Representation of Grammatical Relations*. Cambridge, Massachusetts: The MIT Press.

Bresnan, Joan. 1996. Optimal Syntax: Notes on Projection, Heads, and Optimality. MS. Stanford University.

Bresnan, Joan. 1998. Morphology Competes with Syntax: Explaining Typological Variation in Weak Crossover Effects. In *Is Best Good Enough? Optimality and Competition in Syntax*, eds. Pilar Barbosa, Danny Fox, Paul Hagstrom, Martha McGinnis, and David Pesetsky. Cambridge, Massachusetts: The MIT Press, 241–274.

Bresnan, Joan. 2000. Optimal Syntax. In *Optimality Theory: Phonology, Syntax and Acquisition*, eds. Joost Dekkers, Frank van der Leeuw, and Jeroen van de Weijer. Oxford: Oxford University Press, 334–385.

Bresnan, Joan. 2001. *Lexical Functional Syntax*. Oxford: Blackwell.

Bresnan, Joan and Jonni Kanerva. 1989. Locative Inversion in Chicheŵa: A Case Study of Factorization in Grammar. *Linguistic Inquiry* 20:1–50.

Bresnan, Joan and Lioba Moshi. 1990. Object Asymmetries in Comparative Bantu Syntax. *Linguistic Inquiry* 21(2):147–186.

Büring, Daniel. 1997. Towards an OT Account of German Mittelfeld. MS., Universität Köln.

Büring, Daniel. 1999. Let's Phrase It!: Focus, Word Order, and Prosodic Phrasing in German Double Object Constructions. MS., University of California at Santa Cruz.

Choi, Hye-Won. 1996. *Optimizing Structure in Context: Scrambling and Information Structure*. Ph.D. thesis, Stanford University.

Choi, Hye-Won. 1997a. Focus and Binding in Scrambling: An OT Account. In *Proceedings of WCCFL 16*, eds. Emily Curtis, James Lyle, and Gabriel Webster. Stanford, California: CSLI Publications, 81–95.

Choi, Hye-Won. 1997b. Information Structure, Phrase Structure, and Their Interface. In *Proceedings of the LFG97 Conference (on line)*, eds. Miriam Butt and Tracy Holloway King. Stanford, California: CSLI Publications Online: http://csli-publications.stanford.edu/.

Choi, Hye-Won. 1999. *Optimizing Structure in Context: Scrambling and Information Structure*. Stanford, California: CSLI Publications.

Choi, Hye-Won. 2001. Binding and Discourse Prominence: Reconstruction in 'Focus' Scrambling. In *Optimality-Theoretic Syntax*, eds. Géraldine Legendre, Jane Grimshaw, and Sten Vikner. Cambridge, Massachusetts: The MIT Press, 143–169.

Costa, João. 1996. Word Order and Constraint Interaction. To appear in *Seminários de Linguística*, University of Algarve.

Costa, João. 1998. *Word Order Variation: A Constraint-Based Approach*. Ph.D. thesis, Leiden University.

Costa, João. 2001. The Emergence of Unmarked Word Order. In *Optimality-Theoretic Syntax*, eds. Géraldine Legendre, Jane Grimshaw, and Sten Vikner. Cambridge, Massachusetts: The MIT Press, 171–203.

Culicover, Peter W. 1991. Polarity, Inversion, and Focus in English. In *Proceedings of ESCOL '91*. The Ohio State University: Department of Linguistics, 46–68.

Dalrymple, Mary, John Lamping, and Vijay Saraswat. 1993. LFG Semantics via Constraints. Xerox PARC, Palo Alto.

de Hoop, Helen. 1992. *Case Configuration and Noun Phrase Interpretation*. Ph.D. thesis, University of Groningen.

den Besten, Hans. 1982. Some Remarks on the Ergative Hypothesis. In *Groninger Arbeiten zur Germanistischen Linguistik 21*.

Diesing, Molly. 1992. *Indefinites*. Cambridge, Massachusetts: The MIT Press.

Dik, Simon, Maria Hoffman, Jan R. de Jong, Sie Ing Djiang, Harry Stroomer, and Lourens de Vries. 1981. On the Typology of Focus Phenomena. In *Perspectives on Functional Grammar*, eds. Teun Hoekstra, Harry van der Hulst, and Michael Moortgat. Dordrecht: Foris, 41–74.

Givón, Talmy. 1990. *Syntax: A Functional-Typological Introduction*, volume 2. Amsterdam: John Benjamins.

Grimshaw, Jane. 1997. Projection, Heads, and Optimality. *Linguistic Inquiry* 28:73–422.

Grimshaw, Jane. 1998. Constraints on Constraints in Syntax. MS., Rutgers University. Presented at the Stanford Optimality Theory Workshop: *Is Syntax Different?*

Grimshaw, Jane and Vieri Samek-Lodovici. 1995. Optimal Subjects. In *Papers in Optimality Theory*, eds. Jill N. Beckman, Laura Walsh Dickey, and Suzanne Urbanczyk. Amherst, Massachusetts: GLSA, University of Massachusetts, 589–606.

Grimshaw, Jane and Vieri Samek-Lodovici. 1998. Optimal Subjects and Subject Universals. In *Is Best Good Enough? Optimality and Competition in Syntax*, eds. Pilar Barbosa, Danny Fox, Paul Hagstrom, Martha McGinnis, and David Pesetsky. Cambridge, Massachusetts: The MIT Press, 193–219.

Gundel, Jeanette. 1974. *The Role of Topic and Comment in Linguistic Theory*. Ph.D. thesis, University of Texas at Austin.

Haider, Hubert. 1985. V-Second in German. In *Verb Second Phenomena in Germanic Languages*, eds. Hubert Haider and Martin Prinzhorn. Dordrecht: Foris, 49–76.

Halvorsen, Per-Kristian and Ronald M. Kaplan. 1988. Projections and semantic description in Lexical-Functional Grammar. In *Proceedings of the International Conference on Fifth Generation Computer Systems, FGCS-88*. Tokyo: Institute for New Generation Systems.

Herring, Susan C. 1990. Information Structure as a Consequence of Word Order Type. In *Proceedings of the Berkeley Linguistics Society*, ed. Kira Hall et al., volume 16.

Keller, Frank and Theodora Alexopoulou. 1999. Phonology Competes with Syntax: Experimental Evidence for the Interaction of Word Order and Accent Placement in the Realization of Information Structure. MS., University of Edinburgh.

King, Tracy Holloway. 1997. Focus Domains and Information-Structure. In *Proceedings of the LFG97 Conference (on line)*, eds. Miriam Butt and Tracy Holloway King. Stanford, California: CSLI Publications Online: `http://csli-publications.stanford.edu/`.

Kiss, Katalin É. (ed.). 1995. *Discourse Configurational Languages*. Oxford: Oxford University Press.

Kuhn, Jonas. 2001. Generation and Parsing in Optimality Theoretic Syntax – Issues in the Formalization in OT-LFG. This volume.

Kuno, Susumu. 1972. Functional Sentence Perspective: A Case Study from Japanese and English. *Linguistic Inquiry* 3(3):269–320.

Lambrecht, Knud. 1994. *Information Structure and Sentence Form*. Cambridge: Cambridge University Press.

Lee, Hanjung. 1998. Discourse Competing with Syntax: "Misplaced" *que* in Child French. MS., Stanford University. Presented at the Stanford Optimality Theory Workshop: *Is Syntax Different* and at the 1999 Annual Meeting of the Linguistic Society of America, Los Angeles.

Lee, Hanjung. 1999. The Emergence of the Unmarked Order. Online, Rutgers Optimality Archive: ROA-323-0699, `http://ruccs.rutgers.edu/roa.html`.

Lee, Hanjung. 2001. Markedness and Word Order Freezing. This volume.

Legendre, Géraldine. 1998. Why French Stylistic Inversion is Optimal. MS., John Hopkins University. Presented at the Stanford Optimality Theory Workshop: *Is Syntax Different?*

Legendre, Géraldine, Paul Smolensky, and Colin Wilson. 1998. When is Less More?: Faithfulness and Minimal Links in *wh*-Chains. In *Is Best Good Enough? Optimality and Competition in Syntax*, eds. Pilar Barbosa, Danny Fox, Paul Hagstrom, Martha McGinnis, and David Pesetsky. Cambridge, Massachusetts: The MIT Press, 249–289.

Lenerz, Jürgen. 1977. *Zur Abfolge nominaler Satzglieder im Deutschen.* Tübingen: Gunter Narr Verlag.

Li, Charles and Sandra Thompson. 1976. Subject and Topic: A New Typology of Language. In *Subject and Topic*, ed. Charles Li. New York, New York: Academic Press, 457–490.

Moltmann, Friederike. 1990. Scrambling in German and the Specificity Effect. MS., MIT.

Morimoto, Yukiko. 1999. An Optimality Account of Argument Reversal. In *Proceedings of the LFG99 Conference*, eds. Miriam Butt and Tracy Holloway King. Stanford, California: CSLI Publications Online: `http://csli-publications.stanford.edu/`.

Müller, Gereon. 1998. German Word Order and Optimality Theory. In *Arbeitspapiere des Sonderforschungsbereichs 340, #126*. University of Tübingen.

Pesetsky, David. 1997. Optimality Theory and Syntax: Movement and Pronunciation. In *Optimality Theory: An Overview*, eds. Diana Archangeli and Terence Langendoen. Oxford: Blackwell, 134–170.

Platzack, Christer. 1985. A Survey of Generative Analyses of the Verb Second Phenomenon in Germanic. *Nordic Journal of Linguistics* 8:49–73.

Prince, Alan and Paul Smolensky. 1993. Optimality Theory: Constraint Interaction in Generative Grammar. Technical Report RuCCS Technical Report #2, Center for Cognitive Science, Rutgers University, Piscataway, New Jersey. To be published by the MIT Press.

Reinhart, Tanya. 1982. Pragmatics and Linguistics: An Analysis of Sentence Topics. MS., Distributed by the Indiana University Linguistics Club.

Reinhart, Tanya. 1995. Interface Strategies. Technical Report OTS-WP-TL-95-002, Research Institute for Language and Speech, Utrecht University, Utrecht.

Rigau, Gemma. 1988. Strong Pronouns. *Linguistic Inquiry* 19:503–511.

Rochemont, Michael S. and Peter W. Culicover. 1990. *English Focus Constructions and the Theory of Grammar*. Cambridge: Cambridge University Press.

Samek-Lodovici, Vieri. 1996. *Constraints on Subjects: An Optimality Theoretic Analysis*. Ph.D. thesis, Rutgers University.

Samek-Lodovici, Vieri. 2001. Cross-Linguistic Typologies in Optimality Theory. In *Optimality-Theoretic Syntax*, eds. Géraldine Legendre, Jane Grimshaw, and Sten Vikner. Cambridge, Massachusetts: The MIT Press, 315–353.

Sells, Peter. 1998. Syntactic Positioning as Alignment: Object Shift in Swedish. MS., Stanford University. Presented at the Stanford Optimality Theory Workshop: *Is Syntax Different?*

Sells, Peter. 2000. Alignment Constraints in Swedish Clausal Syntax. MS., Stanford University. Online: http://www-csli.stanford.edu/~sells.

Sgall, Petr, Eva Hajičová, and Jarmila Panevová. 1986. *The Meaning of the Sentence in its Semantic and Pragmatic Aspects*. Prague: Academia.

Taraldsen, Knut Tarald. 1985. On Verb Second and the Functional Content of Syntactic Categories. In *Verb Second Phenomena in Germanic Languages*, eds. Hubert Haider and Martin Prinzhorn. Dordrecht: Foris, 49–76.

Uszkoreit, Hans. 1984. *Word Order and Constituent Structure in German*. Ph.D. thesis, University of Texas at Austin.

Uszkoreit, Hans. 1987. Linear Precedence in Discontinuous Constituents: Complex Fronting in German. In *Syntax and Semantics 20: Discontinuous Constituency*, eds. Geoffrey J. Huck and Almerindo E. Ojeda. New York, New York: Academic Press, 406–427.

Vallduví, Enric. 1992. *The Informational Component*. New York, New York: Garland.

Vallduví, Enric and Elisabet Engdahl. 1996. The Linguistic Realisation of Information Packaging. *Linguistics* 34:3:459–519.

Vikner, Sten. 1995. *Verb Movement and Expletive Subjects in the Germanic Languages*. Oxford: Oxford University Press.

Vikner, Sten. 2001. V^0-to-I^0 Movement, and *DO*-Insertion in Optimality Theory. In *Optimality-Theoretic Syntax*, eds. Géraldine Legendre, Jane Grimshaw, and Sten Vikner. Cambridge, Massachusetts: The MIT Press, 427–464.

Webelhuth, Gert. 1985. German is Configurational. *Linguistic Review* 4:203–246.

Webelhuth, Gert. 1992. *Principles and Parameters of Syntactic Saturation*. Oxford: Oxford University Press.

Webelhuth, Gert and Hans den Besten. 1987. Remnant Topicalization and the Constituent Structure of the Germanic SOV-languages. Presented at GLOW, Venice, Italy.

Weerman, Fred. 1989. *The V2 Conspiracy: A Syncronic and a Diachronic Analysis of Verbal Positions of Germanic Languages*. Dordrecht: Foris.

Zubizarreta, Maria Luisa. 1998. *Prosody, Focus, and Word Order*. Cambridge, Massachusetts: The MIT Press.

3

Markedness and Word Order Freezing

HANJUNG LEE

3.1 Introduction

Studies on word order variation in "free" word order languages fall into two major categories.[1] The dominant approach has been one in which "free" word order or scrambling is driven by grammatical features such as Case and Agr(eement) (e.g., Gurtu 1985; Webelhuth 1989; Mahajan 1990; Speas 1990; Saito 1992; Y. Lee 1993; Miyagawa 1997, among others). In this approach, scrambling is a consequence of Case/Agr-driven movement: a phrase is moved to a certain specifier position or adjoined to a specific functional category (e.g., IP) so that its Case can be licensed or its Agr feature can be checked off. Another approach has been suggested in which scrambling is an instance of semantically-driven movement (e.g., de Hoop 1996; Diesing 1992; Neeleman and Reinhart 1997, among others) or happens as a result of the interaction of syntax and discourse/pragmatics (e.g., King 1995; Costa 1998; Müller 1998; Samek-Lodovici 1998; Choi 1999, 2001,

[1]I am grateful to Joan Bresnan and Peter Sells, who made detailed comments and valuable suggestions on earlier versions of this paper. One of the main ideas developed here—word order freezing involves harmonic alignment of morphosyntactic prominence hierarchies—was first proposed to me by Peter Sells. Special thanks and no blame for my use of their input, comments and suggestions should go to Judith Aissen, Jane Grimshaw, Yukiko Morimoto, Elizabeth Traugott, two anonymous reviewers, the participants in the Stanford OT Syntax Research Group, members of the OT syntax seminar led by Judith Aissen and Joan Bresnan, Winter 2000, and particularly to Ashwini Deo, Devyani Sharma and Shiao Wei Tham. Versions of this paper were presented at the 8th International Symposium on Korean Linguistics (ISOKL 8), Harvard University, July 16–19, 1999, the 30th Conference of the North East Linguistics Society (NELS 30), Rutgers University, October 22–24, 1999, the Joint Stanford/UCSC Workshop on Optimal Typology, UCSC, October 30, 1999, and at the 33rd Annual Linguistics Conference, Language Research Institute, Seoul National University, Korea, December 10, 1999. I'd like to thank the audiences for helpful comments and discussion. This material is based upon work supported by the National Science Foundation under Grant No. BCS-9818077.

Formal and Empirical Issues in Optimality Theoretic Syntax.
Peter Sells (ed.).
Copyright © 2001, CSLI Publications.

among others). In this approach the varied word orders are optional from a purely syntactic point of view: they are motivated by semantic factors, such as specific vs. non-specific interpretations and discourse considerations, such as topic and focus.

In many free word order languages, it is not uncommon to find fixed word order phenomena: a certain canonical word order becomes fixed under special circumstances in which the relative prominence relations of different dimensions of linguistic substance—grammatical functions, semantic roles, case, and positions in phrase structure—do not match, or in which morphology is unable to distinguish the grammatical functions of the arguments. Despite their important implications for syntactic theory relating to the formal mechanisms for capturing word order freedom, fixed word order phenomena, referred to as *word order freezing* (Mohanan 1992; Mohanan and Mohanan 1994), have received relatively little attention in recent literature on word order. While the various approaches to scrambling suggested so far can generally account for the free ordering of constituents, none of the previous approaches explain word order freezing effects found in languages like Hindi and Korean, regardless of whether we assume that scrambling is motivated by Case/Agr or by semantic/pragmatic factors.

This paper presents an Optimality-Theoretic (OT: Prince and Smolensky 1993) account of word order in Hindi and Korean that can account for both the free ordering and fixed ordering of constituents. Specifically, the analysis is developed within the OT-LFG framework which embeds LFG's non-derivational system of correspondence between parallel structures within OT theory of constraint interaction (Bresnan 2000a,b, 2001a; Choi 1999; Kuhn 1999, 2001; Sells 1999, 2000, 2001). A theory like OT-LFG which sees simultaneous competition between parallel, co-present structures as pervasive and constraint ranking as the means to resolve it provides an appropriate framework in which to approach the problem of word order freezing.

This paper is organized as follows: Section 3.2 presents the facts on the two types of word order freezing found in Hindi and Korean, and discusses the problems posed by the data for previous approaches to word order variation. Section 3.3 examines basic clause structures in Hindi and Korean. Section 3.4 and 3.5 present the OT-LFG analysis of word order variation in Hindi and Korean that can account for both the free ordering and fixed ordering of constituents. In section 3.4, I show that the OT approach making crucial use of hierarchy alignment (Prince and Smolensky 1993; Aissen 1999) captures the basic generalization about 'the worst of the worst' type of freezing: highly marked argument types occur only in unmarked position. Then in section 3.5, I show that the word order freezing found in sentences with ambiguous case marking can be explained when the constraint system allows an extension to bidirectional competition (Smolensky 1996b, 1998; Wilson 1996, 1997, 2001). Section 3.6 concludes the paper.

3.2 Word Order Freezing in Hindi and Korean

This section presents data from Hindi and Korean illustrating word order freezing effects, and discusses the problems posed by these data for previous approaches to word order variation.

3.2.1 'The Worst of the Worst' Type of Freezing

In this section I will present basic word order facts about Hindi and Korean, and data demonstrating a loss of word order freedom in clauses which contain highly marked argument types.

Word Order Freezing in Nonvolitional Transitives in Hindi

Hindi is a right-headed language with SOV canonical order. However, unlike Japanese and Korean, the surface order of elements is not strictly head-final. The possible permutations of a simple Hindi sentence are shown in (1).[2] The three elements in a simple sentence can appear in any order.[3]

(1) a. Anuu-ne caand dek^{h}aa.
    Anu-ERG moon-NOM see/look at-PERF
    'Anu saw the moon.'
   b. Caand Anuu-ne dek^{h}aa.
   c. Anuu-ne dek^{h}aa caand.
   d. Caand dek^{h}aa Anuu-ne.
   e. Dek^{h}aa Anuu-ne caand.
   f. Dek^{h}aa caand Anuu-ne.

(1a) reflects the 'basic', 'canonical' or 'unmarked' order. The other orders are deviations from this canonical order (Gambhir 1981; Mohanan 1992, 1994a; Mohanan and Mohanan 1994). Such deviations are used to mark a special information structure and are generally associated with shifts in prominence, emphasis and semantic effects (e.g., definiteness effects).

Despite a high level of word order freedom in this language, under certain circumstances, free word order freezes into a fixed, canonical order. For Hindi (Mohanan 1992; Mohanan and Mohanan 1994), and as I will show

---

[2]The abbreviations used in are as follows: ACC 'accusative', ADJ 'adjunct', ASP 'aspect', AUX 'auxiliary', BCK 'background information', CAUS 'causality', COMP 'complementizer', COMPL 'completive information', COP 'copular', DAT 'dative', DECL 'declarative ending', ERG 'ergative', FOC 'focus', FUT 'future', GEN 'genitive', HON 'honorific affix', INST 'instrumental', IO 'indirect object', LOC 'locative', NF 'nonfinite', NOM 'nominative', OBJ 'object', OBL 'oblique', OM 'object marker', PAST 'past tense', PERF 'perfective', PRES 'present', PRON 'pronoun', SENT 'sentience', SUBJ 'subject', TOP 'topic', VOL 'volitionality'.

[3]The canonical case for animate objects in Hindi is ACC, and the canonical case for inanimate objects is NOM. Verbs that are neutral to the animacy of their objects like dek^h 'see' can take either ACC or NOM depending on the animacy of their object (nominative case in Hindi has no phonological realization). This phenomenon of selective case marking on objects is a highly principled and widespread one, found in a variety of languages typologically remote from Hindi. See Aissen (2000) for a formal articulation of the idea that the higher in prominence an object is, the more likely it is to be overtly case marked.

in the next section, Korean, one environment for restricted word order variation occurs when a sentence contains highly marked types of subject and object (i.e. transitive verbs without prototypical agent-patient argument relations). The other environment will be described shortly in section 3.2.2. In Hindi, an example of a verb class that takes marked argument types is 'unaccusative transitives' or 'nonvolitional transitives' (Mohanan 1994a, section 7.1; Mohanan and Mohanan 1994, section 4). Of the two arguments of the nonvolitional transitives one is sentient and the other may be sentient or nonsentient. The obligatory sentient argument of these verbs always has dative case, as in (2) and (3).[4] While the ergative subject in (1) carries the meaning of volitional action, the dative-marked arguments in (2) and (3) are nonagentive and nonvolitional. Unlike the objects of volitional transitives, the theme arguments in (2) and (3) must be nominative even if animate: they cannot be accusative because they do not have the semantic property of being an entity toward which an action or event is directed by a volitional inceptor of the action or event (Mohanan (1994a, section 4.4) contains a more detailed discussion of the nominative arguments of 'unaccusative transitives' or 'nonvolitional transitives').

(2) Anuu-ko caand   dik^{h}ii.
    Anu-DAT moon-NOM appear-PERF
    'Anu saw the moon.'
    (Lit. 'To Anu the moon appeared/became visible.')

(3) Vijay-ko Ravii   milaa.
    Vijay-DAT Ravi-NOM find/encounter-PERF
    'Vijay met Ravi unexpectedly.'

Unlike volitional transitives, nonvolitional transitives in Hindi are subject/object alternating verbs, i.e. either of the two arguments of the verb may be construed to be subject, the other the object.[5] Two syntactic tests for grammatical subjecthood in Hindi, namely the binding of the reflexive and subject obviation of the pronoun to take subject antecedents, can be used to demonstrate that either argument of nonvolitional transitives can be the grammatical subject. As argued in Mohanan (1994a:122–127), the Hindi reflexive takes either a grammatical subject or a logical subject (i.e. the thematically highest argument role) as its antecedent, and the Hindi pronoun cannot take the grammatical subject of its clause as its antecedent.

---

[4]The dative subject construction in Hindi has been studied in detail in Bahl (1967), Davidson (1969), Mohanan (1994a) and Verma and Mohanan (1990), among others. DAT case on the subject may be induced by any of three types of predicates. The first is a small set of 'nonvolitional transitives' as in (2) and (3). Belonging to the second type are noun+verb complex predicates. A third source of DAT case on the subject comes from modality meanings such as 'urge' and 'oblige', derived from complex verbals involving auxiliaries (Mohanan 1994a:142). Only the first type allows its arguments to alternate between subject and object.

[5]The Marathi counterparts of Hindi nonvolitional transitives also show this property; see Joshi (1993) and Asudeh (2001).

The sentences in (4) show that the nonvolitional experiencer argument *Anuu* is the grammatical subject: the reflexive *apnii* takes it as its antecedent (4a); the pronoun *uskii* cannot be coreferent with it (4b).[6]

(4) a. Anuu-ko Niinaa   apnii   bastii-mẽ   dik^{h}ii.
        Anu-DAT Nina-NOM self-GEN neighborhood-LOC appear-PERF
        'Anu$_i$ saw Nina$_j$ in self's$_{i/*j}$ neighborhood.'

    b. Anuu-ko Niinaa   uskii   bastii-mẽ   dik^{h}ii.
        Anu-DAT Nina-NOM PRON-GEN neighborhood-LOC appear-PERF
        'Anu$_i$ saw Nina$_j$ in her$_{j/*i}$ neighborhood.'

In (5a), either the theme or the nonvolitional experiencer can be the eligible antecedent of the reflexive. Given the principle governing the interpretation of the reflexive in Hindi, it follows that the theme *Niinaa* is the grammatical subject in (5a) and that the experiencer *Anuu*, the logical subject in both (4) and (5a), is the grammatical subject in (4). The subject obviation test supports this conclusion; in (5b) the pronoun cannot be coreferent with the theme argument *Niinaa*. Therefore, it is the grammatical subject.

(5) a. Niinaa   Anuu-ko apnii   bastii-mẽ   dik^{h}ii.
        Nina-NOM Anu-DAT self-GEN neighborhood-LOC appear-PERF
        'Anu$_i$ saw Nina$_j$ in self's$_{i/j}$ neighborhood.'

    b. Niinaa   Anuu-ko uskii   bastii-mẽ   dik^{h}ii.
        Nina-NOM Anu-DAT PRON-GEN neighborhood-LOC appear-PERF
        'Anu$_i$ saw Nina$_j$ in her$_{i/*j}$ neighborhood.'

An interesting fact is that the two grammatical function analyses, shown in (4) and (5) above, are consistent only with certain restricted word orders. According to Mohanan and Mohanan (1994:175), the analysis of the nonvolitional experiencer as the grammatical subject in Hindi is required for all word orders except that in which the theme precedes the experiencer preverbally; this word order, shown in (5), can only receive the analysis of the theme as the grammatical subject, and in fact it is the only possible word order when the subject is a theme and the object is a nonvolitional experiencer.[7] This point is illustrated by the sentences in (6), which are acceptable only under the analysis of the experiencer as the subject. In the word orders shown in (6), the pronoun can be coreferent only with the theme because it is not the subject. This evidence suggests that the analysis of the theme as the subject is incompatible with the five orders

---

[6]Evidence for the objecthood of the nominative argument in (4) comes from the facts of gapping in Hindi. In order to be gapped, an element must be identical to the gapper in both grammatical function and case. The nominative argument in (4) can both gap as well as be gapped by uncontroversial grammatical objects. See Mohanan (1994a:142) for further details and examples.

[7]The passive of triadic predicates shows the same word order pattern: the order of the subject and object becomes fixed as SOV order when the subject is a theme and the object is a goal (Mohanan 1992; Mohanan and Mohanan 1994).

in (6) and that the order of the subject and object becomes fixed as SOV order in the marked linking pattern when the subject is a theme and the nonvolitional experiencer is the object.[8]

(6) a. Niinaa uskii bastii-mẽ dik^hii Anuu-ko.
Nina-NOM PRON-GEN neighborhood-LOC appear-PERF Anu-DAT
'Anu$_i$ saw Nina$_j$ in her$_{j/*i}$ neighborhood.'

b. Anuu-ko Niinaa uskii bastii-mẽ dik^hii.
Anu-DAT Nina-NOM PRON-GEN neighborhood-LOC appear-PERF
'Anu$_i$ saw Nina$_j$ in her$_{j/*i}$ neighborhood.'

c. Anuu-ko uskii bastii-mẽ dik^hii Niinaa.
Anu-DAT PRON-GEN neighborhood-LOC appear-PERF Nina-NOM
'Anu$_i$ saw Nina$_j$ in her$_{j/*i}$ neighborhood.'

d. Dik^hii Niinaa Anuu-ko uskii bastii-mẽ.
appear-PERF Nina-NOM Anu-DAT PRON-GEN neighborhood-LOC
'Anu$_i$ saw Nina$_j$ in her$_{j/*i}$ neighborhood.'

e. Dik^hii Anuu-ko Niinaa uskii bastii-mẽ.
appear-PERF Anu-DAT Nina-NOM PRON-GEN neighborhood-LOC
'Anu$_i$ saw Nina$_j$ in her$_{j/*i}$ neighborhood.'

The word order pattern in Hindi nonvolitional transitives discussed so far is summarized in (7). We see that all orders except the OSV order in (a2) are possible with the unmarked linking pattern shown in (7a) where the experiencer is the subject and the theme is the object. In contrast, the order of the subject and the object is frozen in unmarked order (i.e. SOV) in the marked linking pattern when the theme is the subject and the object is a nonvolitional experiencer.

(7) Table 1. Word order pattern in Hindi nonvolitional transitives

a.	SUBJ	OBJ	a1. $S_{exp}O_{th}V$
				a2. *$O_{th}S_{exp}V$
	$\mid$	$\mid$	a3. $S_{exp}VO_{th}$
	exp	th	a4. $O_{th}VS_{exp}$
			a5. $VS_{exp}O_{th}S$
			a6. $VO_{th}S_{exp}$
b.	SUBJ	OBJ	b1. $S_{th}O_{exp}V$
			b2. *$O_{exp}S_{th}V$
	$\times$		b3. *$S_{th}VO_{exp}$
	exp	th	b4. *$O_{exp}VS_{th}$
			b5. *$VS_{th}O_{exp}$
			b6. *$VO_{exp}S_{th}$

---

[8]Examples with the reflexive are not presented here because reflexive binding in Hindi does not refer to the grammatical subject exclusively, and both the theme and the experiencer can bind the reflexive in the word orders shown in (6).

As mentioned above, the arguments of Hindi nonvolitional transitives may be associated with two different grammatical function realizations. Interestingly, a close examination of the word order pattern summarized in (7) reveals that these two grammatical function realizations do not share the same surface string (strictly speaking, the precedence relation of the subject and the object). In other words, the string expressions of Hindi nonvolitional transitives is not ambiguous; they are associated with only one grammatical function structure. For example, the string *Niinaa Anuu-ko dikʰii* receives an SOV analysis in (b1) but not the OSV one in (a2); similarly, the string *Anuu-ko Niinaa dikʰii* is only grammatical for the SOV analysis in (a1) but not for the OSV one in (b2).

The word order pattern in Hindi nonvolitional transitives exhibits intriguing interactions of various types of prominences as well—prominences on the dimensions of grammatical function, thematic role and position in constituent structure. Crosslinguistically, the subject is canonically associated with the highest thematic role (e.g., agent or experiencer), and the object is canonically associated with a non-highest thematic role (e.g., patient or theme). Therefore, it is more marked for a subject to be a theme rather than an experiencer, and for an object to be an experiencer rather than a theme. The most marked situation obtains when the subject and the object are mapped onto marked thematic roles, *and* one (or both) of the subject and the object is in a marked position in the phrase structure. This situation is manifested in the five ungrammatical structures in (7b) in Table 1, where either a theme subject is not occurring in its unmarked clause-initial position as in (b2), (b4), (b5) and (b6), or an experiencer object is not in its unmarked preverbal position as in (b3), (b5) and (b6). In connection with the lack of ambiguity of the Hindi clauses with the nonvolitional experiencer and the theme, what is revealing about this case is the way the universal typological preference for the unmarked structure reveals itself in the Hindi data. As we will see in the analysis part, of the two grammatical function realizations shown in (7) above, the allowed structure is the less marked one in which the linking of arguments to grammatical functions and the relative order of the two arguments is also not marked.

The descriptive generalizations that emerge can be stated as follows:

(8) a. Generalization 1: **Avoidance of the Worst of the Worst**
Canonical SOV order becomes fixed in a Hindi nonvolitional transitive with a theme subject and an experiencer object. That is, such arguments should not be associated both with a marked semantic role and with a marked position.

b. Generalization 2: **Avoidance of Ambiguous Strings**
There is only one grammatical surface realization (i.e. linear order) for the alternative grammatical function realizations of the arguments of a nonvolitional transitive.

'The worst of the worst' (Smolensky 1995) generalization in (8a) is not easily captured by derivational approaches to word order variation. In the GB theory (Chomsky 1981; Lasnik and Saito 1992), free word order results from optional free adjunction and head movement (e.g., Gurtu 1985, Mahajan 1990, Speas 1990; Srivastav 1991, among others). The basic motivation for syntactic movement is based on the idea that word order at a more abstract underlying level of representation is the unmarked one, and that more marked surface word orders are derived from this by transformational derivations, which are encoded by means of indexed traces. In the Minimalist Program (Chomsky 1993, 1995), all syntactic operations are obligatory and take place only if driven by some independent requirement in the grammar (e.g., formal features of Case or Agr). The freezing effects in Hindi pose a problem for these derivational approaches. As pointed out in Mohanan and Mohanan (1994), in order to account for the freezing effects in (6) in an analysis involving movement, it will be necessary to prohibit both NP movement and head movement if the theme is the Spec of AgrSP and the nonvolitional experiencer is the Spec of AgrOP. Explaining word order freezing in a way that can relate derivational markedness to the relative markedness of arguments along various dimensions may not be an impossible task, but it is worth exploring an alternative theory in which markedness is built into grammars in the form of violable universal constraints, not simply a criterion external to the grammar, evaluating its complexity.

In this paper, I put forward an OT analysis of restricted word order variation in Hindi which captures both generalizations stated in (8). It will be shown that generalization (8a) follows from the general model of hierarchy alignment in OT (Prince and Smolemsky 1993; Aissen 1999) (section 3.4.1). The ungrammaticality of (a2) in (7) is part of the generalization about ambiguity avoidance and the preference for the unmarked structure, and the analysis to be developed here has it as a direct consequence without having to stipulate it using further constraints (sections 3.4.1 and 3.5.2).

Honorification and Word Order Freezing in the Dative-Subject Construction in Korean

'The worst of the worst' type of word order freezing is observed in Korean as well, a canonical SOV language where the surface order of constituents is strictly head-final. The freedom of word order in sentences with a ditransitive verb *cwu-* 'give' is illustrated in (9).

(9) a. Mary-ka   ai-eykey   senmwul-ul cwu-ess-ta.
       Mary-NOM child-DAT present-ACC give-PAST-DECL
       'Mary gave a present to the child.'
    b. Mary-ka senmwul-ul ai-eykey cwu-ess-ta.
    c. Ai-eykey Mary-ka senmwul-ul cwu-ess-ta.
    d. Ai-eykey senmwul-ul Mary-ka cwu-ess-ta.

    e. Senmwul-ul Mary-ka ai-eykey cwu-ess-ta.

    f. Senmwul-ul ai-eykey Mary-ka cwu-ess-ta.

With existential-possessive predicates and psych-predicates, the subject is marked with the dative case marker. In the dative subject construction too, either order of the two arguments is allowed as shown in the examples in (10) and (11).

(10) a. Mary-eykey kay-ka   philyoha-ta.
       Mary-DAT   dog-NOM need-DECL
       'Mary needs a dog.'

     b. Kay-ka Mary-eykey philyoha-ta.
       'Mary needs a dog.'

(11) a. John-eykey kohyang-i   kulip-ta.
       John-DAT   hometown-NOM be missable-DECL.
       'John misses his hometown.'

     b. Kohyang-i John-eykey kulip-ta.
       'John misses his hometown.'

However, freedom of word order disappears in the dative subject constructions when the honorified subject cooccurs with the honorific verbal agreement marker -si. This loss of word order freedom is illustrated in the examples in (12) and (13).

(12) a. Lee kyoswunim-**kkey** kay-ka   philyoha-**si**-ta.
       Prof. Lee-DAT.HON   dog-NOM need-HON-DECL
       'Prof. Lee (honorified) needs a dog.'

     b. *Kay-ka Lee kyoswunim-**kkey** philyoha-**si**-ta.
       'Prof. Lee (honorified) needs a dog.'

(13) a. Halmeni-**kkey**   kohyang-i   kuliwu-**si**-ta.
       grandmother-DAT.HON hometown-NOM be missable-HON-DECL
       'Grandmother (honorified) misses her hometown.'

     b. *Kohyang-i halmeni-**kkey** kuliwu-**si**-ta.
       'Grandmother (honorified) misses her hometown.'

Examples (12b) and (13b) are another instances of 'the worst of the worst': the subject referring to an honorified being is neither in an unmarked nominative case nor in an unmarked clause-initial position. In sharp contrast, the usual (di-)transitive clauses with a nominative subject do not show any word order freezing when the subject is honorified. The theoretical point of this discussion that needs to be captured is summarized in (14).

(14) Generalization 3: Canonical word order becomes fixed when the subject triggering honorific agreement on the verb is not in nominative case. That is, the subject triggering honorific agreement on the verb should not be in both a marked case and in a marked position.

As far as I know, no account has been proposed to explain this generalization, and in fact various approaches to scrambling mentioned so far have little to say about this. Here I will briefly discuss the problems posed by the Korean data for derivational approaches to word order variation.

In her dissertation on scrambling in Korean, Y. Lee (1993) developed a very thorough analysis of word order variation with a number of important consequences. Assuming the VP internal subject hypothesis, she proposes that all arguments have to move out of VP and are adjoined to IP to be assigned Case, resulting in an S-structure representation like (15).

(15)

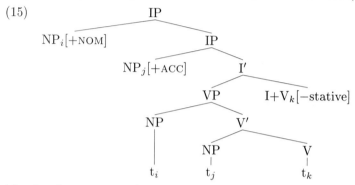

After head movement of the verb to I, both the nominative Case licenser, INFL, and the accusative Case licenser, INFL[−stative], are in the same position (the feature [−stative] is due to the verb) (Y. Lee 1993:68). This leads us to expect that the subject and the object may be arranged in any order, giving rise to scrambling effects.

Y. Lee (1993) assumes that dative case is an inherent case, assigned at D-structure, which looks like (16).

(16)

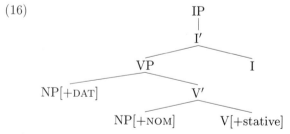

In (16) the subject of the dyadic stative predicates is assigned dative by the verb, and the object is assigned nominative (which is assumed to be the default case in Korean) under government by INFL. Since there is no Case-driven movement here, Y. Lee's (1993) analysis predicts that there will be no scrambling, and therefore wrongly predicts fixed word order for all dative subject constructions in Korean.

The problem is not solved even if we assume that dative case is not an inherent case but a structural Case, as suggested by Yoon (1996). Under this assumption, then, the experiencer or possessor subject NP may be assigned dative Case either in its base-generated position, SpecVP, or in IP-adjoined position just like the accusative objects of non-stative transitive verbs (see (15)). Both the subject and the object move out of VP to be assigned Case, resulting in an S-structure representation like (17).

(17)

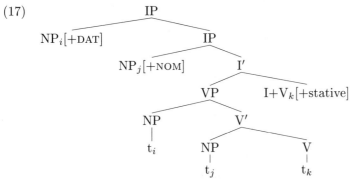

Thus, in this system scrambling is due to the fact that a dative subject can be assigned its Case either in its D-structure position or in IP-adjoined position. Since both the nominative Case licenser, INFL, and the dative Case licenser, INFL[+stative], are in the same position, the subject and the object may now be arranged in any order. However, this analysis predicts free word order for both the standard case frame (nominative-accusative) and the dative-nominative frame, missing the generalization that word order freezing happens in the dative subject construction only in a specific context—when the subject triggers honorific agreement on the verb. The only difference between the frozen and the non-frozen sentences is that only the former (e.g., (12a) and (13a)) contain the honorific marker -si on the verb, but not the latter (e.g., (10) and (11)). Given the lack of any theory neutral evidence for the existence of AgrP and various Spec-head relations in Korean, it is difficult to ascribe the contrast between the frozen and non-frozen sentences to their difference in syntactic structure and derivational complexity.[9]

In sum, the word order freezing phenomena in Hindi and Korean examined in this section strongly suggest that there is another important dimension that constrains word order independently of discourse prominence or formal features such as Case and Agr, namely the relative *markedness* of argument types. A central problem then is how to formally relate the rela-

---

[9]The phrasal head analysis of inflectional morphemes in Korean has been proposed by Whitman (1989), Ahn (1991), and many others. Ahn (1991) also suggests that the honorific marker -si and the negative marker an are syntactic heads of AgrP and NegP respectively. However, consistent with lexicalist theories of grammar, I will assume that Korean lacks functional projections and that verbal inflectional morphemes and case markers are affixes (showing lexical properties), following Han (1991), Sells (1995), Cho and Sells (1995), Kim (1999), and Choi (1999).

tive markedness of arguments along multiple dimensions to word order. In section 3.4, I will show that a nonderivational analysis of syntactic markedness like the one offered by OT captures the markedness generalizations about the freezing effects in Hindi and Korean in a way that acknowledges the universal basis of these effects and at the same time accounts for the language-particular ways in which these effects are realized. As we will see, 'the worst of the worst' type of word order freezing discussed in this section follows naturally from the interaction of markedness constraints derived through hierarchy alignment, constraints on the realization of information structure and constraints on canonical ordering.

3.2.2 Morphological Ambiguity and Word Order Freezing

The data presented in the preceding section have illustrated word order freezing in clauses which contain highly marked argument types. A different type of word order freezing is observed in Hindi and Korean in sentences where case markings on nominal arguments of a single predicate are identical. An example of the double nominative construction in Hindi is given in (18). The subject *patt^{h}ar* 'stone' is nominative because the transitive verb *tod* 'break' is not in perfective aspect, and the inanimate object *botal* 'bottle' is also nominative.[10] The examples in (18) and (19), taken from Mohanan (1992), show that the order of the two nominative constituents is "frozen" in SOV. This happens in a null context and in certain special discourse contexts (e.g., in an all focus context). Reversing the order of the two arguments in (18) yields a new sentence in (19) in canonical SOV order rather than maintaining meaning in an OSV order.

(18) Patt^{h}ar   botal   todegaa.
     stone-NOM bottle-NOM break-FUT
     (i) 'The stone will break the bottle.'
     (ii) *'The bottle will break the stone.'

(19) Botal   patt^{h}ar   todegaa.
     bottle-NOM stone-NOM break-FUT
     (i) 'The bottle will break the stone.'
     (ii) *'The stone will break the bottle.'

The multiple functions of some of the case markers in Hindi provide a further source of word order freezing in sentences with multiple nominals bearing the same case markers. For instance, the dative case marker and the accusative case marker in Hindi are identical: they are both -*ko*. The verb

---

[10]The choice between zero and overt case marking in Hindi is determined not by lexical subclasses of nouns but by their syntactic and semantic properties. Therefore the situation in Hindi double nominative construction is not an instance of case syncretism found in languages such as German and Russian, where certain lexical subclasses of nouns have identical case forms systematically associated with two or more distinct case features (Arnold Zwicky, p.c., April 1999). Word order freezing in Russian sentences with two syncretized arguments will be briefly discussed in section 3.5.2.

sik^h 'teach' in (20) can take either an ergative or a nominative subject. However, when a modal of obligation is superimposed on it, the modal induces dative case on that subject, as in (20).

(20) Raam-ko ilaa-ke bacce-ko gaanaa sik^{h}aanaa hai.
     Ram-DAT Ila's child-ACC music-NOM teach-NF be-PRES
     (i) 'Ram has to teach music to Ila's child.'
     (ii) *'Ila's child has to teach music to Ram.'

In (20) the dative subject *Raam* canonically precedes the two nonsubject arguments, the accusative goal object and the nominative theme object. That is, the initial *-ko* marked NP is interpreted as the agent but not as the goal fronted to the clause-initial position.[11]

Similar facts are found in multiple nominals with the case marker *-se*, which indicates instrument, source, path, the demoted subjects of passive, and so on. In (22), the passive of (21), both the demoted agent and the source bear the case marker *-se*. Grammatical function and thematic role are often closely aligned in Hindi and therefore it is difficult to distinguish which of the two influences ordering. However, the examples in (22) provide justification for the proposal made by Mohanan (1992, 1994a) and others that it is in fact the thematic hierarchy that determines canonical order. In (22a) and (22b), the thematic role of the arguments does not match their grammatical functions in terms of hierarchy: in spite of the fact that the initial *-se* marked NP is an ADJUNCT function, which is lower on the grammatical function hierarchy (i.e. SUBJ > OBJ > OBL > ADJ (Bresnan 1994; Mohanan and Mohanan 1994; Bresnan 2001b)) than the nominative subject, it canonically precedes the subject. Here again, the initial *-se* marked NP is not interpreted as fronted OBLIQUE.

(21) Coor-ne kal Ravii-se paise curaae.
     thief-ERG yesterday Ravi-from money-NOM steal-PERF
     'The/a thief stole money from Ravi yesterday.'

(22) a. Coor-se kal Ravii-se paise curaae gae.
        thief-INST yesterday Ravi-from money-NOM steal-PERF go-PERF
        (i) 'Money was stolen from Ravi yesterday by the/a thief.'
        (ii) *'Money was stolen from the thief yesterday by Ravi.'
     b. Ravii-se kal coor-se paise curaae gae.
        Ravi-INST yesterday thief-from money-NOM steal-PERF go-PERF
        (i) 'Money was stolen from the/a thief yesterday by Ravi.'
        (ii) *'Money was stolen from Ravi yesterday by the thief.'

---

[11]Mohanan (1994b) has proposed a case OCP principle, a constraint that disfavors identical case marking on more than one nominal in Hindi. Multiple occurrences of nominals marked with *-ko* and *-se* allowed in these examples are not subject to the case OCP principle, which is a restriction on case markings only, not on case features. Repetition of a case marking is allowed as long as the markings refer to distinct case features and the nominals marked with the same case markings are not adjacent.

Therefore following Mohanan (1992, 1994a) and also Sharma (1999), I assume that the canonical or unmarked word order in Hindi conforms to the thematic role hierarchy:

(23) Thematic Role Hierarchy
(Bresnan and Kanerva 1989; Bresnan and Zaenen 1990)
agent > beneficiary > experiencer/goal > instrument > patient/theme > locative

A similar phenomenon is found in the Korean double nominative construction. The Korean dyadic stative predicates exemplified in (10)–(13) above allow a different case realization on the experiencer (Gerdts and Youn 1988; Kim 1990; Hong 1991; Yoon 1996). It may be associated with nominative case as in (24)–(25) as well as dative case as in (10)–(13).

(24) Mary-ka   kay-ka   philyoha-ta.
Mary-NOM dog-NOM need-DECL
'Mary needs a dog.'

(25) John-i   kohyang-i   kulip-ta.
John-NOM hometown-NOM be missable-DECL
'John misses his hometown.'

In sentences where the case markings on both the subject and the object NP constituents are identical (i.e. nominative), their order is fixed as SOV. For instance, the two examples in (26) are only grammatical as interpreted in an SO order, and reversing the order of the nominal constituents of (26a) yields a new sentence (26b) in SOV order.

(26) a. Mary-ka   ku kay-ka   coh-ta.
Mary-NOM that dog-NOM like-DECL
(i) 'Mary likes that dog.'
(ii) *'That dog likes Mary.'
b. Ku kay-ka   Mary-ka   coh-ta.
that dog-NOM Mary-NOM like-DECL
(i) 'That dog likes Mary.'
(ii) *'Mary likes that dog.'

The Hindi and Korean examples above reveal the following generalizations, due to Mohanan (1992):

(27) Generalization 4: Canonical word order determined by the grammatical function hierarchy or the thematic role hierarchy becomes fixed if the case markings on two nominal arguments of a single predicate are identical under two alternative thematic role interpretations of the nominals.

Similar freezing effects have been observed in previous studies in various languages with fairly free word order, mostly without an explanatory analysis[12] (e.g., Rudin 1985 and Siewierska and Uhlirova 1998 for Bulgarian; Lenerz 1977 for German; Kuno 1980 for Japanese; England 1983 for Mayan languages; Foley 1986 for Papuan languages; Siewierska and Uhlirova 1998 for Polish; Jakobson 1963, Bloom 1999 for Russian), and occasionally cited as a problem for previous generative approaches to word order and case. One of the problematic aspects of the word order freezing is that it is not absolute but it is always possible to supply a context that brings out the interpretation "disallowed" in a null context (e.g., the OSV reading). In fact, it is usually fairly easy to find real-life examples where preferences for the unmarked word order and interpretation in sentences involving morphological ambiguity are overridden by constraints on the realization of information structure or selectional restrictions on verb arguments, and as a result the "disallowed" interpretation is the intended one. This raises the more general question of what role is played by syntactic constraints and by other sources of "soft" information in the order and interpretation of arguments. Section 3.5 shows that the emergence of the unmarked word order and interpretation in sentences with ambiguous case marking finds a natural analysis in OT, a general theory of constraint interaction which is designed from the beginning to incorporate soft universal constraints.

3.3 Deriving Free Word Order in OT-LFG

So far I have presented data from Hindi and Korean suggesting that theories of word order need to incorporate markedness and express the relation between alternative means of realizing grammatical roles, e.g., word order and case marking. I have also suggested certain generalizations that need to be captured by any general theory of word order. OT is a framework well-suited to the task of formally modeling the markedness generalizations because in this theory markedness is built into grammars in the form of violable universal constraints. In this section, I first briefly discuss the core ideas in OT and present major constraints on word order and basic clause structure, proposed in recent works on constituent ordering.

OT as a general theory of constraint interaction has been applied to a number of areas of linguistic research since its extraordinary success in the domain of phonology. For the domain of syntax, a growing body of work shows that many of the motivations for the OT approach to phonology are paralleled in syntax. Throughout this paper, I assume the formal framework of Lexical-Functional Grammar (LFG) recast within the OT framework (OT-LFG) (Bresnan 2000a,b, 2001a; Choi 1996, 1999; Kuhn 1999, 2001; Sells 1999, 2000, 2001). In this section, for illustrative purposes, we will consider

---

[12]Notable exceptions include Bloom (1999), who proposes an explicit, formal LFG account of word order freezing in Russian, and Kiparsky (1998), who has developed an account of restricted word order variation found in dative subject constructions and double nominative constructions in Hindi, Korean and Icelandic, based on case licensing theory.

how the basic clause structure and free word order in Hindi and Korean are derived in the framework of OT-LFG.

Input

In OT a grammar is a function mapping each linguistic input to its correct structural description or output. Within the OT-LFG framework inputs are taken to be a (possibly underspecified) feature structure representing (i) a predicator, (ii) the proto-role properties (P-ROLE PROP) of its argument(s), Proto-Agent (P-A) and Proto-Patient (P-P) (Dowty 1991), represented with features [VOL(ITIONALITY)], [CAUS(ALITY)], [SENT(IENCE)], etc. (Asudeh, 2001), and (iii) other morphosyntactic and semantic information (e.g., TENSE and ASPECT) in a language independent form (Bresnan, 2001a). The universal input is modeled by sets of f(unctional)-structures. Following Choi (1996, 1999), I further assume that the input also contains a description of the information status of the verb arguments represented with two features [±PROM(INENT)] and [±NEW]. The input that has *Anuune caand dek^{h}aa* 'Anu saw the moon' (=(1a)) in Hindi as its optimal realization would be the feature structure in (28).

$$
(28)\quad
\begin{bmatrix}
\text{GF1} & \begin{bmatrix}
\text{PRED} & \text{'Anu'} \\
\text{PROM} & + \\
\text{NEW} & - \\
\text{P-ROLE PROP} & \begin{bmatrix} \text{VOL} & + \\ \text{CAUS} & - \\ \text{SENT} & + \end{bmatrix}
\end{bmatrix}_x \\
\text{GF2} & \begin{bmatrix}
\text{PRED} & \text{'moon'} \\
\text{P-ROLE PROP} & \begin{bmatrix} \text{VOL} & - \\ \text{CAUS} & - \end{bmatrix}
\end{bmatrix}_y \\
\text{ASP} & \text{PERF} \\
\text{PRED} & \text{'see}<\text{P-A}_x,\ \text{P-P}_y>\text{'}
\end{bmatrix}
$$

(P-A: topic, P-P: discourse neutral)

I assume a four-way distinction of discourse functions based on these two features in (29), following the distinction posited by Butt and King (1996).[13]

---

[13]Choi's (1996) original use of the two discourse features is different from Butt and King (1996) in that she differentiates between contrastive focus and completive focus, as in (i). I do not discuss contrastive focus in this paper.

(i) Sentence = focus, ground

	+Prom	−Prom
−New	Topic	Background
+New	Contrastive Focus	Completive Focus

|| +PROM	−PROM
−NEW	Topic	Background
+NEW	Focus	Completive Information

(29)

Topic and background share the feature [−NEW] since they both express the ground material (i.e. the material that a sentence shares with the preceding sentences), while focus and completive information are classified as [+NEW] information since they both introduce new information into the discourse. The more prominent information units of a sentence, i.e. topic and focus, are differentiated in terms of the feature [PROM] from their less prominent pairs, background and completive information respectively.

In Hindi and Korean topics occur in clause-initial position, which I assume to be a position adjoined to S, following the analysis of scrambling in free word order languages (e.g., Y. Lee 1993; Choi 1999; cf. King 1995 for Russian; Dviwedi 1994, Sharma 1999 for Hindi; Butt and King 1996 for Urdu and Turkish).[14]

Apart from topic, the two most commonly employed discourse functions in Hindi are focus and postposed background (to be described shortly). The major function of focus is to provide new information relevant for the discourse structure. If there is only one focused constituent in the sentence, then it must appear immediately before the verb (Butt and King 1996; Sharma 1999). This is illustrated in (30).[15]

(30) a. Niinaa-ne Mohan-ko [tofii]$_{FOC}$ d-ii.
Nina-ERG Mohan-DAT toffee-NOM give-PERF
'Nina gave TOFFEE to MOHAN.'

b. #Niinaa-ne [Mohan-ko]$_{FOC}$ tofii d-ii.
Nina-ERG Mohan-DAT toffee-NOM give-PERF
'Nina gave toffee to MOHAN.'

Certain syntactic and information structural differences distinguish two types of nonprominent information: preverbal (completive information) and postverbal nonprominent information (background information). Consider the Urdu/Hindi sentences in (31)–(32), taken from Butt and King (1996).

---

[14]The term 'scrambling' here is used to refer to the phenomenon of multiple possibilities of the order of phrasal constituents which carry argument functions rather than to the formal operation.

[15]In Hindi, in addition to the preverbal focus, in-situ focusing of a phrase is possible in a sentence with multiple foci. This in-situ focus is always interpreted as contrastive focus, as illustrated in the example in (i) (taken from Butt and King 1996, footnote 13). I will not discuss multiple foci and in situ contrastive focus in this paper.

(i) (Aadnaan koliye nahii) Naadyaa-ne [Hassan-keliye]$_{CF}$ [tofii]$_F$ xarid-ii.
Adnan-for Nadya-ERG Hassan-for toffee-NOM buy-PERF
'Nadya bought TOFFEE for HASSAN (not for Adnan).'

(31) Naadyaa   kahãã-se   aa   rahii   hai?
     Nadya-NOM where-from come STATE be.PRES
     'Where is Nadya coming from?'

(32) a. Naadyaa   to   abhii [tofii]$_{COMPL}$ [bazaar-mẽ]$_{FOC}$
        Nadya-NOM indeed just toffee-NOM   market-LOC
        xarid rahii t^{h}ii.
        buy   STATE be.PRES
        'Nadya was just buying toffee at the market.'

     b. #Naadyaa to abhii [bazaar-mẽ]$_{FOC}$ xarid rahii t^{h}ii [tofii]$_{BCK}$

Since *bazaar-mẽ* 'at the market' provides the information which answers
the question in (31), it is focused, while the object *tofii* 'toffee' represents
completive information, which expresses purely new information that is neither topicalized nor focused. In this context, the utterance in (32b), where
tofii 'toffee' appears postverbally, is infelicitous because it presumes the toffee to be a familiar entity which represents known background information.

Candidates
Given an underspecified input f-structure (like the f-structure in (28)), a
set of output candidates are generated by the generator GEN. Here I assume that candidate sets consist of pairs of a c(onstituent)-structure and
its corresponding f-structure, which is subsumed by the input f-structure
(Bresnan 2000a; Kuhn 1999, 2001). Candidates are evaluated against the
input with respect to a set of ranked constraints, and all constraints are
universal and violable.

Constraints
Clause structure and word order are constrained by potentially conflicting constraints in several parallel structures of grammar. To derive the
canonical word order and deviations from this order in Hindi, I adopt the
constraints proposed in previous works based on OT-LFG, in particular by
Choi (1999) and Sells (1999, 2000, 2001). Those that are particularly relevant for present purposes are given below. The interaction of two alignment constraints in (33b) and (33c) gives basic subtypes of clause structure
without problematic recourse to complementary Left and Right alignment
constraints (see Sells (1999, 2000, 2001) for details). For example, ranking Spine-R over VHD-L will give right-branching languages. Head-final
languages like Hindi, Japanese and Korean, which lack the structural functional head of I, instantiate fully right-branching, with a single co-head at
the bottom (Sells 1999).

(33) Constraints on Clausal Skeleton (Sells 1999, 2000, 2001):

    a. The co-head of the clause is any node which is part of the Extended Projection (Grimshaw 1991, 1997), including V, V′, VP, I, I′, C and C′.

    b. Spine-R: co-head aligns right in its local subtree.

    c. VHD-L: X^0 verbal head aligns left in its local subtree.

The ordering of a verb's arguments in Hindi results from the interacting competing sets of constraints on word order: constraints on canonical ordering based on the hierarchies of grammatical functions and thematic roles (34); and information structuring constraints (35) distinguishing the contextual dimensions of discourse prominence and novelty, each marked by a binary feature. Here information structuring constraints proposed by Choi (1999) (i.e. PROM and NEW) are reinterpreted as f-structure alignment constraints à la Sells (1999, 2000, 2001b).

(34) Canonical Phrase Structure Constraints CANON (Choi 1999):

    a. CANON$_{GF}$ (f-s/c-s correspondence): Grammatical functions align with their canonical argument positions in c-structure according to the function hierarchy.[16]

       (SUBJ > D.OBJ > I.OBJ > OBL > ADJUNCT (Bresnan 1994; Mohanan and Mohanan 1994; Bresnan 2001b))

    b. CANON$_\theta$ (a-s/c-s correspondence): Non-verbal arguments at c-s align according to the thematic hierarchy.

       (Agent > Beneficiary > Experiencer/Goal > Instrument > Patient/Theme > Locative (Bresnan and Kanerva 1989; Bresnan and Zaenen 1990; Bresnan 2001))

(35) Information Structuring Constraints:

    a. TOP-L: Topic aligns left in the clause.

    b. FOC-L: Focus aligns left in the clause.

    c. BCK-R: Background information aligns right in the clause.

    d. COMPL-L: Completive information aligns left in the clause.

The faithfulness constraints in (36) ensure that the optimal candidate faithfully represents the proto-role information and the discourse information in the input:[17]

(36) Faithfulness Constraints:

    a. IDENT-IO(P-ROLE): The value of the proto-role features in the input (e.g., [VOL], [CAUS], [SENT], etc.) is preserved in the output.

---

[16]Strictly speaking, in Choi (1996, 1999), CANON$_{GF}$ is split into CN1: 'SUBJ should be structurally more prominent (e.g., c-command) than non-SUBJ functions' and CN2: 'Non-SUBJ functions align reversely with the c-structure according to the function hierarchy'.

[17]The MAX-IO class of faithfulness constraints, which penalize the deletion of features in the input, are omitted because they do not crucially distinguish the candidates under discussion here.

    b. DEP-IO(PROM): The feature [PROM] in the output is present in the input.

    c. DEP-IO(NEW): The feature [NEW] in the output is present in the input.

The discourse motivation for locating background information at one end of the clause and other discourse information at the other seems transparent. For Hindi, the dominance ranking is as (37). With this ranking, a topic always more to the left than a focus in the same clause; a background is always more to the right than spine elements in the same clause.

(37) Ranking for Hindi: Faithfulness constraints in (36) ≫
    BCK-R, TOP-L ≫ COMPL-L≫ FOC-L≫ SPINE-R ≫ CANON$_\theta$≫
    CANON$_{GF}$≫ VHD-L

Crucially, the ranking for Hindi in (37) can predict that when the arguments do not differ in informational status, the canonical constraints will take effect, leading to SOV order; when there are differences, the canonical SOV order will however violate information structuring constraints, so that competitors with a noncanonical ordering may win out.

    Korean differs from Hindi in one respect:[18] CANON$_{GF}$ has a stronger effect than CANON$_\theta$. This difference between Hindi and Korean can be handled by modifying the ranking of two types of canonical phrase structure constraints as follows:

(38) Ranking for Korean: Faithfulness constraints in (36) ≫
    TOP-L≫ COMPL-L≫ FOC-L≫ SPINE-R ≫ CANON$_{GF}$≫ CANON$_\theta$≫
    VHD-L

    Now, suppose that the experiencer argument *Anuu* of the Hindi volitional transitive verb *dek^{h}aa* 'saw' is topic (i.e. prominent given information) and the theme *caand* 'moon' is focus (i.e. prominent new information). In this context the input is as in (28) above. This results in the optimal output (39a) (=(1a)), going through the constraint competition in (39) (violations of ordering constraints are computed by counting constituents from the left.[19]). The ranking relation of the constraints separated by the comma is not specified here. CANON$_\theta$ is omitted here, since it has the same effect as CANON$_{GF}$ in this case. The constraints on faithfulness to proto-role information and discourse information in (36) will also be omitted in subsequent tableaux until they play a crucial role in section 3.5, and

---

[18]Another difference is that clause-final backgrounding in Korean is more restricted than in Hindi. I do not include BCK-R in (38) as its effects are not relevant here.

[19]Violations of VHD-L are counted within a local subtree (here VP) (Grimshaw 1997). As argued convincingly in Sharma (1999), no arguments appear within VP in Hindi, whether in specifier or complement position, and all arguments are generated directly under S. In other words, a VP does not contain the verb and its complements. Instead, the only VP-internal elements are those which are preverbally focused.

for our purposes here, we consider only candidates faithfully representing proto-role information and discourse information in the input in (28).

(39) Tableau 1. Volitional Transitives in Hindi

	BCK-R	TOP-L	COMPL-L	FOC-L	Spine-R	CANON$_{GF}$	VHD-L
CANDIDATES:							
☞ a. $[_S\ S_{TOP}\ [_S\ [_{VP}O_{FOC}V\ ]]]$	0			1	0	0	1
b. $[_S\ [S_{TOP}\ [_{VP}V]]_S\ O_{FOC}]$	0			2	1	0	0
c. $[_S\ O_{FOC}\ [_S\ S_{TOP}\ [_{VP}\ V]]]$	1			0	0	1	1
d. $[_S\ [O_{FOC}\ [_{VP}V]]_S\ S_{TOP}]$	2			0	1	1	0
e. $[_S\ [_{VP}\ V]\ S_{TOP}O_{FOC}]$	1			2	2	0	0
f. $[_S\ [_{VP}\ V]\ O_{FOC}S_{TOP}]$	2			1	2	1	0

As noted previously, the varied word orders in Hindi are optional from a purely syntactic point of view: although all orders shown in (39) above are in principle available, each is preferentially brought out by a particular context to mark a particular information structure. In the present framework this can be captured by considering the role of the input (Choi 1996, 1999). For example, the candidate (39c) with OSV order corresponds more faithfully to (40); the candidate (39d) with OVS order, to (41) (in the f-structures below the proto-role properties associated with each argument role are omitted for simplicity). In other words, according to this analysis OSV becomes optimal for expressing the topical status of the object and the newness of the subject under the same ranking that yields (39a) as the optimal output; OVS is optimal for expressing the nonsalient status of the subject as background information.

$$(40) \quad \begin{bmatrix} \text{GF}1 & \begin{bmatrix} \text{PRED} & \text{'Anu'} \\ \text{PROM} & - \\ \text{NEW} & + \end{bmatrix}x \\ \text{GF}2 & \begin{bmatrix} \text{PRED} & \text{'moon'} \\ \text{PROM} & + \\ \text{NEW} & - \end{bmatrix}y \\ \text{ASP} & \text{PERF} \\ \text{PRED} & \text{'see}<\text{P-A}_x,\ \text{P-P}_y>\text{'} \end{bmatrix}$$

(P-A: focus, P-P: topic)

(41)

$$
\begin{bmatrix}
\text{GF1} & \begin{bmatrix} \text{PRED} & \text{`Anu'} \\ \text{PROM} & - \\ \text{NEW} & - \end{bmatrix} x \\[4pt]
\text{GF2} & \begin{bmatrix} \text{PRED} & \text{`moon'} \\ \text{PROM} & + \\ \text{NEW} & - \end{bmatrix} y \\[4pt]
\text{ASP} & \text{PERF} \\
\text{PRED} & \text{`see}{<}\text{P-A}_x, \text{P-P}_y{>}\text{'}
\end{bmatrix}
$$

(P-A: background, P-P: topic)

To summarize, the varied word orders in Hindi and Korean and their related interpretations find a natural analysis in the OT-LFG framework combining the ideas of imperfect correspondence and violable constraints. The next step is to explain why orderings in sentences with more marked types of subjects (e.g., nonvolitional subject and dative subject) are more restricted, and word order is even frozen in SOV order in the most marked situation (see the discussion in section 3.2.1).

3.4 Markedness and Word Order Freezing

This section presents an OT-LFG account of the 'worst of the worst' type of freezing effects in Hindi and Korean. Central to my account is the use of harmonic alignment (Prince and Smolensky 1993; Aissen 1999) and local conjunction in OT (Smolensky 1995). I show that under the analysis I develop here, word order freezing in "free" word order languages is not the exception, but just one of the options allowed by the universal scales of grammatical function, semantic role, case, etc.

3.4.1 Hindi

In this section I demonstrate that the 'worst of the worst' type of the freezing effects in Hindi outlined in section 3.2.1 follows naturally from the general model of harmonic alignment developed in Prince and Smolensky (1993) and adopted in Aissen (1997, 1999). The formal definition of harmonic alignment is given in (42) (Prince and Smolensky 1993:136).

(42) Suppose a binary dimension D_1 with a scale $X > Y$ on its element $\{X, Y\}$, and another dimension D_2 with a scale $a > b > ... > z$ on its elements. The harmonic alignment of D_1 and D_2 is the pair of Harmonic scales:

H_X: $X/a \succ X/b \succ ... \succ X/z$
H_Y: $Y/z \succ ... \succ Y/b \succ Y/a$

The *constraint alignment* is the pair of constraint hierarchies:
C_X: $*X/z \gg ... \gg *X/b \gg *X/a$
C_Y: $*Y/a \gg *Y/b \gg ... \gg *Y/z$

Harmonic alignment is an important source of constraints in OT, and was introduced originally to express the relation between syllable position and sonority: the more prominent position (the nucleus) attracts segments which are more sonorous, while less prominent positions (the margins) attract less sonorous segments. This paper extends an idea first proposed in Aissen (1997) and developed further in Artstein (1998) and Aissen (1999, 2000), that harmonic alignment plays a central role in the domain of morphosyntax to express the relative markedness of different associations of morphosyntactic prominence hierarchies. The basic idea is that subject function plays a role in the clause analogous to that played by the peak in syllable structure: it is the most prominent grammatical function and thereby attracts elements which are relatively prominent on other dimensions such as semantic role (Aissen 1999:9).

Now, we can apply the definition above to the three prominence scales in (43)—the grammatical function (GF) scale, the semantic role scale and the scale on c-structure position. I will adopt the scale Subject > Nonsubject (43a) proposed by Aissen (1999) and the scale Proto-Agent (P-A) > Proto-Patient (P-P) (43b), where ">" means "more prominent than". For present purposes, I use the last two elements of the decomposed prominence scale $P\text{-}A_{vol} > P\text{-}A_{-vol} > P\text{-}P$ proposed by Asudeh (2001). In the predicates I discuss here, the experiencer argument corresponds to a nonvolitional Proto-Agent ($P\text{-}A_{-vol}$), and the theme argument to Proto-Patient (P-P). Furthermore, I use the additional scale of structural position (Lee 1999).

(43) Universal Scales

    a. GF: SUBJ > Non-SUBJ

    b. Semantic Role: $P\text{-}A_{-vol}$ > P-P

    c. Position: Initial > Non-initial

If the scales in (43) are harmonically aligned, we obtain the pairs of combined harmony scales in (44):

(44) Harmony Scales derived through Harmonic Alignment

    a. H_1: SUBJ/$P\text{-}A_{-vol}$ ≻ SUBJ/P-P

    b. H_2: NSUBJ/P-P ≻ NSUBJ/$P\text{-}A_{-vol}$

    c. H_3: SUBJ/Initial ≻ SUBJ/NInitial

    d. H_4: NSUBJ/NInitial ≻ NSUBJ/Initial

The first two harmony scales concern the association between grammatical function and semantic role, and assert that the unmarked situation is for the subject to be Proto-Agent, and for the object to be Proto-Patient (The connective "≻" is read as "more harmonic than"). The last two harmony scales involve the alignment of the grammatical function hierarchy and the structural position hierarchy. The basic insight is that the unmarked situation is for the subject to be in initial position, and for the nonsubject to be in noninitial position. The corresponding constraint alignments are the pairs of structural markedness constraint hierarchies in (45):

(45) Constraint Subhierarchies
    a. C_1: *subj/P-P $\gg$ *subj/P-A$_{-vol}$
    b. C_2: *Nsubj/P-A$_{-vol}$ $\gg$ *Nsubj/P-P
    c. C_3: *subj/NInitial $\gg$ *subj/Initial
    d. C_4: *Nsubj/Initial $\gg$ *Nsubj/NInitial

Each subhierarchy in (45) expresses the universal markedness relation (e.g., a clause with a P-P subject will lose out to a clause with a P-A subject, other things being equal). The important property of the constraint hierarchies in (45) is that while the ranking of constraints within a subhierarchy is fixed (e.g., *subj/P-P always outranks *subj/P-A$_{-vol}$), individually they may be variously ranked with respect to other constraints.

However, showing that a Proto-Patient subject and a subject in noninitial position are more marked than a Proto-Agent subject and a subject in initial position is not enough, because both cases are still allowed in Hindi. In order to capture the idea that if the subject is both a Proto-Patient and in a noninitial position at constituent structure, it is the worst of the worst, we can use the mechanism of *local conjunction* (Smolensky 1995:4).[20]

(46) The Local Conjunction of C_1 and C_2 in domain D, C_1 & C_2 is violated when there is some domain of type D in which both C_1 and C_2 are violated. Universally, C_1 & C_2 $\gg$ C_1, C_2.

To derive the pattern of universal markedness reflected in freezing effects in Hindi, let us consider the conjunction of the subhierarchy C_3 in (45c) with the high-ranked constraint *subj/P-P in (45a). This results in the new constraint subhierarchy in (47). The high-ranked constraint in (47) expresses the basic idea that if the subject is a highly marked Proto-Patient argument, it should not be in marked noninitial position. This most marked configuration excluded by this constraint obtains in sentences like (6b,c,d,e), repeated below as (48a,b,c,d). Recall from section 3.2.1 that these examples are acceptable only under the analysis of the nonvolitional experiencer as the subject, which cannot be the antecedent of the pronoun; the analysis of the theme as the subject in Hindi is compatible only with the theme-experiencer-verb order. This evidence suggests that when the Proto-Patient (e.g., theme) of a nonvolitional transitive verb is the subject and the Proto-Agent (e.g., experiencer) is the object, their order is fixed as sov. This is a clear case of avoidance of the worst of the worst.

(47) Conjoining *subj/P-P with C_3:
    C_5: *subj/P-P & *subj/NInitial $\gg$ *subj/P-P & *subj/Initial

---

[20]Local conjunction was first used in syntax in Legendre, Wilson, Smolensky, Homer and Raymond (1995), and has been extended to various domains of morphosyntax.

(48) a. Anuu-ko Niinaa   uskii   bastii-mẽ   dik^{h}ii.
Anu-DAT Nina-NOM PRON-GEN neighborhood-LOC appear-PERF
'Anu$_i$ saw Nina$_j$ in her$_{j/*i}$ neighborhood.'

b. Anuu-ko uskii   bastii-mẽ   dik^{h}ii   Niinaa.
Anu-DAT PRON-GEN neighborhood-LOC appear-PERF Nina-NOM
'Anu$_i$ saw Nina$_j$ in her$_{j/*i}$ neighborhood.'

c. Dik^{h}ii   Niinaa   Anuu-ko uskii   bastii-mẽ.
appear-PERF Nina-NOM Anu-DAT PRON-GEN neighborhood-LOC
'Anu$_i$ saw Nina$_j$ in her$_{j/*i}$ neighborhood.'

d. Dik^{h}ii   Anuu-ko Niinaa   uskii   bastii-mẽ.
appear-PERF Anu-DAT Nina-NOM PRON-GEN neighborhood-LOC
'Anu$_i$ saw Nina$_j$ in her$_{j/*i}$ neighborhood.'

Another type of structure excluded in Hindi is one like (6a), repeated here as (49), where the subject is in initial position but the object is postposed. Such a structure is marked with regard to the positioning of both the argument and the head, i.e. in that the verbal head is not the final element of the clause.

(49) Niinaa   uskii   bastii-mẽ   dik^{h}ii   Anuu-ko.
Nina-NOM PRON-GEN neighborhood-LOC appear-PERF Anu-DAT
'Anu$_i$ saw Nina$_j$ in her$_{j/*i}$ neighborhood.'

To derive this word order pattern in Hindi, first we need a simple restriction on the positioning of the co-head in (33b) (Sells 1999, 2000, 2001), repeated below in (50):

(50) Spine-R: co-head aligns right in its local subtree.

Now applying the same scheme to the conjunction of the subhierarchy C_2 from (43) with the constraint Spine-R in (50), we get the following new subhierarchy in (51), which concerns the markedness of the nonsubject:

(51) *NSUBJ/P-A$_{-vol}$ & Spine-R $\gg$ *NSUBJ/P-P & Spine-R

The higher-ranked constraint in (51) expresses the basic idea that the most marked situation obtains when the object gets linked to a marked semantic role (i.e. nonvolitional Proto-Agent) *and* the co-head of the clause is not in clause-final position. If this conjoined constraint dominates BCK-R, then marked types of objects would be restricted to the unmarked position, preceding the verb.

The ranking that emerges for Hindi is given in (52).

(52) Ranking for Hindi:
Conjoined markedness constraints:
*SUBJ/P-P & *SUBJ/NInitial, *NSUBJ/P-A$_{-vol}$ & Spine-R $\gg$
Linking constraints: *SUBJ/P-P, *NSUBJ/P-A$_{-vol}$ $\gg$
Information structuring constraints $\gg$ Canonical phrase structure constraints

Note here that the locally-conjoined constraints are ranked higher than their component constraints such as *Nsubj/P-A$_{-vol}$, which penalize the marked linking pattern. Crucially, the higher ranking of the three conjoined constraints on markedness of argument types over the information structuring constraints (e.g., Top-L and Foc-L) has the effect of restricting the word order freedom motivated by discourse prominence and the newness of arguments (see the discussion in section 3.3): marked argument types (e.g., Proto-Patient subject and nonvolitional Proto-Agent object) must occur in unmarked position in the clause.

Now, let us assume a discourse context in which the Proto-Agent is topic and the Proto-Patient is focus. This particular context renders an input like (53). This input then results in the optimal output (a1), going through the constraint competition in (54). The comma in the tableau indicates that there is no crucial ranking between the constraints separated by it. Also, candidates are again schematically represented, and faithfulness constraints, constraints on clausal skeleton and component constraints of the high-ranked conjoined constraints are omitted, as their effects are not relevant here. Candidates (a1) to (a6) are associated with the same f-structure, where the Proto-Agent argument 'Anu' is canonically mapped to the subject, and the Proto-Patient 'Nina' to the object. Similarly, candidates (b1) to (b6) are paired with the same f-structure with the opposite linking. Also, candidates labeled the same number share the same c-structure string. For example, both candidate (a1) and (b1) share the same string *Anuu-ko Ninaa dik^{h}ii*.

(53)   Input:

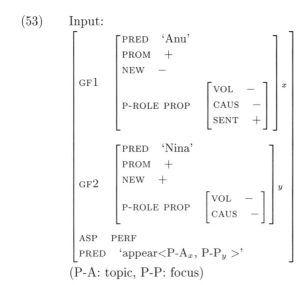

(P-A: topic, P-P: focus)

(54) Tableau 2. Linking and word order in Hindi nonvolitional transitives

CANDIDATES:	*SUBJ/P-P & *SUBJ/NInitial	*NSUBJ/P-A$_{-vol}$ & Spine-R	TOP-L	FOC-L	CANON$_{GF}$
☞ a1. $S_{P-A/TOP}O_{P-P/FOC}V$			0	1	
a2. $O_{P-P/FOC}S_{P-A/TOP}V$			1	0	*
a3. $S_{P-A/TOP}VO_{P-P/FOC}$			0	2	
a4. $O_{P-P/FOC}VS_{P-A/TOP}$			2	0	*
a5. $VS_{P-A/TOP}O_{P-P/FOC}$			1	2	
a6. $VO_{P-P/FOC}S_{P-A/TOP}$			2	1	*
b1. $O_{P-A/TOP}S_{P-P/FOC}V$	*!		0	1	*
b2. $S_{P-P/FOC}O_{P-A/TOP}V$			1	0	
b3. $O_{P-A/TOP}VS_{P-P/FOC}$	*!	*!	0	2	*
b4. $S_{P-P/FOC}VO_{P-A/TOP}$		*!	2	0	
b5. $VO_{P-A/TOP}S_{P-P/FOC}$	*!	*!	1	2	*
b6. $VS_{P-P/FOC}O_{P-A/TOP}$	*!	*!	2	1	

Due to the two high-ranking constraints that penalize highly marked types of arguments occurring in noncanonical position, candidates (b1), (b3), (b4), (b5) and (b6) are ruled out immediately: nonsubject initial candidates (b1), (b3), (b5) and (b6) with Proto-Patient subjects are eliminated by the constraint *SUBJ/P-P & *SUBJ/NInitial. Candidates (b3), (b4), (b5) and (b6) have postverbal arguments, violating the constraint *NSUBJ/P-A$_{-vol}$ & Spine-R.[21] Among (a1), (a3), (a4), (a5), (a6) and (b2), (a1) is the best; it satisfies more higher-ranking constraints than any other candidates.[22]

Now, let's consider a context in which the nonvolitional Proto-Agent is a focus and Proto-Patient is a topic. This is illustrated in the following question-answer examples in (55). Suppose that a speaker A asked another speaker B the question in (55) and that the examples in (56) are possible answers to it in that they provide the hearer with information as to who saw Nina, namely Anu. The *what about Niinaa?* phrase, following Vallduví (1992), is used to identify the topic, namely the prominent old information which is the center of interest in the current discourse. Since *Anuu-ko* 'to Anu' provides the information which answers the question, it is focused.

---

[21] I assume that when gradient alignment constraints like Spine-R are locally conjoined with other markedness constraints, the complex constraint is violated iff both its component constraints are violated at least once. That is, I interpret the conjoined constraint *NSUBJ/P-A$_{-vol}$ & Spine-R as violated by the four candidates (b3), (b4), (b5) and (b6), although (b5) and (b6) are worse than (b3) and (b4) with respect to Spine-R.

[22] The ungrammaticality of (a2) will be explained in section 3.5.2

(55) Aur Niinaa? Niinaa   kisko   dik^{h}ii?
     and Nina?   Nina-NOM who-DAT appear-PERF
     'What about Nina? Who saw Nina?'
     (Lit. 'To whom did Nina appear?')

(56) a. [Niinaa]$_{TOP}$ [Anuu-ko]$_{FOC}$ dik^{h}ii.
        Nina-NOM   Anu-DAT   appear-PERF
        'ANU saw Nina.' (Lit. 'Nina appeared to ANU.')

     b. *Anuu-ko Niinaa dik^{h}ii.

     c. *Niinaa dik^{h}ii Anuu-ko.

     d. *Anuu-ko dik^{h}ii Niinaa.

     e. *Dik^{h}ii Niinaa Anuu-ko.

     f. *Dik^{h}ii Anuu-ko Niinaa.

Among the six examples in (56), only (56a) is an appropriate answer where the topic appears canonically sentence initially, and the focus immediately before the verb. In contrast, in the sentences marked as ungrammatical the topic and focus are not in their canonical position, and as a result they are ungrammatical in the context of (55) as expected given the requirement that topic is clause initial and focus is immediately before the verb.[23]

Suppose that the sentences in (57b,c) are uttered by speaker B as a response to speaker A's question in (57a), followed by (56).

(57) a. Kahan?
        'Where?'

     b. Apnii   bastii-mẽ
        self-GEN neighborhood-LOC
        'in self's neighborhood'
        (Nina (theme) = apnii, Anu (experiencer) $\neq$ apnii)

     c. Uskii   bastii-mẽ
        PRON-GEN neighborhood-LOC
        'in her neighborhood'
        (Nina (theme) $\neq$ uskii, Anu (experiencer) = uskii)

As (57b,c) show, for the Hindi speakers I consulted, Nina is the only eligible antecedent of the reflexive *apnii* within the context of (55) and (57b); it is also the only element in the clause that cannot be coreferent with the pronoun *uskii*. Therefore the facts on word order and coreference in (55)–(57) suggest that the theme argument *Niinaa*, not the experiencer *Anuu*, is the grammatical subject when the former is topic and the latter is focus.

Let us now see how the OT account explains word order freezing in the discourse context in which the nonvolitional Proto-Agent is a focus and Proto-Patient is a topic. In this context the input is as (58). In this

---

[23]The examples in (56c) and (56d) are felicitous only in the context in which the preverbal NP is topicalized with the verb as an informational unit (Devyani Sharma, p.c., September 1999).

context, however, noncanonical linking becomes optimal under the same ranking, as illustrated in (59).

(58)   Input:

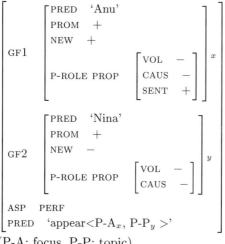

(P-A: focus, P-P: topic)

(59) Tableau 3. Noncanonical linking becomes optimal under the same ranking

CANDIDATES:	*SUBJ/P-P & *SUBJ/Ninitial,	*NSUBJ/P-A$_{-vol}$ & Spine-R	TOP-L	FOC-L	CANON$_{GF}$
a1. $S_{P-A/FOC}O_{P-P/TOP}V$			1	0	
a2. $O_{P-P/TOP}S_{P-A/FOC}V$			0	1	*
a3. $S_{P-A/FOC}VO_{P-P/TOP}$			2	0	
a4. $O_{P-P/TOP}VS_{P-A/FOC}$			0	2	*
a5. $VS_{P-A/FOC}O_{P-P/TOP}$			2	1	
a6. $VO_{P-P/TOP}S_{P-A/FOC}$			1	2	*
b1. $O_{P-A/FOC}S_{P-P/TOP}V$	*!		1	0	*
☞ b2. $S_{P-P/TOP}O_{P-A/FOC}V$			0	1	
b3. $O_{P-A/FOC}VS_{P-P/TOP}$	*!	*!	2	0	*
b4. $S_{P-P/TOP}VO_{P-A/FOC}$		*!	0	2	
b5. $VO_{P-A/FOC}S_{P-P/TOP}$	*!	*!	2	1	*
b6. $VS_{P-P/TOP}O_{P-A/FOC}$	*!	*!	1	2	

The violation patterns for the two top-ranked markedness constraints for (b) candidates in tableau 3 are just like the ones in tableau 2, and they will remain the same for all other tableaux too, because the violations of these conjoined constraints are not sensitive to discourse context. Thus, the constraint ranking proposed here accounts for the fact that in a clause with a Proto-Patient subject and a nonvolitional Proto-Agent object word order is fixed as SOV for expressing the content in (58), capturing the basic generalization that highly marked argument types occur only in unmarked position.

In sum, I have argued that harmonic alignment in OT can fruitfully be applied in word order freezing found in Hindi: the 'worst of the worst' generalization follows naturally from the general model of harmonic alignment. I have also shown that local conjunction of markedness constraints is highly appropriate to dealing with the relative markedness of argument types and its interaction with word order.

3.4.2 Korean

Marked associations of prominence hierarchies also provide an important source of word order freezing in Korean. Before we turn to how harmonic alignment and local conjunction play a role, let us first consider honorification, with which word order freezing is associated in an interesting way.

Korean is a language which has a highly developed system of honorification. The honorification system can be classified into three types, according to who the target of honoring is—subject honorification, nonsubject honorification and addressee honorification. Here I focus only on subject honorification as it is the only type of honorification that is directly relevant to the discussion of word order freezing in Korean.

Subject NP forms and verb forms in Korean vary depending on the relative social relationship among the referent of the subject, the speaker and the addressee. (60) shows six possible contexts according to the relative relationship among the participants of subject honorification, and which subject NP form and which verb form are used in each context.[24] The relative relationship among the participants of subject honorification can be explicitly represented in the input by using the feature honorification LEVEL. Four levels of honorification are represented by the integers 1–4.[25]

---

[24]Subject honorification has been used as a classic test for subjecthood in Korean. Only a grammatical subject—not a logical subject (i.e. a passive agent)—is responsible for *si*-marking on the verb. The object does not trigger *si*-marking even if it is topicalized.

[25]In (60), CASE.HON and -*si* indicate the use of an honorific case form and an honorific subject verb form respectively while CASE represents the use of a nonhonorific (plain) case form and Ø a nonhonorific (plain) subject verb form.

(60) Subject honorification in Korean (based loosely on Han (1991))

Social relationship	Subject NP	Verb form	LEVEL
a. **subj** > speaker,addressee	N-CASE.HON	V-*si*	4
b. addressee > **subj** > speaker	N-CASE.HON/ N-CASE	V-*si*	3
c. speaker > **subj** > addressee	N-CASE	V-*si*/V-Ø	2
d. speaker, addressee = subj	N-CASE	V-Ø	1
e. speaker > **subj** = addressee	N-CASE	V-Ø	1
f. speaker, addressee > **subj**	N-case	V-Ø	1

LEVEL 4 in (60a) corresponds to the context in which the subject referent is socially superior to both the speaker and the addressee. This is the only situation in which the honorific case form and the honorific verbal suffix -*si* are both used, as shown in (61a). In the context (60b), corresponding to LEVEL 3, the honorific case marker is optionally used as in (61b), and in the context (60c) the use of the honorific verbal suffix is optional as in (61c). Word order freezing happens only when the honorific affix is present on the verb in the contexts (60a,b,c) (see examples (12) and (13)).

(61) a. Lee kyoswu**nim-kkeyse** hakkyo-ey ka-**si**-ess-ta.
        Prof. Lee-NOM.HON   school-to go-HON-PAST-DECL
        'Prof. Lee (honorified) went to school.' (LEVEL 4)

     b. Lee kyoswu**nim-i/-kkeyse** hakkyo-ey ka-**si**-ess-ta.
        Prof. Lee-NOM/NOM.HON   school-to go-HON-PAST-DECL
        'Prof. Lee (honorified) went to school.' (LEVEL 3)

     c. Lee kyoswu**nim**-i hakkyo-ey ka-**si**/Ø-ess-ta.
        Prof. Lee-NOM   school-to go-HON/Ø-PAST-DECL
        'Prof. Lee (optionally honorified) went to school.' (LEVEL 2)

     d. Lee kyoswu-ka hakkyo-ey ka-Ø-ss-ta.
        Prof. Lee-NOM school-to   go-Ø-PAST-DECL
        'Prof. Lee went to school.' (LEVEL 1)

Honorific information about the subject of the clause can be represented by the feature HON, and there are three sources of [HON+] information that need to be represented in the input: the honorific verbal suffix -*si*, the honorific form of case markers, and the nominal affix -*nim*. Typically, in the contexts of (60a) and (60b), all of these are used, indicating that the subject's referent is owed honor.

The honorific verb form affixed with the verbal honorific suffix -*si* and the nonhonorific verb form have the feature structure in (62a) and (62b), respectively. In (62a) [HON+] information is contributed morphologically by -*si*. The nonhonorific verb form in (62b) is unspecified for [HON].

(62) a. *-si* marked verb form (honorific subject verb form)

$$
\begin{array}{c}
\text{V} \\
| \\
\textit{ka-si-ess-ta}
\end{array}
\quad
\begin{bmatrix}
\text{TNS} & \text{PAST} \\
\text{SUBJ} & \begin{bmatrix} \text{HON} & + \end{bmatrix} \\
\text{PRED} & \text{`go}<\text{P-A}_x,(\text{P-P}_y)>\text{'}
\end{bmatrix}
$$

  b. *-si*-less verb form (non-honorific subject verb form)

$$
\begin{array}{c}
\text{V} \\
| \\
\textit{ka-ss-ta}
\end{array}
\quad
\begin{bmatrix}
\text{TNS} & \text{PAST} \\
\text{PRED} & \text{`go}<\text{P-A}_x,(\text{P-P}_y)>\text{'}
\end{bmatrix}
$$

I hypothesize the respective representations in (63a) and (63b) for the subject NP form affixed with the honorific case marker and the one with the nonhonorific case marker. [HON+] information is contributed morphologically by the honorific case marker *-kkeyse* in (63a) and the nominal affix *-nim* in (63b). The nonhonorific noun form in (63c) is assumed to be unspecified for [HON].

(63) a. Honorific noun with honorific nominative case marker *-kkeyse*

$$
\begin{array}{c}
\text{NP} \\
| \\
\textit{Lee kyoswunim-kkeyse}
\end{array}
\quad
\begin{bmatrix}
\text{SUBJ} & \begin{bmatrix} \text{CASE} & \text{NOM} \\ \text{HON} & + \\ \text{PRED} & \text{`Prof. Lee'} \end{bmatrix}
\end{bmatrix}
$$

  b. Honorific noun marked with plain nominative case marker *-i*

$$
\begin{array}{c}
\text{NP} \\
| \\
\textit{Lee kyoswynim-i}
\end{array}
\quad
\begin{bmatrix}
\text{SUBJ} & \begin{bmatrix} \text{CASE} & \text{NOM} \\ \text{HON} & + \\ \text{PRED} & \text{`Prof. Lee'} \end{bmatrix}
\end{bmatrix}
$$

  c. Nonhonorific noun marked with plain nominative marker *-ka*

$$
\begin{array}{c}
\text{NP} \\
| \\
\textit{Lee kyoswu-ka}
\end{array}
\quad
\begin{bmatrix}
\text{SUBJ} & \begin{bmatrix} \text{CASE} & \text{NOM} \\ \text{PRED} & \text{`Prof. Lee'} \end{bmatrix}
\end{bmatrix}
$$

Honorific verbal morphology and nominal morphology, which share the [HON+] information, are further classified as in (64) according to the honorification LEVEL information they express.

(64) a. Honorific morphology which is used in the context in which the subject's referent is socially superior to both the speaker and the addressee (LEVEL 4), or to the speaker (LEVEL 3): Honorific case forms.

b. Honorific morphology which is used in the context in which the subject's referent is socially superior to either the speaker or the addressee (LEVEL 4, 3, 2):
Honorific verbal affix and noun forms.

With this classification of honorific morphology we can now formulate three markedness constraints, which apply to the form-content pairings, shown in (65):[26]

(65) HARMONY:

a. HON$_{CASE}$ ⟺ LEVEL 3 ∨ 4: Honorific case forms express honorification LEVEL whose value is 3 or higher.

b. HON$_V$ ⟺ LEVEL 2 ∨ 3 ∨ 4: Honorific verb forms express honorification LEVEL whose value is 2 or higher.

c. HON$_N$ ⟺ LEVEL 2 ∨ 3 ∨ 4: Honorific noun forms express honorification LEVEL whose value is 2 or higher.

The harmony constraints in (65) check the correspondence relations (or harmony relations) between types of nominal and verbal forms and the LEVEL information they are associated with. These constraints are violated by a candidate representation whenever the LEVEL information in the f-structure and the honorific marking of the subject and that of the verb in the c-structure make conflicting indications about the facts of the social relationship among the participants of honorification. This point is illustrated in the table in (66) containing four sentences with the same sentential content 'Prof. Kim left'.

(66)

INPUT: [LEVEL 3]	Constraint violations
a. #Kim kyoswunim-i ttena-Ø-ss-ta. Prof. Kim-NOM leave-Ø-PAST-DECL 'Prof. Kim left.'	(65a,b)
b. #Kim kyoswu-ka ttena-si-ess-ta. Prof. Kim-NOM leave-HON-PAST-DECL	(65a,c)
c. #Kim kyoswunim-kkeyse ttena-Ø-ss-ta.	(65b)
d. #Kim kyoswu-ka ttena-Ø-ss-ta.	(65a,b,c)

(All outputs are LEVEL 3.)

---

[26]The idea on form-function harmony constraints here is drawn from Bresnan (2001a), who has demonstrated convincingly that the pronominal inventories of a language can be derived from interactions of harmony constraints on possible pairings of the pronominal forms and the functional content, faithfulness constraints and markedness constraints on pronominal forms.

Thus the harmony constraints in (65) mark disagreeing candidates like (66a,b,c) or candidates like (66d), in which both the honorific marking of the subject and that of the verb do not correctly indicate the facts of the social context. Candidates like (66d), in which no honorific expressions are present, also violate faithfulness constraints in (67), which require the input feature structures (here the features HON and LEVEL) to correspond to the candidate feature structures to ensure the expressibility of content.

(67) Faithfulness constraints
   a. IDENT-IO(HON): The value of the feature HON in the input is preserved in the output.
   b. IDENT-IO(LEVEL): The value of the feature LEVEL in the input is preserved in the output.

Of course, not all languages have an extensive set of honorific forms, so further constraints are required. The constraints in (68) impose marks against the realization of case markers, nouns and verbs are honorific forms.

(68) Structural markedness constraints
   a. *HON$_{CASE}$: Avoid an honorific form of a case marker.
   b. *HON$_N$: Avoid an honorific form of a noun.
   c. *HON$_V$: Avoid an honorific form of a verb.

The three families of constraints introduced above are ranked in Korean as shown in (69):

(69) Ranking for Korean:
   Harmony constraints in (65) ≫ Faithfulness constraints in (67) ≫ Markedness constraints in (68)

The relative ranking of the harmony constraints and the faithfulness constraints is based on the degree of acceptability caused when they are violated: violations of the harmony constraints are less acceptable than violations of faithfulness constraints. The ranking of the faithfulness constraints above the structural markedness constraints yields an honorific language like Korean, in which specifications for HON and LEVEL in the input are realized at the surface. Conversely, the ranking of the structural markedness constraints above the faithfulness constraints would yield a language like English limited in its expressibility by the absence of honorific expressions.

Now let us return to our original problem, i.e. word order freezing. Recall from section 3.2.1 that in Korean a dative subject triggering honorific agreement on the verb cannot be in a noninitial position. To derive this result we can apply harmonic alignment of the grammatical function scale (70a) with the case scale in (70b) and the structural position scale in (70c).

(70) Universal Scales:
  a. GF: SUBJ > NonSUBJ
  b. Case: NOM > OBL
  c. Position: Initial > Noninitial

The harmony scale in (71), derived through harmonic alignment, expresses the relative markedness of particular associations, for example, the fact that a nominative-marked subject is more harmonic (less marked) than an oblique-marked subject. The constraints that are derived by inverting the rankings of *SUBJ/Initial over *SUBJ/NInitial in (71) and prefixing the Avoid operator "*" are given in (72). For instance, the ranking of *SUBJ/NInitial over *SUBJ/Initial in (72b) means that in the absence of any relevant higher ranking constraint, a clause with a subject in a noninitial position will lose out in direct competition to a clause with a subject in the unmarked initial position.

(71) Harmony Scales derived through Harmonic Alignment
  a. H_5: SUBJ/NOM $\succ$ SUBJ/OBL
  b. H_6: SUBJ/Initial $\succ$ SUBJ/NInitial

(72) Constraint Subhierarchies:
  a. C_6: *SUBJ/OBL $\gg$ *SUBJ/NOM
  b. C_7: *SUBJ/NInitial $\gg$ *SUBJ/Initial

In order to capture the idea that if the oblique subject triggering honorific marking on the verb occurs in a noninitial position, it is the worst of the worst, again we can use local conjunction of existing constraints. Conjunction of the two subhierarchies in (72) results in two new constraint subhierarchies in (73).

(73) a. Conjoining *SUBJ/OBL with C_6:
       C_8: *SUBJ/OBJ & *SUBJ/NInitial $\gg$
       SUBJ/OBL & *SUBJ/Initial
     b. Conjoining *SUBJ/NOM with C_6:
       C_9: *SUBJ/NOM & *SUBJ/NInitial $\gg$
       SUBJ/NOM & *SUBJ/Initial

The high-ranked constraint in (73a) expresses the basic idea that if the subject is in a marked case (oblique case), it should not be in a marked non-initial position. But not every Korean construction with such a highly marked subject is excluded: such a construction is excluded only when the subject cooccurs with honorific agreement on the verb. What is left to do, then, is to make the constraints in (73) apply to the specific construction involving honorification. This is done through the conjunction of the markedness constraint *HON_V in (68c) with the two subhierarchies in (73), as shown in (74).

(74) Conjunction of *HON$_V$ with the two subhierarchies in (73)

        a.   *HON$_V$ &
           [*SUBJ/OBL &
           *SUBJ/NInitial]

  b. *HON$_V$ &
     [*SUBJ/NOM &
     *SUBJ/NInitial]

          c. *HON$_V$ &
             [*SUBJ/OBL &
             *SUBJ/Initial]

        d. *HON$_V$ &
           [*SUBJ/NOM &
           *SUBJ/Initial]

A violation as in (a) represents the most marked situation, and (d) represents the least marked, with (b–c) as intermediate cases. For the current discussion, what is needed to rule out the ungrammatical sentences in (12b) (=(75a)) and (13b) is the topmost constraint in (74). This constraint expresses the idea that in case the verb is realized as an honorific form, the most marked configuration obtains when the subject is in oblique case and in the noninitial position of a clause. This is the only situation in which word order is frozen, and less marked configurations that are penalized by the low-ranked constraints are tolerated in the dative subject construction in Korean. This point is illustrated in (75) containing four sentences with the same sentential content 'Prof. Lee (honorified) needs a dog.'

(75)

	CANDIDATES AND VIOLATIONS:		
a.	*Kay-ka dog-NOM Violation: (74a)	Lee kyoswunim-kkey Prof. Lee-DAT.HON	philyoha-si-ta. need-HON-DECL
b.	Kay-ka dog-NOM Violation: (74b)	Lee kyoswunim-kkeyse Prof. Lee-NOM.HON	philyoha-si-ta. need-HON-DECL
c.	Lee kyoswunim-kkey Prof. Lee-DAT.HON Violation: (74c)	kay-ka dog-NOM	philyoha-si-ta. need-HON-DECL
d.	Lee kyoswunim-kkeyse Prof. Lee-NOM.HON Violation: (74d)	kay-ka dog-NOM	philyoha-si-ta. need-HON-DECL

The constraints introduced so far are ranked in Korean as in (76).

(76) Ranking for Korean: *HON$_V$ & [*SUBJ/OBL & *SUBJ/NInitial] ≫ HARMONY constraints ≫ IDENT-IO(HON), IDENT-IO(LEVEL), TOP-L ≫ CANON$_{GF}$

The higher ranking of the topmost conjoined constraint in (74) over the information structuring constraint TOP-L has the effect of restricting the word order freedom motivated by the topicality of arguments. There is no crucial ranking between the two faithfulness constraints and TOP-L. What this ranking predicts is that in a clause with a highly marked honorific oblique subject in a noninitial position, scrambling of object over subject will not be possible as it results in violation of the top-ranked constraint *HON$_V$ & [*SUBJ/OBL & *SUBJ/NInitial], thus capturing the generalization that marked subject types must occur in unmarked position in the clause.

In a discourse context in which the theme is a topic, that is, [PROM+, NEW−] and the experiencer is nonsalient background information, the input is as (77). This results in the optimal output (78a) with canonical SOV order. (78) schematically represents only candidates which contain at least one element that expresses [HON+] and [LEVEL] and hence satisfy IDENT-IO(HON) and IDENT-IO(LEVEL). Also, only candidates with dative subjects are represented. Though they compete against each other in the universal candidate set, sentences with dative subjects and those with nominative subjects differ in the information status of their arguments, and each is more faithful to a different input. Violations of the top-ranked markedness constraint, which penalizes a highly marked subject, cause ungrammaticality in a strong sense, as indicated in (78e,g) (which are never optimal in any kind of context). On the other hand, examples involving violations of the HARMONY constraints are generally infelicitous: they could be uttered in certain contexts.[27] Among the candidates violating the HARMONY constraints, the candidates (b), (c), (f) and (g) are instances of 'disagreement' because the honorific markers are present only on the subject NP or on the verb, not on both. Hence, the candidate (a) is the best; it satisfies more higher-ranking constraints than any other candidates. As was the case of Hindi, the violation pattern for the top-ranked conjoined constraint for each candidate remains the same for all the other tableaux provided by different inputs, because this constraint is not sensitive to discourse context.

---

[27]Some of them may be appropriate in a context where the social status of the subject referent is placed between that of the speaker and that of the addressee.

(77)   Input:

$$
\begin{bmatrix}
\text{GF1} & \begin{bmatrix} \text{PRED} & \text{'Prof. Lee'} \\ \text{HON} & + \end{bmatrix}_x \\[2ex]
\text{GF2} & \begin{bmatrix} \text{PRED} & \text{'dog'} \\ \text{PROM} & + \\ \text{NEW} & - \end{bmatrix}_y \\[3ex]
\text{TNS} & \text{PRES} \\
\text{LEVEL} & 4 \\
\text{PRED} & \text{'need}{<}\text{P-A}_x, \text{ P-P}_y {>}\text{'}
\end{bmatrix}
$$

(P-A: discourse-neutral, P-P: topic)

(78) Tableau 4. Word order freezing in Korean

CANDIDATES:	*HON$_V$ & [*SUBJ/OBL & *SUBJ/NInitial]	HARMONY	TOP-L	CANON$_{GF}$
☞ a. S-DAT.HON O-NOM V-HON			*	
b. S-DAT.HON O-NOM V-Ø		*	*	
c. S-DAT O-NOM V-HON		*	*	
d. S-DAT O-NOM V-Ø		**	*	
e. O-NOM S-DAT.HON V-HON	!*			*
f. O-NOM S-DAT.HON V-Ø		*		*
g. O-NOM S-DAT V-HON	!*	*		*
h. O-NOM S-DAT V-Ø		**		*

In summary, markedness constraints derived through harmonic alignment and local conjunction in OT provide interesting analyses of word order freezing in Hindi and Korean, a phenomenon which has remained unexplained in generative approaches to syntax. In the current OT account the generalizations about constituent order emerge naturally from interactions among the markedness constraints derived through harmonic alignment and local conjunction, and constraints on the realization of information structure and canonical ordering.

3.4.3 Typological and Theoretical Implications

Word order freezing in the situation of the 'worst of the worst' is not an idiosyncracy of Hindi and Korean. Clauses involving highly marked argument types consistently show restricted ordering possibilities in a variety of languages. For instance, in Kekchi, a Mayan language with canonical VOS order (Pinkerton 1976; Tomlin 1986), all six possible permutations of subject, object and verb are attested. However, when both the subject and object are animate and human, those noncanonical orders in which the object precedes the subject are precluded. When the subject is inanimate and the object is animate or human, those marked orders in which the first NP is the object and the second one is the subject are again precluded.[28]

Some Bantu languages are remarkable in precluding marked order in multiple object constructions. Logooli, a Luhya language spoken in Kenya, has rather free order of a beneficiary NP and a theme/patient NP if no ambiguity results (Morolong and Hyman 1977; Hyman and Duranti 1982; Siewierska 1988). When ambiguity might otherwise arise, for example, if both objects are animate, the thematically preferred beneficiary-theme order is selected. If, on the other hand, the prominence relations between animacy and thematic roles are reversed as beneficiary-nonhuman and theme-human, the animacy hierarchy determines word order: the order of the two is fixed with the theme preceding the beneficiary. Thus the marked association between the thematic role hierarchy and the animacy hierarchy is excluded in the marked order in which the less animate object precedes the more animate one, and surfaces only in the canonical order which conforms to the animacy hierarchy. Shona (Hawkinson and Hyman 1974) is another example which seems to belong in this class.

The effects of morphological case on word order that we have seen in Korean also show up in other languages with rich case morphology. For instance, in Icelandic with canonical SVO order marked orders such as OVS and VSO are permitted. However, not all marked orders are permitted in every case. In cases where the subject is dative and the object is nominative, OVS order is not possible: the dative argument has to precede the nominative one (Holmberg 1998). The impact of case marking on the relative order of arguments is particularly obvious in languages with dative shift (Primus 1998). While there exists considerable variation in factors influencing word order freezing, in all of the languages mentioned here, asymmetries in the word order patterns of arguments reflect exactly the same pattern: highly marked argument types involving the most marked associations of the prominence hierarchies can occur only in unmarked position.

---

[28]Other Mayan languages such as K'iche' (Mondloch 1981) and Kaqchikel (Broadwell 2000) show interesting interactions between word order and the hierarchies of grammatical function and definiteness. See Broadwell (2000) for an analysis of word order variation in Kaqchikel within the OT theory of markedness.

Thus under the markedness approach to word order taken here, word order freezing in languages with fairly free word order is not the exception, but can be derived from more general properties of the grammatical system, namely the markedness of argument types. Further, word order freezing can be seen as an instantiation of the general phenomenon of contextual neutralization often observed in phonology. For example, in some languages nasality is contrastive in vowels, except in the context before a nasal consonant, where all vowels are nasal (Kager 1999). This situation is produced by ranking (79), where the contextual markedness constraint $^*V_{ORAL}N$ dominates the faithfulness constraint IDENT-IO(nasal), which in turn dominates the context-free markedness constraint $^*V_{NASAL}$. This ranking states that nasal realization of vowels before nasal consonants takes priority over preservation of input values of [nasal], which in turn takes priority over the total orality of vowels. In sum, the nasality contrast in vowels is avoided in the marked position, i.e. before a nasal consonant.

(79) Contextual neutralization of nasality in vowels
(taken from Kager 1999:38–39)
Contextual markedness ≫ Faithfulness ≫ Context-free markedness
$^*V_{ORAL}N$ ≫ IDENT-IO(nasal) ≫ $^*V_{NASAL}$

This situation of neutralization of phonological contrasts in the marked position finds an interesting parallel in the syntactic domain of word order freezing. In languages with fairly free word order, noncanonical orderings are preferred options to mark a special information structure. However, as we have seen in the previous sections, under the special circumstances of markedness, they are replaced by the less marked, canonical order. This has been shown to be due to the ranking of the markedness constraints banning marked argument types in the marked positions and the information structuring constraints, which favor realization of contrasting prominence of arguments. The overriding of the information structuring constraints such as TOP-L gives rise to contextual neutralization in word order: realization of contrasts in discourse prominence, even if otherwise preferred in the language, is avoided in the most marked argument types. Under the uniform framework of constraint interaction both in phonology and syntax, this striking parallel can be given a unified markedness explanation.

3.5 Bidirectional Optimization and Word Order Freezing

As mentioned in section 3.2, 'the worst of the worst' is not the only source of word order freezing. Arguments bearing identical case markings can be restricted to unmarked word order position in Hindi and Korean, and if their ordering is reversed, the meaning of the sentence cannot be maintained. In this section, I show that by extending optimization to comprehension as well as to production (Smolensky 1996b, 1998), the bidirectional model of optimization, based on the same constraint ranking, correctly predicts that the type of scrambling leading to irrecoverability of the input content will not occur (section 3.5.1). Furthermore, I show how recovery of marked interpretation is dealt with (section 3.5.2) and address how the existence of ungrammatical and ambiguous strings can be captured (section 3.5.2).

3.5.1 Bidirectional Optimization and Recoverability

As already discussed for the Hindi double nominative examples, repeated below in (80), these sentences can only be unambiguously interpreted with the first NP as the agent, not as the patient (without strong contextual licensing of scrambled word order).

(80) a. Patt^{h}ar   botal   todegaa.
      stone-NOM bottle-NOM break-FUT
      (i) 'The stone will break the bottle.'
      (ii) *'The bottle will break the stone.'
   b. Botal   patt^{h}ar   todegaa.
      bottle-NOM stone-NOM break-FUT
      (i) 'The bottle will break the stone.'
      (ii) *'The stone will break the stone.'

However, this type of word order freezing does not yet follow from the standard generation-based OT grammar sketched above. The obvious problem is overgeneration of ungrammatical scrambling in sentences with ambiguous case marking, more generally generation of structures from which the (original) meaning is not recoverable:[29] the standard OT grammar freely generates outputs like (80b.ii), where the interpretation of the arguments does not conform to the canonical word order. As illustrated in (82), the constraint ranking for Hindi proposed in sections 3.3 and 3.4.1 yields candidate (a2) with the starred reading (=(80b.ii)) as the optimal output from the input in (81) (the [NEW−] is omitted; [PROM+] is abbreviated [P+]).

(81)   Input:

$$
\begin{bmatrix}
\text{GF1} & \begin{bmatrix} \text{PRED} & \text{'stone'} \\ \text{P-ROLE PROP} & \begin{bmatrix} \text{CAUS} & + \end{bmatrix} \end{bmatrix}_x \\
\text{GF2} & \begin{bmatrix} \text{PRED} & \text{'bottle'} \\ \text{PROM} & + \end{bmatrix}_y \\
\text{TNS} & \text{FUT} \\
\text{PRED} & \text{'break} <\text{P-A}_x, \text{P-P}_y> \text{'}
\end{bmatrix}
$$

(P-A: discourse-neutral, P-P: topic)

---

[29]Motivations for developing bidirectional OT in other domains of linguistics will not be discussed here. A growing body of work shows that many of the motivations for the bidirectional approach to syntax are paralleled in phonology and semantics. Especially important among works developing a bidirectional OT for phonology and semantics in recognition of the problems of ambiguity and interpretational preferences are Boersma (1999), Beaver (2000) and Blutner (1999); see also Anttila and Fong (2000).

(82) Tableau 5. Double nominative construction in Hindi

CANDIDATES:	*SUBJ/P-P	DEP-IO(PROM)	TOP-L	CANON$_{GF}$
a1. botal$_{S/P-P[P+]}$ patt^{h}ar$_{O/P-A}$ todegaa	*!			
☞ a2. botal$_{O/P-P[P+]}$ patt^{h}ar$_{S/P-A}$ todegaa				*
a3. botal$_{S/P-P}$ patt^{h}ar$_{O/P-A}$ todegaa	*!	*		
a4. botal$_{O/P-P}$ patt^{h}ar$_{S/P-A}$ todegaa		*		*
b1. patt^{h}ar$_{S/P-A}$ botal$_{O/P-P[P+]}$ todegaa			*	
b2. patt^{h}ar$_{O/P-A}$ botal$_{S/P-P[P+]}$ todegaa	*!		*	*
b3. patt^{h}ar$_{S/P-A}$ botal$_{O/P-P}$ todegaa		*		
b4. patt^{h}ar$_{O/P-A}$ botal$_{S/P-P}$ todegaa	*!	*		*

Intuitively, if we are going to rule out winners in standard generation-based optimization associated with the interpretation that does not match the preferred reading of the string, then we need to have a formal method for allowing the output of generation-based optimization to be checked against the string corresponding to the syntactic parse. This can be achieved by extending optimization to comprehension (or parsing) as well as production (or generation) directions (Smolensky 1996b, 1998). I will call this extended model of optimization the *bidirectional optimization* model.[30] The relation between production-directed optimization and comprehension-directed optimization proposed in Smolensky (1998) is summarized in (83).

(83) Production/Comprehension Chain of /I/:
/I/—Prod → [S] — overt part ⟶ "O" — Comp →/I'/

/I/ is recoverable from "O", where /I/— Prod → [S], if "O" — Comp →/I/

Production-directed optimization starts with an input /I/ and gives the set of structural descriptions [S] of the input /I/ as an output, whereas comprehension-directed optimization starts out from an overt form "O", and gives all structural descriptions the overt part of which is "O" as an output. So, in syntax we can think of production as a function that takes an underspecified f-structure input to a set of fully specified (c- and f-structure) analyses, and comprehension as a function that takes the string

---

[30]The term 'bidirectional optimization' was coined by Wilson (1996, 1997, 2001), who proposes an OT account of anaphora binding, based on 'interpretive' optimization and 'expressive' optimization. Here I use the term bidirectional optimization model to refer to the production/comprehension model proposed by Smolensky.

part of the production output and gives a semantic content as an output (i.e. an underspecified f-structure).

This extended model of optimization has two important properties which play a key role: first, production-directed optimization is based on a candidate set with a common input content, whereas comprehension-directed optimization is based on a candidate set with a common string input. Second, the same grammar can be used for both comprehension and production (Boersma 1999; Hale and Reiss 1998).[31] I will now demonstrate how this extended model of comprehension, based on the same constraint ranking, resolves the problem of generation of structures from which the meaning is not recoverable, thus explaining the emergence of the unmarked effect in word order.[32]

The tableaux in (84) and (85) represent the production and comprehension half of the bidirectional model of optimization respectively. Observe the differences in competitor sets in production and comprehension. As shown in (84), in production, what competes are candidates that share the particular semantic form or input. Hence the candidates where *botal* 'bottle' is the agent and *patt^h ar* 'stone' is the patient are not competitors in production as they are not faithful to the argument structure semantics. Those which are excluded by the high-ranked constraint IDENT-IO(P-ROLE), which requires the value of the proto-role features in the input is preserved in the output feature structure (here [CAUS+]), are shaded out in (84).

In contrast, in comprehension of the string *botal patt^h ar todegaa* (i.e. the overt part of the production output), only the candidates which conform to the input string are competing structures. Such candidates that do not share the same string are shaded out again in the tableau in (85).

---

[31] At first glance, it appears that bidirectional OT might be more complex than unidirectional OT. While the complexity and decidability of bidirectional OT and an OT system as a whole are still open issues, several significant results about these issues have been reported. For a detailed discussion of the formal properties and the issues of the complexity and decidability of OT (both unidirectional and bidirectional), the reader is referred to Jäger (2000) and Kuhn (1999, 2000a,b, 2001). In particular, Jäger (2000) has argued that bidirectional optimization can be modeled by means of finite state techniques.

[32] Kuhn (1999, 2001) independently establishes bidirectional optimization as a formal explanation for word order freezing in German. For recent works applying bidirectional optimization to other ambiguity-related phenomena in syntax, see Asudeh (2001), Donohue (1999), Kuhn (2000a), among others.

(84) Tableau 6. Production-directed optimization

INPUT = (81)	IDENT-IO(P-ROLE)	*SUBJ/P-P	DEP-IO(PROM)	TOP-L	CANON$_{GF}$
a1.	*!				
a2.	*!	*!			*
a3.		*!			
☞ a4.					*
b1.	*!		*		
b2.	*!	*!	*		*
b3.		*!	*		
b4.			*		*
c1.				*	
c2.		*!		*	*
c3.	*!	*!		*	
c4.	*!			*	*
d1.			*		
d2.		*!	*		*
d3.	*!	*!	*		
d4.	*!		*		*

a1. = botal$_{S/P-A[P+]}$ patt^{h}ar$_{O/P-P}$ todegaa
a2. = botal$_{O/P-A[P+]}$ patt^{h}ar$_{S/P-P}$ todegaa
a3. = botal$_{S/P-P[P+]}$ patt^{h}ar$_{O/P-A}$ todegaa
a4. = botal$_{O/P-P[P+]}$ patt^{h}ar$_{S/P-A}$ todegaa
b1. = botal$_{S/P-A}$ patt^{h}ar$_{O/P-P}$ todegaa
b2. = botal$_{O/P-A}$ patt^{h}ar$_{S/P-P}$ todegaa
b3. = botal$_{S/P-P}$ patt^{h}ar$_{O/P-A}$ todegaa
b4. = botal$_{O/P-P}$ patt^{h}ar$_{S/P-A}$ todegaa
c1. = patt^{h}ar$_{S/P-A}$ botal$_{O/P-P[P+]}$ todegaa
c2. = patt^{h}ar$_{O/P-A}$ botal$_{S/P-P[P+]}$ todegaa
c3. = patt^{h}ar$_{S/P-P}$ botal$_{O/P-A[P+]}$ todegaa
c4. = patt^{h}ar$_{O/P-P}$ botal$_{S/P-A[P+]}$ todegaa
d1. = patt^{h}ar$_{S/P-A}$ botal$_{S/P-P}$ todegaa
d2. = patt^{h}ar$_{O/P-A}$ botal$_{S/P-P}$ todegaa
d3. = patt^{h}ar$_{S/P-P}$ botal$_{O/P-A}$ todegaa
d4. = patt^{h}ar$_{O/P-P}$ botal$_{S/P-A}$ todegaa

(85) Tableau 7. Comprehension-directed optimization

INPUT = (84b)	IDENT-IO(P-ROLE)	*SUBJ/P-P	DEP-IO(PROM)	TOP-L	CANON$_{GF}$
a1.			*		
a2.		*!	*		*
a3.		*!	*		
a4.			*		*
☞ b1.					
b2.		*!			*
b3.		*!			
b4.					*
c1.			*	*	
c2.		*!	*	*	*
c3.		*!	*	*	
c4.			*	*	*
d1.					
d2.		*!			*
d3.		*!			
d4.					*

a1. = botal$_{S/P-A[P+]}$ patt^{h}ar$_{O/P-P}$ todegaa
a2. = botal$_{O/P-A[P+]}$ patt^{h}ar$_{S/P-P}$ todegaa
a3. = botal$_{S/P-P[P+]}$ patt^{h}ar$_{O/P-A}$ todegaa
a4. = botal$_{O/P-P[P+]}$ patt^{h}ar$_{S/P-A}$ todegaa
b1. = botal$_{S/P-A}$ patt^{h}ar$_{O/P-P}$ todegaa
b2. = botal$_{O/P-A}$ patt^{h}ar$_{S/P-P}$ todegaa
b3. = botal$_{S/P-P}$ patt^{h}ar$_{O/P-A}$ todegaa
b4. = botal$_{O/P-P}$ patt^{h}ar$_{S/P-A}$ todegaa
c1. = patt^{h}ar$_{S/P-A}$ botal$_{O/P-P[P+]}$ todegaa
c2. = patt^{h}ar$_{O/P-A}$ botal$_{S/P-P[P+]}$ todegaa
c3. = patt^{h}ar$_{S/P-P}$ botal$_{O/P-A[P+]}$ todegaa
c4. = patt^{h}ar$_{O/P-P}$ botal$_{S/P-A[P+]}$ todegaa
d1. = patt^{h}ar$_{S/P-A}$ botal$_{S/P-P}$ todegaa
d2. = patt^{h}ar$_{O/P-A}$ botal$_{S/P-P}$ todegaa
d3. = patt^{h}ar$_{S/P-P}$ botal$_{O/P-A}$ todegaa
d4. = patt^{h}ar$_{O/P-P}$ botal$_{S/P-A}$ todegaa

An additional difference between production and comprehension is that the candidates where [PROM+] is present on *botal* 'botal' are eliminated by DEP-IO(PROM), as this information is not present in the input (now the string, not a morphosyntactic and semantic content). Note that a different candidate from (84) (i.e. the candidate (b1) here), violating none of the constraints under consideration, is selected as the winner in the comprehension direction. Thus by bidirectional optimization we correctly derive the emergence of the unmarked effect (McCarthy and Prince 1994) in word order: the canonical SOV order emerges as the unmarked case in a null or neutral context, where there is no motivation for noncanonical orderings.

The optimal candidate (b1) has the meaning shown in (86), which is different from the input f-structure (81).[33] This means that the input f-structure we started from is not the most harmonic meaning for the string corresponding to the winning candidate in the production direction, and hence we can consider that candidate ungrammatical under bidirectional optimization as it does not provide recoverability for the original input.

(86) Recovered semantic content:

$$
\begin{bmatrix}
\text{GF1} & \begin{bmatrix} \text{PRED} & \text{'bottle'} \\ \text{P-ROLE PROP} & \begin{bmatrix} \text{CAUS} & + \end{bmatrix} \end{bmatrix}^y \\
\text{GF2} & \begin{bmatrix} \text{PRED} & \text{'stone'} \\ \text{PROM} & + \end{bmatrix}^x \\
\text{TNS} & \text{FUT} \\
\text{PRED} & \text{'break}<\text{P-A}_y, \text{P-P}_x >\text{'}
\end{bmatrix}
$$

Similar results can be shown for the double nominative construction in Korean and the constructions containing multiple nominals with *-ko* and *-se* in Hindi (see section 3.2.2): in these cases too, the meaning recovered in the comprehension direction by the output is not identical to the input for the production grammar. Specifically in the case of Hindi, CANON$_\theta$, the constraint ranked lower than TOP-L (but higher than CANON$_{GF}$), emerges as decisive in comprehension-directed optimization, forcing the choice of the canonical order (Agent-Source-Theme-V) determined by the thematic role hierarchy in sentences containing multiple nominals with *-ko* and *-se*. I will not go through these other results here.

---

[33]Several steps are involved in getting (86) from the output c- and f-structures of production-directed optimization. First, the function *yield* (Kuhn, 2001) applies to a c-structure and returns the string of terminal symbols; from the string input to comprehension-directed optimization, the GEN yields a set of candidate c- and f-structure analyses; the underspecified f-structure like the one in (86) is obtained by applying to the candidate f-structure of comprehension the filtering function *F*, which takes a fully specified f-structure to an underspecified f-structure. See Kuhn (1999, 2001) for a more detailed discussion of bidirectional competition and parsing analysis in OT-LFG.

3.5.2   Further Consequences of Bidirectional Optimization

In this section we will examine how contextual effects on recovery of grammatical relations and the ambiguity of a string can be captured in the bidirectional optimization model.

Recovery of Marked Interpretation

In Hindi (and Korean) the order of the two arguments bearing identical case markings is fixed in SOV order in a null or neutral context. Word order can be said to have a disambiguating function: it is the fixed word order that determines which phrase is the subject and which is the object.

This freezing effect operative in sentences with ambiguous case marking, unlike the 'worst of the worst' type examined earlier, is in fact overridden by contextualization. A further consequence of the bidirectional approach is that it makes room for context-directed disambiguation (Joan Bresnan, p.c., March 1999). That is, if discourse context, verb meaning or use of intonation, stress, morphological materials distinct from case markers, etc. disambiguate the grammatical functions or thematic roles of nominals, the recoverability problem is predicted not to arise, and the relevant OT constraints (e.g., TOP-L) come into play in selecting the best candidate. This section examines how the effects of an increase of such information (available clues that activate faithfulness constraints and information structuring constraints) on the construction of grammatical analyses can be integrated into bidirectional optimization and how this integration captures recovery of the marked interpretation of an ambiguous string.

Suppose the following sentence in (87) was uttered in a context where *botal* 'bottle' is highly topical and *patt^{h}ar* 'stone' is a causer. Although case forms on the two arguments are identical, the preceding discourse context clearly overrules the ordering preferences (e.g., basic SOV): the initial nominative argument is interpreted as the topicalized theme object.

(87) Botal   patt^{h}ar   todegaa.
     bottle-NOM stone-NOM break-FUT
     'The stone will break the bottle.'

The input that results in object initial candidates like (87) in production is identical to (81) and EVAL proceeds as in (84). Given the high ranking of the faithfulness constraints and TOP-L above CANON$_{GF}$, the optimal output is always the candidate which correctly parses the argument structure semantics and [PROM+] present on the theme argument in the input.

However, in order for a candidate with noncanonical order (e.g., OSV) to be selected as a winner in the comprehension grammar as well, one modification of Smolensky's model is needed, because bidirectional optimization in Smolensky's model gives only the unmarked order for any string involving ambiguous case marking. The source of the problem is the impoverishment of the input: the input to comprehension, taken to consist of bare strings in Smolensky's production/comprehension model, lacks all information (other than strings) available to language users that activates the constraints on the realization of information structure and the proto-role properties of arguments, and as a result, these constraints can never be active in comprehension, if the input consists solely of bare strings. To solve this problem, we need to assume that the input can no longer be regarded as consisting solely of the string. A representation of the contextual and proto-role information is now also part of this input, and it can be formally modeled as an underspecified feature structure indicating the information status of the string referents. In other words, when context that brings out the marked or scrambled interpretation is supplied to comprehension-directed optimization, the string input to comprehension is enriched with interpretational features, just as the f-structure input to the production direction contains information about each element's discourse status and proto-role information. This additional information plays a role in selecting the optimal analysis of the string, by activating the IDENT-IO(P-ROLE) constraint and the DEP-IO(PROM) constraint.

Another way of treating context-defeating word order freezing would be to say that the SOV restriction on nominal arguments bearing identical case marking may not be syntactic at all[34] and that other overriding factors are also beyond syntactic considerations. However, I believe that there are deep theoretical and empirical motivations for why a theory of linguistic competence needs to model the integration of "nonlinguistic" information.[35] Here I will mention three interrelated but distinct reasons.

First, our refined model of bidirectional optimization provides a highly flexible framework for having syntactic and other extra-syntactic factors interact in constructing grammatical analyses. Research on language processing and learning has suggested that language users and learners are extremely sensitive to information from discourse context, frequency biases and plausibility information and that knowledge of discourse context

---

[34]An argument against the view that freezing effects lie outside the realm of syntax and are merely the result of performance was detailed in Bloom (1999). He demonstrated that in Russian clauses with two syncretized nominal arguments are still frozen into SVO (in non-emotive speech), even when we have enough information from context or verbal morphology to resolve the grammatical roles of the syncretized arguments.

[35]E. Prince (2000) makes a distinction between two kinds of linguistic intuition: 1) the unconscious, inaccessible ability to process utterances of one's language; 2) meta-linguistic intuition, which is conscious, accessible meta-intuition about linguistic intuitions. The latter type includes speakers' knowledge of social/situational and discourse contexts in which an utterance may be used felicitously. The traditional terms 'linguistic' and 'nonlinguistic' information I use here correspond to the kind of information accessed by our linguistic and meta-linguistic intuitions respectively. It should be emphasized that our refined model of bidirectional optimization is not trying to model performance or perceptual strategies. Nor is it proposing to blur the distinction between the two kinds of linguistic knowledge. Rather what it is trying to model are the effects of various kinds of linguistic information in a broad sense including discourse context on the construction of grammatical analyses, which interact in parallel.

and the statistical properties of input is part of linguistic knowledge. So if a grammar is to be compatible with models of sentence processing and learning, then it needs to formally model linguistic knowledge in a way that allows for the dynamic interaction between syntactic and extra-syntactic factors in the construction of grammatical analyses.

Second, another advantage of including a context representation as part of the input is that it allows us to capture the symmetry between the production grammar and comprehension grammar. Research on language processing has shown us that linguistic knowledge is process-independent and that the kind of linguistic description that linguistic theory provides should therefore be a process-neutral grammar.[36] Note that in our model of bidirectional optimization the representation of contextual and proto-role information is part of the input both in production-directed and in comprehension-directed optimization. This refinement of the model has the effect of allowing faithfulness constraints sensitive to contextual and semantic information as well as markedness constraints to apply simultaneously to representations of linguistic structures in both production and comprehension. Thus, in our model of grammar, both production and comprehension can be viewed in terms of a process of satisfaction of the same set of competing constraints. The process-neutrality of our linguistic description seems very suggestive, given that linguistic knowledge is process-independent.

Third, in addition to modeling the symmetry between the production and comprehension grammar, the present model of extended optimization offers the formal integration to syntax and phonology. As Boersma (1999) independently observes, contextual/semantic information is also needed to account for phonological acquisition and the interaction between phonology and semantics. As an example from phonology parallel to the case discussed above, consider the case of final devoicing in Dutch, which causes the two words *rad* 'wheel' and *rat* 'rat' to merge on the surface. Smolensky's comprehension model cannot account for the fact that if the semantic context is 'turn', the recognition of 'wheel' is favored over that of 'rat', as far as the lexicon is concerned—i.e. the fact that infrequent and contextually disfavored items are hard to access. Boersma (1999) therefore proposes to include the semantic context as part of the input to the recognition grammar (e.g., input: [rat], context = 'turn') and to include in the recognition grammar lexical-access constraints whose rankings depend on the semantic context and on frequency of occurrence. So by including a formal representation of the extra-sentential context as part of the input both in comprehension-directed and production-directed optimization, the present

---

[36] For further discussion of how a declarative system of constraints can best ensure process-neutrality, see Bresnan and Kaplan (1982), Halvorsen (1983), Pollard and Sag (1994), Smolensky (1996b) and Sag and Wasow (1999).

model of bidirectional optimization can capture the symmetry between phonology-semantics interactions and syntax-semantics interactions.[37]

Now, let us examine how recovery of marked structure and interpretation is captured in our refined model of bidirectional optimization. Suppose that the argument *botal* 'bottle' of the verb *todegaa* 'break', for instance, is presented prominently in the context where *patt^h ar* 'stone' causes the breaking event. In this context the input to comprehension is like (88).

(88) Input:

Botal	patt^h ar	todegaa
[PROM+] (TOP)	[P-ROLE PROP [CAUS+]]	
	(P-A)	

The input in (88) feeds the EVAL process, shown in (89) (here and in subsequent tableaux, I show only candidates which satisfy the linking constraints, for simplicity). The [PROM+] and [CAUS+] information in the string input then will activate the constraints on faithfulness to proto-role information (IDENT-IO(P-ROLE)) and on discourse information (DEP-IO(PROM)), and the information structuring constraints, which are not in effect when no such information is present in the input string, as we saw above.

(89) Tableau 8. Comprehension-directed optimization in the double nominative construction in a topical context

		IDENT-IO(P-ROLE)	DEP-IO(PROM)	TOP-L	CANON$_{GF}$
	CANDIDATES:				
	a1. botal$_{S/P-A[P+]}$ patt^{h}ar$_{O/P-P}$ todegaa	*!			
☞	a2. botal$_{O/P-P[P+]}$ patt^{h}ar$_{S/P-A}$ todegaa				*
	b1. botal$_{S/P-A}$ patt^{h}ar$_{O/P-P}$ todegaa	*!	*		
	b2. botal$_{O/P-P}$ patt^{h}ar$_{S/P-A}$ todegaa		*		*
	c1. patt^{h}ar$_{S/P-A}$ botal$_{O/P-P[P+]}$ todegaa			*	
	c2. patt^{h}ar$_{O/P-P}$ botal$_{S/P-A[P+]}$ todegaa	*!		*	*
	d1. patt^{h}ar$_{S/P-A}$ botal$_{S/P-P}$ todegaa		*		
	d2. patt^{h}ar$_{O/P-P}$ botal$_{S/P-A}$ todegaa	*!	*		*

---

[37]Enrichment of the input in comprehension is also justified by computational considerations. For parsing/comprehension tasks, a given string is parsed to arrive at possible structures (to which production-directed optimization can apply). To ensure decidability of the parsing/comprehension task and to make constraint violations more detectable, the bidirectional model needs to be further constrained, and one way to do this is to take a context representation into account (Jonas Kuhn, p.c., March 2000).

The crucial constraints here are the faithfulness constraints: any candidate that has *botal* 'bottle' as agent and *patt^h ar* 'stone' as patient eliminated by IDENT-IO(P-ROLE). Candidates (b1) and (b2) show that the [PROM+] information, if present in the input, must be realized in the output, or else offending candidates are eliminated by DEP-IO(PROM). Note here that the same candidates have no violation of DEP-IO(PROM) in (85) since there is no [PROM] feature present in the input that must be realized in a null context. Lastly, candidates (a1) and (a2), ruled out by DEP-IO(PROM) in a null context, incur no violation of DEP-IO(PROM) as they correctly realize the [PROM+] information in the string input on the patient. So, candidate (a2) is the optimal output, under the ranking shown. This recovers the semantic content in (90), which is identical to the input in (81). The reader can also see in tableau (89) that the winner in the comprehension grammar and the winner in the production grammar ((84)) are identical.

(90) Recovered semantic content:

$$
\begin{bmatrix}
\text{GF1} & \begin{bmatrix} \text{PRED} & \text{'stone'} \\ \text{P-ROLE} & \text{PROP} & [\text{CAUS} & +] \end{bmatrix}^x \\
\text{GF2} & \begin{bmatrix} \text{PRED} & \text{'bottle'} \\ \text{PROM} & + \end{bmatrix}^y \\
\text{TNS} & \text{FUT} \\
\text{PRED} & \text{'break} <\text{P-A}_x,\text{P-P}_y> \text{'}
\end{bmatrix}
$$

We have so far paid attention only to sentences which can have both SOV and OSV readings, depending on the context. In some cases, however, only the OSV reading is available. For instance, in the Korean sentences (91) and (92), which involve nominative object scrambling, the bracketed part can only be interpreted with the first nominative NP as theme (mapped onto object) and the second one as experiencer (mapped onto subject).

(91) Computer-ka   philyoha-n-tey, [**VCR-i**   aitul-i
     computer-NOM need-PRES-but VCR-NOM kids-NOM
     philyoha-ta-ko]   hay-se   VCR-ul   sa-ss-ta.
     need-DECL-COMP say-therefore VCR-ACC buy-PAST-DECL
     'I need a computer, but a VCR, my kids said that they need, and therefore I bought a VCR.'

(92) Cinan cwu say coffee shop-i   mwun-ul yel-ess-nuntey,
     last week   new coffee shop-NOM door-ACC open-PAST-and
     ku coffee shop-uy [**coffee-ka** chinkwu-ka coh-ta-ko]
     that coffee shop-GEN coffee-NOM friend-NOM like-DECL-COMP
     hay-ss-ta.
     say-PAST-DECL
     'Last week a new coffee shop opened. Coffee at that coffee shop, my friend said that he/she likes.'

It is important to note that the same constraint system works in these cases. In particular, the constraint ranking IDENT-IO(P-ROLE) $\gg$ CANON$_{GF}$ correctly yields the OSV order as the optimal output in both production and comprehension: due to the high-ranking constraint IDENT-IO(P-ROLE), candidates with the canonical SOV (or experiencer-theme-V) order will be eliminated, since they have a non-sentient argument (i.e. 'VCR' in (91) and 'coffee' in (92)) as the subject and sentient argument (i.e. 'kids' in (91) and 'my friend' in (92)) as the object. Only candidates with the noncanonical OSV (or theme-experiencer-V) order will correctly parse the proto-role property of [SENTIENCE$\pm$] associated with each argument of the predicates used in (91) and (92), satisfying the high-ranked constraint IDENT-IO(P-ROLE) (and also the constraints on the proto-role properties-to-grammatical function linking).

Thus, by enriching the input string with semantic and contextual information, the present OT account captures the fact that with an increase of information that activates the constraints on the realization of arguments and information structure, the recoverability problem observed in a neutral context does not arise when the arguments differ in information status or proto-role properties.

Lastly, let us address the question of how bidirectional optimization can be correctly applied to the examples with unambiguous case marking, and has an effect only with the ambiguous ones. In contrast to the double nominative construction considered above, the recoverability problem does not occur in sentences with unambiguous case marking (e.g., ergative-nominative or ergative-accusative in Hindi) even without taking contextual information into consideration. For example, any permutation of the three elements in (93a) does not change the meaning of the sentence.

(93) a. Anuu-ne caand dek^{h}aa.   (=(1a))
          Anu-ERG moon-NOM see/look at-PERF
          'Anu saw the moon.'

      b. Caand Anuu-ne dek^{h}aa.   (=(1b))
          moon-NOM Anu-ERG see/look at-PERF
          'Anu saw the moon.'

Consider the production half first, illustrated in (94) and (95) below. Tableau (95) shows that candidate (a2) (=(93b)) with OSV order becomes optimal for expressing the topical status of the theme *caand* 'moon' and the volitionality of the experiencer 'Anu'.

(94) Input:

$$\begin{bmatrix} \text{GF1} & \begin{bmatrix} \text{PRED} & \text{'Anu'} \\ \text{P-ROLE} & \text{PROP} & [\text{VOL} \;\; +] \end{bmatrix}^x \\[2ex] \text{GF2} & \begin{bmatrix} \text{PRED} & \text{'moon'} \\ \text{PROM} & + \end{bmatrix}^y \\[1ex] \text{ASP} & \text{PERF} \\ \text{PRED} & \text{'see} <\text{P-A}_x,\text{P-P}_y> \text{'} \end{bmatrix}$$

(P-A: discourse neutral, P-P: topic)

(95) Tableau 9. Production-directed optimization in standard case frame

	IDENT-IO(P-ROLE)	DEP-IO(PROM)	TOP-L	CANON$_{GF}$
CANDIDATES:				
a1. caand$_{S/P-A[P+]}$ Anuu-ne$_{O/P-P}$ dek^{h}aa	*!			
☞ a2. caand$_{O/P-P[P+]}$ Anuu-ne$_{S/P-A}$ dek^{h}aa				*
b1. caand$_{S/P-A}$ Anuu-ne$_{O/P-P}$ dek^{h}aa	*!	*		
b2. caand$_{O/P-P}$ Anuu-ne$_{S/P-A}$ dek^{h}aa		*		*
c1. Anuu-ne$_{S/P-A}$ caand$_{O/P-P[P+]}$ dek^{h}aa			*	
c2. Anuu-ne$_{O/P-P}$ caand$_{S/P-A[P+]}$ dek^{h}aa	*!		*	*
d1. Anuu-ne$_{S/P-A}$ caand$_{S/P-P}$ dek^{h}aa		*		
d2. Anuu-ne$_{O/P-P}$ caand$_{S/P-A}$ dek^{h}aa	*!	*		*

When the string *caand Anuu-ne dek^{h}aa* is uttered in a context in which *caand* 'moon' is topical, the input is like (96). The [VOL+] information can be inferred from the context, but even without any contextual clue, 'Anuu' must be interpreted as the volitional experiencer and *caand* 'moon' as the theme. This is because the ergative case marker -*ne* independently carries volitionality information about the subject of the clause.

(96) Input:

Caand	Anuu-ne	dek^{h}aa
[PROM+]	[P-ROLE PROP [VOL+]]	
(TOP)	(P-A)	

As in the examples involving ambiguous case-marking discussed above, the same constraint system works in comprehension of the string in (96). Observe again the key role played by the high-ranked faithfulness constraints in selecting candidate (a2) with OSV order in (97) as the optimal output.

It correctly realizes the Proto-Agent property of volitionality contributed by the case morphology as well as the topicality of *caand* 'moon'.

(97) Tableau 10. Comprehension-directed optimization in standard case frame

	CANDIDATES:	IDENT-IO(P-ROLE)	DEP-IO(PROM)	TOP-L	CANON$_{GF}$
	a1. caand$_{S/P-A[P+]}$ Anuu-ne$_{O/P-P}$ dek^{h}aa	*!			
☞	a2. caand$_{O/P-P[P+]}$ Anuu-ne$_{S/P-A}$ dek^{h}aa				*
	b1. caand$_{S/P-A}$ Anuu-ne$_{O/P-P}$ dek^{h}aa	*!	*		
	b2. caand$_{O/P-P}$ Anuu-ne$_{S/P-A}$ dek^{h}aa		*		*
	c1. Anuu-ne$_{S/P-A}$ caand$_{O/P-P[P+]}$ dek^{h}aa			*	
	c2. Anuu-ne$_{O/P-P}$ caand$_{S/P-A[P+]}$ dek^{h}aa	*!		*	*
	d1. Anuu-ne$_{S/P-A}$ caand$_{S/P-P}$ dek^{h}aa		*		
	d2. Anuu-ne$_{O/P-P}$ caand$_{S/P-A}$ dek^{h}aa	*!	*		*

Again the production and comprehension processes yield an identical winner, and hence it is predicted that the recoverability problem will not occur in sentences with unambiguous case marking, since the winners in the two processes recover the identical semantic content. Therefore this analysis correctly accounts for the fact that the interpretation of the sentences with unambiguous case marking in terms of thematic roles does not rely on word order, but is driven by the overt case marking.

In summary, I have argued that word order freezing in sentences with ambiguous case marking in Hindi and Korean can be explained when the constraint system allows an extension to bidirectional competition. I have also shown that by enriching the string input to comprehension with semantic and contextual information, the bidirectional approach, based on the same set of constraints, predicts that preferences for canonical ordering are overridden by faithfulness constraints on discourse prominence and proto-role information, which outrank markedness constraints against non-canonical GF order in both the production and comprehension grammars.

Capturing Ungrammatical and Ambiguous Strings

In the current OT constraint system, ungrammaticality arises from a failure to recover the input from the output. Further, the constraint system predicts whether a given string in the language is ambiguous or not. Recall from section 3.2.1 that Hindi avoids a possible (parsing) ambiguity in order to uniquely identify the subject and object of a nonvolitional transitive and that the ungrammaticality of the string in (98b), associated with the marked structure, is part of this larger generalization about ambiguity avoidance. In this section, I discuss how the constraint system can capture this generalization from a bidirectional perspective.

(98) Grammaticality of a string with theme-experiencer-V order

    a. Niinaa   Anuu-ko uskii   bastii-mẽ   dik^{h}ii. (SOV)
       Nina-NOM Anu-DAT PRON-GEN neighborhood-LOC appear-PERF
       'Anu$_i$ saw Nina$_j$ in her$_{i/*j}$ neighborhood.'

    b. *Niinaa   Anuu-ko uskii   bastii-mẽ   dik^{h}ii. (OSV)
       Nina-NOM Anu-DAT PRON-GEN neighborhood-LOC appear-PERF
       'Anu$_i$ saw Nina$_j$ in her$_{j/*i}$ neighborhood.'

Let us first consider the the production-directed optimization in (99). The input is identical to the f-structure in (53) (the two candidates (a) and (b) shown in (99) correspond to (b2) and (a2) in ((54) and (59) respectively)). In this tableau, the high-ranking constraints do not distinguish the candidates[38], and it is the lower-ranking constraint CANON$_{GF}$ that breaks the tie and favors the less marked candidate with SOV order.

(99) Tableau 11. Production-directed optimization in Hindi nonvolitional transitives

INPUT=(53)	*SUBJ/P-P & *SUBJ/N-initial	*NSUBJ/P-A$_{-vol}$ & Spine-R	TOP-L	CANON$_{GF}$
☞ a. Niinaa$_{S/P-P}$Anuu-ko$_{O/P-A}$dik^{h}ii				
b. *Niinaa$_{O/P-P}$Anuu-ko$_{S/P-A}$dik^{h}ii				*

---

[38] One of the key features of grammatical function selection in Hindi (and Marathi) is subject/object alternation in verb classes that do not take a volitional argument. If there is no volitional argument (more precisely, an argument lacking the property of 'conscious choice' (Mohanan 1994a)) and there is more than one argument that has a proto-patient property (e.g., argument not entailed to possess sentience), there will be a subject/object alternation. Here, I am assuming that it is variable constraint rankings as proposed by Asudeh (2001) which yield the subject/object alternation for nonvolitional transitives. I have omitted the floating linking constraints having variable ranking values (Boersma 1997; Asudeh, 2001) in the tableaux in (99) and (100) since they are too complicated to be treated here. It is sufficient to note that these floating constraints on the semantic role-grammatical function linking also equally (dis)favor the two candidates under consideration in the tableaux in (99) and (100).

The tableau in (100) illustrates how the same constraint ranking yields the candidate with SOV order as the optimal output in comprehension. Once again, the CANON$_{GF}$ constraint operates decisively to correctly identify the first argument as the subject and hence serves to rule out the marked structure in the absence of any difference in the volitionality of the two arguments.

(100) Tableau 12. Comprehension-directed optimization in Hindi nonvolitional transitives

INPUT: *Niinaa Anuu-ko dik^{h}ii*	*SUBJ/P-P & *SUBJ/Ninitial	*NSUBJ/P-A$_{-vol}$ & Spine-R	TOP-L	CANON$_{GF}$
☞ a. Niinaa$_{S/P-P}$Anuu-ko$_{O/P-A}$dik^{h}ii				
b. *Niinaa$_{O/P-P}$Anuu-ko$_{S/P-A}$dik^{h}ii				*

Thus, in short, in the tableaux here, we can see that of the available structural alternatives sharing the same string expression of a Hindi nonvolitional transitive, what emerges as the optimal output is the unmarked structure that conforms to canonical SOV order; the ungrammaticality of the OSV analysis of the string in (100) follows from its relative markedness compared to the other parsing alternative that competes with it.

However, while word order, morphology, verb meaning and context can eliminate some ambiguity in the identification of the grammatical role of arguments, they do not remove all ambiguity. Given that all of the cases that we have been examining so far involve only one winning candidate, the existence of ambiguous strings becomes of interest. Before I conclude this section, I exemplify some of the cases where ambiguity still remains with certain verbs.

Passives of ditransitives in Hindi are another example of a verb class that shows an alternation in which the argument can be realized as the subject or object. These verbs are similar to nonvolitional transitive verbs that we have been examining in that the grammatical function realization of their (internal) arguments is also determined by word order in the theme-initial clauses like (101a) (Mohanan 1992; Mohanan and Mohanan 1994). Unlike nonvolitional transitives, however, goal-initial passive sentences as in (101b) do receive more than one grammatical function analysis. That is, they are ambiguous regarding which (internal) argument is assigned to the subject function and which is assigned to the object function, though the sentential meaning is constant.

(101) Parsing ambiguity in passives of ditransitives in Hindi (Mohanan 1992)

a. Baccaa   Mohan-ko   diyaa   gayaa.
child-NOM Mohan-DAT give-PERF go-PERF
(i) 'The child was given to Mohan.' (SUBJ: theme, OBJ: goal)
(ii) *'Mohan was given a child.' (*SUBJ: goal, OBJ: theme)

b. Mohan-ko   baccaa   diyaa   gayaa.
Mohan-DAT child-NOM give-PERF go-PERF
(i) 'Mohan was given a child.' (SUBJ: goal, OBJ: theme)
(ii) 'The child was given to Mohan.' (SUBJ: theme, OBJ: goal)

In some languages, true semantic ambiguity is observed. For example, in the Dogon language Donno Sɔ (Culy 1995), which is both head- and dependent-marking, ambiguity arises in ditransitives under special circumstances. In Donno Sɔ only objects are case-marked but not subjects, with which finite verbs in matrix clauses agree in person and number. Culy (1995) discovered that object case marking in Donno Sɔ is subject to various ordered conditions such as animacy, semantic role, pronominality, definiteness and ambiguity. The strongest condition among these is the animacy restriction: if the goal/recipient and theme objects of a ditransitive verb are both human, it is the goal/recipient that must occur with case marking. Thus, there is potentially some ambiguity if the subject and the theme object of a ditransitive are equal in animacy and both refer to arguments of the same number. In these instances, the clause will be ambiguous as to which arguments are subject and object, as seen in (102) (I am glossing the case OM ('object marker'), following Culy (1995)). In each case, either the first or second NP can be interpreted as the subject. What is somewhat unusual is that such sentences are ambiguous only when the subject and theme object are not separated by the goal/recipient.

(102) Ambiguity in ditransitives in Donno Sɔ (Culy 1995:57)

a. Yaana I   wojinɛ anna pay-ñ tagaa be.
female child stranger male old-OM showed AUX
'A girl showed a stranger to an old man.' or
'A stranger showed a girl to an old man.'

b. Wojinɛ yaana I   anna pay-ñ tagaa be.
stranger female child male old-OM showed AUX
'A stranger showed a girl to an old man.' or
'A girl showed a stranger to an old man.'

Sesotho, a Bantu language spoken in Lesotho and adjacent areas in South Africa (Morolong and Hyman 1977; Hyman and Duranti 1982) is another interesting example of a language that shows semantic ambiguity. In this language, when both objects of a ditransitive verb (or a beneficiary applied verb) are human, both word orders are possible with potential ambiguity, as shown in (103). Both sentences in (103) have two meanings which involve the exact reversal of the thematic role interpretation of the two objects (beneficiary and theme).

(103)   Ambiguity in ditransitives in Sesotho
        (Morolong and Hyman 1977:203)
    a. Ke-bítselítsé morena baná.
       I-called   chief   children
       'I called the children for the chief.' or 'I called the chief for the children.'
    b. Ke-bítselítsé baná   morena.
       I-called   children chief
       'I called the chief for the children.' or 'I called the children for the chief.'

The effect of animacy on the interpretation of arguments shows up in many other languages. Here I briefly discuss the case of Russian, in which the word order is fixed as SVO, as in Hindi and Korean, if the case markings on both the subject and object NPs are identical. The classic examples, taken from Jakobson (1963), are shown in (104).

(104)   Case syncretism and word order freezing in Russian
    a. Mat'   ljubit doč'.
       mother-NOM/ACC loves daughter-NOM/ACC
       'The mother loves the daughter.'
    b. Doč'   ljubit mat'.
       daughter-NOM/ACC loves mother-NOM/ACC
       'The daughter loves the mother.'

Interesting speaker variation in argument interpretation has been reported regarding Russian sentences with syncretized arguments. For some speakers consulted, sentences like (104a,b) with two human arguments are not ambiguous; they can only be unambiguously interpreted with the first NP as the agent, not as the patient. But these speakers accepted sentences like (105) as ambiguous, where both arguments are inanimate, with both SVO and OVS readings.[39] Yet other speakers accepted all the sentences in (104) and (105) with both SVO and OVS readings.[40]

(105) Avtobus   pereexal trolejbus
      bus-NOM/ACC   hit   trolley-NOM/ACC
      'The bus hit the trolley.' or 'The trolley hit the bus.'

Building on Asudeh's (2001) insight that ambiguity can be characterized as a situation in which more than one optimal output is selected in the com-

---

[39]Thanks to Roger Levy for providing the Russian examples and reporting some Russian speakers' judgements to me.

[40]I am grateful to the anonymous reviewer for making this observation and reporting some Russian speakers' judgements to me.

prehension grammar, Lee (2000a, 2001) has shown that bidirectional optimization, coupled with the notion of probabilistically ranked constraints (Boersma 1997, 1999; Boersma and Hayes 2001), provides a simple explanation for cross-linguistic variation in the resolution of ambiguity as to the identity of grammatical relations. Although at present numerous questions raised by the recoverability phenomenon cannot be fully answered, a careful investigation of this phenomenon will show, I believe, that various types of systematic crosslinguistic differences in the treatment of ambiguity and recoverability must lie within the domain of linguistic competence, and are not simply attributable to performance effects.

3.6 Conclusion

This paper has presented an OT-LFG account of word order freezing in Hindi and Korean. Marked associations of morphosyntactic hierarchies, which provide an important source of the 'worst of the worst' type of freezing, have been formally modeled as harmonic alignment: the most marked associations of grammatical function with other prominence hierarchies are expressed in the unmarked word order. I have also shown that word order freezing in sentences with ambiguous case marking can be explained when the constraint system allows an extension to bidirectional competition. Yet these results cannot be achieved in most current formal syntactic frameworks, because they give no theoretical role to markedness, as opposed to purely structural aspects of grammar (e.g., transformational derivations), and the production- or generation-oriented perspective alone is insufficient for explaining the phenomena of recoverability and ambiguity. Furthermore, word order freezing effects in Hindi and Korean show that concepts that have been successfully modelled in phonology—markedness hierarchies, harmonic alignment, contextual neutralization, etc.—also play a key role in the syntactic domain of constituent ordering. These preliminary results suggest that word order freezing phenomena can be subsumed under the universal theory of markedness, although further work is required.

References

Ahn, Hee-Don. 1991. *Light verbs, VP-movement, negation and clausal architecture in Korean and English*. Ph.D. thesis, University of Wisconsin-Madison.

Aissen, Judith. 1997. Person and Subject Choice in Optimality Theory. Paper presented at the Hopkins Optimality Workshop, Baltimore, May 9-12, 1997.

Aissen, Judith. 1999. Markedness and Subject Choice in Optimality Theory. *Natural Language and Linguistic Theory* 17:673–711.

Aissen, Judith. 2000. Differential Object Marking: Iconocity vs. Economy. MS., University of California, Santa Cruz.

Anttila, Arto and Vivienne Fong. 2000. The Partitive Constraint in Optimality Theory. MS., National University of Singapore, Singapore. Online, Rutgers Optimality Archive: ROA-416-09100, http://ruccs.rutgers.edu/roa.html.

Artstein, Ron. 1998. Hierarchies. Online, Rutgers Optimality Archive: `http://www.eden.rutgers.edu/~artstein`.

Asudeh, Ash. 2001. Linking, Optionality, and Ambiguity in Marathi. This volume.

Bahl, Kali Charan. 1967. *A Reference Grammar of Hindi (A Study of Some Selected Topics in Hindi Grammar)*. Chicago, Illinois: University of Chicago Press.

Beaver, David. 2000. Centering and the Optimization of Discourse. MS., Stanford University. Online: `http://www.stanford.edu/~dib`.

Bloom, Douglas. 1999. Case Syncretism and Word Order Freezing in the Russian Language. M.A. Thesis, Stanford University. Online: `http://www-lfg.stanford.edu/lfg/archive`.

Blutner, Reinhard. 1999. Some Aspects of Optimality in Natural Language Interpretation. In *Papers in Optimality Theoretic Semantics*, eds. Helen de Hoop and Henriëtte de Swart. Utrecht University, Utrecht Institute of Linguistics OTS, 1–21.

Boersma, Paul. 1997. How we learn variation, optionality, and probability. In *IFA Proceedings 21*. University of Amsterdam: Institute of Phonetic Sciences, 43–58. ROA-221-109.

Boersma, Paul. 1999. Phonology-Semantics Interaction in OT and Its Acquisition. Online, Rutgers Optimality Archive: ROA-369-1299, `http://ruccs.rutgers.edu/roa.html`.

Boersma, Paul and Bruce Hayes. 2001. Empirical tests of the gradual learning algorithm. *Linguistic Inquiry* 32:45–86.

Bresnan, Joan. 1994. Linear Order vs. Syntactic Rank: Evidence from Weak Crossover. In *CLS 30*. Reprinted in *Formal Issues in Lexical-Functional Grammar*, ed. by Mary Dalrymple, Ronald M. Kaplan, John T. Maxwell III and Annie Zaenen, 241–274. Stanford, California: CSLI Publications.

Bresnan, Joan. 2000a. Explaining Morphosyntactic Competition. In *Handbook of Contemporary Syntactic Theory*, eds. Mark Baltin and Chris Collins. Oxford: Blackwell Publishers, 11–44.

Bresnan, Joan. 2000b. Optimal Syntax. In *Optimality Theory: Phonology, Syntax and Acquisition*, eds. Joost Dekkers, Frank van der Leeuw, and Jeroen van de Weijer. Oxford: Oxford University Press, 334–385.

Bresnan, Joan. 2001a. The Emergence of the Unmarked Pronoun. In *Optimality-Theoretic Syntax*, eds. Géraldine Legendre, Jane Grimshaw, and Sten Vikner. Cambridge, Massachusetts: The MIT Press, 113–142.

Bresnan, Joan. 2001b. *Lexical Functional Syntax*. Oxford: Blackwell.

Bresnan, Joan and Jonni Kanerva. 1989. Locative Inversion in Chicheŵa: A Case Study of Factorization in Grammar. *Linguistic Inquiry* 20:1–50.

Bresnan, Joan and Ronald M. Kaplan. 1982. Introduction: Grammars as Mental Representations of Language. In *The Mental Representation of Grammatical Relations*, ed. Joan Bresnan. Cambridge, Massachusetts: The MIT Press, xvii–lii.

Bresnan, Joan and Annie Zaenen. 1990. Deep unaccusativity in LFG. In *Grammatical relations: A cross-theoretical perspective*, eds. Katarzyna Dziwirek,

Patrick Farrell, and Errapel Mejias-Bikandi. Stanford, California: CSLI Publications, 45–57.

Broadwell, George Aaron. 2000. Word Order and Markedness in Kaqchikel. In *Proceedings of the LFG00 Conference*, eds. Miriam Butt and Tracy H. King. Stanford, California: CSLI Publications Online: http://csli-publications.stanford.edu/.

Butt, Miriam and Tracy H. King. 1996. Structural Topic and Focus without Movement. In *Proceedings of the LFG96 Conference*, eds. Miriam Butt and Tracy H. King. Stanford, California: CSLI Publications Online: http://csli-publications.stanford.edu/.

Cho, Young-mee Yu and Peter Sells. 1995. A Lexical Account of Inflectional Suffixes in Korean. *Journal of East Asian Linguistics* 4:119–174.

Choi, Hye-Won. 1996. *Optimizing Structure in Context: Scrambling and Information Structure*. Ph.D. thesis, Stanford University.

Choi, Hye-Won. 1999. *Optimizing Structure in Context: Scrambling and Information Structure*. Stanford, California: CSLI Publications.

Choi, Hye-Won. 2001. Phrase Structure, Information Structure, and Resolution of Mismatch. This volume.

Chomsky, Noam. 1981. *Lectures on Government and Binding*. Dordrecht: Foris.

Chomsky, Noam. 1993. A Minimalist Program for linguistic theory. In *The View from Building 20: Essays in Linguistics in Honor of Sylvain Bromberger*, eds. Samule J. Keyser and Kenneth Hale. Cambridge, Massachusetts: The MIT Press, 1–52.

Chomsky, Noam. 1995. *The Minimalist Program*. Cambridge, Massachusetts: The MIT Press.

Costa, João. 1998. *Word Order Variation: A Constraint-Based Approach*. Ph.D. thesis, Leiden University.

Culy, Christopher. 1995. Ambiguity and Case Marking in Donnɔ So (Dogon). In *Theoretical Approaches to African Languages*, ed. Akinbiyi Akinlabi. Trenton: Africa World Press, 47–58.

Davidson, Alice. 1969. Reflexivization and Movement Rules in Relation to a Class of Hindi Psychological Predicates. In *CLS 5*. Chicago, Illinois: Chicago Linguistic Society, 37–51.

de Hoop, Helen. 1996. *Case Configuration and Noun Phrase Interpretation*. New York, New York: Garland.

Diesing, Molly. 1992. *Indefinites*. Cambridge, Massachusetts: The MIT Press.

Donohue, Cathryn. 1999. Optimizing Fore Case and Word Order. MS., Stanford University. Online: http://www-csli.stanford.edu/~donohue.

Dowty, David. 1991. Thematic Proto-roles and Argument Selection. *Language* 67:547–619.

Dviwedi, Veena Dhar. 1994. *Syntactic Dependencies and Relative Phrases in Hindi*. Ph.D. thesis, University of Massachusetts at Amherst.

England, Nora C. 1983. *A Grammar of Mam, a Mayan Language*. Austin: University of Texas Press.

Foley, William. 1986. *The Papuan Languages of New Guinea*. Cambridge: Cambridge University Press.

Gambhir, Vijay. 1981. *Syntactic Restrictions and Discourse Functions of Word Order in Standard Hindi*. Ph.D. thesis, University of Pennsylvania.

Gerdts, Donna and Cheong Youn. 1988. Korean Psych Constructions: Advancement or Retreat? In *CLS 25-I*. Chicago, Illinois: Chicago Linguistic Society, 155–175.

Grimshaw, Jane. 1991. Extended Projection. MS., Dept. of Linguistics and Center for Cognitive Science, Rutgers University.

Grimshaw, Jane. 1997. Projection, Heads, and Optimality. *Linguistic Inquiry* 28:73–422.

Gurtu, Madhu. 1985. *Anaphoric Relations in Hindi and English*. Ph.D. thesis, Central Institute of English and Foreign Languages, Hyderabad, India.

Hale, Mark and Charles Reiss. 1998. Formal and Empirical Arguments Concerning Phonological Acquisition. *Linguistic Inquiry* 29:656–683.

Halvorsen, Per-Kristian. 1983. Semantics for Lexical-Functional Grammar. *Linguistic Inquiry* 14:567–615.

Han, Eunjoo. 1991. Honorification in Korean. MS., Stanford University.

Hawkinson, Annie and Larry Hyman. 1974. Hierarchies of Natural Topic in Shona. *Studies in African Linguistics* 5:147–170.

Holmberg, Anders. 1998. Word Order Variation in Some European SVO Languages: A Parametric Approach. In Siewierska, Rijkhoff and Bakker (eds.), 553–598.

Hong, Ki-Sun. 1991. *Argument Selection and Case Marking in Korean*. Ph.D. thesis, Stanford University.

Hyman, Larry and Alessandro Duranti. 1982. On the Object Relation in Bantu. In *Studies in Transitivity (Syntax and Semantics 15)*, eds. P. Hopper and S. Thompson. New York, New York: Academic Press, 217–239.

Jäger, Gerhard. 2000. Some Notes on the Formal Properties of Bidirectional Optimality Theory. Online, Rutgers Optimality Archive: ROA-414-09100, http://ruccs.rutgers.edu/roa.html.

Jakobson, Roman. 1963. Implications of Language Universals for Linguistics. In *Universals of Language*, ed. Joseph H. Greenberg. Cambridge, Massachusetts: The MIT Press.

Joshi, Smita. 1993. *Selection of Grammatical and Logical Functions in Marathi*. Ph.D. thesis, Stanford University.

Kager, René. 1999. *Optimality Theory*. Cambridge: Cambridge University Press.

Kim, Jong-Bok. 1999. *The Grammar of Negation: A Lexicalist, Constraint-Based Perspective*. Stanford, California: CSLI Publications.

Kim, Young-joo. 1990. *The Syntax and Semantics of Korean Case: The Interaction between Lexical and Syntactic Levels of Representation*. Ph.D. thesis, Harvard University.

King, Tracy Holloway. 1995. *Configuring Topic and Focus in Russian*. Stanford, California: CSLI Publications.

Kiparsky, Paul. 1998. Structural Case. MS., Stanford University.

Kuhn, Jonas. 1999. Two Ways of Formalizing OT Syntax in the LFG Framework. MS., Universität Stuttgart. Online: http://www.ims.uni-stuttgart.de/~jonas.

Kuhn, Jonas. 2000a. Faithfulness violations and Bidirectional Optimization. In *Proceedings of the LFG00 Conference*, eds. Miriam Butt and Tracy H. King. Stanford, California: CSLI Publications Online: http://csli-publications.stanford.edu/.

Kuhn, Jonas. 2000b. Issues in the Formalization of OT Syntax. Paper presented at the Syntax Workshop, Stanford University, March 14, 2000.

Kuhn, Jonas. 2001. Generation and Parsing in Optimality Theoretic Syntax – Issues in the Formalization in OT-LFG. This volume.

Kuno, Susumu. 1980. A Further Note on Tonoike's Intra-subjectivization Hypothesis. In *MIT Working Papers in Linguistics 2: Theoretical Issues in Japanese Linguistics*, eds. Yukio Otsu and Ann Farmer. Cambridge, Massachusetts: The MIT Press, 171–184.

Lasnik, Howard and Mamoru Saito. 1992. *Move α*. Cambridge: Cambridge University Press.

Lee, Hanjung. 1999. The Emergence of the Unmarked Order. Online, Rutgers Optimality Archive: ROA-323-0699, http://ruccs.rutgers.edu/roa.html.

Lee, Hanjung. 2000a. Bidirectional Optimality and Ambiguity in Argument Expression. Paper presented at the LFG00 Conference, University of California, Berkeley, July 19-20. MS., Stanford University. Online: http://www.stanford.edu/~hanjung.

Lee, Hanjung. 2000b. The Emergence of the Unmarked Order in Hindi. In *Proceedings of NELS 30*, eds. Masako Hirotani, Andries Coetzee, Nancy Hall, and Ji-Yung Kim. Amherst, Massachusetts: GLSA, 469–483.

Lee, Hanjung. 2000c. Markedness and Pronoun Incorporation. To appear in the *Proceedings of BLS* 26. Berkeley, California: Berkeley Linguistics Society.

Lee, Hanjung. 2001. *Optimization in Argument Expression and Interpretation: A Unified Approach*. Ph.D. thesis, Stanford University.

Lee, Young-Suk. 1993. *Scrambling as Case-Driven Obligatory Movement*. Ph.D. thesis, University of Pennsylvania.

Legendre, Géraldine, Colin Wilson, Paul Smolensky, Kristin Homer, and William Raymond. 1995. Optimality and *Wh*-Extraction. In *Papers in Optimality Theory*, eds. Jill N. Beckman, Laura Walsh Dickey, and Suzanne Urbanczyk. Amherst, Massachusetts: GLSA, University of Massachusetts, 607–636.

Lenerz, Jürgen. 1977. *Zur Abfolge nominaler Satzglieder im Deutschen*. Tübingen: Gunter Narr Verlag.

Mahajan, Anoop. 1990. *The A/A-bar Distinction and Movement Theory*. Ph.D. thesis, MIT.

McCarthy, John and Alan Prince. 1994. The Emergence of the Unmarked: Optimality in Prosodic Morphology. In *NELS 24*, ed. M. Gonzàlez. GLSA, University of Massachusetts at Amherst, 333–379.

Miyagawa, Shigeru. 1997. Against Optional Scrambling. *Linguistic Inquiry* 28:1–25.

Mohanan, K.P. and Tara Mohanan. 1994. Issues in Word Order. In *Theoretical Perspectives on Word Order in South Asian Languages*, eds. Miriam Butt, Tracy Holloway King, and Gillian Ramchand. Stanford, California: CSLI Publications, 153–184.

Mohanan, Tara. 1992. Word Order in Hindi. Paper presented at the Syntax Workshop. Stanford University.

Mohanan, Tara. 1994a. *Argument Structure in Hindi*. Stanford, California: CSLI Publications.

Mohanan, Tara. 1994b. Case OCP: A Constraint on Word Order in Hindi. In *Theoretical Perspectives on Word Order in South Asian Languages*, eds. Miriam Butt, Tracy Holloway King, and Gillian Ramchand. Stanford, California: CSLI Publications, 185–216.

Mondloch, James. 1981. *Voice in Quiche-Maya*. Ph.D. thesis, State University of New York at Albany.

Morolong, 'Malillo and Larry Hyman. 1977. Animacy, Objects and Clitics in Sesotho. *Studies in African Linguistics* 8:199–218.

Müller, Gereon. 1998. German Word Order and Optimality Theory. In *Arbeitspapiere des Sonderforschungsbereichs 340, #126*. University of Tübingen.

Neeleman, Ad and Tanya Reinhart. 1997. The Syntax and Interpretation of Scrambling in Dutch. MS., University of Utrecht.

Pinkerton, Sandra. 1976. *Studies in Kekchi. Texas Linguistics Forum 3*. Austin: University of Texas.

Pollard, Carl and Ivan A. Sag. 1994. *Head-Driven Phrase Structure Grammar*. Chicago, Illinois and Stanford, California: The University of Chicago Press and CSLI Publications.

Primus, Beatrice. 1998. The Relative Order of Recipient and Patient in the Languages of Europe. In Siewierska, Rijkhoff and Bakker (eds.), 421–473.

Prince, Alan and Paul Smolensky. 1993. Optimality Theory: Constraint Interaction in Generative Grammar. Technical Report RuCCS Technical Report #2, Center for Cognitive Science, Rutgers University, Piscataway, New Jersey. To be published by the MIT Press.

Prince, Ellen. 2000. Linguistic and Meta-linguistic Intuition. To appear in the *Proceedings of BLS* 26. Berkeley, California: Berkeley Linguistics Society.

Rudin, Catherine. 1985. *Aspects of Bulgarian Syntax: Complementizers and WH Constructions*. Columbus, Ohio: Slavica.

Sag, Ivan and Thomas Wasow. 1999. *Syntactic Theory: A Formal Introduction*. Stanford, California: CSLI Publications.

Saito, Mamoru. 1992. Long Distance Scrambling in Japanese. *Journal of East Asian Linguistics* 1:69–118.

Samek-Lodovici, Vieri. 1998. OT-interactions between Focus and Canonical Word Order: Deriving the crosslinguistic Typology of Structural Contrastive Focus. Online, Rutgers Optimality Archive: ROA-257-0498, http://ruccs.rutgers.edu/roa.html.

Sells, Peter. 1995. Korean and Japanese Morphology from a Lexical Perspective. *Linguistic Inquiry* 26:277–325.

Sells, Peter. 1999. Constituent Ordering as Alignment. In *Harvard Studies in Korean Linguistics VIII*, ed. Susumu Kuno et al. Seoul: Hanshin, 546–560.

Sells, Peter. 2000. Alignment Constraints in Swedish Clausal Syntax. MS., Stanford University. Online: http://www-csli.stanford.edu/~sells.

Sells, Peter. 2001. *Structure, Alignment and Optimality in Swedish*. To appear, Stanford, California: CSLI Publications.

Sharma, Devyani. 1999. Sentential Negation and Focus in Hindi. MS., Stanford University.

Siewierska, Anna. 1988. *Word Order Rules*. London: Croom Helm.

Siewierska, Anna, Jan Rijkhoff, and Dik Bakker (eds.). 1998. *Constituent Order in the Languages of Europe*. Berlin: Mouton de Gruyter.

Siewierska, Anna and Ludmila Uhlirova. 1998. An Overview of Word Order in Slavic Languages. In Siewierska, Rijkhoff and Bakker (eds.), 105–149.

Smolensky, Paul. 1995. On the Internal Structure of the Constraint Component Con of UG. ROA-86-0000. Rutgers Optimality Archive. http://ruccs.rutgers.edu/roa.html.

Smolensky, Paul. 1996a. The Initial State and "Richness of the Base" in Optimality Theory. Technical Report JHU-CogSci-96-4, Department of Cognitive Science, Johns Hopkins University.

Smolensky, Paul. 1996b. On the Comprehension/Production Dilemma in Child Language. *Linguistic Inquiry* 27:720–731.

Smolensky, Paul. 1998. Why Syntax is Different (but not Really): Ineffability, Violability and Recoverability in Syntax and Phonology. Stanford University Workshop: Is Syntax Different? (December 12–13, 1998).

Speas, Margaret J. 1990. *Phrase Structure in Natural Language*. Dordrecht: Kluwer Academic.

Srivastav, Veneeta. 1991. *WH Dependencies in Hindi and the Theory of Grammar*. Ph.D. thesis, Cornell University.

Tomlin, Russell. 1986. *Basic Word Order. Functional Principles*. Dordrecht: Foris.

Vallduví, Enric. 1992. *The Informational Component*. New York, New York: Garland.

Verma, Manindra K. and K. P. Mohanan (eds.). 1990. *Experiencer Subjects in South Asian Languages*. Stanford, California: CSLI Publications.

Webelhuth, Gert. 1989. *Syntactic Saturation Phenomena and the Modern Germanic Languages*. Ph.D. thesis, University of Massachusetts at Amherst.

Whitman, John. 1989. Topic, Modality, and IP Structure. In *Harvard Studies in Korean Linguistics III*, ed. Susumu Kuno et al. Seoul: Hanshin, 341–356.

Wilson, Colin. 1996. Alignment and Anaphora. Paper presented at the Stanford/CSLI Workshop on Optimality Theory and Its Implications for Cognitive Theory. Stanford University, December 6-8, 1996.

Wilson, Colin. 1997. Absolute Harmony, Relativized Minimality and Blocking. Paper presented at the Hopkins Optimality Workshop, Baltimore, May 9-12, 1997.

Wilson, Colin. 2001. Bidirectional Optimization and the Theory of Anaphora. In *Optimality-Theoretic Syntax*, eds. Géraldine Legendre, Jane Grimshaw, and Sten Vikner. Cambridge, Massachusetts: The MIT Press, 465–507.

Yoon, James Hye-Suk. 1996. Ambiguity of Government and the Chain Condition. *Natural Language and Linguistic Theory* 14:105–162.

4

Verb Raising and Phrase Structure Variation in OT

YUKIKO MORIMOTO

4.1 Introduction

One of the central problems in generative studies on clause structure concerns how phrase structure variation in natural languages is to be characterized.[1] A predominant view within the generative tradition, as represented by the Principles and Parameters (P&P) approach (e.g., Chomsky 1981, 1982, 1986, 1991, 1993, 1995), has assumed a universal hierarchical structure with parameterization of head-directionality. Cross-linguistic variation in surface expression is derived by various types of movement operations. On this traditional view of X-bar theory, it is standardly assumed that hierarchical structure and linear order vary freely—that is, a given hierarchical structure can be associated with more than one linear order. In a recent proposal, Kayne (1994) denies this fundamental assumption and develops what he claims to be a much more "restrictive" theory of word order and phrase structure. His central proposal is that an asymmetric dominance relation (i.e. c-command) invariably maps onto linear precedence. Thus on this view, directionality parameters no longer play a role. Universal Grammar (UG) only permits specifier-head-complement order; adjunction is always to the left; head movement is invariably leftward. Familiar syntactic phenomena such as right-node raising, relative clause extraposition, right-

[1] I am grateful to Paul Kiparsky, Helge Lødrup, Peter Sells, Tom Wasow, and to an anonymous reviewer for detailed feedback and useful discussion on the material presented here, and an additional reviewer for formal details of the proposal. Parts of the paper were presented at WECOL 2000, held at CSU Fresno, October 2000, and at the 32nd Annual Conference on African Linguistics, held at UC Berkeley, March 2001. I thank the audiences for questions and comments. I am solely responsible for any remaining errors or misrepresentations.

dislocation and adjacency relations among constituents must therefore be reinterpreted and reanalyzed.

Kayne's proposal about the antisymmetry of clausal architecture is essentially a generative characterization of universal markedness. Kayne (p.35) notes, for example, that if we consider two ordering possibilities, specifier-head-complement and complement-head-specifier, the former is significantly more common than the latter, and hence makes it a more plausible universal than the latter. While head-complement and complement-head orders are both widely attested, specifier-head order strongly predominates across languages. In other words, specifier-head order is not an absolute universal, but it is cross-linguistically the unmarked order. A notable problem of formalizing markedness generalizations in traditional generative syntax is that the "softness" of such generalizations makes it difficult to integrate into a formal framework that employs inviolable constraints and a restricted set of parameters. Marked configurations are derived from universally unmarked structure, and this requires a series of movements that are often difficult to motivate.

Recent work in Optimality Theoretic Syntax (Samek-Lodovici 1996, Grimshaw 1997, Costa 1998, Sells 2001) has developed an output-based theory of phrase structure by extending the mechanism of Generalized Alignment developed in OT phonology (McCarthy and Prince 1993) to the domain of clausal syntax. As in phonology, an asymmetric alignment has been suggested with greater preference for the left edge than the right edge (allowing only left-alignment), so that the unmarked structure is predominantly right-branching (Sells 1999a,b, 2001). Sells' work takes a pioneering step towards recasting Kayne's antisymmetry hypothesis from the non-derivational view of syntax. As already demonstrated in a growing body of work in OT syntax, the classical notion of morphosyntactic markedness familiar in structuralist linguistics (e.g., Jakobson 1968) and the typological tradition (e.g., Greenberg 1963, 1966) has been successfully integrated into OT grammar, which is designed from the beginning to incorporate the softness of universal markedness.[2] Can the fundamental assumptions and formal machinery that operate within the system of *ranked, violable* constraints on surface representation be fruitfully applied to explain all types of syntactic positioning? Building on earlier work, this paper explores this question and further develops the non-derivational theory of phrase structure within OT-LFG (Choi 1999, Bresnan 2000a,b, Kuhn 2001, Sells 2001).

---

[2]Some representative OT syntax work on markedness includes areas in case/voice systems (Legendre, Raymond, and Smolensky 1993, Sells 2001a, Aissen 1999a,b, Sharma 1999, Deo and Sharma 2000), obviation systems (Aissen 2000), pronominal systems (Bresnan 2000a,b), pronominal incorporation (Arstein 1998, Lee 2000a), word order freezing and noncanonical word order (Lee 2000b, 2001, Morimoto 2000a, Tham 2000), argument linking (Morimoto 1999, Asudeh 2001), and possessive constructions (O'Connor 1999a,b).

From the perspective of an output-based approach like OT, syntactic constituents fall into two types. Constituents such as dislocated topics, sentential adverbs, operators, and core clausal elements like the subject target a privileged position in phrase structure. As noted above, recent OT work (e.g., Grimshaw 1997, Sells 2001) successfully models ordering of this first type by 'edge alignment'. For ease of reference, I will refer to this type as 'edge-attracted' constituents. The second type, which I refer to as 'head-attracted' constituents, exhibits affinity with the head (nominal or verbal). For example, focus is often placed near the verbal head (see Morimoto 2000b for a typological survey based on earlier descriptive work). Negation also tends to appear near the verb (Payne 1985). Some languages exhibit a set of non-projecting X^0 elements (e.g., negation, adverb, pronominal clitics), and they typically form a "cluster" with the verbal head (Sells 1994, 1999, Abeillé and Godard 1998). In the nominal domain, a relative pronoun and the modifying clause generally prefer adjacency with the nominal head. A rather obvious correlating fact is that the position of these head-attracted constituents is dependent on the directionality of heads: head-initial languages typically place the head of the relative clause before the modifying clause, negation before the verb, and focus after the verb; head-final languages, on the other hand, place the head of the relative clause after the modifying clause, negation after the verb, and focus before the verb. The opposite patterns are rare or non-existent. These predictable patterns of syntactic positioning therefore deserve a principled explanation, and should follow from some general, universal constraints on phrase structure.

As will become clearer, restricting alignment to the left-edge of a clause as in earlier proposals imposes serious limitations on the kinds of syntactic positioning and constructions we can explain within the constraint-based, output-oriented model of grammar. In this paper, my goal is to propose a generalized formal mechanism within OT-LFG which provides a unified treatment of head-attracted constituents. The empirical domain to be explored in detail is verb raising in object relativization observed in a subset of Bantu languages. Through the OT analysis of a typology of relativization, I show that the seemingly peculiar properties of Bantu object relativization follows straightforwardly from an interaction of independently motivated universal constraints.

The paper is organized as follows: section 4.2 presents the core facts and a recent transformational analysis of Bantu relativization. Section 4.3 establishes the empirical basis for Bantu clause structure I will assume in this paper. In section 4.4 I outline Kayne's main proposal about the antisymmetry of syntax and major empirical consequences. This will help us identify which part of the proposal is being reconsidered in light of the OT approach to syntax, and what we gain from this alternative characterization of the asymmetry of phrase structure. Section 4.5 discusses some fundamental concepts in OT syntax assumed throughout this work: the nature of INPUT, candidates, and the relation between them, and the properties of the GEN-ERATOR. In section 4.6 I introduce the set of constraints relevant for my analysis. I then introduce the formal device of ABUTMENT (alignment of op-posite edges of two elements) to capture various types of adjacency effects among syntactic constituents, although only relativization will receive full consideration in the present work. Section 4.7 provides an OT-LFG analysis of verb raising and the cross-linguistic variation in relativization. The final section briefly discusses directions for future research.

4.2 Relativization and Verb Raising

It has long been known that object relativization in some Bantu languages (which are canonically SVO) exhibits so-called 'stylistic inversion', where the subject appears postverbally, rendering VS order (e.g., Bokamba 1971 1976, Givón 1972, Kinyalolo 1991, Demuth 1995). This section presents the core facts. I hope to show that the presence of 'stylistic inversion', here analyzed as verb raising, is a natural, expected property once we recognize a wider spectrum of variation in relativization across languages, and the facts follow straightforwardly from a wider typology of relative clauses.

4.2.1 Relativization in Bantu

In Bantu languages, relativization takes one of three forms. Relative clauses can be formed using a prosodically independent relativizer, whose function is similar to a relative pronoun in English. Sesotho falls into this type, as exemplified in (1) (Harford and Demuth 1999). The relativizer *tseo* is analyzed as the head of CP.

(1) di-kobo   **tseo** ba-sadi   ba-di-rekileng kajeno   Ses
    10-blankets 10REL 2-women 2-10-bought   today
    'the blankets which the women bought today'

Other Bantu languages such as Kirundi and Kinyarwanda use a gram-matical tone on the verb to indicate that the verb is in a relative clause (Kimenyi 1980, Sabimana 1986), as shown in (2) from Kinyarwanda (Ki-menyi 1980:67). In the relative clause *the men who returned* in (2b), there is a high tone on the verb stem *-gáruts-*. Contrast that with the verb stem without the high tone in the non-relative clause in (2a).

(2) a. Abagabo b-a-garuts-e.   Krw
       men   2-PAST-return-ASP
       'The men returned.'
    b. N-dá-bon-a abagabo b-a-gáruts-e.
       I-AF-see-ASP men   2PAST-REL.return-ASP
       'I see the men who returned.'

The third type, observed in Dzamba and Chishona, has a bound rela-tivizer attached to the verb in the relative clause. An example of subject relativization is given in (3) (Bokamba 1976). Note that the class 1 subject agreement marker on the verb is *a* (cf. *a-kpa-áki* '1-take-PAST'). In a relative clause, the verb has a relative marker different than the matrix verb class 1 subject marker.

(3) omoto   ó-kpa-áki   imundɔndɔ a-kim-í.   Dza
    the.1person 1REL-take-PAST the.jug   1-feel-IP
    'The person/man who took the jug just fled.'

Among these Bantu languages, this third type exhibits "stylistic inversion" in object relativization, illustrated in (4) (Dzamba; Givón 1972:190). Example (4a) is a simple transitive sentence, and (4b) is object relativization, and the canonically preverbal subject is placed postverbally. Without inversion, the example is ungrammatical (4c).

(4) a. Zaki a-bundaki imo-dondo.   Dza
       Jack 1-caught   the-alligator
       'Jack caught the alligator.'

    b. oPetelo a-nyamozi imo-dondo   i-mu-bundaki Zaki
       Peter   1-sold   the-alligator REL-it-caught Jack
       'Peter sold the alligator that Jack caught.'

    c.*oPetelo a-nyamozi imo-dondo   Zaki i-mu-bundaki
       Peter   1-sold   the-alligator Jack REL-it-caught
                                                    (Givón 1972:190)

Not all the Bantu languages introduced above display such subject inversion. Sesotho, the first type with a free-standing relativizer, is among the languages which do not show subject inversion, as illustrated earlier in (1). Contrast that example with the ungrammatical example in (5) in which the subject appears postverbally.

(5)*di-kobo   tseo   ba-di-rekileng basadi   kajeno   Ses
    10-blankets 10REL 2-10-bought   2women today

A key observation in early work is that the prosodic status of the relative marker correlates with the presence/absence of subject inversion: languages with a prosodically bound relative marker permit (or more accurately, require) inversion as in Dzamba, while those with a free-standing relative pronoun do not, as in Sesotho. The data in (6b) from Kinyarwanda additionally show that languages that employ a grammatical tone to indicate relativization (e.g., Kirundi and Kinyarwanda) do not show subject inversion (Kimenyi 1980, Sabimana 1986; also Morimoto 2000b, chapter 4).

(6) a. Umugabo y a haa yc   umugórc igitabo.   Krw
       1man   1-PAST-give-PERF 1woman book
       'The man gave a book to the women.'

b. N-a-boon-ye   igitabo [umuhuûngu
I-PAST-see-ASP book   boy
y-a-haá-ye   umukoômwa].
1SM-PAST-REL.give-ASP girl
'I saw the book that the boy gave to the girl.'

The category of the relativizer and the presence/absence of inversion across the Bantu languages are summarized in (7). In languages such as Dzamba and Chishona, referred to as Type I, the relativizer is a bound form, and inversion is in fact obligatory, not stylistic. Sesotho and Setswana, referred to as Type II languages, have a free-standing relativizer, and no inversion occurs. Kirundi and Kinyarwanda, Type III languages, make use of a grammatical tone on the verb inside relative clause, and the subject remains in canonical subject position (preverbal).

(7)   The form of the relativizer and 'stylistic inversion'

Languages	REL Form	Inv.
Type I	N-head REL-verb NP_{Su}	Yes
Type II	N-head REL NP_{Su} verb	No
Type III	N-head NP_{Su} REL.verb (tone)	No

Type I: Dzamba, Chishona
Type II: Sesotho/Setswana
Type III: Kirundi/Kinyarwanda

In recent work, Harford and Demuth (1999) (also Demuth and Harford 1999; hereafter H&D and D&H respectively) analyze subject inversion in object relatives as prosodically-driven V-to-I and I-to-C movement. The proposed structure is shown in (8). The V-to-I and I-to-C movement is indicated by the chain of traces indexed t_i; see also Kinyalolo (1991) for a similar verb movement analysis. Harford and Demuth argue that in Type I languages with a bound relativizer, the prosodically weak C "attracts" the V in I, leading to a case where phonology supposedly drives syntactic head movement, contra Pullum & Zwicky (1988) that "syntax feeds phonology" but not vice versa (also Golston 1995 for an OT implementation of this standard assumption). In this type of language, the VP internal subject is assumed to remain in SpecVP; the head noun of the relative clause moves from the original object position to the head of the top NP, leaving the trace indexed t_j. In languages without inversion, the morphologically independent relative pronoun occupies C, and V, having moved to I, stays in I, as shown in (9). The VP internal subject moves to SpecIP, and the relativized noun heads the top NP (leaving the trace indexed t_j).

(8) Type I languages with inversion (e.g., Dzamba)
     (Harford & Demuth 1999)

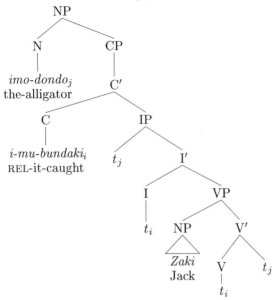

(9) Type II languages without inversion (e.g., Sesotho)
     (Harford & Demuth 1999)

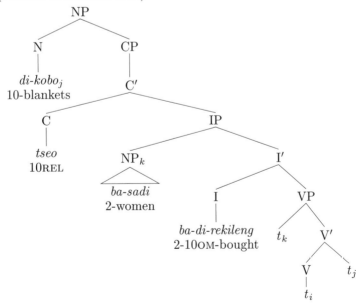

One advantage of D&H and H&D's analysis of object relativization in Bantu languages is that it provides a unified explanation of apparently unrelated phenomena, such as verb raising and stylistic inversion (so-called postverbal subjects) observed in Germanic V2 and Romance languages. Despite this advantage of the above analysis, it faces at least three fundamental problems. First, it is unclear why in Type I languages the prosodically deficient relativizer in C would need a verb as its prosodic host. Sadler (1998) and Nordlinger and Sadler (2000), for example, observe that reduced (non-syllabic) English auxiliaries form a morphological unit with the element to their left, the subject, rather than with the main verb, as shown by the brackets in (10). The bracketing in (10a) shows the (syntactic) phrasing with the unreduced auxiliary *have*, and the bracketing in (10b) shows the phrasing with the reduced auxiliary *'ve*.

(10) a. $[_{IP} [_{DP}$ They] $[_{I'}$ have done $[_{NP}$ their homework]]].
      b. (They've)$_\omega$ done their homework.

Based on data like that in (10) in English and other languages (e.g., Kayardild, Supyire (Niger-Congo), Gui (Khoisan), Chamicuro (Arawak), Pitta Pitta (Pama-Nyungan)), Nordlinger and Sadler argue that nominal elements can be responsible for clause-level information such as tense and aspect that is normally associated with the verbal category. If the Bantu bound relative pronoun in C position in Type I languages were a clitic, then it is not obvious why it would not simply cliticize onto the next available category, the subject, either to form a morphological unit with the subject as in English and the other languages mentioned above, or a phonological phrase with it (though syntactically it may be still part of the verbal projection). If the prosodically weak C requires strict adjacency with the verb across the subject that appears between the relativizer in C and V, this suggests a morphological, rather than prosodic, dependency between these elements.

Secondly, D&H and H&D's analysis requires postulation of two structural positions for subject in these Bantu languages: VP internal position for Dzamba-type languages, and SpecIP for Sesotho-type languages. However, they present no independent evidence for the structural difference in subject position.

Thirdly, there is no evidence in Dzamba or other closely related Bantu languages (e.g., Kirundi, Kinyarwanda) for lexical INFL. For example, in Kinyarwanda, tense and aspect are marked on the verb as a prefix and suffix respectively. Modal verbs that are expressed as auxiliaries in English, such as *-kwii-* 'must' and *-shobok-* 'can' behave like any other main verb: they can be negated like any other verb by a negative prefix; they inflect for tense, aspect, and gender agreement like main verbs. In fact, these modal verbs are analyzed by Kimenyi (1980) as raising predicates which correspond to the English equivalents of 'be necessary' and 'be possible' in the non-raised construction. Similarly for Chicheŵa, Bresnan and Mchombo (1987) conclude that Chicheŵa lacks the category INFL. On the derivational analysis, then, I is only needed for theory-internal reasons, namely to allow V to move through to C, and I is never filled.

In what follows, I explore an alternative analysis of object relativization in these Bantu languages which effectively nullifies D&H and H&D's argument that phonology outranks syntax. In the next section, I motivate the basic clause structure and relative clauses in Bantu languages within the non-derivational framework of Lexical-Functional Grammar (LFG; Bresnan 1982, 2001, Dalrymple et al. 1995). The structures presented here will be the basis for my OT-LFG analysis.

4.3 Bantu Clause Structure

The fundamental assumption underlying proposals about clause structure in LFG is the Lexical Integrity Principle (cf. Bresnan and Mchombo 1995): the internal structure of words is organized by a set of principles different from those that underlie the organization of phrasal structure. Word internal elements are opaque to any syntactic operations. Lexical items are inserted into syntactic structure fully inflected, and are morphologically independent leaves of phrase structure trees.[3] LFG posits two levels of structure relevant in the present discussion, c(constituent)-structure and f(unctional)-structure, which are mutually constrained by correspondence principles. While c-structure represents the surface expressions of phrasal constituents and may vary across languages, f-structure encodes grammatical information and predicate-argument relations, and is largely invariant across languages. In addition, LFG recognizes two types of clausal organization, the endocentric and exocentric type: the former is represented by a familiar X-bar schema where each XP is uniquely headed (e.g., VP, NP, IP). Exocentric clausal organization posits the node S which is not headed in c-structure, and can dominate any XP (or X).

With this background, my goal in this section is to establish the following assumptions about constituency in Bantu languages: (i) Bantu languages exhibit configurational structure with a VP; (ii) the root node is organized around the exocentric category S; and (iii) above S, there is a functional projection CP. Furthermore, due to the absence of evidence to the contrary, I assume that the bound relativizer in Dzamba-type languages is morphologically bound to V rather than being a clitic and heading its own functional projection.

---

[3] As will become clearer, OT takes the view that the lexicon is derived by interaction of universal constraints on the well-formedness of structure, as opposed to the "bottom-up" view that words and morphemes derive (or project) structure.

4.3.1 Elements of the Basic Clause Structure

It is standardly assumed that Bantu languages exhibit configurational SVO structure, and the existence of VP is evidenced by word order and phonological phrasing. Bresnan and Mchombo (1986, 1987) argue conclusively that the verb and object form a VP based on the fact that when the object is not adjacent to the verb, the sentence is ungrammatical unless the object marker is present on the verb. The object marker is argued to be a pronominal argument by Bresnan and Mchombo for Chicheŵa, and appears only when there is no overt NP object in the local structure (= minimal nuclear clause) or when the object NP is a dislocated topic. Bresnan and Kanerva (1989) present corroborative evidence for the existence of VP from phrasal phonology in Chicheŵa. They show that tone doubling, which occurs only phrase-internally, obligatorily applies to the verb and object: the high tone on the last syllable of the verb spreads (or "doubles") onto the object. Although data from phrasal phonology are not available (to me) outside Chicheŵa, the same word order facts hold in Kirundi, Kinyarwanda (Sabimana 1986, Morimoto 2000b, chapter 4), and Sesotho/Setswana (Demuth and Mmusi 1997).

Furthermore, Bantu languages generally lack theory-independent evidence for lexical (morphologically independent) INFL. For this reason, the exocentric category S, which is made available in LFG, has been proposed to be the root node in Bantu languages (cf. Bresnan and Mchombo 1986, 1987 for Chicheŵa; Mugane 1996 for Kikuyu and Swahili; Morimoto 2000 for Kirundi, Kinyarwanda). The existence of C is confirmed by complementizers. In Kirundi and Kinyarwanda, a left-dislocated topic can occupy SpecCP. For example, when an NP is dislocated out of an embedded clause, the dislocated topic can appear before the complementizer, as shown in (11) from Kinyarwanda (Morimoto 2000, chapter 4).

(11) Umwaalimu a-ra-shaak-a   **Sam, abaana,** <u>ko</u>   Krw
     teacher   s/he-FOC-want-ASP Sam, children, that
     a-ba-ha   igitabo.
     he-them-give books
     'The teacher wants that Sam, (to) the children, he gives them the books.'

The sentence in (11) can thus be assigned a structure like that in (12). The existence of SpecCP may vary across the Bantu languages. For example, the Chicheŵa equivalents of the dislocation in (11) are unacceptable (Mchombo, p.c. 7/14/00), as shown in (13bb).[4]

---

[4]Only one NP is dislocated in the Chicheŵa and Swahili equivalents to exclude the possibility that adjunction to CP is bad independently of dislocation before the complementizer.

(12) (= 11)

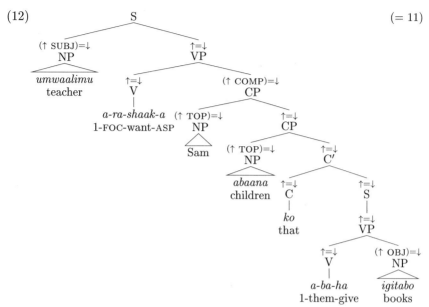

The dislocated NP, *ana*, must be placed after the complementizer, as in (13ba). The facts are the same in Swahili, as shown in (14b) (Mchombo, p.c. 7/16/00; also see Morimoto 2000, chapter 4).

(13) a. mphunzitsi akufuna   kuti **ana,**   Sam awapatse   Chi
          teacher   1.want.ASP that children Sam 1-them-give
          mabuku.
          books
          'The teacher wants that (to) the children, Sam gives them the books."

      b.*mphunzitsi akufuna **ana,** kuti Sam awapatse mabuku.

(14) a. Mwalimu anataka   kwamba **watoto, Sam,** a-wa-pe   Swa
          teacher   1.want.ASP that   children Sam 1-them-give
          vitabu.
          books
          'The teacher wants, (to) the children, that Sam gives them the books."

      b.*Mwalimu anataka, **watoto,** kwamba Sam awape vitabu.

These data suggest that SpecCP is lacking in Chicheŵa and Swahili. The dislocated NPs in the (a) sentences can thus be taken to be adjoined to the embedded S node.

4.3.2 Relativization

The basic clause structure independently motivated elsewhere in Bantu grammar (in the previous work and the topicalization constructions out-

lined above) makes available the structure in (15) for object relativization
in Type I languages: in this structure the bound relativizer and the verb
stem appear in C, and hence we observe "subject inversion".

(15)   Dzamba-type languages ("inversion")

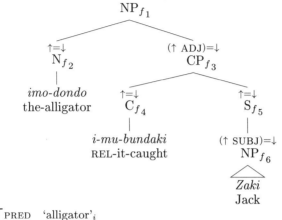

$$f_{1,2}: \begin{bmatrix} \text{PRED} & \text{`alligator'}_i \\ \text{ADJ-REL} & f_{3,4,5}: \begin{bmatrix} \text{PRED} & \text{`catch} <(f_3 \text{ SUBJ}) (f_3 \text{ OBJ})>\text{'} \\ \text{SUBJ} & f_6:[\text{PRED} \quad \text{`Jack'}] \\ \text{OBJ} & [\text{PRED} \quad \text{`pro'}_i] \\ \text{TENSE} & \text{PAST} \end{bmatrix} \end{bmatrix}$$

An uparrow ($\uparrow$) on a node α denotes the f-structure of the mother node
of α, and a downarrow ($\downarrow$) denotes the f-structure of α. In (15), the annotation $\uparrow = \downarrow$ on the head noun (*imo-dondo* 'the-alligator') indicates that
the f-structure of N's mother node is identical to its f-structure. This is the
outermost f-structure labeled $f_{1,2}$. The annotation on the CP adjunct states
that the f-structure of its mother node has an ADJUNCT (more precisely
ADJUNCT-REL) attribute whose value is identified with the f-structure of
CP. The annotation $\uparrow = \downarrow$ on C and S states that their f-structure is identical to the f-structure of the mother node (CP). ($\uparrow$ SUBJ) $= \downarrow$ on the NP
subject *zaki* ('Jack') denotes that the f-structure of the mother node (f_5)
contains a SUBJ attribute whose value is the f-structure of NP (f_6). Note
also that the object pronoun on the verb is represented as having a PRED
value 'pro', which is co-indexed with the head noun.

The structure in (16) represents object relativization in Sesotho-type
languages in which a free-standing relativizer appears in C, the verb in V,
and which has no "subject inversion". Here, the head noun is annotated
$\uparrow = \downarrow$ and thus maps to the same f-structure as that of the mother node
(f_1), which is the outermost f-structure. The adjunct CP is annotated ($\uparrow$
ADJ) $= \downarrow$, stating that the f-structure of the mother node (= the outermost

f-structure) contains an attribute ADJUNCT whose value is identified with the f-structure of CP (f_3). The nodes C, S, VP, and V, annotated $\uparrow = \downarrow$, all map to the same f-structure. ($\uparrow$ SUBJ) = $\downarrow$ on the NP *ba-sadi* 'women' states that the f-structure of the mother node (= the f-structure labeled $f_{3,4,5,7,8}$) has a SUBJ attribute whose value is the f-structure of the NP (f_6). Similarly the annotation ($\uparrow$ ADJ) = $\downarrow$ on XP *kajeno* 'today' indicates that the f-structure of the mother node contains an attribute ADJUNCT and its value is identified with the f-structure of XP (f_9).

(16)   Sesotho-type languages (no inversion)

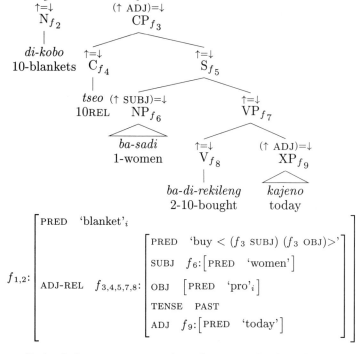

In both language types, the subject inside the relative clause is immediately dominated by the exocentric S node. Under this analysis, no parametric difference in subject position needs to be postulated. As shown, the c- to f-structure correspondence mediated by functional annotations provides the f-structure (grammatical and semantic) information that each c-structure node contributes. Each morpheme contributes relevant semantic and grammatical information in the f-structure; in accordance with the Lexical Integrity Principle, only fully inflected words can be c-structure nodes.

4.3.3 Additional Data from Swahili

Swahili presents additional support for the non-derivational analysis proposed above which posits only one subject position across the Bantu languages regardless of their relativization strategies. Swahili has two relativization constructions (see Keach 1980 for a more detailed discussion on Swahili relativization; all the Swahili examples are taken from Keach 1980): one is where the relative marker *cho* appears on a morphologically independent relative verb *amba*, referred to as the *amba* relativizer here, as illustrated in (17).

(17) kitabu ambacho yule mtu   a-li-ki-soma   Swa *amba* relativization
     book   REL   that person 1-PAST-7-read
     'the book which that person read'

The other relativization strategy is to use a bound relative marker on the main verb. One characteristic of this type of relativization is that, like Dzamba (Type I), when the object is relativized, the subject, normally preverbal, appears after the relativized verb. This is illustrated in (18).

(18) kitabu a-li-cho-ki-soma   yule mtu   Swa REL-V relativization
     7book 1-PAST-REL-7-read that person
     'the book which that person read'

I refer to the former type with the relativizer *amba* as *amba* relativization, and the second type as REL-V relativization. The structural position of the constituents in these relativization constructions is fixed: in *amba* relativization, the subject cannot appear postverbally; by contrast, REL-V relativization does not allow the subject to precede the verb. This is illustrated by the ungrammaticality of the alternative positioning of the relevant constituents in (19a), *amba* relativization, and (19b), REL-V relativization.

(19)   a.*kitabu ambacho a-li-ki-soma   yule mtu   cf. (17)
         book   REL   1-PAST-7-read that person
     b.*kitabu yule mtu   a-li-cho-ki-soma   cf. (18)
         book   that person 1-PAST-REL-7-read

Swahili then exhibits both Dzamba-type relativization with a bound relativizer (and verb raising) and Sesotho-type with a free-standing relativizer (and no verb raising). *amba*-relativization can thus be assigned a structure like that given above in (16), and REL-V relativization can be assigned a structure like that in (15). Positing two subject positions for these different forms of relativization within a single language would be stipulative and unnecessary. More importantly, the above data from Swahili suggest that presence/absence of verb raising in object relativization does not represent a parametric choice which holds for the whole language. Rather, the syntax economically projects the morpho-syntactic features of the lexical resources of the language in question.

One obvious question in examining these data above is how the relativization strategies in these Bantu languages fit into a wider typology of relative clauses. Do the phenomena observed here follow from some general constraints that provide a wider typology of head-modifier constructions? The rest of the paper explores these questions from the OT perspective.

4.4 The Antisymmetry of Phrase Structure

Before I proceed with the above questions, in this section I outline Kayne's (1994) key proposal about the antisymmetry of phrase structure and its empirical consequences. My goal is to highlight the part of the proposal that will be reinterpreted and reanalyzed in light of the OT approach to verb raising and phrase structure variation.

4.4.1 Proposal

Kayne (1994) proposes to abandon the standard assumption in X-bar theory that dominance relations and linear ordering of constituents are independent of each other—that phrase structure is unordered, and directionality of head is parameterized for individual languages. The central idea in Kayne's proposal, known as the Linear Correspondence Axiom (LCA) in the minimalist literature, is that dominance relations directly determine linear order. Crucially, the dominance relation is redefined as *asymmetric* c-command in the proposal in order to derive the antisymmetric nature of linear order (see Kayne, p.4)—that is, not(x>y & y>x).[5] Thus, given two sister nodes, only one (which precedes the other) can c-command the other.

Theoretical implications and empirical consequences of Kayne's key proposal about the direct mapping of the asymmetric domance relation to linear ordering are far-reaching. Although the details of the proposal are omitted here due to space limitations, simple illustrations of his proposal can explicate the idea that X-bar theory is no longer taken to be a primitive component of UG, but is a description of more fundamental antisymmetric properties of phrase structure in natural languages. Put another way, it is those antisymmetric properties that derive the generalizations about syntactic structure encapsulated in traditional X-bar theory. For example, the LCA systematically rules out a structure in which a phrase is headed by two heads, or one which contains non-head sisters immediately dominated by another non-head (e.g., YP and ZP immediately dominated by XP). In other words, the LCA predicts one of the basic tenets of X-bar theory that all phrases are uniquely headed. As Kayne (p.11) points out, X-bar theory states this basic property of phrase structure, but it does not explain it.

The LCA also makes a strong claim about word order typology. In the discussion of word order typology, Kayne further specifies the kind of linear ordering implied by the LCA in terms of precedence/subsequence. He ar-

---

[5]Throughout his work, Kayne takes c-command to be defined in terms of "first node up" rather than "first branching node up" (p.7).

gues that an asymmetric c-command is mapped to *precedence* rather than *subsequence* on empirical grounds.[6] For example, a simple X′ structure with specifier, head, and complement allows six logically possible orderings of these elements. Of those six ordering possibilities, Kayne's theory actually allows only two: specifier-head-complement and complement-head-specifier.[7] Of these two possible orderings permitted by the theory, Kayne argues that the former (spec-head-compl) is cross-linguistically more common, and hence should be postulated as the only order made available by UG. As Kayne (p.35) points out, while ordering between head and complement can vary more widely across languages, ordering of specifier and head is much more uniform. For example, SpecIP, the canonical subject position in many languages, is overwhelmingly initial. He notes that this is evident in SVO and SOV languages, two of the most common basic word order types in the world's languages. Kayne further argues that if we assume that VSO, another commonly attested word order type, is derived by leftward movement of V, then we can say that in VSO languages, subject position (SpecIP) is also initial. Other word order types, OVS, OSV and VOS are exceedingly rare, according to typologists (e.g., Greenberg 1966:76, Comrie 1989:87). These word order types involve linear ordering other than specifier-head-complement order (see Kayne p.36).

Thus, the empirical basis for Kayne's proposal about precedence/subsequence with respect to the ordering of specifier, head, and complement is a typological generalization that specifier-head order is cross-linguistically predominant. The relation between the LCA and the ordering of syntactic elements must therefore be that of precedence. The universality of specifier-head-complement postulated by Kayne's theory of phrase structure therefore has some typological grounding: what is taken to be a universal is essentially the unmarked (or more common) structure typologically.

What does it mean to implement such a hypothesis in a formal framework like that of Kayne's which interprets cross-linguistic tendencies as absolute universals that are inviolable? If the linear order relation must be precedence rather than subsequence and the universal order of specifier, head, and complement is as given, it follows that adjunction, which includes positioning of specifiers in Kayne's approach, must invariably be to the left.[8] More generally, the directionality parameter no longer has a place in the theory, as the dominance relation directly maps onto linear precedence. Such a theory thus requires that any (word order) variation away from a given universal (order or hierarchical structure) is derived

---

[6]Kayne (p.37) also illustrates why the linear order relation must be precedence rather than subsequence based on theory-internal arguments, but this is not taken up in the present discussion.

[7]See Kayne (pp.33–38) for the technical details of his proposal that limits the ordering possibilities of specifier, head, and complement to two rather than six.

[8]In addition to left-adjunction of specifiers, Kayne (chapter 4) motivates leftward adjunction of X^0 elements (e.g., heads, clitics).

by movement of relevant syntactic elements. Furthermore, assuming that lowering is not available at all (e.g., Chomsky 1993), upward movement to a c-commanding position must always be leftward, since asymmetric c-commanding implies linear precedence. For example, complement-head order in SOV languages must be taken as a result of a leftward movement of the complement to a higher specifier position past the verb; postpositional phrases (complement-head) must be derived in a similar fashion from the head-complement order; languages in which IP precedes C^0 must be derived from the C^0-IP order by moving the IP to SpecCP past the C^0; and so forth. A major challenge for the theory then is how to motivate (on theory-external grounds) a series of movement operations necessitated by the proposed UG.

4.4.2 Head Movement

Additional evidence for Kayne's claim that movement of any syntactic element must be leftward comes from verb positioning. Instances of leftward verb movement are well-attested in languages that exhibit verb-second (V2) constructions. In the P&P approach, it is standardly assumed that V2 configurations in languages like German are derived by raising the verb to the highest head position (e.g., V to I, I to C). No languages have been reported which are the mirror image of Germanic V2—namely, languages in which the verb is raised (rightward) to penultimate position (or a sentence-final C^0) in root clauses.

If rightward movement is banned by the theory, it means (in movement analyses) that a V-T-Agr (or V-I-C) sequence cannot be derived by moving the verb rightward to a higher head position. Instead, as briefly noted above, Kayne proposes that in such languages the IP complement of C^0 must move to SpecCP *after* the verb moves from V to I to C, as illustrated in (20).[9] For the present purposes, here and in the subsequent illustration of Kayne's discussion, I take the traditional analysis of specifier position (not the adjunction analysis of Kayne).[10]

Kayne notes an additional favorable consequence of this analysis: if it has to be the case in head-final languages that IP complement moves to SpecCP, this means that *wh*-interrogatives can never fill SpecCP. This supports the observation made by Bach (1971:161) that SOV languages generally lack *wh*-movement to initial position.

---

[9]It is not obvious from Kayne's discussion what triggers these movements. See also the discussion on this point in section 4.4.4.

[10]The diagrams that follow in this section are my interpretations of Kayne's discussion of the relevant structures.

(20)

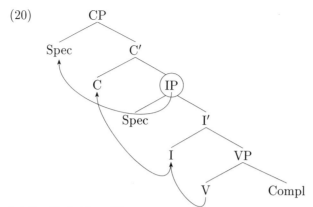

4.4.3 Relative Clauses

Restricting movement to leftward requires reanalysis of familiar right-adjunction constructions. For example, consider the relative clause in (21). Under the proposed approach, *the* takes as its complement *two pictures of John's that you liked*. The phrase *two pictures of John's* must be raised from the lower complement position (sister to the lower V) to SpecCP. D^0 presumably moves to the higher D^0, as diagrammed in (22).

(21) I found [the two pictures of John's] that you liked.

(22)

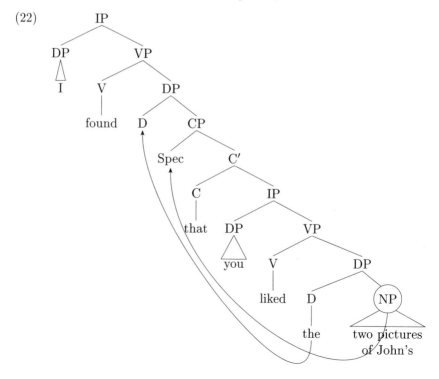

Kayne's analysis of relative clauses in head-final languages takes into consideration two related facts (Kayne, p.93):

(23)   Characteristics of N-final languages

   a. N-final relatives lack relative pronouns.

   b. N-final relatives never display a complementizer that is identical to the normal complementizer of sentential complementation.

The derivation of a relative clause like that in (21) for N-final languages, shown in (24), captures the above facts. The head of the relative clause *picture of John's* first moves to SpecCP, stranding the zero complementizer. The IP complement of covert C moves to SpecDP. D^0 and C^0 are both phonetically unrealized.[11]

(24)

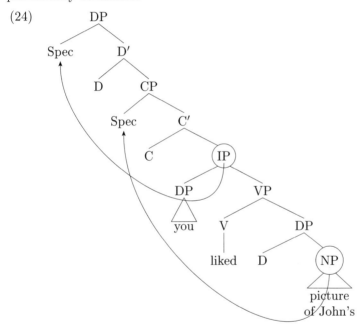

The derivation of an N-final relative clause illustrated in (24) provides an immediate explanation of the generalization in (23b). The constituent that moves to the prenominal position in SpecDP is IP, not the CP that dominates it. Hence the normal C^0 of sentential complementation cannot be present prenominally. According to the above analysis, the phonetically null C^0 follows the head noun.

Now consider *wh*-relatives in English, such as *the picture which the student took* (based on the discussion in Kayne p.95). In (25), within the

---

[11]Presumably, phonetically null D^0 and C^0 in N-final relative clauses are due to parameterized (e.g., 'weak') features on the heads.

DP$_2$ *which picture*, the NP *picture* moves to SpecDP$_2$, yielding the surface order *the picture which* .... Then the whole DP$_2$ moves to SpecCP.

Deriving the N-final structure from (25) would require moving everything following *picture* further up to SpecDP$_1$. But the material following *picture* is not a constituent: DP$_2$ that has moved to SpecCP contains *picture* in SpecDP$_2$ and *which* in D. What has to be moved would be D′; hence this movement would be illegitimate. The presence of a *wh*-relative pronoun is therefore incompatible with N-final relativization. The above analysis then correctly predicts that N-final languages generally lack a relative pronoun, stated earlier in (23a).

(25)

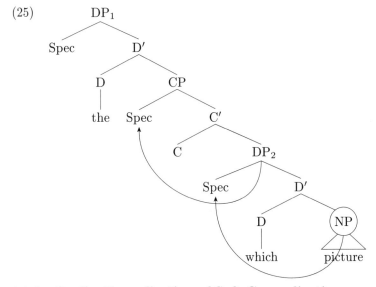

4.4.4 On the Formalization of Soft Generalizations

Now at this point our primary concern is what generalizations we can extract out of the discussion of Kayne's proposal and analysis of specific constructions, independently of technical details that enable us to implement them into the theory.[12] The general claim in Kayne's key proposal, the LCA, is that phrase structure is antisymmetric, and specifically, the left is a more salient position than the right, as asymmetric c-command invariably maps to linear *precedence*: specifier, often the most prominent position (e.g., subject position), is leftmost; the head precedes the complement (= head is left); movement is always leftward; adjunction must also be to the left; the nominal head of a relative clause is universally to the left of the relative pronoun, and the N-finality is derived by movement; and so forth. This "leftness" tendency in structure is also discernible in the fact that structure is predominantly right-branching rather than left-

---

[12]See section 4.6.6 for a summary of Kayne's proposals and a comparison with the alternative approach explored in the present work.

branching. I will return to this last point in section 4.6 in the discussion of the OT constraints on phrase structure.

It is important, however, that this "leftness" condition of (unmarked) structure is not an absolute universal, but is a strong tendency. Such typological tendencies have been frequently noted by functionalists and typologists (e.g., Comrie 1989, chapter 4). And precisely because these generalizations are tendencies rather than rules that apply across the board, the gradient character of typological generalizations has resisted a principled explanation in formal syntax. One of the major challenges for generative syntax is then how to incorporate the "softness" of such generalizations in a way that correctly characterizes universal tendencies (the unmarked properties) and at the same time allows for a range of variation in phrase structure across languages.

Kayne's proposal is insightful in that it explains a number of typological observations noted by others, such as the word order typology, ordering of specifier and head, position of subject, the asymmetry of V2 phenomena, and a set of characteristics shared by head-final languages (e.g., (23)). However, because the system developed by Kayne (and the P&P approach more generally) rests on the assumption that principles are inviolable, and because the universality is represented by common hierarchical structure, all of the "soft" generalizations are taken as absolute. Any instances that do not conform to the generalizations have to be derived by a series of movements. Motivating each and every instance of movement in order to derive cross-linguistic variation will be difficult. One of the most prevalent approaches has been to postulate formal (generally binary) features which are parameterized for individual languages. These formal features supposedly trigger the necessary movements. But the motivation for such formal features can only be theory-internal.

The emergence of Optimality Theory (Prince and Smolensky 1993, Kager 1999, among others) and its successful application to the domain of syntax has enabled us to develop a precise model of the softness of universal markedness that is discernible in various parts of the grammar (see, for example, the references in footnote 2). The basic tenet of OT is that grammaticality is determined by the interaction of well-formedness constraints on output representation. Constraints are universal but violable; instead of serial derivation, constraints on surface representation are evaluated simultaneously. The only source of variation is in ranking of these universal constraints. This radically different conception of grammar is precisely the type of grammatical model needed to capture the softness of typological generalizations.

In the remainder of this paper, I explore the OT approach to phrase structure, building on earlier work (cited above), by providing an analysis of verb raising in Bantu relativization and a typology of relative clauses more generally. First, I provide the basic architectural properties of the OT-LFG model, which augments the parallel grammatical architecture developed in LFG (e.g., Bresnan 1982, Dalrymple, Kaplan, Maxwell, and Zaenen 1995) as the representational basis. After a brief discussion of earlier implementation of 'edge alignment' (cf. McCarthy and Prince 1993) in the modeling of word order, I will introduce the relevant constraints needed to explain the data, along with the discussion of Kayne's generalizations/predictions and how they are captured in OT-LFG (§ 4.6). This is followed by the analysis (§ 4.7) and a brief discussion of extension of the current model to related phenomena for future research (§ 4.8).

4.5 Architectural Properties of OT-LFG

OT grammar has three components: the INPUT, GENERATOR (GEN), and EVALUATOR (EVAL), as schematically shown in (26) (adapted from Kager 1999:9).

(26)   General architecture of OT grammar

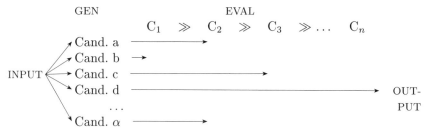

For a given input (briefly discussed below), the grammar generates all and any candidates that are made available by Universal Grammar (cf. FREEDOM OF ANALYSIS; Prince and Smolensky 1993, Kager 1999). The candidate set is therefore the same in all languages. Candidates are then evaluated against a set of ranked constraints simultaneously. The optimal output is one which incurs the least serious violation of the constraint hierarchy. Below, I briefly discuss the nature of the input and candidates as adopted in OT-LFG work.

4.5.1 Input and Candidates

As has been standardly adopted by OT-LFG work to date, OT-LFG takes the INPUT to be minimally a skeletal f-structure in a language-independent form: the semantic content of the predicate and its argument(s), grammatical information such as tense/modality/aspect, etc. Candidates for generation optimization are taken to be pairs of c-structures and their corresponding, fully specified f-structures. Much fuller details of the nature of the input and candidates are discussed, for example, in the work of Bresnan (2000b), Kuhn (2001), Sells (2001), among others.

Given freedom of analysis, and given that in syntax, we are examining much larger structures than in phonology, one of the questions concerning candidates in generation optimization is what constitutes a possible set of candidates—that is, what the relation is between a given input and the candidates that are generated by GEN, and, from a computational point of view, how we can guarantee the computational tractability of OT grammar. In recent OT-LFG work, there have been two proposals regarding the relation between the input representation and candidate generation. One, proposed by Kuhn (2001), is that every candidate produced by GEN must be subsumed by the input. That is, all candidates for a given input must share the same interpretation. Selection of a candidate set of a given input that respects *subsumption* limits the number of possible candidates and, as a result, increases computational efficiency.

The other proposal has more to do with the selection of an optimal analysis: given that any amount of structure is posited in candidate generation, how can the system of ranked constraints guarantee that the optimal analysis under any constraint ranking is one that is attested in some language? There are two options (also pointed out by Grimshaw 2001): one is to admit any possible structural realization of a given input, including those that are never attested in any language. Nonetheless, assuming that constraints are universal and typologically grounded, no ranking of those constraints would yield unattested candidates as optimal. In other words, the correct generalizations and postulation of universal constraints will guarantee that the optimal output is one that is possible in some grammar.

The second option is to assume that there is a set of properties that any well-formed phrase structure in natural language must share, and GEN defines such a set. So only those candidates that are well-formed in some language get generated. This seems to be a computationally more efficient way to achieve the same result (of generating an analysis that is attested in natural language). The latter option is explored in Sells (2001). The present work draws on his proposal about the properties of GEN. Slight modification is made to the original proposal in the present discussion.

4.5.2 General Phrase Structure Properties

General properties of structure discussed in this section include those concerning bar-levels in c-structure, categories, and projection.

First, in accordance with the standard X' structure, we assume three levels of projection, X^0, X', and XP, which will be referred to as projection levels of 0, 1, and 2 respectively. This defines the depth of projections allowed by X' structures.

Second, for a structure to be well-formed, X^0 can only dominate another X^0. Level X^0 does not immediately dominate Y' or YP (levels 1 and 2), where Y may or may not belong to the same category as X. This eliminates ill-formed structures like those in (27) in which the 0-level category X dominates a 1-level category X' (the same category) or Y' (different category).

(27)   Ill-formed X′ structures

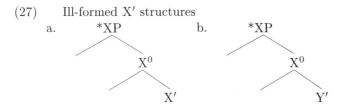

a.   *XP   b.   *XP

Third, a general assumption concerning categories is that there are major lexical categories, N, V, P, and A, and functional categories I and C. Structures are built from these major lexical and functional categories. The lexical and functional categories specified above are potential instantiations of semantic and grammatical concepts available in language. According to the levels of projections allowed in X′ structures, any category X^0 may project X′ and XP.[13]

Lastly, we can assume two types of categories for the root node: the endocentric category XP and the non-projective, exocentric category S standardly assumed in LFG. The endocentric category XP is a projection of its head X, though the head may not always be overtly present (headless XPs are permitted); the exocentric category S, on the other hand, may dominate any category of any levels 0–2.

As standardly assumed in LFG work, in OT-LFG, c-structures represent surface expressions of lexical and phrasal elements, and they are paired with f-structures, which encode functions and grammatical information that words and morphemes carry. All non-root nodes bear one of the functional annotations given in (28). As explained earlier, these annotations indicate the correspondence between the c- and f-structure.

(28)   Functional annotations

    a. $\uparrow = \downarrow$

    b. $(\uparrow \text{GF}) = \downarrow$

    c. $(\uparrow \text{DF}) = \downarrow$

Although c-structure nodes are freely annotated by any of these functional annotations, the properties of structures discussed above filter out annotations that do not conform to those structures.

4.5.3   Two Notions of Head

There are two notions of head that will be crucial in the formation of constraints within the OT-LFG framework: (i) c-(structure) heads and (ii)

---

[13]While the majority of these lexical and functional categories project to X′ and XP, there are some X^0 elements that have been argued to not project. For example, Sells (1994) proposes that verbal elements in Korean such as negation *an*, light verb *ha* 'do' in complex predicates, and certain adverbs like *cal* 'well' do not project a phrase; unlike phrasal elements that can freely scramble, these elements have fixed ordering. Abeillé and Godard (1998) discuss some elements in French which have similar non-projective properties as those in Korean (see also Sadler and Arnold (1994)).

functional co-heads. The c-heads are the familiar notion of heads in the sense of X^0 categories in phrase structure. For example, the c-head of VP is V^0, that of IP is I^0, and so forth. Co-heads, on the other hand, are any c-structure nodes within the same (extended) projection that map to a single f-structure. For example, consider the structure in (29).

(29)

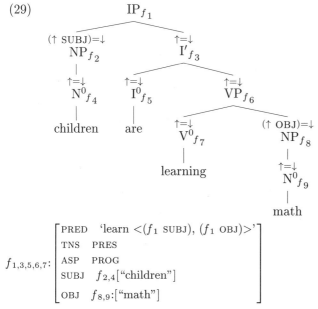

$$f_{1,3,5,6,7}: \begin{bmatrix} \text{PRED} & \text{'learn} <(f_1 \text{ SUBJ}), (f_1 \text{ OBJ})>\text{'} \\ \text{TNS} & \text{PRES} \\ \text{ASP} & \text{PROG} \\ \text{SUBJ} & f_{2,4}[\text{``children''}] \\ \text{OBJ} & f_{8,9}:[\text{``math''}] \end{bmatrix}$$

Here the c-structure heads are the X^0 categories, the I^0, V^0, and the N^0s. The co-heads of IP (f_1) are I' (f_3), I (f_5), VP (f_6), and V (f_7), those that are annotated $\uparrow = \downarrow$. These c-structure nodes all map onto the same outer f-structure nucleus. Inside the SUBJ constituent, the pre-terminal node N^0 (f_4) is a co-head of the mother node (NP_{f_2}), and therefore the two nodes unify in the f-structure. Similarly, inside the OBJ constituent N^0 (f_9) is a co-head of the mother node (NP_{f_8}) and maps onto the same f-structure as that of the mother node.

The hierarchical structures that represent head and co-head relations are assumed to have two properties (discussed in Sells 2001). First, if Y^m immediately dominates X^n, where $m \leq n$, and if X^n and Y^m are different categories $(X \neq Y)$ but both are co-heads, then the hierarchical relation must conform to the 'clausal spine hierarchy' CP-IP-S-VP that share the categorial features with the verbal head (Sells 2000). For example, looking back at the structure in (29), we have a 1-level category I' (Y^m) and a 2-level category VP (X^n); hence $m \leq n$. I' and VP are of different c-structure categories, and both are co-heads. Thus, the local structure in (29) is well-formed. This property also covers the case where IP immediately dominates VP where they are in a co-head relation. On the other hand, VP and CP cannot be co-heads if the former immediately dominates the latter. This is illustrated in (30). In (30a) the annotations $\uparrow = \downarrow$ on VP and CP indicate that they are co-heads and hence map to the same f-structure. In the above definition of the well-formed hierarchical relation, VP corresponds to X^n and CP corresponds to Y^m; both are of level 2 (XP) so $m = n$; they are co-heads. However the structure does not conform to the spine-hierarchy CP–VP, as VP dominates CP. In (30b), VP and CP are not co-heads. The CP bears a COMP function; thus the corresponding f-structure is inside the outer f-structure that V and VP map to. This structure is therefore well-formed.

(30)   a.   b.

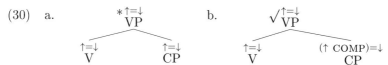

Note that the CP-IP-S-VP hierarchy does not require that all four nodes be present. It only requires that if any two or more of these nodes are present, then they have to conform to the hierarchy.

Another important property of head and co-head structures concerns categorial uniformity of elements that enter into the co-head relation: given a co-head Y^m, and a co-head X^n which it immediately dominates, where $m \geq n$, then X and Y are of the same category. For example, in the structures in (31), the lower V^0 in (31a) and V' in (31b) correspond to X^n; the higher V^0 and VP are Y^m; in (31a), m (higher V^0) = n (lower V^0); in (31b), m (VP) > n (V'); in each structure, X and Y are co-heads, and they are of the same category.

(31)   a.   b.

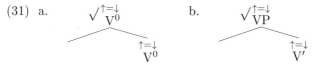

Similarly, I' and I which it immediately dominates are of the same category, where the former is a 1-level category and the latter a 0-level category. On the other hand, the structure in (32) is ill-formed due to the fact that NP (Y^m) and V' (X^n) are co-heads, $m > n$, but X $\neq$ Y.

(32)

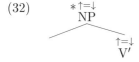

This property also covers adjunction structures where Y^m immediately dominates X^n and $m = n$ (e.g., VP-over-VP in VP-adjunction; IP-over-IP in IP-adjunction).

Lastly, S and X' dominated by XP are assumed to never bear GF. They are thus, always annotated $\uparrow = \downarrow$ and never $(\uparrow GF) = \downarrow$.

4.6 OT Clausal Syntax

Having established the properties of structures and well-formedness of hierarchical relations that are assumed to be part of GEN in OT-LFG, I now turn to the constraints needed to model a typology of word order and head directionality of structure. Unless any modification/extension is specifically discussed, the constraints on word order and hierarchical structure presented in sections 4.6.2–4.6.4 are taken from previous work, drawing primarily on Sells (2001).

4.6.1 Word Order as Edge Alignment

In phonology and morphology, there is often overt or covert reference to edges of constituents: e.g., edges of a prosodic word and a foot coincide; an affix is placed as close as possible to the left edge of the stem; an affix falls on the right edge of the head foot, and so forth. McCarthy and Prince (1993) propose that such phonological/morphological conditions that make reference to constituent edges can reduce to a single family of well-formedness constraints referred to as *Generalized Alignment*, formally defined in (33).

(33)   Generalized Alignment
   Align(Cat_1,$Edge_1$, Cat_2,$Edge_2$) $=_{def}$
   $\forall\, Cat_1\, \exists\, Cat_2$ such that $Edge_1$ of Cat_1 and $Edge_2$ of Cat_2 coincide.
   Where Cat_1, $Cat_2 \in$ ProsCat $\cup$ GramCat
   $Edge_1$, $Edge_2 \in$ {Right, Left}

In the definition, Cat_1 and Cat_2 are the sets of prosodic and grammatical categories (ProsCat and GramCat in (33) respectively). $Edge_1$ and $Edge_2$ range over two values, left or right. Generalized Alignment demands that $Edge_1$ of Cat_1 and $Edge_2$ of Cat_2 coincide.[14] For example, consider the alignment constraint given in (34a); the interpretation of the constraint is given in (34b) (Kager 1999:119, ex (69a)).

(34)   a.   ALIGN (Stem, R, σ, R)
   b.   For every stem there must be some syllable such that the right edge of the stem matches the right edge of the syllable.

The constraint in (34a) is satisfied by candidate (35a) because there is a syllable for the stem, and the right edge of the stem matches the right edge of that syllable. Candidate (35b) also satisfies the constraint because for the stem, there is a syllable whose right edge matches with the right edge of the stem, namely σ_2. Candidate (35c), on the other hand, violates the constraint: there is a syllable in the stem, but the right edge of the stem does not match the right edge of that syllable. The constraint is also violated by candidate (35d) in which the stem contains no syllable (Kager, p.120, ex (70)).

---

[14] As Kager (1999, 119) notes, most phonological/morphological work implicitly assumes that $Edge_1$ and $Edge_2$ are identical edges (both left or both right).

(35)　a.　$[\;\sigma\;]_{Stem}$　　　satisfied
　　　b.　$[\;\sigma_1\;\sigma_2\;]_{Stem}$　satisfied
　　　c.　$[\;\sigma\;\ldots\;]_{Stem}$　　violated
　　　d.　$[\;\ldots\;]_{Stem}$　　　violated

Researchers working in OT syntax have extended this generalized formal mechanism of alignment to positioning of core syntactic elements like heads and complements (Grimshaw 1997, Sells 1998, 1999b, 1999c, 2001) as well as discourse-related constituents such as topic and focus (e.g., Costa 1997, 1998, Grimshaw and Samek-Lodovici 1998, Samek-Lodovici 1998a, 1998b). Some of the relevant constraints in an early proposal by Grimshaw (1997) are shown in (36). The constraints on head-positioning in (36a,b) prefer the (c-structure) head to be at the specified edge within its maximal projection. The assumption is that HEAD-LFT will be relatively high-ranked, necessarily above HEAD-RT, in head-initial languages; HEAD-RT will be relatively high-ranked and is ranked above HD-LFT in head-final languages. Similarly, SPEC-LFT and SPEC-RT in (36c,d) state that the specifier is at the specified edge within the maximal projection that dominates it. Ranking SPEC-LFT above SPEC-RT effectively prefers a structure in which the operator in the specifier position is left-most in the clause, as in English. These alignment constraints are taken to be gradient, measuring the distance between the left/right edge of the relevant projection and the head/specifier position.

(36)　a.　HEAD-LFT: The head is leftmost in its projection (X′, XP).

　　　b.　HEAD-RT: The head is rightmost in its projection (X′, XP).

　　　c.　SPEC-LFT: The specifier is leftmost (in XP that dominates it).

　　　d.　SPEC-RT: The specifier is rightmost (in XP that dominates it).

In Kayne's proposal, the relation between dominance and linear ordering in terms of precedence rather than subsequence is motivated in part by the ordering of specifier and head across languages. Given that the theory permits only two orderings, specifier-head-complement and complement-head-specifier, Kayne proposes the former as the universal order, because specifier-head order is strongly predominant cross-linguistically. Grimshaw's SPEC-LFT is precisely the constraint that characterizes this universal tendency. Furthermore, in Kayne (1994), head-complement order is taken to be the only order permitted by UG, and the complement-head order is derived by movement (see Kayne, p.33–35). Although both orders are well-attested in many languages, given that specifier-head order is a more plausible universal, and specifier and complement must be on opposite sides of the head (in Kayne's theory), it follows that head-complement order must be postulated as the universal order of these elements. Grimshaw's HEAD-LFT expresses this same idea.

Grimshaw's proposal, however, loses Kayne's insightful observation that phrase structure has asymmetric properties. Constraints that refer to complementary edges like those in (36) imply that structure is symmetric. In effect, the set of these constraints as a whole says nothing about universal tendencies and relative markedness of structure.[15] Sells (1998a, 1999c) makes a similar point, who shows that rankings of the above constraints in (36) that refer to complementary edges would produce unattested patterns of head and specifier positioning. Morimoto (2000b, Chapter 3) also points out a similar problem of overgeneration that results from earlier proposals of focus positioning constraints that refer to complementary edges (e.g., FOCUS-RIGHT, FOCUS-LEFT).

In order to solve these problems that arise by assuming constraints that refer to both edges and to effectively restrict the generative power of the constraint system with respect to constituent ordering, Sells (1998a, 1999c, 2001) develops a system within OT-LFG in which all alignment constraints make reference to only left-edges (of clauses), and two constraints on the clausal skeleton determine the directionality of heads. His work provides a precise sense of the notion of alignment in syntax, in part to reformulate alignment constraints proposed earlier such as those given in (36). From the OT-LFG perspective, Grimshaw's alignment constraints (36a,b), for example, are alignment of c-structure elements, whereas the alignment constraint proposed by Samek-Lodovici and others on focus positioning (references cited earlier) is alignment of f-structure elements (e.g., FOCUS) in c-structure. Sells (1998, 20) formulates these two types of alignment as in (37), assuming only left-alignment.

(37) a. C-structure: Align (Cat, L, α, L).

  b. F-structure: Align (GF, L, β, L).

Alignment of c-structure elements in (37a) states that the left edge of a given c-structure category (Cat) shares a left edge of α; similarly, f-structure alignment in (37b) states that the left edge of a given f-structure element (GF) shares a left edge of β in c-structure. α and β are a 'natural domain' for Cat and GF respectively, as defined in (38) (Sells 1998:20).

(38) The immediate mother M of an element E in representation R is the immediately superior constituent domain containing E. M constitutes the natural domain for E.

For example, if Cat is V^0, then α is VP (if there is no V'); if GF is SUBJ, β is the immediately outer f-structure nucleus that contains SUBJ as an attribute.

The present work builds on the notion of alignment in (37). The next section discusses alignment of c-structure elements that derive clausal skeleton and head directionality.

---

[15] In her recent work, Grimshaw (2000, 2001) acknowledges this problem and proposes to take Kayne's observation into consideration in (re)formulating alignment constraints. In particular, the constraint SPEC-RT is no longer postulated in her constraint system.

4.6.2 Clausal Skeleton

Two alignment constraints are proposed by Sells to apply to the clausal skeleton and determine head directionality: left-alignment of heads ('Head-Left') is applied within an immediate projection of the head. Importantly, there is no Head-Right constraint. This essentially recaptures Kayne's proposal about the universal order of head-complement structure. Here, this is a soft constraint on representation; it is violated by head-final structure. The only right-alignment constraint admitted in the present approach is Spine-R(ight): this requires that any head (e.g., V) and its extended heads (V', VP, I, I', IP), or co-heads (= spine), be final in each of their local subtrees, preferring a fully right-headed, right-branching structure.

(39)   Head positioning constraints ("VO" as ranked)
   a. Head-L(eft): X^0 is left in its immediate constituent.
   b. Spine-R(ight): A co-head aligns right in its immediate constituent.

To illustrate how these constraints figure in OT-LFG grammar, let us consider a schematic SIVO structure in (40).[16] First, starting from the bottom, within the local tree of V', there is 1 Spine-R violation at V, as this node, annotated $\uparrow = \downarrow$ is a co-head but does not align right within its immediate projection. V is also a c-structure X^0 head, and aligns left in its local subtree, so this respects the Head-L constraint. Second, going up one level in the structure within the subtree dominated by VP, there is no violation of Spine-R or Head-L: the co-head V' aligns right (respecting Spine-R), and there is no X^0 at this level. Within the next higher subtree, I and VP are co-heads. The configuration given here thus violates Spine-R once for I but there is no Head-L violation. Note in passing that if the head is rightmost, and the VP co-head is leftmost in the structure, then this configuration would violate both Spine-R (degree of 1) and Head-L; consequently, having functional projections is more preferrable in head-initial languages than in head-final languages. In sum, in this structure, there are 2 Spine-R violations and no Head-L violation, as indicated in (40). As will be seen, in order to yield this structure as optimal, Spine-R must be ranked lower than Head-L.

Sells' proposal on the derivation of a clausal skeleton makes a number of important typological predictions relative to a given ranking of these constraints. For example, let us assume the basic clause structure for a head-final language to be the mirror-image of the SIVO structure in (40) with respect to head positioning.

---

[16]The structure in (40) and the subsequent trees representing different word order types are originally discussed in Sells (2001).

(40)   SIVO structure

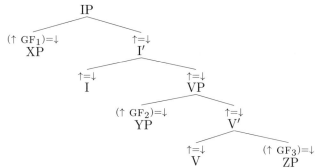

    a. Spine-R violations: 2 (I and V).
    b. Head-L violation: 0.

(41)   SOVI structure

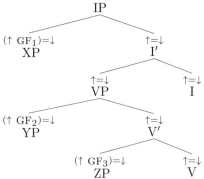

    a. Spine-R violation: 1 (VP).
    b. Head-L violations: 2 (I and V).

The structure in (41) violates Spine-R once at VP (a co-head) and Head-L twice, at I and V. More generally, whenever the structure contains a functional head (F^0), which is also a co-head (annotated $\uparrow = \downarrow$), the sister node will always be a co-head also; therefore whether F^0 is left or right, this local structure will violate Spine-R once. Having F^0 in a head-final structure also means Head-L violations will be more severe.

Is there a more optimal head-final structure than (41) that GEN can generate? Recall that in addition to the endocentric XPs, OT-LFG also allows the exocentric category S. If we posit a structure like that given in (42) where there is a single functional head above S, there are fewer violations of high-ranking Spine-R. This structure is observed in German, where SpecFP is reserved for a discourse function (e.g., TOPIC).[17]

---

[17]It has been argued that the only functional projection available in German is CP rather than IP, as there is no evidence for lexical INFL (cf. most recently Choi 1999, Berman 2000).

(42)   SIOV structure (e.g., German nonsubject-initial clause)

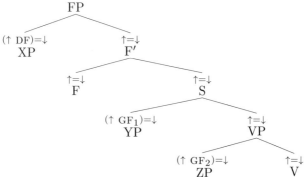

a. Spine-R violation: 1 (I).
b. Head-L violation: 1 (V).

Importantly, unless a functional head is forced to be present (e.g., by V2, as observed in German), the most optimal structure in head-final languages would be one in which the root node has the exocentric organization (S) and has no functional head above it, as shown in (43). In this structure, each co-head (annotated $\uparrow = \downarrow$) aligns right in its local subtree. The degree of Spine-R violation is therefore 0. The structure has one lexical head (V) at the bottom of the structure, aligning right. This incurs 1 violation of Head-L.

(43)   SOV structure

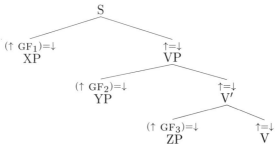

a. Spine-R violation: 0.
b. Head-L violation: 1 (V).

In fact head-final languages typically lack lexically independent functional heads. That is, tense/aspect and complementizer are typically morphological affixes on the verb; see for example, Cho and Sells (1995), Sells (1995) for Korean and Japanese. As noted earlier, Kayne's theory predicts that there is no V-I-C rightward movement. Instead, V universally moves to I and to C leftward; in head-final languages, the IP complement of C moves leftward to yield the verb-final structure. The OT constraints on clausal skeleton derive exactly this asymmetry: Head-L ≫ Spine-R optimally yields a head-initial language; the presence of functional projections (at least one violation of Spine-R) would be tolerated. Spine-R $\gg$ Head-L optimally yields a head-final language; Spine-R being high-ranked, the presence of any functional projection will be dispreferred, as there is an alternative in head-final languages of having bound inflectional elements morphologically attach to a verb. This view of phrase structure is also suggested and formally implemented by Haider (1997a, 1997b) in a different framework.

In this connection, Kayne (p.93) also observes that "many N-final languages lack any equivalent of English *the* so that D^0 will not be visible". Under the present approach, the presence of D would also be dispreferred in head-final languages for the same reason that the presence of verbal functional heads are dispreferred: the NP complement of D would be a co-head (annotated $\uparrow = \downarrow$), and hence this local structure would violate Spine-R, high-ranked in V-final languages.

As Sells (2001) points out, Spine-R also prefers specifiers and adjunctions to be leftward: specifier is sister to a bar-level category, necessarily a co-head, and the node sister to an adjoined element will always be a co-head also, whether adjunction takes place at XP, X', or X^0. No other constraints or movements need to be postulated to capture this 'leftness' tendency observed and modeled by Kayne.[18]

4.6.3 Constraints on Hierarchical Structure

Now we turn to constraints on hierarchical structure. First, two dominance constraints will partially determine the structural 'height' of the head. OB-HD(XP) in (44a), adopted from Grimshaw (1997), requires XP to be headed. On the other hand, *F in (44b), a generalized version of *C and *I proposed by Sells (2001), penalizes the presence of a functional head. These constraints are therefore in mutual conflict for functional heads: for example, if there is an IP, OB-HD(XP) will require the IP to be headed, but *F will penalize the presence of the head. OB-HD(XP) $\gg$ *F will therefore prefer an IP structure in which any verb, including a main verb, appears in I. *F $\gg$ OB-HD(XP) will prefer the verb to appear in V.

(44)   Dominance constraints

    a. OB-HD(XP): XP must have head.

    b. *F: Avoid F

Clearly, some other constraints must interact with these to yield a cross-linguistic variation with respect to the positioning of different classes of verbal heads. For instance in English, only auxiliary verbs appear in I, as in (45a), while lexical verbs appear in V, and in the absence of I, IP is headless, as in (45b). In languages like Swedish, on the other hand, all finite

---

[18]For other word order types not illustrated here, see Sells (2001); also Morimoto (2000b, chapter 3).

verbs appear in I in a main clause if the subject is the first constitutent, and in C if a non-subject appears as the first constituent (the subject is SpecIP in both cases).

(45) a.   b.

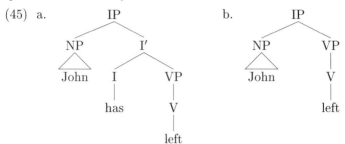

One constraint that has been proposed in Bresnan (2000b) and also used by Sells (2001) in order to model variation like this in the exact position of a verbal head is *Lex-in-F, stated in (46).

(46) *Lex-in-F: Avoid lexical head in F.

Ranking *Lex-in-F above OB-HD(XP) will prefer XP to be headed but disprefer a lexical head in the F^0 position. So the only time OB-HD(XP) is satisfied is when there is an inflectional element that can occupy F^0 that does not violate the high-ranking *Lex-in-F constraint (e.g., English). Reversing the ranking of these two constraints will allow any verbal head to be in F^0 in order to satisfy OB-HD(XP) (e.g., Swedish).

4.6.4   GF Alignment in OT-LFG

As noted earlier, from the OT-LFG perspective, GF alignment (as well as alignment of discourse functions such as TOPIC and FOCUS) is alignment of f-structure elements according to their c-structure positioning. But linear order is a relation only on c-structure; elements in f-structure are unordered, and hence cannot enter into linear precedence relations. We can allow f-structure elements to be in linear ordering relations through the correspondence function ϕ, which induces the f- to c-structure inverse mapping function ϕ^{-1}. Within OT-LFG, Sells (1998, 11) proposes the notion of f-alignment (being analogous to *f-precedence*; cf. Bresnan 1995), defined in (47). F-alignment can be taken as an instantiation of Generalized Alignment that is generalized to allow for alignment of various syntactic constituents.

(47)   F-alignment

        For two f-structure elements f_1 and f_2, f_1 *left-aligns* with f_2 if and only if the left edge of the maximal node that maps onto f_1 shares a left edge with the maximal node that maps on to f_2.

To illustrate how f-alignment is applied to constituent ordering, let us suppose the constraint on subject in (48) and consider a simple transitive sentence in (49). As defined in (38) β in (48) refers to the immediately outer f-structure that contains SUBJ as an attribute.

(48) ALIGN (SUBJ, L, β, L)—abbreviated as SUBJ-L: Subject aligns left in the clause.

In (49), f_1 is the f-structure that corresponds to IP, the 'natural domain' (as defined in (38)) for f_2, the f-structure of SUBJ. So for two f-structure elements f_1 (the outermost f-structure) and f_2 (SUBJ), the maximal node that maps onto f_1, the IP, shares a left edge with the maximal node that maps onto f_2, the subject NP. The structure therefore satisfies the SUBJ-L constraint stated in (48).

(49) $[_{IP}\ [_{NP}\ \text{The boy}]\ [_{I'}\ \text{has}\ [_{VP}\ \text{eaten an apple}]]]$

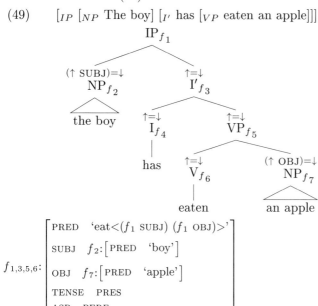

As we see above, all the ordering constraints proposed thus far in OT are stated in terms of alignment rather than the relative order of two elements (e.g., 'X precedes Y'). In the present work, I adopt the constraint SUBJ-L from Sells' work, alignment of subject using the mechanism of f-alignment:[19] SUBJ-L reinforces Kayne's observation that left-specifier strongly predominates across languages, where the specifier position is assumed to be occupied by subject (see Kayne, p.35). Given that OT-LFG makes available the exocentric category S, which lacks Spec, here Kayne's observation is taken to apply to the position of subject, hence the constraint in (48). As I noted earlier in section 4.6.2, another independently

---

[19] As we will see, alignment of complement functions (e.g., OBJ) will be treated differently in the present work.

motivated constraint in the OT-LFG system, Spine-R, also prefers specifiers (and adjunction) to be leftward.

4.6.5 Abutment

While earlier proposals on syntactic positioning based on the idea of alignment (here strictly interpreted as aligning identical edges) have been successful in capturing some typological generalizations about word order, headedness of phrases, and realization of grammatical information that correlates with clausal organization, it is not clear if alignment alone can explain all types of syntactic positioning. There is a rather wide range of syntactic elements that prefer adjacency with their respective heads (referred to as 'head-attracted' constituents in section 4.1): negation, focus, and (XP/X^0) adverbs typically appear near the verbal head; a relative pronoun and possessor prefer adjacency with their respective nominal head. Moreover, positioning of these constituents correlates with head directionality: verb-initial and verb-final languages often (though not always) exhibit the mirror image with respect to positioning of these constituents. In this respect, these head-attracted constituents thus deserve a unified treatment. In this section, my goal is to propose a formal mechanism that provides a unified explanation of this type of constituents.[20]

The formal mechanism for adjacency proposed in the present work, referred to as *abutment*, is modeled on Generalized Alignment of McCarthy and Prince (1993). Abutment is alignment of *opposite*, rather than identical, edges. According to (50), there exist some categories C_1 (e.g., focus, adverb, relative pronoun) and C_2 (e.g., V-head, N-head); abutment is satisfied if, for example, the left-edge of C_1 is adjacent to the right-edge of C_2. Crucially, the constraint does not specify particular edges of the elements; the only requirement is that two edges be opposite.

(50) $\text{Abut}(C_1, \text{Edge}_1, C_2, \text{Edge}_2) =_{def}$
         C_1 abuts with C_2 if and only if Edge_1 of C_1 shares Edge_2 of C_2;
         where $\text{Edge}_1 \neq \text{Edge}_2$.
         Abbreviated as $\text{Abut-}C_1(C_2)$.

The constraint in (51) thus prefers the relativizer to be adjacent to the nominal head (N-HD). The table in (52) shows the evaluation of this constraint. The constraint is violated simply when there is any material between the node filled by a relativizer and the nominal head (e.g., (52c,d)).

(51) Abut-REL(N-HD): Abut E_1 of REL with E_2 of N-HD.

---

[20]The idea of abutment was initially inspired by the work of Sells (1999a) on ordering of non-projective X^0 elements in Korean that exhibit affinity with the verbal head. In his work, Sells extends alignment to cover cases where X^0 aligns with the head. Abutment is an attempt at a precise formalization of essentially the same idea.

(52)   Evaluation of Abut-REL(N-HD) in (51)

		ABUT-REL(N-HD)
a.	[N]$_R$ $_L$[REL]	√
b.	[REL]$_R$ $_L$[N]	√
c.	[N]$_R$ ... α ... $_L$[REL]	*
d.	[REL]$_R$ ... α ... $_L$[N]	*

In earlier proposals (e.g., Sells' work cited above), all GF positioning is handled by left-alignment, as in SUBJ-L in (48) as well as DO-L ("direct object aligns left in the clause") and IO-L ("indirect object aligns left in the clause"). Motivation for the constraint SUBJ-L shares the insight of Kayne (1994), or more generally, that of the traditional generative view in which left-specifier is taken to be a predominent pattern. On the other hand for non-subject arguments, traditionally reference is made to the relation with the verb in terms of government rather than some privileged position in a clause (e.g., left-peripheral), and those non-subject arguments appear within a verbal projection in an unmarked case in most commonly attested word order types such as SVO, SOV, and some VSO languages. As noted earlier, the other three word order types, OSV, OVS, and VOS in which object precedes subject are rare. To reflect this asymmetry of subject and object positions (that subject tends to precede object cross-linguistically), in the present work, I propose that phrase structure position of non-subject arguments should be handled by abutment to the V-head.

As we saw with alignment of subject, in the case of non-subject GF abutment, C_1 in (50) will be an f-structure element (e.g., OBJ) and C_2 is a c-structure node. So in order to abut C_1 with C_2, we need the inverse mapping of f-structure to c-structure, as in (53):

(53)   GF Abutment in OT-LFG

For F ∈ F-Cat, C_1, C_2 ∈ C-Cat; Edge$_1$ ≠ Edge$_2$

Abut(F, Edge$_1$, C_1, Edge$_2$) = $_{def}$

F abuts with C_1 if and only if (i) ∃ C_2 ∈ ϕ^{-1}(F), and (ii) Edge$_1$ of C_2 shares Edge$_2$ of C_1 (abbreviated as Abut-F(C_1)).

To illustrate the abutment constraint in (53) more concretely, consider OBJ abutment in (54) and the simple transitive sentence in (49), repeated here in (55): in (54) F is instantiated by OBJ (f_7), and C_1 by a verbal head (V-HD). C_2 will be the NP that corresponds to OBJ. According to GF abutment defined in (53), the verb-object configuration in (55) satisfies the (abbreviated) constraint (54): there exists a node NP$_{f_7}$ (= C_2 in (53)) which is the inverse (f to c-structure) image of OBJ (= F in (53)), and the left edge of that node meets the right edge of V (= C_1 in (53)).

(54) Abut-OBJ(V-HD): Object abuts with V^0.

(55)   [$_{IP}$ [$_{NP}$ The boy] [$_{I'}$ has [$_{VP}$ eaten an apple]]]

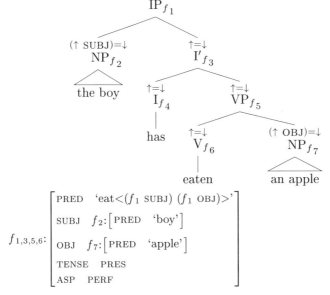

Importantly, Abut-OBJ(V-HD) would also be satisfied by a head-final structure, where the verb *eaten* in (55) follows the object NP, as edges of OBJ and V-HD are not specified by the constraint in (54). What gives us the head-complement order in (55) is the interaction of the abutment and head positioning constraints: {Head-L ≫ Spine-R}, Abut-OBJ(V-HD), where Head-L crucially outranks Spine-R and interacts with Abut-OBJ(V-HD) to prefer (55).

In order to allow abutment of either a c-structure node or the c-structure node that corresponds to a particular grammatical function in f-structure, we can now define abutment in a generalized form where the first category can be either c-structure or f-structure category. If it is the latter, abutment of that category with C_2 is mediated by inverse mapping of f- to c-structure of that category.[21] Cat(egory)$_1$ is an element of f- and c-structure categories (F-Cat ∪ C-Cat), Cat$_2$ is an element of c-structure categories. The generalized definition of abutment requires that the designated edges of Cat$_1$ and Cat$_2$ be opposite (Edge$_1$ ≠ Edge$_2$).

(56)   **Abutment** (generalized)
Abut(Cat$_1$,Edge$_1$, Cat$_2$,Edge$_2$) $=_{def}$
∀ Cat$_1$ ∃ Cat$_2$ such that Edge$_1$ of Cat$_1$ shares Edge$_2$ of Cat$_2$.
Where Cat$_1$ ∈ F-Cat ∪ C-Cat, Cat$_2$ ∈ C-Cat
Edge$_1$, Edge$_2$ ∈ {Right, Left} & Edge$_1$ ≠ Edge$_2$.

---

[21] The definition of generalized abutment models that of Generalized Alignment in McCarthy and Prince (1993).

By modeling the positioning of non-subject arguments by abutment to the verbal head rather than left-alignment in a clause, we can explain the mirror-image distribution of direct and indirect objects across languages: in head-final languages, DO *follows* IO; in head-initial languages, DO *precedes* IO, as schematically shown in (57).[22]

(57) a. Head-final languages: IO – DO – V
      b. Head-initial languages: V – DO – IO

The obvious generalization with respect to the positioning of these arguments is that DO is typically closer to the verb than IO in the unmarked situation. If we model the positioning of these elements by constraints such as DO-L ("DO aligns left in the clause") and IO-L ("IO aligns left in the clause"), we lose the generalization that their precedence relation is predictable in terms of the directionality of the verbal head. Choi (1999) proposes a constraint on ordering of nonsubject arguments for head-final languages stating that ordering corresponds to inverse ordering in the grammatical function hierarchy (DO ≻ IO). Such a constraint makes it an accident that this ordering is attested only in head-final languages, and that in head-initial languages the ordering is reverse: the unmarked order of nonsubjects directly correspond to their order in the relational hierarchy (V – DO – IO). In the current approach, the precedence relation between DO and IO can be modeled by a universal ranking of Abut-DO(V-HD) ≫ Abut-IO(V-HD). This ranking prefers adjacency between DO and V-HD over adjacency between IO and V-HD. Of course, some other constraint can be interpolated between these ranked constraints or interact with them in order to produce the non-canonical IO-DO ordering in some context (e.g., heavy NP shift).

It should be noted that generalized alignment proposed by McCarthy and Prince (1993) does allow two edges to be opposite as to produce "abutment" effects. So in this sense, abutment stated in (56) is not an entirely new proposal. Abutment is nonetheless considered distinct from alignment as it figures in syntax for the following reasons. First, in OT-LFG syntax, alignment is restricted to left-alignment (with the exception of Spine-R), as that correctly captures the antisymmetric properties of phrase structure. Alignment allows syntactic constituents to be placed in some privileged position such as left-most in the clause, where some elements (e.g., TOPIC, SUBJ, operators) tend to appear. Abutment, on the other hand, does not designate specific edges of Cat$_1$ and Cat$_2$ but requires them to be opposite edges. For abutment, interaction of head alignment constraints (Head-L and Spine-R) will therefore be crucial.

Second, alignment takes two elements both of which are either f-structure categories or c-structure categories. For GF alignment (e.g., TOPIC-L, SUBJ-L) the two elements being aligned are both f-structure elements: for example, SUBJ is aligned with its natural domain (defined in (38)) via f-

---

[22]Thanks to Peter Sells for discussion of this point.

to c-structure inverse mapping. For head alignment (Head-L and Spine-R) two elements being aligned are both c-structure elements: for Head-L to be satisfied, left-edge of X^0 head must share the left-edge of the c-structure node which immediately dominates X^0; for Spine-R to be satisfied, the right edge of every co-head (X^0 head and its extended heads in Grimshaw's (1991) sense) must share the right edge of the node which immediately dominates it. Abutment, on the other hand, allows either f- or c-structure category to abut with a c-structure category. If we allow left-alignment of one category (e.g., F-Cat) with another (e.g., C-Cat), there is a risk of overgenerating phrase structure configurations, as it would enable us to align virtually any two elements on c-structure. In this connection, it may be necessary to restrict Cat_2 of abutment to be a c-structure head (e.g., N-head, V-head).

4.6.6 Summary

Below are the constraints introduced in this section that will figure in the OT modeling of relative clauses and verb raising. Two additional constraints that will be discussed in the next section are also listed here.

(58)   Summary of Constraints

Alignment:	SUBJ-L	(48)
	Head-L	(39a)
	Spine-R	(39b)
Abutment:	Abut-REL(N-HD)	(51)
	Abut-OBJ(V-HD)	(54)
Hierarchical Structure:	OB-HD(XP)	(44a)
	*F	(44b)
	*Lex-in-F	(46)
	*S-node	discussed below
	ECONOMY	discussed below

The place of abutment in relation to Generalized Alignment and the family of syntactic alignment constraints is shown in (59). Generalized Alignment is taken to be a general family of alignment constraints in OT grammar. Alignment in syntax instantiates constraints that exclusively make reference to left edges. The only right-alignment constraint is Spine-R, which plays a key role in deriving the clausal skeleton, preferring a right-branching structure. Abutment in syntax requires that edges of two elements be opposite: opposite edges of focus and V-head; object and V-head; negation and V-head; relativizer and N-head; possessor and N-head, and so forth.

(59)

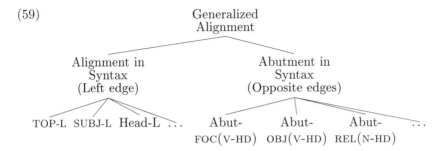

The alternative approach to the antisymmetry of phrase structure explored here explains the following generalizations discussed by Kayne.

1. The presence of functional projections (D, I, C) is preferred by head-initial languages over head-final languages: Spine-R, Head-L, and their interaction explain this, particularly high-ranked Spine-R (relative to the ranking of Head-L) in head-final languages.

2. Left-specifier and leftward adjunction are universally preferred over right-specifier and right-adjunction: Spine-R prefers right-branching structure and any co-head (the sister node to specifier and adjoined elements) to align right.

3. There is no rightward V-to-I, I-to-C movement: Spine-R ensures that the most optimal structure for head-final languages (for which Spine-R is high-ranked) is a fully right-branching structure with no functional projection on the right. If the structure is forced to have a functional projection (e.g., due to verb-second), then the functional head is preferred to be on the left than right, given Head-L (Spine-R is irrelevant). Furthermore, the availability of the exocentric category S makes possible the existence of head-final structure with no functional projection (on the right).

4. There is a class of syntactic elements whose exact positioning is dependent upon the directionality of heads (= directionality parameter derived by movements in Kayne's approach): Abutment.

4.7 OT Modeling of Relative Clauses and Verb Raising

Having established the constraints on word order and hierarchical structure, I now turn to the analysis of the data discussed earlier. I first lay out a typology of relative clauses to show how the relativization strategies observed in Bantu languages fit into a wider typology. Different rankings of the constraints introduced in the previous section will derive the cross-linguistic variation in relative clauses. From this perspective, verb raising in object relativization in a subset of Bantu language (e.g., Dzamba and Chishona) is a natural, expected consequence of constraint interaction.

4.7.1 A Typology of Relative Clauses

The typology of relative clauses presented here is by no means exhaustive. For simplicity, the discussion will be limited to simplex sentences. Furthermore, I will confine my discussion to those relative clauses in which the nominal head is external to the relative clause, and exclude head-internal relative clauses. Nonetheless, I hope to illustrate how the set of constraints introduced above derives some cross-linguistic variation in relativization, and how verb raising in Bantu object relatives can be derived without additional constraints or parameterization of subject positions suggested in earlier work (cited in section 4.2).

Additionally, as is well-known, relativization is subject to the 'accessibility hierarchy' (Keenan and Comrie 1977). The relational hierarchy subject > direct object > indirect object > possessor defines ease of accessibility to relative clause formation: it is easier to relativize an element higher on the hierarchy than one lower on the hierarchy; if relativization is possible with a given element on the hierarchy, the language allows relativization with all the elements to the left of that element on the hierarchy. While this is a potentially fruitful domain to explore within an OT approach, it is beyond the scope of this paper, and I will be concerned mainly with object relativization, and hence with languages which allow such relativization.

In addition to Types I–III in the Bantu languages examined earlier in section 4.2, I consider two other language types here: the English type with either the complementizer *that* (e.g., *the book that you lent me the other day*) or a relative pronoun (e.g., *the picture which my mother took*), and head-final (SOV) languages with a morphological relativizer on the verb. An example of the latter type is shown in (60b) from Korean.

(60) a. John-i   Mary-lul   manna-ss-ta.   Korean
John-NOM Mary-ACC meet-PAST-DECL
'John met Mary.'

   b. John-i   manna-**n** salam
John-NOM met-REL person
'the person that John met'

The table in (61) provides a summary of the forms that object relativization can take across languages. From left to right across the columns, the table lists the language type (referred to as Type I–V below), positions of the nominal head, relativizer, the verb, and the subject NP, and the category of the relativizer (e.g., affixal, relative pronoun).

(61)

Lang.	Positions	REL Category
I.	N-head REL-verb NP$_{su}$	V$_{aff}$ bound to V in C
II.	N-head REL NP$_{su}$ verb	C, free-standing
III.	N-head NP$_{su}$ REL.verb	high tone on V
IV.	N-head REL.PRON NP$_{su}$ verb	DP (or *that* in C)
V.	NP$_{su}$ verb-REL N-head	V$_{aff}$, bound to V

I. Dzamba, Chishona, II. Sesotho/Setswana
III. Kirundi/Kinyarwanda, IV. English, V. Korean

In order to model this variation in the constraint system with a fair number of candidates, we need two additional constraints: one that determines the category of the minimal clause inside the relative clause, and the other that determines the category of the relativizer. As we saw earlier, OT-LFG makes available two types of clausal organizations, endocentric IP and the exocentric S node. Interaction of two constraints plays a role in deriving these clause types. The constraint in (62a) penalizes the exocentric structure S. As shown in (63), the ranking *S-node ≫ OB-HD(XP) prefers the clause to be endocentric (IP); OB-HD(XP) ≫ *S-node prefers the exocentric clausal organization (S), assuming that subjects cannot be VP-internal.

(62)   a. *S-node: Avoid exocentric structure.

b. OB-HD(XP): phrases must have overt head (repeated from (44a)).

(63)   Clause Types

a. Endocentric IP: *S-node ≫ OB-HD(XP)

b. Exocentric S: OB-HD(XP) ≫ *S-node

Besides the set of constraints introduced earlier that determine hierarchical structure and the position of the verbal head, what else is at work that determines, for example, whether a relativizer is realized as an X^0 element (e.g., complementizer) or XP (e.g., relative pronoun)? I pursue the idea that it is a constraint on economy of expression. The economy constraint in (64) penalizes any structure: the fundamental premise is that the best output is the most economical struture—i.e. no structure, and only faithfulness drives overt expression. Economy constraints previously proposed in the OT syntax literature penalize an empty node (DON'TPROJ; Bresnan, 2000b) as well as X^0 elements ("Avoid X^0"; Sells 1998). ECONOMY in (64) collapses these previously preposed economy constraints.[23] Thus, if the relativizer is the head of the relative adjunct CP, this will incur fewer violations of ECONOMY. If the relativizer is realized as relative pronoun (a D^0 in a DP), this incurs an extra mark.

---

[23] In Bresnan (2000b, footnote 30), DON'TPROJ is interpreted as a constraint that penalizes an empty node. Here, the constraint ECONOMY is interpreted more broadly as a constraint against any structure, and hence every XP and X^0 is penalized.

(64) Economy: Economical structure is preferred (every xp and X^0 is penalized).

The crucial constraint interaction that derives the variation in relative clauses summarized in (61) is given in (65). The relevant constraints are given at the top. Other constraints will be considered in the tableaux that follow when we add structure to each candidate.

(65) a. Head-L   b. Spine-R
      c. Abut-REL(N-HD) d. *Lex-in-F
      e. Economy

I. $a \gg c \gg e \gg d \gg b$
II. $a \gg c \gg d \gg e \gg b$
III. $a \gg e \gg d \gg c \gg b$
IV. $a \gg c \gg d \gg b, e$
V. $b \gg a; e \gg d \gg c$

Type I–Type IV are all head-initial languages, so Head-L ranks above Spine-R ($a \gg b$) in all these language types. Rankings of c–e yield cross-linguistic variation in the realization of the relativizer: in **Type I** languages (e.g., Dzamba, Chishona) that exhibit verb raising in object relatives, the Abut-REL(N-HD) constraint that requires the relativizer to be adjacent to the head noun is high-ranked. The next higher constraint Economy forces the verb to appear in C at the cost of *Lex-in-F. In **Type II** languages (e.g., Sesotho/Setswana) the ranking of *Lex-in-F (d) and Economy (e) is reverse: a morphologically independent relativizer occupies C, and the verb stays in V. **Type III** languages (e.g., Kirundi/Kinyarwanda) mark a relative clause by a grammatical tone on the verb inside the relative clause. This language type thus has the most economical structure syntactically. This is ensured by ranking Economy above the other two constraints c and d.[24] In **Type IV** languages (English) the constraints Spine-R and Economy "float" to yield more than one optimum (see, for example, Boersma (1997), Asudeh (2001) for floating constraints; also briefly explained below).[25] As will be clearer in the tableaux, the ranking Spine-R $\gg$ Economy ($b \gg$ e) will yield a relative pronoun DP, resulting in one extra projection. The reverse ranking will yield the relativizer in C: this is one fewer projection, but since C, a co-head, will be left-most in its local structure, this violates Spine-R more severely. The high-ranking *Lex-in-F ensures that for English, no lexical head appears in a functional head position. In **Type V** languages (e.g., Korean) the ranking of head positioning constraints (a and b) and the other three is not crucial. Spine-R $\gg$ Head-L ensures the head-final structure.

---

[24]Here, the high tone on the verb that indicates relativization is taken to be the realization of REL for the abutment constraint.

[25]The floating constraints are indicated by a comma between them rather than a '$\gg$' that indicates strict domination.

4.7.2 Deriving Object Relativization

The only input considered in the present discussion is (the relevant part of) object relativization, given in (66), which corresponds to a relative clause like *the blanket that/which the woman bought*. All arguments/adjuncts are unspecified for their grammatical functions (hence $GF_{1,2,3}$). One of the two arguments indexed as y is associated with TOP_{rel}, and is coindexed with the head noun 'blanket'.

(66) Input for object relativization

$$
\begin{bmatrix}
\text{PRED} & \text{'blanket'}_i \\
\text{ADJ-REL} &
\begin{bmatrix}
\text{PRED} & \text{'buy} <x,\ y> \text{'} \\
\text{GF}_1 & \begin{bmatrix} \text{PRED} & \text{'women'} \end{bmatrix}_x \\
\begin{array}{c} \text{GF}_2 \\ \text{TOP}_{rel} \end{array} & \begin{bmatrix} \text{PRED} & \text{'pro'}_i \end{bmatrix}_y \\
\text{GF}_3 & \begin{bmatrix} \text{PRED} & \text{'today'} \end{bmatrix} \\
\text{TENSE} & \text{PAST}
\end{bmatrix}
\end{bmatrix}
$$

The set of candidates that are considered in the tableaux is shown in (67). For expository purposes, I make four simplifying assumptions. First, all candidates show only the relevant part of object relativization, and are maximally faithful to the input information except for the topicality of the head noun (to be made clearer below). Second, as demonstrated in recent OT work (e.g., Asudeh 2001, Morimoto 1999, Lee 2000a), association of the unspecified GF_n in the input to a particular GF results from constraints on mapping between arguments and grammatical functions. Here, in order to avoid complication, I simply assume the desired mapping between the input GFs (GF_n) and output GFs (e.g., SUBJ, OBJ). No constraint makes reference to the matter of argument-function mapping. Third, note that Head-L and Spine-R are also responsible for the positioning of the nominal head; however, since no candidate violates the higher-ranked constraint (Head-L in a–e; Spine-R in f–g) with respect to the nominal head, 0 violation will not be indicated in the tableaux for Head-L or Spine-R in reference to the nominal head. Fourth, the 'REL' in each candidate indicates some realization of relative clause marking—e.g., a morphologically independent relativizer, a bound relativizer, or a grammatical tone, but exactly how REL comes to each realization (presumably with additional constraints) is not addressed here.[26]

---

[26]Additionally, it should be noted that for Bantu languages, *F is probably the more relevant constraint than *Lex-in-F. *Lex-in-F is used in the tableaux simply because that is clearly the right generalization elsewhere in the English grammar (for tableau (80)) but either would work for the exposition of Bantu relatives: presumably in Bantu languages both these constraints are high-ranked.

(67)   Candidates

N-head	Verb/Rel
a. initial	REL+V in C
b. initial	REL in C, V in V
c. initial	REL+V in V; SUBJ right-most
d. initial	REL+V in V
e. initial	REL-PRON (DP) in SpecCP, V in V
f. final	V+REL in V
g. final	V in V; REL in C

In the tableaux, for candidate α, $\alpha1$ represents one in which the minimal clause inside the relative clause is S, and $\alpha2$ represents the one with IP. For example, candidate a1 and a2 are identical except that in a1, the minimal clause is S, and in a2 it is IP. Below are some notes on how constraint violations are counted in the tableaux for the alignment constraints, Abut-REL(N-HD), and ECONOMY.

(68)   Counting constraint violations

a. **Alignment constraints**: count the number of intervening elements between the element and the edge that are specified in each constraint:

Spine-R: between a co-head and the right edge in its local structure. The degree of violation for each co-head is added to the total number of violations for each candidate.

Head-L: between the (verbal) head and the left edge in its local structure.

SUBJ-L: between SUBJ and the left edge of the clause containing the SUBJ.

b. **Abutment constraints**: count the number of intervening elements between the element and its head specified in each constraint:

Abut-REL(N-HD): between REL and N-head.

c. ECONOMY: penalize every node X^0, XP, or S. X^0s not shown in the tableaux (e.g., SUBJ NP and relative pronoun DP, whose internal structures are abbreviated) are equally subject to the ECONOMY constraint.

The tableau in (69) represents object relativization in Dzamba, Type I, with verb raising. The high-ranking constraint Head-L eliminates the head-final candidates in f–g. Note in passing that Head-L can be ranked lower, as long as it is above ECONOMY (as f incurs fewer violations of ECONOMY than the winner).

Type I: e.g., Dzamba (V raising; REL-V in C)

	*S-node	Spine-R	OB-HD(XP)	*LEX-in-F	ECONOMY	Abut-Rel(N-HD)	SUBJ-L	Head-L
a1. ☞ $[_{NP}$ N $[_{CP}$ REL-V $[_{S}$ NP$_{Su}]]]$	*	2		*	7		0	0
a2. $[_{NP}$ N $[_{CP}$ REL-V $[_{IP}$ NP$_{Su}]]]$		2	*!	*	7		0	0
b1. $[_{NP}$ N $[_{CP}$ $[_{C'}$ REL $[_{S}$ NP$_{Su}$ $[_{VP}$ V]]]]]$	*	2	*		9!		0	0
b2. $[_{NP}$ N $[_{CP}$ $[_{C'}$ REL $[_{IP}$ NP$_{Su}$ $[_{VP}$ V]]]]]$		2			9!		0	0
c1. $[_{NP}$ N $[_{S}$ $[_{VP}$ REL-V] NP$_{Su}]]$	*	2	*		7		1!	0
c2. $[_{NP}$ N $[_{IP}$ $[_{VP}$ REL-V] NP$_{Su}]]$		2			7		1!	0
d1. $[_{NP}$ N $[_{S}$ NP$_{Su}$ $[_{VP}$ REL-V]]]$	*	1	*		7	*!	0	0
d2. $[_{NP}$ N $[_{IP}$ NP$_{Su}$ $[_{VP}$ REL-V]]]$		1			7	*!	0	0
e1. $[_{NP}$ N $[_{CP}$ RELPRON $[_{S}$ NP$_{Su}$ $[_{VP}$ V]]]]$	*	1	*		10!		0	0
e2. $[_{NP}$ N $[_{CP}$ RELPRON $[_{IP}$ NP$_{Su}$ $[_{VP}$ V]]]]$		1			10!		0	0
f. $[_{NP}$ $[_{S}$ NP$_{Su}$ $[_{VP}$ V-REL]] N]$	*	0			7		0	1!
g. $[_{NP}$ $[_{CP}$ $[_{IP}$ NP$_{Su}$ $[_{VP}$ V]] C] N]$		1	*		9		0	2!

(69)

(70)

	Structure	*S-node	Spine-R	OB-HD(XP)	ECONOMY	*LEX-in-F	Abut-Rel(N-HD)	SUBJ-L	Head-L
a1.	$[_{NP}$ N $[_{CP}$ REL-V $[_S$ NP$_{Su}]]]$	*	2		7	*!		0	0
a2.	$[_{NP}$ N $[_{CP}$ REL-V $[_{IP}$ NP$_{Su}]]]$		2	*	7	*!		0	0
b1. ☞	$[_{NP}$ N $[_{CP}$ $[_{C'}$ REL $[_S$ NP$_{Su}$ $[_{VP}$ V]]]]]$	*	2		9			0	0
b2.	$[_{NP}$ N $[_{CP}$ $[_{C'}$ REL $[_{IP}$ NP$_{Su}$ $[_{VP}$ V]]]]]$		2	*!	9			0	0
c1.	$[_{NP}$ N $[_S$ $[_{VP}$ REL-V] NP$_{Su}]]$	*	2		7			1!	0
c2.	$[_{NP}$ N $[_{IP}$ $[_{VP}$ REL-V] NP$_{Su}]]$		2	*	7			1!	0
d1.	$[_{NP}$ N $[_S$ NP$_{Su}$ $[_{VP}$ REL-V]]]$	*	1		7		*!	0	0
d2.	$[_{NP}$ N $[_{IP}$ NP$_{Su}$ $[_{VP}$ REL-V]]]$		1	*	7		*!	0	0
e1.	$[_{NP}$ N $[_{CP}$ RELPRON $[_S$ NP$_{Su}$ $[_{VP}$ V]]]]$	*	1		10!			0	0
e2.	$[_{NP}$ N $[_{CP}$ RELPRON $[_{IP}$ NP$_{Su}$ $[_{VP}$ V]]]]$		1	*	10!			0	0
f.	$[_{NP}$ $[_S$ NP$_{Su}$ $[_{VP}$ V-REL]] N]$	*	0		7			0	1!
g.	$[_{NP}$ $[_{CP}$ $[_{IP}$ NP$_{Su}$ $[_{VP}$ V]] C] N]$		1	*	9			0	2!

Type II: e.g., Sesotho (no "inversion"; REL in C, V in V)

Candidates c1–c2 have the subject on the right, and hence are eliminated at the point they violate SUBJ-L. Candidates d1–d2 violate the next constraint Abut-REL(N-HD), as relativization is marked on the verb and is not adjacent to the head noun. Candidates b1–b2 and e1–e2 violate ECONOMY more severely than a1–a2 and are eliminated at this point: a1–a2 incur seven violations of ECONOMY (top NP, relativized head noun, CP, C^0, S, SUBJ NP, and N^0); b1–b2 additionally incur two more violations for having VP and V^0; in e1–e2, REL is realized as a relative pronoun, DP under CP. This makes it one additional violation of ECONOMY (DP and D^0) compared to the b candidates with just a C^0 under CP. Between the remaining candidates a1 and a2, a1 is more optimal since OB-HD(XP) ranks above *S-node. Spine-R can be anywhere below Head-L and ECONOMY. The optimal output a1 represents the grammatical object relativization in (4b), repeated in (71).

(71) oPetelo a-nyamozi imo-dondo   i-mu-bundaki Zaki   Dza (= 69a1)
     Peter   1-sold   the-alligator REL-it-caught Jack
     'Peter sold the alligator that Jack caught.'   (Givón 1972:190)

The tableau in (70) represents Type II languages such as Sesotho/Setswana that exhibit a relativizer in C and the verb in V. The ranking of the first three constraints is the same as Type I; candidates f, g, c1, c2, d1, and d2 are eliminated by those constraints. As shown schematically in (65) above, the difference between Type I and Type II is the ranking of *Lex-in-F and ECONOMY: in Type II, the former outranks the latter. Therefore there is no verb raising; the verb occupies V and REL is realized as a morphologically independent relativizer in C, even though this structure incurs two more marks for ECONOMY than candidates a1–a2 due to the presence of VP. The rest of the constraints are ranked the same as in Type I, so the candidate where the minimal clause inside the relative claues is S is optimal. The data presented earlier from Sesotho, repeated below in (72) confirm the result of the constraint interaction. (72a) corresponds to the optimal analysis in b1, and (72b), the suboptimal in a1.

(72) a. di-kobo   **tseo** ba-sadi ba-di-rekileng kajeno   Ses (= 70b1)
        10-blankets 10REL 2-women 2-10-bought   today
        'the blankets which the women bought today'

     b.*di-kobo   tseo   ba-di-rekileng basadi   kajeno   (= 70a1)
        10-blankets 10REL 2-10-bought   2women today

Now we saw earlier (§ 4.3.3) that Swahili (also Lingala; see Bokamba 1985) has two types of relative clause, one with a bound relativizer like Dzamba (Type I), and the other with the free-standing relativizer *amba*, like Sesotho (Type II). These types are exemplified in (73) again ((73a) from Keach 1980:101, ex. (16c)). So our constraint system needs to be able to yield both as optimal.

(73) a. sigara   zilizovuta   mvulana   Swa REL-V relativization
cigarettes REL.smoked boy
'cigarettes which the boy smoked'

    b. sigara   ambazo mvulana alivuta   Swa *amba* relativization
cigarettes REL   boy   smoked
'cigarettes which the boy smoked'

The problem of deriving multiple optima can be dealt with formally by adopting the system of 'floating constraints' proposed and developed by Boersma (1997, 1998, 2000) and Boersma and Hayes (2001), and further explored by Asudeh (2001) in the syntactic domain to explain optionality. In this system, each constraint is assigned a ranking value along a continuous scale. During each constraint evaluation, some stochastic noise (constrained by a normal distribution with a small value for the standard deviation) is added to determine the actual ranking of a constraint (its "disharmony"). If two constraints are closely ranked, this means that the difference in ranking values is minimal, and hence the probability of the constraint with the higher ranking value outranking the other (with the lower value) is high. On the other hand, if the ranking difference is high, then the probability of the one with the higher ranking value outranking the one with the lower value is low. In other words, optionality can arise when the ranking difference is small. This system also predicts which one of the two constraints outranks the other more frequently and hence which output is rendered optimal more frequently (for the mathematical details to illustrate this point, see Boersma 1997).

Adopting this probabilistic constraint ranking, if we assume that the two constraints ECONOMY and *Lex-in-F are closely ranked and thus "floating", we allow both Type I and Type II relative clauses observed in Swahili to be optimally chosen. The crucial constraint interaction is shown in (74). The reader may refer to the tableau for Type I or Type II in (69)/(70) for concreteness.

(74)   a.   Head-L   b.   Spine-R
           c.   Abut-REL(N-HD)   d.   *Lex-in-F
           e.   ECONOMY
      Swahili (Types I & II):   a ≫ c ≫ d, e ≫ b

A slight digression is necessary here for an additional note on relativization using an analytic form of the relativizer. Bokamba (1985) presents data from another Bantu language, Lingala, which also exhibits two types of relative clauses analogous to those in Swahili. According to Bokamba (p.32), in object relativization, the bound relative pronoun requires verb raising (75) as in Dzamba and Swahili, but the free relative pronoun optionally allows verb raising (76) (hence traditionally referred to as 'stylistic inversion'). This fact is claimed to hold for Swahili as well.

(75) a. mo-paya á-sómb-ákí li-tɔkɔ líí-tóng-áki pɔ́sɔ lɛlɔ́.
the-1guest 1-buy-PERF the-mat REL-weave-PERF 1Poso today
'The guest bought the mat which Poso weaved today.'

b.*mo-paya á-sómb-ákí li-tɔkɔ pɔ́sɔ líí-tóng-ákí lɛlɔ́.
the-1guest 1-buy-PERF the-mat 1Poso REL-weave-PERF today

(76) a. mo-paya a-sómb-ákí li-tɔkɔ li-ye pɔ́sɔ á-tóng-ákí lɛlɔ́.
the-1guest 1-buy-PERF the-mat REL 1Poso 1-weave-PERF today
'The guest bought the mat which Poso weaved today.'

b. mo-paya a-sómb-ákí li-tɔkɔ li-ye li-tóng-ákí pɔ́sɔ lɛlɔ́
the-1guest 1-buy-PERF the-mat REL 1-weave-PERF 1Poso today

We might speculate that the choices available in (76) do not represent optionality, but rather (76b) is a different construction. It is well-known in Bantu literature that a subset of Bantu languages including Dzamba, Swahili, and Lingala exhibits a construction referred to as 'subject-object reversal', in which the focal subject appears postverbally, and topical object appears preverbally, rendering the non-canonical OVS order.[27] In this construction, the preverbal topical object triggers "subject" agreement. Notice that in (76b), the verb *weaved* has the agreement prefix *li*- which corresponds to the class marker of *mat*, not of *Poso*. This is exactly what is expected in subject-object reversal. In (76a), on the other hand, the prefix on *weaved* agrees with *Poso* in class 1. If this is correct, then the relative clauses in (76a,b) are assigned structures like those in (77a,b). In (77a), the subject inside the relative clause (*Poso*) is dominated by S, while in (77b), it is sister to V, which is the designated focus position in the majority of Bantu languages. In short, in terms of the current analysis, the apparent optionality in (76) may, in fact, represent different inputs, one (76a) that is discourse-neutral, and the other (76b) in which the agent (postverbal subject) is focal and patient (preverbal object) is topical. Of course this would have to be verified by discourse-pragmatic evidence.

---

[27]—cf. Bokamba 1976, 1979, 1985, Keach 1980, Kimenyi 1980, 1988, Sabimana 1986, Kinyalolo 1991, Ura 1996, 2000, Whaley 1996, Ndayiragije 1999, Morimoto 2000b on subject-object reversal.

(77) a.

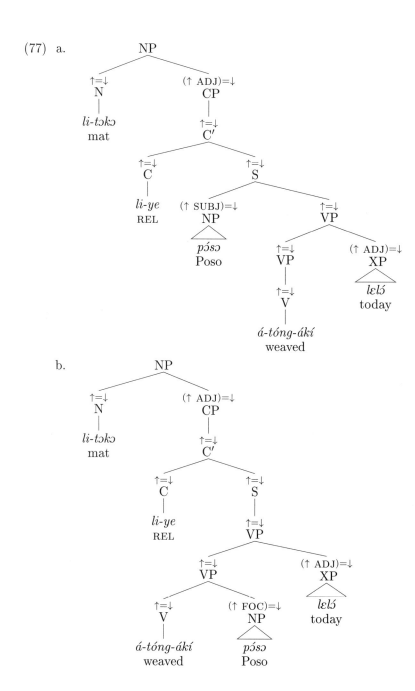

b.

The tableau in (79) represents Type III languages like Kirundi/Kinyarwanda; a relative clause is marked by a grammatical tone on the verb.[28] Here the ranking of the first two constraints, Head-L and SUBJ-L, remains the same as Types I and II, and as we already saw, candidates f, g, c1, and c2 are eliminated by these first two constraints. In Kirundi/Kinyarwanda, ECONOMY and *Lex-in-F take priority over Abut-REL(N-HD). Candidates b1/2 and e1/2 lose to a1/2 and d1/2 as the former group of candidates violates ECONOMY more severely than the latter. The next-highest constraint *Lex-in-F penalizes a1 and a2. Between d1 and d2, again like other Bantu languages, OB-HD(XP) prefers d1 as optimal. Thus in this language type, a more economical structure (with the verb in V) is preferred over one in which the relativizer and head noun respect adjacency.

The optimal structure is exemplified in (78) from Kinyarwanda (Kimenyi 1980:68, ex. (62)).[29]

(78) a. Umuhuûngu **y-a-haa-ye**   umukoôbwa igitabo.   Krw
        1boy   1-PAST-give-ASP 1girl   7book
        'The boy gave the book to the girl.'

     b. N-a-boon-ye   igitabo umuhuûngu **y-a-haá-ye**
        I-PAST-see-ASP 7book   1boy   1-PAST-REL.give-ASP
        umukoîbwa.
        1girl
        'I saw the book that the boy gave to the girl.'

     c. N-a-boon-ye   umukoôbwa umuhuûngu
        I-PAST-see-ASP 1girl   1boy
        y-a-haá-ye   igitabo.
        1-PAST-REL.give-ASP 7book
        'I saw the girl to whom the boy gave the book.'

---

[28]It should be noted that the form REL-V in the candidates is interpreted as either a bound relativizer or some other marking, such as tone, on the verb. The exact form of REL must be derived by a (set of) constraint(s), not pursued here to avoid further complication with the constraint system.

[29]Note that Kinyarwanda allows relativization of subject and direct object only (Comrie 1989:157), but it is a symmetric object language, so either object can be relativized in double object constructions as in (78).

(79)

	*S-node	Spine-R	OB-HD(XP)	Abut-Rel(N-HD)	*LEX-in-F	ECONOMY	SUBJ-L	Head-L
a1. $[_{NP}$ N $[_{CP}$ REL-V $[_S$ NP$_{Su}]]]$	*	2			*!	7	0	0
a2. $[_{NP}$ N $[_{CP}$ REL-V $[_{IP}$ NP$_{Su}]]]$		2	*		*!	7	0	0
b1. $[_{NP}$ N $[_{CP}$ $[_{C'}$ REL $[_S$ NP$_{Su}$ $[_{VP}$ V]]]]]$	*	2				9!	0	0
b2. $[_{NP}$ N $[_{CP}$ $[_{C'}$ REL $[_{IP}$ NP$_{Su}$ $[_{VP}$ V]]]]]$		2	*			9!	0	0
c1. $[_{NP}$ N $[_S$ $[_{VP}$ REL-V] NP$_{Su}]]$	*	2				7	1!	0
c2. $[_{NP}$ N $[_{IP}$ $[_{VP}$ REL-V] NP$_{Su}]]$		2	*			7	1!	0
d1. ☞ $[_{NP}$ N $[_S$ NP$_{Su}$ $[_{VP}$ REL-V]]]$	*	1		*		7	0	0
d2. $[_{NP}$ N $[_{IP}$ NP$_{Su}$ $[_{VP}$ REL-V]]]$		1	*!	*		7	0	0
e1. $[_{NP}$ N $[_{CP}$ RELPRON $[_S$ NP$_{Su}$ $[_{VP}$ V]]]]$	*	1				10!	0	0
e2. $[_{NP}$ N $[_{CP}$ RELPRON $[_{IP}$ NP$_{Su}$ $[_{VP}$ V]]]]$		1	*			10!	0	0
f. $[_{NP}$ $[_S$ NP$_{Su}$ $[_{VP}$ V-REL]] N]$	*	0				7	0	1!
g. $[_{NP}$ $[_{CP}$ $[_{IP}$ NP$_{Su}$ $[_{VP}$ V]] C] N]$		1	*			9	0	2!

Type III: e.g., Kirundi (no inversion; REL-V in V)

	OB-HD(XP)	ECONOMY	Spine-R	*LEX-in-F	*S-node	Abut-Rel(N-HD)	SUBJ-L	Head-L
a1. $[_{NP}$ N $[_{CP}$ REL-V $[_S$ NP$_{Su}]]]$		7	2	*	*!		0	0
a2. $[_{NP}$ N $[_{CP}$ REL-V $[_{IP}$ NP$_{Su}]]]$	*	7	2	*!			0	0
b1. $[_{NP}$ N $[_{CP}$ $[_{C'}$ REL $[_S$ NP$_{Su}$ $[_{VP}$ V]]]]]$		9	2		*!		0	0
b2. ☞ $[_{NP}$ N $[_{CP}$ $[_{C'}$ REL $[_{IP}$ NP$_{Su}$ $[_{VP}$ V]]]]]$	*	9	2				0	0
c1. $[_{NP}$ N $[_S$ $[_{VP}$ REL-V] NP$_{Su}]]$		7	2		*		1!	0
c2. $[_{NP}$ N $[_{IP}$ $[_{VP}$ REL-V] NP$_{Su}]]$	*	7	2		*		1!	0
d1. $[_{NP}$ N $[_S$ NP$_{Su}$ $[_{VP}$ REL-V]]]$		7	1			*!	0	0
d2. $[_{NP}$ N $[_{IP}$ NP$_{Su}$ $[_{VP}$ REL-V]]]$	*	7	1		*!	*!	0	0
e1. $[_{NP}$ N $[_{CP}$ RELPRON $[_S$ NP$_{Su}$ $[_{VP}$ V]]]]$		10	1				0	0
e2. ☞ $[_{NP}$ N $[_{CP}$ RELPRON $[_{IP}$ NP$_{Su}$ $[_{VP}$ V]]]]$	*	10	1		*		0	0
f. $[_{NP}$ $[_S$ NP$_{Su}$ $[_{VP}$ V-REL]] N]$		7	0				0	1!
g. $[_{NP}$ $[_{CP}$ $[_{IP}$ NP$_{Su}$ $[_{VP}$ V]] C] N]$	*	9	1				0	2!

Type IV: English (no inversion; RELPRON SpecCP, V in V)

The tableau in (80) represents English relative clauses, a Type IV language that uses either the complementizer *that* or a relative pronoun. These two forms of relativization are derived by floating Spine-R and Economy. In English, *S-node ranks above OB-HD(XP), yielding IP rather than S. Again the first two constraints remain the same as the others discussed above, and so f, g, c1, and c2 are immediately eliminated. Abut-REL(N-HD) eliminates d1 and d2, and *S-node eliminates the rest of the candidates in which the minimal clause has the exocentric organization. Among the remaining candidates, a2, b2, and e2, b2 violates *Lex-in-F, as REL-V is realized in C. The next lower constraints, Spine-R and Economy float, and yield both b2 and e2 as optimal. This is illustrated in (81).

We see that in b2, Spine-R is violated twice, where the co-heads, the head noun and the complementizer *that*, align left (respecting Head-L); e2 violates it only once at N. In b2, Economy is violated for each node, a total of 9; in e2, the DP, the projection of the relative pronoun D^0, makes it an additional violation. Thus, if Spine-R outranks Economy, then e2 is rendered optimal; if Economy outranks Spine-R, then b2 is optimal.

Note also in passing that the topicality of the head noun in the relative clause is not faithfully represented by *that*-relatives in English: there is no relative pronoun that bears the TOP_{rel} that is identified with the GF (in our discussion, OBJ) indexed with the head noun. Presumably this can be modeled by allowing violation of faithfulness to the topicality information (e.g., Max(TOP)).[30]

(81) b2

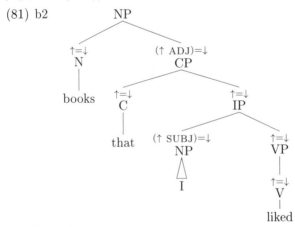

Violations

---

[30] Note the difference in acceptability between (i-a) and (i-b) below. This suggests that relative clauses with a relative pronoun (TOP_{rel}) indeed require the head noun to be referential/topical, as pointed out by Peter Sells (p.c., 1/23/01).

  (i) a. Nothing that Mary has to say matters to John.
       b. ??Nothing which Mary has to say matters to John.

a. Spine-R: 2 (at N and C).
b. ECONOMY: 9 (NP, N^0, CP, C^0, IP, NP_{Su}, N^0_{su}, VP, and V).

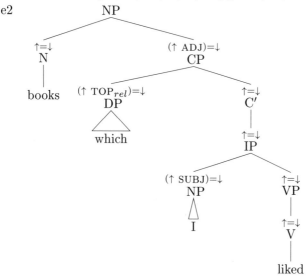

Violations
a. Spine-R: 1 (at N).
b. ECONOMY: 10 (NP, N^0, CP, DP, D^0, IP, NP_{Su}, N^0_{Su}, VP, and V).

Lastly, in English, there is another possible expression of object relativization, namely the reduced relative clause, as in *the book I gave to Mary*. This can be derived by extending the stochastic ranking to also include Abut-REL(N-HD), thereby making candidate d2 a potential winner as well.[31] It should be noted that the distribution of these different forms of relative clauses does not vary freely (see footnote 30). Within the current system, an additional (set of) constraint(s) may rank above the floating constraints to yield one of them as optimal in a given (discourse) context.

4.7.3 The Role of Abutment in Head-Final Languages

We have seen above in the modeling of relative clause formation in head-initial languages that the interaction of Head-L and the abutment constraint (Abut-REL(N-HD)) prefers REL to be realized to the left of the verb in the relative clause in those languages, closer to the nominal head (ideally adjacent). In head-final languages, the crucial interaction of Spine-R and Abut-REL(N-HD) prefers REL to be realized to the right of the verb, closer to the nominal head. The positioning of REL is, therefore, predictable in the current approach in terms of the directionality of the nominal head, as it should be.

---

[31]—suggested by an anonymous reviewer.

(82)

	*S-node	OB-HD(XP)	Abut-Rel(N-HD)	*LEX-in-F	ECONOMY	Head-L	Spine-R	SUBJ-L
a1. $[_{NP}$ N $[_{CP}$ REL-V $[_S$ NP$_{Su}]]]$	*			*	7	0	2!	0
a2. $[_{NP}$ N $[_{CP}$ REL-V $[_{IP}$ NP$_{Su}]]]$		*		*	7	0	2!	0
b1. $[_{NP}$ N $[_{CP}$ $[_{C'}$ REL $[_S$ NP$_{Su}$ $[_{VP}$ V]]]]$	*				9	0	2!	0
b2. $[_{NP}$ N $[_{CP}$ $[_{C'}$ REL $[_{IP}$ NP$_{Su}$ $[_{VP}$ V]]]]]$		*			9	0	2!	0
c1. $[_{NP}$ N $[_S$ $[_{VP}$ REL-V] NP$_{Su}]]$	*				7	0	2	1!
c2. $[_{NP}$ N $[_{IP}$ $[_{VP}$ REL-V] NP$_{Su}]]$		*	*		7	0	2	1!
d1. $[_{NP}$ N $[_S$ NP$_{Su}$ $[_{VP}$ REL-V]]$	*		*		7	0	1!	0
d2. $[_{NP}$ N $[_{IP}$ NP$_{Su}$ $[_{VP}$ REL-V]]]$		*			7	0	1!	0
e1. $[_{NP}$ N $[_{CP}$ RELPRON $[_S$ NP$_{Su}$ $[_{VP}$ V]]]]$	*				10	0	1!	0
e2. $[_{NP}$ N $[_{CP}$ RELPRON $[_{IP}$ NP$_{Su}$ $[_{VP}$ V]]]]$		*			10	0	1!	0
f. ☞ $[_{NP}$ $[_S$ NP$_{Su}$ $[_{VP}$ V-REL]] N]$	*				7	1	0	0
g. $[_{NP}$ $[_{CP}$ $[_{IP}$ NP$_{Su}$ $[_{VP}$ V]] C] N]$		*			9	1	1!	0

Type V: V-final languages (V-REL in V)

(82) represents verb-final languages which typically mark relative clauses by a bound relativizer on the verb. In this language type, Spine-R crucially outranks Head-L. As we saw earlier in section 4.6.2, the presence of functional projections always results in Spine-R violation because both the functional head and its structural complement are co-heads. Therefore regardless of whether the head is left or right, this local structure would violate Spine-R once. For this reason, ranking Spine-R highly eliminates not only those candidates in a1–e2 with head-initial structure, but also candidate g with functional projections. Though not relevant in the evaluation, g also violates other relatively high-ranked constraints such as ECONOMY and OB-HD(XP) more severely than candidate f. As I noted briefly in the schematic crucial ranking in (65), {Spine-R ≫ Head-L} can be ranked below all the other constraints, and we still get f as optimal. The optimal structure in f is exemplified in (83), repeated from an earlier example (60b).

(83) John-i   manna-**n** salam
     John-NOM met-REL preson
     'the person that John met'   Korean

At a more general level, the basic claim in this analysis of verb-final languages is that the grammatical structure in (82f) is derived by interaction of the constraints that are independently observed elsewhere in the syntax of verb-final languages (e.g., Spine-R ≫ Head-L) or cross-linguistically (economy constraints such as ECONOMY; Abut-REL(N-HD)). Given the structure derived by these constraints, the characteristics of N-final languages that Kayne (1994:93) noted earlier in (23) find immediate and obvious explanation. He notes that (i) N-final relatives lack relative pronouns (23a), and (ii) N-final relatives never display a complementizer that is identical to the normal complementizer of sentential complementation (23b). Under the present analysis, in these languages there are no functional projections that can host either a relative pronoun or a relativizer/complementizer. In fact, some verb-final languages (e.g., Japanese, Korean) that lack a relative pronoun or complementizer of sentential complementation used in a relative clause also lack an analytic form of the complementizer or any other elements that mark clause types (e.g., conditional marker equivalent to *if*). Other verb-final languages do have a relative pronoun (e.g., German, Gujarati, Hindi), and these languages also have an analytic form of the complementizer.[32]

For Korean-type N-final languages, under the P&P approach that treats constraints as inviolable, committing onself to correctly characterizing the

---

[32]These verb-final languages show a structure similar to candidate g. In German, the head noun and C are on the left; in Hindi and Gujarati, the head noun is rightmost, and the complementizer is either left or right: the left complementizer functions as a quotative marker, and the right complementizer functions much like the complementizer *that* in English (P.J. Mistry, p.c. 12/30/00).

antisymmetric properties of phrase structure forces one to assume a uniform structure like that given earlier in (24) and derive the surface form below in (24′). Thus in order to explain the characteristics of N-final languages mentioned above, the analysis requires that the head noun and the relative clause move upward and D and C that are left behind be null. D and C are indeed never filled, and hence not motivated anywhere else in the grammar.

(24′)   Surface structure of (24)

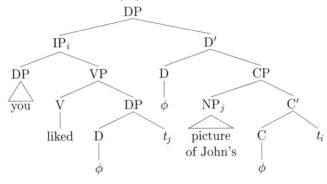

Furthermore, if the apparent symmetry of phrase structure (i.e. the directionality parameter) were to be derived by a series of movements from a common head-initial structure, it becomes unclear how a set of correlating facts elsewhere in the grammar of a head-final language is to be explained in a uniform way: e.g., the fact that in head-final languages, object is before the verb; focus is before the verb; negation is predominantly after the verb (but see Payne 1985 for discussion of verb-final languages such as Hindi that have preverbal negation)—in addition to the set of N-final properties mentioned by Kayne (23). A similar point is raised by Haider (1997b:21) as a potential problem for Kayne's (also Chomsky's 1994) proposal. The output-based account in which a constraint on surface representation such as abutment crucially interacts with head-positioning constraints to yield the directionality parameter seems to provide a much more straightforward explanation of these correlating facts without losing Kayne's insight about the antisymmetry of phrase structure.

4.7.4   Summary

The analysis presented in this section has highlighted the following points: on the empirical side with respect to Bantu relativization, what has been referred to as 'stylistic inversion' is obligatory verb raising, and once we examine a larger typology of object relativization, there is nothing peculiar about the type of relativization found in the subset of Bantu languages. Having examined a rather small typology of relative clauses, it seems unnecessary to posit two different subject positions across the Bantu languages only to accommodate verb raising in object relativization.

From the theoretical perspective, I have proposed the additional formal mechanism of abutment within OT-LFG that can produce adjacency effects (e.g., head-modifier, head-complement). Unlike alignment, abutment does not specify edges of two elements, but requires that two opposite edges coincide. By the interaction of abutment and head positioning constraints (Head-L and Spine-R), we can effectively derive the directionality parameter with respect to various syntactic elements. This is demonstrated in the present paper for relativization: the abutment constraint that requires adjacency between the relativizer and the head noun interacts with the head-positioning constraints to yield parametric differences with respect to the position of the relativizer relative to the N-head. The use of abutment can be extended to other adjacency effects not discussed in the present work, such as positioning of negation, focus, and adverbial elements that tend to appear within a verbal projection on a given side relative to the head.

More generally, I hope to have shown that cross-linguistic variation in relative clause formation can be modeled by interaction of constraints that are motivated both across languages and elsewhere in the grammar of a particular language without stipulation of formal features and multiple empty categories. Constraints are motivated cross-linguistically because they are largely statements about universal tendencies: specifier (or subject) is left-most (SUBJ-L); structure is predominantly right-branching (Spine-R); hence head is leftmost (Head-L); economical structure is preferred (ECONOMY); the relativizer is adjacent to the head noun (Abut-REL(N-HD)); object is adjacent to the verb (Abut-OBJ(V-HD)). And because these constraints are violable, language-particular variation (or marked structure) is easily modeled by ranking of these constraints without any stipulation on movement or additional restriction/assumption about the phonological realization of syntactic categories (e.g., "(the stranded) D and C must be null"). Furthermore, these constraints are often motivated language-internally because of the generality of the constraints: a particular ranking of Spine-R and Head-L and the effects of constraints like ECONOMY and *Lex-in-F are all quite easily discernible elsewhere in the grammar. On the other hand, the presence of D and C in languages like Japanese, for instance, is difficult to motivate especially if these functional heads are always phonetically null. It is not obvious if/how a series of movements necessary to derive N-final relative clauses can be motivated elsewhere in the syntax of head-final languages. Such assumptions/mechanisms can be eliminated if the scalar and the gradient nature of universal markedness is statable in the system of highly general, violable constraints.

4.8 Directions for Future Research

The scope of this paper has been limited to the presence/absence of verb raising across a (restricted) typology of relative clauses and phrase structure variation within that typology. But if the current approach to verb raising and phrase structure variation is correct—in particular, the idea that positioning of certain syntactic elements (e.g., focus, relative clause, negation) can be derived by an interaction of head-positioning constraints and a constraint that prefers adjacency between a given syntactic element and its respective head—I believe that it can be successfully extended to explain a broader typology of various other adjacency phenomena and head positioning.

For example, as discussed in Morimoto (2000b), focus positioning is clearly dependent on the position of the verb in a given language: verb final languages typically place focus before the verb; verb medial (SVO) languages place focus after the verb. For each language type, the exact position of focus varies from VP-adjoined position to the position immediately adjacent to the verb (object position). In verb initial languages, focus is predominantly clause initial, again, adjacent to the verb; when there is a topic NP in addition to a focused element, verb initial languages typically have the focus closer to the verb, and topic is more peripheral. If we model focus positioning by left- and right-alignment as proposed in earlier work (cited above), we lose the obvious correlation between focus and head position. I show in Morimoto (2000b) that the approach that makes crucial use of abutment (Abut-FOC(V-HD)) and its interaction with Head-L and Spine-R correctly predicts the focus typology.

Abeillé and Godard (1998) report that while ordering of some XPs (e.g., direct and indirect object, adverbial phrases) is flexible in French, ordering of non-projective X^0 ("light") elements, such as pronominal clitics, bare nouns, X^0 adverbs, is not. Instead this latter group of constituents observes rigid ordering relative to the verbal head. The templatic generalization about the order of X^0 elements within VP is given in (84), from Abeillé and Godard (1998). (α "<" $\beta = \alpha$ precedes β.)

(84) V^0-Head < Past Participle < V_{inf} < Bare Noun

Head-final languages, on the other hand, show the mirror image with respect to ordering of X^0 elements within VP. Sells (1999) presents data from Korean that confirm this generalization. In Korean, there is a set of X^0 elements that may not project a phrase of their own, including verbal nouns (VN^0), adverbs (Adv^0), negation *an* (Neg^0), and light verbs ($V_\mu{}^0$). Even though Korean is a scrambling language and generally allows phrasal elements to freely scramble, these X^0 elements observe rigid ordering. The template that shows the order of these elements is given in (85).

(85) VN^0 < Adv^0 < Neg^0 < $V_\mu{}^0$ < V^0-Head

The fixed ordering of these X^0 elements can be derived by abutment of these elements to the head. Abutment constraints (e.g., Abut-VN(V-HD), Abut-Adv(V-HD), Abut-Neg(V-HD)) can be (possibly universally) ranked relative to one another, and the constraints on head-positioning (Head-L,

Spine-R) can achieve the desired result with respect to the position of the head relative to the X^0 elements ordered by abutment.

Variation in verb positioning and of elements such as focus and other X^0 elements that show rigid ordering relative to the head therefore can and should be derived by the interaction of constraints on head positioning (e.g., Head-L), clausal skeleton (Spine-R) and abutment that prefers adjacency with the head, which are all independently motivated across and within languages. The OT-LFG approach explored in the present work thus seems to provide a promising framework for a unified treatment of the wider typology of these adjacency phenomena and clausal syntax.

References

Abeillé, Anne and Danièle Godard. 1998. A Lexical Approach to Quantifier Floating in French. In *Lexical and Constructional Aspects of Linguistic Explanation*, eds. G. Webelhuth, J.-P. Koenig, and A. Kathol. Stanford, California: CSLI Publications, 81–96.

Aissen, Judith. 2000a. Another look at *yi* and *bi*: Proximate and obviative in Navajo. MS. University of California, Santa Cruz.

Aissen, Judith. 2000b. Differential Object Marking: Iconocity vs. Economy. MS., University of California, Santa Cruz.

Aissen, Judith. 2001. Markedness and Subject Choice in Optimality Theory. In *Optimality-Theoretic Syntax*, eds. Géraldine Legendre, Jane Grimshaw, and Sten Vikner. Cambridge, Massachusetts: The MIT Press, 61–96.

Asudeh, Ash. 2001. Linking, Optionality, and Ambiguity in Marathi. This volume.

Bach, Emmon. 1971. Questions. *Linguistic Inquiry* 2:153–166.

Berman, Judith. 2000. *Topics in the Clausal Syntax of German*. Ph.D. thesis, Universität Stuttgart.

Boersma, Paul. 1997. How we learn variation, optionality, and probability. In *IFA Proceedings 21*. University of Amsterdam: Institute of Phonetic Sciences, 43–58. ROA-221-109.

Boersma, Paul. 1998. *Functional Phonology: Formalizing the interactions between articulatory and perceptual drives*. The Hague: Holland Academic Graphics.

Boersma, Paul. 2000. Learning a grammar in Functional Phonology. In *Optimality Theory: Phonology, Syntax and Acquisition*, eds. Joost Dekkers, Frank van der Leeuw, and Jeroen van de Weijer. Oxford: Oxford University Press.

Boersma, Paul and Bruce Hayes. 2001. Empirical tests of the gradual learning algorithm. *Linguistic Inquiry* 32:45–86.

Bokamba, Eyamba Georges. 1971. Specificity and definiteness in Dzamba. *Studies in African Linguistics* 2:217–238.

Bokamba, Eyamba Georges. 1976. *Question Formation in Some Bantu Languages*. Ph.D. thesis, Indiana University.

Bokamba, Eyamba Georges. 1985. Verbal agreement as a noncyclic rule in Bantu. In *African Linguistics: Essays in memory of M.W.K Semikenke*, ed. Didier L. Goyvaerts. Amsterdam: John Benjamins, 9–54.

Bresnan, Joan (ed.). 1982. *The Mental Representation of Grammatical Relations*. Cambridge, Massachusetts: The MIT Press.

Bresnan, Joan. 2000. Optimal Syntax. In *Optimality Theory: Phonology, Syntax and Acquisition*, eds. Joost Dekkers, Frank van der Leeuw, and Jeroen van de Weijer. Oxford: Oxford University Press, 334–385.

Bresnan, Joan. 2001a. The Emergence of the Unmarked Pronoun. In *Optimality-Theoretic Syntax*, eds. Géraldine Legendre, Jane Grimshaw, and Sten Vikner. Cambridge, Massachusetts: The MIT Press, 113–142.

Bresnan, Joan. 2001b. *Lexical Functional Syntax*. Oxford: Blackwell.

Bresnan, Joan and Jonni Kanerva. 1989. Locative Inversion in Chicheŵa: A Case Study of Factorization in Grammar. *Linguistic Inquiry* 20:1–50.

Bresnan, Joan and Sam A. Mchombo. 1986. Grammatical and anaphoric agreement. In *Papers from the Parasession on Pragmatics and Grammatical Theory at the Twenty-Second Regional Meeting*, eds. Anne M. Farley, P.T. Farley, and K.-E. McCullough, volume 22(2). Chicago, Illinois: Chicago Linguistic Society, 278–297.

Bresnan, Joan and Sam A. Mchombo. 1987. Topic, pronoun, and agreement in Chicheŵa. *Language* 63(4):741–782.

Cho, Young-mee Yu and Peter Sells. 1995. A Lexical Account of Inflectional Suffixes in Korean. *Journal of East Asian Linguistics* 4:119–174.

Choi, Hye-Won. 1999. *Optimizing Structure in Context: Scrambling and Information Structure*. Stanford, California: CSLI Publications.

Chomsky, Noam. 1981. *Lectures on Government and Binding*. Dordrecht: Foris.

Chomsky, Noam. 1982. *Some Concepts and Consequences of the Theory of Government and Binding*. Cambridge, Massachusetts: The MIT Press.

Chomsky, Noam. 1986. *Knowledge of Language: Its Nature, Origin, and Use*. New York, New York: Praeger.

Chomsky, Noam. 1991. Some notes on economy of derivation and representation. In *Principles and Parameters in Comparative Grammar*, ed. Robert Freidin. Cambridge, Massachusetts: The MIT Press, 417–454.

Chomsky, Noam. 1993. A Minimalist Program for linguistic theory. In *The View from Building 20: Essays in Linguistics in Honor of Sylvain Bromberger*, eds. Samule J. Keyser and Kenneth Hale. Cambridge, Massachusetts: The MIT Press, 1–52.

Chomsky, Noam. 1994. Bare phrase structure. *MIT Occasional Papers in Linguistics 5*.

Chomsky, Noam. 1995. *The Minimalist Program*. Cambridge, Massachusetts: The MIT Press.

Comrie, Bernard. 1981[1989]. *Language Universals and Linguistic Typology*. Chicago, Illinois: The University of Chicago Press, second edition.

Costa, João. 1997. Word order typology in Optimality Theory. Online, Rutgers Optimality Archive: ROA-220-0997, http://ruccs.rutgers.edu/roa.html.

Costa, João. 1998. *Word Order Variation: A Constraint-Based Approach*. Ph.D. thesis, Leiden University.

Dalrymple, Mary, Ronald M. Kaplan, John T. Maxwell, and Annie Zaenen (eds.). 1995. *Formal issues in Lexical-Functional Grammar*. Stanford, California: CSLI Publications.

Demuth, Katherine and Carolyn Harford. 1999. Verb raising and subject inversion in Bantu relatives. *Journal of African Languages and Linguistics* 20(1):41–61.

Demuth, Katherine and Sheila Mmusi. 1997. Presentational focus and thematic structure in comparative Bantu. *Journal of African Languages and Linguistics* 18(1):1–19.

Deo, Ashwini and Devyani Sharma. 2000. Typological Variation in Ergative Marking and Verb Agreement. In *Proceedings of WECOL 2000*. Fresno, California.

Givón, Talmy. 1972. Pronoun attraction and subject postposing in Bantu. In *The Chicago Which Hunt: Papers from the Relative Clause Festival*, eds. Paul M. Peranteau, Judith N. Levi, and Gloria C. Phares. Chicago, Illinois: Chicago Linguistic Society, 190–197.

Golston, Chris. 1995. Syntax outranks phonology: Evidence from Ancient Greek. *Phonology* 12(3):343–368.

Greenberg, Joseph. 1966. *Language Universals*. The Hague: Mouton & Co.

Greenberg, Joseph H. 1963 [1990]. Some universals of grammar with particular reference to the order of meaningful elements. In *On Language: Selected Writings of Joseph H. Greenberg*, eds. Keith Denning and Suzanne Kemmer. Stanford, California: Stanford University Press, 40–70.

Grimshaw, Jane. 1991. Extended Projection. MS., Dept. of Linguistics and Center for Cognitive Science, Rutgers University.

Grimshaw, Jane. 1997. Projection, Heads, and Optimality. *Linguistic Inquiry* 28:73–422.

Grimshaw, Jane. 2000. The Syntax of Matrix and Subordinate Clauses. Talk given at the Stanford colloquium, November.

Grimshaw, Jane. 2001. Clause structure. Talk given at plenary presentation, Annual Meeting of the Linguistic Society of America, Washington D.C., January 4–7, 2001.

Grimshaw, Jane and Vieri Samek-Lodovici. 1998. Optimal Subjects and Subject Universals. In *Is Best Good Enough? Optimality and Competition in Syntax*, eds. Pilar Barbosa, Danny Fox, Paul Hagstrom, Martha McGinnis, and David Pesetsky. Cambridge, Massachusetts: The MIT Press, 193–219.

Haider, Hubert. 1997a. Precedence among predicates. *Journal of Comparative Germanic Linguistics* 1:3–41.

Haider, Hubert. 1997b. Typological implications of a directionality constraint on projections. In *Studies on Universal Grammar and Typlogical Variation*, eds. Artemis Alexiadou and T. Alan Hall, volume 13 of *Linguistik Aktuell*. Amsterdam: John Benjamins, 17–33.

Harford, Carolyn and Katherine Demuth. 1999. Phonology outranks syntax: An Optimality approach to subject inversion in Bantu relatives. MS. University of Zimbabwe and Brown University.

Jakobson, Roman. 1968. *Child Language, Aphasia and Phonological Universals*. The Hague: Mouton de Gruyter.

Kager, René. 1999. *Optimality Theory*. Cambridge: Cambridge University Press.

Kayne, Richard. 1994. *The Antisymmetry of Syntax*. Cambridge, Massachusetts: The MIT Press.

Keach, Camilla Nevada Barrett. 1980. *The Syntax and Interpretation of the Relative Clause Construction in Swahili*. Ph.D. thesis, University of Massachusetts at Amherst.

Keenan, Edward L. and Bernard Comrie. 1977. Noun phrase accessibility and universal grammar. *Linguistic Inquiry* 8:89–123.

Kimenyi, Alexandre. 1980. *A Relational Grammar of Kinyarwanda*. Berkeley, California: University of California Press.

Kimenyi, Alexandre. 1988. Passives in Kinyarwanda. In *Passive and Voice*, ed. Masayoshi Shibatani. Amsterdam: John Benjamins, 355–386.

Kinyalolo, Kasangati Kikuni Wabongambilu. 1991. *The SPEC-Head Agreement Hypothesis in KiLega*. Ph.D. thesis, University of California, Los Angeles.

Kuhn, Jonas. 2001. Generation and Parsing in Optimality Theoretic Syntax – Issues in the Formalization in OT-LFG. This volume.

Lee, Hanjung. 2000a. The Emergence of the Unmarked Order in Hindi. In *Proceedings of NELS 30*, eds. Masako Hirotani, Andries Coetzee, Nancy Hall, and Ji-Yung Kim. Amherst, Massachusetts: GLSA, 469–483.

Lee, Hanjung. 2000b. Markedness and Pronoun Incorporation. To appear in the *Proceedings of BLS* 26. Berkeley, California: Berkeley Linguistics Society.

Lee, Hanjung. 2001. Markedness and Word Order Freezing. This volume.

Legendre, Géraldine, William Raymond, and Paul Smolensky. 1993. An Optimality-Theoretic typology of case and grammatical voice systems. In *Proceedings of the 19th Annual Meeting of the Berkeley Linguistics Society*, eds. J. Guenter, B. Kaiser, and C. Zoll.

McCarthy, John and Alan Prince. 1993. Generalized alignment. In *Yearbook of Morphology*, eds. Geert Booji and Jaap van Marle. Dordrecht: Foris, 79–153.

Morimoto, Yukiko. 1999. An Optimality Account of Argument Reversal. In *Proceedings of the LFG99 Conference*, eds. Miriam Butt and Tracy Holloway King. Stanford, California: CSLI Publications Online: `http://csli-publications.stanford.edu/`.

Morimoto, Yukiko. 2000a. *Discourse Configurationality in Bantu Morphosyntax*. Ph.D. thesis, Stanford University.

Morimoto, Yukiko. 2000b. The role of animacy and associational harmony in Bantu. Paper presented at the 31st Annual Conference on African Linguistics, March 2–5, Boston University.

Mugane, John. 1996. *Bantu Nominalization Structures*. Ph.D. thesis, University of Arizona.

Ndayiragije, Juvénal. 1999. Checking economy. *Linguistic Inquiry* 30(3):399–444.

Nordlinger, Rachel and Louisa Sadler. 2000. Tense as a nominal category. In *On-Line Proceedings of the LFG00 Conference*, eds. Miriam Butt and Tracy Holloway King. Stanford, California: CSLI Publications Online: `http://csli-publications.stanford.edu/`.

O'Connor, Catherine. 1999a. Harmonic alignment of participant hierarchy features and the structure of possessive DPs in Northern Pomo. Talk handout from the Joint Stanford/Santa Cruz Optimal Typology Workshop, October 30, University of California, Santa Cruz.

O'Connor, Catherine M. 1999b. Harmonic Alignment of the Animacy Hierarchy and the Structure of Possession DPs in Northern Pomo. Talk handout from the Lexical Functional Grammar Conference 1999 (LFG99), University of Manchester.

Payne, John R. 1985. Negation. In *Language Typology and Syntactic Description*, ed. Timothy Shopen, volume 1. Cambridge: Cambridge University Press, 197–242.

Prince, Alan and Paul Smolensky. 1993. Optimality Theory: Constraint Interaction in Generative Grammar. Technical Report RuCCS Technical Report #2, Center for Cognitive Science, Rutgers University, Piscataway, New Jersey. To be published by the MIT Press.

Pullum, Geoffrey and Arnold Zwicky. 1988. The syntax-phonology interface. In *Linguistics: The Cambridge Survey*, ed. Frederick Newmeyer, volume 1. Cambridge: Cambridge University Press, 255–280.

Sabimana, Firmard. 1986. *The Relational Structure of the Kirundi Verb*. Ph.D. thesis, Indiana University.

Sadler, Louisa. 1998. English auxiliaries as tense inflections. MS., University of Essex. Online: http://clwww.essex.ac.uk/~louisa.

Sadler, Louisa and Doug Arnold. 1994. Prenominal adjectives and the phrasal/lexical distinction. *Journal of Linguistics* 30:187–226.

Samek-Lodovici, Vieri. 1998a. Opposite constraints: Left and right focus-alignment in Kanakuru. *Lingua* 104:111–130.

Samek-Lodovici, Vieri. 1998b. OT-interactions between Focus and Canonical Word Order: Deriving the crosslinguistic Typology of Structural Contrastive Focus. Online, Rutgers Optimality Archive: ROA-257-0498, http://ruccs.rutgers.edu/roa.html.

Sells, Peter. 1994. Sub-phrasal syntax in Korean. *Language Research* 30(2):351–386.

Sells, Peter. 1995. Korean and Japanese Morphology from a Lexical Perspective. *Linguistic Inquiry* 26:277–325.

Sells, Peter. 1998. Optimality and Economy of Expression in Japanese and Korean. In *Japanese/Korean Linguistics*, ed. Noriko Akatsuka et al., volume 7. Stanford, California: CSLI Publications, 499–514.

Sells, Peter. 1999a. Constituent Ordering as Alignment. In *Harvard Studies in Korean Linguistics VIII*, ed. Susumu Kuno et al. Seoul: Hanshin, 546–560.

Sells, Peter. 1999b. Order as generalized alignment. Handout of the talk given at Gothenburg University, Department of Swedish Language, May 19, 1999.

Sells, Peter. 2000. Alignment Constraints in Swedish Clausal Syntax. MS., Stanford University. Online: http://www-csli.stanford.edu/~sells.

Sells, Peter. 2001a. Form and function in the typology of grammatical voice systems. In *Optimality-Theoretic Syntax*, eds. Géraldine Legendre, Jane Grimshaw, and Sten Vikner. Cambridge, Massachusetts: The MIT Press, 355–391.

Sells, Peter. 2001b. *Structure, Alignment and Optimality in Swedish*. To appear, Stanford, California: CSLI Publications.

Sharma, Devyani. 1999. Sentential Negation and Focus in Hindi. MS., Stanford University.

Ura, Hiroyuki. 1996. *Multiple Feature Checking*. Ph.D. thesis, MIT.

Ura, Hiroyuki. 2000. *Checking Theory and Grammatical Functions in Universal Grammar*. Oxford Studies in Comparative Syntax. Oxford: Oxford University Press.

Whaley, Lindsay J. 1996. Kinyarwanda topics and object-subject reversal. In *Proceedings of the Twelfth Eastern States Conference on Linguistics*, eds. Marek Prezezdziecki and Lindsay Whaley. Ithaca, New York: Department of Linguistics, Cornell University, 354–363.

5

Optimal Order and Pied-Piping in San Dionicio Zapotec

George Aaron Broadwell

5.1 Order and PS-rules

The phrase structure rules of standard theory encode both dominance relationship and precedence relationships.[1] It has been clear for some time that these two ideas can be disentangled so that the PS-rules describe only the dominance relationships, while a separate set of rules or principles tell us what the linear order should be. Within Lexical Functional Grammar, such ideas have been proposed by Falk (1983). They also figured prominently in GPSG (Gazdar, Pullum, Klein, and Sag 1985), continuing into HPSG (Pol-

---

[1]Earlier versions of this paper were given at the Chicago Linguistic Society and at LFG99. Thanks are due to Peter Austin, Lee Bickmore, Joan Bresnan, Yehuda Falk, Javier Gutierrez Rexach, Ed Keer, Jerrold Sadock, Peter Sells, and Robert Van Valin for helpful discussions of this paper. Special thanks to Luisa Martínez, who supplied all the data.

The orthography for SDZ is adapted from the practical orthographies for other Zapotec languages spoken in the Valley of Oaxaca. In the SDZ orthography, <x> = /ʒ/ before a vowel and /ʃ/ before a consonant, <xh> = /ʃ/, <dx> = /ʤ/, <ch> = /tʃ/, <c> = /k/ before back vowels, <qu> = /k/ before front vowels, <eh> = /ɛ/ and <ehh> = /ɛɛ/. Doubled vowels are long. SDZ is a language with four contrastive phonation types: breathy <Vj>, creaky <V'V>, checked <V'>, and plain <V>. High tone is marked with an acute accent, low with a grave. Nominal tones are affected by position within the intonational phrase, and so that nouns may show slightly varying tones from example to example.

Ordinary affixes are separated from the stem by the hyphen; clitics are separated by =. Glosses use the following abbreviations: an = animative, com = completive aspect, hab = habitual aspect, in = inanimate, neg = negative, loc = locative, p = possessed, pot = potential aspect, q = question, 1s =1st person singular, 3 = 3rd person human (ordinary respect level), 3i = 3rd person inanimate.

Formal and Empirical Issues in Optimality Theoretic Syntax.
Peter Sells (ed.).
Copyright © 2001, CSLI Publications.

lard and Sag 1987). Within older styles of government-binding theory, such ideas were proposed by Farmer (1980, 1984) and Stowell (1981).

More recent work in the Minimalist Program (Kayne 1994), however, rejects this view in favor of the hypothesis that linear order is strictly determined by X-bar theory and that apparent variation in linear order across languages is the result of movement.

In this paper, I will argue in favor of the position that PS-rules encode only dominance relationships. Linear precedence, I will suggest, is the result of violable optimality-theoretic constraints. My account will be framed within the optimality-theoretic implementation of Lexical Functional Grammar proposed by Bresnan (2000).

5.2 Word order and Constituency in San Dionicio Zapotec

The following sections discuss the overall syntax of San Dionicio Zapotec (hereafter SDZ), an Otomanguean language spoken in Oaxaca, Mexico, before moving on to a more detailed optimality-theoretic treatment.

5.2.1 Overview

The basic word order of SDZ is VSO, with head initial NPs and PPs:

(1) Ù-dííny Juààny bèh'cw rè' cùn yààg.
    com-hit Juan dog that with stick
    'Juan hit that dog with a stick.'

I will adopt a non-endocentric analysis of the minimal clause for SDZ, suggesting that it has a flat S structure.[2] However, there are two endocentric categories above S, namely NegP and CP. See (3) for the overall clause structure proposed for SDZ.

Unlike some other VSO languages (e.g., Welsh, Bresnan 2001), SDZ shows no evidence for inflectional phrases. Following Bresnan (2001), I will assume that functional categories are only posited when there are lexical items that instantiate them. SDZ has no plausible candidates for Infl, and indeed no distinguishable class of auxiliary or modal verbs. Thus I do not posit IP for this language.

The phrase structure may initially seem somewhat unusual in positioning specifier positions after the heads that introduce them.[3] However, note that this structure assigns parallel structures to the maximal projections S, NegP, and CP; they all conform to the following schema:

---

[2]As suggested by King (1995), Bresnan (2000, 2001), Universal Grammar allows clauses with both endocentric (IP) and lexocentric (S) organizations. Some VSO languages are best analyzed with the LFG analogue of head-movement to Infl; others show a flatter syntax.

[3]As a consequence, Spec refers not to a configurationally distinguished phrase structure position, but to the position typically occupied by elements with a discourse function (for S, NegP, and CP) or the POSS function (for NP).

(2) XP ⟶   Y   ZP   WP
          ↑=↓   (↑ DF)=↓   {(↑ CF)=↓, ↑=↓}

The first element in the phrase is its head (in either x-bar theoretic terms or in terms of feature-sharing). It is immediately followed by a phrase carrying a discourse function (SUBJ, TOPIC, or FOCUS), then by a constituent which carries a complement function (if Y is lexical) or is a cohead (if Y is functional).

There are two preverbal positions for elements with special discourse functions. Topics and foci (contrastive or interrogative) appear in one position, negative foci occur in a second position. The overall phrase structure of SDZ is shown in (3).

(3)   Proposed clause structure for SDZ

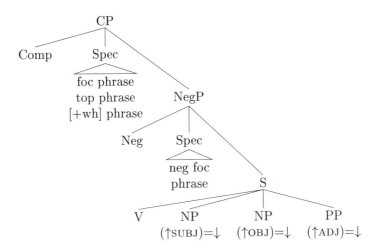

5.2.2 [Spec, CP] and Comp

Any NP or PP may appear in [Spec, CP] when it bears a special discourse function such as contrastive focus or topic (cf. Russian, King 1995).

(4) Juáàny ù-dííny bèh'cw cùn yààg.
     Juan   com-hit dog   with stick
     'Juan (TOPIC/FOCUS) hit the dog with a stick.'

(5) Bèh'cw ù-dííny Juààny cùn yààg.
     dog   com-hit Juan   with stick
     'Juan hit the dog (TOPIC/FOCUS) with a stick.'

(6) Cùn yààg ù-dìny Juààny bèh'cw.
     with stick com-hit Juan   dog
     'Juan hit the dog with a stick (TOPIC/FOCUS).'

Wh-phrases appear in the same [Spec, CP] position. Wh-movement is obligatory, as shown by the following contrast:

(7) a. ¿Túú ù-dííny Juàany cùn yààg?
      what com-hit Juan with stick
      'What (anim.) did Juan hit with a stick?'[4]

   b. *¿Ù-dííny Juàany túú cùn yààg?
      com-hit Juan what with stick

Since only one phrase may appear in [Spec, CP], the material following an wh-element is normally verb-initial:

(8) a. ¿Cálóò b-gwíí Juáàny?
      where com-go Juan
      'Where did Juan go to?

   b. *¿Cálóò Juáàny b-gwíí?
      where Juan com-go

The ungrammaticality of (8b) follows from the fact that there is only one [Spec, CP] position; if it is filled by a wh-element, then it cannot also be filled by a preposed subject.

However, one might also suppose that the word order in (8a) is derived through repositioning the verb so that it follows an initial preposed wh-element. This analysis would be somewhat like a common account of English (e.g., which places the wh-element in [Spec, CP] and then moves an auxiliary from Infl to Comp).

Such an account is not tenable in SDZ. We can see this from the occurrence of examples like the following:

(9) ¿Túú xtéh'cà gèhht ù-dàù?
      who in:neg tortilla com-eat
      'Who didn't eat any tortillas?'

Here the occurrence of the Neg head and the focussed negative phrase show clearly that the main verb ùdàù is still in its basic position. Thus the fact that moved wh-elements are accompanied by verb-initial order is not the result of verb movement, but of competition for the [Spec, CP] postion. From this I will conclude that fronted NPs with TOPIC or FOCUS functions occur in [Spec, CP].

While many elements occur in [Spec, CP], Comp itself is generally empty. In yes-no questions, it may be filled by the particle lá, which cliticizes to the following word:

---

[4]SDZ uses the wh-words xhíí 'what, which' for inanimates and túú 'who, what, which' for animates (both people and animals). I've glossed the examples with the appropriate English wh-word.

(10) ¿Lá Juáány gù Móòny zè'èh   lò ìnyá'?
q   Juan   or Ramón com:go to field
'Was it Juan or Ramón (TOPIC/FOCUS) who went to the field?'

(11) ¿Lá bèh'ty   Juáány bzììny?
q   com:kill Juan   rat
'Did Juan kill the rat?'

Examples like (10) show that the question particle precedes an element in [Spec, CP].

Embedded clauses generally show no overt complementizers in SDZ:

(12) R-cá'z-à'   [$_{CP}$ ì-gú'ì Màrìì bzíàá].
hab-want-1s pot-cook Maria bean
'I want Maria to cook the beans.'

(13) Sàlà's Juàány [$_{CP}$ ííty bèh'cw ny-àùyà'náà-èhby].
believe Juan   not   dog   neg-bite hand-3
'Juan believes that the dog won't bite his hand.'

However, some verbs select embedded interrogatives, and then *lá* appears in the Comp of the lower clause:

(14) ¿Túú gáàn lá Juáány bèh'ty   bzììny?
who   know q Juan   com:kill rat
'Who knows if Juan killed the rat?'

5.2.3   NegP

The Neg position in SDZ is filled with a negative item, followed by the negative focussed item in [Spec, NegP]. The negative agrees in animacy with the item in [Spec, NegP]—*rútèh'cà* is used with an animate focus; *xtéh'cà* is used with an inanimate focus; and *cátèh'cà* is used with a locative focus. The negative focussed NP is preceded by an interrogative/indefinite pronoun, glossed 'any'. *Túú* is for animates; *xhíí* is for inanimates.

(15) Juáány rútèh'cà túú bzììny be-'ty-bí.
Juan   an:neg   any mouse com-kill-3
'Juan didn't kill any mice.'

(16) Xtéh'cà xhíí gèhht   ù-dàù-à.
in:neg   any tortilla com-eat-1s
'I didn't eat a single tortilla.'

If the negative focussed item is the simple 'anyone','anything', or 'anywhere' it can be omitted:

(17) Rútèh'cà (túú)   ù-dáù   gèhht.
an:neg   (anyone) com-eat tortilla.
'No one ate any tortillas.'

(18) Cátèh'cà cá-chà'à.
    loc:neg   com-go:1sg
    'I'm not going anywhere.'

In a sentence with negative focus, it is possible to have other sentential items like the subject either fronted to [Spec, CP] or in situ after the verb:

(19) Juáàny xtéh'cà xhíí gèhht   ù-dàù.
    Juan   in:neg any tortilla com-eat
    'Juan didn't eat any tortillas.'

(20) Xtéh'cà xhíí gèhht ù-dàù   Juàány.
    in:neg any tortilla com-eat Juan
    'Juan didn't eat any tortillas.'

Positioning of a negative focus in [Spec, NegP] is obligatory, like the obligatory fronting of wh-phrases:

(21) *Juáány rútèh'cà be-'ty-bí túú bzììny.
    Juan   an:neg com-kill-3 any mouse
    (Juan didn't kill any mice.)

(22) *Xtéh'cà ù-dáù-à   xhíí gèhht.
    in:neg   com-eat-1s any tortilla
    (I didn't eat any tortillas.)

It is also possible to combine negative focus and interrogative focus. Since the interrogative is in [Spec, CP], it must precede the negative:

(23) ¿Túú x-sóóp rútèh'cà túú   ù-dàù?
    who p-soup an:neg anyone com-eat
    'Whose soup did no one eat?'

(24) ¿Túú xtéh'cà gèhht ù-dàù?
    who in:neg tortilla com-eat
    'Who didn't eat any tortillas?'

5.2.4 Coordination and Clause Structure

The possible coordinate structures in SDZ correlate with the phrases suggested so far. Coordination of S, NegP, and CP occurs, as shown in the following examples. The clausal conjunction 'and' is either *chì'í* or null; *gù* is 'or'.

(25) [Ù-zìì   Juáàny gèhht]$_S$ chì'í [ù-dàù Màrìì lèh'èhn]$_S$
    com-buy Juan   tortilla and com-eat Mary them
    'Juan bought tortillas and Mary ate them.'

(26) [Xtéh'cà xhíí   ù-zìì   Juàány]$_{NegP}$ ∅   [xtéh'cà xhíí
    in:neg anything com-buy Juan   and in:neg   anything
    ù-dàù-bì]$_{NegP}$
    com-eat-3
    'Juan didn't buy anything and he didn't eat anything.'

(27) ¿Túú gáàn [lá Juáàny ù-zìì   bzíàá]$_{CP}$ gù [lá Màrìì
who know q Juan   com-buy beans   or q Mary
ù-zìì   lèh'èhn]$_{CP}$?
com-buy them
'Who knows if Juan bought the beans or if Mary bought them?'

5.2.5   Word Order via Constraints

We can express the idea that in the unmarked order heads precede both their complements and specifiers through constraints of the following sort:

(28) Head ≺ Spec: A head must precede its specifier.

(29) Head ≺ Comp: A head must precede its complement.

(30) Obliqueness hierarchy: SUBJ ≺ OBJ ≺ ADJ
     (less oblique arguments precede more oblique arguments)[5]

Some other recent approaches to word order in optimality theory (Grimshaw 1997, Sells 2001) have used alignment constraints in place of direct statements of precedence. For most data, alignment and precedence statements appear to make similar predictions.

The fact that wh-movement is obligatory suggests that SDZ shows the effects of a constraint like the following:

(31) Align (IntF, L, CP, L) = Wh-L
     Align left edge of an interrogative focus phrase with left edge of CP.[6]

When there is no overt complementizer, I assume that the Comp node is also absent from the tree, and that a wh-phrase in [Spec,CP] fully satisfies this constraint. This suggests a simple tableau like the following:

(32)

		Wh-L
a.	☞ ¿Túú ù-dííny Juààny cùn yààg? (What hit Juan with stick?)	
b.	*¿Ù-dííny Juààny túú cùn yààg? (Hit Juan what with stick?)	*!*

---

[5]This alignment constraint is similar in conception to a constraint CANON$_{GF}$, proposed in Choi (1999), which states that grammatical functions align with their canonical argument positions in c-structure according to the function hierarchy (SUBJ>OBJ>OBJ$_\theta$>OBL>ADJ). However, Choi's constraint expresses prominence via c-command rather than simple precedence. If the flat structure proposed for S in SDZ is correct, then clearly c-command will not achieve the desired effect, since all the arguments within S c-command each other.

[6]In what follows below, I have assumed that Wh-L is interpreted in a gradient manner, so that each word that intervenes between the wh-element and the left edge of CP triggers an additional violation.

5.3   Questioning Specifiers of NP

In SDZ, specifiers of NP normally follow the head:

(33) a. x-pèh'cw Juààny
          p-dog   Juan
          'Juan's dog'[7]

      b. bèh'cw re'
          dog   that
          'that dog'

However, when a specifier is questioned, we see a surprising pattern. Compare the following statements and questions.

(34) a. Juààny cù'á   [$_{NP}$ x-pèh'cw Màríí].
          Juan   com:grab p-dog   Maria
          'Juan grabbed Maria's dog.'

      b. *Juààny cù'á   [$_{NP}$ Màríí x-pèh'cw].
          Juan   com:grab Maria   p-dog

(35) a. ¿[$_{NP}$ Túú x-pèh'cw] cù'á   Juààny?
          who p-dog   com:grab Juan
          'Whose dog did Juan grab?'

      b. *¿[$_{NP}$ X-pèh'cw túú] cù'á   Juààny?
          p-dog   who com:grab Juan

These sentences show that the possessor may not precede the possessed in a declarative. But in an interrogative, this is the only grammatical order. This pattern has been labelled 'pied-piping with inversion' (Smith Stark 1988), and it is found in all Zapotecan languages and in many other Mesoamerican languages as well, e.g., Tzotzil (Aissen 1996, Trechsel 2000) and Quiegolani Zapotec (Black 1994).

The following sentences make the same point for demonstratives:

(36) a. Juààny cù'á   bèh'cw rè'
          Juan   com:grab dog   that
          'Juan grabbed that dog.'

      b. *Juààny cù'á   rè'   bèh'cw.
          Juan   com:grab that dog

(37) a. ¿Túú bèh'cw cù'á   Juààny?
          which dog   com:grab Juan
          'Which dog did Juan grab?'

      b. *¿Bèh'cw túú   cù'á   Juààny?
          dog   which com:grab Juan

---

[7]In SDZ alienable possession, the possessed N has a /x-/ prefix, and the initial consonant of the noun stem is devoiced. In a few cases there are irregular changes to the initial consonant, e.g., *yààg* 'stick', *x-cyààg Juààny* 'Juan's stick'.

Note that the interrogative *túú* is the equivalent of both 'who, whose, what (animate)' and 'which (animate)' in SDZ. Within an NP, the 'whose' reading is differentiated by the presence of the /x-/ possessive prefix on the noun. The same is true for *xhíí*, which is the equivalent of both 'what (inanimate)', 'whose (inanimate)' and 'which (inanimate)'.

As in English, it is ungrammatical to attempt to extract either a determiner or a possessive from the NP without pied-piping the NP:

(38) *¿Túú cù'á   Juààny bèh'cw?
  which com:grab Juan dog
  (Which did Juan grab dog?)

(39) *¿Túú cù'á   Juààny x-pèh'cw?
  who com:grab Juan p-dog
  (Whose did Juan grab dog?)

The ungrammaticality of these sentences seems to be due to an undominated constraint that prohibits extraction from argument functions, specifically from the OBJ.

Following work by Kaplan and Zaenen (1989), I will suggest that we formulate this restriction as a constraint on functional uncertainty paths.

(40) *OBJ-Path
  The body of a functional uncertainty path may not contain OBJ.

However, in contrast to the Kaplan and Zaenen (1989) approach, the approach advocated here treats these restrictions as violable universal constraints, rather than language-particular restrictions on phrase-structure rules.

Then the following tableau (for the possessive case) shows how the correct candidate is selected.

(41)

			*OBJ-Path	Wh-L	Head≺Spec
a.	¿Túú cù'á Juààny x-pèh'cw? (Whose Juan grabbed dog?)		*!		
b.	☞ ¿Túú x-pèh'cw cù'á Juààny? (Whose dog grabbed Juan?)				*
c.	¿X-pèh'cw túú cù'á Juààny? (Dog whose grabbed Juan?)			*!	

5.4   Complements of Quantifiers

Quantifiers in SDZ precede the noun and are most plausibly analyzed as the heads of Quantifier Phrases. Like other heads, they are initial in the phrase and they may be used alone or with a pronominal complement.

(42) [$_{QP}$ tyóp gèhht]
     two tortilla
    'two tortillas'

(43) [$_{QP}$ ìrájtè gèhht]
     all   tortilla
    'all the tortillas'

(44) Nàà gù-zíí   tyóp.
     I   com-buy two
    'I bought two.'

(45) Nàà gù-zíí   tyóp=nì.
     I   com-buy two=3i
    'I bought two of them.'

In this respect, they differ from nominal modifiers such as adjectives, which show neither of these properties.

(46) [$_{NP}$ yù'ú   xníáà]
     house red
    'a red house'

(47) [$_{NP}$ gèhht   ró']
     tortilla big
    'a big tortilla'

(48) *Nàà gù-zíí ró'(=nì).
     I com-see   big(=3i)
    ('I saw the big ones (of them).')

Quantifiers and possessives appear on opposite sides of the noun:

(49) tyóp x-cùtóòny JuàÀny
     two p-shirt   Juan
    'two of Juan's shirts/Juan's two shirts'

When the complements of quantifiers are questioned, we find pied-piping with inversion like that seen with possessives and demonstratives:

(50) ¿Xhíí tyóp ù-dàù   JuàÀny?
     what two com-eat Juan
    'What did Juan eat two of?'

(51) ¿Xhíí rájtè ù-dàù   JuàÀny?
     what all   com-eat Juan
    'What did Juan all of?'

As with NPs, extraction without pied-piping is ungrammatical:

(52) *¿Xhíí ù-dàù   Juáàny tyóp?
     what com-eat Juan   two
     (What did John eat two of?)[8]

Since the QP bears the OBJ function, extraction without pied-piping will violate the previously established *OBJ-Path constraint.

However, unlike the previous case of specifiers of noun phrases, inversion is optional with quantifiers:

(53) ¿Tyóp xhíí ù-dàù   JuàÀny?
     two   what com-eat Juan
     'What did Juan eat two of?'

(54) ¿Rájtè xhíí ù-dàù   JuàÀny?
     all   what com-eat Juan
     'What did Juan eat all of?'

We have the somewhat surprising situation that inversion in NPs obligatory, while inversion in QPs is optional.

We can account for this difference by recognizing that there is a different syntactic relationship in the two cases. The possessors of nouns are specifiers, while the noun that follows a quantifier is its complement. If we treat Head≺Comp and Head≺Spec as distinct constraints, it is possible to account for this difference. We may account for availability of two grammatical forms by ranking Head≺Comp and Wh-L equally.

(55)

		*OBJ-Path	Head≺Comp	Wh-L
a.	¿Xhíí ù-dàù JuàÀny tyóp? (What ate Juan two?)	*!		
b.	☞ ¿Xhíí tyóp ù-dàù JuàÀny? (What two ate Juan?)		*	
c.	☞ ¿Tyóp xhíí ù-dàù JuàÀny? (Two what ate Juan?)			*

As suggested by Boersma (1997), Asudeh (this volume), what is shown as a constraint tie in the preceding tableau may better be interpreted saying that the constraints Head≺Comp and Wh-L have overlapping ranges.

While the constraint Wh-L overlaps Head≺Comp, as seen in the tableau (41) above, it outranks Head≺Spec. The varying strength of the preference

---

[8]This sentence is acceptable on an exclamatory reading, approximately translated as *What! John ate two?!*

for head-initial order depending on what follows may argue against a uniform constraint which would favor candidates aligning the head with the edge of the phrase.

5.5 Objects of Prepositions

Pied-piping with inversion is also found with the objects of most prepositions.

(56) ¿Xhíí cùn ù-dííny Juàány bèh'cw?
what with com-hit Juan dog
'What did Juan hit the dog with?'

(57) ¿Xhíí dèjts   zúú bèh'cw?
what behind lie dog
'What is the dog behind?'

Though my consultant reports a preference for the inverted form, the uninverted form is also acceptable for these prepositions:

(58) ¿Cùn xhíí ù-dííny Juàány bèh'cw?[9]
with what com-hit Juan   dog
'With what did Juan hit the dog?'

(59) ¿Dèjts xhíí zúú bèh'cw?
behind what lie dog
'Behind what is the dog?'

Like *cùn* 'with' are *cuèh'* 'beside', *dèhjts* 'behind', *lò* 'to', and *nì'* 'under'.

In contrast to these prepositions, there is a small set of prepositions that show rather different behavior. This group includes *dèhspuèhhs* 'after', *ààxt* 'toward', *áántèhs* 'before', and *zí'cy* 'like'. For prepositions in this group, the uninverted form is found, and inversion is ungrammatical.

(60) ¿Dèhspuèhhs xhíí b-gwíí Juàány lò gyèh?
after   what com-go Juan   to town
'What did Juan go to town after?'

(61) *¿Xhíí dèhspuèhhs b-gwíí Juàány lò gyèh?
what after   com-go Juan   to town

(62) ¿Zí'cy túú r-ù'ùld   Bèhjd?
like who hab-sing Pedro
'Who does Pedro sing like?'

(63) *¿Túú zí'cy r-ù'ùld   Bèhjd?
who like hab-sing Pedro

---

[9]In Broadwell (1999a,b) I cited this form as ungrammatical. On more careful consideration, my consultant reports that she finds this sentence acceptable, but somewhat awkward or unusual. For reasons that are not clear to me, the uninverted forms with *cùn* seem slightly worse than the uninverted forms with other prepositions in this group.

For both types of prepositions, stranding is completely disallowed:

(64) *¿Xhíí ù-dííny Juààny bèh'cw cùn?
     what com-hit Juan dog with
     (What did Juan hit the dog with?)

(65) *¿Túú r-ù'ùld Bèhjd zí'cy?
     who hab-sing Pedro like
     'Who does Pedro sing like?'

The ungrammaticality of (64) and (65) seems to be due to an undominated constraint in SDZ that forbids preposition stranding.[10]

(66) *ADJ-Path: The body of a functional uncertainty path may not contain ADJ

The difference between the two types of prepositions is difficult to characterize. Invertable prepositions are mostly native to Zapotec, while non-invertable prepositions are mainly borrowings from Spanish. However, *cùn* 'with' is borrowed but invertable, while *zí'cy* is native but non-invertable. Most native Zapotec prepositions are homophonous with nouns referring to body parts: *dèhjts* 'behind; back', *nì'* 'under; foot', *lò* 'to; face', *cuèh'* 'beside; side'. And all the prepositions homophonous with body parts are invertable. (But once again, it is puzzling that *cùn* 'with' should fall in this group.) In earlier forms of Zapotec, a prepositional notion like 'behind the house' was expressed through a noun phrase with a possessed body part 'the house's back'.

We might approach an explanation in the following way. Let us assume that the non-invertable prepositions are purely prepositional, while the invertable prepositions show a mixture of nominal and prepositional properties. Pure prepositions obey a constraint Prep-L (defined as Align (Prep, L, PP, L)), and this constraint outranks Wh-L. Invertable prepositions, on the other hand, are capable of two analyses. If treated as nominal, then they show the obligatory inversion found with possessors. If treated as prepositional, then they show no inversion.

Prepositions like *dèhjts* 'behind' and *zí'cy* 'like' will have the following sorts of information in their lexical entries:

(67) dèhjts $[- V]$ zí'cy $[- V]$
     $[\pm N]$ $[- N]$

Exceptionally, *cùn* 'with' has features like *dèhjts* 'behind', despite the lack of a nominal reading.

---

[10] Although the PP carries the ADJ role in these examples, the PP might carry some other role, such as OBJ$_\theta$ in other cases. Preposition stranding is banned no matter what role the PP bears. The approach here will need to posit separate *ADJ-Path and *OBJ$_\theta$-Path constraints, but it is not clear that this is a disadvantage, since constraints on extraction may treat these two types of PPs differently. (See, for example, work in the Principles and Parameters framework focussing on argument/adjunct differences in extraction (Huang 1982).)

Lexical items that are $[-N, -V]$ will obey the Prep-L constraint, yielding a tableau like the following:

(68)

	*ADJ-Path	Prep-L	Wh-L
¿Túú rù'ùld Juáàny zí'cy? (Who does Juan sing like?)	*!		
¿Túú zí'cy rù'ùld Juáàny? (Who like does Juan sing?)		*!	
☞¿Zí'cy túú rù'ùld Juáàny? (Like who does Juan sing?)			*

Invertable prepositions are subject to two analyses. If they are treated as purely prepositional, then they obey the Prep-L constraint, and a tableau like the preceding results, in which the uninverted candidate emerges as optimal. If however, they are treated as nominal, then they are subject to the Head≺Spec constraint, and the inverted candidate will be optimal. The two tableaux are shown below:

(69)

(prepositional analysis)	*ADJ-Path	Prep-L	Wh-L	Head≺Spec
¿Xhíí zúú bèh'cw dèjts? (What lies dog behind?)	*!			inapp.
☞¿Dèjts xhíí zúú bèh'cw? (Behind what lies dog?)			*	inapp.
¿Xhíí dèjts zúú bèh'cw? (What behind lies dog?)		*!		inapp.

(70)

(nominal analysis)	*ADJ-Path	Prep-L	Wh-L	Head≺Spec
¿Xhíí zúú bèh'cw dèjts? (What lies dog behind?)	*!	inapp.		
¿Dèjts xhíí zúú bèh'cw? (Behind what lies dog?)		inapp.	*!	
☞¿Xhíí dèjts zúú bèh'cw? (What behind lies dog?)		inapp.		*

5.6 Inversion in Negative Contexts

We see nearly identical effects in sentences with negative focussed elements. Focus negation is always accompanied by fronting of the focussed object to preverbal position. As discussed above, the focussed element is accompanied by an interrogative/indefinite determiner. *Túú* is for animates; *xhíí* is for inanimates. The following example shows that such a determiner must precede the noun.

(71) a. Juáány rútèh'cà túú bzììny bè-'ty-bí.
        Juan an:neg any mouse com-kill-3
        'Juan didn't kill any mice.'

    b. *Juáány rútèh'cà bzììny túú bè-'ty-bí.
        Juan an:neg mouse any com-kill-3

We also find pied-piping with inversion for the possessive.

(72) a. Rú-tèh'cà túú   x-pèh'cw ù-dííny Màríí.
        an:neg   anyone p-dog com-hit Maria
        'Maria didn't hit anyone's dog.'

    b. *Rú-tèh'cà x-pèh'cw túú   ù-dííny Màríí.
        an:neg   p-dog   anyone com-hit Maria

If the negative focussed element is the object of a preposition, we get pied-piping with inversion, just as in the questions:

(73) a. Rú-tèh'cà túú   lò ù-déhhdy Màríí cààrrt.
        an:neg   anyone to com-give Maria letter
        'Maria didn't give the letter to anyone.'

    b. *Rú-tèh'cà lò túú   ù-déhhdy Màríí cààrrt.
        an:neg   to anyone com-give Maria letter

For the complement of quantification, pied-piping in negative focus contexts is optional, just as it was in interrogatives.

(74) Xtéh'cà rújld xhíí   ù-dàù Màrìì.
     in:neg half anything com-eat Maria
     'Maria didn't eat half of anything.'

(75) Xtéh'cà xhíí   rújld ù-dàù Màrìì.
     in:neg anything half com-eat Maria
     'Maria didn't eat half of anything.'

These facts suggest that there is a constraint[11] which favors candidates in which the left edge of a negative focussed constituent aligns with the right edge of the negative element, along the following lines:

(76) Align(NegF, L, Neg, R): Align the left edge of a negative focussed item with the right edge of the negation.

Substituting this constraint for Wh-L in the tableau above will yield the right word order for these sentences.

5.7 Complex Specifiers and Complements

The constraints posited above correctly account for simple cases of pied-piping with inversion. More complex cases arise when N, P, and Q occur with multi-word specifiers and complements.

5.7.1 Complex Specifiers of N

When the possessor within NP is itself possessed, a straightforward extension of the account so far would lead one to expect the following result:

(77) ?* ¿Túú x-míehgw x-cùtóòny ndé'?
     who p-friend p-shirt this
     'Whose friend's shirt is this?'

This example contains two cases of inverted word order: the possessor of 'shirt' precedes it, and so does the possessor of 'friend'. Unexpectedly, this order is bad, a matter which we return to in section 5.8.2 below.

Instead, the preferred order is the one shown below:

(78) ¿Túú x-cùtóòny x-míehgw ndé'?
     who p-shirt p-friend this
     'Whose friend's shirt is this?'

In this order, the constituency of the possessor 'whose friend' is disrupted.
Also less than acceptable is

(79) *? ¿X-cùtóòny túú x-míehgw ndé'?
     p-shirt   who p-friend this
     'Whose friend's shirt is this?'

Let us categorize these options more precisely.

(80) a. x-cùtóòny x-míehgw Crìstìáàn
        p-shirt   p-friend Christina
        'Christina's friend's shirt'

---

[11]This constraint is not completely parallel to the constraint on interrogative focus, since that constraint aligned the interrogative focus with the left edge of CP.

There do not appear to be any clauses in SDZ with both and overt complementizer and a wh-phrase. If we posit an empty Comp, we could restate the constraint on interrogative focus as Align(IntF, L, Comp, L), but empty nodes are not in keeping with Economy of Expression (Bresnan 2001).

b.   In-situ configuration

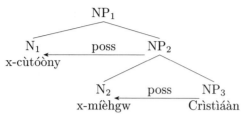

In a normal, non-interrogative, a configuration like that in (80b) obtains. Each possessor follows its head. The possession relationships are indicated via an arrow to highlight the differences between the various possible and impossible configurations.

The grammatical question shows the following configuration, which I label 'disconnected'.

(81)   Disconnected

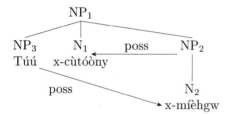

(82)   Double inversion

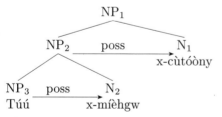

The configuration which is unexpectedly ungrammatical is one I label 'double inversion'.

Both the disconnected and double inversion configurations align the wh-element with the left edge of the constituent, but they do so in different ways. In the disconnected configuration, the constituency of NP$_2$ is disrupted, since N$_2$ and NP$_3$ do not form a c-structure constituent. In the double inversion configuration, the constituency relationships are preserved, but both NP$_1$ and NP$_2$ show marked constituent orders.

The third possibility, not fully grammatical for NPs, is a configuration I label 'lower inversion', in which the order of items in NP$_2$ is inverted, but that of items in NP$_1$ is intact:

(83)   Lower inversion

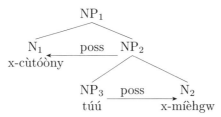

We will see in the following sections that the analogue of the lower inversion configuration is grammatical in QP and PP.

5.7.2   Complex Complements of Q

Quantifiers with complex complements allow both disconnected and lower inversion configurations.

(84) ¿Túú ìrájtè x-cùtóòny gèh'èhcy?   [disconnected]
     who all   p-shirt   com:burn
     'All of whose shirts burned?'

(85) ¿Ìrájtè túú x-cùtóòny gèh'èhcy?   [lower inversion]
     all   who p-shirt   com:burn
     'All of whose shirts burned?'

The in-situ and double inversion candidates are ungrammatical:

(86) * ¿Ìrájtè x-cùtóòny túú gèh'èhcy?   [in situ]
     all   p-shirt   who com:burn
     'All of whose shirts burned?'

(87) * ¿Túú x-cùtóòny ìrájtè gèh'èhcy?   [double inversion]
     who   p-shirt   all   com:burn
     'All of whose shirts burned?'

5.7.3   Complex Complements of P

As discussed in section 5.5 above, prepositions fall into two classes, invertable and non-invertable. There are differences between these two types of prepositions when it comes to inversion and complex complements.

For complex complements of non-invertable prepositions, only the lower inversion configuration is grammatical:

(88) ¿Dèhspuèhhs xhíí   lànìj b-gwíí Juáàny lò gyèh'? [lower inversion]
     after   which party com-go Juan   to market
     'After which party did Juan go to the market?'

(89) *¿Xhíí dèhspuèhhs lànìj b-gwíí Juáàny lò gyèh'? [disconnected]
     which after   party com-go Juan   to market

The in-situ and double inversion configurations are ungrammatical, as in all the other cases:

(90) *¿Dèhspuèhhs lànìj xhíí   b-gwíí Juáàny lò gyèh'?   [in situ]
after   party which com-go Juan   to market
'After which party did Juan go to the market?'

(91) *¿Xhíí lànìj dèhspuèhhs b-gwíí Juáàny lò gyèh'? [double inversion]
which party after   com-go Juan   to market
'After which party did Juan go to the market?'

For complex complements of invertable prepositions, both the disconnected and lower inversion configurations are grammatical.

(92) Ù-dííny JuàÃny bèh'cw cùn yàÃg ré'.
com-hit Juan   dog   with stick that
'Juan hit the dog with that stick.'

(93) ¿Cùn xhíí   yàÃg ù-dííny JuàÃny bèh'cw?   [lower inversion]
with which stick com-hit Juan   dog
'With which stick did Juan hit the dog?'

(94) ¿Xhíí cùn yàÃg ù-dííny JuàÃny bèh'cw?   [disconnected]
which with stick com-hit Juan   dog
(Which with stick did Juan hit the dog?)

Exactly the same facts are found with the possessive:

(95) ¿Cùn túú   x-cyàÃg ù-dííny JuàÃny bèh'cw?   [lower inversion]
with whose p-stick com-hit Juan   dog
'With whose stick did Juan hit the dog?'

(96) ¿Túú cùn x-cyàÃg ù-dííny JuàÃny bèh'cw?   [disconnected]
whose with p-stick com-hit Juan   dog
(Whose with stick did Juan hit the dog?)

We find the same two grammatical possibilities for negative focus:

(97) Rú-tèh'cà túú   lò chèh'   ù-dèhhdy Màrìì càÃrrt. [disconnected]
an:neg   anyone to husband com-give Maria letter
'Maria didn't give the letter to anyone's husband.'

(98) Rú-tèh'cà lò túú   chèh'   ù-dèhhdy Màrìì càÃrrt. [lower inversion]
an:neg   to anyone husband com-give Maria letter
'Maria didn't give the letter to anyone's husband.'

5.7.4 Summary

The following chart summarizes the possible configurations found with complex interrogative complements to N, P, and Q.

	in situ	discon-nected	lower inversion	double inversion
N	no	yes	no	no
Q	no	yes	yes	no
P (invertable)	no	yes	yes	no
P (non-invertable)	no	no	yes	no

5.8 Extending the account to complex complements

Let us assume that there is some penalty associated with breaking up the NP_2 constituent, as is seen in the disconnected configuration. The function associated with this constituent will vary according to the head of the construction.

5.8.1 Restrictions on paths

Within PP, the NP complement bears the role OBJ_θ. Within NP, the NP specifier bears the function POSS. In the unmarked case, both these NPs complements should form c-structure constituents, and I will assume that candidates that violate this trigger a constraint violation.

(99) *POSS-Path/*OBJ_θ-Path: The body of a functional uncertainty path must not contain POSS/OBJ_θ.

The constraint penalizing extraction from the object of a quantifier requires more discussion. There does not seem to be a clearly established name for the function that the quantified noun bears to the quantifier. Dalrymple, Lamping, Pereira, and Saraswat (1999) (hereafter DLPS) examine the type of quantification found in English, where quantifiers occupy a determiner position. They suggest that in an English phrase like *every voter*, *every* bears the function SPEC and *voter* bears the function PRED.

This is not particularly appropriate for languages like SDZ where the quantifier appears to be the main predicating element, taking an NP as its complement. I will instead borrow a term from the DLPS semantic structure and call the complement function within a quantifier phrase RESTR. So the f-str for a phrase like in (100) (repeated from above) will be as in (101).

(100) tyóp x-cùtóòny Juààny
two p-shirt   Juan
'two of Juan's shirts/Juan's two shirts'

(101)

$$\begin{bmatrix} \text{PRED} & \text{'two<(RESTR)>'} \\ \text{RESTR} & \begin{bmatrix} \text{PRED} & \text{'shirt'} \\ \text{POSS} & [\text{PRED} \quad \text{'John'}] \end{bmatrix} \end{bmatrix}$$

Then the constraint that penalizes extraction of the complement to a quantifier can be phrased as follows:

(102) *RESTR-Path: The body of a functional uncertainty path must not contain RESTR

The path constraints *RESTR-Path, *POSS-Path, and *OBJ$_\theta$-Path are low ranked in SDZ, but we will see in the tableaux below that they must be included to penalize disconnected configurations.

5.8.2 The problem with double inversion

For all the cases under consideration, the double inversion configuration is ungrammatical. Consider again the phrase structure tree that results from double inversion:

(103)   Prohibited double inversion structure

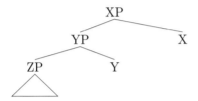

Aissen (1996) shows that analogous examples in Tzotzil are also ungrammatical, despite the fact that a straightforward extension of the movement-based solution proposed there would seem to predict their grammaticality. She appeals to the Consistency Principle initially proposed by Longobardi (1991:98) for Italian, which can be stated as follows:

(104) Consistency Principle: An XP immediately expanding a lexical category on the non-recursive side is directionally consistent in every projection.

The intuition behind this principle is that languages avoid mixed branching structures. Zapotec and Tzotzil are right-branching languages, in which heads prefer positions on the left sides of phrases. As we have seen in the preceding sections, this preference is violable in the presence of higher-ranking constraints, such as Wh-L.

However, as a consequence of their preference for right-branching, the Consistency Principle also places restrictions on any phrasal material that appears on a left branch, namely that such phrases must themselves be consistently right-branching.

While Longobardi restricts Consistency to lexical categories, in Zapotec we see effects of Consistency for non-lexical categories like Q as well. If we conceive of Consistency as a constraint, this suggests that there may be a few distinct variants of the constraint. The relevant constraint for Italian would seem to be Consistency (Lexical), while the variant that is relevant for Zapotec is as follows:

(105) Consistency (X): An XP immediately expanding a category on the non-recursive side is directionally consistent in every projection.

Since examples violating Consistency (X) are all ungrammatical in SDZ, this constraint should be undominated in our tableaux.

The successful candidate shows the disconnected configuration, which incurs a violation of *POSS-Path. Since this is the lowest ranked constraint, however, this candidate wins.

(106)

	Consistency(X)	Wh-L	Head≺Spec	*POSS-Path
a.		*!*		
b.	*!		**	
☞c.				*

a. = ¿X-cùtóòny x-mîehgw túú ndé'?   [in situ]
    (Shirt friend whose this?)
b. = ¿Túú x-mîehgw x-cùtóòny ndé'? [double inversion]
    (Whose friend shirt this?)
c. = ¿Túú x-cùtóòny x-mîehgw ndé'?   [disconnected]
    (Whose shirt friend this?)

5.8.3 Constraints for Q

With the constraints developed in the preceding section added to the constraints already proposed, we are able to account for the distribution of grammatical and ungrammatical configurations. Let us examine the tableau for a QP with a complex complement.

(107)

	Consistency(X)	Wh-L	Head≺Comp	Head≺Spec	*RESTR-Path
a.		*!*			
b.	*!		*	*	
☞c.			*		*
☞d.		*		*	

a. = ¿Ìrájtè x-cùtóòny túú gèh'èhcy?   [in situ]
   (All shirt whose burned?)
b. = ¿Túú x-cùtóòny ìrájtè gèh'èhcy? [double inversion]
   (Whose shirt all burned?)
c. = ¿Túú ìrájtè x-cùtóòny gèh'èhcy?   [disconnected]
   (Whose all shirt burned?)
d. = ¿Ìrájtè túú x-cùtóòny gèh'èhcy?   [lower inversion]
   (All whose shirt burned?)

In this tableau there are two winning candidates. Since, as established before, Wh-L and Head≺Comp are overlapping, the fact that both (c) and (d) candidates are grammatical indicates a second overlap, this time between Head≺Spec and *RESTR-Path.

5.8.4 Constraints for N

Turning to nouns with complex complements, it is easy to explain the unacceptability of lower inversion, as shown in the following example:

(108) *? ¿X-cùtóòny túú x-mîèhgw ndé'?   [lower inversion]
       p-shirt   who p-friend   this
   'Whose friend's shirt is this?'

We can say that since Head≺Comp is not active, a candidate of this sort is suboptimal because it violates Wh-L. As before, the double inversion candidate is ruled out by Consistency (X).

(109)

	Consistency(X)	Wh-L	Head≺Comp	Head≺Spec	*POSS-Path
☞a.				*	*
b.		*!		*	
c.	*!			**	

a. = ¿Túú x-cùtóòny x-míèhgw ndé'?   [disconnected]
(Whose shirt friend this?)

b. = ¿X-cùtóòny túú x-míèhgw ndé'?   [lower inversion]
(Shirt whose friend this?)

c. = ¿Túú x-míèhgw x-cùtóòny ndé'? [double inversion]
(Whose friend shirt this?)

5.8.5 Constraints for P

Recall that for complex complements to non-invertable prepostions, only the lower inversion candidate is grammatical. This follows straightforwardly from the high ranking of Prep-L; any candidate in which the preposition is not initial will be suboptimal.

(110)

	Consistency(X)	Prep-L	Head≺Comp	Wh-L	Head≺Spec	*OBJ$_\theta$-Path
a.		*!			*	*
☞b.				*	*	
c.	*!	**	*		*	

a. = ¿Xhíí dèhspuèhhs lànìj b-gwíí Juáàny lò gy'eh'?
(Which after party went Juan to market?)
[disconnected]

b. = ¿Dèhspuèhhs xhíí lànìj b-gwíí Juáàny lò gy'eh'?
(After which party went Juan to market?)
[lower inversion]

c. = ¿Xhíí lànìj dèhspuèhhs b-gwíí Juáàny lò gy'eh'?
(Which party after went Juan to market?)
[double inversion]

For complex complements to invertable prepositions, the disconnected and lower inversion candidates are grammatical, but the double inversion candidate is not. I suggested in section 5.5 above that invertable prepositions are subject to a dual analysis; they show both nominal and prepositional characteristics. If we construct two tableaux for cases, we arrive at the following results:

(111)

(prepositional analysis)	Consistency(X)	Prep-L	Head≺Comp	Wh-L	Head≺Spec	*OBJ$_θ$-Path
a.		*!			*	*
☞b.				*	*	
c.	*!		**	*	*	

a. = ¿Xhíí cùn yàag ù-dììny Juààny bèh'cw?
     (Which with stick hit Juan dog?)   [disconnected]
b. = ¿Cùn xhíí yàag ù-dííny Juààny bèh'cw?
     (With which stick hit Juan dog?)   [lower inversion]
c. = ¿Xhíí yààg cùn ù-dììny Juààny bèh'cw?
     (Which party after went Juan to market?)
                                              [double inversion]

(112)

(nominal analysis)	Consistency(X)	Prep-L	Head≺Comp	Wh-L	Head≺Spec	*POSS-Path
☞a.		inapp.			*	*
b.		inapp.		*!	*	
c.	*!	inapp.			**	

a. = ¿Xhíí cùn yààg ù-dììny Juààny bèh'cw?
     (Which with stick hit Juan dog?)
     [disconnected]
b. = ¿Cùn xhíí yààg ù-dííny Juààny bèh'cw?
     (With which stick hit Juan dog?)
     [lower inversion]
c. = ¿Xhíí yààg cùn ù-dììny Juààny bèh'cw?
     (Which party after went Juan to market?)
     [double inversion]

5.9 Conclusion

By using a small number of violable constraints, it is possible to successfully model the rather complex data associated with pied-piping and inversion in San Dionicio Zapotec. In particular, the variability of inversion seen in QPs and PPs is easily modeled through the idea of constraint ties.

While it may be possible to construct an alternative account of these facts in which all the word order variation is reduced to movement rules, I believe that the account here catches an essential insight into the true motivation for pied-piping with inversion: a competition between leftmost position for the interrrogative and leftmost position for the head.

References

Aissen, Judith. 1996. Pied-piping, abstract agreement, and functional projections in Tzotzil. *Natural Language and Linguistic Theory* 14:447–491.

Asudeh, Ash. 2001. Linking, Optionality, and Ambiguity in Marathi. This volume.

Black, Cheryl. 1994. *Quiegolani Zapotec syntax*. Ph.D. thesis, University of California, Santa Cruz.

Boersma, Paul. 1997. How we learn variation, optionality, and probability. In *IFA Proceedings 21*. University of Amsterdam: Institute of Phonetic Sciences, 43–58. ROA-221-109.

Boersma, Paul. 1998. *Functional Phonology: Formalizing the interactions between articulatory and perceptual drives*. The Hague: Holland Academic Graphics.

Boersma, Paul and Bruce Hayes. 2001. Empirical tests of the gradual learning algorithm. *Linguistic Inquiry* 32:45–86.

Bresnan, Joan. 2000. Optimal Syntax. In *Optimality Theory: Phonology, Syntax and Acquisition*, eds. Joost Dekkers, Frank van der Leeuw, and Jeroen van de Weijer. Oxford: Oxford University Press, 334–385.

Bresnan, Joan. 2001. *Lexical Functional Syntax*. Oxford: Blackwell.

Broadwell, George Aaron. 1999a. Focus alignment and optimal order in Zapotec. In *Proceedings of the 35th Chicago Linguistics Society*. Online: http://www.albany.edu/anthro/fac/broadwell.htm.

Broadwell, George Aaron. 1999b. The interaction of focus and constituent order in San Dionicio Ocotepec Zapotec. In *Proceedings of the LFG 99 conference*, eds. Miriam Butt and Tracy Holloway King. Stanford, California: CSLI Publications Online: http//csli-publications.stanford.edu/.

Choi, Hye-Won. 1999. *Optimizing Structure in Context: Scrambling and Information Structure*. Stanford, California: CSLI Publications.

Chomsky, Noam. 1995. *The Minimalist Program*. Cambridge, Massachusetts: The MIT Press.

Dalrymple, Mary, John Lamping, Fernando Pereira, and Vijay Saraswat. 1999. Quantification, anaphora, and intensionality. In *Semantics and Syntax in Lexical Functional Grammar*, ed. Mary Dalrymple. Cambridge, Massachusetts: The MIT Press.

Falk, Yehuda. 1983. Constituency, word order, and phrase structure rules. *Linguistic Analysis* 11:331–360.

Farmer, Ann. 1980. *On the Interaction of Morphology and Syntax*. Ph.D. thesis, MIT.

Farmer, Ann. 1984. *Modularity in Syntax: A Study of Japanese and English*. Cambridge, Massachusetts: The MIT Press.

Gazdar, Gerald, Ewan Klein, Geoffrey Pullum, and Ivan Sag. 1985. *Generalized Phrase Structure Grammar*. Cambridge, Massachusetts: Harvard.

Grimshaw, Jane. 1991. Extended Projection. MS., Dept. of Linguistics and Center for Cognitive Science, Rutgers University.

Grimshaw, Jane. 1997. Projection, Heads, and Optimality. *Linguistic Inquiry* 28:73–422.

Huang, C-T. James. 1982. *Logical Relations in Chinese and the Theory of Grammar*. Ph.D. thesis, MIT.

Jackendoff, Ray. 1990. *Semantic Structures*. Cambridge, Massachusetts: The MIT Press.

Kaplan, Ronald and Annie Zaenen. 1989. Long-distance dependencies, constituent structure, and functional uncertainty. In *Alternative Conceptions of Phrase Structure*, eds. Mark Baltin and Anthony Kroch. Chicago, Illinois: University of Chicago Press, 17–42.

Kayne, Richard. 1994. *The Antisymmetry of Syntax*. Cambridge, Massachusetts: The MIT Press.

King, Tracy Holloway. 1995. *Configuring Topic and Focus in Russian*. Stanford, California: CSLI Publications.

Longobardi, Giuseppe. 1991. Extraction from NP and the proper notion of head government. In *The Syntax of Noun Phrases*, eds. A. Giorgi and G. Longobardi. Cambridge: Cambridge University Press, 57–112.

Pollard, Carl and Ivan Sag. 1987. *Information-based Syntax and Semantics*. Stanford, California: CSLI Publications.

Prince, Alan and Paul Smolensky. 1993. Optimality Theory: Constraint Interaction in Generative Grammar. Technical Report RuCCS Technical Report #2, Center for Cognitive Science, Rutgers University, Piscataway, New Jersey. To be published by the MIT Press.

Sadock, Jerrold. 1991. *Autolexical syntax*. Chicago, Illinois: University of Chicago Press.

Sells, Peter. 2001. *Structure, Alignment and Optimality in Swedish*. To appear, Stanford, California: CSLI Publications.

Smith Stark, Thomas. 1988. 'Pied-piping' con inversion en preguntas parciales. MS., Centro de estudios lingüísticos y literarios, Colegio de México y Seminario de lenguas indígenas.

Stowell, Timothy. 1981. *Origins of Phrase Structure*. Ph.D. thesis, MIT.

Trechsel, Frank. 2000. A CCG account of Tzotzil pied piping. *Natural Language and Linguistic Theory* 18:611–663.

6

Kashmiri Case Clitics and Person Hierarchy Effects

DEVYANI SHARMA

6.1 Introduction

The non-random, hierarchical nature of many typological asymmetries in syntactic markedness cross-linguistically has been observed in the literature (Greenberg 1966; Silverstein 1976; Battistella 1990) and has recently been incorporated into the formal framework of Optimality Theory (Prince and Smolensky 1993; Artstein 1998; Aissen 2000, 2001).[1] In this paper, I examine the effect of relative person rank violations on case clitic selection in Kashmiri, and propose a unified analysis of the interaction of the person hierarchy, case marking, and perfectivity by appealing to the notion of universal markedness hierarchies in Optimality Theory (OT).

Clauses in Kashmiri may have either overt pronouns or NPs, both of which are marked for case, or else case clitics which are suffixed to the verb. Direct object clitics in nonperfective clauses are marked with accusative case except when the person value of the object is equal to or higher than that of the subject of the clause. In such situations, dative object clitics appear in place of accusative. This distinctive case marking pattern does not occur in perfective clauses, in which the subject is marked with ergative case and the object is nominative (absolutive). In other words, in the person hierarchy system objects are marked either accusative or dative depending on their person rank relative to the subject, while in the aspectual system

---

[1]I am indebted to Joan Bresnan, Miriam Butt, Paul Kiparsky, Peter Sells, the audience of the Joint UCSC/Stanford Workshop on Optimal Typology (UCSC, October, 1999), three Kashmiri consultants, and an anonymous reviewer for many valuable comments and suggestions on earlier versions of this paper. Any remaining errors are my own.

Formal and Empirical Issues in Optimality Theoretic Syntax.
Peter Sells (ed.).
Copyright © 2001, CSLI Publications.

subjects are marked either nominative or ergative depending on the perfectivity status of the clause. Furthermore, when the subject of a perfective clause carries perfective ergative marking, the split in the person hierarchy system is neutralized and no case marking effects occur on the object. The analysis of these phenomena developed here draws crucially on the alignment of universal markedness hierarchies as well as local conjunction for the representation of relative markedness (Prince and Smolensky 1993; Aissen 2000). The language-particular ranking of these universal markedness constraints derives the interaction found between the two split systems of person markedness and perfectivity in Kashmiri.

After presenting the general phenomena under consideration in section 6.2, I introduce the universal subhierarchy of constraints that applies to the person markedness effect in section 6.3. This is followed by similar discussions of the relevant constraints for case marking and perfectivity in section 6.4 and section 6.5, respectively. These three apparently disparate sets of constraints are brought together in a single ranking for Kashmiri in section 6.6, demonstrating how their interaction results in the candidate selections that were found to hold in the data in section 6.2. Finally, certain typological predictions and residual issues are taken up in section 6.7.

6.2 Kashmiri Case-Marking Patterns

Kashmiri is an Indo-Aryan (Dardic subgroup) language with over four million speakers in North-Western India and Pakistan. Word order is SVO in main clauses and verb-final in subordinate clauses and is relatively flexible, except for a strict verb-second restriction on main clauses (Sayeed 1985; Bhatt 1999:47). Clauses may have either full NPs, case clitics suffixed to the verb, or a combination.[2] The sentences in (1) show an instance of this contrast. In (1a) the object is a free pronoun and in (1b) it is a clitic.

(1) a. tsɨ   chu-kh   su   vucha:n
         you-NOM be-2.SG.NOM   him-ACC   see-PRES.PPL
         'You are looking at him.'

     b. tsɨ   chu-kh-an   vucha:n
         you-NOM be-2.SG.NOM-3.SG.ACC   see-PRES.PPL
         'You are looking at him.'

Although the discussion in this paper is restricted to case clitics on the verb, I present a brief overview of both the NP-marking system as well as

---

[2]This paper does not address the question of competition in realizing full NPs and clitics. See Artstein (1998) for a possible approach to deriving this distinction.

the verbal clitic paradigm in this section.[3] The paradigm of nominal case markers is given in Table 1.[4]

Table 1: Nominal Case Markers [Wali and Koul (1997:151)]

CASE	MASCULINE		FEMININE	
	singular	*plural*	*singular*	*plural*
Nominative	ϕ	ϕ	ϕ	ϕ
Ergative	-an/C′	-av	-i	-av
Dative	-as/-is	-an	-i	-an
Ablative	-ɨ/-i	-av	-i	-av

The pronoun system corresponds broadly to the NP pattern in Table 1, with the exception of some additional suppletive case forms; these occur primarily in the first and second person forms. Furthermore, there is some syncretism across pronominal case forms. Specifically, the ergative and dative pronominal forms for first person and for second person are not distinct (Wali and Koul 1997:200). The more significant contrasts, however, lie between the NP paradigm and the verbal clitic paradigm. Note in Table 1 that nominative/absolutive NPs are null-marked, as might be expected, but direct objects are similarly null marked as there is no case paradigm for accusative. Thus, there is no evidence in the NP-marking system of a nominative-accusative case pattern. This situation is markedly different in the verbal agreement paradigm, which I turn to next.

Suffixation on the finite verb or auxiliary includes (a) obligatory core gender and number agreement with the nominative argument, which may be the subject or the object, and (b) pronominal clitics.[5] The complete verb template is shown in (2):

(2) V-(core nominative gender/number agreement)-Subj-DirObj-IndObj

Some examples of clitic ordering and agreement are given in (3). These clitic forms correspond to the paradigms in Table 2.

---

[3]Wali and Koul (1997) use the terms suffix, clitic, and postposition interchangeably to denote pronominal case markers which attach to the verb; in other work (Wali and Koul 1994), they exclusively use the term clitic. I refer to these markers as clitics here, although nothing in this analysis hinges crucially on this choice.

[4]An alternation based on palatalization is included in the masculine singular paradigm in Table 1. Masculine nouns that mark their plurals by palatalization use this palatalized plural form as their ergative and dative singular forms, instead of -*an* and -*as* respectively (Wali and Koul 1997:151).

[5]The optionality of clitics in Kashmiri and consequently their interaction with null realization of arguments is complicated. Clitic-doubling is forbidden for certain clitics but permitted for others. For example, second person clitics must always be present; nominative clitics for all persons must be present; and dative clitics generally cannot double with overt, coreferential 1st or 3rd person pronouns (Wali and Koul 1994:973).

(3) a. Subject clitic:
    tse   vodu-**th**
    you-ERG cry-2.SG.ERG
    'You cried.'

   b. Subject−Object clitics:
    tse   vichi-**th-as**   bɨ
    you-ERG see-2.SG.ERG-1.SG.NOM me-F.SG.NOM
    'You saw me.'

   c. Subject−Object−Indirect Object clitics:
    bɨ   chu-**s-an-ay**   su
    I-NOM be-1.SG.NOM-3.SG.ACC-2.SG.DAT he-SG.ACC
    tse   hava:lɨ   kara:n
    you-SG.DAT hand-over doing
    'I am handing him over to you.'

[Wali and Koul (1997:253)]

The focus in this paper is on the selection of pronominal clitics which follow the core agreement suffix. The paradigm of pronominal clitic forms is given in Table 2.

Table 2: Case Clitics [adapted from Grierson (1916)]

CASE	1ST PERS	2ND PERS	3RD PERS
Nominative Singular	-s	-h/-kh	ϕ
Accusative Singular	-m	-th	-n
Ergative Singular	-m	-th[6]	-n
Dative Singular	-m	-y	-s
Plural	ϕ	-wa	-kh

The main difference between the paradigms in Table 1 and Table 2 is the inclusion of accusative case-marking in the pronominal clitic paradigm, which shows syncretism with the ergative case forms. The ergative case marker for full NPs does not follow this syncretism; it is not extended to nonperfective NP objects. Thus, for the present analysis I treat this morphological identity as a case of surface syncretism in the clitic paradigm rather than deep neutralization of the two cases in Kashmiri. The syncretism of accusative and ergative results in a shared marking of agentive subjects and nonperfective direct objects with the ERG/ACC pronominal clitics. The dative clitics in Table 2 also perform a range of functions which

---

[6]Grierson (1916) notes that the second person ergative marker may show some variation between the forms -th and -y; however, more recent grammars of Kashmiri cite the second person clitic as exclusively taking the form -th (Wali and Koul 1997:250; Bhatt 1999:48).

are not exclusive to a particular grammatical function; their functions include indirect objects, experiencer subjects, and direct objects in person hierarchy reversal contexts. Finally, both Table 1 and Table 2 exhibit a number of additional instances of morphological identity between various case markers, aside from the clitic ERG/ACC phenomenon; the analysis in this paper does not attempt to provide an account for this intricate morphology of both systems.

Wali and Koul (1997:250) do not include accusative marking in their discussion of the verb clitic paradigm; they only refer to the fact that "nonperfective nominative objects" share the pronominal clitic forms which are otherwise used for ergative subjects.[7] However, since these "nominative" objects (*-m/-th/-n*) do not share the nominative clitic forms (*-s/-kh/-φ*) with nominative subjects, I choose to follow Grierson (1916) here in classifying them as a morphologically different set from nominative subject clitics. As we will see, the nominative case clitics can be linked to direct objects in certain contexts (perfective clauses); hence, retaining the accusative category helps to distinguish those regular nominative objects from the accusative-marked objects and also from the exceptional dative marking of direct objects. This range of object marking alternations is discussed in detail shortly.

The unusual ERG/ACC grouping of agentive subjects and nonperfective objects within a single paradigm of clitic forms will ultimately follow naturally from the general analysis for Kashmiri presented in Section 6.5. Aside from this difference in the clitic paradigm, NPs and clitics in Kashmiri are matched in terms of case when they cooccur. Most importantly, the person-sensitive dative alternation in object marking, discussed in the next section, affects NPs and pronouns in the same way as it affects case clitic selection (Wali and Koul 1994:971).

6.2.1 Person Effects in Case Marking

In the present tense, the default case pattern in Kashmiri is nominative-accusative, as seen in the example in (4).

(4) a. bɨ   chu-s-ath   tsɨ   parina:va:n
      I-NOM be-1.SG.NOM-2.SG.ACC you-SG.ACC teach-PRES.PPL
      'I am teaching you.'

---

[7]Bhatt (1999:35) cites the sharing of the ERG/ACC enclitic forms as an unresolved problem. In Wali and Koul (1994), this set of clitics is referred to as the E-clitic, appearing with perfective transitive subjects and nonperfective objects. I use ERG and ACC to distinguish these two uses, but their terminology could be equally applied to the present discussion. I do not, however, adopt their feature decomposition analysis, in which both perfective subjects and nonperfective objects bear the features [–absolutive, –oblique]. The present paper aims to account for a wider set of related phenomena—person hierarchy effects, case selection and perfectivity—under a unified analysis.

b. tsɨ   chu-h-an   su
   you-NOM be-2.SG.NOM-3.SG.ACC him-SG.ACC
   parɨna:va:n
   teach-PRES.PPL
   'You are teaching him.'

However, this pattern only holds for clauses in which the person of the subject outranks that of the object. Assuming a basic person hierarchy of 1ST PERSON > 2ND PERSON > 3RD PERSON (Silverstein 1976; Aissen 2000:677), if the person rank of the object in a clause is equal to or higher than that of the subject, the object must be marked with dative case instead of accusative. The sentences in (5), when contrasted with (4), demonstrate this alternation. In (4), the rank of subject person is higher relative to that of the object, and the nominative-accusative pattern is maintained. In (5), by contrast, the person rank of the subject is either lower than or equal to that of the object, and a nominative-dative case pattern is required.

(5) a. tsɨ   chu-h-am   parɨna:va:n
        you-NOM be-2.SG.NOM-1.SG.DAT teach-PRES.PPL
        'You are teaching me.'   **(S2–O1)**

    b. su   chu-ϕ-s/*-an   parɨna:va:n
        he-NOM be-3.SG.NOM-3.SG.DAT/*ACC teach-PRES.PPL
        'He is teaching him.'   **(S3–O3)**

                                   [Wali and Koul (1994:977)]

This phenomenon of dative object marking in cases of person hierarchy reversal or leveling is not limited to verbal clitics, and is maintained both in pronoun choice and NP marking, as shown in (6).

(6) a. su   chu-ϕ   təmis   parɨna:va:n
        he-NOM be-3.SG.NOM him-DAT teach-PRES.PPL
        'He is teaching him.'

    b. su   chu-ϕ   Aslam-as   parɨna:va:n
        he-NOM be-3.SG.NOM Aslam-DAT teach-PRES.PPL
        'He is teaching Aslam.'

This distribution of direct object case marking is summarized in the following set of conditionals:

(7) In present tense,
      if OBJ person < SUBJ person, then OBJ case = ACC.
      if OBJ person ≥ SUBJ person, then OBJ case = DAT.

6.2.2 Perfectivity

The second system which is relevant to this phenomenon is an independent split in aspect marking. When a clause in Kashmiri is perfective, the subject must be marked ergative.[8] In nonperfective clauses the subject is nominative, as was seen in the preceding examples. The statement in (7) in fact holds true for all nominative subject clauses, and can thus be reinterpreted as a more general statement about nonperfective clauses, rather than simply present tense contexts.[9] The example in (8) shows ergative subject marking in a perfective sentence.

(8) tse   vichi-th-ϕ (sɔ)
      you-ERG see.f.sg-2.SG.ERG-3.SG.NOM her-SG.NOM
      'You saw her.'   (S2–O3)

In perfective clauses the person hierarchy distinction summarized in (7) no longer holds true, and the ergative-nominative pattern is maintained regardless of the person ranking of the subject and object relative to one another. Thus, in (9) we find that the ergative-nominative pattern is maintained in spite of the lower person rank of subject with respect to object.

(9) tse   vichi-th-as   bɨ
      you-ERG see.f.sg-2.SG.ERG-1.SG.NOM me-F.SG.NOM
      'You saw me.'   (S2–O1)

The data thus present a specialized case of differential object marking (Aissen 2001). Although the differential marking Aissen addresses is primarily a privative opposition of overt and zero marking, the principles of relative prominence and markedness which underlie the choice of default (ACC) and exceptional (DAT) object marking in Kashmiri are comparable. The alternation in this case shows sensitivity along two dimensions: the person hierarchy and perfectivity.

In the next section, I develop an account of the first of the two split systems introduced above—person hierarchy effects in nonperfective clauses—using universal constraint subhierarchies and local conjunction to account for the cooccurrence restrictions. In the subsequent two sections, I provide a similar treatment of case selection and of perfective subject marking. These three sets of subhierarchies are then brought together in a ranking that derives the distinct patterns of clitic-marking found in Kashmiri.

6.3 Preliminary Analysis of Person Hierarchy Constraints

Person-based markedness splits can be manifested in various parts of the grammar, as has been observed in the case, direction, and voice systems of

---

[8] As in most South Asian languages, ergative marking in the perfective in Kashmiri is generally limited to transitive subjects and a restricted subclass of intransitives (Sayeed 1985:10; Blake 1994:129; Mohanan 1994; Bhatt 1999:206). This is presumably related to agentivity (but see Wierzbicka (1981:75) for a discussion of the role of topicality in ergative-accusative patterns). I will not discuss transitivity explicitly; I assume that the constraints in (27) cover the agentivity restriction by virtue of Su/Ag alignment.

[9] As definitions and uses of the term 'imperfective' vary with respect to restrictiveness and defining features, I use 'nonperfective' throughout this paper; the intended category is simply the absence of perfectivity, terminativity, or boundedness.

Dyirbal, Nocte, and Lummi respectively (Aissen 2000). A wide typological range of object marking splits is also surveyed in Aissen (2001), with respect to several prominence scales. Her survey includes differential marking which occurs at different points on these scales; for example, overt marking of definite objects (Hebrew), specific objects (Turkish), personal pronoun objects (Catalan), and animate objects (Dhargari). Since the Kashmiri phenomenon presented here derives from the person markedness of both clausal arguments, it lends itself well to her approach but simultaneously poses certain interesting challenges. One challenge is to account for the relative or contextual markedness of person, and the other is to account for the interaction of this relative person markedness with perfectivity and ultimately with case markedness.

In her discussion of such systems, Aissen proposes eliminating language-particular hierarchies in favor of language-particular rankings of universal constraints. The constraints themselves draw on the alignment of various universal hierarchies. The use of harmonic alignment here is based on the notion developed in phonology for such phenomena as the correlation between the sonority hierarchy and syllable position (Prince and Smolensky 1993:136). Essentially, this operation takes a binary structural scale (e.g., syllable position or grammatical function) and aligns each member of a second scale (e.g., sonority or animacy) with the first. Since such constraint alignments are derived from universal scales, they cannot be mutually reranked within one constraint subhierarchy. An equally important feature, as will become clear in this analysis, is that they can be interleaved with constraints from other hierarchies.

Of the various universal scales presented in Aissen (2000), the person hierarchy effects in Kashmiri make reference to the relational (grammatical function) scale and the person scale. These are shown in the first column in Table 10. The data presented in the preceding section indicate that subjects and objects show reverse patterns for the relative markedness of their person rank. This is an instance of the widely attested phenomenon of markedness reversal, in which precisely those contexts which are marked for objects are unmarked for subjects (Battistella 1990; Croft 1990). This reversal has been developed in terms of harmonic alignment by aligning the highest member of the binary scale directly with the second scale (right to left), and the lower member inversely (left to right) with the second scale (Prince and Smolensky 1993; Aissen 2001. See also Asudeh 2001; Donohue 1999; Lee 2001; and Morimoto 1999 for various implementations of this operation in syntax).

Thus, the markedness of person for the grammatical functions of subject and object is derived from a direct and an inverse alignment with the person scale, respectively. The resulting harmonic alignments are given in the second column in (10). These state, for instance, that it is more harmonic for a subject to be associated with first person than it is for it to be third person.[10] Finally, the universal subhierarchies of actual constraints are shown in the third column. These are derived by prefixing the "Avoid" operator to each alignment and stating the ranking in terms of decreasing markedness.

(10)

SCALE	HARMONIC ALIGNMENT	CONSTRAINT ALIGNMENT
Su>Oj	$Su/1 \supset Su/2 \supset Su/3$	$*Su/3 \gg *Su/2 \gg *Su/1$
1>2>3	$Oj/3 \supset Oj/2 \supset Oj/1$	$*Oj/1 \gg *Oj/2 \gg *Oj/3$

These two constraint alignments are evident in the split systems of various languages. Some examples of the markedness of the highest constraints in these alignments are cited in Aissen's discussion of person-based splits. Dyirbal marks first and second person objects and third person subjects. In Nocte, the same three contexts require inverse verb marking. Finally, in Lummi, first and second person patients and third person agents require passive voice. Kashmiri is an interesting addition to these phenomena in that it requires marking specifically in situations where more than one such marked combination of person and relation occurs. For this reason, the constraint alignments in (10) do not yet account for the pattern found in Kashmiri nonperfective clauses. They only make reference to absolute markedness distinctions within the grammar and not to relative markedness with regard to the person of the cooccurring argument within a given input. In order to represent the intuition that, for instance, a second person object is marked when it cooccurs with a third person subject but not when it cooccurs with a first person subject, it is necessary to extend the constraint alignments to local conjunctions. Smolensky's (1995:4) formulation of local conjunction is as follows:

(11) The local conjunction of C_1 and C_2 in domain D, C_1 & C_2, is violated when there is some domain of type D in which both C_1 and C_2 are violated.

This captures the intuition that "two constraint violations are worse when they occur in the same location" (Smolensky 1995). Aissen (2000:698) further extends local conjunctions to subhierarchies, as in (12).

(12) The local conjunction of C_1 with subhierarchy $[C_2 \gg C_3 \gg ... \gg C_n]$ yields the subhierarchy $[C_1$ & $C_2 \gg C_1$ & $C_3 \gg ... \gg C_1$ & $C_n]$.

Given the Kashmiri generalizations in (7) and the related constraints in (10), we must assume that C_1 may itself be a subhierarchy as well. A set

---

[10]I have expanded Aissen's (2000:673) category of 'local' person into its composite 1st and 2nd person here—as in the original Silverstein (1976) hierarchy—because the split in case marking respects the distinction between the two, i.e. 1st person is considered higher ranked than 2nd person. However, in many languages the distinction within local persons is neutralized; the more general representation of the person scale may be thought of as Local > 3rd (see Aissen 2000:882).

of conjoined subhierarchies can be derived from the pairwise conjunction of the members of the two constraint alignments in (10). This set represents a universal set of decreasingly marked subject-object person combinations. Their ranking is still universal, as it derives indirectly from the scales in (10). The set of possible (symmetric) conjunctions is given below (see Aissen (2000:710); Donohue (1999); O'Connor (1999) for additional cross-linguistic applications of such aligned conjunctions for contextually sensitive subject and object marking).

(13)

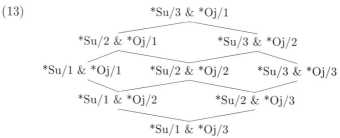

These conjunctions are derived from the pairwise combination of each member of one alignment with each member of the other. Thus, the highest constraint in the first hierarchy (*Su/3) is conjoined with the highest constraint in the second hierarchy (*Oj/1), then with the next highest, and so on. The mutual ranking of these nine pairs results in a partial ordering of constraints. The partially ordered list in (14) is the actual order in which the constraints in (13) emerge when the two constraint subhierarchies are systematically conjoined.

(14)   *Su/3 & *Oj/1 ≫
        {*Su/2 & *Oj/1, *Su/3 & *Oj/2} ≫
        {*Su/1 & *Oj/1, *Su/2 & *Oj/2, *Su/3 & *Oj/3} ≫
        {*Su/1 & *Oj/2, *Su/2 & *Oj/3} ≫
        *Su/1 & *Oj/3 ≫

The mutually unordered members can be thought of as a set of members that are equally distant from the most (or the least) marked conjunction in the whole ordering.

Recall that these conjoined constraints represent configurations that, if realized, must be marked in some way. In other words, we do not want to rule them out entirely; rather, they should be permitted as long as they are morphologically marked. In order to express these combinations as marked rather than prohibited, the constraint $*\phi_c$ is appended to all the constraints in (14).

(15) $*\phi_c$ Avoid absence of morphological case (Aissen 2000:699)

This constraint essentially requires overt case and functions as a sort of MAX constraint, requiring expression of an input feature in the output; it competes with the economy-driven *STRUC (Avoid structure) type of constraints. Conjunction with $*\phi_c$ requires some morphological case marking in the context in question. If $*\phi_c$ is appended solely to a subject constraint, as in the perfectivity constraints discussed later, then a violation can only be avoided by subject marking. Keeping in mind from (11) that these conjunctions must be specific to a particular domain, for instance the nominal or clausal domains, there are in fact several possible alternatives for deriving locally conjoined constraints on relative person markedness in Kashmiri. Since the aligned constraints in (10) in a sense involve clausal subjecthood and objecthood, I will assume that all instances of conjunction ("&") are specified for the clausal domain. Even with this assumption, there are several ways of interpreting local conjunctions of these constraints. I briefly consider three of the main options, in (16), before concluding the discussion of person-markedness constraints.

(16) a. $[*Su/3 \ \& \ [*Oj/1 \ \& \ *\phi_c]]$
      If the conjunction of constraint alignments with $*\phi_c$ is treated as in (16a), the resulting constraint is essentially an object oriented constraint that requires object marking in the presence of certain types of subjects.

   b. $[*Su/3 \ \& \ *\phi_c] \ \& \ [*Oj/1 \ \& \ *\phi_c]$
      The constraint in (b) is balanced in terms of conjunction with $*\phi_c$, but requires that when a given type of subject and object cooccur, both must be marked. This does not reflect the data in question, which represents a strict system of marking either one or the other but not both.[11]

   c. $[\ [*Su/3 \ \& \ *Oj/1] \ \& \ *\phi_c]$
      Finally, the constraint in (c) simply states that when a clause involves a given combination of subject and object, some morphological case marking is required. In other words, it requires that something be marked, but not necessarily everything.

I adopt (c) here as it is the most flexible of the three and can allow either subject or object marking to resolve a particular situation.[12] The

---

[11] There is a small class of 'exceptional transitive' verbs which mark the animate object with dative rather than nominative/absolutive (Wali and Koul 1997:252).

[12] Options (a) and (c) are both possible representations for the data in question, as both can be avoided by object-marking. Option (a) is an object-oriented constraint and would imply that subject marking in perfectivity is unrelated to object marking in person effects, while option (c) can relate the two since perfective subject marking can avoid a violation of this constraint as well. Due to the absence of simultaneous case marking of subjects and objects in Kashmiri, it is difficult to distinguish between the two options.

conjunction of $*\phi_c$ with the set of relative person constraints in (14) derives the local conjunctions shown in (17). The specific bracketing in (16c) is assumed in these constraints, and is omitted for ease of presentation. (17) is identical to (14), except that $*\phi_c$ marks each constraint.

(17)   *Su/3 & *Oj/1 & $*\phi_c$ ≫
        {*Su/2 & *Oj/1 & $*\phi_c$, *Su/3 & *Oj/2 & $*\phi_c$ } ≫
        {*Su/1 & *Oj/1 & $*\phi_c$, *Su/2 & *Oj/2 & $*\phi_c$, *Su/3 & *Oj/3 & $*\phi_c$ } ≫
        {*Su/1 & *Oj/2 & $*\phi_c$, *Su/2 & *Oj/3 & $*\phi_c$ } ≫
        *Su/1 & *Oj/3 & $*\phi_c$ ≫

However, recall from the generalizations in (7) that the requirement to mark certain person combinations only applies to situations in which the person of the subject is lower than or equal to that of the object. A graphic representation of this split is given in (18). This table represents subject/object combinations such that the first number in a pair represents the person value of the subject and the second that of the object. The shaded areas are the marked subject-object configurations which require dative case in nonperfective contexts. These boxes correspond to the first three (higher ranked) rows of marked pairs in (17).[13]

(18)

3/1	3/2	3/3
2/1	2/2	2/3
1/1	1/2	1/3

#/#	= *subject person/object person*
▨	= *dative case marking on objects*
▯	= *accusative case marking on objects*

According to this split, the first six constraints in (17) require special marking while the remaining three do not. In order to ensure this restriction, a general markedness constraint is required to prohibit special marking of the lower person constraints but allow it for the higher ones. The constraint *STRUC penalizes linguistic structure in general (Prince and Smolensky 1993:25). In the interpretation here, as in Aissen (2000), it specifically penalizes case marking. This interpretation may be thought

---

Disambiguating evidence would have to come from a dialect in which, hypothetically, the effect of subject marking on the need for object marking could be directly observed. Adopting (c) allows an integration of the two markedness systems and can explain the absence of dative objects in perfective contexts. Thus, in the absence of further evidence I adopt (c) because it integrates disparate systems in the grammar. The possibility that (a) is a more accurate representation is, however, not ruled out.

[13] I would like to thank Cathryn Donohue for helpful suggestions on describing differential case marking patterns of this nature (see her discussion of the interaction of case-marking and animacy in Fore (Donohue 1999)).

of as *STRUC$_c$—subscripted for case, just as *ϕ_c is a specific instantiation of a more general set of constraints. Constraints ranked above *STRUC may violate it in order to satisfy a higher case requirement. The remaining constraints, which rank lower than *STRUC, remain unmarked as case-marking would violate *STRUC.

(19) *STRUC   Avoid (case specification) structure

The following set of local conjunctions corresponds to the shaded boxes and ranks above *STRUC:

(20) *Su/3 & *Oj/1 & *ϕ_c ≫
      {*Su/2 & *Oj/1 & *ϕ_c , *Su/3 & *Oj/2 & *ϕ_c } ≫
      {*Su/1 & *Oj/1 & *ϕ_c , *Su/2 & *Oj/2 & *ϕ_c , *Su/3 & *Oj/3 &
      *ϕ_c } ≫

This group of constraints will be abbreviated as *SU ≤ OJ for clarity of exposition.[14] The rest will be referred to as *SU > OJ. Thus, the following simple ranking of universal constraints has been derived so far for Kashmiri:

(21) *SU ≤ OJ   ≫   *STRUC   ≫ *SU > OJ

This ranking captures the range of data discussed in this section. The constraints grouped as *SU ≤ OJ are ranked above the constraint *STRUC and therefore require special marking in clauses where subject person is equal to or less than that of the object. The remaining constraints, grouped as *SU > OJ, are ranked below *STRUC and so minimal case-marking is preferable to exceptional marking for those clauses.

6.4   Case Selection

The ranking in (21) isolates the marked combinations but fails to indicate *what* case must appear on *which* of the arguments in order to avoid violating the markedness constraints. To begin addressing these two aspects of the problem, we can first identify three general sets of pronominal case clitics evident in Kashmiri:[15]

(22)   Unmarked: NOM OBJ, NOM SUBJ
              Marked: ACC OBJ
      Contextually marked: DAT OBJ, ERG SUBJ

The problematic distinction to derive is that between accusative marking of objects in general and dative marking of objects which outrank or

---

[14]I follow the convention of capitalization for constraint names, starting with these abbreviated constraints and for all the constraints that follow.

[15]A complication arises when dealing with clitic paradigms rather than nominal case-markers, since the "unmarked" nominative forms do in fact have a morphological realization (see Table 1). The constraint *ϕ_c does not sufficiently distinguish between nominative and other case clitics, since it assumes a null realization for nominative (except marked nominative) in case paradigms. Thus although nominative is treated here as absence of "morphological" case, it points to a need for a careful representation of the interaction of case features and morphology with constraints of the *ϕ_c type.

equal their subjects in person rank (SU ≤ OJ). The fundamental issue is that the constraint conjunctions as they have been stated so far are unable to predict the *form* of case marking that will satisfy the constraint. However, it is clear that accusative object clitics do not satisfy the constraint *SU ≤ OJ; only dative does. What is primarily required to account for the use of marked discriminate case forms is a fully-articulated representation of the alignment of grammatical functions with the case hierarchy. This would independently ensure markedness restrictions on the use of certain cases (cf. Artstein (1998:18) for a discussion of some typological intricacies of case distribution that call for a more refined approach to case in OT). I provide a preliminary approach to this issue here and return to a discussion of additional aspects of the problem in section 6.7.

6.4.1 Core and Noncore Case

For the present analysis, I appeal to the notion of coreness of case and grammatical function in order to account for some of the observed case selection patterns.[16] Wierzbicka (1981) draws on the notion of coreness in regard to the association of cases with meanings. In her discussion of case marking, cases and grammatical functions do not have a one-to-one correspondence:

> Roughly speaking, a case is a set of forms which are mutually substitutable in certain syntactic environments, a subset of which can be used only in those particular syntactic environments. Each such case has a basic (core) meaning which allows us to identify particular cases cross-linguistically (1981:54).

Comrie (1978:35) similarly states that "the function of case systems is often not so much to provide a one-to-one encoding between morphological and syntactic or semantic categories, but rather to enable one to discriminate between different syntactic and semantic categories, especially where these are most likely to be confused".[17] Kashmiri provides a clear instance of contexts where case/GF association may vary systematically, since dative, which is most commonly associated with the indirect object, may also mark the direct object or the subject in marked circumstances. The mechanisms of soft (violable) constraints and universally ranked subhierarchies lend themselves to the alignment of core and noncore case with grammatical functions, deriving increasingly marked combinations that may be exploited in the language under unusual or marked circumstances.

---

[16] I am grateful to Peter Sells for suggesting core/noncore case alignments as a possible domain within which the given case selection patterns might be accounted for.

[17] As quoted in Wierzbicka (1981:52).

(23) a.

SCALE	HARMONIC ALIGNMENT	CONSTRAINT ALIGNMENT
c-arg > nc-arg	c-arg/c-case ⊃ c-arg/nc-case	*C-ARG/NC-CASE ≫ *C-ARG/C-CASE
c-case > nc-case	nc-arg/nc-case ⊃ nc-arg/c-case	*NC-ARG/C-CASE ≫ *NC-ARG/NC-CASE

b. *Core arguments* = Subj, DirObj
Core case = Nom, Acc
Noncore arguments = IndirObj, Obl
Noncore case = Erg, Dat, ...

The alignment of coreness of argument with coreness of case in (23a), along with the corresponding classification of case and argument coreness in (23b), represents one of many possible approaches to case markedness. This is merely the most general classification that captures the distribution of case marking found in the data here; however, it may equally be thought of as a set of groupings of more refined alignments. Thus, core and noncore are used here as useful generalizations. The main function of these constraints is to restrict the use of certain case forms except when needed to avoid a high-ranked markedness violation.

The specific distinction between core and noncore arguments can be drawn within a framework such as Lexical Mapping Theory (LMT; Bresnan and Kanerva 1989). In LMT, an a(rgument)-structure consists of a predicator and a syntactic feature classification of its thematically ordered argument roles. The cross-classification of the syntactic features [±r(estricted)] and [±o(blique)] with grammatical functions captures syntactic differences amongst arguments. On this view, the grammatical functions denoted in (23b) as "core" correspond to thematically unrestricted [–r] functions as opposed to secondary objects and obliques, which are [+r].

Furthermore, the cross-linguistic association of core arguments with structural or core case assumed here is relatively uncontroversial and has been modeled in various frameworks (Chomsky 1981; Blake 1994; King 1995; Bittner and Hale 1996; Woolford 1997).[18] The classification of ergative is somewhat more controversial. A few analyses classify ergative as a core case (Blake 1994; Bittner and Hale 1996), while others identify it with inherent or lexical cases (Mohanan 1994; Woolford 1997).[19] Given

---

[18]In Blake (1994:119), for example, core cases encode S (sole argument of intransitive), A (agent of transitive) and P (patient of transitive) relations, while semantic cases like allative, locative, and instrumental encode peripheral functions. Thus, the S/A/P view of core grammatical case corresponds to the direct functions of "Subj" and "DirObj" in (23b).

[19]Bittner and Hale (1996) analyze ergative as a direct structural case. Although they mention split ergative systems briefly, it is unclear how their analysis of 'raising' ergative (syntactic, e.g. Inuit) and 'transparent' ergative (morphological, e.g. Warlpiri) types

the generalization in (22), ergative subjects appear in the specific context of perfectivity while nominative subjects in a sense represent the default. Thus, for the phenomenon in question, it seems necessary to classify ergative as applying to specific semantic contexts rather than strictly as a default structural case. This is not an unusual assumption; numerous approaches to case theory have either proposed a distinction between ergative and nominative, or else pointed out the affinity between dative and ergative. Mohanan (1994:77) employs the two binary characteristics of semantic/non-semantic and direct/indirect case to address case patterns in Hindi. In her view, ergative and dative share the feature of being semantic in nature.[20] Woolford (1997:184) discusses a similar distinction based on structural and inherent case, whereby ergative and dative may both be viewed as lexical or inherent, unlike nominative and accusative which are treated as structural. Furthermore, in Woolford (2001), inherent cases are treated as more marked than structural cases and the universal hierarchy of *ERGATIVE,*DATIVE ≫ *ACCUSATIVE ≫ *NOMINATIVE is suggested. The proposal here draws on similar notions of case-markedness; in this analysis, however, the markedness of cases only emerges when they are aligned systematically with grammatical functions. In other words, the constraints in (23) follow Woolford's generalizations but do not assume an absolute markedness of case; rather they derive a contextually sensitive hierarchy of case markedness.

---

would apply to these data. Like most Indo-Aryan languages which include ergative in their case systems, Kashmiri behaves like a morphologically ergative language. However, 'transparent' type languages in Bittner and Hale's approach are predicted to show pronominal agreement with the subject, regardless of case, rather than with the nominative argument, which is the agreement pattern predicted for 'raising' ergative languages (1996:25). The data presented in section 6.2 show clearly that the Kashmiri verb template includes both obligatory agreement with the nominative argument as well as additional pronominal suffixes correlating with subject, irrespective of its case. Related languages such as Hindi, which is also morphologically (not syntactically) ergative, follow a strictly nominative agreement pattern, which Bittner and Hale predict as being a consequence of 'raising'/syntactic ergativity. Thus, their description of the structural interaction of pronominal agreement and ergativity cannot be straightforwardly extended to these languages. The interest in the present paper is to integrate the competing influences of perfectivity, subject/object marking, and person-sensitivity in Kashmiri – a combination of factors which does not lend itself easily to a purely structural model such as Bittner and Hale's. In accounting for the complementary distribution of ERG and ACC in Kashmiri, the ACC/DAT alternation, as well as the perfective split in ERG, the analysis presented here furthermore accounts for the typologically more marked position of ergative over accusative, due to the universal markedness of subject case-marking. This is not a natural prediction of an approach which equates accusative and ergative as direct cases, as Bittner and Hale's proposal does.

[20] See also Butt and King (1999) for a detailed discussion of syntactic and semantic reflexes of different categories of case. Ergative is classified as a type of hybrid, semantically conditioned structural case.

The use of core and noncore here is therefore a simplification of far more intricate case/GF relations. The main purpose of these generalizations here is limited to the following:

(24) a. *C-ARG/NC-CASE is violated by DAT direct objects and ERG subjects.

     b. *C-ARG/C-CASE, a universally less-marked alignment, is violated by ACC objects and NOM subjects/objects.

6.4.2 Markedness of Noncore Case

This distinction now allows a refinement of the constraint set *SU $\leq$ OJ & $^*\phi_c$ introduced in section 6.4. As it stands, this constraint permits any case to satisfy the requirement to express case. However, as the data have already shown, only ergative subjects and dative objects appear to avoid a violation of the constraint. Accusative objects, being the default, do not. If we replace $^*\phi_c$ with $^*\phi_{nc}$, the constraint can be reinterpreted as requiring a marked, noncore case form in the given context. This refinement treats $^*\phi_c$ as a family of constraints such that $^*\phi_c$ is the generalized form and $^*\phi_{nc}$ is a more specific subconstraint.

The constraints derived so far begin to cover some of the basic observations regarding Kashmiri person effects. They can account for the markedness of relative person rank between subjects and objects as well as certain aspects of case selection. However, they still fail to predict two crucial aspects of the phenomenon:

(25) a. Why are objects, not subjects, marked when person violations occur in nonperfective situations?

     b. Why are person hierarchy effects absent in perfective sentences?

These two issues are addressed in the next section, after which the set of constraints proposed in sections 6.3–6.5 are joined in a single constraint ranking for Kashmiri and implemented with a range of candidate sets.

6.5 Perfectivity and Ergative Marking

The use of the term perfective in this discussion can be summarized as the denotation of "a single event with a well-defined result or end-state, located in the past" (Dahl 1985:78).[21] Characterizations of perfectivity in the typological literature vary in the degree to which they identify perfectivity as the marked member of the perfective/imperfective opposition. This is partly due to the fact that such studies attempt to accommodate the complex interaction of perfectivity marking with that of other tenses

---

[21] Perfectivity in past time reference in the context of ergative splits is distinct from some uses of the term Perfect. Although both are associated with a completive aspect, perfective represents an action as a whole — sometimes considered a type of Aktionsart — while Perfect indicates relational anteriority and relevance to the present moment, as in the English Perfect (Binnick 1991:161; Bybee et al. 1994:55).

and aspects in a given grammatical system as well as the range of types of expression of perfectivity. However, certain marked characteristics of perfective aspect in relation to imperfective have been repeatedly observed at various points in the literature.

In the markedness patterns of grammatical categories identified by Greenberg, imperfective is considered cross-linguistically less marked than perfective. This is judged on the basis of the relative allocation of functions, such that the imperfective is used for a more heterogeneous and default-like group of functions (Greenberg 1966:49; Croft 1990:93).

Jakobson (1957:6) and Forsythe (1970:347) also address the issue of whether the perfectivity opposition is equipollent, i.e. members are equally marked, or privative, i.e. one member is positively marked and the other represents absence of that member. Both conclude, based on similar criteria to Greenberg's, that perfective is cross-linguistically the more restricted in terms of possible meaning denotation. Comrie (1976:113) suggests further that semantics rather than morphological material may be the most telling of whether one member of an aspectual opposition is unmarked ("more usual, more normal, less specific than the other"). He argues that imperfective generally has a less specific interpretation than perfective, and thus a more default-like distribution. For instance, Slavic perfective forms always convey a specific perfective meaning while imperfectives may or may not have a specifically imperfective meaning. The criterion of extra morphological material might reflect a slightly more equipollent opposition, as verbal morphology cross-linguistically may mark either the perfective or the imperfective.[22] However, at a general level, explicit morphological marking of perfectivity appears to correlate with a positive semantic characterization of perfective, which contrasts with the unmarked, negatively characterized, and underspecified imperfective (see also Battistella 1990:97; Binnick 1991:153; Verkuyl 1993:282).

In keeping with these typological generalizations, aspect-sensitive morphological (case) marking distinctions in South Asian languages appear to favour special marking of perfective clauses rather than imperfective. In the absence of a more detailed depiction of possible universal correlations amongst tense and aspect, I tentatively adopt Nonperf > Perf as a universal scale in (26b), as a basis for the various semantic and morphological markedness tendencies found in perfectivity-based splits, particularly in ergative languages.

(26)   a. Subject > Object
       b. Nonperf > Perf

Returning to the binary structural scale of Su > Oj, we can align the two scales in (26) in a manner similar to that presented in (10), namely

---

[22]Note, however, that when imperfectives are overtly marked, they often convey further aspect distinctions within durativity or habitualness (Bhat 1999; Dahl 1985:72).

that Subject aligns directly with the perfectivity scale and Object aligns inversely to reflect the markedness reversal. This markedness is reflected in perfective-split languages—South Asian and others—which treat the agentive subject as the locus of marking; this markedness pattern has been described in several studies and supports the subhierarchies derived in (27). Masica (1991) suggests that the prevalence of perfective splits in ergative marking is not accidental. He follows the prior work of Hopper and Thompson (1980) and Givón (1984) in suggesting that such splits reflect a universal tendency towards "greater transitivity and more complete affectedness of the patient in perfective predications" (1991:343). De-Lancey (1981) relates the marking of subjects with ergative in perfective sentences to viewpoint. Specifically, he suggests that "the aspectual [split ergative] pattern associates... viewpoint-marking morphology (i.e. nominative/absolutive case and verb agreement) with agent in imperfective aspect, and with patient in perfective" (1981:646). The corollary of these unmarked associations is that perfective agents and nonperfective patients will be marked. This is precisely the complementary distribution of the ERG/ACC case marker we find in Kashmiri.[23]

For clarity of exposition in the present discussion, I only refer to the alignment of perfectivity with grammatical function. (26a) could in fact refer to thematic roles, not grammatical relations, because ergative marking in perfectivity split systems is generally limited to agentive (or A type) subjects, i.e. Su/Ag. A more accurate representation would probably isolate the thematically least marked subject, namely an agentive subject, as being further aligned with perfectivity.[24] I am assuming, therefore, that the alignments in (27) involve agentive subjects in particular, accounting for the restriction of ergative marking to transitives and a subclass of volitional intransitives (referred to by Wali and Koul as "exceptional intransitives").

The table in (27) is similar to those in (10) and (23) but in this case it aligns the relational scale with the perfectivity scale. The resulting harmonic alignments are shown in the second column, and the markedness constraints are shown in the third.

---

[23]Miriam Butt (p.c.) points out that interpreting the relative markedness of agent and patient in perfective clauses on semantic grounds is not entirely straightforward; for example, precisely because of the affectedness of the patient, object alternations in some languages occur only in perfective contexts. The assumptions here are broadly based on morphological and typological markedness observations in the literature; admittedly, many of the finer semantic intricacies of perfectivity effects cannot be adequately accommodated under the present analysis.

[24]Wali and Koul (1994:976) do provide instances of ergative marking in Kashmiri on subjects which are not animate, specific, or definite in order to argue against ergative as a shared marker for any of these features. I do not address their feature decomposition analysis of ergative here; however, I assume that an adequately detailed account of thematic roles with which ergative marking can occur in various South Asian languages could in fact offer a unified account for its occurrence.

(27)

SCALE	HARMONIC ALIGNMENT	CONSTRAINT ALIGNMENT
Subject > Object	Su/Nonperf ⊃ Su/Perf	*SU/PERF ≫ *SU/NONPERF
Nonperf > Perf	Oj/Perf ⊃ Oj/Nonperf	*OJ/NONPERF ≫ *OJ/PERF

As they stand, the constraints in the third column would simply incur a (potentially fatal) violation if perfective subjects appear at all. Since perfective does occur in Kashmiri, these constraints must be further conjoined with $*\phi_c$, as was done with the person constraints, in order to merely require some manifestation of morphological marking in the given situations. The universal markedness constraint subhierarchy for subjects and aspect emerges as in (28):

(28) *SU/PERF & $*\phi_c$ ≫ *SU/NONPERF & $*\phi_c$

The corresponding object subhierarchy treats nonperfective objects as more marked than perfective objects, as shown in (29). This is essentially an OT representation of DeLancey's (1981) association of unmarked viewpoint with the agent in nonperfective sentences.

(29) *OJ/NONPERF & $*\phi_c$ ≫ *OJ/PERF & $*\phi_c$

The most important generalization to be made regarding these alignments is that, if the two higher constraints in the subhierarchies in (28) and (29) are ranked above *STRUC, perfective subjects must be marked and nonperfective objects must be marked.[25]

(30) *SU/PERF & $*\phi_c$, *OJ/NONPERF & $*\phi_c$ ≫
     *STRUC ≫
     *SU/NONPERF & $*\phi_c$, *OJ/PERF & $*\phi_c$

The unusual pattern of employing a single set of clitics to mark perfective ('ergative') subjects and nonperfective ('accusative') objects, presented in section 6.2, appears to be more natural under this representation of constraints on marking arguments. Based on this ranking, case-marking of both arguments will be ruled out by unnecessary violations of *STRUC. I examine some of the typological predictions of this proposal in section 6.7.

Returning to the discussion of person hierarchy violations, we can now reconsider the problem posed in (25a): why are objects, not subjects, marked when person violations occur in nonperfective situations? The second constraint in (30) requires object marking in nonperfective clauses. If the subject were to be marked for a relative person hierarchy violation, the object

---

[25]Recall that the definition I assume here of $*\phi_c$ is that a violation may be avoided by marking any of the arguments identified in the constraint. Thus, subject-specific constraints may only be avoided by subject marking.

would still have to be marked to satisfy *OJ/NONPERF & *ϕ_c . However, using a more marked case form on the object can satisfy this constraint (just as accusative would have) while simultaneously signaling a person hierarchy violation. This accounts for the problem stated in (25a), namely which clitic gets marked when a person hierarchy violation occurs. This will become evident in the implementation in the next section.

The second issue, raised in (25b), is why person hierarchy effects are absent with perfectives. As described earlier, V–ERG–NOM marking is consistent across all person combinations in perfective clauses. Ergative, as a noncore case, satisfies *SU ≤ OJ & *ϕ_{nc} just as dative on nonperfective objects does. These clauses already mark one of the arguments of the verb with a disambiguating noncore case and therefore do not require additional object marking. In a sense, as will be seen below, *SU/PERF & *ϕ_c and *STRUC prevent the evaluation of certain candidates from even 'reaching' the constraints which penalize person hierarchy violations. This resembles an OT incarnation of a bleeding rule, whereby satisfying the requirement of one context removes the conditions which would have made a candidate eligible for restrictions in another context. In sum, the discussion so far has developed a constraint ranking that simultaneously ensures the following:

(a) Subject markedness in perfective (*SU/PERF & *ϕ_c outranks *STRUC);
(b) Object markedness in person asymmetries (*OJ/NONPERF & *ϕ_c and *SU ≤ OJ & *ϕ_{nc} outrank *STRUC);
(c) the absence of (b)-type effects in perfective.

6.6   Implementing Two Split Systems in a Single Grammar

We are now in a position to combine the rankings derived in (21), (23), and (30) for a full picture of the interaction of two split systems in Kashmiri. The full array is presented in (31) and discussed below.[26]

(31) *SU/PERF, *SU ≤ OJ, *OJ/NONPERF ≫
        *STRUC ≫ *C-ARG/NC-CASE ≫
        *SU/NONPERF, *SU > OJ, *OJ/PERF

The three different constraint subhierarchies – person markedness, perfective markedness, and case markedness – are interleaved here such that the more marked set of constraints from the first two subhierarchies are ranked above *STRUC. The constraint *C-ARG/NC-CASE from the third subhierarchy is included in order to show that the use of dative object marking and ergative subject marking is restricted. I assume the lower ranked case alignments from (23) such as *C-ARG/C-CASE and exclude them from the tableaux. The three mutually unranked constraints at the end of the ranking in (31) are included to indicate that the lower constraints in the person and perfectivity hierarchies are below *STRUC and therefore do not require

---

[26] As previously, *ϕ_c is omitted from many of these constraints for clarity of exposition.

morphological marking when those contexts are realized. In fact, the three higher constraints are also mutually unranked; their crucial ranking being with respect to *STRUC and *C-ARG/NC-CASE, not to each other.

The fundamental idea in (31) is that both the perfectivity system and the relative person markedness system are split across *STRUC, and the former essentially supersedes the latter. In (32)–(35), I provide four examples of different inputs. A subset of all possible candidates is evaluated according to the constraint ranking in (31) for each input. The four types of clausal inputs given as examples are: nonperfective with an unmarked 1–2 person combination; nonperfective with a marked 2–1 person combination; perfective with an unmarked 1–2 person combination; and perfective with a marked 2–1 person combination. The five candidates, (a)–(e), in each example carry various combinations of case marking in order to demonstrate the differential evaluation of a single candidate depending on the input.

(32) INPUT: V(nonperf)-S1-O2

	*SU/PERF	*SU ≤ OJ	*OJ/NONPERF	*STRUC	*C-ARG/NC-CASE	*SU > OJ	*OJ/PERF	*SU/NONPERF
a.			*!			*		*
☞ b.				*		*		*
c.			*!	*	*			
d.				*	*!			*
e.				* *!	*			

a. = V-1.nom-2.nom
b. = V-1.nom-2.**acc**
c. = V-1.**erg**-2.nom
d. = V-1.nom-2.**dat**
e. = V-1.**erg**-2.**acc**

In (32), the winning candidate (b) satisfies all the constraints until the morphological case marker incurs one violation of *STRUC. Candidate (a) in nonperfective sentences is a strong contender, but it is ruled out by *OJ/NONPERF, which requires object-marking with nonperfectives. Candidate (c) fails to mark the object as well, and candidate (d) employs a highly marked object case unnecessarily. Finally, the candidate in (e), with two case-marked clitics, is ruled out by an extra violation of *STRUC in perfective sentences. Note that the dative on the direct object in (d) violates *C-ARG/NC-CASE but, as the next example shows, this violation is acceptable when the (marked) dative is required to satisfy a higher constraint.

(33) INPUT: V(nonperf)-S2-O1

	*SU/PERF	*SU ≤ OJ	*OJ/NONPERF	*STRUC	*C-ARG/NC-CASE	*SU > OJ	*OJ/PERF	*SU/NONPERF
a.		* !	*					*
b.		* !		*				*
c.			*!	*	*			
☞ d.				*	*			*
e.				* *!	*			

a. = V-1.nom-2.nom
b. = V-1.nom-2.**acc**
c. = V-1.**erg**-2.nom
d. = V-1.nom-2.**dat**
e. = V-1.**erg**-2.**acc**

The crucial difference between the inputs in (33) and (32) is that the person of the object outranks the person of the subject. Candidates (a), (c) and (e) are ruled out for the same reasons as in (32). However, even though (d) incurs a *C-ARG/NC-CASE violation, this is preferable to violating *SU ≤ OJ. Note that the violation in (b) is incurred because the constraint *SU ≤ OJ requires the expression of noncore case, and accusative is a core case.

(34) INPUT: V(perf)-S1-O2

	*SU/PERF	*SU ≤ OJ	*OJ/NONPERF	*STRUC	*C-ARG/NC-CASE	*SU > OJ	*OJ/PERF	*SU/NONPERF
a.	* !					*	*	
b.	* !			*		*		
☞ c.				*	*		*	
d.	* !			*	*			
e.				* *!	*			

a. − V-1.nom-2.nom
b. = V-1.nom-2.**acc**
c. = V-1.**erg**-2.nom
d. = V-1.nom-2.**dat**
e. = V-1.**erg**-2.**acc**

Examples (34) and (35) involve perfective inputs. As the data showed earlier, both inputs select candidate (c) as optimal, in which the subject is marked ergative and the object is nominative, regardless of the relative person rank between the two. In (34) and (35), candidate (a) violates the high-ranking *SU/PERF constraint, even though it no longer violates *OJ/NONPERF as it did in the previous two examples. Candidates (b) and (d), which were the winners in (32) and (33), are now ruled out due to the unmarked case of their subjects. Contrasting (34) and (35) with (33), we can see that in perfective clauses, all candidates with unmarked subjects are ruled out by a highly ranked constraint, and the person hierarchy constraints play no role in candidate selection. Note that candidate (e) is a strong contender as it includes both the preferred markings for subject and object; however, object-marking is only called for in nonperfective clauses and (e) is therefore excluded by an extra *STRUC violation. To summarize, although the input in (35) includes a higher person object, the noncore case of the subject already satisfies *SU ≤ OJ. Thus, the evaluations in (35) are identical to those in (34) and the same candidate emerges as the winner.

(35)   INPUT: V(perf)-S2-O1

	*SU/PERF	*SU ≤ OJ	*OJ/NONPERF	*STRUC	*C-ARG/NC-CASE	*SU > OJ	*OJ/PERF	*SU/NONPERF
a.	*!	*					*	
b.	*!	*		*				
☞ c.				*	*		*	
d.	*!			*	*			
e.				* *!	*			

a. = V-1.nom-2.nom
b. = V-1.nom-2.**acc**
c. = V-1.**erg**-2.nom
d. = V-1.nom-2.**dat**
e. = V-1.**erg**-2.**acc**

As this analysis draws on a distinction between core and noncore case, it makes an additional prediction regarding dative subjects. Ergative subjects have been treated here as representing a C-ARG/NC-CASE alignment, which can satisfy the noncore marking requirement of *SU ≤ OJ. This explanation simultaneously accounts for the requirement for dative, not accusative, higher person objects when the subject is nominative. As dative is treated as a noncore case, its occurrence with indirect objects is canonical, given that the alignment NC-ARG/NC-CASE is low ranked. However, its occurrence with subjects is equivalent to ergative subject marking, namely it is a C-ARG/NC-CASE alignment and thus should also avoid a violation of *SU ≤ OJ without requiring further marking of the direct object. This prediction appears to be borne out in the data, as can be seen in the example in (36b), which does not show the nonperfective dative object marking despite the person rank reversal.

(36) a. me   cha-kh   tsɨ   pasand
         I-DAT be.f.sg-2.SG.NOM you-NOM like
         'I like you.'

     b. tse   chu-s-ay   bɨ   pasand
         you-DAT be-1.SG.NOM-2.SG.DAT me-NOM like
         'You like me.'

[Wali and Koul (1997:249)]

It must be noted, however, that these dative subject constructions exhibit some interesting additional characteristics, namely obligatory nominative object marking and reversal of clitic ordering. The requirement for the theme arguments of 'non-volitional transitives' such as *like* to be nominative even when animate is found in other Indo-Aryan languages, such as Hindi (cf. Lee 2001), and might be explained under partly independent constraints. However, Marathi in fact shows subject/object alternations for the same class of verbs, as argued convincingly in Joshi (1993) and Asudeh (2001). Given the exceptional clitic reordering requirement for precisely these sentences in Kashmiri, I only tentatively follow prior descriptions of such constructions in Kashmiri as involving dative subjects, in which case they do appear to satisfy *SU ≤ OJ, as predicted. An alternative analysis would treat the nominative argument as the subject and the dative as an exceptional object (Wali and Koul 1997:252), in which case person hierarchy effects would not play a role at all.

6.7 Further issues

The analysis that has been presented here raises some further theoretical issues regarding the cross-linguistic typology of case marking. In this section, I first discuss the typological range predicted by the constraints proposed above, and then consider some implications of the data for the issue of morphological and abstract case in OT syntax.

6.7.1 Typological Predictions

One of the main strengths of the Optimality Theoretic framework lies in its typological foundations, such that all constraints and specifically universal subhierarchies must be supported cross-linguistically. Furthermore, the hierarchical asymmetry of universal constraint subhierarchies restricts the range of systems predicted to be possible. Since the current analysis addresses disparate parts of the grammatical system of Kashmiri, the typological predictions in this section are presented according to the three distinct sets of constraint subhierarchies.

Person Hierarchy

Of the three sets of constraints presented in this paper, the alignment of the person hierarchy with grammatical relations is one which has been previously proposed and examined in some depth. The subhierarchies derived in Aissen (2000:699) are given in (37).

(37) a. *Su/3 & *ϕ_c ≫ *Su/local & *ϕ_c
   b. *Oj/local & *ϕ_c ≫ *Oj/3 & *ϕ_c

As mentioned earlier, data from a wide range of languages appear to support these subhierarchies in their markedness distinctions. In addition, the apparent absence of systems which exclusively mark third person objects or local subjects morphologically, which is a negative prediction of the universal constraint orderings in (37), further supports these subhierarchies. The conjoined subhierarchies that were presented in (17) make more specific claims.

(38) *Su/3 & *Oj/1 & *ϕ_c ≫ ... ≫ *Su/1 & *Oj/3 & *ϕ_c

This set of constraints, repeated in (38), predicts that if certain subject-object person combinations are assigned discriminate marking, the marked combinations will be a subset which must include the uppermost constraints. It precludes marking the object exclusively when its person rank is lower than that of the subject, or conversely marking only higher-person subjects. Although this is a fairly specialized set of predictions, the subhierarchy as it stands is in fact attested in a number of Tibeto-Burman languages discussed by DeLancey (1981:642), including Nocte, Jyarong, and Kham. In Jyarong, for instance, the inverse marker on the verb occurs only when the person rank of the object is higher than that of the subject. The fact that inverse marking, rather than case-marking, avoids a violation of the conjoined constraints in (38) raises the larger question of how broadly *ϕ_c might be interpreted; all the same, the typological asymmetry of relative person markedness is borne out in such phenomena, the inverse of which seems to be unattested.

Case Markedness

As mentioned in section 6.4, the case marking subhierarchy which was derived based on coreness could be reinterpreted as a more refined set of alignments, contingent on whether the notion of coreness and noncoreness is capable of extending to all case/GF associations.

(39) a. *C-ARG/NC-CASE ≫ *C-ARG/C-CASE
   b. *NC-ARG/C-CASE ≫ *NC-ARG/NC-CASE

These constraints predict that core cases are associated with core argument functions, and that languages will not assign noncore cases to core arguments except when a higher constraint calls for discriminate case marking. This brings us to the extension of $*\phi_c$ to $*\phi_{nc}$. This addition aimed at achieving the association of general markedness constraints, in this case relative person hierarchy markedness constraints such as *Su/3 & *Oj/1, with appropriate case forms. In other words, the new subconstraint restricts the actual cases that can satisfy markedness constraints. This is a provisional refinement of the more general case contrast between presence and absence of case allowed by $*\phi_c$, and is necessitated by case alternations such as ACC/DAT in Kashmiri, which cannot be captured by $*\phi_c$ alone.

Perfectivity

Finally, the two subhierarchies that were derived for perfectivity are repeated from (28) and (29) in (40) below.[27]

(40) a. $*\text{SU}/\text{PERF}$ & $*\phi_c \gg *\text{SU}/\text{NONPERF}$ & $*\phi_c$
  b. $*\text{OJ}/\text{NONPERF}$ & $*\phi_c \gg *\text{OJ}/\text{PERF}$ & $*\phi_c$

The ranking for Kashmiri ruled out simultaneous marking by interleaving *STRUC between these two rankings. However, a considerable range of variation occurs across Indo-Aryan languages with regard to the perfective split, many of which can be accounted for with these constraints. Some examples include: Bengali, which has lost ergative marking on perfective subjects; Nepali and Assamese, which optionally extend agentive subject marking beyond the perfective; and Hindi and Gujarati, which permit simultaneous marking of subjects and objects in perfective clauses (Mitra and Nigam 1971; Wallace 1982). Changes in object-marking in these languages have been generally governed by definiteness, specificity or animacy constraints. However, the perfective subject-marking changes in related South Asian languages listed above reflect some of the typological range predicted by (40a). This fluidity of ranking with respect to *STRUC is shown in (41).

(41) $\longleftarrow$ *STRUC (Bengali)
      $*\text{SU}/\text{PERF}$ & $*\phi_c$
                                  $\longleftarrow$ *STRUC (Kashmiri, Hindi)
      $*\text{SU}/\text{NONPERF}$ & $*\phi_c$
                                  $\longleftarrow$ *STRUC (Nepali, Assamese)

In addition, typological gaps in this variation seem to match those rankings predicted to be impossible by (40). The only negative prediction of

---

[27]One concern with the formulation in (40) is whether these constraints are ever evident independent of $*\phi_c$. In other words, do languages actually avoid perfective subjects and nonperfective objects altogether? This reflects a more general tension between the explicit marking of a context ($*\phi_c$) and avoidance of it altogether (absence of $*\phi_c$) and seems to be a typological consideration for any conjunction with $*\phi_c$.

(40) is that no language will exclusively mark nonperfective subjects, but not perfective subjects, and vice versa for objects. Despite the range of historical developments across the Indo-Aryan language group, no attested language appears to have moved in such a direction. Another interesting example comes from Finnish direct objects, which show a partitive/accusative alternation based on perfectivity or boundedness. In this case, although perfective objects are marked, nonperfective objects are as well and the contrast occurs within overt marking of both. In other words, both constraints in (40b) outrank *STRUC. Furthermore, it is interesting to note that the partitive case on nonperfective objects—which satisfies *OJ/NONPERF & *ϕ_c (higher ranked in (40b))—is described as a hybrid case with both structural and semantic patterning (Kiparsky 1998:265). This parallels the hybrid characterization of ergative in Indo-Aryan languages, which in turn applies to *SU/PERF & *ϕ_c (also higher ranked in (40a)). In these two examples, one might argue that 'noncore' cases satisfy both the higher ranked constraints, while structural, 'core' cases apply to the lower ranked subject and object constraints for each language.

6.7.2 Morphological Paradigms and *ϕ_c

I have shown for the Kashmiri data here that *SU $\leq$ OJ & *ϕ_{nc} can only be satisfied by the presence of certain case forms, namely ergative and dative. This case markedness generalization can be summarized as follows: NOM-ACC is the normal unmarked pattern for a transitive. Marked deviations—in which noncore case appears on core arguments—occur in the form of ERG on subjects and DAT on objects. These cases violate the constraint *C-ARG/NC-CASE in order to satisfy a higher markedness constraint. The treatment here has been to integrate the notion of core and noncore case with the constraint *ϕ_c such that markedness constraints may require a range of marked case forms. This is one possible approach; however, the data does point to the need for some such systematic treatment of how case forms are selected in order to satisfy markedness constraints. Various cross-linguistic phenomena indicate this general principle, by which the relative markedness of certain cases with respect to certain grammatical functions can be exploited for either disambiguation or contextual marking.

A related issue that arises out of this discussion is that "morphological case" in the original formulation of *ϕ_c can straightforwardly distinguish between presence and absence of nominal case markers but does not distinguish between nominative clitics that do have a morphological realization, and other case clitics. The distinction between abstract case features and case forms becomes more complex in this situation. The interpretation of *ϕ_c at this point is crucial, as it may need to be interpreted either as a family of more specific constraints, as has been done here, or else as a constraint that in fact stipulates "Avoid absence of morphological case". In terms of the interpretation of clitic forms, using *ϕ_c without modification in order to distinguish amongst case features rather than a more general presence or absence of case remains somewhat problematic.[28]

Finally, a full description of the morphological paradigms in Kashmiri and their interaction with clitic ordering and null arguments has not been provided here. Various details in this analysis suggest, however, that a systematic treatment of the disambiguation of grammatical relations by information provided by other parts of the grammar—in particular the morphology—would complement and possibly share the functional load of the constraints on markedness presented here. For instance, the surface syncretism of ERG and ACC combined with the ϕ form for 3rd person initially seems as though it could lead to the following ambiguity: when only the ERG/ACC form is affixed to the verb, its interpretation could either be V-ERG-(ϕ)NOM or V-(ϕ)NOM-ACC, since the (3P)NOM subject or object is null and ERG and ACC clitics have the same form. However, given the person hierarchy effect, this potential ambiguity is eliminated because the latter form cannot occur. A third person subject always results in dative-marked objects since the object person will always be equal to or higher than that of the subject. Consequently, the apparently idiosyncratic lexical gap in the clitic paradigm for nominative 3rd person pronouns in fact reflects a case of subtle morphological parsimony. Similarly, the detailed restrictions on pro-drop and overt expression of clitics (mentioned in footnote 2) ultimately limit the range of possible interpretations and may therefore have led to the development of certain syncretisms. In this way, the particular characteristics of the morphological system conspire with general, universal markedness constraints presented here to discriminate argument specification as economically as possible.

6.8 Conclusion

The phenomenon examined here poses a challenge insofar as it represents an interaction at the level of case marking of two otherwise relatively distinct aspects of the grammatical system of Kashmiri. The Optimality Theoretic constraint ranking proposed for Kashmiri incorporates constraints on marked person combinations and on perfectivity markedness with general structural restrictions on morphological complexity. The ranking of one split system (perfectivity) relatively higher than the other split system (person hierarchy combinations) with intervening structural constraints results in subject marking to signal one effect and object marking to signal the other. The constraints which address these markedness situations are derived directly from universal subhierarchies and represent a gradient scale of markedness along which different languages may locate a split at different points, if at all. In the Kashmiri scenario here, each system is split at

---

[28]This issue of abstract vs. morphological case with regard to $*\phi_c$ also arises for null ergative marking in Punjabi and Marathi (cf. Deo and Sharma (2000)).

a certain point and the general economy condition *STRUC intervenes at that point ruling out the need to mark lower ranked violations at all.

Consequently, this analysis not only integrates disparate aspects of the grammatical system in order to derive the observed case marking restrictions, it also indicates how other languages may share certain aspects of this particular phenomenon, due to the universality of the subhierarchies involved, while not exhibiting other aspects, in particular, the specific interaction of the subhierarchies. In summary, the fact that the apparently unrelated phenomena of person and perfectivity affect case marking in a linked manner in Kashmiri—insofar as one can prevent the application of the other—can be accounted for directly through the language-specific interaction of locally conjoined constraints with general structural principles and case markedness in the grammar.

References

Aissen, Judith. 2000. Differential Object Marking: Iconocity vs. Economy. MS., University of California, Santa Cruz.

Aissen, Judith. 2001. Markedness and Subject Choice in Optimality Theory. In *Optimality-Theoretic Syntax*, eds. Géraldine Legendre, Jane Grimshaw, and Sten Vikner. Cambridge, Massachusetts: The MIT Press, 61–96.

Artstein, Ron. 1998. Hierarchies. Online, Rutgers Optimality Archive: http://www.eden.rutgers.edu/~artstein.

Asudeh, Ash. 2001. Linking, Optionality, and Ambiguity in Marathi. This volume.

Battistella, Edwin L. 1990. *Markedness: The Evaluative Superstructure of Language*. Albany, New York: State University of New York Press.

Bhat, D. N. S. 1999. *The Prominence of Tense, Aspect, and Mood*. Studies in Language Comparison Series. Amsterdam: John Benjamins Publishing.

Bhatt, Rakesh. 1999. *Verb Movement and the Syntax of Kashmiri*. Dordrecht: Kluwer Academic Publishers.

Binnick, Robert I. 1991. *Time and the Verb*. Oxford: Oxford University Press.

Bittner, Maria and Ken Hale. 1996. The Structural Determination of Case and Agreement. *Linguistic Inquiry* 27(1):531–604.

Blake, Barry. 1994. *Case*. Cambridge: Cambridge University Press.

Bresnan, Joan and Jonni Kanerva. 1989. Locative Inversion in Chicheŵa: A Case Study of Factorization in Grammar. *Linguistic Inquiry* 20:1–50.

Butt, Miriam and Tracy King. 1999. The Status of Case. MS., Universität Konstanz and Xerox PARC, Palo Alto.

Bybee, Joan, Revere Perkins, and William Pagliuca. 1994. *The Evolution of Grammar: Tense, Aspect, and Modality in the Languages of the World*. Chicago, Illinois: University of Chicago Press.

Chomsky, Noam. 1981. *Lectures on Government and Binding*. Dordrecht: Foris.

Comrie, Bernard. 1976. *Aspect*. Cambridge: Cambridge University Press.

Comrie, Bernard. 1978. Genitive-accusative in Slavic: the rules and their motivation. *IRSL* 3:27–43.

Croft, William. 1990. *Typology and Universals*. Cambridge: Cambridge University Press.

Dahl, Östen. 1985. *Tense and Aspect Systems*. Cambridge: Blackwell Press.

DeLancey, Scott. 1981. An Interpretation of Split Ergativity and Related Patterns. *Language* 57(3):626–658.

Deo, Ashwini and Devyani Sharma. 2000. Typological Variation in Ergative Marking and Verb Agreement. In *Proceedings of WECOL 2000*. Fresno, California.

Donohue, Cathryn. 1999. Optimizing Fore Case and Word Order. MS., Stanford University. Online: http://www-csli.stanford.edu/~donohue.

Forsythe, J. 1970. *A Grammar of Aspect: Usage and Meaning in the Russian Verb*. Cambridge: Cambridge University Press.

Givón, Talmy. 1984. *Syntax: A Functional-Typological Introduction*, volume 1. Amsterdam: Benjamins Publishing Co.

Greenberg, Joseph. 1966. *Language Universals*. The Hague: Mouton & Co.

Grierson, George A. 1916. *A Dictionary of the Kashmiri Language*, volume 1. New Delhi: B. R. Publishing Co.

Hopper, Paul and Sandra A. Thompson. 1980. Transitivity in Grammar and Discourse. *Language* 56:251–299.

Jakobson, Roman. 1957. Shifters, Verbal Categories, and the Russian Verb. Harvard University, Dept. of Slavic Languages and Literature. Russian Language Project.

Joshi, Smita. 1993. *Selection of Grammatical and Logical Functions in Marathi*. Ph.D. thesis, Stanford University.

King, Tracy Holloway. 1995. *Configuring Topic and Focus in Russian*. Stanford, California: CSLI Publications.

Kiparsky, Paul. 1998. Partitive Case and Aspect. In *The Projection of Arguments: Lexical and Compositional Factors*, eds. Miriam Butt and Wilhelm Geuder. Stanford, California: CSLI Publications.

Lee, Hanjung. 2001. Markedness and Word Order Freezing. This volume.

Masica, Colin P. 1991. *The Indo-Aryan Languages*. Cambridge Language Surveys. Cambridge: Cambridge University Press.

Mitra, Asok and Ramesh Chandra Nigam. 1971. Grammatical Sketches of Indian Languages with Comparative Vocabulary and Texts. Language Monographs (1961 Series), No. 2. Census of India Publication.

Mohanan, Tara. 1994. *Argument Structure in Hindi*. Stanford, California: CSLI Publications.

Morimoto, Yukiko. 1999. An Optimality Account of Argument Reversal. In *Proceedings of the LFG99 Conference*, eds. Miriam Butt and Tracy Holloway King. Stanford, California: CSLI Publications Online: http://csli-publications.stanford.edu/.

O'Connor, Catherine M. 1999. Harmonic Alignment of the Animacy Hierarchy and the Structure of Possession DPs in Northern Pomo. Talk handout from the Lexical Functional Grammar Conference 1999 (LFG99), University of Manchester.

Prince, Alan and Paul Smolensky. 1993. Optimality Theory: Constraint Interaction in Generative Grammar. Technical Report RuCCS Technical Report #2,

Center for Cognitive Science, Rutgers University, Piscataway, New Jersey. To be published by the MIT Press.

Sayeed, S. M. 1985. Morphological Causatives and the Problems of the Transformational Approach. Indiana University Linguistics Club. Bloomington, Indiana.

Silverstein, Michael. 1976. Hierarchy of Features and Ergativity. In *Grammatical Categories in Australian Languages*, ed. R. M. W. Dixon. New Jersey: Humanities Press, Inc., 112–172.

Smolensky, Paul. 1995. On the Internal Structure of the Constraint Component Con of UG. ROA-86-0000. Rutgers Optimality Archive. http://ruccs.rutgers.edu/roa.html.

Verkuyl, Henk. 1993. *A Theory of Aspectuality*. Cambridge: Cambridge University Press.

Wali, Kashi and Omkar N. Koul. 1994. Kashmiri Clitics: The Role of Case and CASE. *Linguistics* 32:969–994.

Wali, Kashi and Omkar N. Koul. 1997. *Kashmiri*. New York, New York: Routledge.

Wallace, William D. 1982. The evolution of ergative syntax in Nepali. *Studies in the Linguistic Sciences* 12(2):147–209. University of Illinois, Urbana.

Wierzbicka, Anna. 1981. Case Marking and Human Nature. *Australian Journal of Linguistics* 1:43–80.

Woolford, Ellen. 1997. Four-Way Case Systems: Ergative, Nominative, Objective and Accusative. *Natural Language and Linguistic Theory* 3:441–483.

Woolford, Ellen. 2001. Case Patterns. In *Optimality-Theoretic Syntax*, eds. Géraldine Legendre, Jane Grimshaw, and Sten Vikner. Cambridge, Massachusetts: The MIT Press, 509–543.

7

Linking, Optionality, and Ambiguity in Marathi

Ash Asudeh

7.1 Introduction

Optimality theory[1] (OT; Prince and Smolensky 1993) has in a short time proven influential in theoretical phonology, and to a lesser degree in theoretical syntax. One of the main attractions of the theory is its strong commitment to typology. The basic hypothesis is that there is a set of universal constraints and languages differ only in how they rank the constraints. Since constraints are violable,[2] this will result in the same input having a different optimal expression in different languages. The fact that constraint reranking is the *only* difference between languages is a very important assumption in OT and is necessary for its explanatory scope (Smolensky, 1996b; Bresnan, 2000a), its learnability proofs (Tesar and Smolensky, 1998), and most importantly for typology. Once we assume "richness of the base"—as this assumption is often referred to—a natural typology arises. If there are n constraints in a strict ordering then there are $n!$ different ways of ranking them. Since languages differ only in these rankings, it follows then that we predict $n!$ languages. This is called "factorial typology".

[1] This work was supported in part by SSHRC Doctoral Fellowship 752-98-0424 and was completed as a Research Fellow at UCSC, where I was kindly sponsored by Jim McCloskey. I am also very grateful to the following people for discussion, comments, and suggestions: Farrell Ackerman, Judith Aissen, Arto Anttila, David Beaver, Joan Bresnan, Miriam Butt, Ashwini Deo, Alan Gous, Frank Keller, Paul Kiparsky, Chris Manning, Line Hove Mikkelsen, John Moore, Peter Sells, the participants in the Stanford OT Working Group, and the joint Stanford/UCSC Optimality Theory Syntax class. I would like to particularly thank Ida Toivonen, who has influenced my thoughts on OT and optionality through many long discussions. I accept sole responsibility for any remaining errors.

[2] It would be more precise to say that a form can be grammatical and still violate constraints.

Formal and Empirical Issues in Optimality Theoretic Syntax.
Peter Sells (ed.).
Copyright © 2001, CSLI Publications.

Factorial typology is an important, automatic consequence of optimality-theoretic grammars. It is this property that truly sets OT grammars apart from ones in other generative frameworks. However, expressing something easily in a framework often comes at the cost of complicating the formalization of certain other facts. Frameworks in which constraints are inviolable can deal with ambiguity and optionality fairly well. If there are multiple ways of satisfying constraints, then there is optionality (in production) or ambiguity (in comprehension). Similarly, these frameworks have no significant problems with ineffability. This latter term refers to the fact that certain inputs to a grammar have no expression. In frameworks with inviolable constraints, these inputs simply violate one or more constraints and are therefore rejected by the grammar. However, it is precisely the properties of ineffability, ambiguity, and optionality that standard Optimality Theory has trouble expressing.

In this paper, I take steps to accommodate ambiguity and optionality in OT syntax. In particular I examine optionality in linking arguments to grammatical functions in Marathi and give an OT-LFG account of the relevant facts. In doing so, I will illustrate four points. The first is that linking can be achieved with a small set of crosslinguistically plausible, violable constraints. Second, optionality can be captured in OT by modifying the architecture of the theory only slightly. Third, in comprehension directed optimization, the same OT constraints that are used to capture the linking optionality in production can also capture the resulting ambiguity in the Marathi strings that correspond to the winning candidates in production. Fourth, this OT approach to linking has interesting implications for Dowty's theory of proto-roles.

In section 7.2, I briefly present the basic architecture of standard Optimality Theory and how it relates to ineffability, ambiguity, and optionality. Then, in section 7.3, I discuss four possible ways of capturing optionality in OT.[3] In section 7.4, I present the facts about optionality in Marathi linking and review Joshi's (1993) LFG account of these facts. Then, in section 7.6, I present an Optimality Theory account that is considerably simpler in some respects, although it also uses LFG and thus benefits from its formal rigour and representational clarity. I go on to illustrate how the OT analysis deals with ambiguity in the comprehension direction. Lastly, I discuss some new insights into proto-role theory that result from this account.

---

[3]A fifth way, which has not been discussed much in the literature (for example, it is not mentioned in Müller's (1999) rather thorough overview of optionality in OT), is to use underspecification (in the candidates, not the input). I feel that candidate underspecification has severe foundational problems in OT (see Artstein 1998 for a general discussion, as well as Kuhn 2000 for a discussion specific to OT-LFG), but this is not the place to give these issues serious treatment, which they deserve. Therefore, I leave underspecification out of this discussion.

7.2 Ineffability, Ambiguity, and Optionality in OT

The basic architecture of Optimality Theory is as follows (Prince and Smolensky, 1993; Bresnan, 2000a):

(1) **Inputs** The inputs to the grammar are universal. For syntax, the inputs are usually assumed to be semantic forms of some kind (Smolensky, 1998).

   Gen A generator function from an input to a set of candidates which the grammar will evaluate.

   Eval An evaluation function from the set of candidates to a winning output. It consists of:

    1. A universal constraint set.

    2. A language particular ranking of these constraints.

    3. An algorithm for harmonic ordering: the optimal candidate (= the output for a given input) is the one that best satisfies the top ranked constraint on which it differs from its competitors. (Bresnan, 2000a; Smolensky, 1996a)

The last point is the most important one: OT grammars will pick *the most optimal candidate*. As Pesetsky (1997) puts it, an OT grammar only picks winners and it will always pick a winner. However, there are certain cases in which there should be no winners because the input is "ineffable" (i.e. it has no acceptable output). The inability of OT to deal with ineffability led many to initially reject it as a theory of syntax, but steps have been taken to address this problem. Smolensky (1998) presents an OT account of ineffability based on the notion of *production/comprehension chains*. This notion is based on the idea of dealing with production and comprehension using the same constraint ranking. Production takes a semantic input and gives a syntactic parse as an output, whereas comprehension takes the string corresponding to the syntactic parse (i.e. the "overt" part of the production output) and gives a semantic form as an output. The output of comprehension is the same type of form that is the input for production. We can thus talk about bidirectional optimization[4] using a production/comprehension chain:[5]

(2) a. $/I/-prod. \rightarrow [S]-overt\ part \rightarrow$ "O" $-comp. \rightarrow /I'/$

    b. If $/I'/ = /I/$, then $/I/$ is expressible; If $/I/$ is not expressible it is ineffable.

    (Smolensky, 1998)

Once we take this approach into account, although the production grammar still picks a winner, we can formally capture the idea that not all win-

---

[4]For extensive OT-LFG analyses using bidirectional optimization, see Lee (2001) and Donohue (1999).

[5]I is the semantic input; $[S]$ is the syntactic parse; "O" is the string; I' is the output of comprehension, but is also the same type of object as the input in production.

ners are expressible. Thus, bidirectional optimization addresses the charge that OT cannot deal with ineffability and removes a major obstacle in adopting it as a framework for syntax research.

This still does not address the fact that OT picks only one winner.[6] But, there are situations in which more than one candidate should be selected. This occurs when there is either optionality or ambiguity. The latter case is common in semantic comprehension; an example is provided by quantifier scope ambiguity such as in the following sentence, which has the interpretations in (3a) and (3b). An OT grammar that picks only one of (3a) or (3b) has failed to get the facts right.

(3)   Every student read a book.
    a. For every student x, there is a book y such that x read y.
       (wide scope universal)
    b. There is a book y such that for every student x, x read y.
       (narrow scope universal)

This problem is not particular to semantic comprehension. It also occurs in phonological comprehension. In some dialects of North American English, the following phonetic form is ambiguous between the two underlying phonological forms in (4a) and (4b). Again, a properly descriptive grammar should select both the (4a) and (4b) forms.

(4)   [ɹɑjɾəɹ]
    a. /ɹɑjdəɹ/ (= "rider")
    b. /ɹɑjtʰəɹ/ (= "writer")

In Optimality-Theoretic Syntax, ambiguity can be characterized as a situation in which the constraints should pick more than one semantic candidate as optimal (where the semantic candidates are the inputs to production and the outputs of comprehension; see footnote 5). Since optionality can be characterized as a situation in which an input has more than one optimal output candidate as well, it is just the flip side of ambiguity. That is, ambiguity occurs when there is more than one optimal candidate in the comprehension grammar and optionality occurs when there is more than one optimal candidate in the production grammar. Although the focus of this paper is optionality, the ideas presented here can be carried over to deal with ambiguity. In the next section, I present several ways to handle optionality and ambiguity in OT.

7.3   Four Approaches to Optionality

Müller (1999) presents a concise but thorough overview of optionality in OT. He classifies proprosals to deal with optionality into four types: *pseudo-optionality*, *neutralization*, *true optionality*, and *constraint ties*. I will opt

---

[6]There can, in principle, be candidate ties, in which case both candidates will win, but see section 7.3.3 for criticism of this approach.

for a variant of the last approach, but first I will discuss the other three approaches and the reasons for rejecting them.

7.3.1 Pseudo-Optionality

In the pseudo-optionality approach, each option is the winner of a separate optimization competition. Optionality as such does not exist. Müller points out that this predicts that the various options will *never* be in competition, which is too strong. Optionality often breaks down in certain contexts, but pseudo-optionality cannot get only one alternant in such cases, because the alternants are not in competition by hypothesis. Pseudo-optionality approaches will overgenerate in these cases.

One of Müller's (1999) examples will make things clearer. Consider English complementizer drop:

(5) a. I think that John is a fool.
     b. I think   John is a fool.

Leaving details aside, the pseudo-optionality approach would have each of these candidates be the winner for distinct inputs. But, the complementizer cannot always be dropped (Müller, 1999):

(6) a. It surprised me that the earth is round.
     b. *It surprised me   the earth is round.

On this approach, it is impossible to rule out (6b), as the candidate with the complementizer present and the one with the complementizer absent are each the winner of their competition. Therefore, it is not possible for (6a) to block (6b) and the grammar overgenerates.

7.3.2 Neutralization

The second proposal is neutralization. On this approach, the options also belong to different competitions, but in certain contexts a high-ranking constraint will result in the same surface string being selected in each candidate set. Thus, the difference between the two competitions is neutralized, as the candidate that wins in each has the same string yield. Müller reviews the neutralization approach to English complementizer drop given by Baković and Keer (Baković, 1997; Keer and Baković, 1997; Baković and Keer, 2001). I will consider the version presented in Baković and Keer (2001), as this is the most recent statement of this approach.

Baković and Keer make three key assumptions in their analysis. The first is that embedded CPs and IPs are distinguished by the feature COMP. A CP is marked [+ COMP] and an IP is marked [− COMP]. Second, they follow Doherty (1993) and Grimshaw (1997) in assuming that a complement clause is a CP if it has an overt complementizer and an IP if it does not. Third, they assume that an embedded clause in the input to GEN can be freely specified as [+ COMP] or as [− COMP].

The OT analysis they propose is quite simple and elegant. It involves only the two basic OT constraint types: faithfulness and markedness constraints. The faithfulness constraint is based on the feature [± COMP] (Baković and Keer, 2001, (6)).

(7) FAITH[COMP]: The output value of [COMP] is the same as the input value.

The markedness constraints fall into two basic categories. There are constraints that target CP (the MARK-CP family) and ones that target IP (the MARK-IP family).[7]

The analysis works as follows. If FAITH[COMP] outranks MARK-XP, where XP refers to either CP or IP, then the winner is the faithful candidate, as illustrated here:[8]

(8)   Complementizer optionality: FAITH[COMP] ≫ MARK-XP

a.

Input: [+ COMP]		FAITH [COMP]	MARK-CP	MARK-IP
a.	☞ ·CP		*	
b.	IP	*!		*

b.

Input: [− COMP]		FAITH [COMP]	MARK-CP	MARK-IP
a.	CP	*!	*	
b.	☞ IP			*

However, if either type of markedness constraint is ranked higher than the faithfulness constraint, we get neutralization. That is, no matter whether the input is marked [+ COMP] or [− COMP], the same candidate wins. If MARK-IP outranks FAITH[COMP], then the complementizer is obligatory.

(9)   Complementizer obligatoriness: MARK-IP ≫ FAITH[COMP]

a.

Input: [+ COMP]		MARK-IP	FAITH[COMP]
a.	☞ CP		
b.	IP	*!	*

b.

Input: [− COMP]		MARK-IP	FAITH[COMP]
a.	☞ CP		*
b.	IP	*!	

If MARK-CP outranks FAITH[COMP], then the complementizer is absent.

---

[7]In their papers, Baković and Keer spell out the actual constraints that fall into each family of constraints. The Mark-IP and Mark-CP constraints in Baković and Keer (2001) are essentially those used in the complementizer drop analysis of Grimshaw (1997).

[8]All tableaux in this section are adapted from Baković and Keer (2001).

(10)   Complementizer absence: MARK-CP ≫ FAITH[COMP]

a.

Input: [+ COMP]		MARK-CP	FAITH[COMP]
a.	CP	*!	
b. ☞	IP		*

b.

Input: [− COMP]		MARK-CP	FAITH[COMP]
a.	CP	*!	*
b. ☞	IP		

In this fashion, Baković and Keer get the right results for the cases they examine, lending some empirical bite to the neutralization approach.

But, there are various arguments against both the particular analysis that Baković and Keer present and the neutralization approach in general. I will start with considering the problems with this particular analysis. First, there is no independent motivation for the feature [± COMP] beyond its role in the analysis of complementizer drop. Second, this feature is purely a diacritic to indicate whether something is a CP or an IP. That is, CPs are [+ COMP] and IPs are [− COMP]. Therefore, the feature is completely unnecessary, since the category information encodes the required distinction. However, category information is not usually considered to be in the input for a syntactic OT competition. This brings us to the third objection: the input is standardly assumed to be a semantic form of some kind, whether it is a predicate logic argument structure (Grimshaw, 1997), or a partially specified LFG functional structure (Bresnan, 2000b). If this is the case, then the purely formal feature [± COMP] should not and could not occur in the input.

There are also problems with the neutralization approach in general (Müller, 1999). Fundamentally, this approach increases the complexity of inputs, candidate sets, and candidate competition. First, because inputs can differ only on some formal feature, there will be many minimally different inputs. As a direct consequence, there will be more candidate sets to consider. Second, the candidates are allowed to vary from their inputs indiscriminately (at least with respect to these formal features). So, the constraints on GEN must be much weaker than standardly assumed in OT syntax, allowing it to generate all kinds of candidates and "everything competes with everything else in each competition" (Müller, 1999, 7). Third, this approach fosters spurious ambiguities when inputs are neutralized. For one competition the faithful candidate is optimal, while in the other competition (which differs only for the value of the input feature in question), the unfaithful candidate wins. That is, when faced with a neutralized sentence, a language learner cannot determine what the specification of the formal feature is in the input. As neutralization is a common issue in phonology, Prince and Smolensky (1993, 192) propose the mechanism of 'Lexicon Optimization' as a solution for the learnability problem. In OT syntax this term is not appropriate, so Müller (1999, 8) coins the more general term 'Input Optimization'. Informally, the way this works is that the language learner selects the input for the most harmonic output as the correct input. But, as Müller points out, this introduces a notion of second-order optimization into the theory: Input Optimization is selecting the best competition in a set of competitions, where *each competition* is the result of an optimization over a candidate set. This is quite complex from both a computational and learnability perspective.

7.3.3 True Optionality

A third way to select multiple winners in OT is by postulating true optionality, where this means multiple candidates that have exactly the same constraint profile. This is the approach that Grimshaw (1997) uses to account for English complementizer drop. Basically, in the cases where the complementizer is optional, neither optimal candidate violates any of the constraints, or else both candidates violate exactly the same constraints the same number of times. Schematically, the competition looks like this:[9]

(11) IP and CP propositional complements

		C_1	C_2	C_3	C_4	C_5
a.	☞ think $[_{CP}$ that $[_{IP}$ she left $]]$					*
b.	☞ think $[_{IP}$ she left $]$					*

Both candidate (a) and candidate (b) are equally optimal by definition, as they have identical constraint profiles. Thus, there is no way for an OT grammar to pick between them.

This approach has the advantage that it introduces no extraneous mechanisms or features into the theory. But, there are two strong arguments against its adoption. First, it is very unlikely[10] that the two candidates will remain tied in a large OT grammar with many constraints. If *any*

---

[9] I gloss over Grimshaw's actual constraints, as the details of her analysis are not necessary for the arguments I give here. The tableau is based on Grimshaw (1997, 411) and Müller (1999, 4).

[10] In a previous version of this paper I presented an argument against true optionality based on simple probability theory. There are various problems with the argument (as pointed out to me by Chris Manning and Alan Gous), but it is still somewhat instructive. Given a constraint, Constraint$_1$, and two candidates, Candidate$_1$ and Candidate$_2$, there are two possible outcomes: either Candidate$_1$ and Candidate$_2$ are tied for Constraint$_1$ (both candidates have a no marks for this constraint or an identical number of marks), or there is no tie. In general, the probability of two candidates tying on n constraints is $p_{tie}(n) = \frac{1}{2^n}$. It is easy to tell that, even with a small number of constraints, the probability of a candidate tie (i.e. true optionality) is very low. For example, with just twenty constraints, the probability of a tie is $\frac{1}{1048576}$.

There are three problems with this argument, though. First, it requires an assumption of independence between constraints and this is obviously an idealization. In particular, since there will be conflicting faithfulness and markedness constraints in OT grammars, satisfaction of one constraint will often result in violation of another. A related problem

constraint, no matter how lowly ranked, is violated by one candidate but not the other, then the optionality will disappear. It would seem to be an insurmountably difficult task to fine-tune a grammar to the point that no constraint differentiates just the candidates required for optionality. Similarly, a language learner would have to receive no information at all throughout the entire course of acquisition that would differentiate these two candidates according to even just one constraint.

The second argument against this approach, presented in Baković and Keer (2001), is that true optionality makes strange typological predictions. If we assume that the inputs and candidates are universal[11] (Prince and Smolensky, 1993; Smolensky, 1996b) and that the only locus of typological variation is constraint ranking, then the true optionality approach predicts that whatever optionality there is in one language should exist in *all* languages. The reason is simple: if two candidates are not distinguished by their constraint profiles, then no matter how the constraints are ordered they will still be indistinguishable; since the only difference between languages is constraint ranking, by hypothesis, the two candidates will be equally optimal in all languages. Of course, in any given language other candidates could be more optimal than either of the two considered here. However, these two arguments make it clear that the true optionality approach is not a good solution, because it raises more problems than it solves.

7.3.4 Constraint Ties

The approaches considered so far assume a standard OT grammar whose constraint set forms a total order. The final approach to optionality I consider is that of allowing constraint ties,[12] which effectively relaxes the re-

---

is that not all of the constraints in a grammar will apply to all candidates. However, even if we subtract the number of constraints that in principle cannot apply to an input from the total number of constraints and remove markedness and faithfulness constraints that are in conflict for the input in question, we will still be left with a number sufficiently large to make a tie very improbable.

Second, the argument assumes that there is a uniform distribution over ties in the probability model. That is, it assumes that it's just as likely on any given constraint for two candidates to tie as it is for them not to (this is like assuming that the coin is fair when calculating probabilities for coin tosses). This is surely the default assumption, given no further data. But, it is the very lack of this further data that is the third and worst problem. There is no probability model here, as we have no way of replicating the experiment. Although we can calculate probabilities for the competition it is unclear how the probabilities model the real world. That is, the results of the experiment are purely theoretical, and it is difficult to see how they can be tested empirically.

[11]I am not necessarily advocating such assumptions here. Ultimately, I expect both assumptions to be untenable in a more mature version of the theory.

[12]This is also the most widely utilized approach to optionality. Relevant references include Anttila (1997a,b); Boersma (1997, 1998, 2000); Boersma and Hayes (2001); Pesetsky (1997, 1998); Prince and Smolensky (1993). See Müller (1999) for further references and discussion.

quirement of a total order by permitting equally ordered (or unordered) constraints (i.e. constraints that are "tied" for a position in the ordering).

Partial Orderings

One of the properties of a total order is that of connectedness: every constraint must be ranked relative to every other constraint (Anttila, 1997a). If we do not require this property, then we can characterize an OT grammar as a partial order. In this case some of the constraints will not be ranked relative to some others. A schematic view of a total ordering and a partial ordering of three constraints is given in (12):

(12)   Total Ordering   Partial Ordering

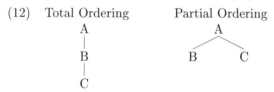

The total ordering states that $A \gg B \gg C$, whereas the partial ordering states that $A \gg B$ and that $A \gg C$. However, in the partial ordering there is no ordering between B and C. It is neither the case that $B \gg C$ nor that $C \gg B$.

Assuming n constraints that are partially ordered, $n!$ possible total orderings of just these constraints can be derived. In this case, we get the two total orderings $A \gg B \gg C$ and $A \gg C \gg B$. Insofar as the total orderings derived will constitute different constraint rankings, different candidates can be selected as optimal on different resulting total orders. Thus, partial orders offer a method for relaxing the total ordering on constraints and deriving some optionality in output.

There are two major problems with general partial orders. To understand the first problem, consider a partial order like the following:[13]

(13)   A
        ╱   ╲
      B   C
              ⋮
              Z

This partial ordering corresponds to twenty-five total orderings, which can be represented with these three schemas:

(14) a. $A \gg B \gg C \gg \ldots \gg Z$
      b. $A \gg C \gg \ldots \gg B \gg \ldots \gg Z$
      c. $A \gg C \gg \ldots \gg Z \gg B$

The problem is evident: since the total ordering from C to Z must be maintained, the various resolutions give radically differing importance to

---

[13]The elide between C and Z indicates a total ordering of twenty-four constraints, with C as the highest-ranking constraint.

the constraint B. The two extreme cases are provided by (14a) and (14c). In (14a), B is very highly ranked and can only be violated in order to satisfy A. However, in (14c), the same constraint B is ranked very low and will not play a significant role in selecting a candidate. This is a very serious conceptual problem with partial orders. Furthermore, it will make modelling optionality very difficult: if the partial ordering is between highly-ranked constraints in a large constraint set, the total orders will be radically different, most likely yielding no optionality after all. Thus, there is not only a conceptual problem, but we also encounter again the problem of constructing a grammar where other constraints do not interfere in the optionality, as is the case with the true optionality account.

The second problem with this approach is that there is no non-exponential learning algorithm for partially ordered OT grammars (Boersma and Hayes, 2001; Boersma, 2001; Kager, 1999). Neither Tesar and Smolensky's (1998) nor Boersma and Hayes's (1999) learning algorithm works for such grammars. In fact, the former learning algorithm only works for totally ordered OT grammars without ties (I return to this point in the following sections). As there are learning algorithms for the other approaches I review below, they are to be preferred to partially ordered grammars.

Stratified Partial Orderings

Anttila (1997a; 1997b) proposes a slightly modified version of partial ordering to handle optionality in Finnish genitive plurals.[14] His approach is essentially a hybrid of total and partial orderings: constraints fall into sets which are totally ordered with respect to each other; however, within the sets there can be partial ordering. I will not go into the details of Anttila's analysis, as it is quite rich and complex, but the three highest ranking sets he proposes are given here.[15]

(15)

Set 1	Set 2	Set 3
*X́.X́	*Ĺ	*H/I
	*H	*Í
		*L.L

This stratified partial ordering corresponds to the following twelve total orderings:

(16) 1. *X́.X́ ≫ *Ĺ ≫ *H ≫ *H/I ≫ *Í ≫ *L.L
      2. *X́.X́ ≫ *Ĺ ≫ *H ≫ *H/I ≫ *L.L ≫ *Í
      3. *X́.X́ ≫ *Ĺ ≫ *H ≫ *Í ≫ *H/I ≫ *L.L
      4. *X́.X́ ≫ *Ĺ ≫ *H ≫ *Í ≫ *L.L ≫ *H/I
      5. *X́.X́ ≫ *Ĺ ≫ *H ≫ *L.L ≫ *H/I ≫ *Í
      6. *X́.X́ ≫ *Ĺ ≫ *H ≫ *L.L ≫ *Í ≫ *H/I

---

[14]The term 'stratified partial ordering' comes from Boersma (2001).

[15]What the constraints mean is not relevant here. The curious reader is invited to consult Anttila's work.

7. $*\acute{X}.\acute{X} \gg *H \gg *\acute{L} \gg *H/I \gg *\acute{I} \gg *L.L$

8. $*\acute{X}.\acute{X} \gg *H \gg *\acute{L} \gg *H/I \gg *L.L \gg *\acute{I}$

9. $*\acute{X}.\acute{X} \gg *H \gg *\acute{L} \gg *\acute{I} \gg *H/I \gg *L.L$

10. $*\acute{X}.\acute{X} \gg *H \gg *\acute{L} \gg *\acute{I} \gg *L.L \gg *H/I$

11. $*\acute{X}.\acute{X} \gg *H \gg *\acute{L} \gg *L.L \gg *H/I \gg *\acute{I}$

12. $*\acute{X}.\acute{X} \gg *H \gg *\acute{L} \gg *L.L \gg *\acute{I} \gg *H/I$

As the partial orderings are only within each set/stratum, this approach does not suffer from the first problem of (general) partial orderings discussed above. In other words, the various total orderings are minimally different from each other and no one constraint varies tremendously in its ranking position.

Using this approach, Anttila (1997a,b) gets very interesting results in both the synchronic and diachronic dimensions of grammar. Furthermore, he makes accurate predictions about the actual distribution of alternants of the genitive plural in Finnish corpora. I contend that it is problematic to expect grammars to predict actual percentages of forms in corpora, as performance factors surely mediate between the forms produced by the grammar and forms listed in a corpus. However, supposing that we do wish to use the grammar to predict actual percentages, we quickly run into a strange consequence of stratified partial orderings. Suppose that a given candidate is optimal under three of the twelve orderings in (16). The prediction is that 25% of the forms attested should be this candidate. Boersma and Hayes (2001) point out that there are cases of free variation in which one variant is considerably more frequent than the other. An example is English words that phonemically end in /... {t,d}ən/. These are normally realized with no schwa and a syllabic /n/, as in *Sweden* [swi:dn̩], but are occasionally realized with the schwa, as in [swi:dən]. Let us assume purely for the sake of argument that the rarely attested form occurs once for every thirty-two times the commonly attested form does. For a grammar with three partially ordered constraint sets, the first and second of which contain two constraints and the third of which contains four constraints, there are 96 (2!·2!·4!) total orderings. Thus, the rarer form would have to be optimal on three of the total orderings. Or, for a grammar with thirty-two constraint sets, each of which contains only one constraint, the rarer form would have to be optimal on one total ordering. In any case, we have a situation in which the frequency of occurrence of the forms produced by the grammar partially determines the *number* of constraints in the grammar and their organization into strata. This is a very peculiar state of affairs, as a grammar with fewer constraints should in principle be preferred to a grammar with more constraints, providing they make identical predictions about grammaticality.

Even if we put this conceptual problem aside, there is a second problem which has to do with learnability (Boersma, 2001; Boersma and Hayes,

2001; Kager, 1999). Tesar and Smolensky's (1998) learning algorithm cannot handle stratified partial orderings: it either fails to acquire them or it never terminates (Boersma and Hayes, 2001). However, as we will see in the next section, stratified partial orderings are just a special case in stochastic Optimality Theory, which uses a modified notion of constraint ranking that associates constraints with a ranking value on a continuous scale. Stochastic OT has an associated learning algorithm: the Gradual Learning Algorithm (Boersma, 2000; Boersma and Hayes, 2001). Since the continuous ranking approach avoids the first problem noted above (see below), is learnable, and can handle stratified partial orderings as a special case, it will be the approach I adopt.

Stochastic Optimality Theory

Boersma (1997, 1998, 2000) and Boersma and Hayes (2001) present a methodology for representing optionality in a stochastic version of Optimality Theory. The method involves assigning a ranking value to each constraint. That is, each constraint has a ranking value along a continuous scale and at constraint evaluation time the ranking of a constraint is randomly distributed around this ranking value (see figure 1 below). The upshot of this is that if two constraints are closely ranked, there will be optionality in which constraint is ranked higher than the other. The frequency of a given ranking (e.g. whether C_1 outranks C_2), depends on the ranking difference. If the ranking difference is high, the constraint with the higher ranking value has a very high probability of outranking the constraint with the lower ranking value. If the ranking difference is 0, each constraint will outrank the other fifty percent of the time.

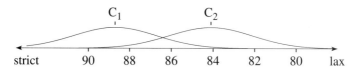

FIGURE 1 Overlapping ranking distributions (Boersma and Hayes 1999:(6))

Thus, constraint evaluation is stochastic in this system. Constraints do not deterministically outrank other constraints, but rather do so probabilistically. This probability is calculated using a Gaussian (i.e. normal) distribution, and the formula is not trivial. For the mathematical details, see Boersma (1997, 1998, 2000). However, the effects for two constraints—C_1 and C_2—are illustrated in the following table (Boersma, 1997):

(17)

$r_1 - r_2$	0	1	2	3	4	5
P	0.5	0.46	0.24	0.14	0.079	0.039

$r_1 - r_2$	6	7	8	9	10
P	0.017	0.007	0.002	$7 \cdot 10^{-4}$	$2 \cdot 10^{-4}$

The top line indicates the ranking difference between the ranking values of the two constraints, r_1 and r_2. The bottom line indicates the probability, P, of the second constraint outranking the first one.[16]

If two constraints are ranked closely enough, on different evaluations one will be ranked higher than the other. This yields optionality. However, if two constraints are ranked fairly far apart, the probability of different rankings becomes small. That is, the ranking becomes close to obligatory (Boersma, 1997). It is important to realize that at evaluation time there will always be a total ordering. Since the probability of the first constraint outranking the second is relative to each evaluation, in any given evaluation the ranking is determinate.

Stratified partial orderings (Anttila, 1997a,b) are simply a special case in this approach. A stratified partial ordering is derived in a constraint ranking where several constraints have exactly the same ranking value. For example, consider the following schematic tableau, which has the ranking value for each constraint indicated below the constraint's name.

(18)

	C_1	C_2	C_3	C_4	C_5
	150	100	100	100	50
⋮					

Bearing in mind that each constraint is associated with the same normal distribution, constraints C_2, C_3, and C_4, are equally likely to occur in any of the six (3!) possible orders. The other two constraints will not enter into the optionality, as their ranking values are too far from the constraints ranked at 100. This is equivalent to a stratified partial ordering with three strata: $C_1 \gg \{C_2, C_3, C_4\} \gg C_5$.

In my analysis of optionality in Marathi linking (section 7.6), I assign the optionally ranked constraints the same ranking value. So I effectively use a stratified partial ordering. The reasons for using the stochastic OT model instead of a simple stratified partial ordering were given at the end of the last section. First, the stochastic model does not depend on a direct relationship between the number of constraints in the grammar (and how they are divided into strata) and the frequency of the optional forms. In the stochastic model, the frequency of forms depends only on the ranking value of the constraints in question.[17] Therefore, on this approach it is possible to have a simpler grammar, with fewer constraints, and still predict the same frequency data.[18]

---

[16] The ranking values assigned to constraints do not have to be integers; finer grained probabilities can be derived using real numbers.

[17] Another relevant factor is the standard deviation of the normal distribution associated with the constraints, but as this is the same for every constraint, it is a constant.

[18] I take this to be a conceptual point about the undesirability of frequency data dictating the number of constraints in the grammar. However, as I stated in section 7.3.4,

The stochastic model also has a learning algorithm—the Gradual Learning Algorithm (GLA; Boersma 2000; Boersma and Hayes 2001)—and grammars stated in this model are therefore learnable. Stratified partial orderings have only been demonstrated to be learnable by the GLA (Boersma, 2001). Until a separate learning algorithm that does not depend on a stochastic model of OT is shown to learn stratifiable partial orderings, there is no choice but to implement them using continous ranking and stochastic Optimality Theory.

Thus, continuously-ranked constraints offer a way to represent optionality which avoids the problems associated with previous approaches. The problem of overgeneration with the pseudo-optionality approach does not arise, because here the various options belong to the same competition. The problem of maintaining identical constraint profiles in the true optionality approach does not arise because the candidates win on different rankings and do not need to have identical constraint profiles. The various problems with the neutralization approach are dispensed with, because there is only one input and it does not require formal features, as will be demonstrated. Lastly, in this section I have demonstrated that this approach is the soundest and most general way of implementing the notion of tied constraints, as it is equivalent to stratified partial orderings as a special case, but is also learnable. In the following sections I review the facts about Marathi that I will be accounting for, as well as Joshi's (1993) insightful LFG account of these facts. In section 7.6, I present my own analysis, which uses continuously-ranked constraints in a stochastic Optimality Theory.

7.4   Subject/Object Alternation in Marathi

Marathi[19] presents an interesting case for studying optionality in Optimality Theory. Certain verbs in this language show an alternation in which argument can be realized as the subject or object. That is, given two arguments, each can be mapped to the subject while the other is mapped to the object. The verb classes that exhibit this property are non-volitional transitives, such as 'saapaḍne' (to find) and 'aawaḍne' (to like), passives of underived ditransitives, such as the passive of 'dene' (to give), and passives of derived ditransitive causatives, such as the passive of causativized 'paaḓzne' (to feed).[20] In the next section I will present examples of all of these verbs and the evidence that Joshi uses to argue for the alternation of their core grammatical functions.

I do not believe that the grammar should ever predict exact frequencies, as there will be many intervening factors which will distort the frequency of forms attested.

[19]Marathi is an Indo-Aryan language spoken in Maharashtra and adjacent states in India. It has roughly 64,000,000 speakers. Ethnographic data from Ethnologue (http://www.sil.org/ethnologue/countries/India.html#MRT; checked 17.03.99).

[20]See appendix A for a list of verbs in these classes.

7.4.1 The Data

Here are examples[21] of the verb classes mentioned in the previous section.

(19) **Non-volitional transitives**

    a. sumaa-laa ek pustak milaale.
       Suma-D/A one book   got
       Suma got a book.
       ('miḷne' (to receive) ∈ 'find' class)

    b. sumaa-laa aait͡saa   upadeš patlaa.
       Suma-D/A mother's advice agreed
       Mother's advice became acceptable to Suma.
       ('paṭne' (to accept mentally) ∈ 'like' class)

(20) **Passive ditransitive**
    baaḷaa-laa kʰaau dilaa gelaa.
    baby-D/A food   given was
    Baby was given food.

(21) **Passive ditransitive causative**
    ramaa-laa dudʰ paad͡zle   gele.
    Rama-D/A milk drink.CAUS was
    Rama was fed milk.

Joshi (1993) separates the non-volitional transitives into the 'find' class (19a) and the 'like' class (19b).

7.4.2 Evidence for the Subject/Object Alternation

Joshi (1993, 37–44) lists three syntactic tests for grammatical subjecthood in Marathi: the conjunction reduction test, the prenominal present participial relative test, and the *un* clause controllee test. She uses all three tests to demonstrate the subject/object alternation in the verb classes under consideration, but in this section I will only review the conjunction reduction test.

The conjunction reduction test is not solely a test for subjects, but rather distinguishes between grammatical functions in general. The phenomenon can be characterized as follows: if two clauses with coreferent arguments are conjoined, the coreferent argument in the second clause must be null, but only if the two arguments have the same grammatical function

---

[21] All Marathi examples are taken from Joshi (1993) and I have used her transcriptions, with one exception. She gives various case feature transcriptions (see footnote 22), for the suffix *-laa*, whereas I normally gloss it as dative/accusative, since the distinctions are never relevant in this paper. See appendix C for example citation information. Relevant gloss abbreviations:

D/A	=	dative/accusative case	ERG	=	ergative case
GEN	=	genitive case	ABIL	=	ability case
CAUS	=	causative	PART	=	participle
ABLE	=	ability verbal morpheme			

(Joshi, 1993, viii)

and have the same case marking (Joshi, 1993, 37–38).[22] For illustration of these requirements on conjunction reduction the reader is invited to consult Joshi (1993). I will show that only subjects can gap subjects, as this will be important in demonstrating the subject/object alternation momentarily.

The following examples have the properties required.[23] Example (22) shows that subjects can gap subjects and must do so if the cases match, example (23) shows that subjects cannot gap objects, and example (24) shows that objects cannot gap subjects.

(22) a. [alkaa-ni mini-laa maarle] paṇ [niilimaa-laa wihirit ḍʰakalle].
Alka-ERG mini-D/A hit   but Nilima-D/A well-in pushed
Alka$_i$ hit Mini, but Ø$_i$ pushed Nilima in the well.

b. *[alkaa-ni mini-laa maarle] paṇ [tini   niilimaa-laa
Alka-ERG mini-D/A hit   but she-ERG Nilima-D/A
wihirit ḍʰakalle].
well-in pushed
Alka$_i$ hit Mini, but she$_i$ pushed Nilima in the well.

(23) a. *[dzaambʰḷi-ci pikleli pʰaḷe kʰaali paḍli] aaṇi [raam-ni
Jamun-GEN   ripe   fruits down fell   and Ram-ERG
goḷaa keli].
collect did
[Ripe fruits of the Jamun tree]$_i$ fell on the ground, and Ram collected Ø$_i$.

b. [dzaambʰḷi-ci pikleli pʰaḷe kʰaali paḍli] aaṇi [ti
Jamun-GEN   ripe   fruits down fell   and those
raam-ni   goḷaa keli].
Ram-ERG collect did
[Ripe fruits of the Jamun tree]$_i$ fell on the ground, and Ram collected them$_i$.

(24) a. *[pustake raam-ni   ṭeblaa-war tʰewli] paṇ [kʰaali paḍli].
books   Ram-ERG table-on   kept   but down fell
Ram put books$_i$ on the table but Ø$_i$ fell down.

b. [pustake raam-ni   ṭeblaa-war tʰewli] paṇ [ti   kʰaali paḍli].
books   Ram-ERG table-on   kept   but they down fell
Ram put books$_i$ on the table but they$_i$ fell down.

These examples have demonstrated how conjunction reduction functions in Marathi. Next I will show how this test provides evidence for the subject alternation.

---

[22] It is important to realize that the two arguments have to have the same case marking, but can have differing case features, or abstract case. For example, the dative/accusative case and the ability case in Marathi are both marked with the suffix -laa, but Joshi (1993, 18–30) argues that they must be distinguished as separate cases.

[23] In all these examples, the case-matching requirement has been controlled for.

7.4.3 Subject Alternation

First, the conjunction reduction test will be used to demonstrate that either argument in non-volitional transitives ('like' and 'find' verbs) can be the grammatical subject. This follows from conjunction reduction because, as demonstrated in (22), "when the subjects of conjoined clauses are coreferent and have matching cases, the second subject is null" (Joshi, 1993, 53). The following examples illustrate that either argument of a non-volitional transitive can be gapped in the second conjunct.

(25) **'like' class**

a. **Dative/accusative argument gapped**
[rajat-laa   aai-laa   exti ṭaakun yewawla naahi]
Rajat-ABIL mother-D/A alone leaving come   able.not
pan [hyaa citrakaaraa-t͡sa maagt͡sa pradaršan kʰup
but this   artist-GEN   last   exhibition much
aawaḍla hota].
liked   had
Rajat$_i$ did not feel like leaving mother alone and coming, but Ø$_i$ had much liked the artist's last exhibition.

b. **Nominative argument gapped**
[sumaa goḍ   hasli] aani [rajat-laa aawaḍla].
Suma sweet smiled and Rajat-D/A liked
Suma$_i$ smiled sweetly and Rajat liked Ø$_i$.

These sentences illustrate that either argument of the non-volitional transitive 'aawaḍne' (to like) can be gapped by a coreferent subject in a preceding conjoined clause. This indicates that both arguments of a 'like' class verb can serve as the grammatical subject.

The following sentences show that the arguments of 'find' class verbs have the same properties.

(26) **'find' class**

a. **Dative/accusative argument gapped**
[raajkumaaraa-laa waaḷwanṭaat soḍla gela] pan [parat
prince-D/A   desert.in   left was but back
d͡zaay-t͡sa rastaa saapaḍlaa].
go-GEN   way   found
The prince$_i$ was left in the desert, but Ø$_i$ found his way back.

b. **Nominative argument gapped**
[raajkumaaraa-ci angtʰi talyaat paḍli] aani [ekaa
prince-GEN   ring lake.in fell and one
koḷyaa-laa   saapaḍli].
fisherman-D/A found
The prince's ring$_i$ fell in the lake and one fisherman found Ø$_i$.

Again, since the subject in the first clause can gap either of the 'find' verb's arguments, this shows that either argument can be the grammatical subject.

The conjunction reduction test can also be used to demonstrate that either argument in a passive of a ditransitive or ditransitive causative can be the grammatical subject.

(27)　**Passive ditransitive**

   a. **Dative/accusative argument gapped**

     [mini-laa k^{h}urcit basawle gele] aani [ek pustak dile　gele].

     Mini-D/A chair.in sit.made was　and one book　given was

     Mini$_i$ was seated in a chair and Ø$_i$ was given a book.

   b. **Nominative argument gapped**

     [ek pustak k^{h}aali padle] aani [mini-laa dile　gele].

     one book　down fell　and Mini-D/A given was

     One book$_i$ fell down and Ø$_i$ was given to Mini.

(28)　**Passive ditransitive causative**

   a. **Dative/accusative argument gapped**

     [mini-laa g^{h}ari nele　gele] aani [te　dud^h paadẑle　gele].

     Mini-D/A home taken was　and that milk drink.CAUS was

     Mini$_i$ was taken home and Ø$_i$ fed milk.

   b. **Nominative argument gapped**

     [te　dud^h taaple]　　aani [mini-laa paadẑle　gele].

     that milk warm.became and Mini-D/A drink.CAUS was

     The milk$_i$ became warm and Ø$_i$ was fed to Mini.

Once again a subject can gap either of the two arguments of these verbs. Therefore, either argument can be the subject.

In this section, I presented Joshi's evidence that either argument in the verb classes with subject/object alternation can be the grammatical subject. In the next section, I will show that either argument can also be the grammatical object.

7.4.4　Object Alternation

Testing for the object alternation in Marathi is slightly more complex than testing for the alternating subject. It involves using a controlled adjunct, the *taanaa* participle adverbial clause, in tandem with conjunction reduction. The basic characterization of the *taanaa* adverbial is that it has an obligatorily null subject which can only be controlled by an argument which has a non-oblique grammatical function (i.e. subjects and objects). Joshi's strategy is to use conjunction reduction to establish that one argument of the relevant alternating verb is a subject and then to show that the other argument can control a *taanaa* adverbial clause. Under the assumption that there can only be one subject per clause in Marathi, and given that only non-obliques can control the gap in these adverbials, it follows that the controller must therefore be a grammatical object.

In the following examples, conjunction reduction is used to establish that one of the alternating verb's arguments is the grammatical subject. At the same time the *taanaa* control test shows that the other argument must be a core grammatical function. Since there is an uncontroversial subject, this other argument must be the object.

(29)   **Non-volitional transitives ('like' class)**
  a. **Dative/accusative object as controller**
     [raajakanyaa rajat-laa   [ang^{h}o$\underline{l}$ kartaanaa] disli] aa$\underline{n}$i
     Princess   Rajat-D/A bath   do.PART   saw and
     [naahiši   dz͡^{h}aali].
     disappear became
     While $\emptyset_{i/j}$ taking a bath Rajat$_i$ saw the princess$_j$ and $\emptyset_j$ disappeared.
  b. **Nominative object as controller**
     [rajat-laa   raajakanyaa [ang^{h}o$\underline{l}$ kartaanaa] disli] aa$\underline{n}$i
     Rajat-D/A princess   bath   do.PART   saw and
     [girafdaar   kele gele].
     imprisoned done was
     Rajat$_i$ saw the princess$_j$ $\emptyset_{i/j}$ bathing and $\emptyset_i$ was imprisoned.

In sentence (29a), *raajakanyaa* is gapped under conjunction reduction as the subject of *naahiši* (disappeared). Therefore, *raajakanyaa* is the subject of *disli* (saw). Since *rajat* can still control the adverbial *kartaanaa*, it must be the grammatical object of *disli*. Likewise, in (29b), *rajat-laa* is coreferent with the gapped subject of *girafdaar* and must therefore be the subject of *disli*. The adverbial *kartaanaa* can be controlled by *raajakanyaa* and *raajakanyaa* is therefore the grammatical object of *disli*. Thus, either argument of the non-volitional transitive 'like' verb *dis$\underline{n}$e* can be the grammatical object.

The test yields the same results for 'find' verbs, passive ditransitives, and passive ditransitive causatives. In each case, conjunction reduction controls for the subject, and either argument can be the grammatical object. The relevant examples follow, but I will not explain each one in detail.

(30)   **Non-volitional transitives ('find' class)**
  a. **Dative/accusative object as controller**
     [kaahi mor   rajat-laa   [janglaat p^{h}ir-taanaa] aad^{h}a$\underline{l}$le]
     some peacocks Rajat-D/A jungle.in roam-PART   came.across
     aa$\underline{n}$i [ekaa kšanb^haraa-t-at͡s naahise   dz͡^{h}aale].
     and one   moment-in-only disappear happened
     Rajat$_i$ came across some peacocks$_j$ while $\emptyset_i$ roaming in the jungle, and $\emptyset_j$ in a moment disappeared.

b. **Nominative object as controller**

[rajat-laa kaahi mor   [janglaat naat͡s-taanaa]
Rajat-D/A some peacocks jungle.in dance-PART

aadʰalle]   pan [tyaancyaa d͡zawaḷ d͡zaawawle naahi].
came.across but they.GEN near   go.ABLE not
Rajat$_i$ came across some peacocks$_j$ when Ø$_j$ dancing in the jungle,
but Ø$_i$ could not go near them.

(31)   **Passive ditransitives**

a. **Dative/accusative object as controller**

[aai-ni   magawleli pustaka sakaaḷ-cyaa ṭapaalaa-ni
mother-ERG ordered   books   morning   post-with

aali] aani [[šaaḷet d͡zaa-taanaa] sumaa-laa daakʰawli geli].
came and school.to go-PART   Suma-D/A shown   were
[The books that mother had ordered]$_i$ came with the morning
post and Ø$_i$ were shown to Suma$_j$ while Ø$_j$ going to school.

b. **Nominative object as controller**

[sumaa-laa madʰya-raatri utʰawla gela] aani
Suma-D/A middle.of-night woken   was and

[hiwaaḷyaa-t͡sa pahila barfa [paḍtaanaa] daakʰawla gela].
winter-of   first snow falling   shown   was
Suma$_i$ was woken up at midnight and Ø$_i$ was shown [the first
snow of winter]$_j$ while Ø$_j$ falling.

(32)   **Passive ditransitive causatives**

a. **Dative/accusative object as controller**

[dudʰ garam d͡zʰaala] aani [raam-laa [d͡zʰoptaanaa]
milk warm became and Ram-D/A sleep.PART

paad͡zla   gela].
drink.CAUS was
The milk$_i$ got warm and Ram$_j$ was fed Ø$_i$ while Ø$_j$ going to sleep.

b. **Nominative object as controller**

[raam-laa bʰuk   laagli] aani [dudʰ [garam astaanaa]
Ram-D/A hunger came and milk hot   be.PART

paad͡zla   gela].
drink.CAUS was
Ram$_i$ became hungry and Ø$_i$ was fed some milk$_j$ while Ø$_j$ hot.

In the last two sections, I have presented Joshi's evidence that in Marathi
non-volitional transitives, passive ditransitives, and passive ditransitive causatives either argument can be the grammatical subject while the other is
the grammatical object. Therefore, these verb classes demonstrate true optionality in linking their arguments to grammatical functions. In the next
section, I outline the relevant aspects of Joshi's LFG analysis, before turning
to my own OT analysis in section 7.6.

7.5 Joshi's Analysis

In her thesis, Joshi uses a combination of Lexical Mapping Theory (LMT; Bresnan and Kanerva 1989; Bresnan and Zaenen 1990), which is a component of LFG, Dowty's proto-role theory (Dowty, 1991), and an unordered argument structure representation to give rules that provide predicates with their required linking properties.

Lexical Mapping Theory provides two syntactic features [± r(estricted)] and [± o(bjective)] which cross-classify grammatical functions. Joshi (1993, 113) assumes the following classification:[24]

(33) SUBJ: [−r, −o], OBJ: [−r, +o], OBL: [+r, −o]

In Joshi's analysis, the LMT features of an argument are determined by the proto-roles associated with the argument. The proto-properties she assumes are:

(34) **Proto-Agent Properties**
   a. volitional involvement in the event or state
   b. sentience (and/or perception)
   c. causing an event or change of state in another participant
   d. movement (relative to the position of another participant)
   e. exists independently of the event named by the verb

(35) **Proto-Patient Properties**
   a. undergoes change of state/location
   b. incremental theme
   c. causally affected by another participant
   d. stationary relative to movement of another participant
   e. does not exist independently of the event, or not at all
   f. not entailed to possess sentience/perception
      (Dowty 1991, 572; Joshi 1993, 80)

I follow Joshi in referring to these properties as PAa, PAb, PPa, PPb, and so forth.

Proto-property PPf is not one of the original Dowty (1991) properties, but is proposed by Joshi (1993). But, this property is quite problematic and I do not adopt it. First, it is not clear what its motivation is. Although, as Joshi (1993, 90) notes, lack of sentience may be a reasonable proto-patient property, the entailment should be non-sentience, in opposition to PAb. The reason Joshi opts for the present formulation instead, is to get certain facts about Marathi linking right (see (39) below). Thus, the problem is a lack of independent motivation.

---

[24]The restricted object, OBJ$_\Theta$, which has the features [+r, +o], is omitted. Joshi argues that Marathi is a symmetric language (i.e. it does not distinguish beween a direct and indirect object).

Second, this proto-property works completely differently from the other ones.[25] In Joshi's formulation, this proto-property will necessarily be present whenever PAb is absent. In other words, any argument of a verb that is not entailed to have the proto-agent property of sentience (PAb) will *automatically* receive property PPf. It is clear, as Dowty (1991) notes, that some proto-properties are related, in particular PAc-d and PPc-d, but they are related positively, not negatively. For example, if one argument is a causer (PAc), then there must also be an argument that is the causee (PPc). Thus, the presence of the first property entails the presence of the second, and vice versa.[26] However, PPf is different because its presence is entailed by the *absence* of another property. Joshi has therefore introduced a completely new dynamic into Dowty's system, changing it considerably.

She then gives two syntactic feature rules for Marathi:

(36) a. an argument with a P-Patient property $\Rightarrow [-r]$
  b. all other arguments $\Rightarrow [-o]$
    (Joshi, 1993, 113)

She also proposes the following function mapping principle:

(37) a. (i)   [+volitional]
       |
      ARG $\Rightarrow$ subject; otherwise:

  (ii)   ARG $\Rightarrow$ subject
       $[-r]$

  b. Other arguments are mapped onto the lowest compatible function on the markedness hierarchy SUBJ > OBJ,OBL.[27]
    (Joshi, 1993, 113)

Finally, she assumes the following well-formedness condition:

(38) The Subject Condition: every predicate must have a single token of the grammatical function SUBJ.
  (Joshi, 1993, 114)

The basic idea of Joshi's analysis is that proto-role information determines syntactic features and these in turn determine grammatical function. I will now give an example of how this works in Joshi's system. The example is for the non-volitional verb *aawaḍṇe* (Joshi, 1993, 117).

---

[25] Farrell Ackerman and his students (p.c.) have made this point to me, in a slightly different manner.

[26] Of course, the argument that receives a certain proto-entailment can be suppressed. For example, a passive of a causative will have the causer suppressed, but the entailments still hold of the base predicate to which the passive is related.

[27] This hierarchy arises from the assumption that, in LMT, negative features are less marked than positive ones (Joshi, 1993, 105).

(39) Mapping of grammatical functions in the verb *aawaḍne* ('like')

	Undergoes change of state (PPa) \	Not E.T.B. Sentient (PPf) /	Semantics
aawaddne 'to like'	$\langle$ARG [−r]	ARG$\rangle$ [−r]	ARG STR by (36a)
	S/O	S/O	by (37aii),(37b)
	S	O	by Subject Cond.
or	O	S	by Subject Cond.

Due to the syntactic feature rules in (36a), the two arguments get the feature assignment [−r], since they have proto-patient properties. Given this feature assignment, either argument can be a subject, according to (37aii). Finally, each argument can equally be an object, according to (37b), since the lowest role in the grammatical function hierarchy that they are compatible with is OBJ (obliques are [+r]). Thus, she successfully accounts for the subject/object alternation using these mechanisms. The other alternating predicates are handled in a similar manner.

This example also illustrates how the problematic proto-patient property, PPf, is necessary for Joshi's analysis. It is clear that the second argument of *aawaḍne* ('like') has no proto-patient properties other than PPf. It does not undergo a change of state or location (PPa). It is not an incremental theme (PPb). It is not causally affected by the other argument (PPc). It is not necessarily stationary relative to the other argument (PPd). Finally, it exists independently of the liking event (PPe). However, if the second argument gets no proto-patient property, it does not get the feature [−r] by (36a), but rather gets assigned [−o] by (36b). If it gets assigned [−o] then it *must* be the subject, since objects are [+o]. But then the optionality is unaccounted for and the analysis would wrongly predict that the verb *aawaḍne* has no subject/object alternation and that the stimulus 'likee' must be the subject (perhaps analogously to English *please*, as in *The food pleased me*). This is clearly not the case, according to the evidence that Joshi presents. This verb exhibits the subject/object alternation and the likee can be the object as well as the subject.

Looking at it another way, Joshi's (1993) theory yields the following two generalizations:

(40) a. If a predicate has a volitional argument, that argument is realized as the subject; otherwise any argument of the verb that possesses a proto-patient property can be the grammatical subject. (Joshi, 1993, 92)

b. If there is no volitional argument and there is more than one argument that has a proto-patient property there will be subject/object alternation.

Both of these principles are somewhat strange. Although Joshi clearly demonstrates the importance of the proto-agent property of volitionality, why should having a *proto-patient* property be the second-most important criterion for subjecthood? The whole point of Dowty (1991) theory is that proto-patient entailments are characteristic of *objects*, not subjects. Instead, (40) proposes that there is one proto-agent property that really matters for subjecthood, and that otherwise subjects are principally characterized by proto-patient properties. This is not at all in accordance with Dowty (1991) and it is extremely hard to see how the different versions of the theory (Dowty (1991) and Joshi (1993)) could possibly both be true.

Joshi (1993)'s analysis is insightful in its use of proto-role information and its avoidance of an ordered argument structure. However, it is a parametric account and the particular instantiation of the parameters she gives are largely parochial to the analysis of Marathi. Thus, her account as such does not make strong crosslinguistic predictions. Furthermore, she stipulates the volitionality of the subject, rather than deriving it from general principles. She also proposes that proto-patient properties characterize subjects. Lastly, her analysis requires the use of the problematic proto-patient property PPf to get the descriptive facts right.

In the following section, I provide an OT account of grammatical function selection in Marathi. This account will use a small set of general, universally viable constraints to derive the correct linking of arguments in Marathi. In addition, it derives the volitionality of the subject from the harmonic alignment of two prominence scales and subsequent constraint interaction, and it does not use proto-patient property PPf.

7.6 An Optimality-Theoretic Analysis

In this section I will provide an OT analysis for the following features of grammatical function selection in Marathi:

(41) a. If a predicate has a volitional argument, that argument is realized as the subject.

b. If there is no volitional argument there will be subject/object alternation.

The principal difference between this formulation and the one in (40) is that proto-patient properties are *not* assumed to be characteristic of subjects. Rather, the alternation facts will be shown to arise from a finer-grained analysis that uses a small set of crosslinguistically viable constraints.

7.6.1 Stochastic Optimality Theory and Harmonic Alignment

Aissen (1999) has motivated the use of prominence scales and harmonic alignment to capture markedness universals. I will adopt her scale Subj(ect) > Nonsubj(ect), where ">" means "more prominent than". I also propose the new scale Proto-Agent > Proto-Patient (P-A > P-P). "Proto-Agent" and "Proto-Patient" should be understood as cover terms for the set of properties listed in section 7.5. Thus, this scale is really a partial ordering, with the P-A properties unordered relative to each other, and likewise for the P-P properties. The idea is that investigating various languages will provide evidence for further ordering these properties. In fact, the importance of volitionality in Marathi indicates that this property is the highest ranked of the Proto-Agent properties.[28] The fully articulated scale I will adopt is P-A$_{vol}$ > P-A$_{-vol}$ > P-P.[29]

Now, I need to express the notion that subjects tend to bear proto-agent properties, and nonsubjects tend to bear proto-patient properties. This will be captured using the prominence scales for proto-role properties and grammatical functions. There is a formal method in OT for aligning two scales (Prince and Smolensky, 1993; Aissen, 1999), called harmonic alignment.

(42)   Alignment: Given a binary dimension D_1 with a scale X > Y on its elements X,Y, and another dimension D_2 with a scale a > b ... > z on its elements, the harmonic alignment of D_1 and D_2 is the pair of Harmony scales:
   a. H_x: X/a ≻ X/b ≻ ... ≻ X/z
   b. H_y: Y/z ≻ ... ≻ Y/b ≻ Y/a
   The constraint alignment is the pair of constraint hierarchies:
   a. C_x: *X/z ≫ ... ≫ *X/b ≫ *X/a
   b. C_y: *Y/a ≫ *Y/b ≫ ... ≫ *Y/z
   (Prince and Smolensky, 1993, 136)

The result of the harmonic alignment is that it is more harmonic for X's to be a's and for Y's to be z's. This is captured in the constraint alignment by having *X/a and *Y/z be the lowest ranked constraints in their hierarchies. It is important to realize that these hierarchies are fixed universally. For example, no language may parochially have the ranking *X/b ≫ *X/z.

---

[28]Davis (1996) postulates that the proto-agent property of causation (PPc) is also a more important factor than the other proto-properties. I leave this aside here.

[29]I have noted the specific volitionality property by subscripting P-A with *vol*. Similarly, I use the label P-A$_{-vol}$ as a shorthand for all the P-A properties except volitionality.

On the other hand the resulting hierarchies may be interspersed, so long as the ordering for particular hierarchies is respected.

The alignment of the two scales that I am using will serve as a more concrete example:

(43)   Subj > Nonsubj
       $P\text{-}A_{vol}$ > $P\text{-}A_{-vol}$ > P-P
   a. Harmonic alignment:
       $Subj/P\text{-}A_{vol}$ ≻ $Subj/P\text{-}A_{-vol}$ ≻ Subj/P-P
       $Nonsubj/P\text{-}P$ ≻ $Nonsubj/P\text{-}A_{-vol}$ ≻ $Nonsubj/P\text{-}A_{vol}$
   b. Constraint hierarchies:
       *Subj/P-P ≫ *$Subj/P\text{-}A_{-vol}$ ≫ *$Subj/P\text{-}A_{vol}$
       *$Nonsubj/P\text{-}A_{vol}$ ≫ *$Nonsubj/P\text{-}A_{-vol}$ ≫ *Nonsubj/P-P

The resulting constraint hierarchies are such that it is worst for a subject to have proto-patient properties and for a nonsubject to have the proto-agent property of volitionality. This does not mean that objects cannot be volitional; it just means that the least preferred situation is one in which a predicate *entails* the property of volitionality for an argument that gets mapped to a nonsubject grammatical function.[30]

With these hierarchies in place, I can now present the constraint set that I will be using in this analysis:

(44)   **Constraints**
   a. MAX(proto): Proto-role information in the input is realized in the output.
   b. DEP(proto): Proto-role information in the output is present in the input.[31]
   c. THEMATIC$_{subj}$: Every clause has a thematic subject.[32]

---

[30] In fact, this is a very important distinction that Dowty (1991) discusses as well. The entire theory of proto-roles is about what the meaning of a predicate entails for that predicate's arguments. Incidental properties of the actual fillers of these argument slots are not under discussion here.

[31] I also assume that there is a markedness constraint, *STRUC(proto), since faithfulness constraints usually have related markedness constraints. However, this constraint plays no role in the analysis presented here.

[32] This constraint is related to the constraint SUBJ, which requires that every clause has a subject, thematic or otherwise (SUBJ is therefore analogous to the Extended Projection Principle of Government and Binding Theory or the Subject Condition of LFG's Lexical Mapping Theory, a version of which is given in (38) above). If a language has SUBJ and either DEP(proto) or *STRUC(proto)—the markedness constraint appropriate for proto-role properties—outranking THEMATIC$_{subj}$, it will realize clausal subjects linked to arguments without proto-role properties as expletives. However, if THEMATIC$_{subj}$ outranks SUBJ, there will be no expletive subjects. Either subjects with no proto-role properties will lead to ungrammaticality, or another argument will be co-opted as subject. The latter case occurs in Marathi verbs that exhibit the subject/object alternation. Marathi does not have expletive subjects (Pandharipande, 1997, 133), so I will assume that THEMATIC$_{subj}$ outranks SUBJ and I do not include the latter constraint in my analysis.

    d. *Nonsubj/P-A$_{vol}$: Avoid nonsubjects with the proto-agent property of volitionality.[33]

    e. *Subj/P-P: Avoid subjects with proto-patient properties.

    f. *Subj/P-A$_{-vol}$: Avoid subjects with proto-agent properties other than volitionality.

    g. *Nonsubj/P-A$_{-vol}$: Avoid nonsubjects with proto-agent properties other than volitionality.

    h. *Nonsubj/P-P: Avoid nonsubjects with proto-patient properties.

The non-stochastic ranking of these constraints is:[34]

(45) **Marathi ranking**

    THEMATIC$_{subj}$ ≫ MAX(proto) ≫ *Nonsubj/P-A$_{vol}$ ≫ DEP(proto) ≫ {*Subj/P-P, *Subj/P-A$_{-vol}$, *Nonsubj/P-A$_{-vol}$, *Nonsubj/P-P}

In order to prove that a ranking is not just sufficient, but also necessary, a set of ranking arguments must be presented. As noted in Prince and Smolensky (1993, 106–107), this constitutes "a potential empirical argument that [Constraint$_1$] dominates [Constraint$_2$]."

The following tableau (Prince and Smolensky, 1993, 106, (160)) will be useful in explaining the form of a ranking argument.

(46)

Ranking Argument		C_1	C_2
⟨input⟩			
a.	☞ *opt*		*
b.	*subopt*	*!	

In this tableau, *opt* is a candidate that is attested in the data set, and is therefore known to be a winning candidate. The higher ranking constraint must not have any violations for *opt*, whereas the lower ranking constraint must have one or more violations. The other candidate, *subopt*, competes with *opt*. The higher ranking constraint must be violated by this candidate, whereas the lower ranking constraint should not be violated. Since it is known that *opt* must be an output, this configuration shows that C_1 must outrank C_2. If the reverse ranking, $C_2 ≫ C_1$, were picked, *opt* would be erroneously rejected in favour of *subopt*. Therefore, ranking arguments are very important in establishing the empirical adequacy of a given ranking and to show that a given ranking is both necessary and sufficient for the data set under consideration. Appendix B contains a full set of arguments for the ranking in (45).

---

[33]Lødrup (1999) uses similar constraints to thematic$_{subj}$ and *Nonsubj/P-A$_{vol}$ in his OT analysis of linking in Norwegian presentational focus constructions. However, he uses thematic roles, such as *Theme* and *Agent*, rather than proto-roles. His paper also contains more extensive discussion of the interaction between SUBJ and THEMATIC$_{subj}$ (see footnote 32).

[34]I present the actual stochastic version in (48) below.

I am using Boersma's probabilistically ranked constraints (see section 7.3.4) to capture optionality, so the constraints in ranking (45) must be augmented with ranking values. There are four constraints that will capture the subject/object optionality in Marathi: *Subj/P-P, *Subj/P-A$_{-vol}$, *Nonsubj/P-A$_{-vol}$, and *Nonsubj/P-P. I will assign these constraints the same ranking value, so that the ranking difference is 0. This yields 4! (= 24) different optional rankings; however, due to the universal hierarchies in (43b), only six of these outcomes are possible without violating either the hierarchy *Subj/P-P $\gg$ *Subj/P-A$_{-vol}$ or *Nonsubj/P-A$_{-vol}$ $\gg$ *Nonsubj/P-P. The six constraint orderings are:

(47) a. *Subj/P-P $\gg$ *Subj/P-A$_{-vol}$ $\gg$ *Nonsubj/P-A$_{-vol}$ $\gg$ Nonsubj/P-P

  b. *Subj/P-P $\gg$ *Nonsubj/P-A$_{-vol}$ $\gg$ *Subj/P-A$_{-vol}$ $\gg$ Nonsubj/P-P

  c. *Subj/P-P $\gg$ *Nonsubj/P-A$_{-vol}$ $\gg$ *Nonsubj/P-P $\gg$ Subj/P-A$_{-vol}$

  d. *Nonsubj/P-A$_{-vol}$ $\gg$ *Subj/P-P $\gg$ *Subj/P-A$_{-vol}$ $\gg$ Nonsubj/P-P

  e. *Nonsubj/P-A$_{-vol}$ $\gg$ *Subj/P-P $\gg$ *Nonsubj/P-P $\gg$ Subj/P-A$_{-vol}$

  f. *Nonsubj/P-A$_{-vol}$ $\gg$ *Nonsubj/P-P $\gg$ *Subj/P-P $\gg$ Subj/P-A$_{-vol}$

Given the ranking value difference of 0, each of these rankings has a $\frac{1}{6}$ probability of occurring.

A note of explanation is in order about the nature of hierarchies and their relationship to the stochastic model of OT that I am assuming here. By definition, hierarchies reduce the number of factorial rerankings to just those that respect the hierarchies, as demonstrated in (47). There are two ways to think about this, both of which are equivalent for my purposes. We could think of the hierarchies as a constraint on the generation of constraint rankings. On this view, the hierarchy-violating rankings would never be generated. Or, we could allow the all factorial rerankings to be generated and then filter out any that violate the hierarchies. With respect to acquisition, this means that when the language learner is reranking her constraints in response to language data, in order to respect the hierarchies the illicit rankings must either not be generated or there must be a filtering of rankings that violate the hierarchies before each evaluation step in learning. Ida Toivonen (p.c.) has pointed out that the hierarchies are not necessarily part of the grammar. They may be functionally/cognitively motivated constraints. Then they do not need to be expressed grammatically at all, but rather constrain the space of possible languages. In that case, no language that violated the constraints would be instantiated, simply because such languages are cognitively impossible. This is an interesting alternative and an important architectural issue, but in the present analysis the hierarchies are to be thought of as purely formal grammatical constraints, with no functional motivation. Thus, I am making the architectural assumption that hierarchies are simply another formal aspect of optimality-theoretic grammars.

This property of hierarchies, that they are effectively meta-constraints on rankings of constraints, is a fundamental one and must be acknowledged by any OT analysis that uses them, no matter whether the analysis uses regular OT or stochastic OT. Thus, hierarchies add a mechanism to OT, but this is *not* particular to stochastic OT. Although we must be cautious in expanding our theories, the descriptive, explanatory, and typologically predictive value of hierarchies are clear, as most notably demonstrated for syntax by Aissen (1999). However, the use of hierarchies and the filtering out of hierarchy-violating constraint rankings—in the manner discussed here—has not been countenanced in the OT learnability literature. Their effect on learnability proofs has yet to be tested thoroughly. In the implementation of the stochastic OT model I am assuming, there is at present no way to implement the filtering effect I have just outlined. The assumption I am making is that although all of the hierarchically ranked constraints have been assigned the same ranking value, on any actual evaluation only one of the hierarchy-respecting rankings in (47) will be instantiated. This is precisely equivalent to Boersma's stochastic OT model augmented with filtering for hierarchies, and gives a similar effect to Anttila's (1997b) stratified partial orderings, but without the problems discussed in section 7.3.4.

With this in mind, (48) presents the constraint ordering again, but marked (with subscripts) for ranking values. There is no evidence for any optionality in the other constraints and they have therefore been assigned values that are far apart. This will have the result that any ordering other than the one stated is extremely unlikely to occur.

(48) **Stochastic Marathi ranking**

$_{100}$THEMATIC$_{subj}$ $\gg$ $_{90}$MAX(proto) $\gg$ $_{80}$*Nonsubj/P-A$_{vol}$ $\gg$ $_{70}$DEP(proto) $\gg$ $_{60}$*Subj/P-P $\gg$ $_{60}$*Nonsubj/P-A$_{-vol}$ $\gg$ $_{60}$*Nonsubj/P-P $\gg$ $_{60}$*Subj/P-A$_{-vol}$

The probability of any of the constraints separated by a ranking difference of 10 switching at evaluation time is 0.0002, (assuming a noise factor of 2).[35] However, the probability of any two of the final four constraints switching is 0.5; so, any of the six rankings in (47) is equally likely to occur.

Now that the constraints are in place, the next step is to characterize the form of the inputs and the candidates. I follow Bresnan (2000b) and Kuhn (2001) in assuming the input to be a basic semantic form, including

---

[35]Recall from section 7.3.4 that there is a random variable with a Gaussian distribution of values associated with each constraint ranking and that this yields a slightly different ranking at each evaluation.

argument structure information. However, I also assume that argument structure is a separate level of representation within LFG grammars, called a-structure, and that it is related to c-structure by the α projection function and to f-structure by the λ projection function (Butt et al., 1997). Since proto-properties pertain to argument structure, they are represented at the a-structure level and are also part of the input. Thus, the inputs I am assuming are pairs of f-structures and a-structures. As an illustration, the input for the sentence in (49) would be the pair in (50), where the first member is an f-structure and the second is an a-structure.

(49) tyaa mulaa-laa te   aaiskrim   aawaḍte.
    that boy-D/A   that ice-cream likes
    That boy likes that ice cream.

(50)

$$
\left\langle
\begin{bmatrix}
\text{PRED} & \text{'aawaḍne'} \\[4pt]
\text{GF}_1 & \begin{bmatrix} \text{PRED} & \text{'mulaa'} \\ \text{PERS} & 3 \\ \text{NUM} & \text{SG} \\ \text{GEND} & \text{MASC} \\ \text{DEIXIS} & + \end{bmatrix}_x \\[4pt]
\text{GF}_2 & \begin{bmatrix} \text{PRED} & \text{'aaiskrim'} \\ \text{PERS} & 3 \\ \text{NUM} & \text{SG} \\ \text{DEIXIS} & + \end{bmatrix}_y \\[4pt]
\text{TNS} & \text{PRESENT}
\end{bmatrix}
,
\begin{bmatrix}
\text{REL} & \text{aawaḍne} \\[4pt]
\text{ARG1} & \begin{bmatrix} \text{P-AG} & \{PAb, PAe\} \\ \text{P-PT} & \{PPa\} \end{bmatrix}_x \\[4pt]
\text{ARG2} & \begin{bmatrix} \text{P-AG} & \{PAe\} \\ \text{P-PT} & \{\} \end{bmatrix}_y
\end{bmatrix}
\right\rangle
$$

I have abbreviated the proto-role properties as PAa–e (i.e. proto-agent properties a to e) and PPa–e, where the letters correspond to the properties listed in section 7.5, (34) and (35), save for the proto-patient property that Joshi added (PPf), which I rejected.

This kind of input is cumbersome in tableaux. So I will instead use inputs that encode the same proto-role information in a more concise manner:

(51) ⟨arg1[PAb,PAe,PPa] arg2[PAe]⟩

This abbreviated format represents only the part of the input that is relevant for my analysis. The correspondence should be clear on inspection. Although I am assuming an unordered argument structure, I will number the arguments so that which grammatical functions they have mapped to will be more obvious.

The inputs I use generally contain the proto-role information attributed to them in Joshi (1993). However, she does not attribute the full set of proto-properties to predicates in all cases, whereas I have endeavoured to include all of a predicate's arguments' proto-properties (except for PPf). Thus, my inputs are in certain respects richer than Joshi's, but only include the necessary proto-role entailments of the predicates in question, as motivated in Dowty (1991). Appendix A gives the proto-properties for each of the alternating verbs listed by Joshi (1993).

The candidates and outputs will be triples of c-structures, f-structures and a-structures.[36] Evidently, this will consist of fixing the underspecified GF feature to a fully specified grammatical function, SUBJ and OBJ in particular. Since I am using the architecture proposed by Butt et al. (1997), this essentially amounts to specifying the λ projection function, which is the linking function.

Once again, though, these large f-structure and a-structure pairs are too cumbersome for tableaux, so I will abbreviate the relevant parts of the candidates like so:

$$\begin{bmatrix} \text{SUBJ} & \begin{bmatrix} \text{arg1} & [\text{PAb, PAe, PPa}] \end{bmatrix} \\ \text{OBJ} & \begin{bmatrix} \text{arg2} & [\text{PAe}] \end{bmatrix} \end{bmatrix}$$
(52)

In this example, one argument has been linked to the subject function, while the other has been linked to the object function. The necessary constraints and ranking are in place now, and I have characterized the form of the inputs and candidates.

7.6.2 Optionality in Marathi Linking

First, I will show how these constraints capture the subject/object alternation in non-volitional transitives. In the tableaux, I have suppressed the constraint ranking values. Instead, I have represented the fact that *Subj/P-P, *Subj/P-A$_{-vol}$, *Nonsubj/P-A$_{-vol}$, and *Nonsubj/P-P can alternate with numerals above these constraints. These numerals are then used to indicate which constraint ranking results in which optimal candidate. For example, the notation $(1 \gg 2 \gg 3 \gg 4)$ next to the pointing finger is shorthand for (*Subj/P-P $\gg$ *Subj/P-A$_{-vol}$ $\gg$ *Nonsubj/P-A$_{-vol}$ $\gg$ *Nonsubj/P-P).

The first case to consider is that of verbs in the 'like' class and the first two verbs in the 'find' class (see appendix A). These verbs all have one argument that is entailed to be sentient (PAb), exists independently of the event (PAe), and undergoes a change of state (PPa). The second argument is entailed to exist independently of the event (PAe) and has no other proto-properties. (*Nonsubj/P-A$_{vol}$ has been omitted in (53) for reasons of space.)

---

[36] Bresnan (2000b) and Kuhn (2001) propose that the candidate set in both production and comprehension directed optimization is actually a set of c-structure, f-structure pairs (i.e. $\{\langle x,y \rangle \mid x \text{ is a c-structure and } y \text{ is an f-structure}\}$). Thus the candidates and outputs assumed here are triples, since they also contain a-structures. However, we can ignore the c-structures in production, since the linking optionality only has to do with grammatical function information in the f-structure. In section 7.6.4, which deals with ambiguity in comprehension, the c-structures will be discussed further.

(53)   **Non-volitional transitives 1**
'like' class
'find' class: saapaḍne (to find)
'find' class: aaḍʰalne (to come across)

		THEMATIC$_{subj}$	MAX(proto)	DEP(proto)	1 *Subj/P-P	2 *Subj/P-A$_{-vol}$	3 *NonSubj/P-A$_{-vol}$	4 *Nonsubj/P-P
a.		*!	****					
b.		*!	***				*	
c.			*!**		*			
d.				*!	**	**	*	
e.	(3 ≫ 1 ≫ 2 ≫ 4) ☞				*	**	*	
	(3 ≫ 1 ≫ 4 ≫ 2)							
	(3 ≫ 4 ≫ 1 ≫ 2)							
f.	(1 ≫ 2 ≫ 3 ≫ 4) ☞					*	**	*
	(1 ≫ 3 ≫ 2 ≫ 4)							
	(1 ≫ 3 ≫ 4 ≫ 2)							

Input: ⟨arg1[PAb,PAe,PPa] arg2[PAe]⟩

a. = $\begin{bmatrix} \text{SUBJ} & [\text{arg1}[\ ]] \\ \text{OBJ} & [\text{arg2}[\ ]] \end{bmatrix}$

b. = $\begin{bmatrix} \text{SUBJ} & [\text{arg1}[\ ]] \\ \text{OBJ} & [\text{arg2}[\text{PAe}]] \end{bmatrix}$

c. = $\begin{bmatrix} \text{SUBJ} & [\text{arg1}[\text{PPa}]] \\ \text{OBJ} & [\text{arg2}[\ ]] \end{bmatrix}$

d. = $\begin{bmatrix} \text{SUBJ} & [\text{arg2}[\text{PAb,PAe,PPa,PPb}]] \\ \text{OBJ} & [\text{arg1}[\text{PAe}]] \end{bmatrix}$

e. = $\begin{bmatrix} \text{SUBJ} & [\text{arg1}[\text{PAb,PAe,PPa}]] \\ \text{OBJ} & [\text{arg2}[\text{PAe}]] \end{bmatrix}$

f. − $\begin{bmatrix} \text{SUBJ} & [\text{arg2}[\text{PAe}]] \\ \text{OBJ} & [\text{arg1}[\text{PAb,PAe,PPa}]] \end{bmatrix}$

Due to the high-ranking THEMATIC$_{subj}$ constraint, candidates (a) and (b) are knocked out immediately, since they have subjects with no associated proto-properties. This also results in several MAX(proto) violations, as these candidates do not realize proto-role information from the input. Candidate (c) does have a subject with a proto-property, thus not violating THEMATIC$_{subj}$, but it is eliminated by MAX(proto). In fact, any candidate that does not realize all of the proto-role information in the input will be eliminated in this manner. Therefore, in subsequent tableaux I do not show such candidates. Similarly, candidate (d) has a fatal violation of DEP(proto), since the proto-property PPb is present on its subject, but is not present in the input. I will also suppress further DEP violators. In subsequent tableaux, I leave out the constraints THEMATIC$_{subj}$, MAX(proto), *Nonsubj/P-A$_{vol}$, and DEP(proto) until the discussion of volitionality in section 7.6.3.

This leaves candidates (e) and (f). In this tableau and any other tableaux with $1 \gg 3$, candidate (f) is the winner. However, on any of the three other legitimate rankings of the optional constraints (where $3 \gg 1$), candidate (e) will be the winner. Thus, these constraints yield subject/object alternation for non-volitional transitives, since the only difference between the candidates is in which argument gets mapped to which grammatical function.[37]

The next case I consider is that of the final two 'find' class verbs, _miḷne_ (to get) and _laab^{h}ṇe_ (to come to possess). These verbs share the same proto-properties as the other 'find' verbs, but the second argument is in addition entailed to undergo a change of location (PPa).

The addition of a single proto-property results in a drastic change in distribution. Now the first candidate is selected on five out of six rankings, while the second candidate is selected only on the ranking $1 \gg 2 \gg 3 \gg 4$. Foreshadowing the discussion in section 7.7 somewhat, there is a difference between candidates (a) and (b) in terms of proto-properties that explains why candidate (a) is favoured. Note that arg2 has one proto-agent property and one proto-patient property; so, it is just as good a subject as it is an object. However, arg1 has two proto-agent properties and one proto-patient properties. This means arg1 is a better subject than object. Candidate (a) has arg1 mapped to SUBJ and arg2 mapped to OBJ, which is what we would

---

[37]It should be noted that nothing in this analysis distinguishes between objects and obliques, which is another important facet of linking in Marathi, since it is a symmetric language. I assume that separate case distribution principles will make the necessary distinctions, as obliques are always marked with oblique case or with a postposition (Pandharipande 1997; Joshi 1993; see section 7.8, example (2c)).

In fact, as suggested by Joan Bresnan (p.c.), in order to capture various generalizations about subjects and objects ranking higher than obliques according to certain criteria, it may be necessary to assume a prominence scale such as Core > Oblique, in addition to the Subject > Nonsubject scale assumed here. We could align the proposed new scale with the proto-role scale as well, thus enabling us to make statements about the realizations of thematic information in obliques. The resulting constraints, along with the constraints for stating the case facts mentioned above, could then be used in accounting for the object symmetry property, as well as possibly related facts, such as the causee in an active causative being realized as an oblique.

A third alternative is to incorporate the OT constraints proposed by Alsina (2000) for distinguishing first and second objects in asymmetric languages and for distinguishing objects from obliques in symmetric and asymmetric languages.

expect according to proto-role theory, as arg1 is a better subject, while arg2 is as good an object as it is a subject.

(54) **Non-volitional transitives 2**
'find' class: milṇe (to get)
'find' class: laab^{h}ṇe (to come to possess)

			1	2	3	4
			*Subj/P-P	*Subj/P-A$_{-vol}$	*Nonsubj/P-A$_{-vol}$	*Nonsubj/P-P
a.	$(1 \gg 3 \gg 2 \gg 4)$	☞	*	**	*	*
	$(1 \gg 3 \gg 4 \gg 2)$					
	$(3 \gg 1 \gg 2 \gg 4)$					
	$(3 \gg 1 \gg 4 \gg 2)$					
	$(3 \gg 4 \gg 1 \gg 2)$					
b.	$(1 \gg 2 \gg 3 \gg 4)$	☞	*	*	**	*

Input: $\langle$arg1[PAb,PAe,PPa] arg2[PAe, PPa]$\rangle$

a. = $\begin{bmatrix} \text{SUBJ} & [\text{arg1}[\text{PAb,PAe,PPa}]] \\ \text{OBJ} & [\text{arg2}[\text{PAe,PPa}]] \end{bmatrix}$

b. = $\begin{bmatrix} \text{SUBJ} & [\text{arg2}[\text{PAe,PPa}]] \\ \text{OBJ} & [\text{arg1}[\text{PAb,PAe,PPa}]] \end{bmatrix}$

Next I turn to the first set of passive ditransitives. These verbs all have one argument (arg2) that is entailed to be sentient (PAb), exists independently of the event (PAe), undergoes a change of state (PPa), is causally affected by the demoted first argument (PPc), and is stationary relative to the movement of the third argument (PPd). The other argument (arg3) is entailed to exist independently of the event (PAe), moves relative to the second argument (PAd), undergoes a change of location (PPa), and is causally affected by the demoted first argument (PPc).

(55) **Passives of ditransitives 1**
    deṇe (to give); paaṭʰawṇe (to send)
    bʰarawṇe (to feed); wikṇe (to sell)

		1	2	3	4
		*Subj/P-P	*Subj/P-A$_{-vol}$	*Nonsubj/P-A$_{-vol}$	*Nonsubj/P-P
a.	$(3 \gg 4 \gg 1 \gg 2)$ ☞	***	**	**	**
b.	$(1 \gg 2 \gg 3 \gg 4)$ ☞	**	**	**	***
	$(1 \gg 3 \gg 2 \gg 4)$				
	$(1 \gg 3 \gg 4 \gg 2)$				
	$(3 \gg 1 \gg 2 \gg 4)$				
	$(3 \gg 1 \gg 4 \gg 2)$				

Input: $<\emptyset$ arg2[PAb, PAe, PPa, PPc, PPd]
     arg3[PAd, PAe, PPa, PPc]$>$

a. $=$ $\begin{bmatrix} \text{SUBJ} & [\text{arg2[PAb, PAe, PPa, PPc, PPd]]} \\ \text{OBJ} & [\text{arg3[PAd, PAe, PPa, PPc]]} \end{bmatrix}$

b. $=$ $\begin{bmatrix} \text{SUBJ} & [\text{arg3[PAd, PAe, PPa, PPc]]} \\ \text{OBJ} & [\text{arg2[PAb, PAe, PPa, PPc, PPd]]} \end{bmatrix}$

Candidate (a) is selected on only one out of six constraint rankings, and candidate (b) is selected on the other five rankings. Again, the candidate that is favoured is the one whose mappings respect the predictions of proto-role theory. Arg3 has two proto-agent properties and two proto-patient properties, while arg2 has three proto-patient properties and only two proto-agent properties. This means that arg2 makes a better object than subject, while arg3 is as good a subject as it is an object. Candidate (b) maps arg2 to OBJ and arg3 to SUBJ,

The second set of passive ditransitives, presented in tableau (56), consists of the semantically similar verbs *linhiṇe* (to write (a letter)) and *saangṇe* (to tell). These verbs have one argument (arg3) that is causally affected by the demoted first argument, which is the writer or teller (PPc), and that does not exist independently of the event (PPe), as the letter or statement comes into existence through being written or told. The other argument (arg2) is entailed to be sentient (PAb), exists independently of the event (PAe), undergoes a change of state (PPa), and is causally affected by the demoted first argument (PPc).

(56) **Passives of ditransitives 2**
   linhiṇe (to write (a letter)); saangṇe (to tell)

			1	2	3	4
			*Subj/P-P	*Subj/P-A$_{-vol}$	*Nonsubj/P-A$_{-vol}$	*Nonsubj/P-P
a.	(1 ≫ 3 ≫ 2 ≫ 4)	☞	**	**		**
	(1 ≫ 3 ≫ 4 ≫ 2)					
	(3 ≫ 1 ≫ 2 ≫ 4)					
	(3 ≫ 1 ≫ 4 ≫ 2)					
	(3 ≫ 4 ≫ 1 ≫ 2)					
b.	(1 ≫ 2 ≫ 3 ≫ 4)	☞	**		**	**

Input: ⟨Ø   arg2[PAb, PAe, PPa, PPc]   arg3[PPc, PPe]⟩

$$\text{a.} = \begin{bmatrix} \text{SUBJ} & [\text{arg2}[\text{PAb, PAe, PPa, PPc}]] \\ \text{OBJ} & [\text{arg3}[\text{PPa, PPc}]] \end{bmatrix}$$

$$\text{b.} = \begin{bmatrix} \text{SUBJ} & [\text{arg3}[\text{PPa, PPc}]] \\ \text{OBJ} & [\text{arg2}[\text{PAb, PAe, PPa, PPc}]] \end{bmatrix}$$

Unlike the other passive ditransitives, arg2 is not stationary relative to the movement of arg3. Therefore, arg2 lacks the proto-patient property PPd. This means that arg2 for these passive ditransitives has two proto-agent properties and two proto-patient properties, meaning there is nothing to distinguish it as an object versus a subject. On the other hand, arg3 *only* has proto-patient properties, making it a good object but a bad subject. We see again that candidate (a) which is preferred on five out of six rankings, is the one where proto-role theory is respected and arg2 is SUBJ while arg3 is OBJ.

This leaves us only with the passives of ditransitive causatives to consider. These are again broken into two sets, according to their proto-properties. The first set has one argument (arg2) that is entailed to be sentient (PAb), exists independently of the event (PAe), undergoes a change of state (PPa), and is causally affected by the demoted causer (PPc). The other argument (arg3) is entailed to exist independently of the event (PAe), but bears no other proto-properties.

(57) **Passives of ditransitive causatives 1**
aikawn̩e (to hear.CAUS)
hungawn̩e (to smell.CAUS)
šikawn̩e (to teach)

			1	2	3	4
			*Subj/P-P	*Subj/P-A$_{-vol}$	*Nonsubj/P-A$_{-vol}$	*Nonsubj/P-P
a.	$(3 \gg 1 \gg 2 \gg 4)$	☞	**	**	*	
	$(3 \gg 1 \gg 4 \gg 2)$					
	$(3 \gg 4 \gg 1 \gg 2)$					
b.	$(1 \gg 2 \gg 3 \gg 4)$	☞		*	**	**
	$(1 \gg 3 \gg 2 \gg 4)$					
	$(1 \gg 3 \gg 4 \gg 2)$					

Input: $\langle \emptyset \quad \text{arg2[PAb, PAe, PPa, PPc]} \quad \text{arg3[PAe]} \rangle$

a. $= \begin{bmatrix} \text{SUBJ} & \text{[arg2[PAb, PAe, PPa, PPc]]} \\ \text{OBJ} & \text{[arg3[PAe]]} \end{bmatrix}$

b. $= \begin{bmatrix} \text{SUBJ} & \text{[arg3[PAe]]} \\ \text{OBJ} & \text{[arg2[PAb, PAe, PPa, PPc]]} \end{bmatrix}$

Notice that the input in this tableau is similar to the one for non-volitional transitives 1 in (53), except that the first non-suppressed argument (arg1 in (53), arg2 in (57)) has one more proto-patient property in (57). In both cases the final argument makes a better subject than object, as its only proto-property is PAe. And the first (non-suppressed) argument is the best object, as it is the only argument with any proto-patient properties. But, the first argument also has more proto-agent properties than the final argument does. So we have a situation in which the same argument is both the best subject and the best object. Since the grammar attempts to assign the same argument to both subject and object, each optimal candidate wins in half the cases, with one winning when $3 \gg 1$ and the other winning when $1 \gg 3$.

Lastly, let us consider the final passive ditransitive causative, *paadzṇe* (to feed), which has slightly different proto-properties from the causatives in (57). Arg2 has the same entailments, but arg3 has additional entailments beyond that of existing independently (PAe). The other entailments are movement relative to the position of arg2 (PAd), undergoing change of location (PPa), being the incremental theme (PPb), and being causally affected by arg2.

(58) **Passives of ditransitive causatives 2**
     paadzṇe (to feed)

		1	2	3	4
		*Subj/P-P	*Subj/P-A$_{-vol}$	*Nonsubj/P-A$_{-vol}$	*Nonsubj/P-P
a.	(1 ≫ 2 ≫ 3 ≫ 4) ☞	**	**	**	***
	(1 ≫ 3 ≫ 2 ≫ 4)				
	(1 ≫ 3 ≫ 4 ≫ 2)				
	(3 ≫ 1 ≫ 2 ≫ 4)				
	(3 ≫ 1 ≫ 4 ≫ 2)				
b.	(3 ≫ 4 ≫ 1 ≫ 2) ☞	***	**	**	**

Input: <∅   arg2[PAb, PAe, PPa, PPc]
         arg3[PAd, PAe, PPa, PPb, PPc]>

a. = $\begin{bmatrix} \text{SUBJ} & [\text{arg2[PAb, PAe, PPa, PPc]}] \\ \text{OBJ} & [\text{arg3[PAd, PAe, PPa, PPb, PPc]}] \end{bmatrix}$

b. = $\begin{bmatrix} \text{SUBJ} & [\text{arg3[PAd, PAe, PPa, PPb, PPc]}] \\ \text{OBJ} & [\text{arg2[PAb, PAe, PPa, PPc]}] \end{bmatrix}$

This presents yet another case of subject/object alternation with preference for one candidate over the other. Arg2 has equally many proto-agent and proto-patient properties, and therefore serves equally well as subject or object. However, arg3 has more proto-patient properties than proto-agent properties, making it a better object than subject. Once again this is reflected in the competition: candidate (a) is selected on five out of six rankings, and this is the candidate with arg2 as subject and arg3 as object.

7.6.3 Volitionality

Tableaux (53) to (58) show that the OT grammar outlined here does indeed get the subject/object alternation in all three relevant cases. Thus, fact (41b) has been accounted for: when there is no volitional argument there is subject/object alternation. The analysis also accounts for fact (41a), which states that if there is a volitional argument, it must be the subject. This is where *Nonsubj/P-A$_{vol}$—the top ranked constraint on the nonsubject grammatical function/proto-role alignment—comes in.[38]

(59)

Volitional transitives

		⟨arg1[PAa, ...] arg2[...]⟩	THEMATIC$_{subj}$	MAX(proto)	*Nonsubj/P-A$_{vol}$
a.		SUBJ [arg2[...]] OBJ [arg1[...]]		*!	
b.		SUBJ [arg2[...]] OBJ [arg1[PAa, ...]]			*!
c.	☞	SUBJ [arg1[PAa, ...]] OBJ [arg2[...]]			

Candidate (a) shows that the property of volitionality, if present in the input, must be realized in the output, or else offending candidates are eliminated by MAX(proto). Candidates (b) and (c) show that once the property of volitionality is realized, it must be realized on the subject, as realizing it on the object results in a violation of *Nonsubj/P-A$_{vol}$. In cases where the input has two arguments marked as volitional, such as in the verb 'khelne' (to play with), the object will be marked for volitionality, even though this violates *Nonsubj/P-A$_{vol}$, because not realizing the property would result in a violation of MAX(proto), which is worse (see tableau (2a) in appendix B).

Thus, this analysis correctly accounts for the fact that subjects in Marathi are volitional, and that in cases where there is no volitional argument, there will be a choice in linking arguments to grammatical functions.

---

[38]In this tableau, I have glossed over all of the proto-roles except that of volitionality, representing them with ellipses (...). Similarly, I have suppressed DEP(proto) and the variable ranking constraints, as these play no role in selecting the winner.

In section 7.7, I compare this approach to Joshi's. But first, let us consider how this grammar deals with ambiguity in the comprehension direction.

7.6.4 Ambiguity

In section 7.2, I argued that optionality and ambiguity in OT can be viewed as opposite sides of the same coin. If we view the difference as one between production and comprehension directed optimization, then the inputs of each kind of optimization correspond to the outputs of the other (Smolensky, 1996c, 1998). Thus, both optionality and ambiguity could be viewed as one input to the optimization having multiple outputs, with the nature of inputs and outputs varying in the appropriate way.

Recall from section 7.2 that one way of handling ineffability in OT is through the use of bidirectional optimization. If we assume Smolensky's (1998) formulation of bidirectional optimization, then the inputs to production are semantic forms (like the f-structure/a-structure pair in (50)) and the inputs to comprehension are strings. The constraints and their ranking are identical in both production and comprehension, though.

From the string inputs to the comprehension directed optimization, the function **Gen** will yield the candidate set of (semantic) f-structures. However, we want to make sure that only those f-structures that match the input string are generated. As mentioned briefly in section 7.6.2 (see footnote 36), a standard assumption in OT-LFG is that the candidate set in both production and comprehension directed optimization is a set of c-structure and f-structure pairs (Bresnan, 2000b; Kuhn, 2001) and I have extended this to include a-structures. In comprehension, we need to consider the string yield of the c-structure members of these triples. Only those triples whose c-structure yields match the input string are generated (Kuhn, 2001).

As motivated in Kuhn (2001) and Johnson (1998), consideration of the string's yield results in an asymmetry between generation and parsing which means further steps have to be taken for parsing. In generation, an input to **Gen** gives candidates with all kinds of (ungrammatical) strings as the yields of their c-structure members. Kuhn (2001) gives the example of the input for a wh-question having as one of the generated strings *She do read what*. Now, if we were to try and parse this string, every candidate in the candidate set will have this string as its yield. So no matter which candidate is optimal, the candidate should actually be ungrammatical and should not be generated.

Kuhn (2001) therefore proposes a filtering function for the resulting optimal candidates of comprehension to get back the kind of input f-structures that are used in generation (i.e. semantic forms). Then a backwards generation step is executed and only the optimal candidate(s) with a string yield that matches the yield of the string being parsed are selected. If no such candidate exists (as in the example), the input string to comprehension is rejected as ungrammatical. This is essentially bidirectional optimization.

Ambiguity in Marathi Linking

The Marathi data that I have been examining does present a case of ambiguity: the strings that display optionality in linking (i.e. non-volitional transitives and passive ditransitives) are ambiguous regarding which noun phrase in the string is assigned to the subject role and which is assigned to the object role. This can be viewed as a kind of structural or parsing ambiguity.[39]

Let us now observe how the constraint system developed for non-volitional transitives in production works in comprehension.[40] Note that I have only presented the two winning candidates (depending on the ranking of the floating constraints, as before).

(60)   **Non-volitional transitives** (comprehension)
       Input: "tyaa mulaa-laa te aaiskrim aawaḍte."

		THEMATIC$_{subj}$	MAX(proto)	*Nonsubj/P-A$_{vol}$	DEP(proto)	1 *Subj/P-P	2 *Subj/P-A$_{-vol}$	3 *Nonsubj/P-A$_{-vol}$	4 *Nonsubj/P-P
a.	(3 ≫ 1 ≫ 2 ≫ 4) ☞					*	**	*	
	(3 ≫ 1 ≫ 4 ≫ 2)								
	(3 ≫ 4 ≫ 1 ≫ 2)								
b.	(1 ≫ 2 ≫ 3 ≫ 4) ☞						*	**	*
	(1 ≫ 3 ≫ 2 ≫ 4)								
	(1 ≫ 3 ≫ 4 ≫ 2)								

---

[39]At first this may not seem like a true semantic ambiguity, since the meaning is constant. But, once we embed these ambiguous sentences in broader contexts which show discourse effects, we should be able to observe the semantic effects of this ambiguity. In particular, SUBJ is a discourse function, whereas OBJ is not. Therefore, in context, the strings under consideration here will be ambiguous, as either NP could be the subject discourse function.

[40]This is example (49) from section 7.6.1:
tyaa mulaa-laa te   aaiskrim aawaḍte.
that boy-D/A   that ice-cream likes
That boy likes that ice cream.

a. =

$$
\left\langle
\begin{bmatrix}
\text{PRED} & \text{'aawaḍne'} \\
\text{SUBJ} & \begin{bmatrix} \text{PRED} & \text{'mulaa'} \\ \text{PERS} & 3 \\ \text{NUM} & \text{SG} \\ \text{GEND} & \text{MASC} \\ \text{DEIXIS} & + \end{bmatrix}_x \\
\text{OBJ} & \begin{bmatrix} \text{PRED} & \text{'aaiskrim'} \\ \text{PERS} & 3 \\ \text{NUM} & \text{SG} \\ \text{DEIXIS} & + \end{bmatrix}_y \\
\text{TNS} & \text{PRESENT}
\end{bmatrix}
, \quad
\begin{bmatrix}
\text{REL} & \text{aawaḍne} \\
\text{ARG1} & \begin{bmatrix} \text{P-A} & \{PAb, PAe\} \\ \text{P-P} & \{PPa\} \end{bmatrix}_x \\
\text{ARG2} & \begin{bmatrix} \text{P-A} & \{PAe\} \\ \text{P-P} & \{\} \end{bmatrix}_y
\end{bmatrix}_x
\right\rangle
$$

b. =

$$
\left\langle
\begin{bmatrix}
\text{PRED} & \text{'aawaḍne'} \\
\text{SUBJ} & \begin{bmatrix} \text{PRED} & \text{'aaiskrim'} \\ \text{PERS} & 3 \\ \text{NUM} & \text{SG} \\ \text{DEIXIS} & + \end{bmatrix}_y \\
\text{OBJ} & \begin{bmatrix} \text{PRED} & \text{'mulaa'} \\ \text{PERS} & 3 \\ \text{NUM} & \text{SG} \\ \text{GEND} & \text{MASC} \\ \text{DEIXIS} & + \end{bmatrix}_x \\
\text{TNS} & \text{PRESENT}
\end{bmatrix}
, \quad
\begin{bmatrix}
\text{REL} & \text{aawaḍne} \\
\text{ARG1} & \begin{bmatrix} \text{P-A} & \{PAb, PAe\} \\ \text{P-P} & \{PPa\} \end{bmatrix}_x \\
\text{ARG2} & \begin{bmatrix} \text{P-A} & \{PAe\} \\ \text{P-P} & \{\} \end{bmatrix}_y
\end{bmatrix}
\right\rangle
$$

Any candidate that does not have a GF SUBJ will be knocked out by THEMATIC$_{subj}$. The interpretation of the faithfulness constraints, MAX(proto) and DEP(proto), is more complex, but unproblematic. Proto-role information essentially concerns entailments from predicate meanings, in this case verb meanings. In lexical look-up, the verb *patlaa* brings along with it these entailments and hence the proto-role information. In other words, to understand the string, a hearer would have to necessarily understand the words in the string. Since the proto-role information is part of the meaning of *patlaa*, or at least directly inferable from that meaning, these faithfulness constraints can operate by comparing the inferable proto-role information to the information present in the candidates. They will thus serve to rule out candidates with the wrong proto-properties (i.e. the wrong inferences).

Therefore, either candidate (a) or (b) will win, depending on how the floating constraints are fixed at evaluation time. Applying Kuhn's filtering function, we get the following semantic form:[41]

---

[41]Technically, this is the recovered semantic form for candidate (a). Candidate (b) would have GF$_1$ and GF$_2$ swapped. However, there is no real distinction here as the features are identical. The index is there only to respect functional uniqueness.

(61)

$$\left\langle \begin{bmatrix} \text{PRED} & \text{'aawadne'} \\ \text{GF}_1 & \begin{bmatrix} \text{PRED} & \text{'mulaa'} \\ \text{PERS} & 3 \\ \text{NUM} & \text{SG} \\ \text{GEND} & \text{MASC} \\ \text{DEIXIS} & + \end{bmatrix}_x \\ \text{GF}_2 & \begin{bmatrix} \text{PRED} & \text{'aaiskrim'} \\ \text{PERS} & 3 \\ \text{NUM} & \text{SG} \\ \text{DEIXIS} & + \end{bmatrix}_y \\ \text{TNS} & \text{PRESENT} \end{bmatrix}, \begin{bmatrix} \text{REL} & \text{aawadne} \\ \text{ARG1} & \begin{bmatrix} \text{P-A} & \{PAb, PAe\} \\ \text{P-P} & \{PPa\} \end{bmatrix} \\ \text{ARG2} & \begin{bmatrix} \text{P-A} & \{PAe\} \\ \text{P-P} & \{\} \end{bmatrix}_y \end{bmatrix}_x \right\rangle$$

The grammatical functions SUBJ and OBJ have been underspecified to GF$_1$ and GF$_2$. By the notational convention discussed on page 287, this is equivalent to:

(62) ⟨arg1[PAb,PAe,PPa] arg2[PAe]⟩

The reader can see by referring to tableau (53) that this is indeed the input for non-volitional transitives in the production grammar. Similar results can be shown for passive ditransitives and passive ditransitive causatives. I will not go through these other results here.

Thus, the OT grammar fragment presented here can account for both the syntactic production optionality in Marathi linking and the comprehension ambiguity for the same constructions. This shows that production optionality and comprehension ambiguity are formally the same in OT grammars. In other words, the system of continuously-ranked constraints that was used to capture optionality can also be used to capture ambiguity. In this paper, I have illustrated this by looking at the same domain. However, I see no principled reason why other types of ambiguity that do not have optionality in the production direction could not be handled in the same manner.

7.7 Comparing the OT Approach with Joshi's Approach

Joshi's analysis not only accounts for the subject/object alternation, it also accounts for the fact that Marathi is a symmetric language, and for several intriguing facts about logical subjects and logical objects. The analysis developed here only accounts for the alternation facts. With respect to just these facts, there are five major differences between my analysis and Joshi's and I will argue that these provide reasons for preferring this analysis.

One major difference is that the OT analysis uses a small number of crosslinguistically viable constraints with an ordering specific to Marathi, whereas Joshi's syntactic feature rules (in (36)) and function mapping principles (in (37)) are part of a parametric approach to language variation, with the relevant parameters set for Marathi. It may seem that the two approaches are more or less equivalent, but while it is not obvious from Joshi's exposition what the relevant dimensions of variation between languages might be, the OT approach makes particular claims (through constraint reordering) about language variation. Of course, this is not a specific problem with Joshi's analysis, but rather an instance of the problem of relating parameters across languages and deciding what the limits of the space of parametric variation are.

The second difference is that in the OT analysis the alternation between subject and object linking and the fact that volitional arguments are realized as subjects are both derived from the alignment of the grammatical function and proto-role prominence scales. This alignment yielded the automatic consequence that volitional arguments are subjects, without ever stipulating it directly. However, Joshi's LFG account does stipulate this property directly (in (37a)).

Third, Joshi's analysis uses proto-patient properties as criteria of subjecthood. Recall the generalizations in (40) from section 7.5:

(40) a. If a predicate has a volitional argument, that argument is realized as the subject; otherwise any argument of the verb that possesses a proto-patient property can be the grammatical subject. (Joshi, 1993, 92)

   b. If there is no volitional argument and there is more than one argument that has a proto-patient property there will be subject/object alternation.

Once the proto-agent property of volitionality does not apply, subject choice is entirely dependent on proto-patient properties. But proto-patient properties were proposed for object selection, not subject selection (Dowty, 1991). Joshi's proposal therefore runs contrary to the theory she presupposes. The OT analysis rejects the proposal that proto-patient properties determine subject choice and thus maintains proto-role theory's original insights.

The fourth difference is that Joshi proposes a new proto-patient property, "not entailed to be sentient" (PPf), which I do not adopt. As discussed in section 7.5, there are two problems with this proto-property. First, it would fit better with proto-role theory if this property was "entailed to be non-sentient", which is a stronger entailment and in direct opposition to the proto-agent property of sentience (PAb). Many of the proto-agent and proto-patient properties are in direct opposition to each other (Dowty, 1991), in particular PAc-d and PPc-d, and this would be another such case. This brings us to the second problem: any argument of a verb that *lacks* the proto-agent property of sentience will automatically have the property of not being entailed to be sentient. The proto-patient property that Joshi proposes is directly entailed by this absence and is superfluous, because its presence is completely predictable. Note that this contrasts with PAc-d and

PPc-d, because these are such that if, for example, one argument has the entailment of the relevant PA property, then a *different* argument gets the opposing entailment. Thus, the new property does not fit into proto-role theory and its motivation is suspect.

The fifth difference between my analysis and Joshi's also has to do with Dowty's proto-role theory and has interesting implications for that theory. Originally, the idea behind Dowty's analysis was that the argument with more proto-agent properties gets linked to the subject function, whereas the argument with more proto-patient properties gets linked to the object function. Any kind of alternation in linking would be predicted to only occur if there is a tie on the number of relevant properties. But, in both Joshi's analysis and this one, this is no longer strictly true. If it *were* true, only the dative-marked argument in non-volitional transitives (e.g., the 'finder' in the 'find' class), could be realized as the subject, for example, since this argument has two proto-agent properties, whereas the other argument only has one (see tableau (54)).

In Joshi's analysis, this feature of Dowty's theory is simply given up. However, in the analysis presented here it is still preserved, but only as a tendency, rather than as an absolute property. Looking back at tableau (54) for a subset of the 'find' class of non-volitional transitives, one alternate is picked five out of six times, whereas the other one is picked only one in six times.[42] The striking fact is that the alternate that is picked most often is the one where the subject has more proto-agent properties than the object.[43] Similarly, the opposing tendency of objects to have more proto-patient properties is illustrated in tableau (55). In that tableau, one candidate is again realized five times out of six, whereas the other is realized only once out of every six times. The candidate that is picked most often is the one in which the object, rather than the subject, has the most proto-patient properties.[44] Thus, the argument with the most proto-agent properties is *preferentially* but not obligatorily linked to the subject, and the argument with the most proto-patient properties is again only preferentially linked to the object.

Another consequence of this analysis is that the optionality in linking is predicted to disappear if there is an asymmetry between arguments on both the number of proto-agent properties and the number of proto-patient

---

[42]How we interpret these predicted frequencies is an open question. It is unrealistic to interpret them as raw frequencies. I believe they should instead be interpreted as encoding the strength of the tendency in question.

[43]The tendency is purely due to the difference in the number of proto-agent properties, since each argument in the winning candidates in (54) has exactly one proto-patient property.

[44]In the same way that proto-patient properties are kept constant across the two arguments in (54), each argument of the winning candidates in (55) has two proto-agent properties. The tendency in argument realization noted in this case is therefore entirely due to the differing number of proto-patient properties.

properties. That is, if the first argument has more proto-agent properties than the second and the second argument has more proto-patient properties, then the first argument must be linked to the subject and the second argument must be linked to the object, as would be the case in Dowty's original theory. This can be demonstrated easily by using similar inputs to the ones that yielded optionality. I will show that adding a proto-patient property to the second argument in the 'find' class of non-volitional transitive would remove the optionality.

(63)

	THEMATIC$_{subj}$	MAX(proto)	*Nonsubj/P-A$_{vol}$	DEP(proto)	1 *Subj/P-P	2 *Subj/P-A$_{-vol}$	3 *Nonsubj/P-A$_{-vol}$	4 *Nonsubj/P-P
a.					**	*	**	*
b. ☞					*	**	*	**

Input: $\langle$arg1[PAb,PAe,PPa] arg2[PAe,PPa,PPb]$\rangle$

$$a. = \begin{bmatrix} \text{SUBJ} & [\text{arg2[PAe,PPa,PPb]}] \\ \text{OBJ} & [\text{arg1[PAb,PAe,PPa]}] \end{bmatrix}$$

$$b. = \begin{bmatrix} \text{SUBJ} & [\text{arg1[PAb,PAe,PPa]}] \\ \text{OBJ} & [\text{arg2[PAe,PPa,PPb]}] \end{bmatrix}$$

According to the hierarchies in (43b), *Subj/P-P must outrank *Subj/P-A$_{-vol}$ and *Nonsubj/P-A$_{-vol}$ must outrank *Nonsubj/P-P. Therefore, either *Subj/P-P or *Nonsubj/P-A$_{-vol}$ must be the highest ranking constraint at evaluation time. Whenever *Subj/P-P is ranked highest, candidate (b) wins. This is the candidate which has the argument with most proto-patient properties linked to the object and the one with most proto-agent properties linked to the subject. And this candidate also wins whenever *Nonsubj/P-A$_{-vol}$ is ranked highest, because it is also the candidate in which the object has the least proto-agent properties.[45] Therefore, there is no optionality: the argument with the most proto-agent properties is linked

---

[45] It is easy to observe in the tableau why this should be true. Since the two candidates have exactly the same constraint violation profile for both *Subj/P-P and *Nonsubj/P-A$_{-vol}$, it does not matter which of these constraints is ranked highest.

to the subject and the argument with the most proto-patient properties is linked to the object.[46]

7.8 Conclusion

In this paper, I have shown how continuously-ranked constraints in a stochastic model of OT can be used to describe optionality and ambiguity in syntax. I argued that this method was preferable to other approaches to optionality proposed in the OT literature. Finally, I applied the method to describing a specific case of syntactic optionality and ambiguity: argument linking in certain Marathi predicates.

The analysis developed here builds on that of Joshi (1993) in using proto-role information. However, while Joshi has to give up certain facts about proto-roles and grammatical function selection originally proposed by Dowty (1991), this analysis preserves those insights as tendencies. Furthermore, this analysis uses crosslinguistically viable constraints and only a simple mechanism of constraint alignment. Thus, the OT analysis of subject/object alternation in Marathi has three attractive features. First, it uses a small number of crosslinguistically viable constraints. Second, one mechanism—harmonic alignment—is used to account for both the subject/object alternation and the fact that volitional arguments must be subjects. Third, and most interestingly, this analysis preserves as a tendency Dowty's observation that the argument with most proto-agent properties is realized as the subject and that the argument with the most proto-patient properties is realized as the object.

I have shown that it is possible to represent linking using a small set of general, violable constraints. I have illustrated how optionality can be handled in OT syntax by using the linking theory developed here to provide an account of the subject/object alternation in Marathi. I have also shown how ambiguity in comprehension grammars can be modelled using the same methods. This gives some indication that Optimality Theory can in fact deal with ineffability, optionality and ambiguity and is a viable syntactic theory.

---

[46]The same effect can be shown using the winning candidates in tableau (55), by adding a proto-agent property (other than volitionality) to arg2.

Appendices

A. Verb Classes[47]

Verbs	Proto-Properties	

Non-volitional transitives ('like' class)	**arg1**	**arg2**
aawaḍne 'to like'	[PAb, PAe, PPa]	[PAe]
samadẑne 'to realize'	[PAb, PAe, PPa]	[(PAe)]
umagne 'to understand'	[PAb, PAe, PPa]	[PAe]
disne 'to notice'	[PAb, PAe, PPa]	[PAe]
patne 'to accept (mentally)'	[PAb, PAe, PPa]	[PAe]
ruťsne 'to agree (aesthetically)'	[PAb, PAe, PPa]	[PAe]
maanawne 'to suit (mentally, medically)'	[PAb, PAe, (PPa)]	[PAe]
kalne 'to hear/learn'	[PAb, PAe, PPa]	[PAe]

Non-volitional transitives ('find' class)	**arg1**	**arg2**
saapadne 'to find'	[PAb, PAe, PPa]	[PAe]
aadʰalne 'to come across'	[PAb, PAe, PPa]	[PAe]
milne 'to get'	[PAb, PAe, PPa]	[PAe, PPa]
laabʰne 'to come to possess'	[PAb, PAe, PPa]	[PAe, PPa]

Passive ditransitives	**arg2**	**arg3**
dene 'to give'	[PAb, PAe, PPa, PPc, PPd]	[PAd, PAe, PPa, PPc]
paatʰawne 'to send'	[PAb, PAe, PPa, PPc, PPd]	[PAd, PAe, PPa, PPc]
bʰarawne 'to feed'	[PAb, PAe, PPa, PPc, PPd]	[PAd, PAe, PPa, PPc]
wikne 'to sell'	[PAb, PAe, PPa, PPc, PPd]	[PAd, PAe, PPa, PPc]
linhine 'to write (letter)'	[PAb, PAe, PPa, PPc]	[PPa, PPc]
saangne 'to tell'	[PAb, PAe, PPa, PPc]	[PPa, PPc]

---

[47]The first column of this table is taken from Joshi (1993, 52–60) and is not meant to be exhaustive. The last two columns are the proto-properties I have assumed.

Passive ditransitive causatives[48] (ingestives)	arg2	arg3
aikawṇe (aikṇe) to hear.CAUS (to hear)	[PAb, PAe, PPa, PPc]	[PAe]
hungawṇe (hungṇe) to smell.CAUS (to smell)	[PAb, PAe, PPa, PPc]	[PAe]
šikawṇe (šikṇe) to teach (to learn)	[PAb, PAe, PPa, PPc]	[PAe]
paadẑṇe (piṇe) to feed (to drink)	[PAb, PAe, PPa, PPc]	[PAd, PAe, PPa, PPb, PPc]

B. Ranking Arguments

(1) a. THEMATIC$_{subj}$ ≫ MAX(proto)

			THEMATIC$_{subj}$	MAX(proto)
⟨arg1[PAa,PAb,PAe,PPa,PPc]⟩				
a.		OBJ [arg1[PAa,PAb,PAe,PPa,PPc]]	*!	
b.	☞	SUBJ [arg1[PAa,PAb,PAe,PPa]]		*

b. output = 'gelaa' (went)

c. raam pail-tiraa-laa   gelaa.
Ram other-bank-LOC went
Ram went to the other bank (of river).
(Joshi, 1993, 24, (30a))

---

[48]The basic verb from which the causative is formed is given in parentheses.

(2) a. MAX(proto) $\gg$ *Nonsubj/P-A$_{vol}$

			MAX(proto)	*Nonsubj/P-A$_{vol}$
	$\langle$arg1[PAa,PAb,PAe] arg2[PAa,PAb,PAe]$\rangle$			
a.		SUBJ [arg1[PAa,PAb,PAe]] OBL [arg2[PAb,PAe]]	*!	
b. ☞		SUBJ [arg1[PAa,PAb,PAe]] OBL [arg2[PAa,PAb,PAe]]		*

b. output = 'kheḷne'[49] (to play with)

c. sudhā   anūśī/barobar   kheḷte
   Sudha.3sf Anu.inst.3sf/with play.pres.3sf
   Sudha plays with Anu.[50]   (Pandharipande, 1997, 295, (847))

(3) a. *Nonsubj/P-A$_{vol}$ $\gg$ DEP(proto)

			MAX(proto)	*Nonsubj/P-A$_{vol}$	DEP(proto)
	$\langle$arg1[PAb,PAe] arg2[PAa,PAe]$\rangle$				
a.		SUBJ [arg1[PAb,PAe]] OBJ [arg2[PAa]]	*	*!	
b. ☞		SUBJ [arg1[PAb,PAe,PPa]] OBJ [arg2[PAe]]	*		*

b. output = 'aawaḍne' (to like)

c. tyaa mulaa-laa te   aaiskrim aawaḍte.
   that boy-D/A   that ice-cream likes
   That boy likes that ice cream.   (Joshi, 1993, 55, (42a))

---

[49] Also bhāṇḍne (to fight with), and bolne (to talk with) (Pandharipande, 1997, 295).
[50] This example is from Pandharipande (1997) and uses her transcription and gloss styles.

(4) a.   DEP(proto) ≫ *Subj/P-P

		MAX(proto)	DEP(proto)	*Subj/P-P
a.		*	*!	
b.	☞	*		*

Input: ⟨arg1[PAb,PAe,PPa] arg2[PAe,PPa]⟩

a. = $\begin{bmatrix} \text{SUBJ} & [\text{arg1[PAb,PAe]}] \\ \text{OBJ} & [\text{arg2[PAe,PPa,PPb]}] \end{bmatrix}$

b. = $\begin{bmatrix} \text{SUBJ} & [\text{arg1[PAb,PAe,PPa]}] \\ \text{OBJ} & [\text{arg2[PAe]}] \end{bmatrix}$

b. output = 'aawaḍne' (to like)

(5) a.   DEP(proto) ≫ *Subj/P-A$_{-vol}$

		MAX(proto)	DEP(proto)	*Subj/P-P	*Subj/P-A$_{-vol}$
a.		**	*!	*	
b.	☞	**		*	**

Input: ⟨arg1[PAb,PAe,PPa] arg2[PAe,PPa,PPb]⟩

a. = $\begin{bmatrix} \text{SUBJ} & [\text{arg1[PPa]}] \\ \text{OBJ} & [\text{arg2[PAe,PPa,PPb,PPc]}] \end{bmatrix}$

b. = $\begin{bmatrix} \text{SUBJ} & [\text{arg1[PAb,PAe,PPa]}] \\ \text{OBJ} & [\text{arg2[PAe]}] \end{bmatrix}$

b. output = 'aawaḍne' (to like)

(6) a. DEP(proto) $\gg$ *Nonsubj/P-A$_{-vol}$

	MAX(proto)	DEP(proto)	*Nonsubj/P-A$_{-vol}$
a.	*	*!	
b. ☞	*		*

Input: $\langle$arg1[PAb,PAe,PPa,PPb] arg2[PAe]$\rangle$

a. = $\begin{bmatrix} \text{SUBJ} & [\text{arg1[PAb,PAe,PPa,PPb,PPc]]} \\ \text{OBJ} & [\text{arg2[ ]]} \end{bmatrix}$

b. = $\begin{bmatrix} \text{SUBJ} & [\text{arg1[PAb,PAe,PPa]]} \\ \text{OBJ} & [\text{arg2[PAe]]} \end{bmatrix}$

b. output = 'aawaḍne' (to like)

(7) a. DEP(proto) $\gg$ *Nonsubj/P-P

	MAX(proto)	DEP(proto)	*Nonsubj/P-A$_{-vol}$	*Nonsubj/P-P
a.	*	*!		
b . ☞	*			*

Input: $\langle$arg1[PAa,PAb,PAd,PAe] arg2[PPa]$\rangle$

a. = $\begin{bmatrix} \text{SUBJ} & [\text{arg1[PAa,PAb,PAd,PAe,PPa]]} \\ \text{OBJ} & [\text{arg2[ ]]} \end{bmatrix}$

b. = $\begin{bmatrix} \text{SUBJ} & [\text{arg1[PAa,PAb,PAe]]} \\ \text{OBJ} & [\text{arg2[PPa]]} \end{bmatrix}$

b. output = 'saaṭʰawne' (to store/collect)

    c. tyaa mulaa-ni kaahi naaṇi saatʰawli.
       that boy-ERG some coins stored
       That boy stored (collected) some coins.
       (Joshi, 1993, 195, (51a))

C. Citation Information for Marathi Examples

	Joshi (1993)			Joshi (1993)	
Example	Page	Example	Example	Page	Example
(19a)	53	(36a)	(19b)	53	(37a)
(20)	60	(51b)	(21)	60	(53b)
(22a)	38	(2a)	(22b)	38	(2b)
(23a)	39	(4a)	(23b)	39	(4b)
(24a)	39	(5a)	(24b)	39	(5b)
(25a)	54	(38b)	(25b)	54	(39)
(26a)	54	(40b)	(26b)	55	(41b)
(27a)	61	(54b)	(27b)	61	(55)
(28a)	62	(56b)	(28b)	62	(56c)
(29a)	59	(48b)	(29b)	58	(48a)
(30a)	59	(49b)	(30b)	59	(49a)
(31a)	64	(61a)	(31b)	65	(61b)
(32a)	65	(62a)	(32b)	65	(62b)
(49)	55	(42a)			

References

Aissen, Judith. 1999. Markedness and Subject Choice in Optimality Theory. *Natural Language and Linguistic Theory* 17:673–711.

Alsina, Alex. 2000. A cross-linguistic theory of object asymmetries. MS., Universitat Pompeu Fabra.

Anttila, Arto. 1997a. Deriving variation from grammar: A study of Finnish genitives. In *Variation, change, and phonological theory*, eds. Frans Hinskens, Roeland van Hout, and W. Leo Wetzels. Amsterdam: John Benjamins, 35–68.

Anttila, Arto. 1997b. *Variation in Finnish phonology and morphology*. Ph.D. thesis, Stanford University.

Artstein, Ron. 1998. The incompatibility of underspecification and markedness in Optimality Theory. *RuLing Papers* 1:7–13.

Baković, Eric. 1997. Complementizers, faithfulness, and optionality. ROA-212-0897.

Baković, Eric and Edward Keer. 2001. Optionality and ineffability. In *Optimality-Theoretic Syntax*, eds. Géraldine Legendre, Jane Grimshaw, and Sten Vikner. Cambridge, Massachusetts: The MIT Press, 97–112.

Boersma, Paul. 1997. How we learn variation, optionality, and probability. In *IFA Proceedings 21*. University of Amsterdam: Institute of Phonetic Sciences, 43–58. ROA-221-109.

Boersma, Paul. 1998. *Functional Phonology: Formalizing the interactions between articulatory and perceptual drives*. The Hague: Holland Academic Graphics.

Boersma, Paul. 2000. Learning a grammar in Functional Phonology. In *Optimality Theory: Phonology, Syntax and Acquisition*, eds. Joost Dekkers, Frank van der Leeuw, and Jeroen van de Weijer. Oxford: Oxford University Press.

Boersma, Paul. 2001. Variation in Finnish phonology and morphology (Review of Anttila (1997)). *GLOT International* 5(1):31–40.

Boersma, Paul and Bruce Hayes. 2001. Empirical tests of the gradual learning algorithm. *Linguistic Inquiry* 32:45–86.

Bresnan, Joan (ed.). 1982. *The Mental Representation of Grammatical Relations*. Cambridge, Massachusetts: The MIT Press.

Bresnan, Joan. 2000a. The emergence of the unmarked pronoun: Chicheŵa pronominals in Optimality Theory. In *Proceedings of the Berkeley Linguistics Society 23, 1997*. Berkeley, California: Berkeley Linguistics Society. ROA-179-0297.

Bresnan, Joan. 2000b. Optimal Syntax. In *Optimality Theory: Phonology, Syntax and Acquisition*, eds. Joost Dekkers, Frank van der Leeuw, and Jeroen van de Weijer. Oxford: Oxford University Press, 334–385.

Bresnan, Joan and Jonni Kanerva. 1989. Locative Inversion in Chicheŵa: A Case Study of Factorization in Grammar. *Linguistic Inquiry* 20:1–50.

Bresnan, Joan and Annie Zaenen. 1990. Deep unaccusativity in LFG. In *Grammatical relations: A cross-theoretical perspective*, eds. Katarzyna Dziwirek, Patrick Farrell, and Errapel Mejias-Bikandi. Stanford, California: CSLI Publications, 45–57.

Butt, Miriam, Mary Dalrymple, and Anette Frank. 1997. An architecture for linking theory in LFG. In *Proceedings of the LFG97 conference*, eds. Miriam Butt and Tracy Holloway King. Stanford, California: CSLI Publications Online: http://csli-publications.stanford.edu/.

Dalrymple, Mary, Ronald M. Kaplan, John T. Maxwell, and Annie Zaenen (eds.). 1995. *Formal issues in Lexical-Functional Grammar*. Stanford, California: CSLI Publications.

Davis, Anthony. 1996. *Linking and the hierarchical lexicon*. Ph.D. thesis, Stanford University.

Dekkers, Joost, Frank van der Leeuw, and Jeroen van de Weijer (eds.). 2001. *Optimality Theory: Phonology, Syntax and Acquisition*. Oxford: Oxford University Press.

Doherty, Cathal. 1993. *Clauses without that: The case for bare sentential complementation*. Ph.D. thesis, University of California, Santa Cruz.

Donohue, Cathryn. 1999. Optimizing Fore Case and Word Order. MS., Stanford University. Online: http://www-csli.stanford.edu/~donohue.

Dowty, David. 1991. Thematic Proto-roles and Argument Selection. *Language* 67:547–619.

Grimshaw, Jane. 1997. Projection, Heads, and Optimality. *Linguistic Inquiry* 28:73–422.

Johnson, Mark. 1998. Optimality-theoretic Lexical Functional Grammar. In *Proceedings of the 11th Annual CUNY Conference on Human Sentence Processing*.

Joshi, Smita. 1993. *Selection of Grammatical and Logical Functions in Marathi*. Ph.D. thesis, Stanford University.

Kager, René. 1999. *Optimality Theory*. Cambridge: Cambridge University Press.

Keer, Edward and Eric Baković. 1997. Have faith in syntax. In *Proceedings of the Sixteenth West Coast Conference on Formal Linguistics*, eds. E. Curtis, J. Lyle, and G. Webster. Stanford, California: CSLI Publications, 255–269.

Kuhn, Jonas. 2000. Faithfulness violations and Bidirectional Optimization. In *Proceedings of the LFG00 Conference*, eds. Miriam Butt and Tracy H. King. Stanford, California: CSLI Publications Online: `http://csli-publications.stanford.edu/`.

Kuhn, Jonas. 2001. Generation and Parsing in Optimality Theoretic Syntax – Issues in the Formalization in OT-LFG. This volume.

Lee, Hanjung. 2001. Markedness and Word Order Freezing. This volume.

Lødrup, Helge. 1999. Linking and optimality in the Norwegian presentational focus construction. *Nordic Journal of Linguistics* 22:205–225.

Müller, Gereon. 1999. Optionality in Optimality-Theoretic syntax. *Glot International* 4:3–8.

Pandharipande, Rajeshwari V. 1997. *Marathi*. London: Routledge.

Pesetsky, David. 1997. Optimality Theory and Syntax: Movement and Pronunciation. In *Optimality Theory: An Overview*, eds. Diana Archangeli and Terence Langendoen. Oxford: Blackwell, 134–170.

Pesetsky, David. 1998. Some optimality principles of sentence pronunciation. In *Is the best good enough?*, eds. Pilar Barbosa, Danny Fox, Paul Hagstrom, Martha McGinnis, and David Pesetsky. Cambridge, Massachusetts: The MIT Press, 337–383.

Prince, Alan and Paul Smolensky. 1993. Optimality Theory: Constraint Interaction in Generative Grammar. Technical Report RuCCS Technical Report #2, Center for Cognitive Science, Rutgers University, Piscataway, New Jersey. To be published by the MIT Press.

Smolensky, Paul. 1996a. Generalizing optimization in OT: A competence theory of grammar 'use'. Stanford Workshop on Optimality Theory.

Smolensky, Paul. 1996b. The Initial State and "Richness of the Base" in Optimality Theory. Technical Report JHU-CogSci-96-4, Department of Cognitive Science, Johns Hopkins University.

Smolensky, Paul. 1996c. On the Comprehension/Production Dilemma in Child Language. *Linguistic Inquiry* 27:720–731.

Smolensky, Paul. 1998. Why Syntax is Different (but not Really): Ineffability, Violability and Recoverability in Syntax and Phonology. Stanford University Workshop: Is Syntax Different? (December 12–13, 1998).

Tesar, Bruce B. and Paul Smolensky. 1998. Learnability in Optimality Theory. *Linguistic Inquiry* 29(2):229–268.

8

Generation and Parsing in Optimality Theoretic Syntax: Issues in the Formalization of OT-LFG

JONAS KUHN

8.1 Introduction

This paper addresses the application of Optimality Theory (OT) in syntax from a computational point of view.[1] The definition of a processing model for OT syntax presupposes a formalization of the notions involved. Here, the work on the OT account based on Lexical-Functional Grammar (LFG) can be used as a basis. In order to guarantee that the processing tasks of generation and parsing with an OT grammar are decidable and computationally tractable, certain restrictions have to be imposed on the formalism. The goal of a computational OT approach is to arrive at a sufficiently restricted formalism that is nevertheless expressive enough to capture the intuitions behind the linguistic OT accounts.

[1]The work reported in this paper has been funded by the *Deutsche Forschungs-gemeinschaft* within the *Sonderforschungsbereich* 340, project B12 (Methods for extending, maintaining and optimizing a comprehensive grammar of German). I'd like to thank Judith Berman, Joan Bresnan, Stefanie Dipper, Christian Fortmann, Anette Frank, Fabian Heck, Ron Kaplan, Frank Keller, Tracy King, John Maxwell, Peter Sells, Christian Rohrer, Jürgen Wedekind, and two anonymous reviewers for comments on various versions of this paper and discussion of related issues. Parts of this work were presented at the GGS conference (*Generative Grammatik des Südens*), Stuttgart, May 1999; at the international SFB workshop "Linguistic Form and its Computation" in Bad Teinach, October 1999; at the poster session of NELS 30 (North-East Linguistic Society), Rutgers University, October 1999; and to audiences in Edinburgh, Saarbrücken, Stanford, Stuttgart, and Xerox PARC. I'd like to thank the audiences for very useful comments and discussion. Some of the issues raised in the present paper have been developed further in Kuhn (2000a,b, 2001a); to keep the reasoning of this paper intact, I only point to these aspects in footnotes.

In the main part of this paper, a particular approach to expressing such restrictions is proposed; although no formal proofs are presented, I point out which directions such proofs would take. The core idea of the approach is to keep the way in which the candidate analyses may differ from the underlying input representation structurally limited.[2] Showing that a restricted formal system is adequate for expressing a linguistic theory is very hard. I will argue that the crucial explanatory mechanisms of OT (in particular the use of "unfaithful" candidates in a Neutralization account) can be applied in the system, arguing that existing accounts can be formulated with the system.

The purpose of this contribution is certainly not to establish formal restrictions once and for all, in particular at this early stage in the enterprise of formalizing OT syntax. Rather the idea is to raise a number of issues in the formalization of OT that are of computational concern. Since many notions of the OT model still seem to be in a state of flux in the linguistic literature, the issue of computational complexity might be taken into account when assessing certain options. The paper is structured as follows: section 8.2 provides motivation for a computational account and some background on OT syntax and OT-LFG. In section 8.3, a processing model of OT is discussed that is based on the idea of modelling the candidate generation function by actual generation with an underlying LFG grammar. Sections 8.4 and 8.5 address the formalization and processing of Markedness and Faithfulness constraints, respectively. Section 8.6 addresses the consequences of the model proposed in sections 8.3–8.5 for the parsing task, in particular a potential complexity problem. Some further formal restrictions are investigated that would allow one to reduce the processing complexity of the original proposal, while the resulting system might still be expressive enough for explanatory linguistic accounts. Section 8.7 contains a brief conclusion.

8.2 Background

After addressing the motivation for a computational or syntactic account in section 8.2.1, I will briefly review the basic concepts and their formalization in the OT-LFG approach in sections 8.2.2 and 8.2.3.

8.2.1 Motivation for a Computational Account

OT as a general framework for linguistic constraint systems has been applied to a number of areas of linguistic research, first in phonology, later also in syntax and morphology. Assuming the grammar of a language to be specified through a particular dominance ranking over a set of conflicting universal constraints provides high explanatory strength, within a conceptually very simple system. The ranking determines which of several

---

[2]In Kuhn (2000b, 2001a) I discuss a less restrictive approach, which requires a different processing strategy.

competing candidate analyses is the most harmonic one (triggering the least serious constraint violations) in the given language. Languages differ only in the relative ranking of the constraints.

It is not only the typological dimension that makes OT attractive to linguists and computational linguists, as the approach may also give rise to more general language-specific accounts: the concept of constraints that may be violated in an analysis in order to satisfy more highly ranked constraints allows for clear and simple formulations of linguistic principles, even in the face of complex constraint interaction as it will occur in any non-trivial syntax fragment.

To date, most work in OT syntax has focused on fairly restricted sets of empirical data, such that little can be said about whether the system does effectively scale up to a realistic amount of constraint interaction. This is in part due to the fact that OT is still a young field of study, but it seems also that there is a limit to the size of an OT analysis that can be mastered on a piece of paper. A thorough assessment of the benefits of OT presupposes computational devices that allow one to manipulate larger sets of constraints and larger candidate sets with more complex candidate analyses. For the application domain of phonology, recent work on formalization (R. Frank and Satta 1998; Karttunen 1998) demonstrates that OT can be integrated in the finite-state tradition of computational phonology. For the syntactic domain, Bresnan proposes in a number of papers (see e.g., Bresnan 1996, 2000, 2001a) to integrate OT with the syntactic framework of Lexical-Functional Grammar (LFG, Kaplan and Bresnan 1982), whose computational properties have been studied extensively (see, e.g., contributions in Dalrymple et al. 1995).[3] LFG's nonderivational system of correspondence between parallel structures lends itself for making assumptions of OT syntax precise. I will refer to the optimality theoretic LFG model as OT-LFG. Even in "pure" LFG, recent work on the general architecture of the mapping from constituent (c-)structure to functional (f-)structure assumes an economy principle (Economy of Expression; cf. the overview in Bresnan 2001b, ch. 6), and thus relies on a comparison between competing candidate analyses. To capture this formally, a mechanism similar to the candidate evaluation in OT is required (see e.g., Kuhn 1999b).

---

[3]With regard to the mentioned perspective of implementing larger OT fragments, an additional consideration is that in the Xerox Linguistic Environment (XLE), there exists an implementation of the LFG formalism that is designed for non-trivial grammar fragments (cf. Butt et al. 1999; King et al. 2000), providing an interface to morphological analyzers and the capability of processing large lexicons. The system even provides a particular OT-style constraint ranking mechanism, as discussed in (A. Frank et al. 2001). It is an interesting question if and how OT approaches from the theoretical literature could be integrated into such a system.

8.2.2 The Basics of OT Syntax

Let us start with an illustrative example of an analysis in OT syntax. It is taken from Grimshaw's (1997) account of inversion in English, which is set in a syntactic framework working with a representational simulation of movement derivations. (Bresnan (2000, sec. 2) shows that Grimshaw's constraint system can be reconstructed in the LFG framework, and the examples I use to illustrate the formalizations in the present paper will also be based on this fragment.) Assume that the constraints in (1) are members of the universal inventory of syntactic constraints Grimshaw (1997, 374).

(1) Op-Spec   Syntactic operators must be in specifier position.
    Ob-Hd   A projection has a head.
    Stay   Trace is not allowed.

For English, the dominance ranking is as follows: Op-Spec ≫ Ob-Hd ≫ Stay, i.e. it is more important that an analysis satisfies Op-Spec than Ob-Hd or Stay, etc. This ranking is considered when for a given underlying representation—the *input*—the grammatical form is determined. Given an input representation, there is a universal range of realization alternatives that compete for the status of the grammatical one. (In different languages, different candidates may win.) The function that takes an input to a set of candidate analyses is called *Gen*.[4] The first column of the table in (2) shows some sample candidates that are contained in the set that *Gen* assigns to the representation underlying the English question *what will she read* Grimshaw (1997, 378).[5]

(2) Candidates

Candidates	Constraint violations
[$_\text{IP}$ she will [$_\text{VP}$ read what]]	*Op-Spec
[$_\text{CP}$ what e [$_\text{IP}$ she will [$_\text{VP}$ read t]]]	*Ob-Hd, *Stay
[$_\text{CP}$ what **will**$_i$ [$_\text{IP}$ she e$_i$ [$_\text{VP}$ read t]]]	*Stay, *Stay

For each candidate it is checked which of the constraints it satisfies; a violation is marked with an '*' (e.g., the first candidate has the *wh*-operator

---

[4]The input that Grimshaw assumes for a verbal extended projection consists of "a lexical head plus its argument structure and an assignment of lexical heads to its arguments, plus a specification of the associated tense and aspect" (p. 376). From this input, *Gen* generates all extended projections conforming to x-bar theory as alternative realizations of this argument structure. The output thus consists of "representational simulations of transformational derivations using chains and traces", as Bresnan (2000) puts it. Bresnan argues for "a more radically nonderivational theory of *Gen*, based on a parallel correspondence theory of syntactic structures".

[5]In this example, I follow Grimshaw's *Government-and-Binding* style notation: 't' marks the trace of the moved *wh* word *what*; 'e' marks an empty head (of the CP projection), '**will**$_i$ – e$_i$' is the chain of *will*'s head movement from I to C.

what in the complement position of the verb, thus failing to satisfy the constraint OP-SPEC in (1)). Formally, the function *marks* assigns a multiset of constraint violations to each analysis.

Based on this marking of constraint violations for all analyses in the candidate set, and the constraint hierarchy for a particular language, the function *Eval* determines the most harmonic, or optimal, candidate: the grammatical analysis. (There may also be a set of equally harmonic candidates.) For two competing candidates the more harmonic one is defined to be the one that contains fewer violations for the highest-ranked constraint in which the marking of the two differs. The result of the evaluation is standardly notated in a *tableau* (3), with the columns for the constraint reflecting the hierarchy of the language under consideration.

(3) Candidates	OP-SPEC	OB-HD	STAY
a. [$_{\text{IP}}$ she will [$_{\text{VP}}$ read what]]	*!		
b. [$_{\text{CP}}$ what **e** [$_{\text{IP}}$ she will [$_{\text{VP}}$ read t]]]		*!	*
☞ c. [$_{\text{CP}}$ what **will**$_i$ [$_{\text{IP}}$ she **e**$_i$ [$_{\text{VP}}$ read t]]]			**

If a candidate loses in a pairwise comparison, the "fatal" mark is highlighted with an '!' (e.g., the first candidate is less harmonic than the second one, since they differ in the highest-ranked constraint OP-SPEC). Note that the score that the losing candidate has for lower-ranked constraints is completely irrelevant. Ultimately, the candidate that remains without a fatal constraint violation is marked with the symbol ☞ as the winner of the entire competition. In the example, the bottom analysis is optimal, although it violates the constraint STAY twice. The other analyses are predicted to be ungrammatical. Different languages are characterized by different relative rankings of the constraints. For instance, a language with *wh*-in-situ may rank OP-SPEC lower than STAY, which will cause the first candidate in (3), to be the winner. Note that there will always be at least one winning analysis for a given (nonempty) candidate set, since optimality is defined relative to the competitors.[6]

After this informal example, we can identify the notions that a formalization of OT must pinpoint—and moreover capture in a computationally tractable way: the input representation, the function *Gen*, the formulation of constraints, the function *marks* checking for constraint violations, and

---

[6]This means that the phenomenon of language-particular ineffability cannot be modelled in the standard OT model. However, Legendre et al. (1998) argue that in an account with candidates that are unfaithful to the underlying logical form, language-particular ineffability can be derived. A different approach to ineffability exploits bidirectional optimization as discussed in section 8.6.2 (Smolensky 1998; Lee 2001).

the function *Eval*.[7] For some of these concepts, the assumptions made in different incarnations of OT vary significantly.

In the bulk of this paper, I adhere to the standard interpretation of optimality as singling out *the* grammatical analysis against its competitors which are throughout ungrammatical (for the underlying representation given in the input). This contrasts with the notion of optimality as preference among several grammatical analysis adopted in A. Frank et al. (2001). I briefly come back to the relation between the two views in section 8.6.2.

Faithfulness Violations

It is generally assumed that in an OT system, the relative ranking of the constraints is the only source of cross-linguistic variation.[8] Thus the following prediction is made: if a well-formed sentence in some language is derived by some OT competition, the exact same competition will take place in any other language as well (possibly with a different winner, of course). *Prima facie* this seems to be contradicted by the situation where one language (L_1) collapses several different feature distinctions into a single realization form, while another language (L_2) contains a fine-grained linguistic distinction. A simple example would be the person and number distinction in verbal inflection (cf. e.g., Holmberg and Platzack 1995): the continental Scandinavian languages constitute type L_1, providing a single form in each tense for any person/number combination, whereas Icelandic is of type L_2, providing practically full morphological distinctions.

Naively, one would tend to assume that in L_1, there is a larger competition, yielding a single winner (illustrated schematically in (4a)), while in L_2, there are a number of separate smaller competitions, each with a different winner (4b).

(4)   *Naive account of cross-linguistic differences in fine-grainedness*

---

[7]I will not say anything about the learning of a constraint hierarchy, which has received much attention in the OT literature, cf. e.g., Tesar and Smolensky (1998). Compare also Kuhn (2001a, ch. 3).

[8]It is an interesting (and, as far as I know, rather open) question how one should envisage the technical organization of the lexicon in OT syntax, which has to encode some residual idiosyncratic, language-specific information. Cross-linguistic variation in the lexicon of functional categories is supposed to follow from differences in constraint ranking (a point already made by Grimshaw (1997), for English *do*). But of course, one still needs to assume a linking of particular bundles of morpholexical features to language-specific phonemic representations (presumably the underlying forms of phonological OT).

a. *Language L_1*

input: X[±F]	M₁	M₂
☞ A[−F]		
B[−F]		*!
A[+F]	*!	
B[+F]	*!	*

b. *Language L_2*

input: X[−F]	M₁	M₂
☞ A[−F]		
B[−F]		*!

input: X[+F]	M₁	M₂
☞ A[+F]	*	
B[+F]	*	*!

But this is incompatible with the OT view of cross-linguistic variation. The different inputs required for the "smaller" competitions in L_2 have to be considered in L_1 as well. The solution in OT is that although there is just one surface realization in L_1, this is the winner of several competitions, one for each of the different inputs that bring out the distinction in L_2 (5a). In order for this to work, the candidate sets must contain analyses that do not render the input information faithfully. The fact that in one language "unfaithful" candidates may win, while in the other, only the faithful ones do, is explained by a conflict between the candidate's goal of being faithful to the input (which is measured by Faithfulness constraints— F in the tableaux in (5)) and the goal of keeping the analysis "simple" in terms of the so-called Markedness constraints (like STAY—M₁ and M₂ in (5)).[9] Now, the difference between L_1 and L_2 is reduced to a difference in constraint ranking again (M₁ ≫ F vs. F ≫ M₁). This type of account is called a *Neutralization* account.[10]

(5) *Neutralization account: in L_1, an unfaithful candidate wins for the input X[+F]*

a. *Language L_1*

input: X[+F]	M₁	F	M₂
☞ A[−F]		*	
B[−F]		*	*!
A[+F]	*!		
B[+F]	*!		*

input: X[−F]	M₁	F	M₂
☞ A[−F]			
B[−F]			*!
A[+F]	*!	*	
B[+F]	*!	*	*

---

[9] The Markedness constraints assumed in this schematic illustration are simply 'Avoid [+F]' (=M₁), and 'Avoid [−F]' (=M₂).

[10] See also Kager (1999, 29), and Bresnan (2001a) as an example from OT-LFG Syntax.

b. *Language L_2*

input: X[+F]	F	M_1	M_2
A[−F]	*!		
B[−F]	*!		*
☞ A[+F]		*	
B[+F]		*!	*

input: X[−F]	F	M_1	M_2
☞ A[−F]			
B[−F]			*!
A[+F]	*!	*	
B[+F]	*!	*	*

Faithfulness violations and the different types of constraints disallowing them have received much attention in the literature. Originally, Prince and Smolensky (1993) proposed to have two types of faithfulness constraints: Fill and Parse, penalizing the addition to and the omission of input information, respectively. In the context of Correspondence Theory, McCarthy and Prince (1995) argue for a richer distinction, working with Max, Dep, and Ident constraints (cf. also Kager 1999).

(6) Max-IO
'No deletion'—Input segments must have output correspondents (i.e. input material to be realized by lexical material).

(7) Dep-IO
'No epenthesis'—Output segments must have input correspondents (i.e. all lexical f-specifications are used in the f-structure).

For present purposes, the exact characterization of Faithfulness constraints is less important than the fact that they play a key role in the theory: when we are formalizing the *Gen* function, we have to make sure that the candidate sets will contain the appropriate unfaithful candidates. In syntax, this means in particular that candidates may contain expletive elements (without corresponding information in the input: violation of Fill or Dep-IO), and conversely input information may be unrealized at the surface (like "null pronouns" in *pro-drop* languages: violation of Parse or Max-IO). Section 8.5 will be devoted to unfaithful candidates, and a more extensive discussion can be found in Kuhn (2000a).

8.2.3 Optimality-Theoretic LFG

Bresnan (2000, sec. 2) presents a relatively close reconstruction of Grimshaw's (1997) OT system with the formal means of LFG.

There may be various reasons for adopting the LFG formalism as the basis for an OT account of syntax, including for instance the fact that a lot of typological research has been conducted in the LFG framework. For present purposes, the main advantage of picking LFG as a base formalism is however that its computational properties have undergone thorough research and that there are highly developed systems for processing the formalism. In fact, one might say that one goal in developing the OT-LFG model is to arrive at a sufficiently restricted formalism for OT syntax in general to allow computational processing—in much the same way as the design of the LFG formalism was guided by the goal of creating a framework that is expressive enough for an explanatory linguistic theory, while at the same time the processing tasks for grammars in that formalism are computationally tractable.

Many design decisions in the set-up of the OT system will have consequences for processing, and some of these issues will be discussed in varying detail in this paper. Before going into such details, it is useful to have a high-level specification of the overall system that abstracts away from processing issues.

Candidates

The candidate analyses that OT-LFG deals with are tuples of structures from LFG, i.e. pairs of c-structure and f-structure (and possibly more levels of analysis) that are in a correspondence relation. All analyses satisfy certain basic inviolable principles, which we can assume to be encoded in an LFG grammar G_{inviol}; thus the set of all possible candidate analyses is defined by the structures generated by this grammar G_{inviol}.

Input

With the candidate analyses being fully specified LFG analyses, an appropriate representation for the input in the OT sense is a partially specified representation of LFG analyses. Bresnan (2000, sec. 1.1) assumes as the input "a (possibly underspecified) feature structure representing some given morphosyntactic content independent of its form of expression". An example (that in English would have *I saw her* as its optimal realization) is given in (8).

(8) Input f-structure: *I saw her*

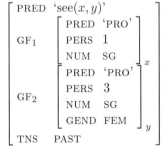

Gen

We can now define the function *Gen*:

(9) Definition of *Gen*

Gen is a function from the set of f-structures to the power set of the analyses in G_{inviol}, i.e. it takes each f-structure to a set of "candidate" analyses, which are contained in G_{inviol}.

Note that this definition does not yet provide a specification how the set of candidates is constructed from the input f-structure. We will certainly expect there to be a systematic specification in a particular system (see section 8.3), but this is intentionally abstracted away from here.

Constraint marking

The constraints come into play when the alternative candidate analyses in the *Gen* image of a given input f-structure are evaluated. The function *marks* assigns a multiset of constraint violation marks to each element of the candidate set.

We distinguish Faithfulness and Markedness constraints. Among the Faithfulness constraints, one subclass refers to the relation between the input structure and the candidate analysis, another subclass addresses the correspondence between various levels of representation within the candidate analysis.[11] The Markedness constraints impose restrictions on allowable structures in the candidate analysis. Formally, for the former subclass of Faithfulness constraints, the *marks* function has to be sensitive to the input, while for the other Faithfulness constraints and the Markedness constraints it suffices to look at the candidate analysis.

Generally, we need the following definition:

(10) Definition of *marks*

Given a set of constraints *Con*, $marks_{Con}$ is a function from a pair of an input f-structure and an LFG analysis to a multiset of constraint violation marks.

A constraint can be defined as a function taking a pair of an input f-structure and an LFG analysis to a natural number, representing the number of times the given input/candidate pair violates that constraint.

Harmony evaluation

Given the multiset of constraint violations for each input/candidate pair, and the language specific constraint ranking, *Eval* determines the most harmonic candidate according to definition (11).

(11) C_1 is more harmonic than C_2 if it contains fewer violations for the highest-ranked constraint in which the marking of C_1 and C_2 differs.

Language Generated by an OT-LFG System

Finally, the language generated by an OT-LFG system can be defined as the set of strings *S* for which there exists an input f-structure such that *S* is the terminal string of the most harmonic candidate for that input.

The abstract specification given above leaves a fairly wide space of possibilities as to how an actual OT-LFG system is defined. Many of these options are presumably rather absurd. In order to meet the linguistic intuitions be-

---

[11]With the assumptions of OT-LFG it will turn out that all Faithfulness constraints can be formulated without explicit reference to a separate input representation (cf. sec. 8.5).

hind an OT theory, further restrictions have to be assumed. Another reason for restricting the formalism comes into play when we want to use a computer for deciding whether a given string belongs to the language generated by a given OT-LFG system: certain restrictions may guarantee decidability, or membership in a certain complexity class.

The remainder of this paper addresses the question whether these two motivations for restricting the formalism converge in some way or other.[12] The strategy pursued here is to ensure that for each conceptual step (in particular candidate generation and constraint checking) in isolation, a decidable procedure exists, building on known results from work outside Optimality Theory. This is not the only conceivable strategy: Tesar's (1995) parsing (or rather, generation) algorithm for OT phonology makes crucial use of an interleaving of candidate generation and constraint checking— the same idea can be applied to OT-LFG syntax Kuhn (2000a,b). For an extensive discussion of both strategies, see Kuhn (2001a).

8.3 *Gen* as Generation with an LFG Grammar

As has been mentioned, one would like to assume that the *Gen* function from inputs to candidate sets has a systematic and simple definition. A conceptually very simple approach would be to define *Gen* as a constant function that takes arbitrary input f-structures to the full set of analyses in G_{inviol}. The constraints—in particular the Faithfulness constraints—would then have to do all the work of filtering out irrelevant analyses. However, it is unclear how such a system could be restricted appropriately to guarantee decidability; one would have to assume very powerful constraints.[13]

An alternative definition of *Gen* builds on the intuition that the candidate analyses are actually *generated* from the input structure by monotonically adding information.[14] With such a definition, it is possible to restrict the expressive power of the constraints quite strongly, still achieving the intended effects. Thus, there is a clear division of labor between *Gen* and the constraints, and further restricting assumptions can be made

---

[12]Learnability considerations as a further restricting factor are not discussed here, but compare (Kuhn, 2001a, ch. 3).

[13]Johnson (1998) sketches an undecidability proof for a similar unrestricted OT system. Note that for the phonological domain—as long as it can be formalized by means of regular relations—this set-up is indeed possible. If one adopts Karttunen's (1998) computational account, the resulting system (a finite-state transducer) will be effectively the same if one assumes (i) a restricted *Gen* with fewer constraints, or (ii) an unrestricted *Gen* with more constraints. Both *Gen* and the constraints are modelled by transducers that are being composed ("leniently").

[14]If it is furthermore assumed that the information relevant for interpretation (predicate-argument structure plus information like tense etc.) is already present in the input, this monotonicity assumption implies that all candidates have the same meaning. In particular an approach assuming LF-unfaithful candidates, like the one in Legendre et al. (1998), is incompatible with these assumptions (but ineffability can be derived in a bidirectional optimization approach).

in a very focused way. Sections 8.3.1–8.4 discuss such a model, basically following Bresnan's (2000) account. What is particularly important here, is that decidability results for generation with LFG grammars can be directly exploited (cf. section 8.3.2).

Quite obviously, under the mentioned specification of *Gen*, by definition no candidates will be unfaithful to the input in terms of PARSE or MAX-IO (in the strict sense that the input structure is not contained in the candidate's f-structure). This means that the intended effect of unfaithful candidates has to be achieved in another way. Section 8.5 addresses this issue.

8.3.1 Generation from Input F-Structures with G_{inviol}

As discussed above, the intuition that *Gen* is generation with an LFG grammar Bresnan (2000) can be captured by restricting the function *Gen* as follows:

(12) Restricted definition of *Gen*

For a given input representation Φ_{input}, the set of candidate analyses $Gen(\Phi_{input})$ is the set of LFG (c- and f-structure) analyses $\langle T, \Phi' \rangle$ generated by G_{inviol}, such that $\Phi_{input} \sqsubseteq \Phi'$, i.e. those analyses whose f-structure is subsumed by the input f-structure.

The task of computing $Gen(\Phi_{input})$ is then exactly the classical task of generation from an underspecified f-structure, given an LFG grammar (G_{inviol}).

To model Grimshaw's fragment of inversion data in English, the LFG grammar G_{inviol} will have to formalize a theory of extended projections. This can be done on the basis of LFG's extended head theory that Bresnan (2001b, ch. 7) discusses in detail. The principles Bresnan assumes can be fleshed out in a set of LFG rules, i.e. context-free rules[15] with f-annotations. Kuhn (1999b) contains a more detailed discussion of how extended head theory can be captured in concrete rule formulations; here it may suffice to assume that the effect of the principles can be envisaged as a set of classical LFG rules like the rules in (13),[16] generating x-bar-configurations with an extension to functional categories (like the verbal functional categories I and C). A lexical category and the corresponding functional categories on top of it form an *extended projection* Grimshaw (1991); Bresnan (2001b).

---

[15]More precisely, a generalization of context-free rule notation which allows regular expressions on the right-hand side.

[16]DF is a generalization over discourse functions (TOPIC, FOCUS and SUBJECT); CF generalizes over complement functions (OBJ, OBL$_\theta$, COMP etc.). The non-endocentric category S that Bresnan (2000, 2001b) assumes is ignored here.

(13)   Some of the rules in G_{inviol}

CP	$\longrightarrow$	(XP)	(C′)
		($\uparrow$DF)=$\downarrow$	$\uparrow$=$\downarrow$
C′	$\longrightarrow$	(C)	(IP)
		$\uparrow$=$\downarrow$	$\uparrow$=$\downarrow$
IP	$\longrightarrow$	(XP)	(I′)
		($\uparrow$DF)=$\downarrow$	$\uparrow$=$\downarrow$
I′	$\longrightarrow$	(I)	(VP)
		$\uparrow$=$\downarrow$	$\uparrow$=$\downarrow$
VP	$\longrightarrow$	V′	
		$\uparrow$=$\downarrow$	
V′	$\longrightarrow$	(V)	(XP)
		$\uparrow$=$\downarrow$	($\uparrow$ CF)=$\downarrow$

There are two crucial points to note about (13): first, the $\uparrow$=$\downarrow$ annotation of both the C and the IP category in the C′ rule, and the I and the VP in the I′ rule. The functional head and its complement (in c-structure) act as "co-heads" on f-structure, i.e. their f-structures are identified. Second, all categories are optional. These points together ensure that a given input f-structure has a wide range of realization alternatives, as required in an OT account like the one sketched in section 8.2: since the f-structures of all heads within the extended projection are identified, each of them is a potential site for a category realizing information from the input f-structure. The structures generated for the underspecified input f-structure in (8) include the LFG analyses in (14a), for example (the correspondence between c-structure nodes and f-structures is illustrated by f-structure subscripts taking up the node numbering).

(14)   Some analyses generated by G_{inviol} for the input in (8)

a.

b.

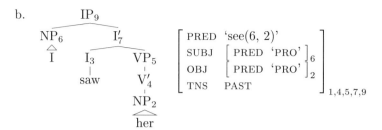

c.

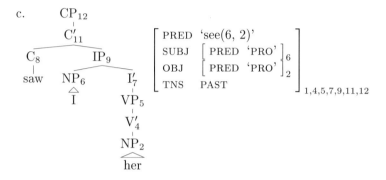

Note that from the assumption of *Gen* being modelled by generation with an LFG grammar it follows that all candidate analyses satisfy the underlying LFG principles, such as functional uniqueness, and completeness and coherence.[17] For example, for the input in (8), no analysis lacking the object altogether and no analyses with two instances of the full verb occurring in two of the head categories will be generated.[18]

It should be noted that although the resulting grammar is formally an LFG grammar, it is certainly unusual since it "overgenerates" vastly, producing all universally possible c-structure-f-structure pairings. This is due to the special role that this LFG grammar plays as part of an OT model: given the different definition of grammaticality, the set of analyses generated by the LFG grammar is not the set of *grammatical* analyses of a particular language (as classically assumed). Rather, it is the union over all possible candidate sets (for any input).

8.3.2 Decidability of the Generation Task

Having restricted the output of *Gen* to candidates with an f-structure subsumed by the input, the computation of $Gen(\Phi_{input})$ amounts to gener-

---

[17] This corresponds conceptually to Grimshaw's (1997) assumption that the candidates conform to x-bar theory and that no illegal movement operations may have applied.

[18] When faithfulness violations are allowed (in particular FILL violations), the situation seems to be different; however, as will be discussed in section 8.5, technically, the f-structure will still respect all LFG principles.

ation from underspecified f-structures. Can this task be performed by a computer?

Wedekind (1995) proves the decidability of generation from *fully* specified f-structures; in contrast, Wedekind (1999) presents a proof that generation from f-structures which are only partially specified is undecidable in the general case (see also Dymetman 1991). However, as Wedekind (1999, 280ff.) discusses briefly, it seems that undecidability arises only with certain non-linguistic grammars in which "semantic" features are used that are structurally unrelated to the remaining f-structure representations and where arbitrarily large portions of recursive f-structure can trigger a single "semantic" feature distinction. The use of features for encoding underlying semantic forms in natural language grammars is more limited: the semantic features will always correspond to some non-recursive portion of other f-structure information in a way defined by the grammar. This property will guarantee that generation from such a semantic feature structure, lacking a full f-structure specification, is decidable after all: the size of the unknown full f-structure corresponding to a given semantic representation is bounded by the size of the semantic representation multiplied with a constant factor determined by the grammar; thus, in adding f-structure features to the underspecified feature structure, only a bounded space of structural possibilities has to be checked against the grammar.

A general "offline generability" condition (analogous to offline parsability) that a grammar has to satisfy to ensure decidability of generation from partial f-structures has yet to be proposed.[19] Still, we can exploit Wedekind's result for the task of generating from an input f-structure like the one in (8). Let us distinguish between two classes of f-structure features, the input and the non-input features. Non-input features are morphosyntactic features that may be added freely in candidate generation without changing the interpretation (which is assumed to be fixed by the input); an example might be the declension class feature of adjectives in German.[20] Note that such features generally have a finite range of values. Input features are specifications like tense and grammatical functions (which are not fully specified in the input leaving the decision between a SUBJ or an OBJ open, but whose configuration of recursive embedding is fixed).

As long as only the addition of features other than such input features is allowed, Wedekind's result implies that the generation task will be decidable. We can put the restriction on the character of features used in the base grammar G_{inviol} in more formal terms (17), disallowing a decoupling

---

[19]For the implementation of XLE's generator, such a condition has been formulated (John Maxwell, p.c., July 2000). The idea is that recursive parts of the grammar may only be passed if some resourced—or instantiated—feature (e.g., a PRED value) is introduced along the way.

[20]However, in a Neutralization account, one might assume that features irrelevant for interpretation are nevertheless present in the input; thus, the set of non-input f-structure features may be very small or even empty in a particular OT account.

of the size of the overall f-structures in the candidate analysis from the size of the input f-structure (by which they are subsumed):

(15) *Addable and non-addable features*
The grammar G_{inviol} distinguishes a set of non-addable (input) features F_{input} and a disjoint set of addable features $\overline{F_{input}}$.
Given an f-structure Φ, the restricted f-structure $\Phi \mid_{F_{input}}$ is defined as the largest f-structure $\Phi' \sqsubseteq \Phi$, such that all features contained in its path are members of F_{input}.

(16) *Restriction on candidate generation*
When generating candidate analyses from an input f-structure Φ_{input}, only features from $\overline{F_{input}}$ may be added.

(17) *Restriction on G_{inviol}*
For any f-structure Φ generated by G_{inviol}, the proportion of the size of the "input feature structure" $\Phi \mid_{F_{input}}$ to the overall size of Φ is bounded by a constant factor.

We may note at this point already that these restrictions do not allow grammars generating "wildly unfaithful" candidate analyses; section 8.5 will address this issue in more detail.

Based on these considerations, the task of generating candidates from an input can actually be performed by LFG systems that implement a generator, like the Xerox Linguistic Environment (XLE) does. The results of Kaplan and Wedekind (2000) tell us that the set of candidates generated from an input f-structure can be characterized by a context-free grammar. This means that we have a way of systematically traversing the space of candidates (this becomes important for harmony evaluation, section 8.4.4).

8.4 Constraint Formulation and Marking

Having suggested a formalization and computational treatment of the input and the *Gen* function, the question has to be addressed of how the constraint violations can be detected in the candidate analyses, to model the function *marks*. In this section, I will focus attention on constraints that can be checked on the analyses directly, without reference to a potentially differing input, i.e. on Markedness constraints and Faithfulness constraints that compare different levels of representation. Input-candidate faithfulness will be addressed in section 8.5.

How should the constraints be specified and checked? In most OT work the constraints are formulated in prose. However, it seems to be a central assumption that the constraints can be formalized as structural descriptions of the type of representations output by *Gen*, i.e. LFG structures in our case.

We find constraints that are expressed purely with reference to f-structure (18). Other constraints make reference to c-structure (19) or to both c-structure and f-structure (20).[21]

(18) OP-SPEC: Bresnan (2000)
"an operator must be the value of a DF in the f-structure"

(19) *LEX-F: Bresnan (2000, (54))
No lexical heads in functional categories.

(20) AGR: Bresnan (2000, (25))
A subject and its predicate in c-structure agree (i.e. a c-structure subject requires that its sister constituent has an agreeing extended head).

The primitive relations in the (c- and f-)structural configurations triggering a constraint violation can be described using little more than the standard specification language of LFG's functional equations (for the c-structure categories, a systematic subclassification has to be assumed, cf. Kuhn 1999b, 4.1).

However, the constraints are not formulated with reference to a particular structure, they typically take the shape of universally quantified implications: whenever a structure satisfies the description A, it should also satisfy the description B (or if the constraint is specified negatively, no structure satisfying A should also satisfy B).

In section 8.4.1, I discuss how this universal quantification could be expressed in the constraint formulations and whether this would affect decidability of the OT system. One might think of simply conjoining all constraints with the grammar G_{inviol}; however, as will be pointed out in section 8.4.2 this would not model the function *marks* correctly, which outputs for each constraint a count of multiple violations.

8.4.1 Universal quantification of constraints

To express universal quantification in the constraints, we need a language that allows universal quantification over the structural objects (f-structures and c-structure nodes), and that contains negation (to express implication). With a feature logic including general negation and universal quantification, we can thus express (18) as (21a). Following B. Keller (1993), one could alternatively use a logic without the universal quantifier, but with general negation and unrestricted functional uncertainty:[22] (21b), which is closer to the standard LFG specification language.

---

[21] An *extended head* of a category is defined to be either the x-bar-categorial head, or a co-projecting category in a c-commanding position Bresnan (2001b, ch. 7.2).

[22] Kaplan and Maxwell (1988) assumed a restricted interpretation of functional uncertainty, excluding cyclic interpretation in proving decidability of the satisfaction problem. However, Ron Kaplan (p.c., August 1999) points out that for functional uncertainty outside the scope of negation, the satisfaction problem is generally decidable (correlate of Blackburn and Spaan 1993).

(21) a. $\forall f.[\exists g.(f\ \text{OP}) = g \rightarrow \exists h.(h\ \text{DF}) = f]$
 b. $\neg[(\uparrow\ \text{GF}^*) = f \wedge (f\ \text{OP}) \wedge \neg(\text{DF}\ f)]$

(21b) is expressed here as if it was an f-annotation at the root node of the grammar, f is a local metavariable for an f-structure, similar to the metavariables $\uparrow$ and $\downarrow$.

For the constraints on c-structure and the c-structure/f-structure correspondence, the language has to refer to c-structure nodes and tree-geometric relations as well. Again, we could assume a logic with quantification over node variables. Alternatively, we could encode the tree structure in a feature structure (maybe as an extra projection from c-structure) and then express functionally uncertain constraints on these feature structures. The constraints at hand could certainly be expressed that way. For current purposes, these general considerations may suffice.

Decidability

Given a candidate analysis and a constraint, is it possible to determine whether the analysis satisfies this constraint? (In section 8.4.4, I will come back to the more general question of whether the same is possible given *all* analyses from a candidate set and *all* constraints.)

Although the general satisfiability problem for feature logics with universal quantification and general negation is undecidable (B. Keller 1993, section 4.4, Blackburn and Spaan 1993, sec. 5), the use of such a logic for expressing constraints being applied to a given candidate analysis is unproblematic, since the expressions are not used constructively.[23] The task performed is not checking satisfiability, but model checking, which is easy: the given candidate structure has a finite number of nodes and f-structures, thus it can be checked for each of them whether it satisfies the constraints by instantiating the variables to the given elements.

8.4.2   Constraint Marking and Multiple Constraint Violations

Although the non-constructive use of the highly expressive feature logic in constraint formulation does not pose a decidability problem, we have to check whether the intuitions behind violable OT constraints are adequately modelled that way.

With the constraints being violable, we cannot simply conjoin all of them with the inviolable constraints specified by G_{inviol}, although the highly general specification would allow us to attach the constraints to the root category of the grammar. But this would have the effect of forcing these constraints on all analyses—as inviolable.

There is a simple way of allowing candidates to violate OT constraints *once* per constraint by specifying the OT constraints as disjoined with their negation, where a constraint violation mark is introduced in case their negation is satisfied: assume constraint C_1 is specified by the feature logic

---

[23]This was pointed out by Ron Kaplan (p.c.) and Maarten de Rijke (p.c.).

formula ψ_1, then we can model its application as a violable constraint as (22), attached to the root node.

(22) $\psi_1 \vee (\neg\psi_1 \wedge `^*C_1' \in (\uparrow\text{MARKS}))$

The idea is that the feature MARKS bears a set of constraint violation marks. In this disjunctive form, the violable constraints can indeed be conjoined with the inviolable constraints. The result will be an LFG grammar that models not only the function *Gen* (when used to generate from an input f-structure), but also the function *marks*. We may thus call the grammar $G_{inviol,marks}$. I briefly come back to this idea in section 8.4.3.

To complete this OT model based on single-time constraint violation, we would merely need a component comparing the MARKS values of the different candidates according to the definition of *Eval*. (This component must quite obviously be located outside the LFG grammar, since it has to operate on several analyses simultaneously.)

Multiple constraint violation

Clearly, the restriction to a maximum of one violation per constraint is not acceptable for modelling OT syntax, even though multiple violations up to a fixed upper bound could be simulated by formulating extra constraints that check for the presence of several instances of the violation in the candidate structure.[24] This may be acceptable when the domain of competition is locally confined to non-recursive structures (cf. section 8.6.6), but it is unnatural for the fully recursive generative system of syntax.

With the universal constraint formulation of section 8.4.1, multiple constraint violations can only be detected by modifying the mechanism checking for constraint satisfaction, i.e. by grammar-external means. Whenever the application of a constraint leads to inconsistency, a violation has to be counted, but the rest of the structure has to be checked for further violations of the same constraint.

The format of constraints

If such a special grammar-external mechanism is required anyway, one may ask whether the conception of formulating violable constraints in the highly general form adopted in section 8.4.1 is justified at all.[25] Moreover, is it clear at all for arbitrary constraints in such a highly expressive logic what constitutes a multiple violation? While for simple implicational constraints with universal quantification over one structural element (an f-structure

---

[24]Karttunen (1998) proposes this for his computational model of OT phonology, which does not allow arbitrarily many violations of a constraint either. (But see Gerdemann and van Noord 2000.)

[25]Ron Kaplan (p.c., August 1999) pointed out for the functional uncertainty based formulation, that the functional uncertainty expressions (assumed in order to be able to reach all configurations in which the constraint at hand is applicable) are somewhat redundant if for detecting multiple constraint violations a structure-walking routine is required anyway.

or a c-structure node) it is intuitively clear what it means to violate this constraint more than once, it seems that expressions involving more than one universal are more problematic. Assume we wanted to work with the following constraint (23a) (the formalization (23c) is closer to how such a constraint might actually be expressed, but (23b) suffices for looking at the logical structure):

(23)   *Hypothetical constraint*
    a. For all DP categories, all their daughters are nominal (i.e. either N or D projections).
    b. $\forall n.[DP(n) \rightarrow \forall m.[M(n,m) \rightarrow nom(m)]]$
    c. $\forall n.[(Cat(n)=nom \wedge Bar(n)=max \wedge Func(n)=+)$
                 $\rightarrow \forall m.[\mathcal{M}(m)=n \rightarrow Cat(m)=nom]]$

Now, the three structures in (24) are evaluated. None of the three satisfies (23). But how many violations does each of them incur? In (24a) and (24b), one DP fails to satisfy the condition that all its daughters are nominal, while in (24c), both do. So, under one interpretation, (24a) and (24b) should violate (23) once, and (24c) twice. On the other hand, (24a) is better than (24b), because only one of the DP's daughters violates the inner implication. Shouldn't one expect then that (24b) incurs two violations?

(24)   a.   b.

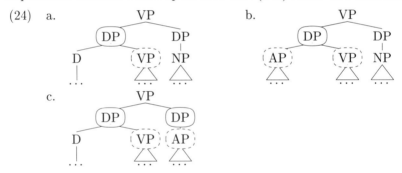

In fact, the modified checking mechanism sketched above, which counts sources of inconsistency, would presumably have this effect (unless the mechanism is explicitly set back to the outermost universal whenever an inconsistency is encountered).

    The problem is also clearly brought out if we look at the following two reformulations of (23):

(25) a. Each daughter of a DP category is nominal.
     b. $\forall m.[\exists n.[M(n,m) \wedge DP(n)] \rightarrow nom(m)]$

(26) a. For every category, if it has a non-nominal daughter, then it is not a DP.
     b. $\forall n.[\exists m.[M(n,m) \wedge \neg nom(m)] \rightarrow \neg DP(n)]$

Both are equivalent to (23) in terms of classical predicate logic, but read with the intuitions behind violable constraints, they clearly differ in the number of violations ascribed to (24b): (24b) violates (25) twice, but it violates (26) only once. This indicates that the use of general formulae of this type of feature logic is inappropriate for modelling the intuitions behind OT constraints, for which we need a precise way of stating what it means to incur multiple violations of a given constraint.

More work on the logic of violable constraints is required, but for the current purposes we may introduce a restriction on the form of violable constraints, which avoids the mentioned problem and which also appears to be in line with the goal of keeping constraints simple (as is argued for example in Grimshaw 1998). The idea is to take out of the constraint formulation the explicit generalization over structures (which makes the constraint recursively applicable on all embedded structures). The universal applicability is now by definition implicit to all constraints and will be made effective in the checking routine that the candidate structures have to undergo after they have been constructed. At every structural object (c-/f-structure), all constraints are applied. This application of the constraints to multiple objects is the only source for multiple violations—a single structural element can violate each constraint only once. The constraints are interpreted classically.

In order for this to work, the structural object which is being checked with a given constraint has to be clearly identified. I will assume a metavariable $\star$ for this (reminiscent of the $*$ used in standard LFG f-annotations of categories to refer to the category itself). (25) will for example take the following shape:

(27) $\exists n.[M(n,\star) \wedge \mathrm{DP}(n)] \rightarrow nom(\star)$

When the constraints are checked, the metavariable $\star$ will be instantiated to one structural element after the other. Thus, the constraints are actually specified as constraint schemata, generating classical constraints.

Note that we could now express (23b) in either of the following two ways, reaching the two different effects for the structures in (24) discussed above:

(28) a. $\mathrm{DP}(\star) \rightarrow \forall m.[M(\star,m) \rightarrow nom(m)]$
b. $\forall n.[\mathrm{DP}(n) \rightarrow (M(n,\star) \rightarrow nom(\star))]$

Thinking of (28b) in the equivalent form (27) may actually be more intuitive (note that now, equivalences of classical logic apply again).

So, we can state the following restriction on constraint formulation, which allows for a simple concept of multiple violations that is compatible with a classical concept of satisfiability, and also seems to meet the intuitions behind violable constraints in OT:

(29) *Restriction on the form of constraints*
Violable constraints are formulated with reference to a unique structural element, which is referred to by a metavariable ($\star$).

Note that it is compatible with this restriction to assume a "scalar" interpretation of alignment constraints like, e.g., HEAD LEFT (30). (Under a scalar interpretation, this constraint is violated twice if there are two intervening elements between a (single) head and the left periphery of its projection.)

(30) HEAD LEFT: Grimshaw (1997, 374)
The head is leftmost in its projection.

The metavariable-based formulation allows a clear distinction between the non-scalar and the scalar version of this constraint (it is assumed that *proj*—'a projection of'—and the relations D—'is a daughter of'—and *precede* are defined appropriately):

(31)   HEAD LEFT
non-scalar interpretation
$$head(\star) \rightarrow \neg\exists n.[D(n, proj(\star)) \wedge precede(n, \star)]$$
scalar interpretation
$$cat(\star) \rightarrow \neg\exists n.[head(n) \wedge D(\star, proj(n)) \wedge precede(\star, n)]$$

The first formulation is stated from the point of view of the head; since the instantiated schema is interpreted classically (i.e. incurring maximally one constraint violation for each structural element), a given head can violate this constraint only once (even if there are several intervening nodes to the left of it). The second formulation is from the point of view of the intervening category; thus if there are several of them, the overall structure will incur several violations of this constraint.

To finish this section, note that Bresnan's formulation of the constraints from the initial example (1) can now be captured as follows:

(32)   OP-SPEC   An operator must be the value of a DF in the
f-structure.   Bresnan (2000)
$$(f\text{-}str(\star) \wedge \exists v.[(\star \; \text{OP}) = v]) \rightarrow \exists f.[(f \; \text{DF}) = \star]$$

       OB-HD   Every projected category has a lexically filled
[extended, JK] head.
                                   Bresnan (2000, (21))
$$(Xbar\text{-}cat(\star) \vee Xmax\text{-}cat(\star)) \rightarrow \exists n.[ext\text{-}hd(n, \star)]$$

       STAY   Categories dominate their extended heads.
                                   Bresnan (2000, (24))
$$cat(\star) \rightarrow \exists n.[ext\text{-}hd(n, \star) \wedge dom(\star, n)]$$

Applying these constraints to the OT-LFG candidate analyses corresponding to the candidates in (2), the picture in (33) arises. Recall that for evaluation, all constraints are applied at every structural element.

In candidate a., the f-structure embedded under OBJ—let's call it '$\star$' for the moment—fails to satisfy OP-SPEC: although it contains a feature OP, there is no f-structure f that embeds $\star$ under a DF feature. Candidate b. contains a node C', which incurs a violation of OB-HD, since there is neither an X-bar-categorial head, nor a co-projecting category in a c-commanding position (thus, no extended head). It furthermore violates STAY.[26] In candidate c., both the I' and the V' nodes violate STAY, since their extended head is C, which neither of them dominates. But with the ranking for English, candidate c. is the winner.

Constraint marking

Based on the constraint schemata just proposed, the marking of constraint violations incurred by a given candidate structure is conceptually straightforward. For each structural element (c-structure node and f-structure), the set of constraints is applied, with the metavariable instantiated to the respective element. When the application of a constraint fails, the candidate is not rejected, but a constraint violation mark is introduced to the multiset of marks.[27]

Since the constraints are applied in a non-constructive manner, as discussed in section 8.4.1, decidability is guaranteed. The task of comparing the different candidates is discussed in section 8.4.4.

(33)   OT-LFG version of the tableau (3)

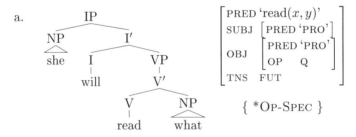

---

[26]I omitted a discussion of the functional-uncertainty-based function specification, which is at work here enforcing the presence of an empty NP in the canonical object position. The analysis displayed here follows the inside-out functional uncertainty analysis of Bresnan (2001b, 66f); in Kuhn (2001a, ch. 4) I illustrate an alternative OT approach based on outside-in functional uncertainty (compare Kaplan and Zaenen 1989).

[27]Another way of viewing this is the following: (the negation of) a constraint is a structural description of a partial structure that should be avoided. When constraint violations are counted, we effectively determine the cardinality of the set of partial structures in the candidate analysis satisfying this description. This set-theoretical view was pointed out by Ron Kaplan (p.c.).

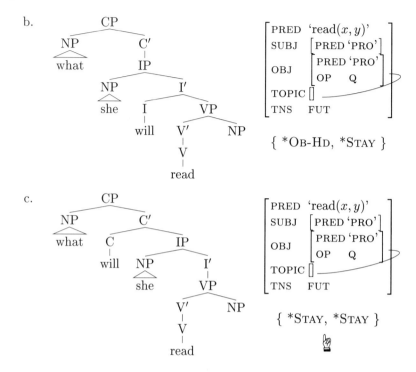

b.

{ *Ob-Hd, *Stay }

c.

{ *Stay, *Stay }

8.4.3 Digression: Constraint Marking within the Grammar

The restriction on the form of constraints introduced in the previous section opens up a possibility of realizing the constraint marking in practical grammar writing. Rather than assuming an extra processing step after the analyses have been constructed, the constraint marking can be coded into the grammar rules specifying the inviolable principles. There is a parallel to different approaches of realizing semantic construction in an LFG grammar: the *description by analysis* approach vs. the *codescription* approach. In the former, semantic construction starts only once the f-structure analysis has been created; in the latter, f-structure and semantic structure are built up simultaneously (see e.g. Kaplan 1995 for discussion). The constraint marking approach introduced above works as description by analysis. But as long as there is a unique place in the grammar/lexicon from which a certain structural element can be introduced, we can attach the constraints it has to meet there already. (This becomes possible since the constraints are formally restricted to be talking about a single structural element.) For c-structure categories, it is true that there is such a unique place: we can attach the constraints in the rules for nonterminals and in the lexicon entries for terminals. With f-structures, we have to be careful, since due to unification, there is not generally a unique source in the grammar/lexicon for an f-structure. (For all PRED-bearing f-structures, the instantiated symbol interpretation of semantic forms Kaplan and Bresnan (1982) guarantees uniqueness however; so, attaching the constraints wherever a PRED-value is introduced would capture this subset of f-structures.[28])

As in the grammar-based constraint marking discussed briefly at the beginning of section 8.4.2, we have to ensure the violability of the attached OT constraints. Like in (22), we can again disjoin the constraints with their negation—this time not just for the root category, but potentially for every category in each rule. As a result we will again have a grammar that performs both the task of candidate generation and constraint marking, thus we can call it $G_{inviol,marks}$.

Constraint violation marks are introduced to the MARKS multiset in the places in the grammar where the structure violating a constraint is created. Since constraint marks can now be introduced into the MARKS multiset in every rule, we have to ensure that all contributions are collected and made available at the root node of the analysis.[29] This is achieved by identifying the MARKS feature of all daughter constituents with the mother's by the equation $(\uparrow \text{MARKS})=(\downarrow \text{MARKS})$, creating a single multiset for the complete analysis. Note that multiple violations of a single constraint fall out from the use of a multiset.[30]

Note that if we now use a special projection o instead of the feature MARKS (and assume implicit trivial equations identifying the o-structure of all constituents) we are very close to the system of (A. Frank et al. 2001), which is built into the XLE system. (The difference in application will be addressed in section 8.6.2.) The XLE system also provides an (extended) implementation of the *Eval*-function, based on the marks introduced to the o-projection, and a dominance hierarchy specified in the configuration section of the grammar.[31]

The practical advantage of the grammar-based constraint marking is that it makes it easy to focus on some specific phenomenon, abstracting away from irrelevant interactions. This allows a linguist to write an ex-

---

[28]One could easily generalize this idea by defining an extended Completeness condition that demands for every well-formed f-structure that there be some feature ID, with an instantiated symbol as its value. Furthermore, whenever a rule or lexicon entry talks about some f-structure, the ID feature is optionally introduced, along with the constraint marking schemata. Hence, it is guaranteed that for each f-structure the constraint schemata are introduced exactly once. (The non-determinism does not affect the result.)

[29]As Ron Kaplan (p.c.) pointed out, the collection of marks need not be realized within the grammar, since evaluation is a grammar-external process anyway; thus, the identification of the MARKS feature is an unnecessary overhead.

[30]An alternative way using a standard set would be to interpret the constraint marks introduced as instantiated symbols (like the PRED values in standard LFG), i.e. as pairwise distinct.

[31]As A. Frank et al. (2001) discuss in detail, XLE distinguishes several types of constraint marks—in particular preference marks as well as dispreference marks. For the purposes of modelling a standard OT account, the dispreference marks suffice.

perimental grammar fragment rather fast: writing the LFG grammar that models *Gen* happens simultaneously with thinking about the constraints. So, in particular one can focus attention on a small set of relevant constraints, generating only the candidate distinctions at stake.[32] Different hypotheses can be checked very quickly. Parts of the grammar that are not at the center of attention can be realized with a classical LFG analysis. (Of course, the fact that the grammar writer herself/himself can decide which constraints to check in which rule runs the risk that interactions are left out that *are* relevant, especially when the fragment grows over time. This is a familiar risk in grammar writing, occurring whenever some underlying generalizations are not made explicit in the grammar code.)

8.4.4 Harmony Evaluation

Having clarified the formalization of constraints, the last step to finish the OT model is to look at the procedure of checking the constraints on a given candidate set, i.e. harmony evaluation. We must make sure that this task is decidable, given the output of generation and the set of constraints.

We know that checking a single constraint on a single candidate analysis (a c-structure/f-structure pair) is feasible (this is the model checking problem addressed in section 8.4.1 and section 8.4.2). there is a finite set of constraints,[33] we can also check all constraints on a given candidate.

The candidate set is not guaranteed to be finite, but we can assume it to be characterized by a context-free grammar Kaplan and Wedekind (2000). Applying the pumping lemma for context-free languages, all strings longer than a fixed bound contain the recursive application of a set of rules in that grammar. Creating extra structure by applying such a recursive cycle can have three types of effects for each constraint C_i: the number of violations that the overall analysis incurs for C_i is either (i) left unchanged; or (ii) increased after a particular number of cycles; or (iii) decreased after a particular number of cycles. Case (iii) occurs when the addition of structure removes a configuration that violates the constraint. For example, assume C_i says that all lexical categories are dominated by three nested functional categories; then the structure generated without using the recursive part of the grammar may incur a number of violations of this constraint. Now, if the recursion permits the introduction of more functional categories, it is possible to decrease the number of violations of C_i.

---

[32] With this strategy, it was relatively easy to implement the entire OT fragment of Bresnan (2000, sec. 2) in the XLE system, i.e. leaving aside instances of constraint violation where they were obviously irrelevant.

[33] If local conjunction of constraints and similar operations are assumed, the situation may get more complicated. Then one can easily get arbitrarily many constraints to be checked, so an algorithm has to be defined that stops the checking as soon as the more and more complex composite constraints fail to make new distinctions between the candidates.

What is important to note here is that quite obviously, the best we can do is to avoid all the constraint violations that there were in the first place—for the structure without the pumping. From this point on, further "pumping" will have the effect of type (i) on C_i violations. So, for case (iii), we just have to look at a finite number of different groups of candidates. Case (ii) will make things worse and worse (i.e. the candidates less and less harmonic); this means that once we have unfolded the effect of case (iii), we can "cut off" the branches in the search tree making use of a recursion containing case (ii) for some constraints. This leaves us just with recursions of type (i), i.e. we have a finite number of possibly infinitely large equivalence classes of candidates that are indistinguishable in terms of harmony evaluation. So, we can simply output the most harmonic equivalence class (again, characterized by a context-free grammar).

Thus, the overall task of determining the set of optimal candidates, given an input f-structure and a ranked set of constraints is decidable.

8.5 Violating Faithfulness to the Input

The discussion of candidate generation and constraint formulation in the previous sections was primarily motivated by the situation of having realization alternatives for a given input that incur violations of markedness constraints. In all such cases, the resulting f-structures are subsumed by the underspecified input f-structure, hence *Gen* can clearly be modelled by monotonically adding information to the input (according to an LFG grammar G_{inviol}).

When the candidate set is supposed to contain candidate analyses that are unfaithful to the input (as motivated in section 8.2.2), there appears to be a problem for this subsumption-based approach. Under a straightforward view, the unfaithful candidate analyses leave out or alter information from the input. Thus, their f-structure cannot be *subsumed* by the input f-structure.

Conceptually, there is a way of allowing more than just the addition of information to the input within a unification-based framework.[34] Counter to the assumption made in section 8.3.1, the input representation could be kept separate from the candidate's f-structure. As in the high-level specification in section 8.2.3, the constraints could then see both the input and the candidate analysis. (Technically, there are different ways of doing this: the input could be represented as an extra projection level, separate from c-structure and f-structure; or one might assume a special feature INPUT

---

[34] Johnson (1998, sec. 3) raises the issue whether a unification-based framework is the adequate setting for OT at all. He suggests that functional uniqueness from classical LFG may not really be required. Rather, a purely resource-based feature interpretation may suffice, as proposed in resource-sensitive LFG (R-LFG; Johnson 1999—a generalization of the linear-logic based semantics for LFG, see the other contributions in Dalrymple 1999). He argues that the full unification machinery might be superfluous ballast.

within the f-structure.) The subsumption of the candidate f-structure by the input structure would then hold only for the faithful candidates.

Without further provisos, this construction is however incompatible with the restrictions (16) and (17) discussed in section 8.3.2, which guarantee decidability of the computational task of candidate generation. As the unfaithful candidates may leave out arbitrary portions of the input structure, the structural relationship between input features and the overall output f-structure is lost; thus, the generation task would be generally undecidable Wedekind (1999).[35]

Does this mean that a full-fledged OT model making use of faithfulness violations cannot be captured computationally? Not necessarily. What the computational considerations suggest is a closer investigation of the degree of unfaithfulness required for explanatory accounts. As Bresnan (2000, sec. 2) demonstrates, the cases of unfaithfulness occurring in Grimshaw's (1997) inversion analysis can be reconstructed with a restriction of unfaithfulness to morpholexical constraints. (Likewise, Bresnan's (2000, sec. 3) analysis of negative contraction in various dialects of English is based on purely morpholexical unfaithfulness.) As I will discuss instantly, this morpholexical conception is in fact compatible with the subsumption-based model of *Gen*, and will thus pose no decidability problems. This adds a computational argument to the conceptual points that Bresnan (2000, sec. 4) makes in favor of a lexicalist setting for OT syntax.[36]

8.5.1 The Lexicalist View on Unfaithfulness

In Grimshaw's (1997) analysis, *do* insertion in English questions is explained with reference to faithfulness violations: the insertion of additional verbs like *do* is only possible under the violation of the (FILL or DEP-IO type[37]) faithfulness constraint "Full Interpretation" (FULL-INT). In unstressed positive clauses of English, such candidates will be less harmonic than their competitors without additional verbs; however, in questions with an operator in CP-Spec, insertion of the additional verb *do* is a way of filling the otherwise empty C position. Thus, these candidates avoid a violation of

---

[35] See also Johnson's (1998, sec. 4.1) sketch of an undecidability proof for unrestricted OT-LFG.

[36] Note that it is not necessarily impossible to formulate a more liberal restriction on the input-candidate relation guaranteeing decidability. However, combining the rather strict subsumption restriction on *Gen* with a more liberal account of lexical insertion appears to be a natural, non-redundant split of the explanatory burden.

[37] Terminology is slightly confusing here. *Do* insertion violates a FILLconstraint in the sense that there is nothing in the input that would get realized by the lexical item. So, in this sense *do* adds to the input, not preserving faithfulness. This means that the contribution (the full verb) *do* would usually make doesn't make it into the candidate's f-structure representation, and in this sense, one can also speak of leaving its lexical conceptual structure "unparsed". This should not be confused with PARSE (or MAX-IO) violations, which occur when material from the input f-structure is not realized by any lexical element, i.e. we have "unparsing" with respect to the input.

OB-HD, which dominates the constraint FULL-INT, such that the unfaithful candidate with the inserted *do* wins the competition.

Bresnan (2000, sec. 2) demonstrates that in an OT-LFG version of this interaction, faithfulness violations can be seen as situations where certain morpholexical constraints are not used for the f-structure of the sentence. In general, the contribution of words is modelled by a set of morpholexical constraints—the lexical annotations of classical LFG as in (34), for the main verb *did*:[38]

(34) *did* V * ($\uparrow$ PRED) = 'do'
$\quad\quad\quad\quad\quad\quad$ ($\uparrow$ TNS) = PAST

Classically, all metavariables $\uparrow$ in the set of morpholexical constraints introduced by a given lexical entry have to be instantiated to the same f-structure—the one projected from the lexical item's category (here V). For the OT-LFG model, Bresnan assumes that some of the metavariables may be instantiated by an element that does not occur in the candidate's f-structure. (In OT terminology, this means that the respective constraint remains "unparsed".) Specifically, for the auxiliary *did* like in *what did she say*, the main verb entry (34) is used, but the morpholexical constraint introducing the PRED value is not instantiated within the candidate's f-structure. (If it was, there would be a clash with the main verb's PRED value—thus this structure is not even contained in G_{inviol} and is not a candidate.) Of course, leaving morpholexical constraints uninstantiated is possible only at the cost of a faithfulness violation, and thus these candidates will only win if the relevant faithfulness constraint is dominated by a markedness constraint (like OB-HD for English).

In the present context, the lexicalist account of unfaithfulness raises two questions: (i) how is the decidability of the overall system influenced by allowing morpholexical constraints to be uninstantiated within the candidate's f-structure; and (ii) what controls the choice of expletive elements (*do* rather than *shout* etc.). Let us consider the latter question first (the former will be discussed in section 8.5.3). It is briefly addressed by Bresnan (2000, sec. 2), adopting the basic idea from Grimshaw (1997, 386): the assumption is that for a verb like *do*, "[t]he unparsing of its semantically minimal PRED feature is a smaller violation of faithfulness than that incurred by unparsing the semantically richer PREDs of *shout, obfuscate*, or any other verb in the English lexicon."

For concreteness, let us assume that this intuition is modelled by a conceptual hierarchy of PRED values—or lexical conceptual structures. More specific sub-concepts will inherit all the information from their super-concepts, plus they will add some information. Now, to evaluate faithfulness constraints on "unparsed" PRED values, the conceptual contribution they would

---

[38] I assume that in OT-LFG, the lexical specification of the PRED-values does not include the subcategorization frame; for some discussion, see Kuhn (2001a, sec. 4.3).

have made is considered piece by piece, i.e. concepts embedded more deeply in the conceptual hierarchy will incur more violations than the more general ones. In effect, everything else being equal, the most general available concept will be picked as an expletive element.[39]

8.5.2 Formalizing Morpholexical Constraints

Before we can address the decidability issue, we have to commit to a formal way of dealing with the (potentially unparsed) morpholexical constraints. Bresnan (2000, sec. 2) assumes that the metavariables in unparsed constraints are instantiated with some arbitrary element not occurring in the output f-structure. To facilitate the application of the faithfulness constraints, I will assume that all morpholexical constraints for a lexical item will be introduced in a separate feature structure projected from the pre-terminal node.[40] Let us call this new projection the λ-projection (for "lexical"), describing a correspondence between c-structure and "l-structure". When faithfulness is met, all elements in this set will subsume the f-structure projected from the same category; however, for unparsed morpholexical constraints, a mismatch occurs.

(35) Full-Int/Dep-IO violation (with PRED 'do' missing in f-structure)

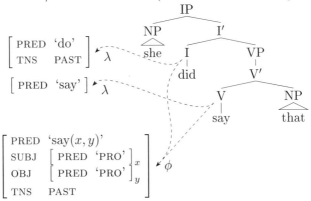

In (35), (a modification of Bresnan 2000, (44)), the idea is illustrated for an example violating faithfulness: the PRED constraint introduced by *did* does not re-appear in the f-structure. In order to reach the intended

---

[39]To turn this idea into an account with reasonable empirical coverage, it clearly has to be complemented by some additional device allowing for conventionalization of the use of a particular lexical item out of a choice of semantically very similar items. For example, most Romance languages use the verb derived from Latin *habere* ('have') as a perfect auxiliary, while Portuguese uses the verb derived from *tenere* ('hold').

[40]In Kuhn (2000a), I adopt an alternative approach, which doesn't assume a representational reflex of the morpholexical constraints in the candidate structures. Rather, faithfulness violations arise directly as a mismatch between the lexical specification of an item and f-structure. (Procedurally speaking, they can be detected at the point of lexical insertion.)

effect, the lexicon entries have to look as follows (recall that ↑ is short for $\phi(\mathcal{M}*)$, i.e. the f-structure projected from the current node's mother, in this case the pre-terminal):

(36) *did* I * $(f_1$ PRED$) = $ 'do'
     $f_1 = \lambda(\mathcal{M}*)$
     $(\ f_1 =\uparrow\ )$
     $(f_2$ TNS$)=$PAST
     $f_2 = \lambda(\mathcal{M}*)$
     $(\ f_2=\uparrow\ )$

  say V * $(f_1$ PRED$) = $ 'say'
     $f_1 = \lambda(\mathcal{M}*)$
     $(\ f_1 =\uparrow\ )$

For every morpholexical constraint, there are three annotation schemata, making use of a distinct local metavariable referring to a feature structure $(f_1, f_2, \dots)$. The three schemata are: (i) the lexical constraint itself,[41] (ii) an f-equation introducing the morpholexical constraint to the l-structure projected from the pre-terminal, and (iii) an *optional* f-equation introducing the constraint at the level of f-structure. The optionality of schema (iii) leads to the presence of unfaithful analyses.

The faithfulness constraint FULL-INT/DEP-IO can now be formulated as follows:

(37) FULL-INT/DEP-IO
  $\forall n, P.[\ \ (atomic\text{-}f\text{-}str(\star) \land cat(n) \land (\lambda(n)\ \ P) = \star)$
    $\rightarrow (\phi(n)\ \ P) = \star\ \ ]$
  "For all categories n and feature paths P, if $\star$ is an atomic value under P in the λ-projection from n, then $\star$ is also the value under P in the ϕ-projection from n."

Since the metavariable $\star$ is generally instantiated to every structural element (cf. section 8.4.2), it is now in particular instantiated to the feature structures in l-structure. Note that the value 'do' of the PRED feature in (35) fails to satisfy this constraint: instantiating n as the I category and P as PRED, we have $(\lambda(I)$ PRED$) = $ 'do', but not $(\phi(I)$ PRED$) = $ 'do'.

8.5.3 Decidability of Generation with Unfaithfulness

We can now ask whether decidability of the generation task, as discussed in section 8.3.2, is affected. Let us first assume that the lexicon is a finite list. For each lexical item, there is a finite set of morpholexical constraints. What is the effect of making the introduction of each piece of morpholexical information to f-structure optional? We can think of the different realizations

---

[41] Note that the assumption is that all constraints are expressed as *defining* equations, rather than *constraining* equations, and that completeness and coherence are checked only on f-structure, not on l-structure.

of an underlying lexical item with a different selection of the morpholexical constraints introduced to f-structure as separate effective lexical entries. Note that there will be a finite number of such effective lexical entries. (Many of them will be synonymous in terms of f-structure contribution, in particular the ones introducing few or no morpholexical constraints to f-structure.) Thus, there are no principled changes in the generation task: the lexicon will be larger, but still finite. (Note that PRED-less lexicon entries do not constitute a problem for decidability of generation.) This means that the decidability results will remain unaffected.

Does constraint evaluation also remain decidable with the addition of unfaithful candidates and the faithfulness constraints? As noted, many of the effective lexicon entries are synonymous in terms of f-structure. Each member of such a set of synonyms will incur exactly the same markedness violations, so they differ only in faithfulness violations. Since there are finitely many synonyms in each set, the least unfaithful one(s) can be easily determined, i.e. we have again reduced the task including unfaithful candidates to the original task.

One may object that it is not correct to think of the lexicon as a finite list, since there are productive processes of compositional and derivational morphology that can create an infinite number of items (e.g., arbitrarily long noun compounds). Recall however that in the discussion section 8.4.4, infinite candidate sets were no problem as they were characterized by a context-free grammar, i.e. the set could be enumerated with the guarantee that from a certain point on, candidates were at least as bad as one that had been enumerated already. The morphological rules provide a similar (presumably simpler) scheme of enumeration, and the organization of PRED-values in a concept hierarchy will also guarantee that with a growing number of 'unparsed' PRED introducing constraints, candidates get less and less harmonic.

8.5.4 Parse or Max-IO Violations

The previous subsection addressed only FILL-type faithfulness violations, i.e. the situation where on the surface it appears as if information had been added to the input.

The symmetrical situation—input information apparently disappearing—is addressed by the PARSE/MAX-IO constraints. To generate candidates that violate such faithfulness constraints according to the view adopted here, we would have to allow for the situation that no lexical element contributes the morpholexical constraints to meet a particular part of the input f-structure. With such an account null pronominals and ellipsis could be modelled. For example, Samek-Lodovici (1996) and Grimshaw and Samek-Lodovici (1998), assume that null subject clauses in a *pro-drop* language like Italian involve this kind of "deletion". An example is given in the structure (39) for (38). Note that neither of the λ-projected (i.e. morpholexical) feature structures introduces the PRED values under SUBJ, which *does* appear in the f-structure.[42]

(38) ha cantato
      has sung

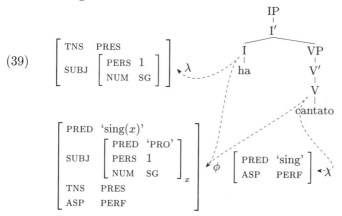

(39)

$$\begin{bmatrix} \text{TNS} & \text{PRES} \\ \text{SUBJ} & \begin{bmatrix} \text{PERS} & 1 \\ \text{NUM} & \text{SG} \end{bmatrix} \end{bmatrix}$$

$$\begin{bmatrix} \text{PRED} & \text{'sing}(x)\text{'} \\ \text{SUBJ} & \begin{bmatrix} \text{PRED} & \text{'PRO'} \\ \text{PERS} & 1 \\ \text{NUM} & \text{SG} \end{bmatrix} \\ \text{TNS} & \text{PRES} \\ \text{ASP} & \text{PERF} \end{bmatrix}$$

$$\begin{bmatrix} \text{PRED} & \text{'sing'} \\ \text{ASP} & \text{PERF} \end{bmatrix}$$

For technically "assembling" the f-structure, there has to be a way of optionally providing "pseudo-lexical constraints" (basically attached to the root node) for each piece of information occurring in the input—in the example, we made use of this option for the PRED-value under SUBJ. These constraints can of course be used only at the cost of incurring a PARSE/MAX-IO violation.[43]

In the generation direction that we have been adopting up to now, decidability is not affected by this move: there is a finite set of "partial" generation tasks (partial because part of the goal structure is given already at the beginning). Interestingly however, this extension of the definition of G_{inviol} requires more thought for the parsing task (the relevance of which will be addressed in section 8.6.1). Up to this point, parsing with G_{inviol} did not involve any departure from classical LFG parsing. Now, parsing with G_{inviol} involves guessing what the part of the input f-structure was that was only realized by "pseudo-lexical constraints" and that therefore has no reflex in the surface string. Without some additional minimality assumptions (or alternatively, a *bidirectional* OT model, section 8.6.2), it is clear that an algorithm for this task will not terminate: the guessed

---

[42]In classical LFG, it is assumed that the inflectional morphology introduces the subject's PRED-value, however, in the OT framework we can assume that this PRED-value arises as a faithfulness violation.

[43]This set-up will generate something similar to a NULL PARSE in every candidate set: the analysis that uses all available pseudo-lexical constraints (and no real morpholexical constraints). Note however that the NULL PARSEs for different inputs will have different constraint profiles. In particular, it is not possible to construct a constraint that is *only* violated by the NULL PARSE, as seems to be required for Johnson's (1998, sec. 4.1) undecidability proof.

structure may grow arbitrarily large.[44] A further exploration of Parse violations is beyond the scope of this paper, but cf. Kuhn (2000a,b).

8.6 Generation and Parsing

So far, we have looked at the application of the LFG grammar G_{inviol} only in the stepwise manner underlying the definition of grammaticality in OT, which took us from an input f-structure via the generation of alternative candidate analyses to the identification of constraint violations, which is input to the evaluation function computing the optimal analysis. While this alone may be illustrative for an experimental system, we expect a little more of the implementation of an OT grammar: it should recognize the strings in the language generated by the OT grammar, and it should moreover assign the structures of the grammatical analyses to the strings. Johnson (1998, sec. 4) formulates the following parsing problem:

(40) *The universal parsing problem for* OT-LFG*:*
    Given a phonological string s and an OT-LFG G as input, return the input-candidate pairs $\langle i, c \rangle$ generated by G such that the candidate c has phonological string s and c is the optimal output for i with respect to the ordered constraints defined in G.

8.6.1 The Parsing Task

It is very important to note the following (cf. also the discussion in Johnson 1998, sec. 4.2): the universal parsing problem cannot be solved by simply applying the grammar G_{inviol} and the harmony evaluation introduced in 8.4 in the opposite direction. Parsing a string with G_{inviol} (rather than generating from an input f-structure) and computing the most harmonic of the alternative parsing analyses has a different effect;[45] the resulting optimal candidates will not satisfy the grammaticality definition of OT (which remains generation-based). To see this, recall that the grammar G_{inviol} was set up to allow for all universally available alternatives. For example, with the G_{inviol}-grammar for the Grimshaw/Bresnan fragment we discussed above, the strings in (41b) are among the ones generated for the input f-structure (41a) (with *What does she read* being the optimal candidate for the English ranking).

---

[44]A situation where one might want to assume an arbitrarily large portion of the underlying f-structure to be unrealized is ellipsis in context as in (i). At an underlying level, B's utterance should have a similar structure of recursive embedding as A's (cf. L. Levin's (1982) analysis of sluicing).

(i)   A: John claimed that Bill saw Sue.
       B: And Ann.

[45]As the parsing-based application of an optimizing competition by A. Frank et al. (2001) shows, this mechanism can be used to model (or approximate) preference among readings of a string.

(41) a.
$$\begin{bmatrix} \text{PRED} & \text{`read}(x,y)\text{'} \\ \text{GF}_1 & \begin{bmatrix} \text{PRED} & \text{`PRO'} \\ \text{PERS} & 3 \\ \text{NUM} & \text{SG} \\ \text{GEND} & \text{FEM} \end{bmatrix}_x \\ \text{GF}_2 & \begin{bmatrix} \text{OP} & \text{Q} \\ \text{PRED} & \text{`THING'} \end{bmatrix}_y \\ \text{TNS} & \text{PRES} \end{bmatrix}$$

b.   Reads she what
Read she what
She reads what
She read what
She do read what
. . .
What does she read
Do she read what
Does she read what

Suppose we try to *parse* one of the ungrammatical strings like *She do read what*, applying G_{inviol}. It will receive at least one analysis; now, we might hope that the optimizing competition will rule out this candidate analysis. However, *all* candidates in the set of analyses constructed in parsing, i.e. our candidate set in this context, are analyses of this very string. So, no matter which one will win according to the optimization, the optimal analysis will trivially have this string as its yield, although this string is ungrammatical.

The same is illustrated by the abstract illustration (42) taken from Johnson (1998, sec. 4.1):

(42)

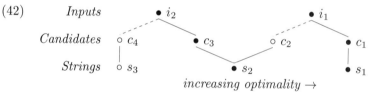

increasing optimality $\rightarrow$

Parsing the string s_2 produces the analyses c_2 and c_3. Being more optimal (i.e. further to the right in this abstract illustration), the candidate analysis c_2 wins the competition if these two analyses sharing the same string form the candidate set. However, for the input underlying c_2 (the predicate-argument structure i_1), there is a more optimal analysis: c_1 (with a different surface string: s_1). Thus c_2 is not a grammatical analysis. The alternative parse c_3 is the optimal candidate for its underlying input representation i_2. But there are strings with no grammatical analysis, like s_3.

These considerations show that more care has to be taken to ensure that the right candidate set enters the competition—even when the processing direction for the overall system is turned around. We should use G_{inviol} in the parsing direction only to find out possible f-structures. Then we can extract from these f-structures the amount of information that forms an OT input. We perform a *backward* generation step, generating from the extracted OT input f-structures, applying the original generation-based competition. For each of these competitions there are two possibilities: (i) the optimal candidate has a different phonological string—this means that the string we started from is not grammatical for that input; or (ii) the optimal candidate has the string we started from—this means we have found one grammatical analysis. If case (ii) occurs for none of the competitions based on inputs extracted from the parsing results, then the string is not contained in the language generated by the OT grammar.

To contrast the two tasks of generation and parsing more clearly, let me put things a little more formally: Assume G to be an LFG grammar together with a *description by analysis* constraint marking routine (cf. the discussion in section 8.4.3). G defines triples $\langle T, \Phi, O \rangle$, where T and Φ are a c-structure/f-structure analysis in the classical sense, and O is a multiset of constraint marks for the constraints violated by this LFG analysis. The grammar of a language L is defined by the constraint ranking R_L. We furthermore assume that a filter F exists taking a fully specified f-structure to an underspecified f-structure, which contains just the amount of information we assume as the input, in accordance with the restrictions discussed in section 8.3.2. The function *yield* applies to a c-structure tree and returns the string of terminal symbols.

Let us first go through the simpler case of *language production*, i.e. the generation task . Here the optimal analysis is determined as follows: the input consists of an (underspecified) f-structure Φ_{in}; first (P-i) we determine all analyses $\langle T, \Phi', O \rangle$ in G with $\Phi_{in} \sqsubseteq \Phi'$; (P-ii) the harmony evaluation mechanism *Eval* computes the set of optimal analyses (often a singleton) based on the constraint violations O and the language-specific constraint ranking R_L. So, we can think of production Π as a function that takes an underspecified f-structure to a set of optimal analyses $\langle T_k, \Phi_k, O_k \rangle$.

Now we can address *language understanding*—the general parsing problem (cf. also the schematic illustration in Figure 1). The system starts out with a string w; first of all (U-i), the parser determines all analyses $A_p = \{\langle T, \Phi, O \rangle$ in G with $yield(T) = w\}$; after (U-ii) filtering the input information $F(\Phi_j)$ out for each analysis $\langle T_j, \Phi_j, O_j \rangle \in A_p$, we (U-iii) apply the production function Π to each of the resulting underspecified f-structures to determine the respective optimal candidates under a generation view: we obtain a set of optimal analyses for each parse of the string (again, often a singleton set); (U-iv) from the union of these winner sets we subtract all analyses for which $yield(T) \neq w$. The result is the set of *grammatical* analyses for the input string w.

Due to the subtraction of those analyses yielding a string different from the input in step (U-iv), the set of grammatical analyses may be empty. This differs from the purely generation-based view, where the set of optimal analyses will always contain at least one candidate (unless the grammar G contains no analysis for the input, i.e. the candidate set is empty).

The complexity of this task, involving "backward generation" will be discussed in section 8.6.3. Note that although processing in both the parsing and the generation direction is involved, optimization is only performed in the production direction. This means that we may call the technique a *bidirectional processing* approach, but not *bidirectional optimization*, which is briefly addressed in the following (for more discussion see Kuhn 2000a).

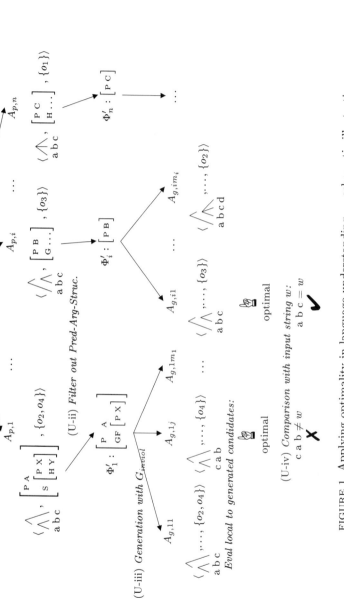

FIGURE 1 Applying optimality in language understanding — schematic illustration

8.6.2 Competition among Parsing Alternatives

The above discussion of the parsing problem with a standard OT grammar suggested that competition between candidates sharing the same surface string does not take us anywhere useful, when we are interested in formalizing the concept of grammaticality. However, A. Frank et al. (2001) show that the ranking of alternative parses can be very useful as a preference mechanism—certainly based on different constraints, and with a different underlying LFG grammar (with a classical concept of grammaticality).[46] With the formalization proposed in the previous subsections at hand, we are in a position to address the question whether constraint systems with generation-based competition are necessarily distinct or even incompatible with systems designed for a parsing-based competition. I will address this point only briefly here, arguing that there are phenomena where using the same constraints in both directions makes the correct empirical predictions.

The basic idea is very simple. The technique sketched in Figure 1 stops at the point where the winners of the generation-based competition—the grammatical analyses—are checked against the original string. In the situation where more than one analysis survives this step, i.e. when the string is ambiguous, we could again apply *Eval* to single out the most harmonic analysis among these alternatives. Note that when used in this disambiguation scenario, optimality models a different intuitive concept: the optimal analysis is the *preferred reading* of a given string (whereas in generation-based competition, the optimal analysis is the only grammatical form expressing the underlying content). The technique of applying an OT-style competition both in generation (based on a candidate set with a common input), and in parsing (based on a common string) is called a *bidirectional competition* technique.[47]

If we find empirical cases where the result of this bidirectional competition (based on the same set of constraints) coincides with the intuitively preferred reading, this shows an interesting generalization of OT. To bring this out, we need to look at an empirical domain which involves a fair amount of realization alternatives and ambiguity. A good example is the

---

[46]Also, Smolensky (1996) proposes to explain the lag of children's production abilities behind their ability in comprehension by assuming that in comprehension a simple parsing-based optimization is performed, which permits processing the strings that the child hears with the same constraint ranking that is applied in production. Thus in comprehension, many analyses are accepted that are not grammatical under the child's current constraint ranking (according to the *Gen*-based definition of grammaticality). The simple parsing task is liberal enough not to filter them out. However in production, the common underlying structure *does* determine the candidate set, and the constraints will have a strong filtering effect. The result is a very reduced production ability for the initial constraint ranking. The simpler parsing task is called *robust interpretive parsing* in Tesar and Smolensky (1998), and plays an important role in the learning algorithm.

[47]See for example (Wilson 2001; Lee 2001), and the discussion in Kuhn (2000a) and Kuhn (2001a, ch. 5). Blutner (1999) discusses different bidirectional OT models in the context of interpretation/lexical pragmatics.

relatively free word order in German, modelled within OT-LFG by Choi
(1999).

In the German *Mittelfeld* (the region between the finite verb in verb second position and the clause-final verb position), nominal arguments of the
verb can appear in any order. However, as has been widely observed (cf.,
e.g., Lenerz 1977; Höhle 1982; Abraham 1986; Uszkoreit 1987), a certain
"canonical" order is less marked than others. Deviations from this canonical order are used to mark a special information structure (or topic-focus
structure), i.e. these non-canonical orderings are more restricted through
context. Sentence (43) reflects the neutral order as it would be uttered in
an out-of-the-blue context. Variant (44a) is used to mark *dem Spion* as the
focus; (44b) furthermore marks *den Brief* as the topic.

(43) dass der Kurier   dem Spion   den Brief
     that the courier (NOM) the spy (DAT) the letter (ACC)
     zustecken sollte
     slip   should

(44) a. dass der Kurier den Brief dem Spion zustecken sollte
     b. dass den Brief der Kurier dem Spion zustecken sollte

Choi (1999, 150) models these data assuming competing sets of constraints
on word order: the canonical constraints, based on a hierarchy of grammatical functions (and, in principle also a hierarchy of thematic roles) (45); and
information structuring constraints (distinguishing the contextual dimensions of novelty and prominence, each marked by a binary feature) (46).

(45) CANON   Choi (1999, 150)
    a.   CN1:   SUBJ should be structurally more prominent
              than (e.g. 'c-command') non-SUBJ functions.
    b.   CN2:   Non-SUBJ functions align reversely with the
              c-structure according to the functional hier-
              archy.
              (SUBJ > D.OBJ > I.OBJ > OBL > ADJUNCT)

(46) Information Structuring Constraints: Choi (1999, 150)
    a.   NEW: A [−New] element should precede
              a [+New] Element.
    b.   PROM: A [+Prom] element should precede
              a [−Prom] Element.

Based on an appropriate ranking of these constraints (PROM ≫ CN1 ≫
{NEW, CN2}), Choi can predict the optimal ordering for a given underspecified f-structure (which in this case will also contain a description of
the informational status of the verb arguments). When the arguments don't
differ in informational status, the canonical constraints will take effect, leading to the order in (43); when there *are* differences, the unmarked order will

however violate information structuring constraints, such that competitors with a different ordering can win out.

Like the Grimshaw/Bresnan fragment, Choi's assumptions about Gen can be formulated as an LFG grammar G_{inviol}. For sentence (43) and its ordering variants, bidirectional optimization does not give results that go beyond what can be reached with generation-based competition alone, since in parsing the NPs can be unambiguously mapped to argument positions. However, if we look at sentences with ambiguous case marking like (47) and (48), the situation changes.

(47) dass Hans   Maria   den
     that H. (NOM/DAT/ACC) M. (NOM/DAT/ACC) the
     Brief   zustecken sollte
     letter (ACC) slip   should

(48) dass Otto   Maria   Hans
     that O. (NOM/DAT/ACC) M. (N/D/A) H. (N/D/A)
     vorschlagen sollte
     suggest   should

Parsing (47) with the appropriate G_{inviol}-grammar will result in two classes of analyses: one with *Hans* as the subject, and *Maria* as the indirect object, and one with the opposite distribution. The latter reading is strongly preferred by speakers of German (i.e. we observe a "freezing effect"). Note that there is no way of avoiding this ambiguity with hard constraints. Neither will the generation-based OT competition predict any difference, since the two readings are not members of the same candidate set. For (48), even more readings become possible: any of the three NPs can fill any of the three available argument positions. Nevertheless, speakers clearly prefer one reading.[48]

If we apply the OT parsing scheme from Figure 1, with the additional preference optimization among the grammatical alternatives, Choi's original constraints predict exactly these observations. Since in this additional optimization the string is fixed for all competing candidates, the analysis that violates the least constraints will be the one that interprets the arguments in such a way that the observed order is in line with the canonical order.

Thus, for the constraints that Choi (1999) assumes, the standard OT generation-based view can be generalized to the parsing scenario if a bidi-

---

[48]Note however that further factors are at work: in (i), which also contains ambiguous case marking, the selectional restrictions of the verb clearly overrule the ordering preferences—the absurd reading of the opera composing Mozart does not occur to a speaker of German (neither does the sentence sound odd).

    dass diese Oper   Mozart   komponiert hat
    that this opera (NOM/ACC) M. (NOM/ACC) composed   has

A similar influence of world knowledge in bidirectional optimization is observed by Lee (2001).

rectional competition is applied.[49] (Nevertheless, there are a number of issues about bidirectional optimization which I cannot go into here; cf. Kuhn 2000a, Kuhn 2001a, ch. 5, and fn. 50 below.)

8.6.3 The Complexity Problem

The computational model for OT presented in sections 8.3-8.5 and section 8.6.1 follows the definition of the notions involved quite closely. In particular, it realizes the specification of the candidate set entering the optimizing competition by actually constructing the analyses. Since the underlying LFG grammar is intentionally kept highly unrestricted (as most restriction is performed by the violable constraints), relatively simple sentences involve already a great number of candidate analyses. The complexity burden of constructing all conceivable candidate analyses is enormous when an OT grammar is compared with a classical grammar covering a similar set of data.

An additional unfortunate circumstance—from the viewpoint of complexity considerations—is the need for parsing and backward generation from every analysis in the parsing task (section 8.6.1). Both subtasks work with the highly unrestricted underlying grammar, and unless the generation task could benefit much from the result of the parsing task, one has to assume that the complexities multiply, to a first approximation.

Note however that for discarding a candidate as ungrammatical in the backward generation step, it suffices to show that there is a more harmonic analysis with the same input but a different surface string. Thus, a more efficient processing strategy might be to start out with the parsing analysis and systematically try to vary the parts of the structure that caused some constraint violation, proceeding from the most highly ranked constraint downwards. As soon as it turns out that a given constraint violation can be avoided by an analysis with a different string, the parsing analysis can be dropped without going through the remaining alternatives. However for the grammatical analyses (if there are any) all competitors which do better in terms of some constraint have to be generated.

An additional point worth mentioning is that with a bidirectional optimization system as discussed in 8.6.2, preferences among analyses based on the same string could be exploited in a control strategy for the backward generation step illustrated in Figure 1 Right after the initial parsing step (U-i), a preliminary ranking of the alternative parsing analyses can be computed (with the generation-based decision about grammaticality pending). Now the order of applying backward generation to the various analyses

---

[10]Under this extended view on possible competitions, the preference mechanism of A. Frank et al. (2001) is just a special case of an OT grammar, in which only the competition in the parsing direction takes place. The determination of the grammatical candidate analyses is based on a classical grammar without OT competition. For this reason, no bidirectional processing is required (which reduces the processing complexity considerably).

follows the parsing-based preference order. Under this regime, the overall average processing complexity is decreased considerably if one is only interested in the most preferred grammatical analysis:[50] one can stop with backward generation as soon as a single analysis has been confirmed to be optimal, and thus grammatical. A garden path effect will occur for cases where the most preferred analysis of the string turns out to be ungrammatical after backward generation and one has to recur to the second best parse etc.

As the considerations just made suggest, there is presumably much room for improving the efficiency of an actual algorithm performing the parsing and generation tasks, without imposing additional restrictions on the formalism.[51] On the other hand, there may be linguistically plausible ways to further narrow down the expressiveness of the formalism. These will be addressed briefly in the following section (see also Kuhn 2000c).

8.6.4 Possible Ways of Reducing the Processing Complexity

In the face of the potentially severe complexity problems of the processing approach based on the OT formalization introduced in sections 8.3-8.5, the question arises if there are further possibilities of expressing plausible restrictions in order to allow for more efficient processing. Intuitively, the explicit construction of entire candidate analyses seems to miss some concept of relative locality inherent to theoretical OT accounts. In this section and in 8.6.5, I attempt to pinpoint this intuition in a more formal way. Furthermore, one intuitively expects that once the language-particular ranking is known, there should be a fairly direct way of determining the optimal candidate for a given string or semantic representation. Can't one anticipate which candidates will be losers, thus avoiding their construction in the first place? In finite-state OT phonology, a compilation of the competition is possible (R. Frank and Satta 1998; Karttunen 1998). In section 8.6.6, I address very briefly how this conception might be extended to syntax, building on the locality restriction I will introduce shortly.

---

[50] Under the *strong* (symmetrical) view on bidirectional optimization Blutner (1999), a well-formed output indeed has to be optimal in both directions independently. The discussion in section 8.6.2 is however also compatible with weaker models, for example an asymmetrical model where in the comprehension-based competition, the most harmonic candidate of all production-based winners is chosen (which need not necessarily be optimal for a purely comprehension-based competition). Blutner (1999) discusses a symmetrical weak concept of bidirectional optimization which relies on mutual determination of the candidate sets for the two competitions (which poses another computational challenge). This weak bidirectional approach is applied to OT syntax in Kuhn (2001a, ch. 5).

[51] For example, an interleaved chart parsing/generation algorithm can be used Kuhn (2000b).

Locally Restricted OT Competition

The apparent reason why candidate analyses of considerable size have to
be constructed prior to optimization (which will typically rule out all but
one analyses) is the following: unlike a system with hard constraints, in OT
one cannot discard an analysis on the basis of a local constraint violation,
since the analysis may still be the best of all possible ones due to more
highly ranked constraints.

Nevertheless, a striking property of OT systems in the literature is the
relatively restricted structural domain to which the competition can be
limited. Let us look at an example which demonstrates this relative locality:
the tableau in (49) illustrates the competition underlying the combination
of a matrix and an embedded clause (the constraint definitions were given
on page 329 and 343).

(49)   Evidence for independence of substructures in an OT competition

Candidates	*LEX-F	AGR	DEP-IO
a. I not think that he not smokes		*!*	
b. I don't think that he not smokes		*!	*
c. I think not that he not smokes	*!	*	
d. I not think that he doesn't smoke		*!	*
☞ e. I don't think that he doesn't smoke			**
f. I think not that he doesn't smoke	*!		*
g. I not think that he smokes not	*!	*	
h. I don't think that he smokes not	*!		*
i. I think not that he smokes not	*!*		

What is striking about tableau (49) is that it wouldn't have been necessary to construct the full amount of candidate analyses. Rather, it would
have been enough to determine the different types of analysis each of the
two clauses can adopt and compute locally for these which is the most
harmonic (as in tableaux (50) and (51)). Combining the two winning local
analyses will have the desired effect (leading to candidate e. in (49)).

(50)

Candidates		*LEX-F	AGR	DEP-IO
a.	I not think CP		*!	
☞ b.	I don't think CP			*
c.	I think not CP	*!		

(51) Candidates		*Lex-F	Agr	Dep-IO
	a. that he not smokes		*!	
☞	b. that he doesn't smoke			*
	c. that he smokes not	*!		

The question is what properties a tableau has to have in order for such a split to be possible. I will here approach this question first formally, proposing an adequate formal property; in section 8.6.5, I will also address the linguistic question what structural objects we can assume to have this property.

Let us assume we have ways of identifying and composing subparts of LFG analyses (like the partial c- and f-structures corresponding to the matrix clause and the embedded clause in (49), respectively). This issue will be discussed briefly, but not exhaustively in section 8.6.5.

- Call two sub-structures R, S of an analysis A **harmonically independent** or **h-independent** with respect to a definition of *Gen* and a given set of constraints, if
  - (i) corresponding substructures R_i, S_i can be uniquely identified in any of the candidate analyses A_i (presumably with reference to the structure of the input), such that any distinctive constraint violation incurred by A_i is also incurred by either R_i or S_i (but not both);
  - (ii) the different possible substructures R_j, S_k combine freely (i.e. the candidates of the overall structure can be formed by taking the cross-product of the substructures).

- *Lemma*
  For h-independent substructures, the computation of the overall winner is equivalent to computing the individual winners (the most harmonic R_j, and the most harmonic S_k) plus putting the substructures together.

Why is this so? Assume we can split an analysis A into h-independent substructures R and S. For computing the most harmonic $Max(R_j)$ ($j \in 1 \ldots n$), a tableau of all local realization alternatives with their respective constraint violations is constructed, likewise for the most harmonic $Max(S_k)$ ($k \in 1 \ldots m$). From these two tableaux, we can construct a new tableau for all pairs $\langle R_j, S_k \rangle$ ($j \in 1 \ldots n, k \in 1 \ldots m$), taking the multiunion of constraint violations of the two components. Since R and S are h-independent, this new tableau is the same as the original tableau for determining the most harmonic A_i directly.

As such, the most harmonic candidate in the composite tableau must be $\langle Max(R_j), Max(S_k) \rangle$. To see this, assume there is a more harmonic candidate A'. Then A' violates some particular constraint fewer times than $\langle Max(R_j), Max(S_k)\rangle$, i.e. either the R part or the S part of A'—call them $R_{A'}$ and $S_{A'}$—violates this constraint fewer times than $Max(R_j)$ or $Max(S_k)$, respectively. But then $R_{A'}$ (or $S_{A'}$) would be more harmonical than $Max(R_j)$ (or $Max(S_k)$), which contradicts the assumption. Thus, $\langle Max(R_j), Max(S_k)\rangle$ must indeed be the winner of the overall competition.

The concept of h-independence allows us to make the difference between "classical" and OT constraints in terms of the locality of processing more precise. Classical, inviolable constraints work in such a way that if any two constraints operate on different substructures (and there is a possibility of satisfying these constraints), then the substructures will be h-independent. For this reason, processing with such constraints can proceed in a strictly local way: if there is a choice of violating such a classical constraint or not when constructing an analysis, the negative alternative can be discarded without looking at any other part of the structure.

In contrast, for OT analyses it is clearly essential for their explanatory impact that the structures on which the violable constraints apply are *not* mutually h-independent. The whole point of assuming that even grammatical analyses may violate certain constraints is to allow for situations in which the lesser of two evils is chosen; this means situations, where there are several ways of expressing a certain part of the input, each of which violates some of the constraints, i.e. there is no "perfect" way of saying it. In other words, if the violation of a constraint C_1 is accepted in the optimal solution, that is only to avoid a violation of C_2, which would have been even worse. The part of the structure that violates C_1 is not h-independent from the part that might have violated C_2. In order to evaluate the competition we have to take all combinations (local to the non-h-independent portion of structure) into account.

8.6.5 Extended Projections as H-Independent Domains

As the example in (49) (and its factorization into (50) and (51)) suggested, despite the inherent interdependence of constraint satisfaction in OT analyses, at some level h-independent substructures may nevertheless emerge. When dealing with substructures that have this property, a potentially exponential amount of processing expense could be saved. This is due to the independence in the determination of the optimal candidate observed in lemma (51): rather than constructing the cross-product of possible analyses for the individual substructures, all but the optimal candidate for the subparts can be discarded. (This presupposes that the competition for each of the substructures can be processed individually.)

The problem is of course how to know in advance when two substructures are h-independent. Here, I will investigate the option of assuming a restriction in the formalism that enforces h-independence of certain structural domains.[52] To arrive at such a restriction, a criterion for separating the relevant substructures has to be found. For an informal characterization of h-independent domains, the concept of an extended projection seems a very good candidate: in many OT accounts, the competition is more or less explicitly restricted to a single extended projection. For instance, Grimshaw (1997) assumes that the candidate sets entering a competition are alternative extended projections (cf. the quotation in fn. 4), and Sells (1998, fn. 2) makes explicit that his analysis hinges on a separate competition for each X^0 item (and, one could add, the extended projection of the X^0).

Intuitively, assuming extended projections to be h-independent structural domains amounts to saying that realization alternatives for a given input structure are fully determined by the realization alternatives for the extended projections of each head that is involved. With Bresnan's (2000; 2001b) LFG account of extended projections, we have a simple way of relating the input—an underspecified f-structure—to the relevant extended projections: the lexical head of the extended projection and the functional co-head(s) are all projected to the same f-structure. Thus, already the structure of recursive embedding in the input determines in first approximation the domains, local to which realization alternatives will compete.

(52) Input underlying the competition in (49)

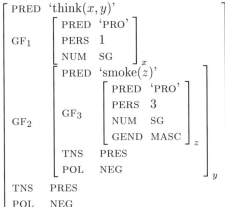

Going back to (49), we will have the input f-structure in (52), for instance. The competition (50) can be computed local to the outermost f-structure with PRED value 'think(x, y)'; the competition (51) will take place

---

[52]Although the problem of deciding whether two substructures are h-independent is presumably undecidable in the general case, there may be less restrictive ways of exploiting h-independence during processing. (For example, it is conceivable that one could devise a technique similar to lazy copying—as used in sophisticated unification procedures in LFG parsing Maxwell and Kaplan (1996)—to take advantage of h-independence where it factually applies, without losing coverage of the cases where it doesn't apply.) On the other hand, it may turn out that such a restriction on the formalism is indeed compatible with the intuitions underlying linguistic OT-accounts.

local to the f-structure indexed y, with PRED value 'smoke(z)'. Strictly speaking, there will be further local competitions for the nominal projections.

If we decide that the restriction of the domain of OT competition to extended projection is linguistically plausible, we can define the interpretation of constraints to be generally local to an extended projection.[53]

(53) *Locality of constraint interpretation*
If a part of a structure violates a constraint and there exists an alternative realization for the underlying input not violating this constraint, then the alternative realization lies within the same extended projection.

With the interpretation fixed in that way, h-independence can be exploited in processing, without making the algorithm incorrect.

Restricting the application of constraint schemata

To make the system fully precise, more would have to be said about details such as how partial structures are generated. Here, I will just sketch how one could make sure that the alternative realizations that are considered do actually lie "within the same extended projection".

We have to restrict the domain of structural elements that are taken into account when checking the constraint schemata, i.e. both (i) the selection of elements that $\star$ is instantiated to, and (ii) the domain of the quantifiers occurring in constraint schemata.[54] The restriction is made relative to an equivalence class of c-structure nodes projected to the same f-structure (and thus forming an extended projection).

Since we are interested in the relation that the nodes in this class bear to other categories (which are themselves extended projections), the domain will include their immediate daughter nodes also, plus the f-structures that these project.[55] If constraints are violated trivially because they require the existence of some structure that is excluded from this domain, they will be violated by all candidates and thus will be non-distinctive.

---

[53] *Prima facie* phenomena like *wh* extraction from embedded clauses seem to be incompatible with this restriction. Note however that the set of alternative "realizations" of an argument NP, for instance, may include non-realization within the clause.

[54] In general, the domains for (i) and (ii) will cover the same elements; a detailed account will however have to restrict instantiation of $\star$ more strictly, to avoid double counting of violations (which would make the system incompatible with the first clause of the definition of h-independence (51)).

[55] Note that it is not possible to "see" the c-structural realization of the embedded f-structures. Thus, these f-structures will become relevant only if they have a bearing on the main f-structure and its c-structural realization. (This is the case, e.g., for the AGR constraint (20), and the OP-SPEC constraint (32). In the former case, the realization of subject agreement features on the verbal head is checked, with different consequences depending on the c-structural location of this head. In the latter case, the fact that a certain embedded phrase is marked as an operator has consequences for possible loci of realization.)

So, we can assume the following restrictions on the application of the constraint schemata and harmony evaluation.

- An evaluation domain is specified by an input f-structure and a corresponding root category.
- In the application of a constraint schema local to a given evaluation domain, the metavariable $\star$ and the quantifiers range over the following elements:

  (i) all co-projecting c-structure categories that have a direct projection line to the root of the evaluation domain (i.e. not intervening elements that are not co-projecting)

  (ii) all daughters of the elements in (i)

  (iii) the f-structures projected by (i) and (ii)

- Harmony evaluation is performed separately for each evaluation domain.

Note that the evaluation domain is specified not just by an f-structure, but also by a c-structure root node. For the matrix f-structure in the input f-structure, this does not make a difference. But the competitions for embedded f-structures will now depend on the outcome of the competition for their matrix f-structure: if the optimal matrix candidate realizes the entire embedded f-structure on a matrix head (like it happens, e.g., with the information about a pronominal subject in a *pro-drop* language), there will be no (relevant) embedded competition at all. But there may be one or even several[56] separate competitions for new "root categories" determined by the matrix competition. The search space for a top-down or head-first routine (proceeding from the matrix f-structure to the embedded f-structures) is thus narrowed considerably.

8.6.6 Exploiting Locality in Processing

Having limited the scope of OT constraints to extended projections, the particular way in which h-independence is exploited in processing is still open. A conceivable option of modifying the parsing routine with "back generation" discussed in section 8.6.1 accordingly might be the following: the input string is parsed as usual (U-i), determining potential underlying forms conveyed by that string. For each reading, the portion of the f-structure analysis that makes up the OT-input is filtered out (U-ii). Now, rather than generating entire candidate analyses for these predicate-argument-structures while leaving the optimizing competition until the end, a sepa-

---

[56]The situation of having two separate competitions for the same underlying (argument) f-structure may be exploited for instance in a doubling analysis of the so-called Split NP construction as proposed in Kuhn (1999a, 2001b) (in a non-OT framework). It is the matrix competition that determines whether or not to realize the argument f-structure discontinuously (presumably based on information structure). The separate local competitions for the separate c-structural loci "know nothing" about this matrix-based decision, and hence also nothing about each other.

rate substructure for each extended projection is constructed based on the respective part of the predicate-argument-structure and a local OT competition is computed, passing on just the winning candidate.[57] The narrowing of search space under a top-down or head-first regime as addressed in the previous subsection can thus be applied.

Another possibility would be to apply compilation ideas from computational OT phonology (R. Frank and Satta 1998; Karttunen 1998) to the (sets of) rules covering an extended projection. Karttunen (1998), extending ideas by R. Frank and Satta (1998) and Hammond (1997), shows that it is possible to compute the OT competition off-line. In this compilation step, a transducer is constructed that composes the violable constraints in a ("lenient") cascade. For the on-line application, i.e. when confronted with an input structure, this transducer determines the optimal candidate for the given underlying form, without effectively computing the candidate structures. The opposite processing direction works in exactly the same way (not requiring any "backward generation"). However, a limitation of this approach is that, similar to the single-violation account discussed and rejected in section 8.4.2, it is not possible to account for (arbitrarily many) multiple violations of a constraint.[58]

In Kuhn (2000c), I discuss how an off-line competition might be incorporated into the LFG set-up, exploiting the h-independence of extended projections.[59] The reasoning is as follows: with the decisions of the previous subsections, the evaluation domain is already quite restricted; so one might go one step further and confine the allowable extended projections formally to partial tree structures that can be described by regular expressions. If futhermore the OT constraints can refer to no more than a finite domain of f-structure "types" projected from these skeletons, the relevant part of *Gen* plus the entire constraint system can be expressed by means of regular languages and regular relations. This means that one can effectively apply the idea of a lenient cascade of precompiled constraints in the syntax as well. Note that the language generated by the overall system is not restricted to the class of regular languages. The recursive structure of the input f-structure and the well-formedness principles applying on f-structure may enforce that the string language generated is contained in a higher class.[60]

---

[57] In a chart-based approach, the difference between these approaches may not be as great as it sounds. Since by assumption the larger structures are derived by forming the cross-product of the substructures, the chart will also ensure that the space of structural possibilities is represented in a compact, non-exponential way. However, book-keeping over constraint violations will be considerably more difficult if interaction across extended projections is allowed.

[58] But see Gerdemann and van Noord (2000).

[59] An earlier manuscript version of the present paper Kuhn (1999c) also contained a more detailed discussion of the off-line approach.

[60] See also Wartena's (2000) extension of R. Frank and Satta's (1998) approach to regular tree languages, making it available as a formal model for OT Syntax.

As with OT phonology, the resulting compiled grammar can be applied in both directions, using standard techniques; no special "backward generation" step is required. Under this view, the use of OT constraints clearly doesn't add anything to the generative capacity of the base formalism; rather, it allows the expression of highly generalized principles whose actual effect is determined by their language-specific priorization. This fact makes the system very attractive for high-level language processing.

8.7 Conclusion

In this paper, I have discussed a formalization of OT syntax in the framework of LFG, following the approach of Bresnan (2000). Particular attention was paid to keeping the system decidable, in order to provide a basis for further computational work. A number of restrictions on the formalism were discussed that will ensure decidability while at the same time being compatible with linguistic intuitions.

Although I presented no formal proofs, I pointed out which directions such proofs would take.[61] The central assumption made was that the candidate generation function *Gen* is modelled by generation with an LFG grammar that incorporates the inviolable constraints. It has to be ensured that the grammar does not allow the addition of arbitrarily large portions of f-structure to a given input. In order to capture the intuition behind violable constraints, ensuring at the same time that they can be effectively checked, I proposed a notation of constraints as constraint schemata, using a single metavariable ($\star$) per constraint. Allowing general faithfulness violations would pose a problem for a computational OT account; however the lexicalized system proposed by Bresnan (2000) avoids this problem while still allowing one to express the relevant conspiracies of constraints. I proposed a formalization making use of an extra "λ-projection".[62]

Beyond the basic formalization of an OT syntax system (section 8.3–8.5), I discussed the universal parsing task for an OT system (section 8.6). In order to be able to apply the same grammar and evaluation component as in generation, parsing has to involve a "back generation" step. Applying optimization both in the parsing and the generation direction (i.e. working with bidirectional optimization) permits the extension of certain constraint systems to a broader range of data, without having to stipulate any further constraints. Besides this linguistic interest, bidirectional optimization seems to have implications for processing that future research may explore: for instance, the order of processing candidates in the second direction may be guided by the outcome of the first processing direction.

---

[61] It cannot be excluded that the actual proofs will have to make some further tacit assumptions explicit, but I hope not to be missing out any substantial assumptions.

[62] Faithfulness issues—in particular PARSE or MAX-IO violations—are discussed more extensively in Kuhn (2000a).

Section 8.6.4 discussed further restrictions which could be imposed on the formalism. The relative locality of constraint evaluation, captured by the concept of "h-independence", could be exploited to avoid a combinatorial explosion of the number of candidate structures to be generated and checked. Taking this idea further, one may even devise an OT syntax system that allows off-line computation of the optimal candidate, given a certain type of input structure (inspired by the finite-state model from OT phonology). Thus, the effective processing tasks of parsing and generation would work without effective construction of candidate analyses.

References

Abraham, Werner. 1986. Word Order in the Middle Field of the German Sentence. In *Topic, Focus, and Configurationality*, eds. Werner Abraham and Sjaak de Meij. Amsterdam: John Benjamins, 15–38.

Blackburn, Patrick and Edith Spaan. 1993. A Modal Perspective on the Computational Complexity of Attribute Value Grammar. *Journal of Logic, Language, and Information* 2(2):129–169.

Blutner, Reinhard. 1999. Some Aspects of Optimality in Natural Language Interpretation. In *Papers in Optimality Theoretic Semantics*, eds. Helen de Hoop and Henriëtte de Swart. Utrecht University, Utrecht Institute of Linguistics OTS, 1–21.

Bresnan, Joan. 1996. LFG in an OT Setting: Modelling Competition and Economy. In *Proceedings of the First LFG Conference*. Stanford, California: CSLI Publications Online: http://csli-publications.stanford.edu/.

Bresnan, Joan. 2000. Optimal Syntax. In *Optimality Theory: Phonology, Syntax and Acquisition*, eds. Joost Dekkers, Frank van der Leeuw, and Jeroen van de Weijer. Oxford: Oxford University Press, 334–385.

Bresnan, Joan. 2001a. The Emergence of the Unmarked Pronoun. In *Optimality-Theoretic Syntax*, eds. Géraldine Legendre, Jane Grimshaw, and Sten Vikner. Cambridge, Massachusetts: The MIT Press, 113–142.

Bresnan, Joan. 2001b. *Lexical Functional Syntax*. Oxford: Blackwell.

Butt, Miriam, Tracy Holloway King, María-Eugenia Niño, and Frédérique Segond. 1999. *A Grammar-Writer's Cookbook*. Stanford, California: CSLI Publications.

Choi, Hye-Won. 1999. *Optimizing Structure in Context: Scrambling and Information Structure*. Stanford, California: CSLI Publications.

Dalrymple, Mary (ed.). 1999. *Semantics and Syntax in Lexical Functional Grammar: The Resource Logic Approach*. Cambridge, Massachusetts: The MIT Press.

Dalrymple, Mary, Ronald M. Kaplan, John T. Maxwell, and Annie Zaenen (eds.). 1995. *Formal issues in Lexical-Functional Grammar*. Stanford, California: CSLI Publications.

Dymetman, Marc. 1991. Inherently Reversible Grammars, Logic Programming and Computability. In *Proceedings of the ACL Workshop: Reversible Grammar in Natural Language Processing*. Berkeley, California.

Frank, Anette, Tracy H. King, Jonas Kuhn, and John Maxwell. 2001. Optimality Theory Style Constraint Ranking in Large-scale LFG Grammars. This volume.

Frank, Robert and Giorgio Satta. 1998. Optimality theory and the generative complexity of constraint violation. *Computational Linguistics* 24(2):307–316.

Gerdemann, Dale and Gertjan van Noord. 2000. Approximation and Exactness in Finite State Optimality Theory. In *Coling Workshop Finite-state Phonology*.

Grimshaw, Jane. 1991. Extended Projection. MS., Dept. of Linguistics and Center for Cognitive Science, Rutgers University.

Grimshaw, Jane. 1997. Projection, Heads, and Optimality. *Linguistic Inquiry* 28:73–422.

Grimshaw, Jane. 1998. Constraints on Constraints in Syntax. MS., Rutgers University. Presented at the Stanford Optimality Theory Workshop: *Is Syntax Different?*

Grimshaw, Jane and Vieri Samek-Lodovici. 1998. Optimal Subjects and Subject Universals. In *Is Best Good Enough? Optimality and Competition in Syntax*, eds. Pilar Barbosa, Danny Fox, Paul Hagstrom, Martha McGinnis, and David Pesetsky. Cambridge, Massachusetts: The MIT Press, 193–219.

Hammond, Michael. 1997. Parsing syllables: modeling OT computationally. Online, Rutgers Optimality Archive: ROA-222-1097, http://ruccs.rutgers.edu/roa.html.

Höhle, Tilman. 1982. Explikation für 'normale Betonung' und 'normale Wortstellung'. In *Satzglieder im Deutschen*, ed. Werner Abraham. Tübingen: Gunther Narr Verlag.

Holmberg, Anders and Christer Platzack. 1995. *The Role of Inflection in Scandinavian Syntax*. Oxford: Oxford University Press.

Johnson, Mark. 1998. Optimality-theoretic Lexical Functional Grammar. In *Proceedings of the 11th Annual CUNY Conference on Human Sentence Processing*.

Johnson, Mark. 1999. Type-driven Semantic Interpretation and Feature Dependencies in R-LFG. In *Semantics and Syntax in Lexical Functional Grammar: The Resource Logic Approach*, ed. Mary Dalrymple. Cambridge, Massachusetts: The MIT Press, 359–388.

Kager, René. 1999. *Optimality Theory*. Cambridge: Cambridge University Press.

Kaplan, Ronald and Annie Zaenen. 1989. Long-distance dependencies, constituent structure, and functional uncertainty. In *Alternative Conceptions of Phrase Structure*, eds. Mark Baltin and Anthony Kroch. Chicago, Illinois: University of Chicago Press, 17–42.

Kaplan, Ronald M. 1995. The Formal Architecture of Lexical-Functional Grammar. In *Formal Issues in Lexical-Functional Grammar*, eds. Mary Dalrymple, Ronald M. Kaplan, John T. Maxwell, and Annie Zaenen. Stanford, California: CSLI Publications. Originally appeared in *Proceedings of ROCLING II*, ed. C.-R. Huang and K.-J. Chen (Taipei, Republic of China, 1989), 1–18.

Kaplan, Ronald M. and Joan W. Bresnan. 1982. Lexical-Functional Grammar: a formal system for grammatical representation. In *The Mental Representation of Grammatical Relations*, ed. Joan W. Bresnan. Cambridge, Massachusetts: The MIT Press, chapter 4, 173–281.

Kaplan, Ronald M. and John T. Maxwell. 1988. An Algorithm for Functional Uncertainty. In *Proceedings of COLING-88*. Budapest. Reprinted in Dalrymple et al. (1995), pp. 177–197.

Kaplan, Ronald M. and Jürgen Wedekind. 2000. LFG Generation Produces Context-Free Languages. In *Proceedings of COLING-2000*. Saarbrücken.

Karttunen, Lauri. 1998. The Proper Treatment of Optimality in Computational Phonology. In *Proceedings of the International Workshop on Finite-State Methods in Natural Language Processing, FSMNLP'98*. ROA-258-0498.

Keller, Bill. 1993. *Feature Logics, Infinitary Descriptions and Grammar*. Number 44 in CSLI lecture notes. Stanford, California: CSLI Publications.

King, Tracy Holloway, Stefanie Dipper, Annette Frank, Jonas Kuhn, and John Maxwell. 2000. Ambiguity management in grammar writing. In *Proceedings of the Workshop on Linguistic Theory and Grammar Implementation, ESSLLI-2000, Birmingham, UK*, eds. E. Hinrichs, D. Meurers, and S. Wintner.

Kuhn, Jonas. 1999a. The syntax and semantics of split NPs in LFG. In *Empirical Issues in Formal Syntax and Semantics 2, Selected Papers from the Colloque de Syntaxe et Sémantique à Paris (CSSP 1997)*, eds. F. Corblin, C. Dobrovie-Sorin, and J.-M. Marandin. The Hague: Thesus, 145–166.

Kuhn, Jonas. 1999b. Towards a simple architecture for the structure-function mapping. In *Proceedings of the LFG99 Conference, Manchester, UK*, eds. M. Butt and T. H. King, CSLI Publications.

Kuhn, Jonas. 1999c. Two Ways of Formalizing OT Syntax in the LFG Framework. MS., Universität Stuttgart. Online: http://www.ims.uni-stuttgart.de/~jonas.

Kuhn, Jonas. 2000a. Faithfulness violations and Bidirectional Optimization. In *Proceedings of the LFG00 Conference*, eds. Miriam Butt and Tracy H. King. Stanford, California: CSLI Publications Online: http://csli-publications.stanford.edu/.

Kuhn, Jonas. 2000b. Processing Optimality-Theoretic Syntax by Interleaved Chart Parsing and Generation. In *Proceedings of the 38th Annual Meeting of the Association for Computational Linguistics (ACL-2000)*. Hongkong.

Kuhn, Jonas. 2000c. Resolving some apparent formal problems of OT Syntax. In *Proceedings of NELS 30*, ed. Masako Hirotani et al. Amherst, Massachusetts: GLSA, 443–454.

Kuhn, Jonas. 2001a. *Formal and Computational Aspects of Optimality-theoretic Syntax*. Ph.D. thesis, Institut für maschinelle Sprachverarbeitung, Universität Stuttgart.

Kuhn, Jonas. 2001b. Resource Sensitivity in the Syntax-Semantics Interface and the German Split NP Construction. In *Constraint-Based Approaches to Germanic Syntax*, eds. Tibor Kiss and Detmar Meurers. Stanford, California: CSLI Publications.

Lee, Hanjung. 2001. Markedness and Word Order Freezing. This volume.

Legendre, Géraldine, Paul Smolensky, and Colin Wilson. 1998. When is Less More?: Faithfulness and Minimal Links in *wh*-Chains. In *Is Best Good Enough? Optimality and Competition in Syntax*, eds. Pilar Barbosa, Danny Fox, Paul Hagstrom, Martha McGinnis, and David Pesetsky. Cambridge, Massachusetts: The MIT Press, 249–289.

Lenerz, Jürgen. 1977. *Zur Abfolge nominaler Satzglieder im Deutschen*. Tübingen: Gunter Narr Verlag.

Levin, Lori S. 1982. Sluicing: A Lexical Interpretation Procedure. In *The Mental Representation of Grammatical Relations*, ed. Joan Bresnan. Cambridge, Massachusetts: The MIT Press, chapter 9, 590–654.

Maxwell, John and Ronald Kaplan. 1996. Unification-based Parsers that Automatically Take Advantage of Context Freeness. MS., Xerox PARC, Palo Alto.

McCarthy, John J. and Alan Prince. 1995. Faithfulness and Reduplicative Identity. In *University of Massachusetts Occasional Papers, Volume 18: Papers in Optimality Theory*, eds. Jill Beckman, Laura Walsh Dickey, and Suzanne Urbanczyk. Amherst, Massachusetts: Graduate Linguistics Students' Association, 249–384.

Prince, Alan and Paul Smolensky. 1993. Optimality Theory: Constraint Interaction in Generative Grammar. Technical Report RuCCS Technical Report #2, Center for Cognitive Science, Rutgers University, Piscataway, New Jersey. To be published by the MIT Press.

Samek-Lodovici, Vieri. 1996. *Constraints on Subjects: An Optimality Theoretic Analysis*. Ph.D. thesis, Rutgers University.

Sells, Peter. 1998. Optimality and Economy of Expression in Japanese and Korean. In *Japanese/Korean Linguistics*, ed. Noriko Akatsuka et al., volume 7. Stanford, California: CSLI Publications, 499–514.

Smolensky, Paul. 1996. Generalizing optimization in OT: A competence theory of grammar 'use'. Stanford Workshop on Optimality Theory.

Smolensky, Paul. 1998. Why Syntax is Different (but not Really): Ineffability, Violability and Recoverability in Syntax and Phonology. Stanford University Workshop: Is Syntax Different? (December 12–13, 1998).

Tesar, Bruce. 1995. *Computational Optimality Theory*. Ph.D. thesis, University of Colorado.

Tesar, Bruce B. and Paul Smolensky. 1998. Learnability in Optimality Theory. *Linguistic Inquiry* 29(2):229–268.

Uszkoreit, Hans. 1987. Linear Precedence in Discontinuous Constituents: Complex Fronting in German. In *Syntax and Semantics 20: Discontinuous Constituency*, eds. Geoffrey J. Huck and Almerindo E. Ojeda. New York, New York: Academic Press, 406–427.

Wartena, Christian. 2000. A Note on the Complexity of Optimality Systems. MS., Universität Potsdam, Online, Rutgers Optimality Archive: ROA-385-03100, http://ruccs.rutgers.edu/roa.html.

Wedekind, Jürgen. 1995. Some Remarks on the Decidability of the Generation Problem in LFG- and PATR-style Unification Grammars. In *Proceedings of the 7th EACL Conference*. Dublin.

Wedekind, Jürgen. 1999. Semantic-driven Generation with LFG- and PATR-style Grammars. *Computational Linguistics* 25(2):277–281.

Wilson, Colin. 2001. Bidirectional Optimization and the Theory of Anaphora. In *Optimality-Theoretic Syntax*, eds. Géraldine Legendre, Jane Grimshaw, and Sten Vikner. Cambridge, Massachusetts: The MIT Press, 465–507.

9

Optimality Theory Style Constraint Ranking in Large-scale LFG Grammars

ANETTE FRANK, TRACY HOLLOWAY KING, JONAS KUHN AND JOHN T. MAXWELL III

9.1 Introduction

Linguistic research in syntactic frameworks like Lexical-Functional Grammar and other syntactic frameworks such as GPSG, HPSG, and TAG is most often focussed on theoretical issues concerning the theory's architecture, its formalism or basic assumptions, or else specific syntactic phenomena that are usually investigated with respect to language-internal and cross-linguistic validation.

Applying high-level syntactic theories in the context of real-life natural language applications brings about two features of language—ambiguity and varying notions of grammaticality. These are often overlooked in linguistic research, but are coming increasingly into focus due to large-scale computational linguistic applications, as well as to linguists taking a fresh look at phenomena like linguistic variation, aspects of language learning, and language change.

Computational LFG grammars can be developed that assign syntactic analyses to real-life texts of considerable complexity, such as technical documentation for highly complex machines or software.[1] An LFG grammar

---

[1] In the Parallel Grammar Development (ParGram) project (for details see http://www.parc.xerox.com/istl/groups/~nltt/pargram/), large-scale LFG grammars are being developed for English (Xerox PARC), French (Xerox Research Centre Europe), German (IMS, University of Stuttgart), and recently Norwegian (University of Bergen), with special focus on technical documentation text types. The grammars are implemented in the Xerox Linguistic Environment (XLE) grammar development platform. See

Formal and Empirical Issues in Optimality Theoretic Syntax.
Peter Sells (ed.).

of this type will cover a significant number of core syntactic phenomena which interact with one another. It will also integrate large-scale lexical resources (that is, thousands of nouns, verbs, adjectives and adverbs), in order to deal with real-life corpora.

While these syntactic and lexical resources are built on the basis of well-established insights from linguistic research, large-scale grammar development raises issues that are not yet well explored in the theoretical framework of syntactic linguistic analysis.

Ambiguity is one of the key problems facing large-scale grammatical analysis. Many ambiguities in broad-coverage grammars arise due to an interference of core syntactic constructions with rather rare constructions that occur in real-life texts. Another important source of ambiguity is lexical ambiguity, again induced by large-coverage lexicons which contain rare alternative readings for many lexical items.

The issue of massive ambiguity arising with broad-coverage grammars and lexicons is not so much an issue of computational grammars in particular: it constitutes a general feature of language. Language is inherently ambiguous—consider only simple PP attachment and lexical ambiguities and how they interact and multiply, giving rise to exponentially many possible analyses. Yet, it is only with computational grammars that these ambiguous structures are identified rigorously. Put slightly differently, language is inherently highly ambiguous, and this ambiguitiy blatantly surfaces in broad-coverage computational grammars, whereas in human language perception most of these syntactic and lexical ambiguities are simply not perceived. Thus, when faced with the full number of ambiguities arising in realistic natural language processing, one will be confronted with a large number of possible analyses which are usually not perceived by humans and which are considered inappropriate in a given context.

Even though in advanced computational systems, exponential numbers of ambiguities can be processed efficiently (see Maxwell and Kaplan 1989, 1993, 1996), the problem of determining which analysis is the desired or appropriate one in a specific context remains to be solved. If we were able to eliminate special or infrequent constructions or rare lexical readings from the grammar, we could filter certain of these non-perceived ambiguities. However, eliminating them from the grammar would mean that some specific sentences that involve such rare constructions would not receive the correct analysis. It is therefore desirable to devise a syntactic formalism that allows the grammar writer to express, for instance, a dispreference for infrequent constructions or rare lexical readings, rather than ruling them out in all cases by "hard" syntactic constraints. In this way, rare or "dispreferred" constructions can still be considered in sentences where none of the standard, or common rules can apply, while they will be disregarded

---

Butt et al. 1999 for more details on the project and large-scale grammar development in general.

whenever a well-formed analysis can be obtained by use of more common constructions.[2]

Robustness is an important aspect of large-scale computational grammars. In real-life corpora, we frequently find minor grammatical mistakes, such as agreement mistakes, misplaced adverbials or punctuation marks. Also, certain text types may come with specific syntactic constructions that would be considered marginal or ungrammatical in a general context, such as the telegraphic-style utterances sometimes encountered in technical instruction manuals. Computational high-level syntactic grammars like LFG are not well-prepared to deal with robustness in terms of ungrammaticality. The classical LFG formalism assigns each natural language sentence, on the basis of a set of rules and lexical entries, a (set of) valid analyses, in accordance with various constraints on syntactic well-formedness (Dalrymple et al. 1995). Whenever a constraint violation occurs, the sentence is judged ungrammatical with respect to the grammar. There is, in the standard LFG framework, no notion of graded grammaticality, or linguistic variation, when dealing with a specific, single grammar. Linguistic constraints must be fully satisfied; constraints defined by the grammar or lexicon cannot be violated.[3]

Generation is, finally, an aspect of large-scale computational grammars which sheds a different light on the same aspects of ambiguity and robustness discussed above. In computational applications that involve generation from abstract syntactic representations, such as Machine Translation, reversible (LFG-)grammars can be used both for parsing (analysis) and generation. Using a single grammar for both processing modes increases consistency and facilitates grammar maintainability. Yet at the same time, the grammar has to fulfill double and incompatible duties: it has to account for a wide variety of constructions in analysis, in order to fare well with a realistic coverage and minor linguistic incorrections in real-life texts; at the same time, generation should be restricted to well-formed sentences and a restricted number of surface realizations when generating from a single f-structure representation. However, a single grammar that accounts for considerable variation of, for instance, adverbial positioning in analysis will also produce a large number of distinct surface realizations for adverbials in generation—whereas in practical applications a small number of appropriate surface realizations would be required.

---

[2]The problem of disambiguation cannot be solved in terms of pure syntactic criteria. Semantics, pragmatics, situational and world knowledge play a crucial role in ambiguity resolution. Yet, we cannot build rule-based systems that could capture the full range of factors that help humans to disambiguate and resolve syntactic ambiguity. Our approach focuses on syntactic preference constraints, and as such is closely related to syntax-based probabilistic approaches (see Section 9.5 for discussion).

[3]Here, OT-LFG (Bresnan 1996, 2000)) is an important breakthrough, in that syntactic constraints are violable. Still, this OT framework of LFG has not yet been explored in a computational setting, but see Kuhn (2001).

To address these various aspects of large-scale LFG grammar processing, we propose an extension of the LFG projection architecture that incorporates ideas from the theoretical literature on Optimality Theory (OT) (see i.a. Prince and Smolensky 1993, Bresnan 1996, 2000) in particular the aspect of ranking competing analyses on the basis of a set of violable, ranked constraints. In our approach, a new projection, o-structure, is defined on top of the classical (non-violable) constraint system of existing LFG grammars. It determines a preference ranking on a set of competing candidates. A relative ranking is specified for the violable constraints that appear in the o-projection, where this ranking determines the winner among the competing candidates. In this architecture the violable optimality constraints are overlaid on the existing grammar without altering the basic tenets of LFG theory.

Most work in Optimality Theory is focussed on using violable constraints to choose among competing ways of expressing an underlying form (such as an underspecified f-structure). The function GEN defining the set of candidates for a given underlying form may thus be viewed as a grammar used to generate full analyses from the underlying form. The grammar modelling GEN will only contain very basic inviolable principles that any candidate has to satisfy. The present paper adopts a parsing perspective instead and uses the mechanisms of OT to choose among competing analyses of a sentence, although we also apply our constraint ranking mechanism to choose among competing candidates in generation from f-structures (section 9.4.3).

The basic idea behind standard Optimality Theory is that constraints are violable. This means that the set of competing analyses usually includes structures that violate a number of constraints. The optimal, most harmonic candidate is typically defined to be the (only) grammatical analysis for the given underlying form or structure (see Choi (1999) on allowing multiple, grammatical analyses to surface). This structure may involve serious constraint violations, but, as long as there is no competing analysis with fewer important constraint violations, it will be considered as grammatical.

In our approach we slightly diverge from this classical OT perspective in that the competing LFG analyses, that is the f-structure representations, do not involve constraint violations in the sense of classical LFG analysis. However, if the LFG analyses are viewed as the output of GEN, then this approach is similar to that of classical OT. The main difference is then that the optimality constraints under our approach determine the likelihood that an analysis is the correct reading, not whether it is the (only) correct analysis.

We show how the basic idea of competing, violable contraints in OT can be incorporated into classical LFG, by defining violable "optimality constraints" in a separate grammar projection, the o-structure, in conjunction with a ranking mechanism to choose among competing analyses on the basis of their associated optimality constraints. This OT-style constraint ranking scheme is proposed as a uniform mechanism for solving typical problems facing large-scale computational grammars, such as pruning undesirable ambiguity, making a grammar robust in the face of marginal constructions and outright mistakes, and allowing a single grammar to be used for both parsing and generation. Section 9.5 provides more detailed discussion about the relation of our work to classical Optimality Theory.

The overlay of OT-style constraint ranking mechanisms on LFG can be very effective in filtering syntactic ambiguity: eliminating an unwarranted ambiguity in terms of hard syntactic constraints typically induces loss of a corresponding valid analysis in a different syntactic context. Defining violable "optimality constraints" in a separate grammar projection, in conjunction with a ranking mechanism to choose among competing analyses, provides a more flexible filtering mechanism. Rare constructions can be marked as "dispreferred" and will thus be outranked by more common constructions in the general case. Yet, they can still be chosen as the winning candidate in cases where no other analysis based on more common constructions is available. Even though in certain cases the constraint rankings are faced with exceptions or counterexamples, they give valuable results and allow a selective and focused approach to particular types of ambiguities.

With the addition of an OT-style constraint ranking mechanism to the LFG architecture, the robustness of a grammar can be increased by introducing some low-ranked grammar rules that allow for the analysis of common grammatical mistakes (e.g., subject-verb agreement mistakes) and marginal constructions (e.g., misplaced adverbials). This potential for increased robustness is invaluable in real world applications of LFG in which the material to be parsed may contain minor grammatical mistakes.

Finally, using the same grammar in parsing and generation can be facilitated by the proposed OT-style preference mechanism: while a grammar must accept a wide variety of alternative syntactic structures in parsing, generation can be restricted to a subset of optimal or 'preferred' alternatives. This use of OT constraints is perhaps the closest to that of classical OT in that the input is an underlying f-structure which corresponds to a number of possible sentences. Which of these sentences is the optimal one is determined by the constraints on the grammar.

The remainder of this paper is organized as follows. Section 9.2 provides a brief introduction to classical OT theory; more detailed discussion can be found in the references cited and in other papers in this volume. Section 9.3 then introduces the implementation of optimality constraints in our system and the place of OT in the projection architecture of LFG. Section 9.4 discusses possible applications for this OT-style constraint ranking in large-scale LFG grammars. Section 9.5 elaborates on the differences between the proposal made here and the standard framework of OT-LFG. Finally, Section 9.6 provides a conclusion.

9.2 Constraint Ranking in Optimality Theory

Optimality Theory, introduced by Prince and Smolensky (1993), assumes a grammar architecture consisting of a universal set of constraints. These constraints may be mutually conflicting and can be violated. The grammar of an individual language is specified by a particular ranking of the violable constraints. The constraints operate on a set of competing candidate representations produced from the input by a function GEN.[4] The computation of the candidate(s) with the least violations of the most highly ranked constraint is performed by the operation EVAL.[5]

To give a simple example of the effect of competing syntactic constraints, assume the violable constraints in (1):[6]

(1) OP-SPEC   Syntactic operators must be in specifier
                position.
     OB-HD   A projection has a head.
     STAY   Trace is not allowed.

The goal is to determine the optimal analysis among the three competing candidates given in the tableau in (2). The relative ranking of the constraints in (1) assumed for English is reflected in the order of the columns in the tableau: constraints that constitute serious constraint violations are stated to the left; those that constitute weaker constraint violations are stated towards the right. If a candidate violates a certain constraint, the violation is marked by '*' in the respective column ('!' marks a candidate's

---

[4]Versions of OT differ, among other things, in the kind of structures they assume as the input and output of GEN (and thus the candidate set in a competition). Grimshaw (1997) assumes the input for a verbal extended projection to consist of "a lexical head plus its argument structure and an assignment of lexical heads to its arguments, plus a specification of the associated tense and aspect" (p. 376). From this input, GEN generates all extended projections conforming to X-bar theory as alternative realizations of this argument structure. The output thus consists of "representational simulations of transformational derivations using chains and traces" (Bresnan (2000:1)). Bresnan argues for "a more radically nonderivational theory of GEN, based on a parallel correspondence theory of syntactic structures" (p. 1). She proposes a reconstruction of Grimshaw's theory within an LFG setting. Here, the input to GEN is "a (possibly underspecified) feature structure representing some given morphosyntactic content independent of its form of expression" (Bresnan 2000: sec. 1.1).

[5]As Karttunen (1998) shows, this conceptual generate-and-test situation need not be reflected in a computational account. For computational phonology, a computational treatment based on the finite-state calculus can be devised that composes the violable constraints "leniently", thus avoiding the need to enumerate the candidate set prior to application of EVAL. However, for most work in OT syntax this is not an option, since the constraints cannot be formalized in the finite-state calculus (but see the discussion in (Kuhn 2001)).

[6]The example is based on Grimshaw (1997:378); cf. Bresnan (2000: sec. 2) for a reconstruction in a purely declarative LFG setting—see also fn. 4.

"fatal" constraint violation). EVAL proceeds stepwise from left to right, to determine the optimal candidate(s), i.e. the one(s) which have the weakest constraint violations. If a unique candidate has the fewest constraint violations for some constraint under consideration, it is the winner. If no unique winner could be determined on the basis of the constraint under consideration, EVAL considers the weaker (lower-ranked) constraints for all the remaining candidates, again identifying the candidate(s) with the weakest constraint violations. '☞' marks the optimal candidate(s) determined by EVAL as the candidate(s) with weakest constraint violations. In our example, the third candidate wins despite two violations of STAY (against one or no violation of STAY), since the alternative candidates violate the higher-ranked constraints OP-SPEC or OB-HD. In OT this means that the third candidate is the only grammatical realization of the input. The unsuccessful candidates are considered ungrammatical.

(2)

Candidates		OP-SPEC	OB-HD	STAY
	a.	*!		
	b.		*!	*
☞	c.			**

a. = [IP she will [VP read what]]
b. = [CP what_j **t**_j [IP she will [VP read t]]]
c. = [CP what **will**_i [IP she **t**_i [VP read t]]]

In the following sections, we propose a scheme of integrating a ranking of violable constraints into the projection architecture of LFG, and show how it can be applied as an add-on to existing large-scale computational LFG grammars. In this approach grammaticality is defined classically. That is, the LFG grammar only provides grammatical analyses of sentences. As such, the integration of OT plays different roles than in classical OT and OT-LFG. For example, under our approach the OT constraints can be used to identify the most likely analysis of a given sentence among multiple grammatical analyses. In this paper, contrary to the original generation perspective of most work in OT, we primarily adopt a parsing perspective. That is, we start with an English sentence and parse it to obtain the possible LFG c-structure and f-structure analyses. However, it is also possible to use the OT mechanisms in generation, more closely resembling classical OT. In this case, we start with a well formed f-structure and determine which sentences it can correspond to, using OT constraints to choose an optimal surface realization from multiple candidates. How our approach relates to standard OT syntax is discussed in more detail in Section 9.5.

9.3   OT within LFG's Projection Architecture

This section discusses the technical implementation of the LFG-based OT account we are proposing. Section 9.3.1 introduces the idea of an optimality projection as the basis for an OT-style preference mechanism. The basic approach is exemplified through a syntactic ambiguity found with PPs. Section 9.3.2 shows how the constraints encoded in the optimality projection are introduced in the grammar and provides more details about the formal interpretation that determines the relative ranking of analyses.

9.3.1 Optimality Projection

The LFG-based implementation of OT-style preference ranking relies on an extra level of representation, which is called *o*-structure, or the optimality projection. For each candidate analysis that the grammar assigns to a given input (sentence), a record is kept of the optimization relevant rules and constraints that were applied. This record, the *o*-structure, is an extra level of representation projected from c-structure.[7]

(3)

In order to know which optimization relevant rules and constraints apply in a given analysis, so-called optimality marks are explicitly introduced in the *o*-structure by *o*-descriptions, stated in the relevant parts of the grammar. Information from these marks is projected into the *o*-structure just as functional annotations project information into the f-structure.[8] This is seen in (4) in which MARK1 will be projected in the *o*-structure if the OBL analysis is chosen, while MARK2 will be projected if the ADJUNCT analysis is chosen.

$$(4) \quad \text{VP} \rightarrow \text{V} \left(\begin{array}{c} \text{NP} \\ (\uparrow \text{OBJ}) = \downarrow \end{array} \right) \left\{ \begin{array}{c} \text{PP}* \\ (\uparrow \text{OBL }) = \downarrow \\ \text{MARK1} \in o* \\ \\ \downarrow \in (\uparrow \text{ADJUNCTS}) \\ \text{MARK2} \in o* \end{array} \right\}$$

With a grammar including such *o*-descriptions, parsing an input sentence amounts to two tasks in the original OT setting. First, the set of candidate analyses is determined; that is, the set of analyses that the LFG grammar specifies for that sentence, ignoring *o*-descriptions. This corresponds to the task of the function GEN. Second, for each analysis, the constraints it satisfies are recorded: they are listed in the *o*-structure. This corresponds to part of the task of EVAL. Based on this information, the set of optimal

---

[7]Formally, it is a multiset of constants ("optimality marks"). The *o*-structure of a phrase is implicitly defined as the multi-union of the *o*-structure of its constituents plus any local optimality marks.

[8]The notation used for this projection is that * refers to the node itself and M* to its mother node (Kaplan 1987).

candidates is determined relative to a ranking of the constraints. This corresponds to the main task of EVAL.

In the specification of the constraint ranking for a grammar, the optimality marks, as used in the *o*-descriptions, are ordered. This ranking marks the satisfaction of certain constraints (i) as positive (and for some more positive than for other positive constraints), or (ii) as negative (and accordingly for some more negative than for others). In (5), MARK1 is the most positive and MARK4 the most negative. All constraints without an explicit marking are treated as NEUTRAL. (As will be seen in the next section, the marks below NEUTRAL are divided into three subfields.)

(5) OPTIMALITYRANKING   MARK1 MARK2 NEUTRAL MARK3 MARK4.

Parsing a sentence produces the set of candidates, comprising c-, f-, and o-structures, that enter the competition under the given constraint ranking. To determine the winner, just the *o*-structures of the candidates are considered: the winning structure(s) will be the one(s) containing the fewest instances of the most negative mark. If this does not produce a unique candidate, the second most negative mark is counted, and so on. If all the negative marks fail to single out a candidate, for the remaining structures the positive marks are considered successively, starting from the most positive mark. Here the candidates with the greatest number of instances win.[9]

Assume, for example, that the disjunction under PP in rule (4) is the only source of optimality marks for a certain sentence (as in the competing analyses (7) and (8) for sentence (6)), and that the constraint ranking is as in (5). Candidate (7) wins over (8), since neither analysis introduces any negative optimality marks, but (7) contains an instance of the highest positive mark, MARK1, while (8) does not.

(6) John waited for Mary.

---

[9]This is a different approach than that of classical OT in which all constraints are negative constraints and the constraints are listed from most negative to least negative. Transforming the ranking of dispreference marks in (5) to the classical OT system would give the ranking in (i).

(i) OPTIMALITYRANKING   MARK4 MARK3 NEUTRAL.

However, the preference marks cannot be directly converted into traditional OT since an analysis is more optimal if it has more preference marks, not less.

The ordering used in our system was developed as an aid in conceptualizing grammar writing. It was tailored to the task of modifying existing large grammars that encode grammaticality in the classical way—i.e. that provide an analysis only for grammatical sentences. This explains why more fine-grained means of dealing with equally well-formed sentences were required.

(7)

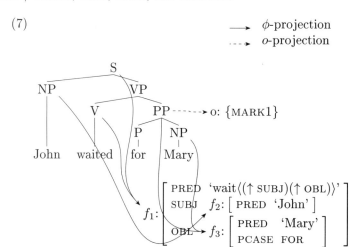

(8)

Note that for this particular example, the effect of excluding the (8) analysis could have been reached by simply removing the respective f-annotation from rule (4), making the exclusion of PP-adjuncts an inviolable constraint. However, the OT-style analysis—employing a violable constraint—has the considerable advantage that the PP-adjunct option is still available for other situations: For instance, with a verb that does not subcategorize for an OBL function, like *sleep* in *John slept for three hours*, the analysis corresponding to (7) will be ruled out by LFG's Coherence condition (which is not violable). It does therefore not enter the set of competing candidates. The (8)-type analysis will have no competitor and will win.

This general pattern of reasoning underlies practically all usages of such OT-style rule formulations: a strict, inviolable constraint on the one hand would get very many cases right, but would fail to provide an analysis for some well-formed data. Imposing no restrictions at all on the other hand would result in incorrect (or unwanted) extra readings in many cases, although it would at least cover all data. A competition-based ranking now opens the third possibility of providing a rule alternative for the case that no better (or less dispreferred) analysis could be generated using other rules or rule parts.

9.3.2 Interpretation of Ranked Constraints

The most common metric used to compare analyses in the OT literature is to compare the (constraint violation) marks on the two analyses from most dispreferred to least dispreferred until there is a mark that has a different number of instances in the two analyses. When there is a mark where the two analyses differ, then the one that has the fewest instances of that mark is chosen.

The implementation discussed here extends Optimality Theory by allowing preference marks. If the dispreference marks do not distinguish between two analyses, then the preference marks are compared from most preferred to least preferred. When there is a mark where two analyses differ, then the analysis that has the greater number of instances is chosen. The extension of OT constraint ranking discussed here also provides for different types of dispreference marks. In particular, UNGRAMMATICAL and NOGOOD subtypes are introduced. These are discussed below in detail.

The constraints introduced in the grammar are ranked from highest to lowest. As such, a sample ranking would look like (9).[10] Note that in traditional approaches to Optimality Theory, marks are listed from most dispreferred to least dispreferred; however, we list them in the reverse order because of the preference marks (cf. also fn. 9).

(9) MARK1 NEUTRAL MARK2 UNGRAMMATICAL MARK3 NOGOOD MARK4

NEUTRAL, UNGRAMMATICAL, and NOGOOD are keywords separating areas in the ranking with different interpretations. The NEUTRAL keyword separates the preference marks from dispreference marks. When NEUTRAL is used as a mark on a constraint, this is equivalent to introducing no mark

---

[10]To facilitate modifications of the ranking without having to edit grammar and lexicon files, it is possible to collect marks into an equivalence class by enclosing them in brackets. A declaration of the form:

OPTIMALITYRANKING (MARK1 MARK1a) (MARK2 NEUTRAL) MARK3
UNGRAMMATICAL MARK4 NOGOOD MARK5

is interpreted in such a way that MARK1a and MARK1 count as preference marks of identical strength and MARK2 is treated as equivalent to NEUTRAL, i.e. it is effectively ignored.

This ability relates directly to a controversial subject in classical OT theory. Namely, are all constraints strictly ranked relative to one another or can some constraints be unranked relative to other constraints? We do not discuss this further here; see Sells et al. (1996), Ackema and Neeleman (1998), and Asudeh (2001) and references therein for details.

at all.[11] Marks listed before NEUTRAL are preference marks (e.g., MARK1 in (9)). Marks listed after NEUTRAL are dispreference marks (e.g., MARK2). The keywords UNGRAMMATICAL and NOGOOD each mark the beginning of sections that we will refer to as the ungrammatical marks (e.g., MARK3) and the nogood marks (e.g., MARK4). These marks are used in specific technical applications. The four types of marks (preference, dispreference, ungrammatical, and nogood) are discussed below, each with a brief example of how it might be used in a large-scale grammar.

Preference Marks

Preference marks are used when one out of two, or more, readings is preferred. Consider the problem of multiword expressions. Typical English examples of multiword expressions are seen in (10), while (11) shows a translation triple in which a noun-noun compound multiword expression is used in English, a morphological compound in German, and a N-P-N multiword expression in French.

(10) a. Xerox DocuColor 70
      b. fast forward

(11) a. print quality
      b. Druckqualität
          print-quality
      c. qualité d' impression
          quality of printing

Multiword expressions pose a number of problems. One is illustrated by the English examples in (10). These forms are nouns. However, their internal structure is not similar to that of regular noun phrases, making it difficult to write phrase structure rules for them. Another is seen by the triple in (11). In certain contexts, a multiword expression in a given language is always translated by the same term in another language. This can be difficult to capture if the internal structure of the multiword expression is examined (e.g., examining the French *qualité d'impression* would result in the incorrect translation 'quality of printing'). These problems can be avoided if the multiword expressions are treated as single words, e.g., there is a lexical entry for 'fast forward' that treats it as a noun.

However, if these are treated as multiword expressions, a different problem arises. What happens if both the analytical and multiword expression analyses are possible, as in (12a)? This sentence would receive two analyses, since 'print quality' can either be a multiword expression or a noun-noun compound. To avoid getting the analytic reading, we might construct the tokenizer in such a way that it will group together any string-adjacent occurrence of 'print' and 'quality', so we will only get the multiword reading.

---

[11] By default, marks that appear in the grammar but not in the ranking are treated as being NEUTRAL.

However, (12b) can be covered only if 'print' and 'quality' can also be analyzed as adjacent individual tokens. Such cases indicate that the grammar needs to accommodate both analyses. In a setting working with inviolable constraints, this gives rise to large number of analyses and hence ambiguity.

(12) a. The [print quality] of this printer is good.
      b. I want to [print] [quality] documents.

To avoid this, preference marks can be used to state a preference for the multiword analysis of these terms: in general, when the multiword expression reading is possible, it is the preferred one. By marking the lexical entries of multiword expressions with a preference optimality mark, the analysis involving the multiword expression will be preferred over the analytic analysis whenever both analyses are possible, as in (12a). However, if there is no valid analysis for the multiword expression, as in (12b), an analysis that uses the individual word entries is still possible. In absence of a preferred multiword analysis, the construction based on individual word tokens is the optimal candidate.

Dispreference Marks

Dispreference marks (those below NEUTRAL and above UNGRAMMATICAL) are generally used to mark rare constructions that are grammatical and as such are to be analyzed by the grammar, but are infrequent. The dispreference mark ensures that the construction surfaces only when no other, more common, analysis is possible. Consider the case of NPs headed by adjectives. A simple example of a valid use of this construction is seen in the German example (13).

(13) Meistens kauft die größere Firma   die kleinere.
     Mostly   buys the larger company the smaller
     'Usually, the larger company buys the smaller one.'

However, once the grammar admits an NP structure that consists of an adjectival head with an optional determiner, such NPs can be built in many places where they are implausible. An example of such a situation is seen in (14), which would be assigned two readings.

(14)   Nachts fallen helle Farben auf.
        at night stand bright colors out
     a. [NP(nom) helle Farben]
        reading = 'At night, bright colors stand out.'
     b. [NP(nom) helle] [NP(dat) Farben]
        reading = 'At night, the colors notice bright ones/bright ones strike colors.'

The reading in (14a) in which *helle Farben* forms an NP is the desired one. However, the reading in (14b) in which *helle* forms an NP headed by an adjective and *Farben* a canonical NP is also possible because the verb *auf-*

fallen can either be intransitive or take a dative object. To constrain this extra, infelicitous reading, a dispreference mark can be introduced in the part of the NP rule which defines the adjective headed structure, as shown in the rule fragment (15).

(15) a. OPTIMALITY RANKING ... NEUTRAL <u>AHEADNP</u> UNGRAMMATICAL NOGOOD.

    b. NP $\longrightarrow$ { ...

$$
\begin{array}{cc}
\text{(DET)} & \text{A} \\
(\uparrow \text{SPEC})=\downarrow & \uparrow\,=\downarrow \\
 & \text{AHEADNP} \in o*
\end{array}
$$

       ... }

Ungrammatical Marks

It is also possible to have UNGRAMMATICAL marks. These are used to mark rules which parse ungrammatical constructions. This is useful for building robust grammars (see Section 9.4.2). A simple example of this is relaxing the subject-verb agreement constraint.

Ideally, a grammar would only parse grammatical sentences. However, when dealing with sentences from real texts for certain applications, it is desirable to also parse slightly ungrammatical sentences in order to extract basic information from them, such as the intended predicate-argument structure. One of the most common errors encountered in these texts is incorrect subject-verb agreement where a third singular verb is used with a subject that is not third singular, as in (16).

(16) The boxes on the train arriving early in the morning is delivered before noon.

This type of sentence can be parsed by a grammar if the grammar explicitly relaxes agreement constraints, by allowing plural subjects with singular verbs. However, it is undesirable to allow such parses in the general case, especially in situations in which another analysis leads to a parse with correct subject-verb agreement. In addition, the fact that the original sentence is ungrammatical should be indicated in some way in the analysis.

This problem can be solved using the UNGRAMMATICAL optimality marks. A basic form of this is shown in (17) for the English third singular verbal ending -*s*. In cases where subject-verb agreement is observed, the first disjunct delivers an analysis where no optimality mark is introduced. However, when subject-verb agreement is violated, only the second disjunct can be chosen, which introduces an UNGRAMMATICAL mark NOSVAGR. According to the interpretation of UNGRAMMATICAL marks, this structure will only surface if there is no competing grammatical analysis, and an asterisk will be placed before the solutions to indicate ungrammaticality. Similar constraints could be added for other person and number combinations.

(17) a. OPTIMALITYRANKING NEUTRAL UNGRAMMATICAL
   NoSVAGR NOGOOD.

   b. -s { (↑ SUBJ NUM)=SG
          (↑ SUBJ PERS)=3
        | NoSVAGR ∈ o* }

Nogood Marks

The NOGOOD marks indicate that the analysis is never chosen/taken into account, even if there is no alternative analysis.[12] This is useful for marking constructions specific to a particular language register or corpus.

For instance, suppose the same grammar of German is used for parsing newspaper texts and instruction manuals. In instruction manuals, count nouns frequently appear without a determiner, a style which is deviant within full sentences in standard German. Examples are shown in (18).

(18) a. Unterer Hebel nach links gestellt: die Lüftung   ist
       lower   lever to left put   the ventilation is
       geöffnet.
       opened
       Lower lever in left-hand position: the ventilation is open.

   b. Zündschlüssel abziehen.
      ignition key   remove
      Remove the ignition key.

It would be possible to write a grammar with no requirements on singular count nouns to have determiners. However, there is a problem in that in other contexts, e.g., newspapers and novels, the appearance of count nouns without a determiner indicates ungrammaticality. As such, allowing these noun phrases to be parsed allows ungrammatical sentences to be parsed by the grammar.[13]

The use of NOGOOD marks allows the grammar writer to formulate the NP rule as in (19), allowing the absence of DET[14] in the following situations: (i) generally, if the noun is *not* a singular count noun, or (ii) in instruction manuals, also if the noun *is* a singular count noun. This latter case is marked by introducing the optimality mark INSTR-MANUAL.

---

[12] Technically, NOGOOD marks are treated like an inconsistent constraint. So, if one of these marks occurs conjunctively in a rule or lexical item, then the rule or lexical item will still appear in the output, but the mark will appear as an inconsistent constraint and no further structure will be built.

[13] Presumably, one would not apply the ungrammaticality analysis of sec. 9.3.2 for lacking determiners in these text types either, since this is not necessarily a typical error that speakers make.

[14] Note that ε marks the empty string, not a null category. In this case, the annotations are interpreted as if they were on the head N.

(19) NP $\longrightarrow$ {   DET
                              $(\uparrow \text{SPEC})=\downarrow$

          | ϵ
                              $\{\sim \begin{bmatrix} (\uparrow \text{NTYPE})= \text{COUNT} \\ (\uparrow \text{NUM})= \text{SG} \end{bmatrix}$
                              $| (\uparrow \text{NTYPE})= \text{COUNT}$
                              $(\uparrow \text{NUM})= \text{SG}$
                              INSTR-MANUAL $\in oM*\}$

          }
          $\vdots$
          N
          $\uparrow =\downarrow$

The intended effect is obtained if the grammar configuration for parsing general text uses the ranking in (20a), and the configuration for instruction manuals uses that in (20b). Note that with the ranking in (20b), determinerless singular nouns are still dispreferred, but possible.

(20) a. OPTIMALITYRANKING NEUTRAL NOGOOD <u>INSTR-MANUAL</u>.

      b. OPTIMALITYRANKING NEUTRAL <u>INSTR-MANUAL</u> NOGOOD.

Thus, NOGOODs can be used to restrict certain parts of a rule to the sublanguage of a particular corpus. This is useful for constructions that are not acceptable in the "core" language. For normal use of the grammar, the relevant marks are placed in the NOGOOD section of the ranking, but for parsing sentences belonging to the sublanguage the marks are re-ranked into the sections discussed above.[15] The use of NOGOOD marks to deactivate parts of rules introduces a range of possibilities for the systematic manipulation of a grammar in an experimental context, as discussed in Kuhn and Rohrer (1997) and, in the context of lexicon creation, in Kuhn, Eckle-Kohler and Rohrer (1998). Another usage is discussed in Section 9.4.3 below: namely, a bidirectional grammar can be tuned to allow a certain construction only in parsing, but not in generation, by marking this construction with a NOGOOD mark and using different rankings for parsing and generation.

Preference vs. Dispreference Marks

The existence of preference and dispreference marks introduces a problem not found in classical OT which only has dispreference marks. In particular, it can be difficult to decide whether to use a preference or dispreference mark to express a preference for one of two analyses. There are two issues here: the possible interaction between the preference or dispreference

---

[15]The same effect could be reached by maintaining different copies of the grammar for different sublanguages; but keeping rule alternatives in a single rule, marked by o-descriptions, has considerable advantages from a practical point of view: all rule modifications that are orthogonal to the sublanguage distinction will automatically generalize to all variants of the grammar.

marked analyses and other, unrelated analyses, and what happens when one of the analyses is missing. If a preference mark is added to the preferred analysis, then it will be preferred over all unmarked analyses, whether they are related or not. On the other hand, if a dispreference mark is added to the dispreferred analysis, then it will be dispreferred even when the preferred analysis is not present.[16]

For instance, recall the example of PP ambiguities from Section 9.3.1, where obliques were preferred over PP adjuncts in order to handle the syntactic bias for obliques in sentences like (21).

(21) John waited for Mary.

There are two ways to do this: add a preference mark to obliques or add a dispreference mark to PP adjuncts. If a preference mark is added to obliques, as shown in Section 9.3.1, then the oblique analysis will be preferred over all unmarked readings, even those that are completely unrelated to the two competitors we have in mind. For instance, suppose we have the ambiguous input in (22) from a speech recognizer.

(22) John waited {for | four} {hours | ours }.

This has the readings in (23), among others.

(23) a. John waited [PPobl for ours].
      b. John waited [PPadj for ours].
      c. John waited [PPobl for hours].
      d. John waited [PPadj for hours].
      e. John waited [NPadj four hours].

A preference mark on obliques would cause the first and the third readings to be preferred. If there was a more sophisticated preference scheme, then the preference mark on the third reading could be avoided since the PP is a time expression. However, there would still be the unintended result that the first reading would be preferred over the fifth reading, which is otherwise unrelated.

On the other hand, if PP adjunct readings are dispreferred, then there is an unintended dispreference when the preferred reading is missing, such as in (24).

(24) a. [NP Fruit flies] [V like] [NP a banana].
      b. [NP Fruit] [V flies] [PP like a banana].

In (24a), *fruit flies* is treated as a compound noun subject, *like* as a transitive verb, and *a banana* as the direct object. Since there is no PP, no

---

[16] Another consideration when deciding between preference and dispreference marks is which analysis is easier to mark. For instance, it is easier to mark a multi-word expression (Section 9.3.2) with a preference mark than it is to mark its components with a dispreference mark that would only occur when *all* of the components are used in a particular way. However, this causes multi-word expressions to be preferred even when compared to unrelated analyses.

dispreference mark is incurred. In (24b), *fruit* is the subject, *flies* the verb, and *like a banana* is an adjunct PP. As such, (24b) incurs a dispreference mark and will be outranked by (24a) even though in this case it is as preferred a reading as (24a).

In this case, it would be better to use a preference mark on the obliques, since intuitively there is a preference for obliques rather than a dispreference for PP adjuncts. That is, the preference for obliques can even override pragmatic considerations, as in (25).

(25) He painted the wall with cracks.

Here, many people prefer the reading that the result of the painting is that cracks appear on the wall, even though this is pragmatically dispreferred.

9.4 Applications in Large-Scale Grammars

In this section, we discuss in more detail how the basic mechanism introduced above can be successfully exploited within large classical LFG grammars. This discussion is based on our experience with large-scale implemented grammars for English, French, and German.

One of the major problems facing large-scale grammars is ambiguity, both spurious and intended. In Section 9.4.1 we discuss when optimality marks can be used to control ambiguities. In particular, we argue that true syntactic and lexical ambiguities can be successfully filtered by optimality marks, whereas spurious ambiguity is usually not appropriately constrained in this way. Other uses include low-ranked constraints that mark special rules devised either for marginal input (often found in spontaneous speech, misspellings, etc.), or for constructions not covered systematically (e.g., guessing that a word with a capital first letter is a proper name). These uses increase the robustness of the grammar (Section 9.4.2). Finally, an additional application of constraint ranking is the parameterization of a single grammar used both in parsing and generation, by specifying distinct constraint rankings for these two processes (Section 9.4.3).

9.4.1 Ambiguity

There is a limitation on the use of OT to filter syntactic ambiguity: for many kinds of ambiguities we will always find counterexamples, i.e. we will always find some case in which the optimality constraints prefer the incorrect reading. However, despite this drawback the inclusion of optimality constraint ranking has proven very useful in large-scale grammar applications.

Filtering of Syntactic Ambiguity

First, consider an example that to our knowledge does not suffer from counterexamples. In French, some verbs allow for optional complex predicate formation. The verb *laisser* in (26) is of this type: (26a) is a non-complex control construction, where the controlled NP object is placed between the main predicate and the embedded verb. (26b) is the complex construction, where the embedded verb's external argument is realized as a postverbal NP object. (26c), where the external argument of *venir* is a pronominal clitic, is structurally ambiguous: the sentence can be analyzed as involving a non-complex construction or a complex construction (involving "clitic climbing"). Since in other syntactic configurations the two construction possibilities are clearly disambiguated by the grammar, we can introduce an optimality mark for either the complex or non-complex verb entry of ambiguous verbs like *laisser*. This mark will filter the ambiguity in configurations like (26c), thus producing a single optimal analysis.

(26) a. Jean laisse le conducteur venir.
      John lets   the driver   come

    b. Jean laisse venir le conducteur.
      John lets   come the driver

    c. Jean le   laisse venir.
      John him lets   come

However, for most types of ambiguities, like the oblique/adjunct ambiguity, it is possible to find counterexamples. There are several possible conclusions to draw from such observations. One is to be aware of the problem of 'false guesses', but make use of these preference constraints nevertheless. A first, pragmatic reason for this is to help grammar writers by preventing them from being overwhelmed with too many analyses. In addition, experience has shown that if the application is limited to specific domains,[17] counterexamples are infrequent. To an extent, then, certain types of preferences can be fine tuned for specific types of corpora. This is especially the case for lexical ambiguities, to be discussed below.

Occasional mistakes in preferences are also less harmful if the application incorporates an interactive disambiguation tool where first the optimal analyses are presented to the user, but where lower-ranked analyses can be accessed, stepwise, by exploiting the relative ranking of the analyses. Even in a fully automatic setting, different modes of application can be used, allowing various strengths of reliance on the preference modules, so that a limited number of additional lower-ranked analyses can be admitted and transferred to subsequent processing modules. Given the number of ambiguous analyses produced by large-scale grammars, there is considerable gain in such a relaxed model of application.

Ultimately, the most promising approach is to incorporate more external knowledge sources into the definition of preferences. In the case of PP ambiguities this could be selectional restrictions on verb arguments. That is, a second "level" of preference constraints could be added to the existing system, which marks analyses as preferred if they are in accordance with the verbs' selectional restrictions. Below is a sketch of how this could be

---

[17]In the ParGram project, grammar development mainly focuses on technical documentation.

defined in the verb entries that contain oblique arguments. (We assume an additional r-projection, in which for each argument a set of possible semantic classes is specified.) For the verb *wait* the lexicon would thus encode selectional restrictions to assign the oblique argument slot a concept class that subsumes the concept class of *Mary*, but not that of *three hours*.

(27) wait: V ($\uparrow$ PRED)= 'wait$\langle$($\uparrow$ SUBJ)($\uparrow$ OBL)$\rangle$'
  ($\uparrow_r$ ARG1-CL)= { cl1 cl2}
  ($\uparrow_r$ ARG2-CL)= { cl1 cl5}
  { (($\uparrow$ OBL)$_r$ CL) $\sqsubseteq$ ($\uparrow_r$ ARG2-CL)
  | (($\uparrow$ OBL)$_r$ CL) $\not\sqsubseteq$ ($\uparrow_r$ ARG2-CL)
  NOSELRES $\in$ $o*$ }.

Sentences where the concept class of the PP argument is not subsumed ($\not\sqsubseteq$) by selectional restrictions of the corresponding verb argument slot are assigned a dispreference mark NOSELRES. In the case of *John waited for Mary*, where the selectional restrictions are satisfied, no dispreference mark is introduced. Due to the general preference mark for obliques, the oblique reading is the optimal one. In the example *John waited for three hours*, where the concept class of *three hours* is not subsumed by the selectional restriction classes for the oblique argument, NOSELRES is added to the set of optimality constraints. In this case, the oblique analysis is assigned two optimality marks: NOSELRES and OBLIQUE (the preference mark for obliques), whereas the adjunct analysis is treated as neutral. Due to the dispreference mark NOSELRES, the oblique analysis is correctly dispreferred.

This setup is, however, still not perfect. Consider the following example from French, with the verb *renoncer* which optionally subcategorizes for a PP argument. In (28a) the oblique reading, in which the journey is given up, is correctly preferred over the competing adjunct analysis, in which he gives up (some unspecified activity or object) on the journey. In contrast, (28b) is a case that is truly ambiguous. Even taking into account selectional restrictions, the preference mechanism would still disprefer a correct analysis: in (28b) there is no violation of selectional restriction classes for the oblique argument, so OBLIQUE will be the only optimality mark, yielding a preference for the oblique reading.

(28) a. Il renonce au   voyage.
      he give up at the journey
      He gives up (abandons) the journey.

    b. Il renonce au   premier essai.
      he give up at the first   attempt
      He gives up on the first attempt./He abandons the first attempt.

A better solution is therefore to drop the original general preference mark for oblique PPs (OBLIQUE) completely and to retain a dispreference for oblique arguments (as well as for diverse types of adjuncts) in case the arguments' selectional restrictions are not met, as proposed in (27).

However, even a perfectly ranked combination of all possible linguistic sources of information would never completely compensate for the additional extra-linguistic information a human language user can easily exploit in the disambiguation task.

Lexical Ambiguities

Another frequent source for ambiguities in large grammar systems is lexical ambiguity. The XLE grammar development platform provides the LFG grammars with a direct interface to rich morphologies for English, French, and German. As a consequence, for many types of categories, especially nouns, there are no explicit LFG lexicon entries. Instead, the entries are built by exploiting the information delivered by the morphological entries.

Consider the formation of the lexical entry for the French noun *utilisation* assuming that there is no entry for it in the full form dictionary. A typical tree defined by so-called *sublexical rules* for nouns, interfacing to morphological entries, is shown in (29a). This tree matches the morphological entry for a noun, which is composed of a noun stem (N_STEM), followed by a morphological tag indicating its gender (GEND_TAG), one indicating its number (NBR_TAG), and finally one indicating the part of speech (N_TAG). These morphological tags are defined as (sub)lexical entries, annotated with appropriate functional descriptions, to define the corresponding functional features, as seen in (29b). The lexical entry in (29c) defines the stem as the value of the PRED feature. Together these rules define the f-structure in (29d) for the French "unknown" noun *utilisation*.[18]

(29) a.

```
                              N
          ┌──────────┬────────────┬──────────┐
        N_STEM     GEND_TAG     NBR_TAG    N_TAG
          |           |            |          |
      utilisation    +FEM         +SG       +NOUN
```

b. +FEM   GEND_TAG $(\uparrow \text{GEND})= \text{fem.}$
    +SG   NBR_TAG $(\uparrow \text{NUM})= \text{sg.}$
    +NOUN   N_TAG $(\uparrow \text{PERS})= 3.$

c. +LUNKNOWN N_STEM $(\uparrow \text{PRED})= \text{'%stem'.}$

d.
$$\begin{bmatrix} \text{PRED 'utilisation'} \\ \text{GEND fem} \\ \text{NUM sg} \\ \text{PERS 3} \end{bmatrix}$$

---

[18] The intuition behind the use of the "unknown" mechanism with the N_STEM (29c) in the syntax/morphology interface is to avoid having to list all the forms covered by the morphological analyzer in the interface lexicon: the context of 'utilisation' in (29a) (being followed by the typical noun tags) restricts the form *utilisation* sufficiently to identify it correctly as a noun. So, the syntactic lexicon need not have seen this particular form before—thus the term "unknown". This mechanism allows one to maintain morphology and syntax in a very modular way (see also Butt et al. 1999:166ff).

Since the morphologies are very rich, this provides a powerful lexical device for the LFG grammars, allowing them to be of large scale lexically as well as syntactically. Correspondingly, this constitutes a significant source of lexical ambiguity. For example, the French morphology has noun entries for many forms that are homonyms of function words: *est* 'is/east', *si* 'if/B (music)', *la* 'the (fem)/A (music)', *a* 'has/letter 'a'', *été* 'been/summer', *être* 'be/human being', etc. In many syntactic configurations it is possible to derive analyses that make use of these noun entries, in addition to those for the intended function words. An example is given in (30), where *est* can be analyzed as the third person form of the auxiliary verb *être* 'be' or as the noun *est* 'east' in a compound noun phrase *défaut est* 'error east'.[19]

(30) a. [s [NP Le défaut] [VP [AUX est] [V corrigé]]]
          the error   is   corrected
         'The error is corrected.'

     b. [NP Le [NMOD défaut est] [VPAP corrigé]]
          the   error east   corrected
         'the corrected east error'

OT can be used to disprefer such alternative analyses by assigning the rare readings a dispreference mark RARE-NOUN. Still, with a dispreference mark on *est* as a noun, the intended analysis for sentences like (31) is available.

(31) Il faut   orienter l' imprimante vers   l'   est.
     it necessary orient   the printer   towards the east
     'You must orient the printer towards the east.'

The presence of the determiner enforces the NP analysis, ruling out a verbal analysis. Since this is the only syntactic possibility, the NP analysis is optimal in this case despite the dispreference mark.

Spurious Ambiguity

Besides the filtering of syntactic and lexical ambiguities, it is tempting to utilize OT to constrain spurious ambiguity as well. However, under the parsing-based perspective on OT competition that we adopted spurious ambiguity is almost always best constrained by other means.

     A prime example of spurious ambiguity appears with coordination. As the data in (32) illustrate, the c-structure rules for NPs have to accommodate a number of different levels of coordination. With such rules and no ranking, the analysis of coordinated plural NPs like *cats and dogs* give rise to spurious ambiguity. In this case, there are the three analyses in (33).

(32) a. the numerous [friends]$_N$ and [relatives]$_N$ of Peter's
     b. a [brilliant singer]$_{N'}$ but [mediocre guitarist]$_{N'}$
     c. [the cousins]$_{NP}$ and [a sister]$_{NP}$

---

[19]Note that for header phrases the grammar has to admit both noun phrases and sentences without punctuation.

(33) a. N: [[[[cats] and [dogs]]]]

    b. N′: [[[[cats]] and [[dogs]]]]

    c. NP: [[[[cats]]] and [[[dogs]]]]

Introducing hierarchically ranked optimality marks for the different levels of coordination at first appears to solve the problem. This is demonstrated in the small NP grammar in (34) which prefers structurally low coordination.

(34) OPTIMALITYRANKING LEVEL1 LEVEL2 LEVEL3 NEUTRAL.

$$N \rightarrow \quad \begin{array}{ccc} N & \text{CONJ} & N \\ & \text{LEVEL1} \in o* & \end{array}$$

$$N' \rightarrow \quad \left\{ \begin{array}{ccc} \text{AP}* & N & \\ N' & \text{CONJ} & N' \\ & \text{LEVEL2} \in o* & \end{array} \right\}$$

$$NP \rightarrow \quad \left\{ \begin{array}{ccc} (\text{DET}) & N' & \\ \text{NP} & \text{CONJ} & \text{NP} \\ & \text{LEVEL3} \in o* & \end{array} \right\}$$

However, if this is done, a coordinated NP such as that in (35) is no longer ambiguous even though this is an instance of *true* ambiguity.

(35) a. [old [men and women]]

    b. [[old men] and women]

The OT grammar in (34) will determine (35a) to be the optimal analysis since the optimality mark LEVEL1 prefers this structure over one assigned in (35b). However, in this case both analyses are equally possible and only context can determine which one is preferred. Filtering out *just* the spurious cases of ambiguity is not possible on the basis of a competition between parsing alternatives as we are using it in the other cases. Instead, the instances of spurious ambiguity should be constrained by more judicious writing of the c-structure rules, such as ruling out N′ → N when N is coordinated.[20]

---

[20] Alternatively, the optimizing competition involving the constraints in (34) could be performed with respect to generation alternatives sharing a common underlying predicate-argument structure, rather than on parsing alternatives sharing the same form. The former view on the candidate set is the one adopted in most of the theoretical OT literature. Under this perspective, (35a) and (35b) would not be competitors in the same candidate set, thus both could be optimal candidates (arising from different competitions). However, to implement this an additional generation step would be required after parsing is finished (see also sec. 9.5.1 and (Kuhn 2001)).

Some cases of spurious ambiguity can, however, be successfully filtered by OT constraints. For example, because French has relatively fixed word order, the VP rule encodes the order of dependent constituents. To allow for the frequent alternation of object NP and PP order, however, there is a PP position preceding the object NP, besides the one that follows it. This leads to spurious ambiguities for verbs with a single oblique or dative object PP, like (36).

(36) Le livre appartient à Jean.
     the book belongs   to John

Either PP-constituent position can derive the dative object. Annotation of the first PP-constituent with a dispreference mark PREOBJ-PP successfully filters the unwarranted ambiguity.

9.4.2 Robustness

Another useful aspect of optimality constraint ranking is to increase the robustness of the grammar. There are a number of ways in which this can be done. Parsing texts and speech unfortunately involves input which is not always strictly speaking grammatical. By marking rules which parse such input with an UNGRAMMATICAL constraint mark, it is possible for the grammar to assign the best possible analysis under the circumstances, while still indicating that the sentence is not well-formed. This was seen for subject-verb agreement in Section 9.3.2.

Not all issues affecting robustness involve ungrammatical constructions. Sometimes, it is virtually impossible to write a grammar which encompasses all the possibilities of a construction. An example of this is the use of labels whose source can be practically any part of speech, as in (37).

(37) a. the print button
     b. the reload button
     c. the fast forward button

The "label" construction in (37) is basically of the form *the X button* where X can range over a large number of parts of speech.[21] A special c-structure rule can be written to allow for the unusual labels but to disprefer them in relation to more conventional parses. This avoids odd parses of simple NPs such as *the red button*. Thus, the grammar is able to parse such constructions when necessary, thereby increasing robustness, but these constructions will not interfere with more common analyses when they are available.

Another example where OT-constraint ranking is profitably used to improve robustness of a grammar is in cases of lexical gaps. As discussed in Section 9.4.1, morphological lexicons can be used to define large LFG lexicons. However, this is only possible for word classes with fixed subcate-

---

[21] This construction can even involve non-constituents as labels, as in (i).
(i) the save as button

gorization properties, like nouns, adjectives, prepositions, and adverbs. For verbs, and certain nouns and adjectives, large subcategorization lexicons are needed. To account for missing entries in such subcategorization lexicons, we can provide generic subcategorization assignments in sublexical rules, as in (38) (see Section 9.4.1).

(38) +LUNKNOWN V_STEM
          GUESSED-SUBCAT ∈ $o*$
          { (↑ PRED)= '%stem⟨ (↑ SUBJ)⟩'
          | (↑ PRED)= '%stem⟨ (↑ SUBJ)(↑ OBJ)⟩'
          ...}

If these fall-back lexical entries are marked with an ungrammatical mark GUESSED-SUBCAT, they will only be considered in a real case of lexical gap, i.e. if no valid analysis is available on the basis of regular LFG lexicons. As such, they increase the robustness of the lexicon and grammar without adding incorrect subcategorization frames to known verbs.

9.4.3 Generation

A final use of OT which we discuss here involves the difference between grammars used for parsing and those used for generation. This problem is applicable to more technical contexts, but is also relevant in considerations of speaker competence vs. performance. The basic issue is that there are many sentences which a grammar needs to be able to parse but which do not necessarily need to be generated. Optimality marks allow the marking of rules which are used only in parsing and not in generation. To do this, distinct constraint ranking hierarchies are specified for parsing and generation. Optimality marks which occur in constructions which should not be generated appear below NOGOOD in the constraint ranking hierarchy for generation. This is shown abstractly in (39b) in which the ungrammatical MARK3 appears below NOGOOD. In addition, a new mark MARK4 which plays no role in parsing has been introduced as NOGOOD.

(39) a. parsing: MARK1 NEUTRAL MARK2 UNGRAMMATICAL
          MARK3 NOGOOD

      b. generating: MARK1 NEUTRAL MARK2 UNGRAMMATICAL NOGOOD
          MARK3 MARK4

Optimality constraints that mark ungrammatical constructions are a clear instance of when a reranking is needed for generation (Section 9.3.2). Even though it may be desirable to have the grammar parse ungrammatical sentences to improve robustness, such ungrammatical structures should not be produced.

Finally, certain constructions may be grammatical but may not be ones that should be generated. This is where the introduction of optimality marks just for generation comes in (e.g., MARK4 in (39)). Consider, for example, punctuation. In general, punctuation should be parsed in a large number of positions but generated in a more restricted manner. So, although commas appear with reckless abandon in many texts, they can be generated in a more controlled fashion. Next consider an example involving syntactic constructions. It is possible to place a *when* clause after the subject and before the verb in English, as in (40a). However, the grammar can be restricted to only generate *when* clauses in sentence-initial and sentence-final positions, as in (40b). Similar restrictions can be defined, in generation mode, for the positioning of adverbials and PP-adjuncts.

(40) a. The rear burner, when left on for too long, will overheat.

b. S $\longrightarrow$ (CONJPsub)   NP
                 $\downarrow \in$ ($\uparrow$ ADJUNCT)   ($\uparrow$ SUBJ)=$\downarrow$

(CONJPsub)   VP   (CONJPsub)
$\downarrow \in$ ($\uparrow$ ADJUNCT) $\uparrow =\downarrow$ $\downarrow \in$ ($\uparrow$ ADJUNCT)
PARSEONLY $\in o*$

Thus, the specification of distinct constraint ranking hierarchies for parsing vs. generation provides an effective mechanism which allows us to use one and the same grammar in parsing and generation, thereby facilitating the maintainability of the grammar, whereas at the same time it allows us to define slightly distinct grammar coverage for parsing and generation in a simple, effective fashion.

9.5 Relating our Approach to Theoretical OT Work

As seen above, there are a number of differences between our application of OT in parsing with large-scale grammars and theoretical work on OT-LFG. We elaborate on some of these here: the parsing (vs. generation) perspective; what constitutes the candidate set; the nature of the optimality constraints; and the relation between grammaticality and ambiguity.

9.5.1 The Parsing Perspective

An obvious difference between our account and most work in OT syntax is that in the construction of the candidate set we adopt a parsing perspective, in the classical sense, rather than a generation perspective. That is, the constraint ranking is applied to find the optimal candidate in a set of competitors sharing the same surface form, rather than in a set of analyses sharing a common underlying predicate-argument structure (see Johnson (1998) for a closely related discussion). While this is the appropriate viewpoint for work with large-scale grammars, the technical difference may lie only in the direction in which the underlying grammar with o-descriptions is used. Kuhn (2001) discusses the option of formalizing constraint systems like Bresnan's (2000: sec. 2), in which the optimal candidate is to be interpreted as the (only) grammatical realization for an (underspecified) input f-structure, by applying the same EVAL mechanism that we propose on a candidate set produced by the LFG generator for an underspecified f-structure.[22]

9.5.2 The Candidates

As already pointed out, in our account the constraint ranking mechanism of OT is overlaid on existing classical LFG grammars, which work with a classical definition of grammaticality. That is, the core grammatical phenomena have been accounted for already making use of classical, inviolable constraints. Thus, for determining grammaticality we do not employ the typical conspiracy of constraints assumed in standard OT syntax, where the constraints are set up in such a way that the language-specific ranking singles out just the right candidate as grammatical. With all candidates being grammatical in the first place, we can use the ranking mechanism for more fine-grained distinctions, in particular for the prevalent problem of ambiguity in broad-coverage grammars. From the set of possible grammatical analyses of an input form, an "optimal" candidate is chosen on the basis of optimality constraints that are primarily designed to discriminate among, or disambiguate, competing grammatical analyses.

Although in OT syntax, in particular in the OT-LFG model, one may also assume an underlying classical grammar formalizing the function GEN (i.e. determining the candidate set), the restrictive role such a grammar plays is quite different: it will only enforce very basic inviolable principles,

---

[22]Using such "real" OT grammars for the parsing task—i.e. to determine the optimal grammatical analysis for a given string—requires a two-way application of the grammar: parsing and then generating from each predicate-argument structure of the obtained analyses. The reason for this is that the optimal analysis chosen from competitors with a common input string may be a non-optimal analysis (and thus ungrammatical) when compared with alternative strings realizing the same underlying predicate-argument structure. For example, if the string to be parsed is s_2 in the abstract illustration (i) taken from Johnson (1998: sec. 4.1), the candidate analysis c_2 is the optimal one with that string; however, for its underlying predicate-argument structure i_1, there is a better analysis: c_1 (with a different surface string: s_1). Thus c_2 is in fact not a grammatical analysis, and c_3, being the best parse of s_2 that is also optimal with respect to alternative realizations of its predicate-argument structure (i_2), ultimately wins.

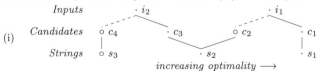

(i)

As Johnson (1998: sec. 4.1) argues, this "universal parsing problem for OT LFG" is not decidable if unrestricted classical LFG grammars are used; that is, stronger restrictions on the formalism have to be found (cf. also Wedekind's (1999) undecidability proof for generation from semantic structures (underspecified f-structures)). These results however do not affect our use of constraint ranking in parsing, which builds on a classical concept of grammaticality determined by the hard constraints of the underlying grammar, and thus does not require (re-)generation. For processing our grammars it suffices to solve what Johnson (1998: sec. 4.2) calls the much simpler "revised universal parsing problem for OT LFG".

such as some variant of x-bar theory etc. Most of the task of ruling out
ungrammatical candidates in particular languages is left to the system of
violable constraints. Here, OT filters out the "optimal", most harmonic
candidate as the only grammatical analysis for the underlying input.

Thus, while in standard OT syntax the grammar that generates the candidates is relatively unrestricted, generating vast numbers of ungrammatical analyses, which end up being unoptimal, in our context the grammar
generating the candidates is already highly restricted. With the exception
of weakening introduced for robustness, the grammar generates only grammatical candidates.

9.5.3 The Nature of the Optimality Constraints

As a consequence of both the parsing perspective and the nature of the
competing candidates, the rankable constraints we assume are quite different in nature from the violable constraints assumed in theoretical OT. In
our context the purpose of competition is not so much to single out the
only grammatical analysis in a set of universal generation alternatives, but
rather to determine which analysis of a given sentence is the most plausible one, among a set of candidates that primarily consists of grammatical
candidates.

Using a classical LFG grammar in parsing mode will associate a unique
sentence with distinct f-structures. To a certain extent one can try to reduce this ambiguity problem, which surfaces with large-scale grammars, by
encoding more and more syntactic or semantic constraints into the classical LFG grammar.[23] However, given the scale of ambiguities that arise with
large-scale grammars, there are limits where even fine-grained constraints
cannot provide enough criteria for disambiguation. A unique sentence can
potentially map to many distinct f-structure representations, and in parsing, as opposed to generation from a fixed input structure, we have to
"guess" which f-structure representation the sentence was intended to express.

With our addition of a constraint ranking mechanism to a classical LFG
grammar we induce a ranking on all the possible and perfectly valid f-
structure candidates for a sentence. This ranking determines what could
be characterized as its "most likely" f-structure representation—in the absence of any further syntactic or semantic constraints that could guide
disambiguation. Examples of this include syntactic or lexical ambiguities.
Assigning an optimality dispreference mark to rare syntactic constructions
or certain readings of lexical items that are competing against other readings in a parsing ambiguity, and which are less frequent, and thus less likely
to contribute to the intended, "optimal" f-structure of the sentence, comes

---

[23]In the generation direction, this has been done, in the OT-LFG framework, e.g., in
Choi 1999.

down to determining an "optimal" candidate among a set of competitors—not in terms of degrees of grammaticality, but in terms of probability.

9.5.4 Grammaticality and Ambiguity

While one of the most important aspects of our usage of constraint ranking is to filter ambiguities arising in large-scale grammars, this architecture allows us to admit minimal amounts of ungrammaticality, and thus improve the robustness aspect of these grammars.

To a limited degree and in a controlled way, the LFG grammar can be weakened to admit certain violations of grammatical constraints that would appear as constraint violations in OT-LFG syntax, such as agreement constraints. In the underlying unification-based LFG framework, such constraint violations are admitted by relaxation (i.e. violation) of grammatical constraints, and marked in terms of UNGRAMMATICAL constraints.

It is the division between preference and dispreference marks on the one hand, and ungrammatical marks on the other hand, then, which in our constraint ranking scheme encodes the basic distinction between grammaticality and ungrammaticality.[24] This extension of the space of ranking from the grammaticality determining constraints to further aspects of ranking—to choose among competing grammatical structures—constitutes an important difference between standard OT syntax and the OT-inspired c̲ ̲ ̲ ̲ ̲nt ranking scheme proposed in this paper.

9.6 Conclusion

In this paper we introduced a way to integrate central ideas from theoretical OT with LFG such that we maintain a classical LFG grammar and overlay OT mechanisms to select the optimal analysis from a set of competitors. We then discussed a number of ways in which OT can be used to facilitate the writing of large-scale LFG grammars. These included preference marks for specific constructions, dispreference marks for rare constructions, ungrammaticality marks to increase robustness in parsing, and NOGOOD marks to allow specialized corpus rules to be turned off.

We discussed cases of syntactic ambiguities where the usage of OT to express syntactic preferences between otherwise grammatical analyses was problematic. One reason for this was that it is almost always possible to construct a context in which the dispreferred reading is the best one for semantic or pragmatic reasons. Another reason is that OT assigns a global ranking over all analyses. This means that expressing a preference between two different analyses often results in expressing preferences between these analyses and other unrelated analyses. However, in some cases it is possible to state preference constraints in a way to avoid such interaction problems.

---

[24]However, see section 9.2 for the basic distinction between the classical notion of grammaticality in terms of f-structure constraint solving and the notion of grammaticality adopted by OT syntax.

In spite of these problems, we believe that syntactic preferences can be useful as a component of a larger scheme for disambiguation and more generally in large-scale grammar writing.

References

Ackema, Peter and Ad Neeleman. 1998. Optimal Questions. *Natural Language and Linguistic Theory* 16(3):443–490.

Asudeh, Ash. 2001. Linking, Optionality, and Ambiguity in Marathi. This volume.

Bresnan, Joan. 1996. LFG in an OT Setting: Modelling Competition and Economy. In *Proceedings of the First LFG Conference*. Stanford, California: CSLI Publications Online: http://csli-publications.stanford.edu/.

Bresnan, Joan. 2000. Optimal Syntax. In *Optimality Theory: Phonology, Syntax and Acquisition*, eds. Joost Dekkers, Frank van der Leeuw, and Jeroen van de Weijer. Oxford: Oxford University Press, 334–385.

Butt, Miriam, Tracy Holloway King, María-Eugenia Niño, and Frédérique Segond. 1999. *A Grammar-Writer's Cookbook*. Stanford, California: CSLI Publications.

Choi, Hye-Won. 1999. *Optimizing Structure in Context: Scrambling and Information Structure*. Stanford, California: CSLI Publications.

Dalrymple, Mary, Ronald M. Kaplan, John T. Maxwell, and Annie Zaenen (eds.). 1995. *Formal issues in Lexical-Functional Grammar*. Stanford, California: CSLI Publications.

Grimshaw, Jane. 1997. Projection, Heads, and Optimality. *Linguistic Inquiry* 28:73–422.

Johnson, Mark. 1998. Optimality-theoretic Lexical Functional Grammar. In *Proceedings of the 11th Annual CUNY Conference on Human Sentence Processing*.

Kaplan, Ronald. 1987. Three Seductions of Computational Psycholinguistics. In *Linguistic Theory and Computer Applications*, ed. P. Whitelock et al. London: Academic Press, 149–181. Reprinted in: M. Dalrymple, R. Kaplan, J. Maxwell, and A. Zaenen, (eds.) (1995) *Formal Issues in Lexical-Functional Grammar*. Stanford, California: CSLI Publications, 339–367.

Karttunen, Lauri. 1998. The Proper Treatment of Optimality in Computational Phonology. In *Proceedings of the International Workshop on Finite-State Methods in Natural Language Processing, FSMNLP'98*. ROA-258-0498.

Kuhn, Jonas. 2001. Generation and Parsing in Optimality Theoretic Syntax – Issues in the Formalization in OT-LFG. This volume.

Kuhn, Jonas, Judith Eckle, and Christian Rohrer. 1998. Lexicon acquisition with and for symbolic NLP-systems – a bootstrapping approach. In *Proceedings of the First International Conference on Language Resources and Evaluation (LREC98)*. Granada, Spain.

Kuhn, Jonas and Christian Rohrer. 1997. Approaching ambiguity in real-life sentences – the application of an Optimality Theory-inspired constraint ranking in a large-scale LFG grammar. In *Beiträge zur 6. Fachtagung der Sektion Computerlinguistik, Deutsche Gesellschaft für Sprachwissenschaft (DGfS-CL), Heidelberg*.

Maxwell, John and Ronald Kaplan. 1989. An Overview of Disjunctive Constraint Satisfaction. In *Proceedings of the International Workshop on Parsing Technologies, Pittsburgh, PA*. Reprinted in: M. Dalrymple, R. Kaplan, J. Maxwell, and A. Zaenen, (eds.) 1995, *Formal Issues in Lexical-Functional Grammar*. Stanford, California: CSLI Publications.

Maxwell, John and Ronald Kaplan. 1993. The Interface between Functional and Phrasal Constraints. *Computational Linguistics* 19(3):1–19.

Maxwell, John and Ronald Kaplan. 1996. Unification-based Parsers that Automatically Take Advantage of Context Freeness. MS., Xerox PARC, Palo Alto.

Prince, Alan and Paul Smolensky. 1993. Optimality Theory: Constraint Interaction in Generative Grammar. Technical Report RuCCS Technical Report #2, Center for Cognitive Science, Rutgers University, Piscataway, New Jersey. To be published by the MIT Press.

Sells, Peter, John Rickford, and Thomas Wasow. 1996. An Optimality Theoretic Approach to Variation in Negative Inversion in AAVE. *Natural Language and Linguistic Theory* 14(3):591–627.

Wedekind, Jürgen. 1999. Semantic-driven Generation with LFG- and PATR-style Grammars. *Computational Linguistics* 25(2):277–281.

Subject Index

Name Index